Newtown's History And Historian, Ezra Levan Johnson

Ezra Levan Johnson, Jane Eliza Camp Johnson

Nabu Public Domain Reprints:

You are holding a reproduction of an original work published before 1923 that is in the public domain in the United States of America, and possibly other countries. You may freely copy and distribute this work as no entity (individual or corporate) has a copyright on the body of the work. This book may contain prior copyright references, and library stamps (as most of these works were scanned from library copies). These have been scanned and retained as part of the historical artifact.

This book may have occasional imperfections such as missing or blurred pages, poor pictures, errant marks, etc. that were either part of the original artifact, or were introduced by the scanning process. We believe this work is culturally important, and despite the imperfections, have elected to bring it back into print as part of our continuing commitment to the preservation of printed works worldwide. We appreciate your understanding of the imperfections in the preservation process, and hope you enjoy this valuable book.

Johnson

NEWTOWN'S HISTORY

AND

HISTORIAN
Ezra Levan Johnson

With Additional Material

PREPARED BY

JANE ELIZA JOHNSON
The Historian's Life Companion

NEWTOWN, CONNECTICUT, 1917

THE NEW YORK
PUBLIC LIBRARY
21540A
ASTOR, LENOX AND
TILDEN FOUNDATIONS
R   1921   L

Jane E. Johnson

82 years of age

FOREWORD

It was the fond desire and studied purpose of the late Ezra Levan Johnson, to publish and preserve the early history of his native town and in this labor of unrequited love he gave unstintedly of time, travel and research.

The Newtown Bee furnished him opportunity to reach the public and this memorial volume to Mr. Johnson's memory aimed to gather and perpetuate some of his published articles. It by no means includes the wealth of material at his disposal for additional articles, which would have been published had his life, strength and faculties been prolonged. It is but the plain truth that no man was so well equipped for the task which Mr. Johnson set for himself with such unflagging zeal, both in his own knowledge of Newtown's past and in his painstaking search into local records, as well as those of the Colony, State and Nation.

Connecticut Colony, formed by the union of Hartford and New Haven in 1665, appointed a committee at the May session at Hartford in 1711, to lay out such divisions of land within the said Newtown as shall be agreed upon by the proprietors thereof. At the October Session at New Haven in October of 1711, this committee reported to the General Assembly that, "having lately had a general meeting of the said proprietors and their agreement or order for laying out a certain division, or sundry lots of lands within the said town of Newtown, the said committe have thereupon proceded and laid out the same." William Junos, Justice Bush and Samuel Hawley had bought this Newtown land, a tract six by eight miles of the Indians, July 25, 1705. Junos sold half of a third interest in this land to John Glover, making him a large landholder in the early settlement, which he served as town clerk.

Glover's purchase from Junos took place Dec. 6, 1708 and the deed of sale was copied by Glover from the records of Stratford, to which town Newtown then belonged. Dec. 19, 1710, two years after Glover's purchase, Samuel Hawley, who had a third interest in this six-by-eight-mile Newtown tract, united with his father, Joseph Curtis, Rev. Charles Chauncey (the Stratford minister) and 38 others, with "Richard Bryan's heires," to buy Junos' remaining sixth interest and Bush's third for £22,10s, "currant silver money of the Colony of Connecticut." This deed was copied into Newtown records from those of Stratford by Joseph Curtis, one of those buying out Junos and Bush.

There were 48 rights in this land so bought, Richard Hubbell Sr. having three rights, John Glover, John Reed, Benjamin Fayerweather two each and the rest one apiece. This land was not all parcelled out at once, nor all held at the same value. The swamps, open glades made by annual Mohawk fires that swept all this country in the Housatonic valley, in which meadows the early settlers cut coarse native grass for winter fodder, were most valued and were cut into four-acre strips. In 1717 the Great Bogs, as swamp land near the Horatio Northrop place was called, and the Little Bogs a half mile below on the stream running out of Great Bogs were parceled out. The hills were mainly timbered and were cut into larger pieces; 20, 30 and 40-acre divisions are frequently spoken of. An allotment of 30 acres to each of 48 rights was voted in 1721; in 1717, the record speaks of a 100-acre division and the common or undivided land continued to be parceled out until the Revolution. Land was rated then, as lists show, as pasture land, or plow-land or meadow land, and different kinds of lands were returned distinct and separately. The custom was to divide the land into the given number of acres and then draw lots for each man's "pitch" as they called it. A committee was appointed to see that each one got his rights, but some were so slow in drawing lots that the proprietors passed votes to spur the delinquents up to the mark.

This volume further illuminates the history of this Newtown land, so honestly gotten from the red man, as well as of the men who bought and settled here, mostly from Stratford.

The preparation of this volume has been a labor of love, as was the material from which it was prepared, and thanks are due all who have encouraged and aided the enterprise whether by suggestion, advice or purchase of this tribute to the effort of an unselfish, high-minded, patriotic American.

Additional material seeks to make it a more complete Newtown history, to which have been added names of descendants of Newtown's early settlers, an account of Mr. Johnson's death and burial, with some of the many tributes paid his memory.

Reuben Hazen Smith.

MR. JOHNSON'S OWN FOREWORD.

How time does fly! Here we are well agone in March and the third month of the new year will soon be gone. Before we realize it, turtles will be peeping, frogs will be croaking, woodchucks will be waking from their long winter nap and crawling from their holes will, with blinking eyes, be on the lookout for some sneaking, hungry dog. Soon bluebirds and robins will be looking for nesting places and the phoebe bird will build its nest of moss and mud and hair, perhaps over your front door and mine, where it was built last year and when she has lined it carefully with feathers, deposited her eggs, will sit the allotted time for the young life to appear, all unconcerned of danger, for she will remember the warm welcome that was hers from us all through her brooding season of one year ago. With the coming of the birds will also come the earliest of our wild flowers, the arbutus, the anemone, the trillium, the hepatica, the wind flower, the adder tongue, dutchman's breeches, columbine, cowslip, spring beauty and a wealth of others. Only a few short, swiftly going weeks and the nooks and crannies, now so silent under their winter garb, will echo and re-echo with the sound of voices of our younger people, who are the vanguard, soon to fill the breach made by the passing on of their elders. Well, so goes the time and old fellows like myself may as well realize that Time's clock for us is almost run down, and the striking of the last hour must be very near at hand. But there is no use sitting down to wait for its coming, better far to keep busy and though we cannot care for so large a piece of fallow ground as once we could, it will be far better to keep on sowing, even though some other one shall do the reaping.

In these days of restlessness, how small the percentage in our rural communities of those who are the descendants of first settlers of their native town, and Newtown is no exception. True it is, that there are a few exceptions where can be found those of the fifth, sixth and seventh generation of those who had a hand in the first purchase of the land from the Indians and there are a few instances of those still living in the house built and on the farm purchased by their ancestors over one hundred years ago. And when those belonging to the class above mentioned, who have lived all their life in one community, get to talking about the early days as they remember them and as they have heard about them from their elders, there is bound to be something said that makes us sorry ofttimes that we did not take note more carefully of the stories handed down to us, for the sake of future generations. What a large percentage of the traditions of any community remain unwritten, ignored or carelesly forgotten; they now lie buried on the page of unwritten history. Not criminally careless, though culpably negligent. The new people care but little about the old days, though it will not be long before those who are now in middle life will care, and there will be no one to tell them. Put forty years upon the lives of men and women in middle life, and those of them still living will be past their four-score years. To whom can they go outside of their circle to get their memories refreshed as to happenings at the time of early childhood? Put sixty years additional upon the ages of boys and girls of to-day, who are in the Newtown High School, and who can they consult as to the ancestry, work and helpfulness, individually and collectively, of those who are to-day a part of the web and woof in the making of our town history. Too apt are we to think as we look about us, if we don't speak it, "It is by my might and by my power have I gotten to myself this great wealth," instead of calling to mind that "others have labored and we have entered into their labors."

These papers lay no claim to literary merit, but are plain statements of incidents and happenings, by a plain man in a plain way, in the hope that our youg people, with those of maturer years, may find at least momentary pleasure in the retrospect.

Friends prophesied for the writer that in his announcement he "had bitten off more than he could chew," and the writer has had occasion many times to recall a little experience he had the first winter he taught school and boarded 'round 60 years ago. Comparing notes one evening with a brother teacher, of our experiences in boarding 'round, he said he was at the supper table, one night and was waited upon to a plate of meat, as he supposed, but the more he chewed upon it, the bigger it grew, and he mustered courage to ask the hostess what kind of meat it was. The answer came, "We butchered our old cow, yesterday, and so we cooked the udder for to-night's supper." And so with my historical work attempted, the more I chewed upon it, the bigger it has seemed to grow, until instead of reaching a finish, it really seems but just begun.

On the farm where I was born and where is still my home, there is a spring whose waters flow out from underneath a granite rock. In my early boyhood, it was made my duty in harvest time to go there with the water jug for cool, fresh water for the harvesters at luncheon hour. Ever and anon some fisherman, huntsman, farmer boy or nut gatherer would stop there to get a drink, the squirrel to wet its tongue and the little bird panting under the burning summer sun stop for a bath before soaring skyward to pour forth its sweetest notes, but to the great outside world it was all unknown. In Summer heat and Winter cold, its flow is uniform and perpetual. It is a little spring. A six-quart bowl inverted would cover it from sight, and yet, in the great economy of Nature, it has its part to perform and performs it well. But a short distance from its source its waters lose their identity as they mingle with the water of the northwest branch of Pootatuck brook. On they flow, into Housatonic River and from thence into Long Island Sound, and so on into the broad ocean on whose bosom float the navies of the world.

I go there in these later years and as I sit on the moss-covered rock from underneath which the waters flow, and in the shadow of the old birch tree that has marked off more than a century of growth, I muse over the bygone days. And musing there it sometimes comes to me that that spring is in a way typical of one phase of Newtown's life. Typical in this, that from our town, for more than 100 years, a steady, never ceasing flow of young life has been going out from us into the great ocean of human endeavor and still the stream flows on until there is hardly a country on the globe in which there is not some one Newtown born, or a descendant, helping to Christianize communities and mould public opinion along lines of virtue and good living. And who dare question the truth of the statement that the New England stock of this country is the backbone of the nation?

On land and sea, wherever our flag floats, nine-tenths of them, including the gentler sex as well, have made, and are still making, good their ancestral training in the old New England homes.

We are glad when our young people marry and settle in the ancestral homes, or take the homes of those whose family name has died out, and, with the co-operation of mother, wives or sisters and in the home life, help to build and strengthen the nation, for in the homes of its people rests the prosperity and perpetuity of the nation.

REUBEN HAZEN SMITH'S TRIBUTE.

> Who for their fellows live and die,
> They the immortals are. O, sigh
>   Not for their loss, but, rather, praise
> The God who gave them to our days.
>   Richard Watson Gilder.

In the going home of Mr. Johnson, Newtown loses, not only its most widely known citizen, but its best beloved and most esteemed. I feel sure that no citizen of his generation will be laid at rest in Newtown more widely and sincerely mourned.

"Hebrews of the Hebrews," Mr. Johnson was, in ancestry, linked by blood to many of Newtown's early families, and it was a happy Providence that turned his patient industry, his unrequited toil, his faithful research to the early, musty records of his native town. Who is left that carries in memory so much of Newtown's history, and who knows the intimate family details of Newtowners scattered far and near in our modern widening world? Who has the ardent zeal to carry on his valuable labors with a zest and perseverance that invested even his columns of names, and quotations from documents painfully and carefully searched out, with an aroma and halo all their own? He was Newtown's first and most devoted historian, and a prophet too little honored by those for whom he toiled so unselfishly.

No pent-up Utica shut in Mr. Johnson's searching gaze and so he knew not only his native town, but his native State, and native land as well. He was Newtown's most informing traveler and what he saw, the columns of The Bee circulated to eager and admiring readers far and near. Many of The Bee's readers learned geography anew and with an unwonted interest, when Mr. Johnson traveled and wrote. Even a broken hip, with a stiff leg and a cane, could not check his excursions or his overflow. How many a Newtown man or women in distant spot had memory thrilled and information furnished, as Mr. Johnson and his loyal wife stopped in with words of cheer and good will! Mr. Johnson never forgot that he was from Newtown, and that earliest affections and impressions are gladly recalled and give fresh life and motive power. Mr. Johnson seemed to have drunk from the fountain of perennial youth, so active his mind, so general his interest in to-day and the fresh innocence of childhood. His fellow citizens recognized this unfailing bouyancy of mind and honored themselves by keeping him on the School Board, in spite of four-score years, and the Church of his adoption was glad to honor him in an official way. Large and commanding in person, his qualities of mind and heart matched his frame. This made him a most excellent correspondent, for there was that upward look, that warmth of friendship, that half-concealed wit that made his letters so welcome. "I'm on 'tother side of 80," he wrote in May, "and on a steep down-hill grade. I do not forget that life, in its length, has been most lavishly dealt out to me, and the five senses are still in running order, although the axletrees are becoming worn and wobbly and all the while demanding more and more axle grease. I cannot be thankful enough that I still have my eyesight and reason, and wife and children still spared to me." In another cherished letter his unrequited spirit expressed itself: "How Time does fly! Eighty years have gone with me, and still there is a silver lining to each cloud, should one happen to be covering the sun when the evening shades are gathering." It often occurs to me that the world lost a brilliant writer when Newtown gained an indifferent farmer.

But Mr. Johnson's hold upon us was not so much of the brain as of the heart. Faithful he was. It was "Once a friend, always a friend" with him. Others might misunderstand and cast you off, but he—never. To meet him was to come into the sunshine. Others might repel and distress you. He understood and comforted you with that rare psychology more divine than human, because patient, unselfish, inspiring. I recall, riding with him as a big boy and meeting a man who had been under Mr Johnson's instruction, in the days when Cupid was playing pranks with him and his assistant, Miss Camp. How the man beamed as Mr. Johnson recalled those school days. Mr. Johnson, and his good wife as well, has been an uplift, a compelling force, in more lives than the world knows of. I may quote his own words of another, as applicable in his own case: "I am sure that he has the blessing of God upon his work, for he is so warmly welcomed in everybody's home, regardless of nationality, sect or social standing. He may, and does, make mistakes, but they are those of the head, not of the heart." Is it any wonder that such a man gave such a successful selectman to his town and a bishop to his Church?

The mind is cold, critical, the heart warm, bounding, and so Mr. Johnson's generosity overflowed to so many and in so many ways that he was like a fountain in the desert, a well-spring in the wilderness. Heaven alone will reveal what he and his have been to me and mine. I am not competent to speak here, but I know that I am not alone in sharing his royal bounty. How kindly and unostentatiously, how unselfishly he gave, whether it was a glad word and a welcome smile to a child that he had met, perhaps, in visiting the Newtown schools, or some relief in distress, gem set in memory like a diamond in its kingly crown! I remember once saying how poorly I felt myself able to repay some helpful act and his reply, "Pass it on to someone else." If earth is richer, sweeter, for such spirits in this harsh, relentless world, surely his Master must be glad to say, "Well done," to these cups of cold water in His name. The generous nature is tolerant and so was he. Holding his own opinion with firm reliance in his own integrity of purpose, he granted a like honesty of intent in others. He was easily Newtown's most loving servant, ready for his own part in the home, in the schools, in The Bee, in whatever helped to advance the town at present and to preserve the best in its past. Hence we not only esteem this memory but love it, and join in the general acclamation to the wealth and uprightness of his character.

THE BRIDGEPORT FARMER

Ezra Levan Johnson, who died at 82, is best known to the younger generation as the bard, historian and educator of Newtown, where he served upon the School Board for many years. But his contributions to the commonwealth were unusual, and to the older men he is known as one of the fathers of free education in this State, as a pioneer in the movement to secure instruction by trained teachers, as one of the foremost laymen of the Episcopal Church. He was a rugged, honest, intellectual man of the Lincoln type, advanced in his views, fearless in expression of his opinions and determined in any public effort that he undertook. His loss is to the town in which he lived and labored. He passed on in the peace of a certain and comfortable faith.

THE NEWTOWN BEE'S TRIBUTE.

Ezra Levan Johnson, Newtown's historian, and its most widely known and best beloved citizen, entered into rest, Sunday, Dec. 27, 1914, about 1.30 p. m. For some days previous, it was seen that the end was not far distant, but he passed peacefully away, as one lying down to sleep.

Throughout the early Fall, he had been active as usual and, in September, made his customary visits on the Dodgingtown, Hopewell, Pootatuck and Half Way River schools and the primary department of the Sandy Hook school, over which Mr. Johnson had immediate supervision. He was also able to attend church and enjoyed meeting friends. He took a deep interest in the Bi-Centennial services of the Congregational church, and was present at almost every session. In November, he began to fail and his decline from that time was rapid.

Ezra Levan Johnson was born Nov. 11, 1832, son of Charles and Julia Merritt Johnson. Mr. Johnson's ancestors, so far as Newtown records show, were as follows: Ichabod Johnson, great-great grandfather; John Johnson, great-grandfather; Ezra H. Johnson, grandfather; Charles Johnson, father.

Ezra H. Johnson died in 1857 and Charles Johnson in May, 1871. Ezra Levan Johnson received his early education in Newtown schools. He took a course at the State Normal school in New Britain and at Medina Academy, Medina, N. Y. He began teaching in Stony Hill district in Bethel at the age of 17. He also taught for a year at Clinton, Middlesex county. With these exceptions, Mr. Johnson gave his services to Newtown, teaching in South Center and Sandy Hook districts. So thoroughly were his services appreciated that older boys and girls from other districts in town came to have the benefit of his instruction. In 1856, he was elected to the Board of School Visitors and served continuously from that date to his death, a period of 58 years, a record unparalleled in this State of Connecticut. Up to the last his interest and sympathy in the work of the public schools continued unabated. His attitude toward all the teachers was helpful, rather than critical. And from his own experience, he was able to point the way out of difficulties and to give the word of encouragement, when needed and deserved.

In his young manhood, Mr. Johnson was an active member of the

Congregational Church, and superintendent of its Sunday school. He was also superintendent of a district Sunday school maintained for years in Huntingtown district. Later in life, he became a communicant of Trinity Church and at the time of his death was its honored senior warden.

Mr. Johnson's work as a local historian stands forth pre-eminently. At the Bi-Centennial of the town in 1905, Mr. Johnson was chairman of the executive committee having the celebration in charge, and was historian of the day. The citizens of the town are indebted to Mr. Johnson for painstaking work in local historical writing, which appeared from time to time in the columns of The Bee. To the editor and business manager of The Bee, he has always been a sympathetic and helpful friend, and it is with sorrow we are compelled to note the "passing on" of Mr. Johnson. To a large degree, it may be truthfully said, his outlook on life was unselfish, and in this lies the great secret of his success. Shortly after its organization, Mr. Johnson became a member of the Men's Club and served a term as president.

October 10, 1858, Mr. Johnson married Jane Eliza, daughter of Beach and Catherine Foote Camp, who survives him, with four sons: William Camp Johnson and Charles Beach Johnson of Newtown, Levan Merritt Johnson of Painesville, O., and Bishop Frederick Foote Johnson of St. Louis, Mo. To an unusual degree Mr Johnson has been blessed in his family relations and this first great break in the domestic chain must cause the deepest grief.

The funeral took place on Wednesday Dec. 30, at 2 p. m., from Trinity Church, and was one of the most largely attended in recent years. Rev. James Hardin George, rector of Trinity Church, officiated. With the rector in the chancel were Rev. George Thomas Linsley, rector of the Church of the Good Shepherd, Hartford, who read the lesson; Rev. George H. Buck of Derby, who read the creed and prayer, and Rev. Charles J. Sniffen of South Lee, Mass.

The two hymns sung were: "Jesus, lover of my soul," and, "O God, our help in ages past." For a recessional, this hymn was used: "Abide with me, fast falls the eventide."

Members of the vestry of Trinity Church, and of the Board of School Visitors, occupied seats together in the center of the church.

The pallbearers were the four sons. At the service at the grave, the rector was assisted by Rev. Mr. Sniffen. At the service at the house, before the start for the Church, Mr. George was assisted in the prayers by the Rev. F. W. Barnett.

There was a profusion of beautiful floral tributes from loving friends, including wreath from the vestry of Trinity Church, wreath from the Board of School Vistors, wreath from the Men's Club, floral piece from the teacher and pupils of Pootatuck school, flowers from the girls of Walnut Tree Hill, floral piece from Messrs Smith of the Bee and many others.

Among those present at the funeral from out of town were: Percy L. Johnson of Bridgeport, Mr. and Mrs. John C. Keeler of Seymour, Mrs. George Welch of Meriden, Miss Jennie Clark of Bethel, Frederick Maguire of Litchfield, A. C. Innis of New Milford,

1832 EZRA LEVAN JOHNSON 1856

1837 JANE ELIZA CAMP 1856

Camp Fam Name
many camp

EZRA L. JOHNSON 1866

JANE E. JOHNSON 1868

Mr. and Mrs. George Russell, of Southbury, Mr. and Mrs. Fred H. Beers of Brookfield.

Resolutions Adopted by the Vestry of Trinity Church on the Death of Ezra Levan Johnson.

The Vestry of Trinity church, speaking in behalf of all, old and young, in the parish, feels that in the death of Ezra Levan Johnson, our Senior Warden, we have sustained a great loss.

By birth and training not a member of our communion, Mr. Johnson came into it in the ripeness of his middle life, and was confirmed under the rectorship of Dr. Marble, by Bishop Williams, August 11, 1871. He at once took an active part in the parish work, and business and was chosen a Vestryman, April 14 1873. The record shows him constant at the meetings and faithful in the duties laid upon him. For more than 40 years he served the parish in this capacity. He was chosen Junior Warden at Easter, 1904, and Senior Warden at the annual parish meeting in 1913.

Because of his knowledge of town history, he was chosen the historian of the parish at the celebration in Sept., 1907, of the 175th anniversary of the beginning of Rev John Beach's ministry. It was his knowledge of tradition which located the spot where Mr. Beach's first service was held, the place now marked by the memorial boulder.

Mr. Johnson had a deep interest in the work of the Church at large, and for many years represented the parish in the diocesan convention, and became well known to leading churchmen throughout the State.

In church worship he had an unfailing joy. He was constant in his attendance, and the prayers and praises of divine service became a part of his life as their words were ever fresh in his memory. His presence at the Church's services and his regular family devotions, brought him a growing love of the Prayer Book and the Church's ways.

Loyal in his devotion to the Church, he yet had a broad sympathy for all Christians and an especially kind and loving feeling towards the communion in which he was born and reared; and he had the respect and good will of its members.

By his upright life before the world and his faithfulness to his religious duties he commemded to all men the Church which he loved.

We shall greatly miss his familiar form at the Church's services, and his wise council in our business deliberations. His example of a sober, righteous and godly life will have its lasting influence upon the parish and community, and his memory is blessed.

To his bereaved family we extend our sincere sympathy, and commend them to the God of all comfort and consolation.

HIS EPITAPH.

"The children loved him!" That was what they said
    When a kind man lay dead!

Ah, yes! and when he slept serene and still,
    From every glade and hill

The children brought bright flowers, pink and white,
    For his last day and night.

They loved him through their young untroubled years.
    They loved his smiles; his tears,

His sorrows and his loss they knew not of—
    They only knew his love,

For he was kind and he was gentle; best
    And surely happiest

When little children left their games and play
    To follow his glad way.

"The children loved him!" for he made them laugh.
    O! splendid epitaph!

              Selected by
                  Julia and Cynthia Merritt.

COPY OF DEED
Newtown's Purchase from the Indians.

Know all men by these presents, yt we Mauquash, Massumpas, Nunnawauk all belonging to Pootatuck in ye Colony of Connecticut for and in consideration of four guns, four broad cloth coats, four blankets, four ruffelly coats, four collars, ten shirts, ten pair of stockings, forty pounds of lead, ten of— ten pounds of powder and forty knives, to us promised to be paid as by these bills underhand and one may more fully approve, we say we have Given, Granted, Bargained and sold, alienated, Conveyed and Confirmed and by these presents do freely, fully and absolutely Give, Grant, Bargain, sell alienate, convey and confirm unto William Junos, Justus Bush and Samuel Hawley all now resident in Stratford in ye Colony aforesaid, a Certain Tract of land situate, lying and being in the Colony of Connecticut Butted and Bounded as followeth, viz. Bounded South upon pine swamp and land of Mr. Sherman and Mr. Rositer, South West upon Fairfield bounds, North West upon the bounds of Danbury, North East by land purchased by Milford men at or near ovanhonock and South East on land of Numaway an Indian, the line running two miles from the river right against pootatuck the sd tract of land Containing in length eight miles and in breadth five miles but more or less with all appurtenances, privileges and conditions thereunto belonging or in any wise appertaining to them, the said William Junos, Justus Bush and Samuel Hawley their heirs and assigns to have and to hold forever to their own proper use, benefit and behoof forever, and, we the said Mauquash, Massumpas and Nunnawauk for us our heirs and administrators do covenant promise and grant to and with the said William Junos, Justus Bush and Samuel Hawley their heirs and assigns yt before ye ensealing thereof, we are the true, sole and lawful owners of the above bargained premises and possessed of ye same in our own Right as a good, perfect and absolute estate of inheritance in fee simple, and have in ourselves good Right, full power, and authority to grant, bargain, sell, convey, alien and confirm the same and all the priviledges and particulars before mentioned in manner as above said, yt ye said Wm. Junos, Justus Bush and Samuel Hawley their heirs and assigns shall and may from time to time and at all times hereafter by virtue of these presents lawfully, peaceably and quietly, Have, hold up, occupy, possess and enjoy the said bargained premises with ye appurtenances free and alone and freely and clearly acquitted, exonerated and discharged of, and from all and all manner of former and other Gifts, Grant, Sales, losses, Mortgages, Wills, Intails, Joyntures, Dowries, Judgments, Enventory, Incumbrances, or other incumbrances whatsoever. Furthermore, we ye sd Mauquash, Massumpas and Nunnawauk, for ourselves, heirs, executors and administrators do covenant and engage the above described premises to them, the said William Junos, Justus Bush and Samuel Hawley, their heirs and assigns against the lawful claims or demands of any person or persons whatsoever forever hereafter, to warrant and defend. Moreover, we, Washunawanian, Wasuabye, Moctowek, Awashkoeum, Annuminobe, Mallocksqua, Jennohumpisho, Wompocowash, Munnaposh, Punuanta, Wannonio, Mosunksio, Tacoosh, Morammoo, Slickanungus, Susoouso, we and every one of us doth for ourselves and each of us by ourselves, do freely give grant and of our own voluntary mind resign to the said William Junos, Justus Bush and Samuel Hawley, all our right title and interest by possession, heirship or by any other way or means whatsoever. Witness our hands and seals July ye 25 in the fourth year of her Majesties Reign, Anno Domino, 1705. Signed Sealed and delivered in presence of Jacob Walker, Daniel Denton, Edward Hinman, Indian witnesses Obimosk, Nunako, Maquash and Musumeas.

Personally appeared at Potutuck and acknowledged ye above written instrument to be thare free and voluntary act and deed before me this 12th September 1705. Jon Minor Justice. Witness, Ebenezer Johnson.

The above written is a true copy of the original on file.

Test, Eleazor Kimberly, exactly entered and compared Jan. 22, 1710 per me. Joseph Curtis, one of the committee for Newtown.

QUIOMPH'S PURCHASE—1723

Several years passed after the Indians had sold the English, land eight miles in length and five miles or more in breadth, which in due time was to become the township of Newtown, "bounded easterly on Stratford and part of Fairfield, westerly upon Danbury and a line running from the southeast corner of Danbury parallel to the east line of said town to Fairfield bounds, northerly upon New Milford purchase, and the Great River, shall be one entire town known by the name of Newtown." In March, 1710, 22 proprietors took their pitch in the first allotment of land and other allotments were made from time to time as the years went by, with nothing appearing to disturb the even tenor of the settlers' way until about 1720, when there appeared upon the scene an Indian, Quiomph by name, who made claim to being sole owner of all land not sold to the English, claimed to be a strip of mountain land lying along the line of the Pootatuck brook at the base of Pisgah. The town records show the adjustment made between the land proprietors and Quiomph, as regards the land to which he laid claim. Interesting it should be, showing the friendly feeling between the whites who were getting possession by honest purchase. At a lawful town meeting of the inhabitants and landed proprietors of Newtown, Sept 1723, to consider what method to take for purchasing land lying southerly and westerly of Pootatuck river offered upon sale by Quiomph, Indian:

First, voted at above said meeting that all the land lying southerly and westerly of the Great or Pootatuck River, to be purchased of Quiomph shall be equally divided by heads of families, to each their equal proportion of purchase money, namely, each proprietor as above said.

Secondly, voted at said meeting that Mr. Thomas Bennitt and Johathan Booth shall be a committee in behalf of the proprietors aforesaid to purchase the said tract of land of Quiomph.

Thirdly, voted that the purchasers shall pay by next Wednesday, the 7th day of this instant, one shilling apiece; upon the neglect of payment of one shilling they are to lose their right of purchase.

Fourthly, voted that the whole purchase money that the above said committee shall agree upon shall be paid by the first week ensuing, which will be the fourteenth day of October, 1723. Upon the neglect of such payment to be made they shall lose their right in said tract.

Fifthly, no former grant or division shall be taken up within the boundary of the above said tract of land, purchased of said Quiomph.

Recorded by Joseph Peck, town clerk. The deed in folio form reads: "The proprietors of Newtown deed from Quiomph, Recorded January ye 21st, 1726, in ye 3d Book of Newtown Records, folio 74."

Per Joseph Peck, town clerk.

The leaves that contained the record are lost from the record book; the original deed is carefully preserved in the town clerk's office:

"Know all men by this instrument, bearing date this seventh day of August, in ye tenth year of his Majesties' reign, Anno Domine One thousand seven hundred and twenty-three, that I, Quiomph, an Indian of Pootatuck, do declare myself ye sole heir of all land that is not purchased by ye English before this date in ye boundaries of Newtown, in ye County of Fairfield within his Majesties colony of Connecticut, in New England. Now, in ye performance of ye convenant of ye one part, bargain and quit claim made between me ye sd Quiomph of ye one part and John Glover and Abraham Kimberly, purchasers for ye proprietors of Newtown, being their committee, and Thomas Bennitt being assisting with them of ye other part, witnesseth, that I Quiomph aforesaid, for, and in consideration of sixteen pounds in hand paid or promised to be paid where in I do acknowledge myself fully satisfied, have given, granted bargained, sold, allienated, made over and forever quit claim and confirmed and by these presents, do give, grant, bargain, sell, make over and forever quit claim unto John Glover and Abraham Kimberley, ye above said purchasers for the proprietors of Newtown in ye county of Fairfield and colony of Connecticut, all lands in ye boundaries of Newtown not purchased by ye English before ye date of these presents, except a corner of intervale land lying by ye river where Cock shures fence is bounded easterly by ye river and ye other side by a brook called Hucko by ye Indians, from ye river until ye brook comes down between ye hills, and from ye said brook where it comes down between ye hills a straight line direct to ye River, and ye reversion and reversions, ye remainder and remainders and rights, titles, interests, claims and demands whatsoever of me, ye sd Quomph, of, in, and to ye same to have and to hold all ye said grant, all which land claimed said Indian in ye boundaries of Newtown aforesaid except yt intervale land above expressed and all and singular ye premises with their and every of their appurtnances before to be mentioned to be granted to ye said John Glover and Abraham Kimberly, committee for ye proprietors of Newtown according to ye grant of ye General court to them as on record and to their heirs to ye use of said proprietors their heirs and assigns forever. And I, ye said Quiomph, of Pootatuck in Connecticut, have granted for me and my heirs that we will grant, warrant and defend unto ye sd John Glover and Abraham Kimberly, committee for ye proprietors of Newtown above sd their heirs executors, adminstrators, assigns, the above said land except ye intervale land and promises with and for their attorney against all people laying any lawful claim to ye same forevermore, by these presents. In witness of ye sd promises ye aforesaid Quiomph hath hereunto sett his hand and put to his seal, the day and year above written.

Quiomph his (x) mark.

Signed, sealed and delivered in presence of Robert Seeley, Euniss Bennitt, Indian witnesses: Mauchoro, Wahuncop, Machocomp, Mausumpus.

Quiomph, the above subscriber to this instrument personally appeared in Newtown the day and date above said and acknowledged the same to be his own free act and deed. Before me, Thomas Bennitt, Justice of the Peace."

Although the land was purchased, the deed made out and the money paid in 1732, before any measurements were taken or the land laid out, it evidently was shared in by the then proprietors of the town, who at that time numbered 51 and so there were 51 equal proprietors in what became known as the Quiomph purchase. After the purchase, this wild mountain land lay undivided and unmeasured until 1742. In the meantime, Peter Hubbell, a land proprietor, had bought at different times 49 rights of the fifty-one, and a proprietors' committee was appointed to lay out the Quiomph purchase, January 25, 1748.

"Then laid out to Peter Hubbell, Esq., his heirs and assigns, or to his or their assigns according to ye several parcels of land which they hold by deeds from him, or his heirs or assigns according to ye several proportions expressed by sd deeds of ye lands known by ye name of Quiomph's last purchase ye sd Hubbell having formerly bought at several different times ye rights of 49 out of 51 equal proprietors in sd Quiomph purchase and ye same as not being laid out or divided according to ye vote of ye proprietors of Newtown, therefore we ye subscribers at ye desire of ye sd Peter Hubbell have laid out ye greater part of ye 49 rights in ye following manner: Beginning at a black oak tree marked and stones put to it, which is commonly known to be ye bounds for ye southwest corner of ye aforesaid Quiomph purchase, and then running north 5 degrees west in ye west line of sd purchase 426 rods to a heap of stones laid to a small spier then east five degrees north 75 rods to a heap of stones, then north 5 degrees west 11 rods to a heap of stones laid betwist a bunch of large alder bushes, then east to 5 degrees north one hundred rods to black oak spier marked and stoned, then north five degrees west sixty rods to a large black oak tree standing on ye bank of ye Great Pootatuck River, then easterly and southeasterly and southerly by sd Great River in all 295 rods to a white oak spier marked and in or near ye dividing line of ye Indians land, and ye land of Mr. Read of Boston, 71 rods at ye brook near to ye sd Hubbell's dwelling house and then due west 33 rods to ye southeast corner of Samuel Towner's land, then westerly by sd Towner's land 60 rods to a black oak spier marked, then south 6 degrees east 30 rods to a pine at ye top of ledge of rocks known by ye name of second Pisgah towards the easterly part thereof, then went 15 degrees south 72 rods to ye southeast corner of Mallery land, then southwesterly by ye top of sd Pisgah to Sanford's mill land and then westerly by said mill land to ye northwest corner thereof, and from thence in a straight line to ye black oak began at within which limits and boundaries is contained one hundred and ninety-one acres and a half, twenty acres of which is allowed for ye highways that is already laid out through ye said tract, above said, land which we look upon as necessary yet to be laid out in ye same. Completed ye day and date above said by us.

John Glover, Junr.
Joseph Botsford,
Peter Hubbell,
Proprietors Committee.

And to ratify and confirm ye doings as above set forth we, John Glover and Daniel Foot who were chosen a committee to lay out ye above sd purchase, have hereunto set our hands.

Daniel Foot,
John Glover.

Recorded ye day and date above by me Job Sherman, Proprietors' clerk. January 26, 1748.

The original deed was placed on file with the Town Clerk and was by him recorded as "The Proprietors of Newtown deed from Quiomph. Recorded January ye 21st, 1726, in ye third Book of Newtown Records, folio 74.

Per Joseph Peck Town Clerk.

The first three record books of those early days, dating back of 1730, became coverless many, many years ago, although the first volume remained well intact, but the greater part of the leaves of the second and third volumes were lost, and among the leaves were those which contained the record of Quiomph's deed. Between 1873 and 1880, Charles Henry Peck was Newtown's town clerk, and being extremely interested in the town history and a persistent student of it, he was so troubled in mind, when he saw the dilapidated condition of the three coverless volumes of records of those early days, that he gathered the remains of the three volumes and had them rebound within one cover. It has been from his thoughtfulness as to their preservation that so much can be gathered of the doings of those earliest days. Not content with having the remnants of the these first volumes bound into one, he also had the original deed from Quiomph bound between covers for preservation, to be handed down to coming generations. It is a wonder that the deed could have been preserved in folio form, among other loose papers, for 100 years or more. Of the two deeds that passed between the Indians and the English, the original of the first transaction has been lost, but the recorded deed can be found, commencing on Page 48, Volume 1, and of the second deed, the original is well preserved in the Town Clerk's office, but the recorded deed was lost when the third volume fell to pieces.

"BEARING EACH OTHER'S BURDENS"

In the early part of my study of town history, before I had become much interested therein, my attention was arrested by a line sentence close to the very edge of the top of a page in Vol 1, Newtown records, which made no particular impression upon my mind at the time. It read, "A Court of election at Hartford, May 9, 1678." Following out the clue, it proved the key to open an interesting bit of history closely related to individual and family life. The transaction referred to dates back to May, 1678 and reads:

"A court of Election at Hartford, May 9, 1678. This court grants John Hubbell in consideration of his loss of one of his fingers and one ear, etc., one hundred acres of land provided he takes it upon where it may not prejudice any former grant to a plantation or particular person. Extracted out of the Court Record.

Per John Allyn Secretary.

Transferred as in ye copy. December ye 25th, 1712. Per me John Glover, Recorder.

Reading carefully, we see that the grant of land referred to was given no definite location, nor was there any stated time within which it must be taken up. The grantor could take it up in any part of Connecticut colony he might choose. Not until 32 years had passed do we hear anything more about it, when it appears that John Hubbell's two sons, acting in their father's stead, took up the 100-acre grant in Newtown and sold it to John Glover, who was fast becoming an extensive land owner. The following record of the sale forms interesting reading and we wish we could also transfer the "annexed figure" as the pen picture looks upon the old record, giving the lines and angles with their geometrical disproportions.

"Newtown, March ye 7th, 1710.

The Court was pleased to grant to Mr. John Hubbell in consideration of his loss of his finger and ear, etc., one hundred acres of land. Mr. John Glover hath bought sd grant of Mr. John Hubbell's sons as may appear from these bonds and seals on ye back side of ye copy of Court Grant and I being at Mr. John Glover's house ye day above in Newtown he desired me to assist him to lay out sd hundred acres near his own land where he had about 60 acres formerly laid out by persons appointed and there being a slip of land between Mr. Glover's land and a mountain, (NE) also sd Glover has a great part of this 100 acres yt taken up within fence and for pasturage land.

The manner and form as it lies and distance is showed in ye annexed figure or plott which quantity is not above one hundred acres.

As per me, William Thompson, Surveyor.

Recorded December 25, 1712, per me John Glover, Recorder."

Following the record of the sale of the land to John Glover, we have the declaration of John Hubbell's sons that they have sold for a valuable consideration this land.

"We, Richard Hubbell and Josiah Hubbell, the sons of John Hubbell, within mentioned in ye grant of ye election court in May ye 9th, 1678, we say we do for a valuable consideration by us in hand received sell and make over all our right, title and interest in ye said grant of ye aforesaid Court unto Mr. John Glover of Newtown, his heirs and assigns forever.

Witness our hands and seals, October 10, 1710.

Signed, sealed and delivered in presence of Joshua Judson and Caleb Galpin.

October ye 2nd, 1710, Richard and Josiah Hubbell personally appeared before me and acknowledge this instrument to be their free act and deed.

James Judson, Justice.

Recorded on ye backside of ye copy of sd Court Grant, December 25, 1712, per me, John Glover, recorder."

In this brief space is collected all that can be gathered as to that land transaction so long ago. To the writer it has a deep interest not devoid of pathos. It is one of many instances that crop out from the silent pages of Newtown's unwritten history. The grant of land was given for the loss of a finger, an ear, etc.

We would like to know what the "and so forth" included. We would like to know how the misfortune came. Was it from skirmishing with a hostile foe?

Whatever the cause, a sympathy corresponding to the misfortune showed itself by a substantial acknowledgement from the colony, verifying the Scriptural adage, that "when one member suffers, all the members suffer with it."

QUANNEAPAGUE,
The Home of The Pootatucks.

The oldest people in Newtown, Newtown born, are of the sixth generation in direct line of descent from the first settlers, so that information they can give of the town's earliest history must be from reminiscenses or as gathered from the earliest of the town records. When Jeremiah Turner and Samuel Sanford were each in turn given liberty to set a grist mill in the west part of town on "Quanneapague Brook," and were to have two parcels of land, one of which was a sixteen-acre tract "lying in ye crotch of Quanneapague pond," we have the evidence that our beautiful inland lake, nestled down between the hills for aught we know "since the morning stars first sang together," was known by that name when the white man looked upon it for the first time. If it was handed down to the first and second generation of our ancestors, it long since became obsolete, but when the land now comprised in the town of Newtown was purchased it was known by the Indian name, Quanneapague. To prove this, we copy from the first volume of town records five separate transactions of sale of petition rights, each independent of the others in 1710 and 1711. The question may arise, "What is meant by 'petition rights?'" In 1708, the General Court of the colony of Connecticut granted to certain petitioners "that all that tract of land lying on the west side of Stratford and part of Fairfield, westerly by Danbury and a line running from the southeast corner of Danbury to Fairfield bounds, northerly by New Milford Purchase, shall be one entire town, called by name of Newtown."

QUANNEAPAGUE
TAUNTON POND
From the South End
See Page 18

QUANNEAPAGUE
TAUNTON POND
North End
See Page 18

SOUTH MAIN STREET
Looking North

SCUDDER—SMITH RESIDENCE
South End Newtown Street

Among the Privileges Granted

Among the privileges granted those who might become inhabitants was that of free liberty to purchase by petition a parcel or tract that might be claimed by any Indian or others, and a right and privilege at all times in all lands that should be common in the town. An individual wishing to purchase a piece of land independently of "pitch" or general division would petition the General Court of the colony, which held two sessions yearly, in May and October, for the privilege, and, if the Court consented to the request, the petition was granted and he was given what was called in law a "petition right" by which he could take land where he chose that was common land, subject only to the requirements of the General Court. To illustrate:

Upon the request of Captain Ebenezer Johnson, this Court grants him liberty to purchase of the Indians about one acre and half of the land that was set out to them by the town of Milford, it being unsuitable for the Indians and very advantageous to said Johnson to set his fence upon it, also having some meadow in it. This Court grants said Captain Johnson's request. Colonial Records, Vol. 4, of Connecticut.

That land was bought by a "petition right" and a person having from the Court a petition right could sell the right to any person, if he did not care to use it himself. These several recorded sales of "petition rights," taken from Vol. 1 of Newtown's Records, each say: "In that tract of land called by ye name of Quanneapague and now known by ye name of Newtown."

DEED 1.—Be it known unto all men by these presents yt I, ye sd John Minor of Woodbury in ye county of Fairfield in Her Majesty's Colony of Connecticut have by these presents, given, granted, alienated, sold and confirmed to yt sd John Burrowsh, his heirs and assigns forever, my right in ye sd Newtown or Quanneapague in virtue of our petition to ye late General Court at Hartford, the which petition right for several reasons and particular for two (undecipherable) in hand received, or good security for ye same, peaceably to have, hold and occupy and improve ye sd premises, with all ye privileages and conveniences therof from ye date hereof for ever and for ye confirmation thereof, to all intents and purposes I hereto subscribe this 16th day of January, 1710,   John Minor.

Witnessed by us: Daniel Beardsly, Thomas Sherwood.

The above named John Minor ye same day of ye date of ye above written deed and acknowledged it to be his free act and deed. John Minor, Justice.

Exactly entered from ye original deed and compared. September 7, 1710. Joseph Curtis, assistant clerk.

DEEDS 2 and 3—These may signify to whom it may concern that we whose names are underwritten have sold unto Richard Hubbell of Stratfield one petition right (by grant from ye General Court) at Newtown, (alias) Quanneapague, dated in Stratfield, April 1st, 1709. Witness our hands,
    Samuel Hubbell, Jr.
    David Whitlock, Jr.

Exactly recorded from ye original and compared March 6, 1710, per me, Joseph Curtis, one of ye Committee for Newtown.—Vol. 1, Page 44, Town Records.

Know all men by these presents yt I, John Burross of Stratfield in ye County of Fairfield, have by these presents given, granted, bargained and sold from me and my heirs, executors and administrators and assigns, forever, all my right, titles and interest in and unto a petition right I purchased of Captain Minor of Woodbury of land granted by ye General Assembly to sd Minor lying in ye bounds of Quanneapague or Newtown I say I have sold unto Richard Nichols of Stratford in ye County of Fairfield to him, his heirs and assigns forever for a valuable consideration to pay 10 pounds in money at eight shillings ye ounce troy weight ye which

I acknowledge ye receipt of to my full satisfaction and for ye confirmation of ye above sd, I have hereunto set my hand and seal, at Stratfield, April 27, 1710. John Burross.

Deed 4—To all Christian people to whom these presents shall come, greeting. Know ye, that whereas I, Benjamin Nichols, inhabitant in the town of Stratford, in ye county of Fairfield, Colony of Connecticut in New England, being one of ye petitioners to ye General Assembly of this province for a right in ye tract of land commonly called by the name of Quanneapogue, and now by the name of Newtown, sd petition being granted, I, having a certain right therein, I, ye sd Benjamin Nicolls have sold, and do by these presents alienate, set over, and sell to Joseph Fairchild of ye above town, county and colony, ye whole of my above sd right with all of ye appertenances and privileges thereto belonging both as to ye present and future ye are or may be here to belonging for him ye sd Joseph Fairchild, his heirs, executors or assigns for ever to hold, occupy, possess and enjoy and yt without any let, molestation, hindrance or disturbance from me, my heirs or assigns forever, hereby acknowledging to have already received in full satisfaction therefore. In testimony of ye above written I have hereunto set to my hand and seal in Stratford, June 14, 1710. Benjamin Nicholls.

Benjamin Nicolls, ye subscriber to ye above instrument personally appeared in Stratford on ye 21st day of December, 1710, and acknowledge ye above instrument to which he had signed and sealed to be his own free act and deed.

Joseph Curtis, assistant clerk.

Deed 5 INDENTURE—This indenture made this fifth day of November, in ye tenth year of her Majesty's reign, Anno Domini, one thousand seven hundred and eleven, between Joseph Botsford of Milford, planter, in ye county of New Haven, within Her Majesty's Colony of Connecticut in New England of ye one party, and Joseph Peck of Milford aforesaid ye other party, witnesseth that Joseph Botsford of aforesaid, for and in consideration of a certain parcel or division of land situate in Milford aforesaid being ye fifty-second lot in ye second shoot, containing twelve acres, more or less lying on ye race bounded with Timothy Baldwin's land northward, and a high-way, and east and westward, and John Merwin's land southward to him, ye sd Botsford made over by a bill of exchange under ye hand and seal of ye sd Peck being equal date and indentured with these presents which to ye full satisfaction of ye sd Botsford hath granted, bargained and exchanged and by these presents doth freely, firmly and absolutely grant, bargain, exchange, alienate and make over unto Joseph Peck aforesaid, and to his heirs and assigns forever, one moity or half a right, sometimes called a "petition right" in that tract of land called by ye name of "Quanneapogue" and now known by ye name of Newtown in ye County of Fairfield and Colony aforesaid, ye whole right being a forty-ninth part of ye whole tract of land, ye other moity of ye sd right being for a valuable consideration already sold by ye sd Botsford to sd Peck and his heirs forever, is hereby ratified and confirmed however hereafter it may be butted and bounded when it shall be divided and a petition made of ye whole or any part of ye aforesaid tract of land, together with all ye present and future privileges and to have and to hold both ye moities or whole of ye aforesaid right or forty-ninth part of ye aforesaid tract of land to him ye sd Joseph Peck, his heirs and assigns as a free, absolute and indefeazable estate of inheritance to his and their proper use, behoofe and benefit forever, and further, ye sd Joseph Botsford doth for himself and his heirs covenant and promise to and with ye sd Joseph Peck and his heirs and assignees that he and they shall quietly and peaceably have, hold, use and enjoy ye aforsaid right or forty-ninth part of ye aforesaid tract of land called Newtown with ye privileges and appurtenances therein to belonging from person or persons whatsover, that shall lay any legal claim thereunto or any part thereon forever.

In witness of ye above premises ye aforesaid Joseph Botsford has hereunto set his hand and put to his seal ye day and year first above written.

Joseph Botsford, seal

Milford, November 5 1711.

Joseph Botsford of Milford, subscriber to ye above written instrument personally appeared and acknowledged ye above writen instrument to be

his act and deed before me.
Jonathan Law,
Justice of the peace.

Signed, sealed and delivered in the presence of Richard Baldwin, Thomas Baldwin. Exactly entered from ye original sigment, November 28, 1711, by me, Peter Hubbell, recorder.

FIRST GRIST MILL

About six years after the land had been purchased from the Indians, although they had been busy all the time, a wilderness still surrounded them, and they were practically cut off from the outside world. Sickness was soon to come, and sorrow and death might follow. What more natural than that they should feel lonely with no well regulated method of "assembling of themselves together," for the one common purpose of religious sympathy and helpfulness?

Next to the settling of a minister and the building of a meeting house, the getting of a grist mill that would grind the town's grain was matter for serious consideration, being an absolute necessity. The records show no action to give any one liberty to take water for power until 1711. No artificial ponds had been made, but there was the "Great Pond," as spoken of, the Indian name of which was "Quanneapague." With no mill for grinding grain, the pioneers had from the first been obliged to use a mortar and pestle as the Indians did, or go to Stratford on horseback (for they had no wagons) for the nearest mill.

At a town meeting at the house of Daniel Foot, 1711, it was " voted that Benjamin Sherman, Ebenezer Prindle and Samuel Sanford should view ye pond and see if it would contain a grist mill."

"Voted that Jermiah Turner should have liberty to build a grist mill, and ye inhabitants do promise to give ye sd Turner 40 square acres adjoining to ye mill."

At a town meeting Dec. 24, 1711, at the house of Daniel Foot it was "voted for Poodertook brook to get a grist mill on Poodertook brook."

In the meantime, negotiations had got so far along with Jeremiah Turner that the inhabitants chose Abraham Kimberly and Turner chose John Platt to pick out the 40 acres he was to have for building the mill on Pond Brook, but Turner for some unexplained reason did not build the mill.

At another town meeting Feb. 12, 1712, it was "voted that Samuel Sanford shall have the liberty to get a grist mill upon ye Pond Brook that Jeremiah Turner had."

"Voted that Abraham Kimberly, Ebenezer Prindle and John Griffin be instructed to draw articles of agreement with sd Sanford as fast as may be."

The articles of agreement: "To all people to whom these presents shall come, we agents for ye Town of Newtown, in ye county of Fairfield and Colony of Connecticut in New England, authorized by ye sd Town by a vote of ye sd Town at a meeting of ye sd town on ye eleventh day of January last past, as by ye record doth appear, do sign, seal and deliver an instrument of ye sd Town's behalf for ye conveying and passing over unto Samuel Sanford and his heirs and assigns forever, two parcells of land hereafter described upon this condition. That ye aforesaid Sanford of Newtown, aforesaid, and his heirs and assigns do erect and maintain a grist mill on Quanapague brook in Newtown aforesaid or such other place as sd Town shall assign and convey for such an improvement and so attend ye same as that sufficient stores may be thereby ground for 50 families of Newtown, allowing reasonable time for repairing and rebuilding as occasion shall require, and grinding. Know ye that whereas by instrument bearing date of ye 15th of March, 1712, the sd Town did convenant to convey and confirm unto ye sd Sanford and his heirs and assigns on ye conditions therein mentioned and ye sd Sanford being now in a fair way to accomplish ye erecting of a grist mill, for ye further encouragement we ye aforesaid agents for ye town of Newtown, do on ye sd Town's behalf, by virtue of ye above sd authority above recited by these presents firmly and absolutely grant, make over, and confirm on ye conditions above described, unto ye sd Samuel Sanford and his heirs and assigns forever two parcells of land situated in Newtown afore sd, one of which parcells containing 16 acres lying in ye notch of Quannapague Pond aforesaid bounded with an highway on ye northwest, ye other parcel containing 24 acres lying on ye northwest side of ye aforesaid highway and bounded on all other sides with common land, together with all the privileges and appurtenainces unto them belonging, to have and to hold to him, his heirs and assigns forever, on ye conditions above exprest as free land upon all accounts whatsoever excepting only non-performance of ye conditions above sd indefeazable estate of inheritance to his and their own use and benefit forever. Reserving only to ye sd Town, liberty upon ye failure of sd Sanford and his heirs or assigns in any part of ye conditions aforesaid to enter and take ye above granted lands and premises. And further, we the aforesaid agents on ye behalf of ye sd Town and their successors, do, to, and with ye sd Sanford, his heirs and assigns covenant and promise ye sd Sanford, his heirs and assigns in ye quiet and peaceable possession of ye above granted land appurtenances during ye whole time and term of his and their performances of sd conditions according to ye true intent and meaning thereof against all and every person or persons whatsoever that shall lay and legal claim unto ye premises or any part thereof to warrant and defend forever.

Witness whereof we have hereunto sett our hands and seal.

    Samuel Sanford   (Seal)
    Abraham Kimberly   (Seal)
    Ebenezar Prindle   (Seal)
        his
    John (X) Grifin   (Seal)
       mark

Witness,
Jno. Leavenworth,
John Foote,
September 12, 1713.

    John Peck, Recorder.

A year or more passed and as neither Turner nor Sanford entered into agreement with the town to build a mill on Pond or Quannapague brook another town meeting was called to take further action in regard to getting a grist mill.

At a lawful town meeting, December 14, 1714, of ye settled and aproved enhabitants of Newtown being duly notified met and assembled together made choice of Thomas Bennitt, Abraham Kimberly and Daniel Foot a comity in behalf of ye town to agree with Samuel Sanford about ye land and stream laying under Mount Pizza and to draw articles of agreement with him for ye building and erecting a grist mill there for ye youse of ye Town and what land sd Samuel Sanford takes up about sd stream he is to lay off as much from his 40 acres of land at ye Pond."

Recorded per me
    Joseph Peck, Town Clerk.

In accordance with the vote of the town, the committee conferred with Samuel Sanford; these articles of agreement were drawn up between the town of Newtown and Sanford, to which Samuel Sanford agreed:

"To all Christian people to whom these presents shall come. We agents for ye town of Newtown in ye County of Fairfield and Colony of Connecticut in New England authorized by ye sd Town by vote on December 14, 1714, to sign, seal and deliver an instrument on ye sd Town's behalf unto Samuel Sanford and his heirs and assigns forever, that is to say a certain parcell of land lying under a mountain known by ye name of Pisga, that is to say, all ye land lying under sd mountain to ye bend of ye brook commonly called Pohtertuck Brook, so called, with all ye land belonging to us southward of ye sd mountain to ye farms called Old Farms all sd land thus granted bounding eastwardly on ye eastward bank of ye aforesaid brook to him ye sd Sanfor, his heirs and assigns forever, provided ye sd Sanford throw up with sizer in quantity out of his forty acres of mill land ye sd Sanford hath Liberty to take up ye same for part of his 60 acres pitch, provided that ye sd Sanford erecteth and buildeth a good grist mill sufficient for ye supply of ye Town of Newtown at or before ye 20th of August next, upon Pohtotuck Brook, provided that ye sd Sanford maketh a good mill seasonably, allways allowing suitable time for repairing or rebuilding, we ye above sd agents, in ye Town's behalf, engage yt no other grist mill shall be erected to ye damage of sd Sanford so long as he sd Sanford doth supply ye sd Town with good mills and for ye full performance of ye above sd premises we bind ourselves, our heirs, executors or administrators or assigns forever. In witness hereof we have set our hands and seals in Newtown, this 14th day of December, 1714, in ye first year of our sovereign Lord George.

Signed, sealed and delivered in presence of us.

        Joseph Gray   (Seal)
        Peter Hubbell   (Seal)
        Samuel Sanford (Seal)
        Thomas Bennitt (Seal)
        Abraham Kimberly (Seal)
        Daniel Foot   (Seal)

September 21, 1715.
  Joseph Peck, Recorder.

The articles of agreement were duly signed and witnessed, work on the foundation was immediately commenced and in due time the mill, with a limited assortment of machinery, was announced as ready for use. What a real treasure a good picture of the first mill would be to the antiquarian of today! No need that it be large, for the town called for one only large enough to furnish 50 families and it could be enlarged as necessity required. The records give no account of public celebration over its completion, but we can have no doubt that in the homes of those godly families prayers of thanksgiving were offered to the Giver of all good that, in addition to the blessings in their personal and family life by having a minister settled among them, they were also to have the means wherewith the grain they raised could be the more easily and effectually transformed into the "staff of life."

It may be a surprise to some that the first grist mill was located where the building long known as the Niantic mill stands. It served its purpose well during Samuel Sanford's life and for many years after his death, the town took entire charge of running the mill.

Samuel Sanford was about 30 years of age when he came to Newtown from Milford, Conn. In 1711, the year Newtown was incorporated a town, he was one of three chosen as selectmen at the first annual town meeting, Dec. 4, 1711. William Atwater Sanford, sixth generation in direct line of descent, who has compiled a book of the Sanford family, has this to say of him: "He was the father of ten children, seven of them born in Milford and three in Newtown." Of John, second grandson of John Sanford, the writer says: "He was one of the largest landholders in Sandy Hook. He was called 'Squire John." Leaving considerable property to his heirs, his son Elijah received the major part, which included the cotton mill erected on the site of the grist mill built by Samuel Sanford, that still stands on the banks of the stream flowing through the village; also a grist mill several hundred feet below, which is still used for the purpose for which it was originally built.

When Elijah Sanford died, the mill property passed into the hands of his son, David Sanford, and from him to his son, William, grandson of Elijah. A long stretch of years it stood in the Sanford name and is owned now by Patrick Campbell. Oft repaired and somewhat dull from age, it serves the public, though not exactly as of old, when all the work was custom work, as the farmers raised the grain they used and the miller got his living from the toll he took for grinding, and laid by some cash for a rainy day. Now most of the grain for grinding, coming from the West, the farmer goes to mill with an empty wagon and money in his pocket, to return with his wagon full but pockets empty and, perchance, an increase of the debit side of the account.

The motive power of the old mill has not yet been superseded by steam or electricity, as the power still comes from the sparkling waters of the Pootatuck, the same old stream, with the same old Indian name, which, though differently spelled than of old, is a name musical in our ears, whose waters, ever beautiful to look upon as they ripple along in sunshine or in shade, until lost in the quiet restfulness of the pond below, are again let loose to move the great machinery of the rubber works and from thence pursue checkered, fascinating wanderings through wooded glen and quiet meadows, to find outlet in the waters of our beautiful river, the Housatonic.

THE FIRST SAWMILL

Almost as imperative as the necessity for a Grist Mill, was the necessity for a Sawmill.

March 17, 1712, the town voted, that Mr. Benjamin Sherman and Capt. John Holley and John Sely shall have Liberty to get a Saw mill on ye deep Brook South of ye Town Reserved and ordered four Rods on ye west Side of ye Sawmill for A gangway and ordered that iff any man draws any Log or Logs into sd Gangway ys sd Log or Logs to be forfitt to ye Town, Except sd Logs are drawn or put into sd Gangway to be sawed forthwith before any other Logs at sd mill.

Dec. 24 1713. Voted and agreed upon yt ye proprietors of ye town do freely give and grant liberty to Ebenezer Smith, James Hard, Jerimiah Turner, John Seely and Joseph Gray of Newtown, to build and erect a sawmill on ye Half Way River, so called, North west of Darby road down near Stratford, or on Pohtatook River, and as much land as shall be needful for ye use of sd saw mill so long as sd persons shall erect a mill there, provided they will saw for ye town to ye halves all such timber and logs as ye inhabitants shall bring to this mill and for two shillings six pence per hundred in pay for Whitewood and Chesnut, it is also granted yt they shall have liberty of a convenient passage to ye Great River yt ye owners of sd mill and ye inhabitants of ye town may have ye advantage of ye transportation of their timber, plank, boards and slit work where they shall see cause to make sail of ye timber—and sd partners are to build ye sawmill in two years time or else expect to lose ye sd stream. Also voted Joseph Gray and Jeremiah Turner are chosen a Committee to lay out concerning ye land for sd Mill and a Highway to ye Great River called Stratford River.

Voted and agreed and ordered four rods on ye west side of ye sawmill for a gangway and ordered yt if any man draws any log or logs into sd

gangway yt sd log or logs to be forfitt to ye town except sd log or logs are drawn or put into sd gangway to be sawed forthwith before any other logs at sd mill.
             John Glover
              Town Clerk.

December 24, 1713

John Glover enters caution upon ye land he hath taken up on ye north side of ye Half Way River so called at ye mouth of sd River where it emptieth into ye Great River, that it be not taken from him for no use or pretense whatsoever.
             Test John Glover
              Town Clerk.

The same year as above, the town Voted that Thomas Bennitt, John Burr and Peter Hubbell shall have liberty to set a sawmill on Potatuck Brook any where near ye Great River, within 60 Rods of ye Great River Provided they ye above sd persons build ye sd mill in ye space of three years.
          Test John Glover town Clerk.

In 1712 it was voted and agreed That Joseph Dudley shall have liberty to get a fulling-mill on the Deep Brook above the saw-mill and the use of half an acre about his mill so long as he maintain a sufficient fulling-mill thereon the Deep Brook provided he do not damnify the saw mill.

Deep brook is the stream that crosses the highway in South Center district.

GRANTING TOWN RIGHTS

Power to choose Town Officers. Compulsory Attendance at Town Meeting Settling Bounds With Indians. First Pitches of Land.

Town rights were granted Newtown by the General Court of Connecticut colony in May, 1708.

At a general assembly holden at New Haven, Oct. 11, 1711: Whereas ye general assembly of this colony holden at Hartford in May last, upon ye petition of ye inhabitants of Newtown did appoint Capt. John Hawley and Mr. Benjamin Sherman of Stratford and Mr. John Platt of sd Newtown to be a committee to lay out such divisions of land within ye sd Newtown with ye advice of Mr James Beebie and Mr Thomas Taylor of Danbury as should be agreed upon by ye proprietors thereof, and to make a return of the findings therein to this assembly at this time, and ye sd committee in persuance of ye sd act or order, having lately had a general meeting of ye sd proprietors and their agreement in order for laying out a certain division on sundry lots of land within ye sd town of Newtown, have thereupon proceeded and laid out ye same and have now made their return thereof to this Assembly which sd return having been now considered ye same is allowed and approved by this assembly and ordered to be kept on file. And whereas ye above sd committee by ye desire and on ye behalf of ye proprietors and inhabitants of sd Newtown have now petitioned to this assembly to have all such town liberties and privileges granted to them as all other towns in this colony generally have and enjoy, and a figure for a brand mark for their horses to be appointed for them, upon consideration whereof this assembly do give and grant unto sd proprietors and inhabitants of ye sd town of Newtown all such liberties, privileges and powers in all respects whatsoever as all other towns in this colony generally have and do enjoy, and do order and appoint ye figure 7 to be ye town "Brand Mark" for their horses, and it is ordered and enacted by this assembly that the present committee of sd Newtown shall give seasonable notice and warning to all ye proprietors and inhabitants thereof to convene together in a general town meeting within ye sd town some time in ye month of December next upon a day and at a place by him appointed for ye choosing of all town officers as ye law directs.

A true copy of ye record.
  Caleb Stanley, Clerk of Court.
Entered by me, December ye 23, 1711.
        Stanley Glover, Recorder.

Oct. 2, 1911, Newtown held its 200th annual town meeting. Of more than 800 electors enrolled in the town, 649 ballots were cast, showing that the wheels of town government set in motion 200 years ago have continued to revolve under varying conditions.

The year 1911 marked 200 years from the time when the town was given power by the General Court of the Colony to elect minor officers, and a town clerk, constable, surveyor of highways, field driver and fence viewer were chosen, each of whom had to journey to Danbury to take the oath of office, after which such business as would not conflict with the laws of the General Court could be legally transacted in anticipation of the time when full privileges would be granted. The election of these officials was in May 1711. The first allotment of land was made in March, 1710. The second allotment of land was made easterly and adjoining the first in the summer of 1711, and on this second plot the village of Newtown was laid out. It was in 1711, too, that by vote of the proprietors, one acre and a half of land was set apart in which to bury their dead. Newtown's first business meeting was held at the house of Peter Hubbell. The attendance could not have been large, because in 1716, Newtown had 30 families; allowing one voter to a family, the show of hands must of necessity have been few. The meeting was held on the 24th day of September, 1711, when it voted that Peter Hubbell should be Newtown's first town clerk, which office he held until 1714.

"Voted, yt Abraham Kimberly should be constable for ye year ensuing."

"Voted, yt Ebenezer Prindle and Thomas Sharp should be surveyors of highways for ye year ensuing."

"Voted, yt Johathan Booth shall be field driver or hayward for ye year ensuing."

"Voted, yt Joseph Gray and Daniel Foot shall be fence viewers."

"Voted, yt Thomas Lake shall slip his 20 acre division and take it on the west side of ye rhoad against ye heither part of New Haven plain westerly of sd plain to be laid out by ye committee upon ye sd Lake's charge."

"Voted, yt each proprietor containing ye number of 48 shall forthwith as soon as can conveniently be done have four acres of meadow apiece laid out by ye committee, ye sd committee to lay out ye same in ye great meadow at ye south end of ye town lying on ye Deep Brook, and ye meadow at ye north end of ye town where it may be as convenient either under Mount Tom or elsewhere, as also four acres of meadow for ye ministry as ye rest are laid out, and it is to be understood and it is voted, yt swamp land that is suitable is accepted as meadow and so to be laid out, ye sd committee to size ye whole meadow and swamp land and ye proprietors to draw for ye lots as hath been usual, unless they order otherwise.

Peter Hubbell, clerk.

The first annual town meeting, held at the house of Daniel Foot.

"Voted, yt Ebenezer Pringle should be selectman or townsman ye year ensuing, and again voted, yt Samuel Sanford and John Platt should also be townsmen for ye year ensuing."

"Voted, that Peter Hubbell should be town clerk."

"Voted, that John Griffin and Benjamin Dunning should be surveyors of highways.

"Voted, yt Daniel Foote and Joseph Gray should be fence viewers for ye year and Jonathan Booth should be hayward."

"Voted, yt Ebenezer Prindle and John Platt and Samuel Sanford should be listers and collectors for ye year and Abraham Kimberly should be brander of horses."

"Voted, yt Peter Hubbell, Ebenezer Prindle, Benjamin Sherman, Abraham Kimberly and Joseph Gray shall be a committee to lay out divisions of land and highways for ye year ensuing."

"Voted, that Benjamin Sherman, Ebenezer Prindle and John Griffin should view ye pond and see if it would contain a grist mill."

"Voted, yt Jeremiah Turner should have liberty to build a grist mill and ye inhabitants do promise to give ye sd Turner 40 acres of land adjoining ye sd mill. The proprietors do also ask for Mr. Phineas Fisk to come and give them another visit. John Glover protests against it."

"Voted and it is enacted ordered and declared by authority of ye same, that all and every person or persons truly and legally notified to give their attendance at ye several and respective town meetings yt hereafter shall be and shall refuse or neglect to attend on ye sd town meetings at time and place, shall pay ye sum of three shillings to ye treasury of ye town except ye fine be remitted and released by ye town."

"It is further enacted and ordered by this Assembly aforesaid, that it is and shall be, for ye time being and from time to time, true and legal notice for all town meetings to any person or persons, to be notified by ye selectman or ye constable or by any other meet or fit person constituted or empowered by them, or yt ye town shall impower, which notice shall be given with ye time and place to ye person or persons, given or left at ye place or ye usual abode and a certificate or declaration from ye person so notifying as above expressed is and shall be a sufficient warrant for ye Recorder to record ye meeting lawful and lawfully convened."

Peter Hubbell, town clerk.

Later on it was voted and agreed upon "that ye warning for town meetings for ye future shall be given by setting up notifications by ye selectmen at three certain places ten days before ye sd meeting, namely at or near ye oak tree near Sargeant Joseph Botsford, one at ye pound, and one at ye oak tree near Jonathan Booth's house, which shall be sufficient warning to ye inhabitants of Newtown."

At the same meeting it was further agreed that ye inhabitants aforesaid should make choice of John Glover, James Hard, Jeremiah Turner and John Platt, a committee to measure ye land and settle ye bounds with ye Indians of that purchase which William Junos purchased of ye Indians with his associates in ye boundary of Newtown and to request Col. Johnson and Captain Minor's assistance to declare to ye Indians what land they sold by ye deed.

"Also to procure four gallons of rum to treat ye Indians and to refresh themselves and charge ye town for ye same and all other charges and trouble necessary in completing ye same."

It was further "voted to lay out 60 acres of land for every right or rights of ye sd inhabitants of ye town two miles distant from ye center of ye town and as far further as any man shall please to lay by way of pitches according to ye following lay or draft: Daniel Foot ye first pitch, Edward Fairchild ye second, Job Sherman ye third, John Lake ye fourth, Widow Sharp ye fifth, John Dunning ye sixth, Ebenezer Prindle ye seventh, Peter Hubbell ye eighth, John Glover ye ninth, John Burr ye tenth, John Seely ye eleventh, Freegrace Adams ye twelfth, Matthew Sherman ye thirteenth, Benjamin Dunning ye fourteenth, Samuel Ferris ye fifteenth, Jeremiah Turner ye sixteenth, Jonathan Booth ye seventeenth, Abraham Kimberly ye eighteenth, John Platt ye nineteenth, Samuel Sanford ye twentieth, and the balance of those who drew the 60 acre pitches, in the order their names are writen up, to the number of 42, viz: Josiah Burritt, John Griffin, Joseph Gray, Stephen Parmalee, Daniel Jackson, James Glover, John Blackman, Thomas Bradley, Joseph Miles, Jonathan Hubbell, Stephen Parmalee, Capt. John Holly, Ebenezer Smith, Nathan Baldwin, Josiah Curtis, John Bardslee, Samuel Beers, Alice Brions heirs, Thomas Bennitt, Mr Rood, Ebenezer Booth."

It should be remembered that these 60 acre "pitches" were made two miles or more from the center of the town and, Jan. 29, 1712, it was voted in town meeting to lay out ten acres of land, which was done. Because of unfair means used, another town meeting was held on February ye second, 1712, which was held at the house of Daniel Foot, when it was voted to revoke and disallow of ye lot that was drawn, January 29, 1712, for ye ten acre division within ye two miles because of some unfair dealings by some persons in drawing ye same and ye town for ye reasons aforesaid judged ye lot aforesaid to be unlawful and came to a new draft. Peter Hubbell protests against it, yet notwithstanding his protests, he, ye aforesaid Hubbell, voted as usual when it was put to a vote to know whether ye first lot should stand, and ye town at ye above sd town meeting above written came to a new draft for pitching for ye ten acre division, which is to be laid out within ye two miles, which is as followeth in the order in which the pitches were drawn, viz: John Glover, John Burr, Ebenezer Smith, Widow Sharp, Samuel Sanford, Stephen Parmalee, John Glover, Thomas Braase, Jonathan Mills, James Brisco, James Hard, Peter Hubbell, Jeremiah Turner, Abraham Kimberly, Daniel Foot, Samuel Ferris, John Blackman, Edward Fairchild, Jonathan Booth, John Lake, Joseph Osborne, Josiah Burritt, Samual Beers, Mrs Alice Bryan's heirs, Eben Booth, Joseph Peck, John Platt, Joseph Dudley, Abram Storo, Joseph Miles, Ebenezer Prindle, Freegrace Adams, John Seeley, Benjamin Dunning, Mrs Rood, Josiah Curtis, Matthew Sherman, Job Sherman, John Morris, Daniel Jackson, John Dunen, Capt. Halley, Jonathan Hubbell, John Griffin, Nathan Baldwin, Joseph Gray, Thomas Bennitt, John Bardslee. The town voted to allow to ye ten acres for distance from ye center of Newtown, two acres a man for two miles, one acre and a half for one mile and a half, and one acre for one mile.

These early pioneers, coming to Newtown from Milford, Stratford, Guilford, New Haven, Derby and elsewhere, pitched for land not only to make themselves homes, but also to become tillers of the soil and nation builders as well.

As announcements were made of drawings for "pitches" of land on certain dates the freeholders were expected to be present. At the "pitch" made Dec., 1712, 42 pitches were taken. These were 60-acre pitches, two miles and over outside the center of the town, only one man drawing two pitches, determining the number present to have been 41.

In Jan. 1713, a second pitch was announced, this time to be a ten-acre pitch within two miles of the center, at which 49 pitches were taken, one man taking three pitches, showing there were 47 freeholders present, qualified to meet the requirements necessary to have the right to draw a number for a "pitch." How long "pitching" for land continued is not certain, but there came a time when the town sold tracts of common and undivided land, which continued until the township at large became individual property.

To raise money to meet town expenses, a town meeting held, Aug. 18, 1713, "voted, determined and agreed and settled to levy all their town charges and rates both town and minister's rates upon each petition rate proportionably. Voted to make choice of Mr. Thomas Bennitt to cite all those that hold tracts of farm land within ye boundaries of Newtown to appear before ye next General Court to be held ye next October at New Haven to give ye reason why they ought not to pay rates in Newtown to ye ministers and school, except they will agree to pay, and will pay without their being cited."

John Glover, Town Clerk.

Another town meeting, two weeks later, Sept. 1, 1713, "voted and agreed to give ten shillings per head for those wolves that were killed by ye inhabitants before this date, and for further encouragement after ye date of those presents, if any inhabitant shall kill or destroy any grown wolf or wolves within ye bounds of Newtown he shall have 15 shillings per head and half as much for a wolf's whelp yt suck."

It was also voted and agreed that every right or allotment shall bear an equal proportion of ye charge ye proprietors have been at from ye time when sd proprietors had town privileges granted by ye General Court, to January, 1714.

Also voted that every right or allotment for defraying ye charge ye proprietors have been at to ye above mentioned date of January, 1714, shall pay ye sum of 17 shillings as money.

PITCHING FOR LAND.
Proposition of John Glover. Proprietors' Meetings. Settling disputed Boundary Line Between Stratford and Newtown.

For the first 75 years of Newtown's life, town meetings were frequent. The laws of the General Court made it obligatory to hold the annual town meeting in December, at which time town officers were chosen and provisions made for the management of town affairs. Politics cut no figure in any department of the town's business life.

There were also proprietary rights considered at what were called proprietors' meetings, that were held when, by petition, they were called for. The care, the use and the disposal of common land was a frequent theme for discussion and plans were devised by which proprietors' meetings would act in harmony with town officials. The first business was to settle a long disputed claim in regard to the line between Stratford and Newtown, which was run by the county surveyor after the land had been purchased from the Indians. Up to this time their chief concern had been to pitch for land, and settle disputes and differences that might arise.

My grandfather, born in 1772, used to tell me in my younger days, and others of his time told me the same, that land holders as far down as 1800 looked upon swamp land as being more valuable than upland, as they depended so much upon swamps for their hay for winter use, while they turned upland to corn, wheat, flax, buckwheat, potatoes and oats; that too rocky to plow was sheep pasture. Swamp land was called meadow land.

At a proprietors' meeting, Sept. 24, 1711, it was voted that Thomas Lake shall slip his 20 acre division and take it on ye west side of the road against ye neither part of New Haven Plain westerly of sd plain to be laid out by ye sd committee at sd Lake's charge and that each proprietor containing ye number of 48 shall forthwith as soon as can conveniently be done, have four acres of meadow apiece laid out by ye committee, ye sd committee to lay out same in ye great meadow at ye south end of ye town lying on ye Deep Brook and ye meadow lying on ye north end of ye town where it may be as convenient, either under Mount Tom or elsewhere, and also four acres of meadow for ye ministry as ye rest are laid out, and it is understood and it is voted that swamp land that is suitable is accepted as meadow and so to be laid out. The sd committee to size ye whole meadow and swamp land and ye proprietors to draw for ye lots as hath been usual, unless they order otherwise.

Peter Hubbell, Town Clerk."

March 4, 1712, it was also "voted for ye committee to begin on ye north side of Mr. Sherman's mile square, (Queen street divides it now, 1910) for ye four-acre division so far as it will hold out, and as near elsewhere as it may be found to make up ye number of 49 lots."

It was also voted, March 10, 1712, that ye land on ye north side of Mr Sherman's mile square shall be laid out in a general field and for every petitioner to have an equal share in ye "general field," be it more or less, and that after lots are laid out timber and stone shall be free for any man till improvement be made by ye owners of such lots. The improvement is to be understood fencing and ye committee shall have three pence per acre for laying small divisions.

April 2, 1712, it was "voted for to take ye four-acre divisions that is to be laid out in "pitches" and that ye proprietors shall go eight in a company and draw by figures, 1, 2, 3, 4, 5, 6, 7, 8, 9, and so on until the whole number of 49 lots be drawn, and laid out. Also voted that John Glover shall have his "pitch" at ye rear of his home lot, to ye east and north of ye highway, so far as it will hold out, and ye sd Glover will pay to ye town treasurer twelve shillings for his "pitch."

Voted that if any of ye proprietors don't agree when ye time comes for to "pitch" they shall lose their pitch and ye next shall take it successively, and ye seventh day of April shall be ye day for ye first company to pitch, and successively till they have done, excepting foul weather hinders.

Peter Hubbell, Recorder."

In February, 1712, a ten-acre pitch for 49 pitches meant 490 acres additional ownership. The act was carried out under a vote passed "to lay out ten acre of land to each petition right any where within two miles from ye center of ye town by way of pitches. except ye land lying on ye north side of ye Deep Brook from Abraham Kimberly's point to where ye brook runs into Mr. Sherman's farm to ye south end of ye town. Also at ye northwest end of ye town from ye north corner of John Glover's 20 acre lot to Mr Rood's 12 acre lot, ye line to be south of Bear swamp from thence to ye north corner of Josiah Burritt's 20 acre lot, according to ye following draft, except any man fail when it comes to his pitch, then the next man to fall in and take his pitch by possession. Ye sd ten acres of land is to begin to be pitched for, and laid out ye February second 1712, and to be sized by ye committee.

Ye pitches, Josiah Curtis ye 1, Job Sherman ye 2; Peter Hubbell, ye 3; Joseph Gray, ye 4; John Dunning, ye 5; Joseph Miles, ye 6; Abraham Kimberly, ye 7; Ebenezer Booth, ye 8; Jeremiah Turner, ye 9; Nathan Baldwin, ye 10; Samuel Ferris, ye 11; John Glover, ye 12; minister, ye 13; Daniel Foot, ye 14; Freegrace Adams, ye 15; James Hard, ye 16; John Glover, ye 17; John Platt, ye 18; Mathew Sherman, ye 19; Mr. Rood, ye 20, 22, 26; Benjamin Dunning, ye 24; John Burns, ye 25; Capt. Halley, ye 27; Widow Sharp, ye 28; Ebenezer Prindle, ye 29; John Beardsley, ye 30; Thomas, ye 31; Jonathan Booth, ye 32; Daniel Jackson, ye 33; Samuel Sanford, ye 34; Joseph Osborn, ye 35; Ebenezer Smith, ye 36; Jonathan Hubbell, ye 37; Joseph Peck, ye 38; John Morris, ye 39; John Griffin, ye 40; James Bisco, ye 41; Stephen Parmalee, ye 42; Joseph Dudley, ye 43; Jonathan Mills, ye 44; John Seely, ye 45; John Blackman, ye 46; Edward Fairchild, ye 47; Samuel Beers, ye 48; Thomas Bennitt, ye 49.

This offer from John Glover was laid before the proprietors' meeting; I, John Glover, of Newtown, County of Fairfield in Connecticut, do declare yt I do give liberty for 48 families with myself to take up and settle all that tract of land I bought of William Junos as ye deed on record will show what land I, ye sd Glover, have, which land sd Glover gives liberty to be settled at will forever, or to loan with reference what ye town shall give for ye fee simple of sd land, except what sd Glover has taken up according to court grant, and my petition rights, ye fee simple thereof reserved to myself.

John Glover."

The proprietors made choice of Capt. John Halley of Stratford and Peter Hubbell of Newtown and empowered them to act, and to represent ye town and also to choose a man to arbitrate and make up all contrivences between ye town and John Glover aforesaid, and John Glover to choose another man, which arbitrators are to determine what ye town shall pay to sd Glover for his native rights in Newtown as offered, and the town at a town meeting agreed to and with John Glover to bind themselves and heirs in a bond of ten thousand pounds to John Glover and his heirs, to stand by ye award of ye arbitration of ye two arbitrators which are to be indifferently chosen.

Entered John Glover, Town Clerk."

Call of the proprietors of Newtown to elect a proprietors clerk:

"At a meeting of the proprietors of Newtown warned by authority as the law directs for such cases, holden May ye 4, 1724, the bisness to be attended att sd proprietors' meeting is to make choice of a proprietors' clerk to consult about a pattent for the Township of Newtown, to pitch upon a time when to begin to lay out ye 30 acre division, and to do something about ye land yt Mr John Reed has laid out in ye neck so-called above ye Pond Brook. Peter Hubbell by ye vote of the proprietors chosen proprietors' clerk and sworn by Thomas Bennitt, justice. This meeting adjourned to ye 13th day of instant May at 5 of ye clock afternoon. At an adjourned meeting agreed and voted held May 13, 1724, to warn ye proprietors' meeting in Newtown by notifications set up in writing to be set up in three several places in Newtown, one at ye north end of ye town near Capt Thomas Bennitt's and on, at or near Abraham Kimberly's shop and ye other near Joseph Botsford's house which notifications are to be set up by ye proprietors' clerk as the law directs six days before ye meeting and ye proprietors are to be assembled or to convene together at ye beat of ye drum at time and place appointed, which methods are to stand good till ye proprietors see cause to alter ye same.

Peter Hubbell, Clerk."

"Newtown, April ye 3, 1725, att a proprietors' meeting legally called and warned by ye proprietors' clerk to make choice of some persons to meet Stratford committy at the head boundary between Stratford and Fairfield on ye fifth day of instant April att tenn of ye forenoon. Then made choice and elected Reverend Thomas Tousey, Mr. John Glover, Mr. John Leavenworth, Mr. Joseph Peck and Mr. Ephriam Peck a committy to settle ye head line between Stratford and Newtown and to use any leagale measures for ye accomplishing the same, and in case there shall arise any dispute between Stratford agents and above said committee yt we do empower the committee above named or any three of them agreeing to leave ye desition of that matter to three uninterested gentlemen that shall be mutually chosen by both partys, and upon their award to sett down forever satisfied as they in their wisdom shall think fitt. To be understood that the work of choosing three uninterested gentlemen to determine as above exprest, is refered to ye above sd committy for ye proprietors of Newtown as far as it concerns ye part of Newtown. This meeting adjourned to ye ninth day of April at five of ye clock afternoon.

Peter Hubbell, Clerk."

"Agreement as to the lines between Stratford and Newtown. This writing witnesseth that Mr. Thomas Tousey, Mr. John Glover, Mr. Joseph Peck and Mr. Ephriam Peck, proprietors and committee and agents for Newtown and Mr Joseph Curtiss, Capt. James Lewis, Mr. John Wilcokson, Mr Joseph Judson, Selectmen of Stratford and committee for sd town to settle the line between Stratford and Newtown for final issue and determination of all differences between said towns have mutually agreed respecting sd bounds of Stratford and Newtown as followeth. Begining at the northwest corner bounds betwixt Stratford and Fairfield a due cross line as already run by Ensigne Edmund Lewis, County surveyor, which line runs upon a due cross line from sd northwest corner on the south or southerly side of ye swamp called Monkantick swamp and so upon a strait line to ye brook or river called ye Half Way River and there the said river until it emptieth itself into the Grate River, which river and straight line from the northwest come aforesaid to be the north bounds of Stratford and ye fixed bounds between Stratford and Newtown, according to means and bounderies now erected by said Edmund Lewis, county surveyor. A straight due cross line as bounds are set by sd surveyor from the northwest corner bounds aforesaid to the half way brook and from thence the sd brook to be the bounds between the sd town as aforesaid. In witness whereof and for confirmation of ye above boundaries betwixt the sd town of Stratford and Newtown is confirmed by the committee of each town subscribing as agents for sd towns, this 19th day of April, 1725.

On this 29th day of April, 1725, I declare by my subscription hereunto my concurrence in and with above sd agreement.

Committee for Stratford.
Joseph Curtis,
James Lewis,
John Wilcokson Jr.,
Joseph Judson.
Committee for Newtown.
John Glover,
Thomas Tousey,
Joseph Peck.

Entered this 28th day of December, 1725, per me, Peter Hubbell, Clerk.

PITCHING FOR MEADOW LAND,
In ye Great Boggs and ye Little Boggs and Elsewhere.

Pitching for land means drawing by lot. At the town meeting in September, 1711, it was voted to take two pitches for meadow land, the one to be under Mount Tom, and the other to be below Deep brook.

Mount Tom is the name given more than 200 years ago to the highest point in the range of hills running northerly from Walnut Tree hill to Hanover. Through the intervale at the base of the hill's western slope flows the stream that feeds what is known as Foundry Pond (the town's skating rink every mid-winter) flowing on in serpentine course until it enters the Pootatuck near the village of Sandy Hook still remembered by its old name, Tom brook.

The other drawing by lot arranged for at this meeting was to be south of Deep brook. That swamp land lay and still lies as swamp, part of which is still mown, and the balance is a maple swamp. It lies on the west side of the railroad, as you round the rock curve about a mile south of Newtown station. Forty eight proprietors (and that was all the town numbered in 1711) were to draw lots, and the lots were to contain four acres each.

At a town meeting, Sept. 24, 1711, it was voted that each proprietor to the number of 48 shall forthwith as soon as can conveniently be done have four acres of meadow apiece laid out by ye committe, the said committee to lay out ye same in ye great meadow at ye south end of ye town lying on ye Deep Brook and ye meadow at ye north end of ye town where it may be convenient either under Mount Tom or elsewhere. Also four acres of meadow for ye ministry as ye rest are laid out, and it is understood and it is voted that swamp land that is suitable is accepted as meadow and so to be laid out, ye sd committee to size ye whole meadow and swamp land and ye proprietors to draw for ye lots as hath been usual unless they order otherwise.

Voted that for to take ye four acre division that is to be laid out by "pitches."

Voted, that the proprietors shall go eight in a company and draw by figures as 1, 2, 3, 4, 5, 6, 7, 8, till ye whole number of 48 lots be laid out. Voted yt Abraham Kimberly shall draw for all of ye proprietors of ye town.

Voted that if any of ye proprietors of ye town don't agree when ye time comes for to pitch they shall lose their pitch and ye next shall take it successively.

Voted yt ye 7th day of April, shall be ye day for ye first company to pitch and successively till they have done, excepting foul weather hinders.

In 1716 the town voted another drawing of meadow lots at ye Great Boggs and ye Little Boggs. As we drive from Newtown street to Bethel, by what is known as the lower road, when we have driven a half mile or so we drop into a valley of swamp land on either side of the road, passing through maple swamp and open swamp, some of which is still mown, while on either side is as fertile upland meadow and pasture as one need rest their eyes upon. We drive on a little further and enter another strip of low land thickly wooded, until we come to what is still known as Morgan's four corners. We enter this long strip of swampy land at what is known on the records as the Head of the Meadow from which the school district, first called on the records Scoschia, then Sugar Street. The records tell us that the drawing for meadow land was made at the head of the meadow in the Great Boggs and the Little Boggs.

At a town meeting, Jan. 12, 1716, "It was voted to lay out ye Great Boggs lying at ye head of ye northwest sprain of Pootatuck brook sou'west from ye town, in ye bounds of sd town, and ye little meadow also lying about half a mile easterly on ye stream that comes out of ye great bogs.

Also voted that ye above sd two pieces of meadow land above mentioned shall be equally divided to each proprietor by a Sizer, what is wanting in quality to be made up in quantity.

Voted also at sd meeting that James Hard, Jeremiah Turner, Daniel Foot, and Peter Hubbell be a committee and are empowered to lay out ye above granted division of meadow land by Sizure according to their best judgment.

Joseph Peck, Recorder."

Feb. 5, 1716, "It was voted that John Lake and John Bristol shall be and are empowered to lay out ye above granted divisions of meadow land with ye committee above named.

Joseph Peck, Clerk."

February 8, 1716, "Agreed and voted to draw ye meadow lotts laid out in ye great Boggs and Little Boggs. This division of land was granted January 12, 1716, February 11, 1717. We ye subscribers hereof a committee for laying out ye Great Boggs and ye Little Boggs near adjoining according to ye trust reposed in us have been upon and accomplished sd work in manner following: The lot on ye north side of ye brook in ye Great Boggs, ye most eastward lot of ye tier of lots lies on ye side of ye Brook bounding eastwardly on land of John Griffin, north on ye upland, south on ye brook and after ye manner ye rest on ye tier. The division ye first column of figures showing ye number of ye lots, ye second ye width at ye upland or swamp, ye third ye width at ye brook. The number in all being 50 according to ye number of rights. The lots on ye south side of ye Brook begining on John Griffin's land, there being allowance for private highways through all ye lots on ye south brook till it comes to a highway between ye 28th and 29th lots and where any lots do not join to ye upland there is allowance in ye next lots to get along from ye cross highway to ye upland. Att ye north easterly corner of ye Great Boggs laid out two lots against ye northerly end of ye 29th, 30th, 31st lots, ye 34th joining upon them and ye 35th joining upon ye 34th so yt between them there is liberty for a private highway."

Then follow the names of those who draw lots, in the order in which they drew, up to the number of 50, the whole number of proprietors.

Joseph Blackman, 1; Samuel Prindle, 2; John Glover, 3; Mr Glover, 4; John Read, 5; Edward Fairchild, 6; John Read, 7; Jehew Burr, 8; Ephriam Peck, 9; Daniel Jackson, 10; Samuel Samp and John Golot, 11; Daniel Fott, 12; Daniel Baldwin, 13; Samuel Beers, 14; Ebenezer Prindle, 15; John Grffin and John Treadwell, 16; Mathew Sherman, 17; John Read, 18; John Seely, 19; Joseph Peck, 20; Hullhens and James Hard, 21; Job Sherman, 22; Thomas Bracy and Jeremiah Northrupp, 23; Peter Hubbell, 24; Jonathan Hubbell, 25; Thomas Bennitt, 26; Jonathan Booth, 27; Benjamin Dunning, 28; Ephraim Osborn, 29; Freegrace Adams, 30; Moses Johnson, 31; Abraham Kimberly, 32; Samuel Ferris, 33; Ebenezer Johnson, 34; Samuel Sanford, 35; John Read, 36; Josiah Bennitt, 37; Thomas Toucey, 38; John Lake, 39; Jeremiah Turner, 40; Mr Tousey, 41; Thomas Sharp's heirs, 42; Joseph Gray, 43; Capt. Halley, 44; Capt. Curtis, 45; Ebenezer Booth, 46; John Platt, 47; Eleazer Morris, 48; Joseph Bristol, 49; Stephen Parmalee, 50.

Peter Hubbell,
Daniel Fott,
Joseph Bristol,
Committee.
Recorded March 25, 1717.
Joseph Peck, Town Clerk."

Aug. 1, 1717, following the lay out of meadow land, a town meeting was called and the following resolutions adopted:

"Whereas there was a division of meadow land granted to each Right or Proprietor of Newtown, January 12, 1717 (viz) to each Petition Right, their equal proportion of land by sizure, the two tracts of meadow land lying at ye head of ye nor'west sprain of ye Pohtatuck brook sou'west from ye town in ye bounds of sd Newtown, which is called ye Great Boggs and ye Little Boggs, lying about half a mile down ye same stream, also a committee appointed to lay out ye same and ye committee have finished their work and made return of their doings, and each proprietor's lot is recorded, as now fully appears on reccord. Whereas, Mr. Daniel Burr, Senr. of Fairfield, and Mr. Samuel Burr, ye son of Major John Burr, deceased, do lay claim to ye aforesaid Boggs, therefore at a lawful meeting of ye proprietors of Newtown this August 1, 1717, then agreed and voted that if any of ye aforesaid Burrs, or any person or persons representing sd gentlemen, shall molest any particular proprietor or proprietors in ye improvement of their meadow lots and prosecute any proprietor in a court of law that each proprietor having in either of ye above sd tracts of meadow a lott shall pay his or their equal proportion of all ye charges yt shall arise in going through ye law to try title of land with ye Burrs in defending of ye aforesaid tract of meadow land.

Entered August ye 1st, 1717, per Joseph Peck, Town Clerk."

As no law-suit followed the drawing of the meadow lots, the owners held them in peaceable possession free to dispose of them by sale or otherwise.

NEWTOWN'S FIRST MEETING HOUSE

A Brief History of its Building, Furnishing and Moving, with Sketch of the Present Church Edifice.

Could we dissociate the past from the present and see Newtown Street as it was when the meeting house was built and when the Town House was built, I am sure we could the more readily enter into the spirit of those times and realize more fully how things were, but that is difficult especially for those in middle life or younger. Children are thinking of the present, young people of the near future, while those in middle life, busy with the cares increasing about them, are ever looking forward to the time when they may hope to lay down life's greater burdens and engage in retrospection. It is left to the aged to find their greatest pleasure in dwelling upon the past, and recalling forms and faces of those who started on life,s journey with them, and of happenings of childhood, of early life, and of later years, if, perchance, their lives have been lived in or near the ancestral home.

The first action taken about building a meeting house was at a town meeting Nov. 23, 1713. when it was "Voted, that John Glover, James Hard and Ebenezer Smith be a committee to hire workmen on ye town's account to build a meeting house to serve God in, 40 foot long and 32 foot between Joynts."

We find nothing further referring to the matter until Dec. 26, 1717, and on the day following. No written agreement was entered into and for some unknown reason it fell through. Naught appears again on record about a meeting house until Nov. 18, 1718.

In the spring of 1718, the Colonial Court, convened at Hartford, came to the aid of the proprietors in their attempt to build a meeting house, by laying a tax of one penny an acre yearly for four years. The vote:

"The proprietors of farm to pay at that rate for so many acres as they have by grant, and every proprietor of a right to pay for 400 acres proportionately for any part of a right, and all that have purchased any quantity of land in sd town to pay according to ye number of acres expressed in their deeds, all ye money to be raised by this tax to be improved for building a meeting house."

May 15, 1719, the town "voted that ye committee for ye care of erecting a meeting house shall have power to defer ye time for ye completion of ye sd house according to agreement until June in ye year of 1720."

In the meantime Thomas Scidmore, inhabitant and landed proprietor in Newtown, came forward with an offer to build a meeting house on certain conditions which led to the calling of a town meeting on Nov. 18, 1718, to act upon the proposition of Thomas Scidmore, the result being as follows:

'Voted, that whereas Thomas Scidmore hath made offer to this town for ye sum of 45 pounds to get and hew all ye timber for a meeting house of dimensions as followeth and to frame it workmanlike, viz., In length, 30 foot, in breadth 36 foot and between joynts 20 foot, and also to cover it, the sides with clabbord and the ruff with short shingles, the town finding nails and boards to shingle on, and to do all ye carting, and whereas the Town doth comply with his motion, it is by this meeting voted Mr John Glover, Mr Thomas Bennitt and Mr Joseph Peck shall be a committe and shall have full power to concert all matters necessary with sd Scidmore relating to sd work in behalf of ye town. Draw writing with sd person consarning aforementioned work, thereby to bring him under due obligations and to render him secure with respect to ye payment of ye aforesaid 45 pounds, upon his answering of ye engagement, also that sd committee shall have full power to oversee sd work and to do and get done whatsoever shall be necessary to the carrying on or perfecting of it until sd Scidmore shall have answered the proposals above mentioned."

Joseph Peck, Town Clerk.

With the contract let for building the meeting house, the next matter was its location. At a town meeting Jan. 8, 1719, it was "voted and agreed that the Cross Lane or that by John Platt's or rather where the lane that runs easterly and westerly intersects the maine town street or the street that runs northerly and southerly shall be ye place to set or erect the meeting house or house for carrying on ye public worship of God that is already agreed upon to be built."

Joseph Peck, Town Clerk.

January 27, 1720, another town meeting was called when it was "agreed, concluded and voted that an addition of 20 feet should be made to ye meeting house, which was agreed upon now, to be 50 feet in length. Further voted that Thomas Bennitt, James Peck and Jeremiah Turner should be and are appointed by this vote in behalfe of this town to covenant and agree with Thomas Scidmore to frame and cover ye above 20 feet added to ye meeting house, also to take ye whole care and oversee of getting ye shingles, clabboards and other stuff."

One can readily see that for 45 pounds, which in our money would be less than $225, the building, finished according to contract, must have been not much more than a barn, and even 20 feet added to its length, making its entire length 50 feet, would not add to its comfort, while it would add much to the aggregate expense. We will show from the records that making the interior comfortable and convenient was the slow work of years.

The records show that, though unfinished, it was ready to occupy before Rev. Thomas Toucey resigned in 1724, because one pew was built for ye use of ye Rev. Mr. Toucey's family.

When Mr Toucey's successor, Rev. Elisha Kent, came, a pew was built for ye Rev. Mr Kent's family. With these exceptions there were nothing but wide benches for seats and no other furnishings save an open fire place where they could roll on logs for bodily comfort.

Things remained in this way until 1735, when at a town meeting April 22, 1735, it was "voted and agreed that ye Presbyterian society shall as soon as may be, erect and set up in ye Presbyterian meeting house on ye north side six fationable pews, three on either side of the pulpit, and ye tax to defray ye charge of building ye same if there be money enough, to be paid by ye town but if not, then ye sd society to defray ye charge of ye above sd pews." Also "voted that there is liberty to build two pews more, one on ye west side of Mr Kent's pew and ye other on ye east side of Mr Tousee's pew, so as not to damnify ye gallery stairs, which pews are to be built at ye cost of ye particular persons that ye committy shall allow, they bearing their proportion of ye charges of finishing ye meeting house notwithstanding."

Joseph Peck, Town Clerk.

Nothing more was done towards making the interior of the meeting house more comfortable or attractive until after the installation of the Rev. David Judson in 1743.

December 9, 1745, the society "voted to proceed so far in ye finishing of our publick meeting house as to lay ye gallery floor and erect a fore seet and also ye gallery stairs. A rate of three pence on the pound was laid and Heth Peck, Donald Grant and Deacon Bennitt were appointed to look after the work, to whom Abel Booth, Alexander Bryan and Caleb Baldwin were added later. Within two months £230 was raised which decided the society, January 30, 1746, to lay it out, "in rectifying ye underpinning, in rectifying ye gable ends and in puting on good fine boards and if subscription shall be more than sufficient for doing all ye aforesaid outside work, with glass and nails, that what remains shall be laid out on ye inside of ye house so far as it is consistent with ye prudent and advantageous management, and whatever more was necessary to ye outside of ye house to make it fationable."

In the spring of 1746, it was voted to build a "bellfree." The galleries were still without seats and April 24, 1749, "a rate of 12 pence on the pound was laid for finishing ye meeting house as to ye galeries and plastering over head or any other work in sd house which shall be seen needful. Jeremiah Northrop, Abram Bennitt, John Botsford and Caleb Baldwin were in charge of the work.

In 1762 Captain Amos Botsford, Lieutenant Nathaniel Brisco, Gideon Botsford, Ebenezer Ford, and Caleb Baldwin 3rd were appointed a committee "to build a steeple at ye east end of ye meeting house if there shall be money enough signed to build ye same." At a society's meeting, Sept. 6, 1762, Captain Amos Botsford and Lieutenant Nathaniel Brisco promised " that at their own cost and charge they would procure a good bell of about 500 pounds weight fit to hang in ye steeple and that it shall be for ye use of sd society as long as there shall be a Presbiterian society to meet in ye above sd meeting house, that is to say, if ye above sd society will go on to complete ye steeple, fix ye outside of ye meeting house and culler it and culler ye pulpit and ye society voted to go on and finish ye steeple and culler ye house and culler ye pulpit according to ye proposal."

January 4, 1763, "Voted that ye work of fixing ye meeting house should be completed by November 1, 1763, at which vote passed, Captain Amos Botsford and Lieutenant Nathaniel Brisco made open declaration that they freely and frankly gave ye bell, which they had procured for ye use of ye society so long as there should be a Presbiterian society to meet in sd house."

Up to this time Stephen Parmalee had been hired to beat the drum for religious meetings, town meetings and public gatherings but the spirit of progress was developing and at a meeting Jan. 9, 1764, it was "voted that Abel Botsford should be bell ringer for ye year ensuing and shall ring ye bell on ye Sabbath and on all other public times and at 9 o'clock at night and shall have for his services for ringing ye bell and sweeping ye meeting house 40 shillings a year."

The bell was used until May, 1787, when it was "voted to get a new bell in sd meeting house" and the meeting was adjourned to ye first Monday after ye new bell should arrive in Newtown. It is on record "that on ye first day of July, 1767, ye committee for ye bell took ye old bell to Fairfield, got it recast, brought it back and it was hung on the 3rd day of july, 1767," and the society's records further gratefully adds, "it is always to be understood that ye inhabitants of ye church of England society in Newtown signed of ye above money of £27-4s-7d and provisions, ye sum of five pounds 12s-9d, nearly a fifth of the whole cost."

January 9, 1769: "Voted that ye time of intermission between meetings on ye Sabbath shall be one hour and one quarter to the tenth of March next."

"Voted, that ye meeting house bell shall be rung at all seasons needful, at deaths and funerals, and other occasions of lectures and religious meetings of a religious nature."

"Voted, that Abiel Botsford is chosen to ring ye bell at all times and seasons as above and that he is to have for his services three pounds per year to be paid out of ye town treasury."

It makes a long story even to give an outline of the history of the building of "the first meeting house." At this time, Newtown contained three hundred and fifty families. Our fathers, where are they? And do the children live forever? But the old bell that has done continuous service for 143 years still hangs in the belfry sending forth its peal over the hills and adown our valleys, calling new forms and new faces "not to forget the assembling of themselves together as the manner of some is," but to join in the service of devotion, adoration and praise, and though the old bell is cracked, its tones are still sweet music to him who has been hearing them for nearly four score years.

This inscription is cast on the bell, "The Gift of Capt. Amos Botsford and Lieutenant Brisco, 1768."

During the Revolutionary war the society fell into sore straits, a wide divergence of opinion prevailed, many of its members were Tories, although their minister espoused the cause of the colonies. The time had passed when the society was depending on the town to pay the minister's rate and funds ran low. Those who would not take the oath of fidelity to the cause of the colonies absented themselves from public worship on the Lord's day, and to win them back the society called a meeting for Oct. 9, 1781, under the following warning:

"Notice is hereby given to the first society in Newtown, that a society's meeting will be held on Tuesday ye 9th at 2 o'clock p. m. at the meeting house in said district to transact ye business (viz) of ascertaining ye number and strength of sd society, of making sale of ye parsonage lott, belonging to sd society, of disposing of ye floor of sd meeting house, so much as is sufficient for 12 pews, of repairing said meeting house and new painting of ye outside of ye same, of removing some dificultys in sd society heretofore existing, of appointing a committee to supply ye desk for six months, next coming, of hiring a master of Music to instruct sd society in singing psalms, hims and spiritual songs, and to do any other business necessary and proper to be done at sd meeting and it is desired that ye society will punctually attend by order of committee.

Abel Botsford, Society's Clerk. Newtown, Oct. 1, 1781.

October 9, the meeting met according to notification, chose Mr. George Terrill moderator and voted as follows: "That it is the opinion of this meeting that all those that belong to this society notwithstanding they have nott taken ye oath of fidelity as required by law in political matters, in society matters have the same privileges with those who have sworn and that the excuses of many for not attending legal meetings on that account are groundless."

Also "voted that the three penny rate laid on the society in April last past for ye support of preaching the gospel, shall be collected and applied to the use of paying the debts or arrearages of the society and if there be any overplus, it shall be for the use of hiring a minister."

Also "voted that the meeting house shall be repaired and that Mr Jabez Botsford, Amos Tirrill and Joseph Wheeler be a committee to see what repairs are necessary for said house and report at an adjourned meeting and Jabez Botsford and Abram Bennett were appointed a committee to procure flax seed to exchange for oil to paint the meeting house."

In 1786 there seems to have been an awakening of things temporal and at a society's meeting, April 3, 1786, it was "voted to procure by donation shingles sufficient to cover the back roof of the meeting house and to take care that the same be laid on as a free donation and John Sherman, Nathanial Northrop, Capt. Silas Fairchild, Capt Joseph Wheeler, Asa Cogswell and Hezekiah Booth be committee."

In May of the same year it was "voted that this society will sell and convey to the purchasers an exclusive right to that part of the lower floor of the meeting house where the body seats now are, except the front seats on each side of the main alley." The floor space for pews on the broad alley nearest the pulpit was appraised at 9 pounds English money each, the next two at 7 pounds, the next two at 6 pounds. The front pews on the side alleys at 5 pounds, 10 shillings each, the next two at 5 pounds, the next two at 3 pounds. The pews when built were to be constructed according to specifications, fixed by vote of the society.

May 1786, at a meeting of the first society in Newtown, "voted that this society will sell and convey to the purchasers an exclusive right to that part of the meeting house on the lower floor where the body seats now are, except the front seats on each side of the main alley. Voted, that on each side of the broad alley there may by the purchasers be built six pews of equal bigness provided they be built all on one construction. (Viz) to be raised not exceeding four inches from the present floor, that they be built of equal height, panel work thus, one panel of proper length perpendicular, over which one panel of proper width horizontal, a handsome rail on the top, the door equivelent and painted a proper color for the inside of such a building. Voted, that said pews shall be built within nine months of this time or the purchaser shall forfeit his right which shall be sold again for the benefit of said society.

Voted, that the purchasers immediately on bidding off said floor for the purpose aforesaid shall give their obligation with surety to the society's clerk payable the first of March next. Voted, that said ground floors for pews be set up in the following manner: The two front pews nearest the pulpit on the broad alley be set up at 9 pounds each, the next two at 7 pounds each, the next two at 6 pounds each, the front pews on the other alleys at 5 pounds, 10 shillings each, the next two at 5 pounds each, the next 2 at 3 pounds each. That the persons that bid these several prices unless some person or persons bid higher shall be entitled to said ground to build on as aforesaid, at his own expense, but in case any person or persons jointly bid higher for any or every ground floor for a pew, the highest bidder to be entitled as aforesaid."

"Voted that the society's clerk make record of those who purchase or bid off said pews and what number beginning at the front pew on the women's side, No. 1, the opposite No. 2, the next on the women's side No. 3, the opposite No. 4, and so on according to the dignity or rank, and said clerk being thereunto requested, is hereby directed to give a copy of these votes to the proprietors or purchasers which shall be to them a sufficient title to all intents and purposes, they having first complied with and fullfilled the several articles and directions contained in these votes, so be it the whole of the ground is sold.

Voted, that John Chandler be appointed and he is hereby appointed to make sale of said ground floor for the purposes aforesaid and that he begin on Tuesday of next week at 3 of the clock at this place and use his descretion until he hath bid off the whole provided he finish with a reasonable time and that he have good right to bid for himself."

So it came about that a considerable amount of floor space was sold for pews, a goodly number of pews were built, money flowed into a depleted treasury, for ministers' salary and building improvements. Nothing more appears on the society minutes about the meeting house, either for its adornment or repairs, until 1792, when the Church of England people having the consent of the town to build a church for public worship on the ground where the town house was standing, provided they would remove the Town house to some other site, without expense to the town. The meeting house standing near to, and in front of, the Town house made an objection to putting the Church of England house there without removing the meeting house also, and it was proposed to them that their house be removed to the opposite side of the north and south road, which led the Presbyterians to call a society's meeting under the following warning, to act upon the proposition:

NOTIFICATION.

"Warning is hereby given to ye first society in Newtown that there is a meeting of sd society to be holden at the meeting house of sd society on Monday, ye 7th day of May, 1792 at five of ye clock afternoon to determine the matter respecting ye moving of ye meeting house and to do all other business necessary to be done at sd meeting. All persons who belong to sd society are desired to attend.

Notified by order of ye committee.
Newtown, May 1, 1792.
Abel Botsford, Society's Clerk.

The meeting met as warned and adjourned to May 10.

At the adjourned meeting, May 10, 1792, it was "voted that to render it more convenient for ye Episcopal society in Newtown to erect a church or house of public worship on the ground where the town house now stands we are willing that said Episcopal society or any individual of them remove our meeting house to the west side of the street so that the east end of the steeple fall in a line drawn from the north east corner of Gen. John Chandler's dwelling in said Newtown and the southeast corner of Josiah Curtis' store, provided the same can be done without any risk, damage, or expense to this society, and that said meeting house, when removed, be put in a good repair in every respect as the same now is."

Voted, "that said meeting house in its present state be estimated and valued at 700 pounds, lawful money and that sufficient surety be taken by this society's committee for the payment of the same in case of damage. Voted that Jabez Botsford, Esq., Mr Abel Booth, Roger Terrill, Capt. Moses Sheapard and Capt. Elijah Botsford be a committee to transact all business relative to the foregoing vote.

Test   Abel Botsford, Society's Clerk."

At the rooms of the Connecticut Historical Society, at Hartford, can be seen a bound volume of the Connecticut Journal of the year 1792, a weekly newspaper then printed in New Haven, in which under date of June 6, 1792, is the following:

"On Wednesday, the 13th of June inst., at one o'clock p. m., if the weather be fair, and if the weather is not good at the same time of day on on the first fair day following, an attempt will be made to remove the meeting house, together with the steeple entire, belonging to the Ecclesiastical society in Newtown, about eight rods west of its present site. As this will be the greatest movement ever attempted in this part of the state, the subscribers by whom the business is to be performed have been requested to give this public notice to their friends.

Solomon Glover,
Andrew Beers,
Daniel Tomlinson.

Fortunately for us we are not left in the dark as to the result of such a "great movement," for in the same paper under the date of June 27, 1782, we are given the result:

"On the 13th instant the meeting house in Newtown was removed about eight rods; the removal was effected in one hour and a half, after previous preparations had been made. The house is between 70 and 80 feet long, and about 50 feet wide, with a steeple at one end, the whole of which was removed without the least injury to any part.

Solomon Glover,
Andrew Beers,
David Tomlinson

We have only to measure a distance of eight rods directly east from where the Congregational church now stands to get the exact location of the first meeting house in Newtown, and the buildings it was in line with. Gen. John Chandler's house stood where the Grand Central Hotel is, and the store of Josiah Curtis stood where R. H. Beers & Co.'s. store now stands.

The old building must have grown rapidly into disfavor, for only eleven years passed before, at a society meeting at the meeting house, October 3, 1803, at 3 o'clock afternoon it was —

"Voted that we prefer a memorial to the General Assembly to be holden at New Haven on the second Thursday in October, 1803, in behalf of said society, praying for a grant of a lottery to raise the sum of $4000 to enable the society to build a meeting house for said society where the meeting house now stands, or for such other sum as the Assembly may think it expedient to grant."

Hon. William Edmond was appointed a committee to prefer a petition to the General Assembly for the grant. The assembly granted the petitioners the sum of $3,000.

March 2, 1808, "Voted that the society go forward the present season to build a meeting house with all convenient speed where the old meeting house now stands, 60 feet in length, and 40 feet in breadth, with posts of a proportionable length, to have a belfry and cupola or dome thereon, in lieu of a steeple upon the east end; that the avails of the lottery granted by the General Assembly and the materials of the old meeting house be appropriated for the purpose aforesaid."

Isaac Scudder did the work of building by contract for $1138.48 and the completed building left the society in debt. In Feb., 1810, a tax of 17 cents on the dollar on list of 1808 was laid to apply on the debt. Arnold Foot was collector.

With no money left with which to finish the interior, funds for building slips and pews were raised by carrying out a society vote passed Feb. 1, 1812.

"To dispose of the pew grounds adjoining the wall on the north and south sides of the meeting house to the highest bidder belonging to said society. The purchaser of the pew to be at the expense of building the same. The money for which the pew ground shall be sold to be paid down or secured by note payable to the society's treasurer within six months and appropriated to pay the expense of building the slips or pews on the ground not disposed of; and every purchaser shall hold the pew ground so purchased to himself and heirs forever and shall have right at any time to sell and assign the same to any other person or persons, a member or members of said society, and not otherwise."

Michael Parks auctioned off the pew grounds, No. 1, on the north side to Silas Fairchild and Philo Fairchild, $15; No. 1 on the south side to David Peck and Chauncey Botsford, $20; No. 2, north side, Lamson Birch and Ebenezer Turner, Esq., $9; No. 3, south side, William Edmond, $26; No. 2, south side, Samuel C. Blackman, Esq., $14; No. 3, north side, Moss K. Botsford and James Terrill, $20; No. 4, south side, Timothy Shepard, Esq., $22; No. 4, north side, Caleb Bennitt, $21; No. 5 south side, Ezra H. Johnson, $20.50; No. 5, north side, Ziba Blakslee $12; No. 6, south side, Arnold Foot, $15; No. 6 north side, Thomas B. Botsford, $10.50; No. 7, south side, Daniel Morehouse, $5; No. 7, north side, Rev. Jehu Clark, $2; No. 8, south side, Levi Jackson, $1; No. 8, north side, Timothy Shepard, Esq., $1; $215 was raised from the sale of pew ground.

The pews once sold, became the family possessions and were sold as such, as far down as 1839.

A deed that Horace M. Shepard gave to 'Squire John Dibble for one dollar (as I have it) describes the pew as situated in the "Presbyterian meeting house on the south side of the house, being the fourth pew from the west end, formerly owned by and occupied by my father, Timothy Shepherd, deceased April 7, 1825."

Witnessed by Samuel C. Blackman.

Charles Johnson (father of the writer) held a deed for a pew he bought of Czar Keeler in the year 1839, for which he paid $5. The deed described it as being bounded on the north by the south alley, east by pew of Ezra H. Johnson, south by the wall and west by pew owned by Hon. William Edmond.

That box pew was usually my Sunday home during the hours of "meeting" and by resting my chin on the top cap piece I could see all about. In those days ministers wrote long sermons and I soon learned that there was time for a good long nap before he would reach "eighthly," "ninthly" and "finally." I would stretch on the long seat and go to sleep, to be awakened by the singing of the last hymn, in time to hear the benediction pronounced.

The committee appointed to build the pews were Lamson Birch, Timothy Shepard and Ziba Blakeslee, and they were to lay out the residue of pew ground money partly finishing the galleries. May 10, 1813, another petition was sent to the General Assembly for the grant of $4000 to defray the expenses of the society in building their meeting house and in support of public worship in the society. The petition was not granted. During the Rev. Jason Atwater's ministry, between 1845 and 1852, the exterior of the building was very much improved, the belfry was closed in, a new steeple was built, the building newly covered and painted.

Twelve hundred dollars were spent in renovating the exterior and in 1852 the basement was fitted up, the main floor raised to its present level, new seats and a pulpit were provided for the audience room, at an expense of $500. Down to the present time the people have kept pace with the needs of the times and this building compares well in its furnishing, conveniences and adornment with those of any country edifice in the Fairfield County Consociation.

The writer regrets exceedingly that he finds nothing on record of the history of the "weather vane." That it was on the steeple at the time of the Revolutionary war is well known, for it bears the marks of bullets fired by French soldiers, as, by order of Gen. Washington, they passed through Newtown on their way from Hartford to the Hudson River in 1781.

When the old building was torn away to make room for the present structure, the weather vane was transferred to it.

When a little boy, my father took the rooster to Bridgeport to have it re-gilded and I had the honor of riding to the city with it. It was nearly as high as I and its long spurs, its high comb, and the dents the bullets had made on its body were all part of a history lesson which I have never forgotten. It was a catch story of those early days told to us children that whenever the old rooster on the Presbyterian meeting house steeple heard Judge Blackman (who lived on the corner close by) call his hens to feed them he always flew down and ate with them. Judge Samuel C. Blackman lived in a house on the ground where the Grand Central Hotel stands. He was a lawyer and proverbially known as a truthful man. Even little children knew it, and the mother had to solve the puzzle telling the reason, "The rooster could not hear the call."

NEWTOWN'S TOWN HOUSES

In two hundred and more years of our town history, the town has built but two town houses. Not until 1717 do we find in Newtown town records allusion to the building of a town house. The business meetings of the town were held at dwelling houses, for which rentals were paid. At a town meeting, October 9, 1717, it was "Voted by ye inhabitants of the town that a schoolhouse or town house shall be forthwith or with all possible speed erected of ye following dimensions: 25 foot square and eight foot between joists, and whereas Joseph Gray and Peter Hubbell have undertaken to build ye sd house (viz) to get, draw ye timber, make ye frame, get all ye shingles and clabbords and lay them, ye town finding nails. It is agreed and voted to give sd workmen for sd work, 10 pounds money, to be paid upon their accomplishing or compleating sd work, workmanlike." Entered, Joseph Peck, Town Clerk.

On Jan. 8, 1718, another town meeting was held, to fix the location for the town house that the town had voted to have built. It was "voted, that the place for building ye school or town house or house for holding town meetings in, and for teaching school in, shall be on ye main street or town street near unto Abraham Kimberley's betwixt sd Kimberley's and John Lake's house." (Abraham Kimberley's house stood on the corner opposite Trinity.)

In 1733, the population had increased so that as new conditions arose, a larger town house was needed. By vote of the town, the town house was removed to become the schoolhouse for Middle district, the neighborhood moving it at their own expense. The second town house was not built until 1766. In the meantime, business meetings of the town were held, sometimes in the north and sometimes in the south schoolhouse, and at other times in the meeting house. Thirty-three years passed and then a town meeting was called for Dec. 8, 1766, at which meeting it was "voted, that there shall be a town house built for ye use of ye town and that Johnathan Booth, Ebenezer Ford and Nathanial Nichols shall be a committee to examine into what place is most convenient to set the house and what ye house will cost, and make report at an adjourned meeting." The second town house was located on what was the site of the first one and at a town meeting held Dec. 22, 1766, it was "voted, that the town house shall be built 32 feet long, 24 feet wide and nine feet between joists and that Oliver Tousey shall build it at ye price of 66 pounds and that he shall give bonds to ye committee for ye building of sd house and that there shall be a rate of three farthings half farthings on ye pound raised to build sd house and also voted that Jonathan Booth and Caleb Baldwin shall be a committee to obligate sd Tousey and take his obligations for ye completing sd house and shall make and collect a rate." Also "voted, that sd Tousey shall cause to be made in sd town house good seats as are generally made, in form as in ye State House at Hartford. Sd house to be finished by ye first day of December, 1767." Also "voted, that ye sd Tousey shall light ye house with 30 windows, 15 squares of glass in a window size of ye glass 7 x 9."

The house was finished as per contract and the first meeting was held in it, Dec. 7, 1767. Nothing further is said of the building until, at a town meeting in 1789, it was "voted that the selectmen should, as soon as convenient, repair ye town house in a manner as shall seem to them most prudent and best for ye advantage of ye town."

When the third Episcopal church was to be built, the ground on which the town house stood was needed as part of the site of the Church building, and the town gave the Episcopalians liberty to remove the building. Capt Solomon Glover bought the old Episcopal church building (the second one) in 1799, and the town voted to give him five pounds in money, yearly rental, provided he would purchase for it a plot of ground on which to set the building, which was then standing on the west side of the north and south highway and a little south of where now stands Newtown Inn. The old Church building was removed to the westward off the highway, fitted up for the use of the town for a town house, and was rented by Solomon Glover for a long term of years to the town at an annual rental of $20. In the early part of the last century the building now used as a tin shop, stood where the store of R. H. Beers & Co. is and was used for a general merchandise store by the firm of Baldwin & Beers, which, with the two-story building joined on the north end, covered the ground now occupied by the present building. The second floor of the main building was rented for many years by the town, and, when Norman B. Glover put up a building for a store on the ground near the house now owned by Mrs. S. F. Schermerhorn, somewhere in the "70s," the town rented the upper floor, until it burned down, for a town house, owning no building for town use, until it bought the present town house, which was originally built by the Universalists for religious purposes, and afterward became the property of St. Rose's parish, and so remained until the building of this present edifice, when, in 1883, it was sold to the town of Newtown and is now a large and commodious building, that is likely to continue (except in case of fire) Newtown's town house for at least a century to come.

SABBATH DAY HOUSES

The Sabbath Day house was a place in which to take refreshments between the two Church services and for social and religious worship as the occupant might be inclined. It was built in two divisions, one for males and the other for females. They were located on the highway, permission being given by vote of the free holders in Town meeting. They were necessary because the meeting houses were not warmed.

Dec. 9, 1740, "voted and agreed that Jeremiah Northrop shall have liberty to set a small Sabbath Day house in ye lane by or against Capt. Baldwin's orchard."

Dec. 3. 1750, "voted that Jonathan Sanford shall have liberty to build a small Sabbath Day house at ye westerly end of John Platt's Sabbath Day house."

Dec. 30, 1754, "voted that Captain Amos Botsford shall have Liberty to Build a small house for Sabbath Days not Doing Damage to ye Highway nor any other person."

Dec. 23, 1751, "voted that Benjamin Northrop shall have liberty to building a Sabbath Day house for his use in ye Lane of Captain Baldwin's fence of his home lott below or something west of Caleb Baldwin's Sabbath Day house."

DISPUTES OVER TOWN LINES

Reference has been made to the dispute between Stratford and Newtown regarding lines between the two towns, a dispute that arose in 1725 and was not amicably adjusted and confirmed by the General Court until 1761. About the same time, disputes arose between Newtown and Danbury and Newtown and New Milford from the same cause, creating uneasiness, friction, and contention, from which, in the case between New Milford and Newtown, litigation arose.

NEW MILFORD—NEWTOWN TOWN LINE

"At a town meeting held March 28, 1727, at sd Newtown, Mr. Thomas Tousey and Capt. Thomas Bennett by vote were appointed a committee to meet ye gentlemen from New Milford upon Thursday, ye 13th instant of March, at westerly end of ye supposed line between New Milford and Newtown to declare to sd gentlemen the dissatisfaction of sd Newtown with respect to sd line and to propose to them with respect to sd line, and to propose to them whether some method of accommodation and what might be pitched upon for ye removing of ye difficulty, and that speedy and effectual care be taken in that matter, yt those who are not only neighbors, but christian neighbors, may dwell as such.

Entered Joseph Peck, Town Clerk."

"April 6, 1731, John Leavenworth is chosen and empowered in behalf and in room of Newtown to appear at ye county court to be holden in New Haven on ye seventh day of April to implead ye town of Newtown at New Milford in an action or plea of debt as it is by New Milford termed, commenced against Newtown as they say, for neglecting to perambulate according to law between ye two towns of Newtown and New Milford and that ye sd Leavenworth shall have full power in ye affair to employ any attorney and to review or appeal as ye case may require, making firm and good what ye Leavenworth shall do in ye premises.

Joseph Peck, Town Clerk."

At a lawful town meeting of ye inhabitants of Newtown, held, August 17th, 1735, "voted by ye inhabitants of Newtown that Capt. Thomas Tousey should be moderator to carry on ye business of sd meeting.

Voted that Capt. Thomas Tousey should be agent in ye behalf of ye town of Newtown to appear at ye Superior Court to be holden at New Haven on ye first Tuesday in September, 1730, and is fully impowered to emplead ye town of New Milford in an action or plea of debt commenced against Newtown, as they say, at ye County Court held at New Haven, April 7, 1730, for neglect to perambulate according to law, etc. The town ratifying and confirming what ye sd Capt. Tousey shall do in ye premises.

Joseph Peck, Town Clerk."

"At a lawful meeting of ye inhabitants of Newtown held April 9, 1731, appointed to consult what method to take to get or have ye dividing line atwixt New Milford and Newtown settled, first voted that Capt. Thomas Tousey should be moderator to carry on ye business of sd meeting.

Secondly, agreed and voted to send a prayer or petition to ye General Assembly to be holden at Hartford in May next, to intreat ye favor of ye honorable assembly for a committee of their appointment to settle ye above sd line that further trouble may be prevented.

Thirdly, agreed and voted that Capt. Thomas Tousey be Committee or agent in ye behalf of ye town to prepare and present to ye General Assembly to be held in Hartford in May next, a memorial, and to take ye whole care of ye business aforesaid.

Joseph Peck, Town Clerk."

"At a lawful town meeting held in Newtown, September 17, 1731.

Whereas ye General Assembly have appointed a committee with ye assistance of ye surveyor of ye county of Hartford to run and ascertain of ye dividing line between New Milford and Newtown, it was voted that Capt. Thomas Tousey and Lieut. John Northrop were chosen and appointed a committee in behalf of ye town of Newtown when sd committee, shall come upon sd work, to appear to do and act whatsoever shall be proper in order to bring said affair to a good conclusion and to take thorough care that ye return of sd committtee shall be presented to ye General Assembly in order to the ratification and confirmation thereof.

Joseph Peck, Town Clerk."

At a town meeting held March 23, 1732, it was voted that Captain Thomas Tousey, John Leavenworth and Jeremiah Northrop shall be a committee to discourse and conclude with ye committee chosen by New Milford upon terms of accomodations between the two towns respecting ye charges yt have arose upon Newtown by virtue of New Milford having commenced an action against Newtown for not perambulating and what sd committee shall do in ye premises shall be held as valid and that ye sd committee shall have power this spring to perambulate ye line between New Milford and Newtown, late established by ye General Assembly.

Joseph Peck, Town Clerk."

New Milford, Dec. 10, 1734.

"To ye inhabitants or to ye moderator of your meeting which is to be held on ye 12th day of this instant in Newtown, greeting.

"Gentlemen, these are to propose conditions of people with you in consideration you will let all former contentions in ye law be laid aside from this time, which hath been about ye line, between New Milford and Newtown, about perambulating with you on ye new line or boundary line. Be pleased to return by the bearer how or what you will do refering to this matter. Wishing you peace and prosperity,

James Prime,
Theophilus Baldwin,
Selectmen.

Recorded December 12, 1734, Joseph Peck, Town Clerk."

The above seems to have been an "olive branch of peace" sent from New Milford to Newtown. Nothing further appears upon the records in regard to the matter.

DANBURY—NEWTOWN TOWN LINE

In 1758, the boundary line between Newtown and Danbury having become so obscure, the town took action in regard to making the establishment of the line the better understood and appointed a committee to act with a committee appointed by the town of Danbury to report at a future meeting. The result of that action was embodied in a report made at a town meeting held on the 17th day of April, 1758, which reads as follows:

"These may certify whom it may concern, that we, ye subscribers hereunto being chosen appointed by and impowered by ye selectmen of Newtown a committee appointed to meet ye selectmen or a committee of Danbury to perambulate, renew and erect ye boundaries or monuments in ye line between ye township of sd Danbury and Newtown if any of them were unknown on this 17th day of April, 1758, proceeded and performed in manner and for following:

Viz. First, we reported to and made our appearance at ye N. W. corner bounds of sd Newtown and there joined with Danbury committee, who were Capt. John Benedict, Capt. Ebenezer Hecock and Phineas Judd. We agreed to renew sd boundaries or monuments by putting stones to it which was and is a small ditch, and a heap of stones about one foot on ye east side of ye sd ditch. Then we went S. by E. to ye next monument, added stones to it which is red or black oak tree with stones to it, then moving southeasterly about 80 rods where we erected a new boundary or monument which is a black oak tree with stones to it, then on ye same course about 89 rods to a heap of stones, adding to it more stones, from thence to a rock near Lyon's orchard, from thence to a rock with stones boundary, which is a large rock with a heap of stones on it, and from thence to Garshum Botswick's shop, a little south, where we erected a new on it at the corner of Mr. Northrop's lot, and then running ye same line 80 or 90 rods, where we erected a new boundary or monument, which is a heap of stones where ye southard side of sd Northrop's lot or land, then to a large rock with stones on it gainst Ebenezer Blackman's land adding stones to it.

Performed per us on ye 17th day of April, 1758.
        Caleb Baldwin,
        James Hard, Jr.,
        H. Peck,
          Committee.

This return of ye committee received for record May ye 8th, 1758. Recorded per John Northrop, Town Clerk.

STRATFORD—NEWTOWN TOWN LINE

Until 1761, there were frequent disputes between the towns of Stratford and Newtown in regard to the line established by the duly appointed committees as the records plainly show, causing suits at law, expense and general uneasiness. At a proprietors' meeting held on the 15th of Sept., 1761, Messrs. Esquire Caleb Baldwin, Capt. John Glover, Capt. Henry Glover, Mr. Benjamin Curtis and Theodore Leavenworth were chosen a committee in behalf of ye proprietors in ye affair or case about ye dividing line betwixt Stratford and Newtown, and empowered "to prefer a petition to the General Assembly in ye name of ye proprietors of common and undivided land in such manner and form as said committee shall judge best, praying said assembly to establish ye antient agreement made between ye townships of Stratford and Newtown, or in some other way relieve ye sd proprietors from the force of ye judgment of ye Superior Court held at Fairfield in August last."

"At a town meeting of the inhabitants of Newtown held January 30, 1761, it was voted and agreed that at the charge of ye proprietors of Newtown with ye assistance of a proper County surveyor of ye county of Fairfield that the east or easterly line of ye township of Stratford according to their patent shall be procured with all proper speed. To be run and at ye extent of 12 miles from ye sea a fair monument be there erected and from sd monument a straight or due cross line be run to ye northeast corner of ye township of Fairfield and that Thomas Tousey, Esq., Capt. John Glover and Mr. Benjamin Curtis shall be a committee in all respects to take care that ye above said work be thoroughly affected.
        John Glover, Town Clerk."

At a town meeting, May 11, 1761, "It was voted that Capt. John Glover and Mr. Daniel Booth shall be agents in behalf of the inhabitants of Newtown to prefer or persue the petition at the General Assembly to be held at Hartford on the second Thursday of May, praying sd Assembly to appoint a committee to ascertain the dividing line between the township of Stratford and sd Newtown and that sd agents are hereby either of them fully empowered to act in ye premises. Another town meeting held on October 8, 1761. It was voted that Richard Fairman and Capt. Henry Glover be agents and they are hereby impowered to act in the name and behalf of the town at the next General Assembly at their present session to prosecute and persue their petition now depending at sd Assembly. Voted also that Capt. John Glover shall have the like power as above mentioned.
        John Northrop, Town Clerk."

The committee appointed in Oct. 1761, acted in conjunction with that appointed in Sept. 1761, and the General Court accepted and confirmed the action of inhabitants of Newtown and established the line and monument and declared the same to be the dividing line between the towns of Stratford and Newtown. This line is now the dividing line between Monroe and Trumbull on the south and Newtown on the north, those two towns having been set off from Stratford in the early part of the last century.

"At a general assembly of the governor and company of the Colony of Connecticut holden at New Haven on the second Thursday of October, 1761, upon the petition of Daniel Booth, Caleb Baldwin and Benjamin

Curtiss, all inhabitants of Newtown and proprietors of the common and undivided land in sd Newtown and ye rest of ye inhabitants of sd Newtown and ye rest of ye proprietors of ye sd common and undivided land in sd Newtown, representing to this assembly that ye dividing line between yt town towards Stratford was for a long time unsettled and uncertain, which occasioned teadius and unhappy disputes and controversies between sd towns, the same lasting and continuing until ye year 1725, when ye sd towns and ye proprietors of ye common and undivided lands in sd towns by their respective committees, in order to prevent any further disputes and contentions respecting such dividing line and to settle and make ye same known, did honestly and in an amicable manner did agree to settle and establish a dividing line between said towns, that the sd agreement was put into writing and duly executed and that the same was accepted and approved of by ye inhabitants of said towns and at last by the proprietors of ye common and undivided lands in sd Stratford. But such acceptance, etc., not being entered upon record, rendered such agreement week and not a lawfull evidence of such dividing lines. But said agreement being so honestly made as aforesaid said line therein contained ought to be deemed and accounted ye dividing line between sd towns as to jurisdiction and propriety. Praying that sd agreement may be confirmed and established and that sd line may be the dividing line between said towns both as to jurisdiction and propriety, etc., as on file."

"Resolved by this assembly that the sd agreement mentioned in sd petition be confirmed and established and that the sd line and monument mentioned and contained therein shall be and the same is hereby declared to the dividing line between said towns both as to jurisdiction and propriety, etc., as petition on file."

Recorded per John Northrop, proprietors' clerk a coppie of ye bill in form at Hartford past at New Haven, October, 1761.

A true cope of record examined by George Willeys, secretary of state.

BROOKFIELD'S ORIGIN

Less than 20 years after Newtown was incorporated, some living in the north end of town, more particularly at the "West farm," the local name of which was "Whiskenere," wanted to be set off with part of Danbury and part of New Milford as an ecclesiastical society.

"At a town meeting called in Oct. 1751, it was voted to appoint agents in behalf of ye town in ye case of ye people of ye west farm belonging to Newtown making application to ye honorable Assembly to be held at New Haven, Oct. 9, 1751, in order to be set off with ye other parts of ye neighboring towns as an Ecclesiastical society." And it was also "voted that ye professors of ye Church of England in Newtown shall be freed from any charge in that affair above mentioned." That meeting being declared illegal another was held as soon as the law would allow, at which "Messrs. Joseph Smith, Daniel Booth and Joseph Botsford were appointed agents in behalf of the town to oppose in ye case of ye west farm belonging to sd Newtown and others, making application to ye Honorable Assembly to be held at New Haven, October 9, 1751, in order to be set off with some parts of ye neighboring towns as an Ecclesiastical Society, therefore voted that whereas a committee May last was by ye Honorable Assembly authorized to view ye circumstances of part of ye town of Danbury, Newtown and New Milford, all adjoining, in order to ye forming of an Ecclesiastical Society and to make report to ye Assembly in this month of October with instructions to notify ye several parties concerned of ye time and place of their meeting upon that affair that they might have opportunity of making their pleas that ye Honorable General Assembly to be held this month be made acquainted that ye town of Newtown by sd committee or any form or under them, were never notified with relation to ye premises whereby they are debarred of their first privilege and exposed to suffer great wrong and many are aggrieved. Voted in ye affirmative.

John Northrop, Town Clerk."

Though thus far disappointed, the people of the north end of Newtown were not discouraged. Released by vote in town meeting from their tax toward the support of the Newtown minister, provided they would support one in the "north end," they hired Rev. Thomas Brooks in 1757, the parish of Newbury having been incorporated in 1754.

Warning concerning Newbury being opposed by Newtown at the General Court for a town, in 1772:

"Whereas the town of Newtown is called to answer to Newbury parish at ye General Assembly to be holden at Hartford Instant May, concerning said Parish being granted town privileges and ye selectmen, not having power invested in them to oppose or not oppose unless by agreement with sd Newbury to ye maintainance of their proportionable part of ye poor, which they refuse to comply with. Therefore at ye desire of ye selectmen warning is hereby given to ye inhabitants of Newtown in Fairfield County that there is to be a town meeting holden at ye Town house in sd town on Monday, ye 18th day of May, 1772, at 5 of ye clock, afternoon, to consider and determine ye matter above mentioned.

Caleb Beldwin, Town Clerk."

At a town meeting held in accordance with this notification "it was voted that the town shall oppose ye parish of Newbury at ye General Court now sitting at Hartford in regard to sd parish being set off for a township."

Voted that Mr. Oliver Tousey shall be agent in behalf of ye town of Newtown to oppose sd Newbury at ye General Assembly.

Caleb Baldwin, Town Clerk.

We are not able to find that further action was taken by Newtown in regard to the matter until 1779. The seven years between the action taken by vote of the town in 1772 "to oppose the parish of Newbury from being set off as a town" and that taken by Newtown at the annual town meeting in 1779 showed a decided reaction in feeling in relation to the matter, and again at the annual town meting in December, 1781. Still matters were held in abeyance for some reason until 1785, when it was voted in town meeting that "all objection and opposition on the part of Newtown should be withdrawn," as will be seen by these votes:

At Newtown's annual town meeting in Dec. 1779, "it was voted that ye inhabitants of ye parish of Newbury that belong to the limits of Newtown shall have liberty to apply to ye General Assembly next coming to be set off as a district town without any opposition made by this town."

Again at the annual town meeting held in Dec. 1781, the town voted "that this town will not oppose the inhabitants of the parish of Newbury at the General Assembly in May next for town privileges."

Again at a special town meeting in Newtown, March 29, 1785, to determine the matter concerning town privileges for the parish of Newbury it was voted "that this town, considering ye difficulties ye parish of Newbury labors under in lying in three towns and two counties, have no objection nor shall we oppose them at ye General Assembly in their memorial for town privilege, they ye sd parish of Newbury bearing their proportion of ye town debts already contracted or that shall be contracted as a town at any time before ye confirmation of sd parish in town privileges."

As to the line to be established between Newtown and Newbury, the town voted at the same meeting, "that the line between the Township of Newtown and the proposed Township of Newbury shall begin in the line between the Township of Danbury and Newtown 80 rods southerly of the known monument called the "bound hollow" which was the ancient parochial bounds of the said parish of Newtown. Thence a straight line to a monument 30 rods southerly of a white oak tree at the southeasterly corner of Capt Richard Smith's garden, sd tree being an old boundary line between the sd parish of Newbury and Newtown, thence a straight line to the Great River at the riding place about 120 rods northerly from the mouth of Pond Brook.

Although Newtown did not oppose the people of the "north end" having parish privileges to the finish, yet their opposition long delayed the time of its incorporation as a town. Time, the mollifier of long continued disputes, at last brought about the wished for result and, in 1788, Newbury was incorporated as a town. From 1757 to 1788 Rev. Thomas Brooks had had the pastoral care of all Newbury, and it was known far and wide as "Brooksfield," and what more natural than the name Newbury being dropped to make way for the proposed new name of "Brookfield," a name to be retained, we hope, until it shall be proclaimed that "Time shall be no more."

In deference to the towns from which Newbury was formed, its name was taken from the first part of the name of Newtown and New Milford and for the last part of Danbury, from which came Newbury. The parish of Newbury was incorporated in 1754. In 1759 the General Court, upon petition, annexed the section of the parish taken from New Milford town to Fairfield county, and in March, 1788, it petitioned for its incorporation with town privileges and it was granted 34 years intervening. In June, 1788, the town of Brookfield held its first town meeting, at which the following vote was passed.

"Thanks to the gentlemen spectators from neighboring towns for the respect shown to the town of Brookfield in attending their first town meeting and in particular to Col. Samuel Canfield, Esq., appointed first moderator for said town of Brookfield by the General Assembly for his care and service in said office."

LAY OUT OF COUNTRY ROADS IN YE OLDEN TIMES

Fifty years ago or so, a little boy of eight or ten years of age was trudging along on his way home from the school in Taunton, when he was overtaken by an elderly man, a stranger, who, instead of asking "Where does this road lead to?" accosted him with the query, "Say, bub, where does this road go to?" The boy, with a quick wit replied, "Don't go nowheres, zi knows on, it's been here ever since I've been here." The questioner, together with a listener, who related the epsiode to me, died long time since, but the lad of the years long gone is still living and a grandfather. That same question is one of to-day with some, who, upon pleasure bent, drive along the lanes, the by-ways and the highways of our extensive township, forming as they do a complete net work of mysterious complications, which, at the same time, are a delight to the artist, the naturalist and the botanist, though a burden to the tax payers and a perplexity to the town fathers. A conservative estimate of those best informed, as to the mileage of Newtown's roads to be kept in repair at town expense, is not less than 400 miles. While it is true that none of our roads "go" anywhere, it is equally true that in their circuitous courses and serpentine windings they have a continual series of surprises for tourists, to whom it is the height of pleasure to drive along our country roads.

HOUSE BUILT BY EZRA H. JOHNSON
E. L. Johnson's grandfather, in 1795

BIRTHPLACE OF EZRA L. JOHNSON
Built in 1830, reconstructed in 1876.

The most reasonable opinion that the student of history can arrive at in regard to their extreme crookedness is that in the early days the pitching for land and the building of homes, "shacks," if we please to call them, took precedence of the laying out of highways, a long time intervening before the coming of wheeled vehicles, so that footpaths for man or horse were all needed for the first few years of pioneer life. There seems not a doubt that the highway leading from the center of Newtown to Bridgeport follows the trail of the Scatakooks and Pohtatucks who wandered all over the Housatonic valley from the Massachusetts line down through Kent, New Milford, Newtown and Stratford to the shore of the great salt sea.

My grandfather, born in 1772, died in 1854 and lived his life alongside this road. My father, born in 1799, lived alongside the same road all his life, dying in 1871. The writer, born in 1832, has lived all his life on the ancestral farm, and has seen the summer migrations of the Indians along this road on their way to "salt water." Year after year they dwindled in numbers, a natural result of the coming of the "pale face," so that the last of their migratory trips ended about 1860.

Newtown's bi-centennial celebration fixed permanently in our minds the fact that the township of land was purchased from the Indians in 1705. In course of time, settlers began to come in. It was decided, after careful investigation, where the center of the town should be fixed and a certain routine line of business affairs moved along, controlled by regulations laid down by the General Court, which held semi-annual sessions in May and Oct. alternately at Hartford and New Haven.

The layout of highways in the early years of Newtown life was in striking contrast to the scientific methods along the same lines at the present day. We are having a daily object lesson of the laying out and also of the building of highways, not only as regards survey and easy grades by cutting down the hills and filling the valleys, but also by widening the road bed and the elimination or the lessening of heavy and dangerous curves.

The first recorded lay-out of a highway the writer has been able to find in his researches of the town's records is dated Nov. 14, 1715. It is called "Ye lay-out of ye country road toward Stratford."

We will need to keep in mind that the present boundary line separating Newtown from Monroe and Trumbull is the same line that separated Newtown from Stratford in 1715, Monroe and Trumbull having been set off from the north part of Stratford long time afterward, so that it was only six miles from the center of our town to the boundary line between Stratford and Newtown. That the earliest lay-out of roads followed the foot paths or trails that led from one central point to another is especially true of the lay-out toward Stratford, toward Woodbury and toward New Milford and Danbury.

"Jonathan Hubbell hath pitched for his ten acre pitch at ye swamp at ye north corner of Mr. Rood's lot now in ye improvement of Stephen

Parmalee and on ye southeast side of ye path which goes from Nototuck to Danbury. Entered this fourth day of Nov. 1714.

Joseph Peck, Town Clerk."

Of the lay-out of highways in Newtown, first in order is the road leading southerly to the town line, the whole distance now a State road that will become a section of a "trunk line" extending from New York City to Berkshire Hills in Massachusetts.

We, the committee that are to lay out highways whose names are underwritten have ye 14th day of November, 1715, laid out ye country road towards Stratford as far as Pototuck brook and measured it from Joseph Peck's house two miles. Sd road is eight rods wide from Ebenezer Johnson's and crooks as ye path to ye Deep Brook does and there we crost ye east corner of Ebenezer Booth's land, which he had of Samuel Beers, which quantity he takes and joyns to his other land. We clypt ye northeast corner of Jeremiah Northrop's twelve acre lott from his eastward corner which is a white oak tree, and by ye side of ye next brook we marked a black oak tree. Ye highway down stream eight rods from sd tree. Ye first mile goes 16 to 18 rods southard to a crooked white oak, marked. We clypt ye east corner of Joseph's Peck's 20 acre lott as marked by a black oak standing on his part. He then consented to it. Betwixt this and ye next swamp we began to lay out ye highway 10 rods wide. Eastward of ye cart parth it goes to Joseph Peck's 60 acre lot as marked trees will discern, the eight rods until over sd Pohtatuck brook ye two miles. Here is a white oak tree marked against sd Peck's land. When we laid out ye highway eight rods wide over Pohtatuck brook across ye southern end of John Glover's 60 acre lot, and up a valley between New Haven Plain and Long Swamp, eight rods wide, and so crossing ye old road at a little brook as ye marked trees will show, and rocks with stones and homeward to ye place where we began to make ye road 10 rods wide sd highway comes in.

Thomas Bennitt,
John Glover,
Ebenezer Booth,   Committee.

Recorded per Joseph Peck, Town Clerk, November 25, 1715.

A lay-out, a few days later, from the center to what became Sandy Hook and on toward Woodbury:

"We that are ye committee for to lay out highways whose names are underwritten have this 18th day of November, 1715, laid out a highway or country road two miles from ye middle of ye town down by ye north side of ye old farm over Pohtatuck Brook and so toward ye Single Pine to a bunch of stones upon a rock which was two miles. The highway is 20 rods wide according as ye common or undevided land will allow. We removed Daniel Foot's southwest corner of his four acre lott northwest six rods and we gave him seven rods at his east corner. Sd Foot was preasant and consented to ye same. We lay out a road for to go to Woodbury. We began it at ye First Meadow in ye above sd road eastward of ye Pohtatuck Brook turning of it more North till we come to some pines. We lay it 20 rods wide. We laid out Darbee road from ye going over sd brook by ye side of it upon ye east side of ye Old Farms till we come to a path that leads to Fregrace Adamses 60 acre pitch. Also that path we laid 20 rods wide except when there is a meadow.

Thomas Bennitt,
John Glover,
Ebenezer Booth,

Recorded November 28, 1715, Joseph Peck, Clerk. Committee.

The Great Boggs, in Head of Meadow district:

"We whose names are under written have, this 23rd day of November, 1715, laid out a road southward of ye town towards ye Great Boggs two miles, ten rods wide, joining upon ye west side of Ebenezer Smith's home lott, and Ebenezer Johnson's four acres, and Samuel Ferris' 20 acre lot, in ye east side of ye home meadow until we get to Stephen Parmalee's 20 acre lot, it turns more eastern to a marked black oak tree and then to a white oak tree which stands by ye west side of a swamp against Samuel Beers, 20 acre and other trees we have marked till we come to ye top of ye hill which is on ye east side of ye highway and so to ye place where ye paths part to ye Little and Grate Boggs, as ye path goes, 10 rods wide."

Layout in South Center district, Nov. 23, 1715:

"Also we have laid out a road this same day round ye east corner of Mr. Peck's nine acres over Deep Brook and so on ye northwest side of Ebenezer Smith's 20 acre lott or 14 acres, and on ye west end of Joseph Peck's 20 acre lot, and Samuel Prindle's land on ye eastern part of Bushy Hill as ye trees will decifer, being marked on each hand till we come to a small swamp which goes down to Prindle's land or 20 acre lott, so up a valle till we come near to a swamp, near to Joseph Botsford's 30 acre lott, ye north corner of it, then turns more eastward as ye marked trees will show till we come to a swamp and cross it, which is near to Joseph Botsford's east corner and then round it upon ye eastward side down to a little brook, yt enters itself into ye west sprain of Pohtatuck brook, as markd trees will show. We have also laid out ye road eight rods wide cross ye Deep Brook at ye north corner of Ebenezer Smith's lot, which corner we have clypt for ye straightening of ye rode, and so to ye center at ye northwest corner of Mrs. Widow Toucey's lot. We have laid out a highway to Ebenezer Booth's 60 acre lott 10 rods wide as his part goes, only he crosses ye brook 10 rods hier to get akross a swamp until he comes to his path again.

Thomas Bennitt,
Ebenezer Booth,
Committee.
Joseph Peck, Town Clerk.

As the reader, enjoying the comforts that come from a well-ordered, well-cared-for home, ponders over the crude ways of those early days, let him give a tender thought to those to whom we are so much indebted under the providence of God, who, in perilous times, crossed the ocean to make for themselves homes in a new world, and later to join in laying foundations for a "Government of the people, by the people and for the people," the like of which exists nowhere else upon the earth. Let us not only think of these things, but may it be our daily desire and our daily endeavor to make principle, honesty of purpose and virtue our guiding stars, so that our form of government shall not perish from the earth.

NEWTOWN'S FIRST CALL FOR A MINISTER
MR. PHINEAS FISK—1711.

For many years the ministers of the several towns in the colony were hired at the annual town meeting and the salary was paid by a tax levied on the taxable property of the freeholders and was considered a part of the town expenses, and there was no getting away from payment of the tax when once levied. Although the settlement of Newtown commenced in 1705, it was not until six years after that the first move, town-wise, was made toward calling a minister, who was to be a non-conformist, and settled upon the Presbyterian foundation.

The first town meeting for that purpose was on September 24, 1711, at the house of Peter Hubbell. It was then voted that Peter Hubbell be town clerk for the year ensuing, and it was at this meeting that the calling of a minister was first taken up.

"Voted, that Mr. Phineas Fisk be invited to come to this place to preach a sermon amongst us, and that we may discuss him about settling amongst us as a minister of the gospel for half a year or some other space of time as may be agreed upon for a trial. And Lieutenant William Adams be the person to wait upon him here as soon as can be conveniently attended upon." December 24, 1711, it was "Voted, that if Mr. Phineas Fisk will come and settle in Newtown and preach ye ministry to us he shall have a petition right." February 12, 1712, Ebenezer Prindle, Samuel Sanford, John Platt, Abraham Kimberley and John Griffin were made a committee "to discourse a minister in order for settling him in Newtown."

May 30, 1712, it was voted "to give the minister that settles as a minister that right of land that was laid out to the ministry. "Voted by the major part for Mr. Phineas Fisk to be minister for Newtown." "Voted to give the minister that comes and settles amongst us, as a minister of the Gospel to preach the Gospel amongst us, that he shall have a petition right in full with said petitioners of Newtown."

August 12, 1712, it was voted in town meeting "that if Mr. Phineas Fisk carry on ye work of ye ministry amongst us we will for his encouragement, besides ye petition right, before granted him build him and finish a sufficient dwelling house of 40 feet in length, and 20 feet in breadth, two stories high, 16 feet between joists, frame and cover a lean-to, 12 feet wide ye whole length of ye house and provide him at our cost a comfortable house until we have built as above sd, and give him his wood yearly and to be at ye charge of ye removal of his family and goods, fence, clear and sow his home lot with wheat, ye first year, and in like manner fence, clear, and sow four acres of his land a year for three years following, give him for a salary 30 pounds for ye first year, 40 pounds a year the three following years, fifty pounds ye fifth year, 60 pounds ye sixth year in money or wheat at a shilling a bushel, and Indian corn at 20 pence a bushel and so much upon ye yearly after ye sixth year as 60 pounds shall amount to upon ye pound on ye list of rateable estate sd year."

Joseph Peck, Town Clerk.

After the town had held six town meetings in regard to calling Mr. Phineas Fisk and all of no avail at a town meeting Oct. 1, 1712, it was "voted: "That Mr. John Glover request ye Rev. Mr. Charles Chauncey and ye Rev. Mr. Joseph Weed and some other ministers of ye county, if they think needful, that one or two, or as they see meet, come and assist and carry on and advise us at Newtown and keep a day of humiliation with us, that God in His mercy would direct us and prosper us with a man to preach the Gospel to us, and that God would continue the Gospel to us."

It might seem to a thoughtful person that disrespect was shown by the Town Clerk in not entering the name of the one called with his title, but at the time the call came, Mr. Fisk was still tutor at Yale College at Saybrook, and had not been ordained minister of the Gospel. From 1706 to 1713 he was tutor at Yale.

As the correspondence was all on one side, nothing came of it. It was learned many years later that he settled in Haddam.

NEWTOWN'S FIRST SETTLED MINISTER
REV. THOMAS TOUSEY—1714-1724.

At a lawful meeting of ye inhabitants of Newtown, April 29, 1713, voted and agreed for Ebenezer Smith to go to Wethersfield to treat with Mr. Tousey of Wethersfield and request him to come and give us a visit and preach a Sabbath or two with us that we may have opportunity to discourse him in order to carry on ye work of ye ministry amongst us.

John Glover, Recorder.

May ye 21, 1713, "voted and made choice of John Glover, Mr. Ebenezer Smith and Mr. Benjamin Sherman, a committee to discourse and treat with Mr. Tousey of Wethersfield in order to settle amongst us to carry on ye work of ye ministry in this place. This meeting is adjourned until tomorrow night, sun half an hour high, from ye date above."

John Glover, Recorder.

May ye 22d, 1713. "At ye said adjourned meeting the inhabitants voted and agreed to give Mr. Thomas Tousee thirty pounds in money and also to sow all ye minister's home Lott with Wheat that is suitable, Mr. Tousee to have ye crop provided ye sd Mr. Tousee preach ye Gospel Amongst us a year. The Inhabitants Aforesaid voted and agreed and made choice of Mr Thomas Tousee to preach ye Gospel Amongst us for ye space of a year, upon Probation in order to settlement." John Glover, recorder.

November 16, 1713. The town "voted and agreed and made choice of Abraham Kimberly, John Glover, Ebenezer Prindle and John Griffin a committee to discourse Mr. Tousey in order to settlement, to know whether he is willing to carry on ye work of ye ministry in this place as long as God shall grant him life and health on ye salary yt ye town and he shall yearly agree for." Voted, "to give Josiah Burritt 20 shillings in pay or two-thirds money for meeting in his house on ye Lord's Day from this date until next May ensuing." John Glover recorder.

December 14, 1713. "Voted ye inhabitants of Newtown on ye Date above written, Have made and in our place and stead, Put and Empowered our trusty and loving friends Abraham Kimberly, John Glover, Ebenezer Smith Ebenezer Prindle and John Griffin our true and lawful attorneys, agents or trustees for us and in our name to indorse and agree with ye Reverend Mr. Tousee respecting his settlement and maintainance so long as he shall continue to carry on ye work of ye ministry in this place or town Aforesaid. Ratifying, Allowing and Confirming and holding firm and effectual all, and whatsoever our sd Attorneys or Trustees shall Lawfully do in and About ye Premises as we ourselves had Personally indented and Agreed. Entered verbatim as voted. Attest John Glover, Town Clerk."

At a town meeting called and held three days later, Dec. 16, the following vote was passed. "The householders and Inhabitants of Newtown by their vote Accepted ye agreement of Town's committee, Attorneys or Trustees made with ye Reverend Mr Thomas Tousee as to his settlement and sallary and ordered yt sd agreement to be recorded.
John Glover, Town Clerk.

May 6, 1714: "At a lawful town meeting of ye householders and Inhabitants of Newtown by their vote accepted the agreement ye town's committee, attorneys or trustees made with ye Rev. Mr. Thomas Tousey as to his settlement and sallary and orders ye sd agreement to be recorded."
John Glover, Town Clerk.

At a town meeting held February 24, 1718, the question of salary came up when the following vote was passed: "Voted, Whereas it is concluded Between Mr. Tousey and ye selectmen of ye town of Newtown that for ye greater convenience of paying ye sd Mr. Tousee his sallary that the year shall begin with Him as to his ministeriall work on ye 8th day of March next, and so shall continue year by year. It is concluded yt all yt is behind or remaining due of sd Mr. Tousey's salary from ye first of his ministry to ye 8th of March, next is 43 pounds, 16 shillings, three pence, shall be Payed by sd Day or with all convenient speed and that ever after ye 8th of March Shall be ye time on or by which ye sd Mr. Tousee shall be cleared or that shall be promised therefor."

Thomas Toucey,

Thomas Bennitt,
Joseph Peck,
Selectmen.

Attest, Joseph Peck, Town Clerk.

March 7, 1718: "At ye above sd town meeting the Inhabitants aforesaid did consent to, and by their vote confirm ye agreement between ye Reverend Mr. Tousee and ye selectmen of ye town of Newtown, February 24, 1718, and ordered sd agreement to be recorded,"—Attest Joseph Peck, Town Clerk.

"Whereas, in the articles of agreement between the town of Newtown and myself, particular prices are specified of grain and provisions, I do hereby declare that as to the grain and provisions that I shall receive of the town for the use of my family or for my own necessity or occasion to be improved in this place, that I will receive it at the common and current price that it shall go at in this place of Newtown from man to man and as to what I shall receive over and above what is above mentioned, that I will receive it at the price that it will fetch at the market at the seaside where I shall cause it to be transported. The price of transportation being to be subtracted. That is, that I will give as much here as it shall fetch me at any of the near seaboard towns where I shall carry it, except the charges and expense that I shall be at in conveying of it down and the loss that I may sustain by shrinkage of grain before such sale or rather at the reception of such grain or provision I will allow how as it will fetch at the same time at the next seaport town or towns excepting the common and usual price of transportation from here thither.

In witness whereof I do hereunto set my hand this 18th day of November A. D. 1718.—Thomas Toucey."

Joseph Peck, Town Clerk.

"At a lawful town meeting of the inhabitants of Newtown held on February 9th 1714, it was agreed and voted that the inhabitants aforesaid shall pay four pence per pound of the List to the Rev. Mr. Toucey's salary for the year 1718 to the 8th of March, next, and then the years begin again according to agreement as appears on record."

Joseph Peck, Town Clerk.

At a lawful meeting of the Inhabitants of Newtown held December 26, 1720, "It was unanimously agreed upon and voted to pay Mr. Toucey his salary and all the provisions he shall name of the above inhabitants as is specified in the instrument to be seen on Page 79."

Three years of apparent prosperity pass, and for the greater encouragement of the minister the town "voted and agreed by ye Inhabitants aforesaid to get Mr. Tousee his fire wood the year 1721 by a rate leavied out of ye list of ye estate of ye inhabitants afore sd at one penny per pound; ye price of a load of wood, walnut wood is to be 2 shillings, 6 pence; a load of oak or other good wood is 2 shillings a load; ye aforesaid wood is to be carted or sledded by ye last of January or ye first of February next, and if any man shall neglect to give in his account of his wood into ye Collector of ye Wood Rate, Shall by virtue of this vote be as Liable to be strainde upon for his wood rate, as he yt has got no wood for ye aforesaid Mr. Tousee." "Voted that Daniel Foot shall be and is appointed collector for to take care of and collect ye above sd wood rate according to vote or as the law directs for ye gathering of other town rates." Attest, Joseph Peck, Town Clerk.

Two years pass and the conditions between the town and the minister are again discussed at a town meeting March 12, 1823. It was voted: "that Capt. Thomas Bennett, Sergt. Peter Hubbell, Samuel Beers and Ephraim Peck be a committee in ye behalf of ye town to discourse with ye Reverend Mr. Tousee by reason of uneasiness of ye major part of ye inhabitants of sd town, they being willing to pay himself for ye time he has continued in ye work of ye ministry till this Instant and no further, provided he will lay down ye work of ye ministry among us."—Recorded, Joseph Peck, Clerk.

In the fall of 1723, Mr. Tousey prefers a memorial to the General Court complaining that his salary is not forthcoming. The General Court, upon complaint of Mr. Tousey issues an order that the "Inhabitants of the town of Newtown in compliance with the agreement with Mr. Tousey shall pay to the sd Mr Tousey 60 pounds of money beside a reasonable consideration for his fire wood for ye year 1723, which ended ye 8th of March last, and it is further enacted that a rate of five pence on ye pound on all ye polls and rateable estate within ye sd Town and collect and gather the same and pay it to ye sd Mr. Tousey on or before ye third Tuesday of July next year, and still further, should this fail, ye secretary of ye colony is ordered to issue a warrant or distraint to ye sheriff of Fairfield County, who is to be allowed 15 shillings fee; and is to send forthwith a copy of this act to Mr. Thomas Bennitt, Justice of ye peace, who is hereby required to see it properly served." —Joseph Peck, Town Clerk.

July 10, 1723, "It was put to vote whether or no ye inhabitants of ye town would abide contented and sitt still under Mr. Tousey's ministry and pay him a salary of 60 pounds ye year and find him fire wood for ye time to come. Voted in ye negative."—Joseph Peck, Town Clerk.

March 12, 1724, "it was voted whether ye inhabitants of ye town would pay Mr Tousee a sallary of 60 pounds and find him his fire wood under ye consideration of ye sircumstances of ye place and as Mr. Tousee hath and now doth carry on ye work of ye ministry. Voted in the negative." At ye above sd meeting ye persons underwritten Entered their protest against paying Mr. Tousee any Money by way of rate, declaring themselves to be of another persuasion, namely: Mr. John Glover, Sergt. John Seely, Robert Seely, Daniel Jackson, Samuel Henry and John Foot, because they could not sit easy under him.—Joseph Peck, Town Clerk."

At a town meeting, March 19, 1724, it was "Voted for to discuss with Mr. Toucey about laying down the work of the ministry among us, hoping to have some answer from him about the same thing, but we had none. Then we put to vote whether or no Capt. Bennitt, Peter Hubbell, Samuel Beers, and Ephraim Peck should be a committee to act and write in behalf of the town to the Reverend Mr Toucey, and to the rest of the elders and it was a clear vote that they should."

Samuel Beers,
Ebenezer Booth,
Nathan Baldwin,
Selectmen.

Recorded March 27, 1724, per Joseph Peck.

"At a lawful town meeting of the Inhabitants of Newtown held May 14, 1724, tried by vote separating one from another, whether the inhabitants would send an agent or an attorney to the General Court to be holden at Hartford on May 14, 1724, to show reasons why a petition to be preferred to the General Assembly aforesaid by Mr Tousey should not be granted as set forth in the writ, and it was voted in the affirmative and at the above said meeting the inhabitants by their votes authorized the selectmen in the town's behalf to assist in the matter depending between Mr. Toucey and the town relating to a petition to be preferred to the General Assembly to be holden at Hartford, May 14, 1724, according to that decision either by an attorney, agent or by writing."

Recorded, Joseph Peck, Town Clerk.

December 28, 1724, "it was voted by the inhabitants of the town in town meeting that the selectmen should discourse with Mr. Toucey concerning an account of salary and rearages and see what his demands are and make report to the town."

From the State records at the October Assembly of 1725: "Upon the memorial of the town of Newtown showing to this Assembly that sd town is at present under pressing circumstances occassioned by ye removeal of ye former minister (Mr. Toucey) and the settling of another (Mr John Beach) being weakened by ye dissension in opinion which hath been and is still among them, and remarkably cut short in their crops this present year by ye frost by ye which they are much straightened and incapacitated to pay a rate to ye publick, this Assembly therefore for ye special reasons aforesaid, do see cause to free and do hereby exempt and free the Inhabitants of sd town from paying any county rate for ye next year ensuing, provided ye town of Newtown draws no money for ye schools nor sends representatives to this Assembly during ye exemption."

"Whereas, In the Engagement of the town of Newtown by their committee to myself for my encouragement and for them In the work of the ministry bearing date July the 27th, 1714, there is in it an article as this expressed in these words: 'And also if by the Providence of God the Reverend Mr Tousey should be disinabled from his work in the ministry through sickness, infirmity, or age, he is notwithstanding to have his salary of sixty pounds a year yearly during life.' This article being to some distrustful, be it known to all men to whom this present shall come, That I do that is, I the said Tousey do accept said agreement of the Town as though the above said article had never been mentioned, always reminded that there be never any but confidence on this act of mine as though I did, in such losses as above said cut myself from the common privileges of ministers of the Gospel, or from reasonable subsidence being adminstered. In witness whereof I do hereunto set my hand and seal this fifth day of October, Anno Domini 1715." Thomas Tousey.

In presence of us
    Abraham Kimberley,
    Samuel Beers.

At a lawful town meeting of ye inhabitants of Newtown, held by adjournment on ye 8th day of February, 1725, then agreed and voted by ye inhabitants "aforesd at sd meeting to pay a rate of two pence half penny upon ye pound of ye inhabitants of Newtown per year to recompense Mr Toucey for ye time he served in ye work of ye ministry in ye year 1724.

Differences were at last amicably adjusted, all arrearages paid and soon after Mr Toucey went to England, accepted a commission of Captain in the King's Army and on his return to America came back to Newtown, retired from the ministry, but retained his residence in Newtown through life, always taking an active part in religious, social, civic and business matters and holding many high offices of public trust.

Soon after Rev. Mr. Toucey was hired, the town began to take necessary steps towards building a house for the minister, which was speedily carried to completion. It stood on ground opposite Newtown Inn.

A meeting house was also built during his ministry. The matter began to be agitated soon after Mr. Tousey was settled, but the town moved slowly in the matter and it was not until after 1720, that the work had progressed so far as to encourage them to hold meetings in it, and it was used in an unfinished state for many years.

The location of the meeting house was fixed beyond dispute by vote of the town "to be where the lane that runs easterly and westerly intersects the main street, or the street that runs northerly and southerly." There it was placed and so remained until 1792, when it was moved 80 feet directly west, where it is recognized as the Congregational church of to-day, remodeled without and within, and the home church of a goodly congrgation. "The groves were God's first temples," and although the town by vote in town meeting paid a rental to such families as would open the doors of their crude log houses for Sunday worship, we can easily believe that, when the warm mid-summer days came, they held their meetings out of doors, oft-times in the shade of native trees that were then abundant all through what is now our beautiful village street.

Rev. Thomas Toucey was born in Wethersfield, Conn., in 1688, graduated from Yale College in the class of 1707, and was hired to become the minister for Newtown in December, 1713, and was ordained as a minister of the Gospel and commenced his work as such in the early part of the year 1714. He was married to Hannah Clark of Milford, November 12, 1717. They had a family of 11 children: Hannah, born September 25, 1718; Arminal, born Apr. 15, 1720; Elizabeth, born November 26, 1721; Oliver, born April 26, 1726; Mehitable, born March 16, 1728; Sarah, born October 16, 1730; John, born June 15, 1731; Ann, born May 4, 1733; Thomas, born December 5, 1736; Zalmon, born February 20, 1738; Amaryllis, born September 11, 1739. Rev. Mr. Toucey died in Newtown, March 14, 1761, in the 74th year of his age. A blue slate stone slab marks his grave in the old part of Newtown cemetery, with this epitaph:

> "Down to an impartial Graves' devouring shade,
>   Sink human honors and the Hoary Head
> Protract your years, acquire what mortals can
>   Here see with deep concern ye end of man."

NEWTOWN'S SECOND SETTLED MINISTER
REV. JOHN BEACH—1724-1732.

At a town meeting July 27, 1724, it was "voted, that Capt. Thomas Bennitt should be moderator to put to vote what was then in consideration to be acted for ye hireing a young minister to preach ye gospel to ye town of Newtown. At ye above meeting Mr John Beach of Stratford was made choice of by vote of ye inhabitants of ye above sd town to come and preach ye gospel to sd town for ye space of two or three months, and it was further agreed and voted also yt if Mr Beach cannot be obtained by ye messenger or messengers that shall be empowered in behalf of ye town, then ye messengers are to apply themselves to Mr Andrews of Milford, Mr Gould of Stratford and Mr Cook of Stratfield for counsel and advice when they had best applied themselves for a man." "Voted also at ye above meeting that Capt. Thomas Bennitt and Mr Freegrace Adams shall also be messengers in ye towns behalf to act in ye business above written according to act of ye town. Robert Seely, being of another persuasion, entered his protest against ye vote passed concerning a minister." "Voted, that Mr Beach should be paid for his salary, sixty pounds a year for the first two years, and so rise ten pounds a year, yearly, until it should make one hundred pounds per annum and that to be Mr Beach's salary, all which payments are to be truly paid to him in money or provisions as they shall pass from man to man. Besides his standard salary he is to be paid in pork, beef, rye, wheat, flax, and Indian corn, also to give him fire wood when he is settled, also erect and build for him a two story house, Mr Beach to furnish ye glass and nails, ye house to be 40 feet long and 21 feet wide, and in height as generally two story houses are built, and erect a chimney in ye midst of ye house, of three funnels, two fire places below and one in ye chambers, Mr Beach finding glass and iron; also agree to give him ye improvement of a four acre home lot, during life, and also make to him 123 acres of land besides." "At a lawful town meeting of ye inhabitants of Newtown, held October 8, 1724, ordered and appointed for ye making choice of a gospel minister in order to settlement, the voters were ordered to bring in their votes for ye man's name whom they desired should be their settled minister with ye man's name fairly written on a piece of paper with their own names to it also, and Mr John Beach of Stratford was made choice of for ye Gospel minister in Newtown. Those whose names are underwritten declaring themselves to be of another persuasion, dissented or entered their protest against their doing anything for ye settling of any dissenting minister, namely John Glover, Robert Seely, Daniel Jackson, Samuel Henrix, James Hard, Senr, Moses Lyon. Received for record ye date above."—Joseph Peck, Town Clerk.

At a lawful meeting of ye proprietors of Newtown, Nov. 9, 1724, voted: "Whether Mr John Beach shall have the improvement of four acres of paster land lying south on ye land of Thomas Sharpe's home lott, westerly on Samuel Ferris, southerly on common land or highway, duering ye sd Mr Beach his natural life, viz. if he, ye sd Beach shall settle in ye work of ye ministry, in this place of Newtown. Voted in ye affirmative." "Voted, that those proprietors which have or shall give by subscription to Mr. John Beach for his encouragement, to settle in ye work of ye ministry in Newtown, according to ye conditions of this Government, that is to say, ye persons so subscribing shall have liberty to lay what they have subscribed out of their thirty acre divisions, in one or two entire tracts—that is to say, part on Brushy Hill, near ye south end of ye town, on ye westerly side the other part or tract without ye sequesterment. Voted in ye affirmative. Entered per me, Peter Hubbell, Town Clerk."

November 9, 1724: We, ye subscribers do freely give for ye encouragement of Mr. John Beach's settlement in ye ministry in Newtown, that is to say, out of ye thirty acre divisions already agreed upon to be laid out, money sufficient to pay for ye number of acres subscribed to our respective names the same to be combined in two or more larger tracts:

Subscribers: Capt. Thomas Bennitt, 5; Samuel Beers, 5; Ebenezer Booth, 6; Joseph Peck, 5; Ebenezer Prindle, 2½; Stephen Parmelee, 5; Samuel Sanford, 5; Ephraim Peck, 5; Mathew Sherman, 5; John Northrop, 2;

Josiah Burritt, 4; Jeremiah Northrop, 2; Joseph Botchford, 2; Nathan Baldwin, 4; Benjamin Dunning, 3; Jonothan Hubbell, 2; Lemuel Camp, 3; Hugh Stillson, 5; Adonijah Morriss, 2; Peter Hubbell, 5; Joseph Gray, 5; Jonathan Booth, 4; Joseph Bristol, 2; John Gillett, 7½; John Plat, 5; Andrew Wheller, 1; Thomas Sharp, 1; Benjamin Northrop, 1; John Griffin, 4; Moses Stillson, 4; Samuel Bryan, 6; Thomas Skidmore, 4; John Lake, 2.

In addition to these acres, at a town meeting April 6, 1725, "It was voted that Mr. John Beach shall have liberty to take up 30 acres of land that was given to him out of ye 30 acres as it appears on the records, viz. at ye end of one mile from ye meeting house to be taken in two or three places at his election, provided it be taken so that it damnify no highway."

Peter Hubbell, Clerk.

One of the first propositions made Mr Beach, in case he would become Newtown's minister, assured him that he was, at the outset, to be ranked among the town's largest landed proprietors. That settled there was to follow the matter of salary and the perquisites.

"The agreement entered into between Rev. John Beach of Stratford, in ye County of Fairfield, and Colony of Connecticut in New England, on ye one part, and Peter Hubbell, Samuel Beers and John Leavenworth of Newtown, in ye County and Colony aforesaid, on ye other part, witnesseth as followeth—

The above sd Mr Beach doth covenant with ye above sd Peter Hubbell, Samuel Beers and John Leavenworth, as they are a committe in ye behalf of ye town of Newtown abovesaid to settle in ye ministry of Newtown aforesaid, as soon as may be with conveniency comformable to Providence only excepted and allowed to continue during my life if ye Providence of God shall allow ye same, and furthermore I, ye sd Mr Beach, do promise to find all ye iron work, nails and glass for ye building me a house in Newtown, this house after exprest.

Peter Hubbell, Samuel Beers and John Leavenworth as a committee in ye behalf of ye town of Newtown above sd do covenant with ye above sd Mr. John Beach that upon his settling in ye work of a ministry in Newtown aforesaid, therefore ye sd Mr. John Beach shall have paid him for his salary ye sum hereafter mentioned, sixty pounds per year for ye two first years, after ye first day of this instant January, and allow to rise ten pounds per year yearly, until make one hundred pounds per annum, and then to be Mr Beach his standing salary, all which payments are to be truly paid to Mr Beach in provisions as they shall pass from man to man here in Newtown on ye first day of January, also to erect and finish a two story house for Mr Beach, he finding glass and nails as above exprest, and to find Mr Beach in his fire wood yearly and also to give Mr Beach ye improvement of four acres of pasture land lying near Shay's home lots as appears by record during his life, also we, Peter Hubbell, Samuel Beers and John Leavenworth as a committee for ye town of Newtown do make over unto Mr John Beach sundry parcels of land containing one house and 23 acres, and also four acres home lot, in Newtown above sd as may appear by deed executed under my hands and seal, bearing date with this instrument in confirmation of every one of above articles ye above mentioned parties have enterchangeably sett to their hands and seals in Newtown, ye date above mentioned."

John Beach (Seal)

Note: That ye above house is to be finished on or before the first day of November next ensuing the date above mentioned.

Peter Hubbell   (Seal)
Samuel Beers   (Seal)
John Leavenworth (Seal)

Signed, sealed and delivered in the presence of Thomas Bennitt, Joseph Peck.

This instrument received for record January ye 25th, 1725.

Recorded per me, Joseph Peck, Town Clerk.

"At a lawful meeting held May 14, 1725, it was agreed and voted by ye inhabitants at sd meeting that Peter Hubbell, John Leavenworth, and Nathan Baldwin shall be, and are appointed a committee in ye behalf of ye town to take efficient care yt ye sd town answer those obligations to and for Mr. John Beach and ye sd town as appears in ye article of agreement between Mr. Beach and ye sd town and by votes of sd town as appears on record, or by subscription under hand by particular persons; also take special care ye work be done, ye town ratifying and confirming what ye aforesaid committee shall do in ye premises."—Joseph Peck, Town Clerk.

"At a town meeting held, June 8, 1725, it was voted to recompense Rev. Mr. Beach for ye time he preached in Newtown before ye town agreed with Mr. Beach for settlement. Further voted that if ye selectman of ye town cannot gather money enough to pay ye purchase of ye house lot bought of Daniel Foot for Mr. Beach, then ye selectmen are to make or levy a rate upon ye list for ye payment of what money is wanting of ye sum of 40 pounds.

"At a lawful meeting held December 30, 1726: Voted to pay a rate of four pence on ye pound upon ye list of ye inhabitants to pay Mr Beach his salary for ye year 1726. Also agreed to vote to pay one-half penny on ye pound to get Mr Beach his fire wood. Voted that ye price of walnut wood is four shillings six pence a load, and of oak wood is three shillings and six pence a load: also voted to give the two collectors of the town and minister's rates, fifteen shillings apiece for one year."—Joseph Peck, Town Clerk.

April 6, 1727: The town voted and agreed that they should pay a tax of 10 pence on ye pound for to defray ye charges of erecting and furnishing a house for ye Rev. Mr. John Beach.—Joseph Peck, Town Clerk.

December 18, 1727: "Voted that Capt. Thomas Bennitt, Dea John Botsford, Lieut. John Northrop, Joseph Peck and Peter Hubbell shall be a committee in behalf of ye town to audit the accounts with Nathan Baldwin and John Leavenworth, committee for ye erecting and building a house for Mr Beach and make returns to ye town. Further voted and agreed that the committee appointed to erect and build the house for Mr Beach shall have 40 shillings apiece for their labor and trouble in sd service, which is six pounds."

January 8, 1728, the town "voted to pay a rate of three pence half penny half farthing upon ye pound of ye list to pay Mr Beach his salary for ye year 1727, and further agreed and voted to pay a rate of one-half penny upon ye pound to defray ye charges of Mr Beach's fire wood for ye year 1728 and voted to give ye collectors fifteen shillings apiece for collecting ye minister's and ye town rates (viz.) thirty shillings."—Joseph Peck, Town Clerk.

December 10, 1730, the town "voted that Samuel Henry and his son, Nathaniel Henry, be freed from paying any church minister's rate ye year ensuing, provided that ye sd Samuel and Nathanial Henry pay their proportion according to their list to a preaching Presbyterian minister at Redding at ye place known by ye name of Redding Ridge."

Mr. Beach was dearly beloved by the people, but he was so strongly fortified in his conscience in regard to the invalidity of ordination, and the necessity of being consecrated to the ministerial office by a duly chosen Bishop that after a few short years had passed he made known his views and that because of his strong convictions he felt it to be his duty to resign the pastoral office. In no way can the proceedings that culminated in the severing of the ties by which he and his people were so closely knitted together be so clearly portrayed than from compilations from the records of the more important town meetings that were held in relation to the matter. A town meeting was called for January 12, 1732, "to consult what was proper to be done with ye Rev John Beach under ye present difficulties of ye town by sd Mr Beach, who hath declared himself to be in communion with ye church of England. Ye meeting is adjourned until ye 19th day of January at 3 o'clock in ye afternoon." At ye aforesaid adjourned meeting "voted by ye inhabitants above sd to keep a day of solemn fasting and prayer under ye present difficult circumstances. Also to call in ye Ecclesiastical Council of ye County of Fairfield to direct and do what they shall think proper under ye present difficult sircumstances of ye sd town respecting ye Rev John Beach and ye inhabitants of ye town of Newtown. Also ye first Wednesday of February next is ye day appointed for ye fast. Also voted by ye inhabitants aforesaid that Captain Thomas Toucey, Mr Peter Hubbell and Mr John Leavenworth be a committee in ye behalf of ye town to write to ye Reverend Elders of ye County as above said, for their assistance." The following protest was entered at the same meeting against its action: "Protest—Whereas there being a town meeting held in Newtown on ye instant January 19, 1732, it is voted in sd meeting to keep a fast and to send out for ye Council of Elders to consult what methods to take in ye present difficulty of ye town above sd. We whose names are hereunto subscribed do enter our protest against sd vote: James Hard, Benjamin Glover, James Hard, Jr., John Glover, Samuel Sherman, Robert Seely, Henry Glover, John Fabrique." —Joseph Peck, Town Clerk.

January 31, 1732, it was voted in town meeting that Capt Thomas Bennitt Capt. Thomas Toucey and Deacon John Botsford be a committee to lay before ye Ecclesiastical council this work expected here, the present difficulties of ye town for that ye Rev. John Beach declareth himself to be partly reconciled to ye Church of England, that he questions the validity of the Presbyterian ordination, that he cannot, in faith, administer the Sacrament and refuseth to administer them, and declares that though there is a possibility, yet, not ye least probability that he shall return to us again upon his former principles, and to begg that ye said venerable Council would conclude and determine for this place with respect to ye premises as they shall think most regular." A protest was made by those whose names are entered below, "declaring themselves to be of another persuasion and protesting against the meeting doing anything for ye settlement of any dissenting minister: John Glover, Robert Daly, Daniel Jackson, Samuel Hawley, James Hard and Moses Lyon." —Joseph Peck, Town Clerk.

The town voted February 28th, 1732, "that Capt. Thomas Bennitt, Deacon John Botsford, Lieut. John Northrop and Mr John Leavenworth be a committee in behalf of ye town to discourse with John Beach with respect to ye estate made by settlement here and to know of him his terms (if any) that he will be upon with respect to the signification of ye whole or a part of what as above he hath received and to make report to ye town at an adjourned meeting."

Reply of Rev. John Beach to the above request: "Whereas a committee appointed by the inhabitants of the town of Newtown have made this proposal, viz: That if I will quit claim all ye land which I do now possess by virtue of a deed from ye proprietors of sd town and any of their acts, then I shall hold ye house and home lot, as my own estate and have ye use of that under Mount Tom, and ye use of that lot near Nathaniel Parmalee's until November next, and be paid by sd town for ye fences about ye above lots. To ye above sd proposal I consent, as witness by hand this 8th day of March, 1732." John Beach.

In presence of us: Thomas Bennitt, John Northrop, John Leavenworth, John Botsford, Committee.

"At a lawful meeting held by adjournment, this 13th day of March, 1732, upon condition that Mr Beach shall amply quit claim unto all ye lands referred to by ye town committee in their proposal to ye sd Mr Beach as on ye other side bearing date March 8, 1732, that is to say, shall quit claim ye same to ye Presbyterian part of ye town of Newtown considered as in distinction from that of the Episcopal persuasion, the town of Newtown by their vote concur with sd proposal made by their committee accepted."

"Voted, that the town committee shall take a quit claim of Mr Beach of ye land according to ye proposals above expressed."—Joseph Peck, Town Clerk.

"In ye stead, behalf and name of ye town of Newtown and their successors forever, unto ye aforesaid Mr John Beach, his heirs and assigns forever, devise, release, relinquish and quit claim with ye house and homestead on which sd house is now erected, containing four acres, east on ye main street, north on ye home lot of Daniel Foot, south and west by ye heirs of Hugh Stillson, deceased. Recorded April 8, 1732, by Joseph Peck, and signed by John Gregory, Justice of ye Peace."

In the first settlement of New England the preachers introduced the practice of having their congregation rise as they entered the meeting house. The males and females being separate, the one on the left and the other on the right, the moment the minister entered the broad aisle, the whole congregation rose. The minister, with a slow and solemn pace proceeding up the aisle, inclined his head first to the ladies, and then to the gentlemen. After entering his pulpit, all standing, he first bowed to the ladies, who returned the compliment by a decent courtesy, then he turned to the gentlemen and bowed to them, they also returning the compliment. Rev. Mr. Beach, finding the practice had been introduced in the congregation, requested them not to rise and bow to him, but worship God. saying that kneeling meant prostration and that we were told by the Apostle that at the name of Jesus "every knee shall bow."

Rev. John Beach, successor to Rev. Thomas Toucey, was the second settled minister in Newtown. He was born in Stratford, Conn., Oct. 6, 1700, and was a graduate of Yale College of the class of 1724. He was married in Stratford in 1726 and became the father of eight children, all of whom were born in Newtown. He died in Newtown in 1782. When he resigned as minister of the first Ecclesiastical society in Newtown in 1732, it was from his conscientious convictions of duty and he publicly informed his people of a change in his views and declared his readiness to receive orders in the Church of England. His resignation came in March, 1732. He soon sailed to England for Holy Orders, returning in September of the same year. He was appointed by the Society for the propagation of the Gospel in Foreign Parts missionary over the towns of Newtown and Redding, which work he carried on until his death in 1782. He was much loved by his congregation and, though the sundering of the ties that bound them caused many a heart ache, it did not weaken friendship, nor cause a bitterness of feeling that was long continued.

The Ministry of Rev. Elisha Kent.

An Association of ye County of Fairfield met in Newtown, Feb.2, 1732: "It is agreed that it is advisable, and accordingly advise ye good peolpe in Newtown to be speedy in their application to some meet person for steady information in order to a settlement in ye ministry among them and recomend to them for that purpose Mr Samuel Sherman of New Haven or Mr Hinsdall of Deerfield.

Ye above advice offered to ye town at ye above sd meeting and accepted by vote of ye inhabitants, James Hard Junr., entered his protest against ye advice above sd at sd meeting. The meeting is adjourned until Tuesday at sun an hour high in ye afternoon ye 8th day in Februray inst."

The meeting convened according to ye adjournment Feb. 8th. Then was ye judgment of ye venerable Council concerning Mr. Beach published in ye sd town meeting."—Joseph Peck, Town Clerk.

At a meeting held Feb. 8, 1732, "it was voted by ye inhabitants yt Capt. Thomas Toucey, Deacon John Botsford, Lieut. John Northrop, Mr. Joseph Peck and Mr. John Leavenworth shall be ye committee in ye behalf of ye advice of ye Rev. Association Late Given to ye town of Newtown with respect to ye obtaining if it may be, either Mr. Samuel Sherman of New

Haven or Mr. Hinsdale of Deerfield to come and carry on preaching in this place in order to a settlement in ye gospel ministry here in case there be a good liking and agreement to that end between those calling and him called, and in case that neither of those gentlemen can be obtained that ye sd committe shall have power with good advice to apply themselves to any other suitable persons for ye end aforesaid."—Joseph Peck, Town Clerk.

"At a lawful meeting of ye inhabitants of Newtown held May 11, 1732, appointed to consider and conclude upon proper measures to be pushed under our present circumstances, to ye end that we may have ye greater reason to hope for ye blessing of God in and upon our proceedings and endeavors for ye obtaining a Gospel Minister of ye Presbyterian persuasion to be settled among us in Newtown. Captain Bennett appointed moderator. Agreed by vote at above meeting: That ye next Thursday, ye 18th of this instant, be in this place religiously observed as a day of fasting and prayer. To seek of God a right way for us and ye smiles of his contenance upon us and to make application to two or three neighboring elders for assistance in carrying on ye work of sd day."

"Agreed and voted that at or towards ye close of ye fast, that ye town be brought to vote respecting ye choice of ye men whom they would have to be ye minister as above said. The meeting is adjourned to this day ye 18th instant May, until ye exercises of ye fast be concluded. Capt. Toucey voted moderator for ye present meeting."

At a lawful town meeting of ye inhabitants of ye town of Newtown held June 30, 1732, appointed to vote for a minister. Lieut. John Northrope appointed moderator, for ye business of ye meeting. "Voted, that ye voters should bring in their votes with their names written to their votes, which was done and brought in and Mr. Elisha Kent was by a fair and clear vote of ye inhabitants of ye town of Newtown made choice of for their minister, upon ye Presbyterian foundation." Voted also, by ye inhabitants of Newtown at above sd meeting that if Mr Elisha Kent shall if he see cause to settle to settle in ye ministry in Newtown upon ye Presbyterian foundation, (by Presbyterian foundation is to be understood that in opposition to ye Episcopal persuasion,) that Mr. Kent so settling and continuing, that for his encouragement he shall have all of ye land quit claimed by Mr Beach unto those of ye Presbyterian foundation in Newtown, and one hundred and ten pounds per year during his continuing in ye ministry, provided that Mr Kent shall give good security that if he shall see cause to alter his principles from his foundation on which he shall be settled to pay unto ye above Presbyterian party ye sum of four hundred pounds lawful money. It is to be understood by Mr Kent, his salary is to be paid in provisions or other such as we raise at ye prices as they pass among ye neighborhood in Newtown. Voted That Capt. Thomas Bennitte, Mr Peter Hubbelle and Ensign Thomas Skidmor should be added to ye committee that were appointed to seek out for a minister in behalf of ye town of Newtown above as appears upon record (namely) Captain Thomas Toucey, Deacon John Botsford, Lieut. John Northrop, Joseph Peck, and John Leavenworth, and are empowered by this vote in behalf of ye town, to represent ye towns affairs to Mr. Kent, respecting to his settlement and salary in Newtown and make report to ye town. This committee was adjourned until the 6th day of July, 1732, at sun and hour high in ye afternoon." Joseph Peck, Town Clerk.

"At a lawful town meeting of ye inhabitants of Newtown holden June 30, 1732, appointed to vote for a minister, etc., ye names of those that voted for Mr. Elisha Kent to be their minister at sd meeting are as followeth: John Leavenworth, Moses Johnson, Ephraim Hawley, Johoial Hawley, Henry Botsford, Henry Botsford Jr., Daniel Foot, Jedediah Prindle, Ebenezer Johnson, Joseph Peck Jr., Joseph Peck, James Brisco, Nathaniel Brisco, Jeremiah Johnson, Thomas Pearce, John Platt, Ebenezer, Platt, Stephen Parmelee, Joseph Benedick, Joseph Benedick Jr, Gideon Benedict, Samuel Pearce, Samuel Griffin, John Lake, Daniel Booth, Capt. Thomas Bennitt, John Golot, Abraham Bennitt, John Griffin, Joseph Botsford, Noah Parmelee, Joseph Murray, Samuel Parmelee, Thomas Northrop, Johnathan Hubbell, James Baldwin, Benjamin Northrop, Mathew Sherman,

Deacon John Botsford, Nathan Baldwin, Caleb Baldwin, Caleb Baldwin, Jr., Capt. Thomas Toucey, Samuel Summers, Benjamin Dunning, Stephen Burritt, Jehosaphat Prindle, Edward Fairchild, Stephen Hawley, Ephraim Prindle, Joseph Prindle, John Blackman, Thomas Skidmore, Jeremiah Northrop, Lieut. John Northrop, Joseph Bristol, Moses Botsford, Ebenezer Prindle, Benjamin Dunning, Jr., Samuel Sanford, Lemuel Camp, Mr. Peter Hubbell, John Hull, Job Sherman, Abel Booth."

"At a lawful meeting of ye inhabitants of Newtown, held July 21, 1732, Lieut. John Northrop, moderator, it was agreed and voted to give Mr. Elisha Kent for his encouragement and settlement in ye work of a gospel minister in Newtown one hundred pounds money to be paid (viz.) one-third part of ye one hundred pounds sometime in November next ensuing, ye second part of sd one hundred pounds in November in ye year 1733, and ye last third part sometime in November, 1734.—Joseph Peck, Town Clerk."

"Understood thus by ye town that Mr Elisha Kent is to pay Mr John Beach for ye fence that Mr Beach hath erected on some of ye lands which Mr. Kent is to have if he see cause to settle in Newtown in ye ministry. The meeting is adjourned until Thursday ye 25th of July. Ye meeting convened ye 25th of July and by reason of having no direct answer of Mr. Kent's acceptance of ye town's proposals as above exprest, ye meeting is adjourned until Tuesday ye first day of August at sun an hour high in ye afternoon."

"Ye meeting convened August ye 1st, 1732: Voted by ye inhabitants of Newtown at sd lawful town meeting that Mr. John Leavenworth should be moderator of sd meeting, Agreed and voted at said adjourned meeting that Mr Peter Hubbell, and Ensign Thomas Skidmore shall be, and are by this vote, appointed committee and are empowered with ye committee that took a quit claim of Mr. Beach in ye behalf of ye Presbyterian part of ye town so distinguished in opposition to Episcopal, namely, Captain Thomas Toucey, Deacon John Botsford, Lieut. John Northrop and John Leavenworth, which appears of record, as to ye lands, quit claimed by Mr. Beach and before named committee power to act in ye behalf of ye town as above sd. The above named committee are by this vote empowered to make ample conveyance of sd land unto Mr Elisha Kent, according to agreement and vote of ye town." Entered per Joseph Peck, Town Clerk.

"At a lawful town meeting of ye inhabitants of Newtown, held by agreement August 1st, 1732, Agreed and voted at sd meeting that Captain Thomas Toucey, Captain Thomas Bennitt, Deacon John Botsford, Lieut. John Northrop, Mr John Leavenworth, Mr Peter Hubbell and Ensign Thomas Skidmore, shall be, and are appointed a committee and are empowered by this vote in ye behalf of ye town to give sufficient security, to Joseph Murray for ye sum of one hundred pounds in current bills of credit which hundred pounds is to be understood the hundred pounds which is voted to Mr. Elisha Kent in order to his settlement in the ministry. The town holding firm and good whatever the above sd committee shall lawfully do in ye premises. Further voted at above sd meeting that there shall be a rate, a tax levied upon ye list made in ye year 1731, that amounts to ye sum of thirty-three pounds, seven shillings. Voted also at sd meeting that Joseph Bristol and Abraham Bennitt shall be collectors to gather sd tax of thirty-three pounds, seven shillings and deliver it to ye above named committee. Meeting adjourned till ye 24th day of August, 1732—Joseph Peck, Town Clerk."

"At a lawful town meeting held by adjournment August 24th, 1732. Then by vote of ye inhabitants Captain Thomas Toucey was chosen and appointed committee or agent in ye behalf of ye town to take ye bond of Mr Elisha Kent of sum of four hundred pounds money, which sd Mr Kent is to pay to ye Presbyterian part of ye town so distinguished from ye Episcopal, in case sd Mr. Elisha Kent falls from ye principles he shall be settled upon in ye work of a gospel minister in Newtown. Also voted at sd meeting that ye ordination of Mr Kent should be attended on ye last Monday of September next, which will be ye 27th day of ye month.—Joseph Peck, Town Clerk."

"December 19, 1733, voted by ye inhabitants yt there shall be a rate of four pence farthing half farthing levied on ye list of aforesaid inhabitants to pay ye ministers their salary (viz.) to ye Rev. Mr. Kent his salary, and those of ye Episcopal persuasion to ye Rev. Mr. Beach his salary on what is levied upon their list."

"December 24, 1733: Voted, that there shall be a rate levied upon ye Presbyterian party, so-called, to defray ye extraordinary charges of ye council and Rev. Mr. Kent's ordination, to be under stood thus, that ye Presbyterians shall pay three pence on ye pound upon their list, and ye church of England, so distinguished, shall pay two pence halfpenny upon ye pound levied upon their list."

"December 24, 1734: Whereas, ye worshipful Mr. Thomas Toucey and ye Rev. Mr Elisha Kent have petitioned for liberty to build upon their own charge each of them a pew in ye meeting house in Newtown for ye use of themselves and families as they shall have occasion ye one on ye one side of ye great or south door, and ye other on ye other side thereof, at ye above sd meeting, voted in ye affirmative that their petition be granted and is hereby granted.—Joseph Peck, Town Clerk."

"December 19, 1737: Agreed and voted that ye Rev Mr Kent shall have one hundred and eighty pounds for his salary for ye year past in ye work of ye ministry."

"December 11, 1738: Agreed and voted that a rate or tax shall be levied upon ye list of ye rateable estates of ye Presbyterian society, that shall amount to ye sum of two hundred pounds, to pay ye Reverend Mr. Kent his salary for ye year 1738."

Rev Mr Kent gave time among the Indians still living in the town during his ministry, for in 1742 the Colonial Court of Connecticut voted 13 pounds lawful money to be delivered out of the treasury of the Colony to Rev. Elisha Kent, who shall improve it for the instruction and Christianizing of the Indians at a place called Pohtatuck.

December ye 2d, 1742: "Voted that two of ye Reverend Council shall be called into our assistance. Voted and aggreed they being brought in, that ye committee chosen and appointed by ye Society in Newtown shall be empowered and are hereby empowered to lay all such reasons as they shall think proper why Rev Mr Kent should be removed from ye ministry in this place, before ye Venerable Consocation now sitting in Newtown as a Judicial Council for their judgment and determination and to manage sd act in that affair in behalf of this society according to their best prudence and judgment and discretion. The above mentioned vote clearly passed. Caleb Baldwin, Clerk."

"At ye desire of ye subscribers hereof these are to give notice to ye Presbyterian society in Newtown in ye County of Fairfield to meet at ye North School house in Newtown on Monday, ye 20th instant at nine of ye clock in ye morning for ye following reasons. That is to say to know ye minds of ye society relating to ye Reverend Mr Kent and also to make a rate for ye defraying of charges that hath or may necessarily occur or for any other business that may be thought proper.

Job Sherman, Obadiah Wheeler, Heth Peck, John Shepherd, Joseph Peck, Dated December 6, 1742. Per me, Caleb Baldwin, Clerk."

"The above said meeting opened and convened on ye 20th of December, 1742, Deacon Job Sherman chosen moderator and Caleb Baldwin clerk, and it was fairly tryed by poles whether sd society would further proceed to have ye Council proceed in ye case in which they have been heretofore engaged in referring to ye differences between ye Reverend Mr. Kent and ye above society and it is voted in ye affirmative. Voted also that ye above Council shall convene on ye first Tuesday of January next ensuing. Voted also that ye Rev. Mr Kent should sign a note to ye moderator of sd meeting if he is pleased with the committee appointed. Meeting adjourned to first Wednesday of January at one of clock, afternoon, at ye same hour. Caleb Baldwin, Clerk."

The adjourned meeting convened on ye fifth day of January, 1743 and "Voted yt whereas ye Reverend Council sat in Newtown on ye third day of December, 1742, their final determination was considering ye circumstances of this church and society ye Council concluded it not proper to determine suddenly yt ye union between ye Reverend Mr Kent and this people should be disturbed, or to say he shall still continue their minister, without ye concurring advice of ye neighboring consociation which said council declared they were willing to attend when called upon. Wherefore, we of Ecclestiastical society, in Newtown, do by this vote desire the speedy attendance of sd Council to determine ye difference between ye Reverend Mr. Kent and ye people whose affections are very much alienated from him as hath already or shall be made to appear before sd council when convened and yt ye Reverend Moderator would be pleased to signify to this society or any one of their committee when he shall think proper, for ye calling sd Council, and this society desires ye moderator be as expeditious as in His wisdom shall think fit. The above mentioned vote clearly passed.—Test, Caleb Baldwin, Clerk."

January 14, 1743: Unaminously voted yt ye moderator of this District be forthwith sent to, to call in ye Council of this district to gather with ye neighboring consociations in this County to appear in Newtown on ye fourth Tuesday of February next at one of ye clock in ye afternoon at ye meeting house in Newtown, then and there to hear and determine ye matters of difference between ye Reverend Mr. Kent and ye Society under his present care and finally to determine ye same according to ye rules of justice and equity.—Caleb Baldwin, Clerk.

"At ye desire of ye subscribers hereof they are to give notice and warn ye Ecclesiastical Society in Newtown, in ye County of Fairfield, to meet at ye North schoolhouse in Newtown on Thursday, ye tenth day of January, 1745, at two of ye clock, afternoon, for ye following reasons: To consult in and to agree upon some proper measures whereby we may be able to answer ye Reverend Mr. Kent, our former minister, in his further demands upon sd Society for his service in times past, among us.

Job Sherman, Nathan Baldwin, Joseph Smith, Abraham Bennitt, John Botsford, members of committee.

Caleb Baldwin, Clerk."

January 10, 1745: "Voted at meeting of ye Society yt we will give ye Reverend Mr Kent for his two last months services in ye ministry in sd society after ye rate of one hundred and ten pounds per year, old tenure money or provisions according to former agreement with ye lawful interest for ye year which is to be levied on ye list of rateable estates in ye year 1744. Voted: Deacon Job Sherman, Lieut John Northrop, Captain Ephraim Peck and Capt. Wheeler shall be a committee to make ye above rate and to discors and agree with ye Rev. Mr. Kent as there shall be further occasion.—Caleb Baldwin, Clerk."

"A vote passed by ye proprietors of the Common and undivided land in Newtown in ye County of Fairfield at their meeting legally warned and held by adjournment on ye 19th day of March, A. D. 1744.

Forasmuch as divers persons of ye Presbyterian persuasion did formerly sign or subscribe to give to ye Rev. Mr John Beach divers peaces of land out of ye thirty acre division and other divisions them to themselves granted to be laid out in ye bounds of sd Newtown as appears on Record, on consideration of said Mr Beach settling in ye work of ye ministry in sd town and sd lands so signed to be given was laid out to Mr. Beach and afterward sd Mr. Beach declare himself to be of ye church of England pursuasion in matter of Religion and thereupon did resign up to ye town of Newtown all his right, title and interest in the lands to him laid out as aforesaid and thereupon sd town did by its committee excute a deed in due form of law dated August ye first 1732 of one hundred and four acres and half of land to Mr. Elisha Kent in consideration of his settling in ye work of ye ministry according to ye Presbyterian persuasion and sd signers not having conveyed ye sec. of sd lands by any legal deed or deeds did afterwards lay out their full right in sd division to themselves and to their heirs, and therefore sd lands laid out to Mr Beach as aforesaid and supposed to be conveyed to Mr Kent by sd deed and then by right belong to ye proprietors of ye common and undivided land in sd Newtown, several of which sd proprietors was and did then profess themselves to be of ye church of England persuasion and not willing to contribute towards a settlement of a Presbyterian minister and whereas part of sd lands was laid out nearer than ye limits of ye 30 acre division therefore to secure to sd churchmen ye proportionable right in ye common and undivided lands for ye use of a church of England ministry equal both in quantity and quality to those of ye Presbyterian persuasion whose rights are devoted to Mr Kent, his heirs and assigns forever.

It is voted and agreed in sd meeting that those proprietors of said common and undivided land that were and did profes themselves to be of ye church of England persuasion have two acres and forty three rods of land, and so in proportion for half rights, etc., three eighth parts to be laid out within one mile from ye meeting house, ye remainder to be laid in ye limits assigned for ye thirty acre division to be laid out for a parsonage for a church of England clergy for ye use of ye Rev. Mr John Beach and his lawful successors forever.

Always provided that nothing in this vote shall be conserved to brake ye sequesterment.

Recorded ye day and date above per me, Job Sherman, Clerk.

Voted in ye affirmative."

"Copy of a writ put into the hands of the collector of the minister's rate for the Town of Newtown in the County of Fairfield for the year 1747."

"Whereas by the Selectmen of the town of Newtown aforesd a certain rate or tax leavied according to law upon the inhabitants of the town of Newtown for defraying the publick charges of the ministry for the year 1747 which hath been for collection committed unto you. In his Majesties name you are hereby required of the several persons named in the sd Rate to Collect the Respective sum or sums to their names annexed in sd rate and upon any or all such person or persons refusing or neglecting to make payment of the respective sum or sums at which they are in sd rate asesed you are to leavie by Distress of the Goods or Chatels of sd persons if to be found by you for ye respective sum or sums as above with your own fees and two shillings more for the writ, and the same dispose of as the law directs for the satisfying the above said sum or sums and fees and ye overplus, if any, be returned to ye proper owners thereof, and for want of such goods or chattels by you to be found, you are to take the body of him, them any or all of them so refusing or neglecting as above, and him, them any or all of them to receive and safely keep until he or they shall have satisfied the above sd sum or sums his, the sd Gaoler's fees, all charges and be by due order of law discharged hereof fail not and make Due return of this writ with your doing thereon as the law directs.

Dated in Newtown, this sixth day of April, A. D. 1748.

Job Sherman, Justice of ye peace."

December 27, 1757, whether this society will do anything as a society in order to reward ye Rev. Mr. Kent for his past services in sd society.

Voted in ye affirmative.

Voted in sd meeting whether the society will give ye Reverend Mr Kent fifteen pounds money, New York currency for his past services in ye society.

Voted in ye affirmative

Mr. Obadiah Wheeler chosen to gather ye 15 pounds and pay it in to some certain place as Mr. Kent shall appoint, which is Abiel Botsford's house.

Voted that Abiel Botsford shall deliver ye same 15 pounds when collected to ye Reverend Mr. Kent and take of him a final discharge from ye society.

Caleb Baldwin, Clerk.

Mr Kent was 25 years of age when he took up ministerial work in Newtown. No record can be found as to his family, but he must have had one for the town gave him liberty to build upon his own charge a pew in the meeting house for "ye use of himself and family as they shall have occasion for themselves on one side of ye great south door." There was some delay in the final settlement between the society and the minister, but at last all was amicably adjusted, as the following receipt will show.

February 22, A. D., 1763, there received of Mr. Obediah Wheeler, collector ye full of ye 15 pounds rate granted by ye society in Newtown in ye year 1757 which I very freely acknowledge is ye full of my demands upon sd society on ye account of my ministerial labors amongst them, and assure this people I retain a gratified remembrance of ye many favors received from them as witness by hand, —Elisha Kent.

Mrs. Emily H. Denslow of Marbledale, Conn., a descendant of the Rev. Elisha Kent, writes of the Kent family:

"The first of the Kent name in this country was Thomas Kent, who, with his wife cme from England to Gloucester, Mass., prior to 1643, and was one of Gloucester's original proprietors. He died April 1, 1658. His widow died at Gloucester, Mass., Oct. 16, 1671. Their children, Thomas, Samuel and Josiah, were probably born in England. Samuel was married Jan. 17, 1654, to Frances Woodal. They had nine children, of whom the youngest son Elisha, was born in Suffield, Conn., July 9, 1704. He was graduated at Yale college in 1729 and was married, April 3, 1732, to Abigail Moss, daughter of Rev. Joseph Moss, of Derby, Conn., granddaughter of Rev. M. Russell, a graduate of Yale, 1702. He left his charge in Newtown, conscientiously opposed to the existing religion there, and in 1743 was installed first pastor of Fairfield East Association, Dutchess Co., N. Y. Southeast Carmel, East and West Phillippi were under his charge, but in 1750 he confined his labors to East Phillippi, where he had in 1743 purchased a farm of 500 acres. He became one of the most influential men of his section. His wife died in 1751 and his own death occurred at Phillippi, N. Y., July 17, 1776. They are buried in the old Southeast cemetery. His children had settled near by, the daughters and their families within a few miles of East Phillippi parsonage. The sons-in-law were royalists, and the fortunes of war scattered the family, whose members became prominent in civil, religious and scientific circles. The children of Elisha and Abigail Kent: Moss Kent, born March 25, 1733. Elisha Kent, born July 6, 1736. Abigail Kent, born July 6, 1736. Sybil Kent, born July 9, 1738. Lucy Kent, no date. Mary Kent, born Dec. 10, 1744.

The oldest son, Moss Kent, married Hannah Rogers and was father of James Kent, Chancellor of New York. Abiel Botsford married the oldest daughter, Abigail Kent, and they have several descendants in this vicinity, among whom are Mrs James A. Sperry and Dr. M. H. Denslow. Mrs. M. H. Denslow (nee Kent) is descendant from Rev. Elisha Kent through his second son, Elisha. The Arctic explorer, Elisha Kent Kane, was also descendant of Rev. Elisha Kent of Newtown.

The Calling and Settlement of the Rev. David Judson as Minister of the "Presbyterian Foundation." 1743—1776.

With the going of Rev. Elisha Kent and the incoming of Rev. David Judson, there came a change in the business methods of the calling and settlement of a minister. Whether the change came by mutual consent of the taxpayers or by an enactment of the General Court of the Colony, the writer does not know, but we find no further allusion in the town records to the hiring of ministers after the discharge of Rev. Elisha Kent, although the meeting did fix a tax for the minister's rate, as far along as 1752. For information as to calling and settling Rev. Mr Judson, it is fortunate that the first book of records of the First Ecclesiastical Society takes up the history where the town records leave off, and from that we gather the business relations between the society and minister during the 33 years of his ministry.

Upon the retirement of Rev. Elisha Kent in 1743, the society was again in dire straits for a minister. On March 8, 1743, the society convened at the North schoolhouse in Newtown at 2 of the clock in the afternoon by order of Job Sherman, John Northrop, Moses Stillson, Joseph Bristol and Nathaniel Brisco, members of the society:

"So to make choice of a committee in our desolate state to take all proper measures in order for procuring some suitable person upon probation to supply ye pulpit in this place for a season. In order for ye settlement, if to ye good choice of sd society, sd committee so to proceed from time to time as there shall be occasion until sd society shall be satisfactorily supplied even to settlement. Also to take all proper measures at sd meeting for ye levying and gathering such sum or sums of money or other species as shall be thought needful for ye defraying or answering ye past or coming charges of ye society and any other affairs yt shall be thought needful to ye real advantage of sd society as though they were herein particularized. Caleb Baldwin Society's clerk."

At the above sd meeting it was "voted that Lieutenant John Northrop, Seargent Joseph Botsford, Capt. Obadiah Wheeler and Heth Peck shall be a committee to proceed in calling in some suitable person on probation for settlement in ye ministry and so to proceed from time to time if there be occasion until there is a settled minister in sd society." May 3, 1743: "Upon ye desire of ye persons hereafter subscribing that there is to be a meeting of ye Presbyterian society in Newtown on ye ninth day of May at four of ye clock, afternoon, at the north schoolhouse, then and there to take some proper measure with ye worthy Mr. David Judson, for his continuance among us in ye Gospel ministry, in order for settlement and such other business as may be thought proper at sd meeting to be done."—John Botsford, Johnathan Booth, Nathan Baldwin, Job Sherman, Free Grace Adams, members of Society.

May 9, 1743, it was voted, "whether so far as they had made trial of ye Worthy Mr. David Judson in his work as by ye committee he was invited to this place in order to probation for ye Gospel ministry here he was to their good satisfaction voted very fully in ye affirmative."—Caleb Baldwin clerk.

"Voted at ye above meeting whether this society will call ye Worthy Mr David Judson to ye Gospel ministry in this place, and it was voted fully in ye affirmative. Also voted whether this society will give ye Mr. David Judson four hundred pounds settlement old tenure to be paid three years from this date and it was voted fully in ye affirmative." Voted at a meeting held on the 23rd day of May, 1743, "to give to ye worthy Mr. David Judson if he shall see cause to settle in ye Gospel ministry as above—the sum of three hundred pounds old tenure towards or for his ye sd Mr. Judson's settlement in manner and form as followeth: One hundred pounds at or before ye first day of December next, and one hundred pounds per year to be paid annually by ye first day of December annually, until ye three hundred pounds above sd be paid. All ye above unanimously voted. There is also promised by signature to ye worthy Mr. David Judson if he shall settle in ye ministry in this society one hundred pounds old tenure to be paid at or before ye 23rd day of December, A. D. 1743."

At a society's meeting held by adjournment at ye Presbyterian meeting house, August 15, 1743, it was voted "that whereas ye vote by this society of fifty pounds lawful money per annum for Mr David Judson, his support upon his settlement in ye ministry in sd society is considered dissatisfactory to many and fearing it mayn't be for ye health of sd society, and, understanding from ye committee of sd society upon conference with ye sd Mr. Judson that ye sd Mr. Judson for ye peace of sd society was willing to forgo sd vote provided his support might by sd society be voted in manner and form as hereunto immediately annexed: Voted, that upon ye worthy Mr Judson's settlement in ye Gospel ministry in this Presbyterian society upon ye Presbyterian foundation and so long as he shall faithfully continue their minister upon sd foundation yt for his annual support they will give him year by year ye sum of fifty pounds lawful money or two hundred pounds according to bills of credit of ye old tenure of Connecticut, ye which is now equivalent to what it now is if there shall be any falling of ye currency of ye above mentioned two hundred pounds of bills of credit according to old tenure in Connecticut the above sum to be answered in bills of credit of New England, or provisions as they shall currently pass at ye market price in Newtown.—Caleb Baldwin Clerk."

"I, David Judson, referred to in ye above sd vote declare in case of my settlement in ye Gospel ministry in Newtown, I will never take ye advantage of ye vote of ye society in fifty pounds per annum lawful money proposed May ye 23, 1743, for my support, there being later provision made by sd society and it is my desire yt this with ye former go upon ye public record of sd society, as witness my hand in Newtown above sd, in this 15th day of August, A. D. 1743.—David Judson."

"Voted at this same meeting that ye standing committee so-called for this society for ye calling in a probationer for ye Gospel ministry and proceeding from time to time in ye affair till there shall be a minister settled here to be seen as of record, that they are hereby authorized in ye behalf of this society in conjunction with ye committee of ye Presbyterian church in this place to send forth letters of request to ye neighboring churches to cause their help that their reverend pastors with a messenger from each church would be pleased on ye third Wednesday of September next with ye leave of Providence attend ye solemn affair of ye ordination of ye Worthy Mr. David Judson to ye pastoral office in and over this society and church yt sd committee in behalf of sd society are authorized to take care yt ye sd gentlemen of yt affair are provided for, and that a day of fasting and prayer be solemnly attended by this society on ye first Wednesday of September next, to implore ye Divine blessing in that great affair and yt ye help of ye Rev. Mr Graham and Mr Judd be sought on yt occasion."—Caleb Baldwin, Clerk.

From the first book of records of the First Ecclesiastical Society of Newtown Jan. 30, 1746, we find the first allusion to the first repairs on the meeting house as follows: At a legal meeting of ye Presbyterian Society in Newtown, held on ye 30th day of January, 1746, Thomas Toucey, Esq., moderator of sd meeting, Caleb Baldwin, Clerk. Voted at above sd meeting that ye several sums above subscribed or that shall be subscribed to a certain instrument dated Newtown, December 30, 1745, already ammounting to two hundred and thirty pounds old tenure for repairing and completing ye Presbyterian meeting house which shall be laid out in new shingling sd meeting house, in putting in new window frames and windows of sash glass, in well siding sd house, in well securing and rectifying ye underpinning, in rectifying ye gable ends, and in putting on good floor boards, and if sd subscription shall be more than sufficient for doing all ye above sd outside work with glass and nails, that what remains shall be laid out upon ye inside house. All to be under ye direction of sd committee yt shall be chosen for sd business, always to be understood yt ye committee shall as far as is consistant with ye prudent and advantageous management of above sd affairs improve several subscriptions in said business as they ye committee shall think best and ye above sd committee is to cause to be done to ye outside of ye sd house what further they shall see to be needful to make it fationable. Voted: That Heth Peck, Donald Grant, Deacon Bennitt, Abel Booth, Alexander Bryan, and Caleb Baldwin are appointed committee to take ye oversight of, and carry on ye work according to ye above described vote. Voted: That ye above sd committee shall have ye care of all ye old shingles and clapboards and lead window frames and all ye other furniture of sd house and dispose of it all to ye best advantage of sd society.—Caleb Baldwin, Society's Clerk.

"At ye desire of ye subscribers hereof these are to notify and warn ye Presbyterian Society of Newtown, in ye County of Fairfield, to meet at ye north school house in sd Newtown on Thursday ye 13th day of March, at three of ye clock afternoon, for ye following reasons: That we may know ye minds of sd society respecting our erecting or building a convenient belfry on ye public meeting house of sd society in order for a bell when sd society is able to purchase one. Ye subscribers are Job Sherman, Nathan Baldwin, Abraham Bennett, Donald Grant, John Botsford, members of society,—Caleb Baldwin Clerk, March 7, 1746. Voted at sd meeting: Yt there shall be a convenient belfry built upon ye meeting house of sd society. We ye subscribers being members of ye Presbyterian society in Newtown, being sensible of ye neglect of ye house of God in this society for want of being furthur finished as to seats in ye galleries and all other work necessary to be done in sd house for necessary convenience at public meetings, notice is hereby given to ye society to meet at ye North school house on Monday, ye 24th day of April, at three of ye clock, afternoon, for reasons above mentioned. Dated April 17, A. D. 1749. Thomas Toucey, Ephraim Peck, Nathan Baldwin, Joseph Botsford, Nathaniel Peck, members of Society."

"Voted at above meeting: That a rate of 12 pence on ye pound old tenure on ye list of rateable estates of ye Presbyterians which is to be improved for ye further finishing of ye meeting house as to ye galleries and plastering overhead or any other work in sd house that shall be thought needful.—Caleb Baldwin, Clerk."

At a meeting Jan. 6, 1762, it was "Voted that there shall be a steeple built on ye east end of ye meeting house if there shall be money enough signed to build the same, and that Captain Amos Botsford, Lieutenant Nathaniel Brisco, Mr Gideon Botsford, Mr Ebenezer Ford, and Mr Caleb Baldwin shall be the committee to receive the money so signed and to lay out ye same in building sd steeple to ye best of their judgment."

"At a legal meeting of ye Presbyterian society in Newtown, Fairfield County Conn., holden on ye 6th day of September, A. D., 1762, Richard Fairman chosen moderator, proposed at sd meeting by Captain Amos Botsford and Mr. Nathaniel Brisco, that they will on their own cost and charge procure a good bell of 500 pounds weight, fit for to hang in ye steeple of aforesaid society and that it shall be for ye use of sd society so long as there shall be a Presbyterian society to meet in ye above sd meeting house, that is to say, if ye above sd society will go on to complete ye sd steeple, fix ye outside of ye meeting house, culler it and culler ye pulpit proposed for to vote whether ye sd society will concur with ye sd Botsford and Brisco in their proposals will go on to finish sd steeple and house according to sd proposals. Voted in ye affirmative. It was voted that there should be a rate laid out in finishing ye steeple and cullering ye meeting house and pulpit."

"At a meeting held in January, 1763, Captain Botsford and Nathaniel Brisco made open declaration that they freely and frankly gave ye bell which they had procured for ye use of ye society so long as there should be a Presbyterian society to meet in sd house, and ye society gave them hearty thanks."

For some reason not given in the record, the first bell did not meet expectations, and at a society meeting, May 28, 1767, it was "Voted whether they would do anything in order to get a new bell, and it was voted in ye affirmative and sometime in ye month of June was made out by way of signation ye sum of twenty-seven pounds, four shillings and seven pence, lawful money or provisions, and ye same being gathered on or about ye first day of July, ye committee for ye bell took ye old bell and conveyed it down to Fairfield, got it recast and brought up ye new bell and delivered it up and it was hung on ye third day of July, A. D. 1767. Always to be understood that ye inhabitants of ye Church of England society in Newtown signed of ye abovesaid moneys and provisions ye sum of five pounds twelve shillings and nine pence."

"Voted, yt Gideon Peck shall sweep ye meeting house twelve times in ensuing year and shall have twelve shillings for his services. Voted, yt time of intermission between meetings on ye Sabbath Day shall be one hour and one quarter from ye time of this meeting to ye first of next March.—Caleb Baldwin, Society Clerk."

In 1773, the agitation over what was known as the Saybrook platform came up, which neither Mr. Judson nor his congregation favored. A meeting of the church was held October 6, 1773, when it was proposed whether it be the minds of this church to stand in the consociated connection according to the Saybrook platform, and it was voted in the negative. It was then put to vote "whether this society will choose a committee to send for a council of the churches or not," and it was voted in the negative. January 12, 1774, a meeting of the ecclesiastical society was called, when it was put to vote "whether this society will agree to what the first church in Newtown does respecting their renouncing their connection with Consociated churches or not and it was voted in the affirmative."

In January, 1775, it was voted to raise Rev. Mr. Judson's salary for the year by subscription, provided £50 could be subscribed, which was done. The subscribers:

John Botsford, £2; Richard Fairman, £2; Amos Botsford, £2; Abel Botsford, £1 10s; Abraham Bennett, £1 10s; Josiah Beardsle, £2; John Sherwood, £1 10s; Caleb Baldwin, £1 10s; Jonathan Northrop, £1 5s; Benjamin Curtis, 18s; Joseph Botsford, 15s; Moses Platt, 10s; Ichabod Fairman, £1; Abel Baldwin, £2; Nathan Burritt, £1; Joseph Wheeler, £1 10s; Joel Bassett, 10s; Asa Cogshall, 12s; Nathaniel Northrop, 10s; Joseph Peck Jr., 10s; Nathan Sherman, 15s; Jonathan Baisley, 10s; Ezra Peck, 8s; Abraham Bennett Jr., 18s; Henry Fairman, 15s; Gideon Botsford, £1 10s; Gideon Botsford Jr., 13s; Silas Fairchild, 10s; Andrew Wheeler, 6s; James Fairchild, £1; Timothy Shepherd, £1 10s; Abel Botsford Jr., £1 5s; Jared Botsford, £1; Jerusha Baldwin, 6s; John Sterling, £1 15s; Widow Anna Baldwin, 15s; Joseph Platt, 12s; John Chandler, £1; Amos Terrill, £1 2s 6d; Abraham Botsford, 12s; Jabez Botsford, 18s; Moses Platt, Jr., 1£; Abraham Shepherd, 1s; John Bassett, 6s; Moses Botsford, 15s; Jonathan Booth's wife, 6s; Thomas Bennitt, 10s; Deacon Northrop, 6s; Ebenezer Beers, 5s; Henry Wood, 6s; Samuel Beardsley Jr., 5s; Roger Terrill, 15s; Mathew Curtis, 15s; Moses Gillett, 6s; John Gillett, 6s.

Voted that the above subscription be paid by the first of next April, 1776.
Richard Fairman, Clerk of society.

When Rev. David Judson was called to become minister in Newtown on the Presbyterian foundation, it was at a salary of three hundred pounds, old tenure, which at that time would be equal to about 50 pounds, English money. Bills of credit were in a fluctuating condition. Not later than December, 1753, it was voted in the Presbyterian society's meeting that for that year Mr Judson's salary should be six hundred pounds, old tenure, or in provisions at the market price as they currently pass in Newtown. They became tired of a flunctuating salary and in 1755 a vote was passed that the society would pay ye Rev. Mr Judson for his services ye year past, ye full sum of fifty pounds lawful money and that if any of sd society shall pay him in grain it shall be at ye several prices hereafter named: Wheat at three shillings six-pence per bushel; rye at two shillings four-pence per bushel; Indian corn at one shilling nine-pence per bushel; flax at five-pence per pound; and if any shall work it shall be at one shilling nine-pence per day.

Later the salary was raised to sixty pounds, then again to seventy pounds, and at the time of Mr Judson's death in 1776 it was fifty pounds. When Rev. Mr Judson became minister, the rateable assessment of the Presbyterians was 7693 pounds and six pence.

During the whole of Rev. Mr Judson's ministry of 33 years, he kept a continuous record of his ministrations, which is still intact and carefully preserved by the Newtown Congregational church. There were 30 families in Newtown in 1716. In 1738, there were 60 families, and, by a census taken in 1752, the town's population was found to be 1230 and in 1770 the number of families had increased to 350. Mr Judson says that about one-half of them were of the Church of England, and that his own congregation numbered 150 families and over 200 church members. From his manuscript record of official acts, we find that he solemnized 226 marriages, officiated at 887 baptisms, of which only eight persons were adults, 13 were children of slaves and only one Indian; 378 deaths where his ministrations were given.

Mr Judson was married by Rev. Mr Gould of Stratford, Conn., October 20, 1743, to Mary Judson, daughter of Joshua Judson, also of Stratford, and took his bride to Newtown when he entered upon his work. Their children were Mary, born July 4, 1744; Phoebe, born August 16, 1746; David, born May 17, 1748; Hannah, born June 10, 1750; Mary, the second, born June 7, 1752; David, the second, born August 25, 1757; Betty, born February 22, 1762. His death came Sept. 24, 1776, from dysentery, contracted while visiting soldiers in camp less than four months after the signing of the Declaration of Independence. A red sandstone slab marks his grave on the west side of the old part of the Newtown cemetery, alongside the graves of the two children, David and Mary, who died in early childhood.

The Church of England as a corporate body was acknowledged by the General Court, sitting in Hartford, in May, 1752, which then gave the Church of England parish privileges. Until then the people of the town were obliged to pay taxes to support the Presbyterian minister. From that time on, for many years, the Presbyterian part of the people were taxed for support of their own minister and the Church of England people were taxed to aid in the support of the missionary placed in charge over Newtown and Redding Church of England people, then under the supervisions of the Society for the Propagation of the Gospel in Foreign Parts, with its headquarters in England and Rev. John Beach minister in charge.

During the Rev. Mr Judson's ministry, the records show that the best of relations existed between the Church of England people and the Presbyterians.

MIDWAY CHAPTER IN THE HISTORY OF THE FIRST ECCLESIASTICAL SOCIETY OF NEWTOWN, CONN.

The First Ecclesiastical Society of Newtown has made extensive improvements in the interior of their house of worship, enlarging their conference room, adding to their conveniences for social enjoyment, installing an up-to-date plant with modern fixtures, and other improvements that follow lines conforming to the demands of the times in which we live. Three score years ago, the perplexing question with the little band of the faithful few was whether to disband their organization, struggle along as they were, or take up a site and start anew in Sandy Hook. A study of our town and the society records show that the growth in numbers increased continuously until after the death of Rev. David Judson in 1776. Mr Judson left on record that in 1770 Newtown numbered 350 families. His own congregation numbered 150 families and over 200 church members. For ten years after his death they were without a settled pastor and they were as sheep without a shepherd. The society no longer kept up its numbers. From 1786 to 1798, Rev. Zephaniah Smith was minister on a salary of 75 pounds lawful money and 30 loads of wood.

Rev. Jehu Clark was Rev. Z. Smith's successor from 1799 to 1816, resigning in August of that year. When he was installed pastor, in so dilapidated a condition was the meeting house that the installation services were by invitation held in the Episcopal Church.

What stronger evidence is needed to show the friendly feeling between the two Christian bodies.

He was settled at a salary of $400 a year and, when he left, the society was in debt to him $1,232.78. A tax of six cents on the dollar was laid on the grand list of 1815 to make up arrearages, but the sum fell short and a subscription was circulated to raise a balance of $240. From an old manuscript in my possession the names of subscribers are copied, which probably represent the families interested in the Presbyterian society at that time:

William Edmond, $10.00; Moss R. Botsford, $8.00; Samuel C. Blackman, $6.00; Timothy Shepherd, $6.25; Daniel Botsford, $3.00; Abel Botsford and son, $8.00; Gould St. John, $4.00; William H. Fairchild, $8.00; James Sears, $2.00; Arnold Fott, $2.00; Lamson Burch, $5.00; Caleb Bennitt, $4.00; Michael Parks, $2.50; Charles Burroughs, $4.00; John Clark, $7.00; John Skidmore, $1.00; Rebecca Glover, $3.00; Abiel Booth, $8.00; Thomas Botsford, $2.00; Philo Botsford, $3.00; Philo Beardslee, $3.50; David Sterling, $10.00; Amos B. Fairman, $7.50; Abraham Bennitt, $3.00; Luther Harris, $3.00; Joseph and Joseph B. Wheeler, $8.00; Miles Johnson, $3.00; Daniel Colburn, $1.00; David Peck, $5.50; Israel C. Botsford, $6.00; James Terrill, $3.50; Daniel Peck, $2.00; Benjamin Fairman, $2.00; Jacob Johnson, $1.50; Abraham Botsford, $1.50; Mehitabel Botsford, $2.00; Molly Curtis, $2.00; James Thomas, $1.00; Silas Fairchild, $6.00; Samuel Beardslee, $6.00; James Fairchild, $3.25; John Johnson, $2.00; Asabel Booth Jr., $3.00; Samuel Northrop, $2.00; Philo Johnson, $1.00; Abel Botsford, $0.50; Clement Fairchild, $2.00; Job S. Terrill, $1.00; Moses Shepherd, $3.00; Jabez Fairman, $2.00; Reuben Terrill, $3.00; Amos Terrill, $2.00; Philo Fairchild, $6.00; John Rogers, $3.00; John Blackman, Jr., $3.50; Roger Terrill, $2.00; Moses Beardslee, $5.00; Billy Hall, $2.00; Ziba Blakeslee, $2.00; Philo Baldwin, $1.00; Riverius Prindle, $0.50; Abel Johnson, $2.00; Obadiah Wheeler, $1.00; Adoniram Fairchild, $1.00; Ezra H. Johnson, payable in tailor work, $4.50; Truman Fairchild, $1.00; Zalmon Beers, $1.00; Joseph Fairchild, $2.00; Elijah Jennings, $1.50.

From 1816 to 1825, the people were without a settled minister. Those were times when candidating was in vogue and services were irregularly held. What were called "deacon's meetings" were occasionally held, when the good deacons would take the devotional part and some lay reader would read an acceptable sermon. January 14, 1825, Rev. William Mitchell was installed pastor, and continued in that relation until his resignation was accepted, May 31, 1831. He died of yellow fever in Corpus Christi, Texas, Aug 1, 1865. The two maple trees still standing at the rear of the Congregational Church were placed there by his own hands. "Woodman, spare those trees!"

December 5, 1833, Rev. N. M. Urmston was installed pastor and remained until 1838 when the Consociation of Fairfield East met in Bethel and by request of all parties concerned the relation was dissolved and the following resolution adopted by the Consociation: "To the church and society again destitute of a pastor we would extend our sympathies and hope they will not be discouraged, though feeble, but make every proper effort to sustain the interest of religion among them and as soon as practicable seek another pastor, relying as in times past, upon such aid as is extended to feeble branches of our Zion. Bethel, April 17, 1838.

From 1839 to 1842, Rev. Alexander Leadbetter was in charge and so difficult was it to pay his salary, the church at that time having a membership of only 45, that a special subscription paper was circulated outside of the society, to which members of the other Christian bodies, as well as non-communicants, contributed. At this time there were four houses of worship in the village: The house of the ecclesiastical society, then called the Presbyterian meeting house, the Episcopal church standing its width north of the present Trinity, the Universalist meeting house, now the town hall, and the Methodist, that stood on the open lot just north of Mrs Marcus Hawley's residence, the building later used as a blacksmith and wagon shop near the Newtown railroad station.

In order to show the kindly feeling on the part of the townspeople, other than those who were members of the society, I include a copy of a subscription paper that shows the contributions raised to keep the society from becoming defunct. The original subscription came into my possession more than 50 years ago, and reads: "We, the subscribers, do hereby promise to pay Elizur W. Keeler, treasurer of the First Ecclesiastical Society of Newtown or his successor in office, the sums annexed to our names respectively, for the purpose of employing Rev. Alexander Leadbetter to officiate as pastor of the first Congregational church and society of Newtown for one year from the 1st day of May, 1841, payable on the 1st day of November next. Newtown, March 27, 1841.

Eben Beach, $6.00; Samuel C. Blackman, $5.00; Lyman Beers, $5.00; Henry Fairchild, $5.00; Joseph D. Wheeler, $4.00; E. W. Keeler, $4.00; Rufus Somers, $4.00; George B. Peck, $2.00; George Scott, $2.00; Lucas Barnes, $3.00; William Beard, $8.00; Russell Wheeler, $3.00; Reuben B. Burrows, $4.00; Hiram Parmelee, $10.00; Philo Northrop, $2.00; Reuben Beach, $1.50; William Fairchild, $2.50; Edwin A. Lum, $2.00; Charles W. Coe, $1.00; Rufus L. Parmelee, $3.00; Jesse Hoyt, $3.00; John Johnson, $5.00; Charles Johnson, $5.00; Legrand Bennett, $2.00; Esther Ferris, $4.00; Grandison Parmelee, $0.50; Theodocia Peck, $2.00; Emily A. Sanford, $10.00; Ambrose Stillson, $1.00; Meeker Hoyt, $2.00; Ladies Society, $50.00; Wooster Peck, $4.00; Mary Tomlinson, $1.00; Almon Miller, $1.00; Alva B. Beecher, $2.00; Zalmon Griswold, $1.00; Sidney Middlebrook, $1.00; John Glover, $1.00; George Curtis, $1.00; Royal O. Gurley, $0.50; William Sherman, $0.50; George C. Peck, $2.00; A. Judson, $1.00; Daniel S. Hawley, $1.00; H. W. Tucker, $2.00; Widow Sanford, $0.50; Mary E. Parsons, $1.00; Graham Hurd, $2.00; Charles Dick, $1.00; Doctor Dutton, $2.00; J. S. Tomlinson, $1.00; Dr. Erastus Erwin, $1.00; Norman Hoyt, $0.50; Dr. George Judson, $0.50; Ammon Shepherd, $1.00; Hannah Shepherd, $1.00; David W. Jones, $1.00; Isaac M. Sturges, $1.00; Abel Botsford, $6.00; Abigail Marshall, $2.00; S. B. Fairchild, $2.50; William H. Fairchild, $1.50.

Encouraged by the response of people in contributing funds, Rev. Mr. Leadbetter was content with what could be raised by subscription, but that method had its day and when the stipend became too small to live upon, he resigned.

From a secular standpoint it looked as if the end of organized action was close at hand, so feeble numerically and financially had they become. The small fund they had depended upon had nearly been swept away by the failure of the Eagle Bank of New Haven, and but for the aid received from the Connecticut Home Missionary Society, which began in 1817, the organization might have ceased to exist. In addition to all other drawbacks, the meeting house itself had become so dilapidated that it seemed almost beyond repair.

A meeting was called, June 3, 1844, adjourned to June 15, when it was voted "that the committee of this society take such measures as they may deem proper for the purpose of building a meeting house in Sandy Hook." Two days later it appears by the record the following notice was sent out: "Notice is hereby given to the citizens of the village of Sandy Hook that the Congregational society of Newtown have instructed their committee to take such measures as they may deem proper to build a house for public worship in Sandy Hook. The committee hereby call upon all the friends of the enterprise to meet with them in the Temperance hall, June 29, 1844, at 4 o'clock p. m., to take the subject into consideration and to devise ways and means for the accomplishment for said object."

Samuel C. Blackman,
Eben Beach,
Joseph D. Wheeler,
Hiram Parmelee,
Society's Committee.

The meeting was held as appointed, the matter was discussed, it did not appeal very strongly to Sandy Hook people, people in the west part of the town did not fall in with it. The meeting was adjourned for six weeks and the matter dropped indefinitely.

Those were dark days for the few, at the head of whom were the worthy deacons, Eben Beach and Rufus Somers, while the venerable Samuel C. Blackman, Hiram Parmelee, Wooster Peck, Elizur W. Keeler, Charles Johnson, Henry Fairchild, Joseph D. Wheeler, William Fairchild, with their wives and a few others, helped whereever duty seemed to call them. Then it was that came the most perplexing question, "What must be done?" and one question that gained prominence again was: "Shall we change the site and go to Sandy Hook?" Up to this time no house of worship had been built in Sandy Hook. The only one in town, outside the center, was the Baptist meeting house in Zoar on the corner near what is now known as Snake Rock farm. At this juncture, a spirit of local pride seized upon the town's people, for they did not want the society to become defunct and the meeting house obliterated. Subscription papers were circulated until $1200 was raised and laid out in repairs. One of the subscription papers fell into my hands more than 40 years ago. Some will find the names of their ancestors here.

We, the subscribers, hereby severally agree and promise to pay to Eben Beach, treasurer of the First Ecclesiastical Society in Newtown, the sums annexed to our names, respectively for the purpose of repairing the Presbyterian meeting house in Newtown, provided the sum subscribed shall amount to the sum of $1,000. This subscription to be paid Dec. 1, 1845. Newtown, August 2, 1845.

Abel Botsford, $50.00; George Botsford, $25.00; Abigail Marshall, $10.00; Oliver Peck, $5.00; Elliot M. Peck, $5.00; Wooster Peck, $10.00; Hezekiah B. Fairchild, $3.00; John B. Wheeler, $5.00; Ezra H. Johnson, $15.00; Charles Johnson, $20.00; Henry Fairchild, $15.00; William Fairchild, $15.00; Hiram Parmalee, $20.00; Samuel C. Blackman, $10.00; Rufus Somers, $10.00; Eben Beach, $10.00; Lewis S. Brisco, $7.00; Robert N. Hawley, $5.00; Philo J. Marsh, $5.00; Sinclair Tousey, $5.00; Abner Beers, $5.00; Isaac Hawley, $3.00; Charles H. Beers, $3.00; Sallu P. Barnum, $10.00; Lemuel Beers, $5.00; Alexander Hall, $2.00; Isaac Nichols, $2.00; Reuben Beach, $5.00; Baldwin and Beers, $20.00; D. N. Belden, $10.00; Theophilus Nichols, $4.00; Charlotte Glover, $2.00; Henry B. Glover, $10.00; Henry Baldwin, $5.00; Abigail Walker, $5.00; George Scott, $2.00; Ambrose Stillson, $2.00; J. B. Nichols, $2.00; Isaac Marshal, $10.00; Joseph Wheeler, $2.00; Abel T. Peck, $1.00; Levi Peck, $2.00; Phoebe Booth, $3.00; Naomi Booth, $5.00; William Blakeslee, $5.00; Amos S. Treat, $3.00; Amos G. Peck, $5.00; James P. Geeler, $3.00; Walter and Isbell, $4.00; George A. Townsend, $20.00; Lyman Beers, $5.00; Charles Fairman, $3.00; Hepsa Foote, $2.00; Lucus M. Hard, $2.00; Jabez B. Peck, $3.00; Joseph Blackman, $2.00; Simeon B. Peck, $2.00; Eli Bennett, $3.00; Daniel Skidmore, $1.00; Isaac Foot, $1.00; Mary Tomlinson, $5.00; Ann R. Peck, $5.00.

To help determine the feasability and propriety of changing the site to Sandy Hook it was decided to have Sunday services alternate between Newtown Street and Sandy Hook. The upper room of a three story building near the bridge was rented, where, for a few months, services were held every other Sunday. The writer, a boy of 10 years, was a regular attendant with his father and mother and the remembrance of those experiences comes vividly to mind in these later days. This experiment caused a reactionary movement from the other end of the line. Voluntary offers were made of money to help put the meeting house in repair, which, with other reasons, led to the abandonment of the proposed project.

Coming of Rev. Jason Atwater.

In 1846, Rev. Jason Atwater offered his services gratuitously for five Sabbaths, an offer gladly accepted. In three years; $1200 was raised, the meeting house put in repair and re-dedicated in January, 1847. Rev. Mr Atwater resigned the pastorate in 1856. His salary was $500 a year. The following well deserved testimonial is inscribed on the society's record: "Like the Good Samaritan he came to us in the time of our greatest necessity, when days were dark and friends were few and hopes were faint and he has thereby exhibited the spirit of his Master, the Great Shepherd himself, who gathered the lambs in His arms and carried them in His bosom."

As we look backward from the standpoint of 1845 and then forward to the standpoint of to-day, it would seem that the year 1845, marked the point of the Great Divide with this church and society, as the past 60 years seem to have been years of most uninterrupted prosperity.

Here our chapter will close, but not so this society's history. From 1856 to 1914, 58 years of additional history has been making and awaiting the pen of some ready writer. There are but three persons besides himself, who were connected with the society and congregation between 1840 and 1850, and those are Mrs Lucy Beers, Mrs Elizabeth Fairchild and Mrs Adeline J. Fairchild, each of whom is now well past 80 years of age. (1914)

Note: Since the above was written in 1914, Mrs. Elizabeth Fairchild died June 7, 1915, aged 89 years and Mrs Adaline Fairchild died Aug. 4, 1916 aged 88 years.

At this writing Aug. 1917, Mrs Lucy Beers is more than 94 years old.

Rev. Wm. H. Moore succeded to the pastorate the same year. He was a godly man and an earnest and efficient pastor. Mrs. Moore an invalid for many years died in 1861. In 1862 he resigned to become State Missionary of the Missionary Society of Connecticut but retained his residence in Newtown for some time. In 1863 he married Miss Jeanie Sanford and removed to Berlin, Conn.

Rev. Wm. M. Arms became pastor in 1863, but remained only a year and a half. Rev. Daniel W. Fox was his successor. He was installed in 1865. In that year the church celebrated its 150 anniversary, and the parsonage was bought that same year. He resigned in February 1867. In June the same year the Rev. Henry Bagg Smith was installed, Mr. Smith was a faithful pastor, visiting his people scattered about the town, holding Sunday afternoon or evening services in school-houses at stated intervals. He was especially noted for efficient work in the Sunday School. In May 1873 he resigned to accept a call to Greenfield Hills. Miss Scudder

REV. WM. H. MOORE

See Page 78

REV. HENRY BAGG SMITH

See Page 78

REV. JAMES P. HOYT

See Page 79

REV. OTIS W. BARKER

See Page 79

REV. EDWARD O. GRISBROOK

CONGREGATIONAL CHURCH

pays a beautiful tribute to the family who made so large a place in the life of the church, "the pastor's good wife, a woman possessing rare gifts of heart and mind and a tender sympathy so that all those in trouble turned to her for consolation and counsel, the charming daughters who gave in unstinted measure of their time and gifts to their father's work in the church. Five of the seven sons have at various times returned to the town and to the church to do valued services as deacons, superintendents in the Sunday School and various activities in the church.

In May, 1874, Rev. James P. Hoyt accepted a call on condition that the pews be free. His pastorate was one of the longest in the church covering a period of sixteen years. Many improvements were made in his time the greatest being in the lecture room. One hundred and fifty new members were received during his pastorate, the benevolences tripled and the fund increased from $2,200 to $5000, $2000 being a legacy from Miss Sarrah Blackman, a daughter of Judge Samuel C. Blackman.

Mr Hoyt resigned in 1890 accepting a call to Cheshire Conn.

In August 1890, Rev. Samuel W. Delzell became pastor. He was a faithful pastor and an earnest preacher and it was with sincere regret that the church parted with him after a three years pastorate. He left to affiliate himself with the Baptist denomination.

Rev. Otis W. Barker was ordained Oct. 24, 1893, and installed, October 1894. Many improvements were made; a new chandelier costing $90, also the vocalion organ. Monthly missionary concerts were held and many notable workers from various fields all over the world came to tell us of their work. A Christian Endeavor Society was organized in 1899. It was with a feeling akin to dismay that we learned in 1905, that our beloved leader must lay down the work so dear to him and to us.

In October 1905 Rev. Ralph Danforth accepted a call from the church. He remained only until September 1907, when he left to study at a western university. Rev. Alexander Steele came from the Methodists, with the understanding that he should pursue his theological studies at Yale University. He organized and led the Boy Scouts. He left in August 1912 to return to his own denomination.

Rev. T. J. Lee took up the work of the church and the parish, February 1913.

Miss Susan Scudder, from whose historical address, the largest part of the record from the days of Rev. Mr. Atwater down, have been taken, says. "He is known and loved by all as he goes out and in amongst us, rejoicing with those who rejoice, comforting those who sorrow, and breaking to us the Bread of Life on the Lord's Day"

October 18th, 19th and 20th 1914, were given up to celebrating the two hundredth Anniversary of the Congregational Church.

THE EPISCOPAL CHURCHES IN NEWTOWN STREET.

Nothing can be found in Newtown records regarding the location of the place of worship built in 1732, after the adherents of the church of England had withdrawn from the "standing order," which in the colony was Presbyterian, and for the support of which taxes were levied on all freeholders of the town. Their first public service was held in the open under a large button-ball or sycamore tree at the foot of the hill to the south of the village. In 1907 a boulder suitably inscribed was placed to mark the nearby spot and in that vicinity it is supposed was their first building in which to meet for worship. We know nothing further about it, but however small, crude or unpretentious it may have been, it served their purpose until 1746, when they asked for a grant of land on the hill to the northward. A town meeting was held at the north schoolhouse, March 27, 1746, "to take action for ye setting up a public meeting house for ye church of England so-called in Newtown," when it was "voted that whereas those of ye church of England people in this place are now upon building a new meeting house for ye public worship of God, that sd people of ye Episcopal Communion shall have liberty to erect sd house on ye west side of ye town street southward of ye Presbyterian meeting house 28 rods, ye south end of ye termination of ye church of England meeting house to be ye termination of 28 rods, said house to set northward and southward fronting to ye street, and ye back or westward side of sd house to be 10 feet distant from ye front of ye house lot on which it stands against, and that they and their successors shall never be molested by this town from this time forward and forever in ye enjoyment of sd place for ye use aforesaid.

Attest John Northrop, Town Clerk."

After the building was erected and covered the Presbyterians, troubled lest the vote of the town had not been complied with in locating the building, called out Edmond Lewis, county surveyor, who "being assisted by chain bearers as the law directs," found that the Church of England meeting house had not been located quite as ye town directs, as ye 28 rods south of ye Presbyterian meeting house terminated 19 feet southward of ye south sill of ye Church of England meeting house as they are now laid."

The same day John Glover, Jr., Thomas Skidmore and James Hard, committee of the Episcopal church, apologized for the mistake:

We ye subscribers, members of ye church of England in Newtown, being sensible that we have not fully complied with ye vote of sd town in respect to building ye Church, in that we did not lay ye foundation of sd Church as far southward as it ought to have been by sd vote, by about 20 feet and in so doing have so far done contrary to good order and ye agreement of ye town by sd vote and hereby desire that those who are aggrieved to forgive us that rong. —John Glover, Thomas Skidmore, John Glover, the Committe.

"Ye subscribers hereunto received ye above acknowledgment and accepted it to put on record, April 12, 1746.

John Northrope, Town Clerk."

OLD NEWTOWN ABOUT 1800

JOHN BEACH MEMORIAL TABLET

See Page 87

As the building was erected at the expense of the Church of England people, and not at the expense of the town, nothing appears on the town records as to the expense of the work or as to its dimensions or the time of its completion. All we know about the building is what we are told by Dr E. Edwards Beardsley in his history of the Church in Connecticut:

"It was a strong, neat building 46 feet long and 35 feet wide and 25 feet to the roof."

To make clear to the reader its exact location with reference to the meeting house of the Presbyterians, we need to bear in mind that the meeting house was on the east side of the street exactly opposite where the Congregational church now stands, and this location of the Church of England house of worship was by vote of the town exactly 28 rods to the south of that, but on the opposite side of the road. The building was used by the Episcopalians until 1793, when it was sold to Solomon Glover, who moved it off the highway and rented it to the town for a term of years for a town house.

In 1752, the Church of England people in Newtown began to show signs of uneasiness at being made to pay taxes to help pay the Presbyterian minister's salary and petitioned the authorities to call a town meeting to answer this Church of England people preamble:

Whereas ye professors of ye Church of England, Newtown, in ye county of Fairfield have cited ye inhabitants of sd town to appear at ye General Court to be held at Hartford on ye second Thursday of Instant, may it please to show reasons, if any they have, why said court should not grant sd professors parish privilege, etc.

The town meeting was held, May, 1752 at 6 in the afternoon, at the north schoolhouse in the town street to do what shall be thought proper in sd affair.

Capt. John Glover was appointed moderator and put to vote whether they would make choice of any meet person to be an agent to appear at Hartford on ye second Thursday of May of ye General Court sitting to oppose or give reasons why ye professors of ye Church of England in Newtown should not have their prayer granted unto them and it was voted in ye negative.

Also voted that we have no reasons to offer against ye motion of the Church of England in Newtown prayer to ye Assembly.
Voted in ye affirmative.

John Northrop, Town Clerk.

Up to this time the Church of England people had had no parish privileges independently of the town authorities. At the annual town meeting, a man was chosen to collect the minister's rates which were paid by tax. Two collectors, one to collect rates for the Presbyterian minister, who was at that time Rev. David Judson, and one to collect for the Church of England minister, who was Rev. John Beach. The population of Newtown in 1752 was 1250, 23 of whom were slaves.

REV. JOHN BEACH

The Rev. John Beach after his ordination in England officiated alternately at Newtown and Redding. During the Revolutionary War he was forbidden to pray for the King, but like Daniel of old he persisted in doing what he considered his duty.

Attached to a memorial tablet near the pulpit in Christ Church, Redding, is a bullet, which had it reached its mark would have ended the career of this brave pioneer of the Church. The inscription reads:

"This bullet was fired at the Rev. John Beach while officiating in the Ante-Revolutionary Church of this parish, and was found lodged in the sounding board when that church was taken down and the present edifice erected. Pausing for a moment the venerable pastor repeated these words to the alarmed congregation: 'Fear not them which kill the body but are not able to kill the soul, but rather fear Him who is able to destroy both soul and body in Hell.' The bullet is preserved here as a relic of his loyalty to the Church."

To the Blessed Memory of Rev. John Beach, A. M., Founder of this Parish.

Born at Stratford, Conn., A.D. MDCC., graduated Yale College A. D. MDCCXXI. At great sacrifice upon thorough investigation and deep conviction conforming to the Church of England he was admitted to Holy Orders in England, A. D. MDCCXXXII and appointed missionary at Newtown and Redding of the Venerable Society for the Propagation of the Gospel. He was a scholar thorough—a reasoner cogent—a controversialist able—a preacher persuasive—a pastor untiring—a Christian hero undaunted. He was of all most effective in laying deep and broad the foundations of the Church in the Colony of Connecticut. From the begining of his ministry assailed by bitter intolerance and pursued by malicious plottings he patiently endured in the added perils of a cruel war remaining with his flock he continued his ministrations at the constant risk of threatened violence and death. Full of years and labors he entered into rest, March XIX, A. D., MDCCLXXXII.

In 1790 the Church of England people made known to the town they desired to secure a new location on which to build. A town meeting was held Dec. 23, 1790, and the town voted "that the people of the Episcopal Church and society in this town have liberty to erect a house for public worship on the place where the Town house now stands, placing the west part of the steeple in a line with the building on the east side of Town street, they being to the expense of moving the Town house to some proper place that shall be agreed upon by the town."

The only objection the Episcopalians had to that site was the nearness of the meeting house which was on the east side of the main street and near the town house. The Episcopalians made a proposition to move the meeting house to the west side of the main street at their own risk. This proposition was acted upon at a Presbyterian Society's meeting, Jan. 9, 1792, when it was voted "that the Presbyterian society give their free and full consent that their meeting house for public worship may be removed westward and placed in such position as shall be further directed, provided it shall be done without subjecting the society to any expense and that the society shall be indemnified for all damages the said house shall sustain in consequense of such removal as shall be hereafter estimated and agreed to by said society and that a committee be appointed to confer with the Episcopal society's committee to hear and report their terms at the next society's meeting or adjournment of the present meeting. Voted Mr William Edmond, Jabez Botsford and Roger Terrill be a committee for the above business."

Caleb Baldwin, Clerk."

After the death of Rev. John Beach in 1782, we have no record of a settled rector until 1787, when Rev. Philo Perry was called.

During his rectorship the third church house was built. The first record is dated Nov. 2, 1790. At a parish meeting that day "it was voted that we build a new Church house." On the 25th day of the same month another meeting was held, at which it was moved "to rescind the vote of the previous meeting." The motion did not prevail, and a committee was appointed "to inspect and search where it is most convenient to set the new church and to make inquiry how the several plots of ground that have been proposed can be purchased."

December 30, 1790, at another parish meeting it was voted "that if we do build a new church it shall be erected where the town house now stands." It was also voted "that a committee be appointed to prefer a petition to the General Assembly now sitting in New Haven for permission to raise by a lottery the sum of one thousand pounds lawful money by a deduction of 12 per cent for the purpose of building a new church, or as much short of the sum mentioned as the committee after further consideration shall think proper; and that the committee shall have descretionary power to form a scheme of said lottery and to make report of their proceedings at the next meeting." Capt. David Baldwin, Messrs. Andrew Beers and Solomon Glover were appointed lottery committee.

As the records show no report from the lottery committee we infer the scheme was abandoned and at a meeting in Oct., 1791, it was—

Voted "that we will build the Church by subscription provided we can get one thousand pounds subscribed by the second Tuesday in Nov. Messrs David Beers, Samuel Ferris, Abraham Booth, Ebenezer Beers and Josiah Fairchild were appointed a committee to obtain subscriptions and David Fabrique, Abijah Curtiss and Jonathan Sherman committee to examine and propose the bigness of the church." At a meeting, Nov. 8, 1791, "it was voted that the bigness of the church shall be 68 by 48 feet and that Daniel Booth, David Beers, Solomon Glover and Jonathan Sherman be a committee to contrive carry out and complete the building of the Church."

March 5, 1792, it was "voted that the price for common timber for building the Church should be 4 pence the square foot, brought to the place of building and well dressed." April 23, 1792, it was "voted that Andrew Beers, Josiah Tomlinson, Solomon Glover, Josiah Fairchild, Capt. John Glover, Zalmon Toucey and Ezra Booth be a committee to inspect and make further search for the most convenient place to set the new Church house and make a report at our next meeting." A week later a meeting was held when it was "voted whether we will do anything in regard to moving the Church from the plot of ground where it was formerly voted."

It was decided in the negative by a large majority and the meeting decided to adhere to the selection first made. In April, 1793, Henry Glover, Cyrenius Hard and Joseph Ferris were appointed a committee to dispose of the old Church and it was also voted to give the reading desk and the pulpit to the Episcopal Church in Brookfield. At a parish meeting June 17, 1793, it was "voted that the new Church be called Trinity." In September, 1793, the Church was consecrated by Bishop Seabury, first Bishop of the Episcopal Church in America. The annual convention of the Diocese of Connecticut met in this Church three times, 1801, 1806 and 1826. May 18, 1795, it was "voted that the thanks of the parish be returned to Messrs. Richard Nichols and Philo Norton for the donation of a bell for the society's use." The bell was cast in London in 1793.

Mr Perry died in 1798. A tablet bearing this inscription is inserted in the wall of the stone church: "In Memory of the Rev. Philo Perry. Born in Woodbury, Conn., A. D. 1752. Graduated at Yale

College in 1777. Admitted to Holy Orders by Bishop Seabury, June 3, 1787, from which time until he was called to the rest of Paradise, A. D. 1798, he was the devoted and efficient Rector of this Parish and a Clergyman of eminence in the Councils of the Church."

Rev. Daniel Burhans, D. D., became rector in 1799 and remained in charge of the parish until 1830, when he resigned and became rector of St. James Church. At that time he reported belonging to the parish 214 families and 300 communicants. "In my 30 years ministry, I have admitted by baptism 1350, for confirmation 400, admitted to Holy Communion 203." He remained in Zoar two years and accepted a call to Plymouth. During his later years, it was his custom to visit his dear old parish each year and preach a farewell sermon.

Mr. and Mrs. Beach Camp were the last couple married while rector at Newtown in 1830. Their daughter, Mrs. E. L. Johnson, born in 1837, heard him preach several farewell sermons and attended his funeral at Trinity Church. He died Dec. 30, 1853.

The tablet in the wall of the stone church bears this inscription: "To perpetuate the blessed memory of the Rev. Daniel Burhans, D. D., for thirty-one years the zealous and efficient Rector of this Parish, adorning his life with the fruits of the Spirit and his ministry with faithful diligence. He was the last survivor of those ordained by the first Bishop of Connecticut, having for more than half a century contended for the faith once delivered to the Saints as this church hath received the same. He was born at Sherman, Conn., July 7, 1762. Entered into rest Dec. 30, 1853, in the ninety-second year of his age and the sixtieth of his ministry."

Immediately succeeding Rev. Burhans was Rev. Samuel C. Stratton, a godly man and much beloved. Some appreciative friends placed a beautiful window to his memory in the new stone Church. He was rector from Oct. 1, 1831, to Oct. 1. 1839, being succeeded, Sept. 11, 1841, by Rev. S. S. Stocking, who remained untli Sept. 24, 1848. A good man and loved by his peaple. Rev Horace Hills became rector, Jan. 7, 1849, resigned Nov. 11, 1849.

Rev. Dr. Wm. M. Carmichael became rector, Nov. 6, 1850, re signed Nov. 6, 1852. The death of his wife by small pox and other events made his rectorship a period of sorrow and unrest.

The parish was greatly blessed during the ministry of Rev. Benj. W. Stone, D. D., from Nov. 20, 1852, to Nov. 17, 1856, when to the regret of his people he answered a higher call.

At the suggestion of Jonathan E. Goodhue, a student for the ministry while Principal of Newtown Academy, the parish, with the Bishop's permission, called Rev. Dr. Newton E. Marble, of Concord, N. H., who became rector, April 1, 1857. In June, he brought his bride, Miss Mary Gillis, great-grand-daughter of Maj. Gen. John Stark of Revolutionary fame, to be the mother of the motherless Frances, the gracious mistress of the new rectory built the same summer, and the always loyal and efficient help-meet in a singularly useful and blessed ministry of more than twenty-one years.

Their two children: Mary Gillis, born 1858, died 1874; Frederick

REV. DANIEL BURHANS, D. D.

See Page 84

REV. NEWTON E. MARBLE D. D.
See Page 85

TRINITY P. E. CHURCH

See Page 85

SILAS N. BEERS
See Page 85

SHOWING RELATIVE POSITION OF THE TWO
CHURCHES 1793 and 1870

Parker, born 1859, is an eminent lawyer of Lowell, Mass.

In 1866, the parish bought the homestead of Isaac Beers, just south of the old church and separated from it by a branch road connecting at the rear of the Church with the road leading to Sandy Hook The town relinquished its right to this road. The strip of road, together with the homestead bought of Isaac Beers, made ample room for the site and building of the new Church, without disturbing the old Church building. After the completion of the stone Church, the old building was sold at auction for $100 and torn down.

The building committee were, Mr. Henry Sanford, Simeon B. Peck, David H. Johnson, Henry B. Glover, Aaron Sanford. Dec. 28, 1867, Walter Clarke, Daniel N. Morgan, Silas N. Beers, Legrand Fairchild and Frederick Chambers were added to the building committee.

The architect was Mr. Silas Norman Beers, one of Newtown's gifted sons. He, with Mr. Henry Sanford and others of the committee, gave time and strength in unstinted measure to the work, and it was a proud day in February, 1870, that saw the completion of the fourth Church edifice since the first Rector, Rev. John Beach, preached his first sermon in 1732 under the button-ball tree at the four corners below the Street.

The last service was held in the old Church, Jan. 30, 1870. The text of the last sermon, "It is the last time," struck a note of sadness in the heart of many in the well-filled Church.

After a service of thirteen years in the old Church, and eight in the new, whose building he had watched from corner-stone to turret, Dr. Marble was obliged, because of physical infirmities, to offer his resignation, May 1, 1878, to take effect, Sept. 1, 1878, that date being his 70th birthday and the 36th of his entering the ministry. He had been unable for several weeks to walk or stand and strong men of the parish took him in a wheel-chair across the Street, up the steps and to the chancel for his last service in the parish he had served so faithfully for more than twenty-one years. With heavy hearts, we heard him say, "I have finished my course." The precious body never entered the portals of the Church again, until after two years of patient suffering it was released, and strong men again bore it to the chancel where he had been wont to proclaim Jesus' words: "I am the Resurrection and the Life," for the comfort of sorrowing ones, then bore it to its last earthly resting-place in "God's acre."

In 1882 during the rectorship of Rev. Gouverneur Morris Wilkins, a beautiful and costly tablet was placed in the south wall of the Church, bearing this inscription:

Sacred to the memory of the Rev. Newton E. Marble, D. D., for twenty-one years the faithful and beloved Rector of this Parish. This Church, eretced during his rectorship, stands as his monument; but a nobler and more enduring one will be found in the souls he won to Christ. Born, Sept. 1, 1808, slept in Jesus, Sept. 28, 1881, having lived on earth seventy-three years.

Rev. Thomas W. Haskins was made rector, Sept. 30, 1878, and resigned in October, 1880, being succeeded by Rev. Gouverneur

Morris Wilkins at Easter, 1881. He found the parish in sore straits; but young blood, earnestness of purpose and persistence in accomplishing a purpose wrought wonderful results.

A debt of $8,000 rested upon the parish.

A committee appointed to canvass for subscriptions was successful, not only in raising sufficient to wipe out the debt, but for re-decoration and re-furnishing. The four tablets, to the memory of Rev. John Beach, Rev. Philo Perry, Rev. Dr. Burhans and Rev. Dr. Marble, are said to be the finest in the country.

June 8, 1882, the long-wished-for event was accomplished. Trinity Church was consecrated by Rt. Rev. John Williams, Connecticut's beloved Bishop. A record from which we quote says:

"In conneceion with the building and construction of the Church will stand side by side the names of Rev. Dr. Marble and Rev. G. M. Wilkins. Dr. Marble's part was to see the beautiful structure rise from foundation to turret during his ministry and to enjoy the pleasure of ministering to his people in it eight years. Rev. Mr. Wilkins' satisfaction will be to see the parish free from debt through his efficiency in less than one year after coming among us"

That fact assured, Mr. Wilkins took a much desired vacation of a year in Europe, during which time the parish was most acceptably served by Rev. J. Addison Crockett.

REV. GEORGE THOMAS LINSLEY

Rev. George Thomas Linsley succeeded Rev. Mr. Wilkins in Feb., 1890.

During his rectorship the organ, built by Andrews in 1853, was rebuilt by Geo. Jardine and Son in 1896, and moved from the gallery at the west end of the Church to the north-east corner. Under the direction of Prof. Charles S. Platt, one of Newtown's sons, as organist, and the instruction of his talented wife, the musical talent of the young people of the parish was discovered and developed, and a good choir was formed, adding very materially to the beauty and the dignity of the Church service.

Those who were young people at that time remember the happy social events in connection with Trinity Guild, organized under the guidance of the rector and his capable sister, Miss Martha Linsley. In January, 1895, Miss Mary Chauncey became the bride of the rector and the rectory continued to be the center of much literary and social activity. The Women's Auxiliary did valient service and the twelve years were peaceful and prosperous. In March, 1902, the higher call to the Church of the Good Shepherd, Hartford, proved too strong to be resisted, and reluctantly the connection was severed.

REV. JAMES HARDIN GEORGE

Rev. James Hardin George, who had been several years rector of St. John's Church, Salisbury, was called in May, 1902.

The large family of children just blossoming into manhood and womanhood formed an interesting accession to the life of the parish.

The sick and sorrowing soon learned to look for visits of the

REV. GEORGE T. LINSLEY

See Page 86

REV. JAMES H. GEORGE

See Page 87

REV. WILLIAM C. CRAVNER
Elected Rector June 1918

BEACH CAMP

Elected Vestryman 1836
Junior Warden 1843
Senior Warden 1853
Died July 8th 1885

DANIEL G. BEERS

See Page 262

Elected Clerk of Trinity Parish	1876
Vestryman	1877
Junior Warden	1883
Senior Warden	1889
Died Feb. 12th	1913

rector, and Mrs. George won all hearts. A notable event occurred Nov. 2, 1905, when Rev. Frederick Foote Johnson, who had left Redlands, California, to be General Missionary in Western Mass., had been elected to become assistant Bishop to Bishop Hare of South Dakota, was consecrated to that office in Trinity Church. The Bishops present were, the Presiding Bishop, Rt. Rev. Daniel S. Tuttle, Bishops Whitaker of Penn., Vinton of Mass., Brewster of Conn., Lines of Newark, Jagger of Boston, Courtney of N. Y. More than 100 clergy were in the procession, besides Divinity School students and crowds from adjacent towns. Rev. Mr. George received great praise for having so successfully engineered the interesting but difficult situation.

Another notable event was the celebration, Sept., 1907, of the 175th anniversary of the founding of the parish, and the unveiling of a boulder in which was imbedded a bronze tablet, which stated that under a sycamore tree which stood near that place, the Rev. John Beach preached, in 1732, his first sermon as rector of the Church.

A few years after their coming, an accident occurred which it was thought produced only a slight injury to Mrs. George, but proved to have very serious results. Her hitherto active life was for a long time restricted to the movements of a wheel-chair, yet she was still a power in the home and in the parish. She had the joy of witnessing the ordination to the diaconate of James Hardin, Jr., the son who remembered no other mother. He was ordained by Bishop Johnson, Ascension Day, May 28, 1908.

The choir were vested for the first time Easter Day 1909.

Slowly and insidiously the disease progressed, until in May 1911, the release came. Miss Theodora, occupying a good position in N. Y. and Miss Bertha having become the wife of William R. Curtis, Miss Caroline was the solace and comfort of the rector and the young sister Marilla, until in July, 1914, he took to wife, Miss Jane Fitch Beers, eldest daughter of Daniel G. and Arabella Fitch Beers. The new wife at once entered into all the activities of the parish and endeared herself to every family, being in truth a help meet, not simply to the rector, but to the whole parish. In the Autumn of 1916, the large basement room was divided, making a much smaller and more attractive room, suitable for parish activities; many kitchen improvements were also added, Trinity Guild being responsible for the improvements. It was first used before Christmas for a Guild sale.

Soon after Christmas the rector seemed to be very weary, but performed his customary parish duties, until prostrated by pneumonia early in January. He entered into rest, Jan. 18, 1917. The large congregation that filled Trinity Church at the last sad service testified to the affection of the people for their rector, and their sympathy for the bereaved family.

Resolutions Adopted by the Vestry of Trinity Church on the Death of Charles S. Platt, who died Oct., 1908.

"Whereas God in His wise providence has seen fit to take our beloved friend and fellow worker, Chas. S. Platt from the scene of his early life to the rest of Paradise, therefore, Resolved, that we place on the record of this vestry our sincere appreciation of his true worth as an earnest communicant of our Church, a consistent member of our Parish and an efficient organist and leader of our choir.

For 25 years he has presided at our organ with skill and ability, thereby adding much to the beauty and dignity of the worship of the Church. Untiring in his faithful and devoted attendance, with not only an unflagging interest in the musical part of the service, but a true reverence for all parts of the Church's worship.

Though his hands no longer touch the keys to sound forth a hymn of praise, a wedding chime, or a funeral dirge, the memory of his faithfulness and his devotion will live always in the hearts of those who associate him with the organ and with the Church, where we feel so keenly a sense of great loss."

RECTOR'S ASSISTANTS.

Rev. Wm. Ackley, the first of Trinity's assistants to Rev. Dr. Marble, also officiated at St. John's Church from Aug. 1870, to December, 1873.

Rev. Thomas Mallaby was assistant from April 6, 1874, to June 10, 1875.

These two long since "entered into rest."

Rev. Francis W. Barnett, who commenced his ministerial labors in June, 1876, as assistant to Rev. Dr. Marble and minister at St. John's, Sandy Hook, resigned in April, 1879, and became rector of St. Matthew's Church, Wilton, Conn. His next charge was Christ Church, Canaan, Conn., from which place he went to St. Luke's, South Glastonbury, Conn. His whole ministry, until ill-health made it necessary to relinquish charge of a parish, was singularly useful and fruitful. Each parish grieved when he left them.

He married Miss Mary F. Blackman, one of Newtown's daughters and when he must retire from active duty, they made a home for themselves in the home town.

Having regained sufficient health for occasional service, he was chosen after the death of Rev. Mr. George as minister in charge of the parish, until a rector should be secured.

Of Mr. Barnett's three sons, to whom by great self-sacrifice he gave a college education, the eldest, Rev. F. B. Barnett served acceptably a few years at St. Mary's, Mitchell, South Dakota, then removed to Ridley Park, Pa., from which place, on the entering of the United States into the world war, he enlisted to go as Chaplain to France. Rev. Joseph is curate at St. George's Church, New York, and Edward is at Plattsburg awaiting orders. Miss Mary, the daughter, is the stay and comfort of the parents.

Since this writing, Rev. Joseph Barnett has enlisted in the Army and is now Lieut. Barnett in U. S. service.

Lieut Edward is in France and has been decorated for heroic service.

REV. FRANCIS W. BARNETT

See Page 88

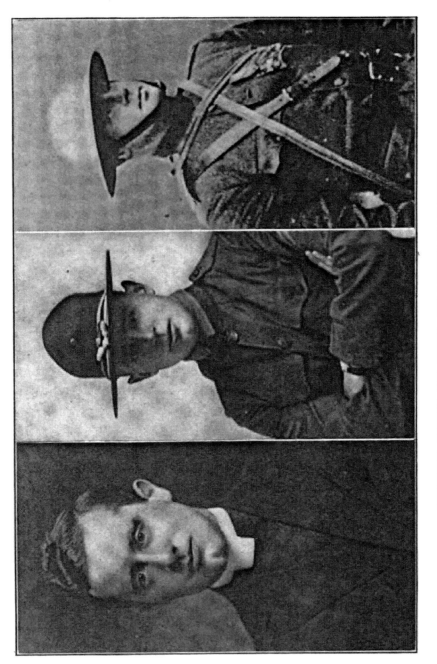

THREE SONS OF REV. FRANCIS BARNETT

REV. GEORGE L. FOOTE
See Page 89

REV. DAVID BOTSFORD
See Page 89

THOSE NEWTOWN BORN WHO BECAME MINISTERS OF THE GOSPEL.

REV. DAVID BOTSFORD.

Rev. David Botsford, son of Gideon and Pulcrea Fairman Botsford born at Newtown, March 5, 1797, graduated from Yale, 1818, was ordained by Bishop Brownell, 1821. He preached at Wallingford, Conn., for a while but because of ill-health he was obliged to return to his father's home at Newtown, where he died 1823, respected and beloved by all who knew him.

REV. ABEL NICHOLS

Rev. Abel Nichols, fifth son of Lucy Beach and Capt. James Nichols, a direct descendant of Rev. John Beach, was born at Newtown, May 23, 1807, died Dec. 16, 1859. He was going to the Bermudas to take charge of a Divinity School. He sailed on the "Silas Marner." A most fearful storm arose and the vessel sprung a leak. The life-boats were lowered and the passengers and crew taken off. Mr. Nichols stood by the Captain and assisted him to maintain order. At the last moment it was found that there was room for only one more, and he insisted that the Captain's life was of more value than his own, besides his being responsible to the agent for his passengers; and so the fact remains that the Rev. Abel Nichols was then and there translated to the reward of heroic self-sacrifice.

The Beach-Sanford Book.

REV. GEORGE L. FOOTE.

Rev. George Lewis Foote, was born in Newtown, Conn., March 3, 1812. When only fifteen years old, his father died. For a few years he worked as apprentice to a shoemaker, but deciding to study for the ministry, he obtained a situation at Elizabeth, N. J., with Rev. Birdsey G. Noble, as assistant teacher, still studying and preparing for college. He was graduated from Washington (now Trinity) College in 1837, and founded Newtown Academy the same year. April 28, 1839, he married Minerva Tuttle. During the latter part of his teaching in Newtown Academy he was lay-reader at Christ Church, Roxbury, Conn. After his ordination as deacon in 1840, and as priest in 1841 by Bishop Brownell, he became rector and remained in charge ten years. He was also principal of Roxbury Academy.

In 1850 he resigned and became rector of Zion Church, McLean, N. Y., where he remained six years. He also had charge of missions in Homer, Courtlandt, and Truxton, N. Y. In 1856, he removed to Sherburne, but at the end of two years, realizing the need of better education for his growing family, he became rector with Rev. Richard Whittingham, of St. Andrew's Church, New Berlin, N. Y. and principal of St. Andrew's School. At the end of three years, finding the burden of the school too great, he resigned and in 1860 became rector of Zion Church, Morris, N. Y. For two years he devoted himself with untiring patience and fidelity but with impaired health to his parish work. May 13, 1862, he was prostrated by Paralysis and after lingering in partial helplessness for eighteen months he passed away in the 52nd, year of his age.

Of the nine children born to them two died in infancy. Of the seven who reached maturity, two of the sons became clergymen, Rev. G. W. Foote and Rev. Henry L. Foote, and two of the daughters married clergymen. One who died in 1899 became the wife of Rt. Rev. Daniel S. Tuttle, now, in 1918, Bishop of Missouri and Presiding Bishop of the Protestant Episcopal Church in the United States, at 81 years of age. Another went with her husband, Rev. G. D. B. Miller, as missionary to Japan. They returned and since the death of her husband she has been for many years private secretary to Bishop Tuttle. Another, Mrs. S. K. White, was many years principal of the Diocesan School for girls at Tacoma, Washington, but is now engaged in missionary work in St. Louis, Missouri.

REV. SYLVESTER CLARK, D. D.

Rev. Sylvester Clarke, D. D., was born in Newtown, Sept. 26, 1833, son of Betsy Ann Fairchild and Charles Clarke. His early education was received at the district school and at the private school of Harry Peck. While preparing for the ministry he did duty with several banking instiutions, entering Berkeley School in 1855. He was ordained to the diaconate in 1858, and to the priesthood in 1859, by Bishop Williams, who gave him charge of St. Peter's, Oxford and Christ Church, Quaker Farms. In 1861, he resigned charge of those parishes and became assistant to Rev. Dr. Gurdon Coit, rector of St. John's Church, Bridgeport. In the summer of 1863 he became rector of the new Trinity Church, Bridgeport. In 1870, he founded the Coit Memorial Chapel, now St. Luke's, East End, Bridgeport.

He was elected Professor of Church History at the University of the South, Sewanee, Tenn., to the same professorship at Seabury Divinity School, Fairibault, Minn. At the Berkeley Divinity School, Middletown, Conn., he was Professor of Homiletics and Pastoral Theology, and of Christian Evidences. As a member of the Committee on Constitution and Canons and for several years its president, the greater part of the present Canon Law of the diocese was formulated by him. He was for many years one of the examining Chaplains of this diocese.

Of a singularly modest and retiring disposition, Dr. Clarke was not wont to push himself into prominence; but the clearness and balance of his judgment and the purity of his character made his influence positive and weighty. Men accepted him and supported him in offices that called for the higher qualities of intellect and character. Unfaltering in his loyalty to his own Church, his friendship could not be bound by denominational lines. He displayed a tender fraternal spirit, toward all who like himself were set for the preaching of the Gospel, to whatever denomination they belonged.

The same fraternal spirit seeking ample outlet led him to membership in the Masonic order, of which he was a Master Mason.

He was past grand of Pequonnock Lodge, I. O. O. F., and one of its Trustees. He served many years as a member of the Board of School Visitors. His influence in the Church life will be felt

REV. SYLVESTER CLARK D. D.
See Page 90

RT. REV. FREDERICK F. JOHNSON D. D.

See Page 91

through coming years by many who will not know its source; the example he set and the words he spoke as a Christian man and pastor will continue to enrich many lives. The truth of the statement that though "he rests from his labors, his works still follow" is exemplified in the fact that in 1917, thirteen years since he entered into rest, $50,000 are being raised for a new St. Luke's Church and "The Sylvester Clarke Parish House Memorial," to take the place of the outgrown chapel he founded in 1870.

ARTHUR THOMAS PARSONS.

Arthur Thomas Parsons, born in Sandy Hook, Dec. 2, 1847, attended public schools, was fitted for college in St. Paul's School, Brookfield, Conn., entered Trinity College in 1867, was graduated in 1871, a member of the Delta Upsilon and the Phi Beta Kappa fraternities, entered Berkeley Divinity School in 1871, was graduted in 1874. the ordination to the Diaconate by Bishop Williams taking place on May 27. The class of 1874 was the first to be ordained in the new Church (Holy Trinity) in Middletown, and, as Mr. Parsons was senior candidate, he has the honor of being the first man ordained in that building. Mr. Parsons was advanced to the Priesthood in St. Andrew's Church, Meriden, by Bishop John Williams, Feb. 21, 1875.

Rectorships: St. Alban's Church, Danielson, Conn., May 27, 1847, to March 1, 1880; St. George's Church, Central Falls, R. I., March 1, 1880, to Jan. 1, 1885; St. Stephen's Church, East Haddam, Conn., Jan. 1, 1885 to Jan. 1, 1890; Trinity Church, Thomaston, Conn., Jan. 1, 1890, to June 1, 1909; Christ Memorial Church, North Brookfield, Mass., June 1, 1909, to April 1, 1912; Christ Church, Sheffield, Mass., April 1, 1912, to October 1, 1914. Retired from active service, Oct. 1, 1914. Has since lived in Northampton, Mass.

In 1878 married Sarah E. Peck, of Brooklyn, N. Y., daughter of Richard W. and Sarah (Mather) Peck. One child, Jessie A. Parsons, is secretary to the Librarian of Smith College, Northampton, Mass.

REV. EDWARD J. EGAN.

Born in Newtown, Dec. 12, 1861, graduated from Newtown Academy, 1879. Graduated from St. Charles College, Ellicott, Md., 1883; entered St. Joseph's Seminary, Troy, N. Y., the same year, and was ordained, Dec. 19, 1885.

Son of Edward and Eliza Gordan Egan. Pastor of St. Philip and James Church, Phillipsburg, N. J.

RT. REV. FREDERICK FOOTE JOHNSON, D..D.

Rt. Rev. Frederick Foote Johnson, D. D., born at Newtown, Conn., April 23, 1866, son of Ezra L. and Jane E. Camp Johnson; educated at public school, Newtown Academy, St. Stephen's College, Annandale, N. Y., Cheshire Episcopal School and Trinity College, Hartford, Conn., from which he was graduated with degree of B. A. in 1894, M. A. in 1897. Theological course at Berkeley Divinity School, Middletown, Conn.; ordained deacon at Newtown,

Conn., Nov. 11, 1896, by Bishop White of Indiana, ordained priest, 1897, by Bishop Spalding at Denver, Colorado. Was minister at Glenwood Springs, Colorado, 1897; curate at St. Stephen's Church, Colorado Springs, 1897-98; rector Boulder, Colorado, 1898; rector Trinity Church, Redlands, California, 1899-1904; Diocesan Missionary, Western Mass., 1904-05; elected assistant to Bishop Hare, South Dakota, 1905; consecrated Bishop at Newtown, Conn., Nov. 2, 1905. Given D. D. degree by Trinity College, 1906; D. D. by Berkeley, 1909. After the death of Bishop Hare, Oct. 23, 1909, he was elected Bishop of South Dakota, Oct. 11, 1910; elected Bishop Coadjutor of Missouri in May, 1911. Feb. 4, 1899, he married at Redlands, California, Susan Lynn Beers, daughter of Silas Norman and Sarah Nichols Beers, of Newtown. She died, June 23, 1901, at Redlands, California. June 26, 1915, married Elizabeth L. Beers, daughter of Daniel G. and Arabella Fitch Beers, of Newtown. Son by first marriage, born at Redlands, California, July 17, 1900, Frederick Foote Johnson, Jr.

REV. JAMES HARDIN GEORGE, JR.

Though born Nov. 21, 1884, in Salisbury, Conn., Rev. James Hardin George has a right to be called a Newtown boy by virtue of his descent in a direct line from Rev. John Beach, through his mother, Harriet Emma Sanford, deceased wife of Rev. James H. George, for fifteen years rector of Trinity Church, Newtown.

His early schooling was at Salisbury, followed by a course at the Hotchkiss School, a large preparatory school for Yale. He entered Trinity College in 1902, and evidently made good use of his time, for he was graduated in 1905, one year ahead of time. Perhaps it was due to his having acquired "a thirst for strange tongues" through his close companionship during his college course with Dr. W. A. Martin, Professor of Oriental languages, that the same year he was sent to Shanghai, China. to teach history in St. John's University there. He spent a vacation in Japan, then because of ill-health it seemed best to return home. Having decided to study for the ministry he entered Philadelphia Divinity School. While pursuing his studies he was a member of the Philadelphia City mission. Ascension Day, 1908, he was ordained deacon at Trinity Church Newtown, by Bishop Johnson, and went that summer to do mission work in South Dakota, returning to Philadelphia in the fall to complete his seminary work, and was made second assistant to the work in the parish of St. Simeon.

As soon as he was free from that duty, he returned to his former field in the extreme northwest section of South Dakota, in the new territory about Lemmon, which was a new town still having the "smack of the wild West." A new Chapel was built while he was in charge.

During his stay in China he became devoted to Miss. Carrie Mason Palmer, then a laborer in the mission field. He reported coming east in time to prevent the return of Miss Palmer to China, and they were married, Sept. 28, 1910. He accepted a call then to St. Alban's, Danielson, where he remained until October, 1916, when he became rector of Calvary Church, Columbia, Missouri. While at

WM. B. PRINDLE

Elected Chorister of Trinity Church, from 1835 to 1875.
Elected Junior Warden 1880
" Senior Warden 1883
Died May 23rd 1903

Danielson he founded St. Paul's Mission, Plainfield, and by the aid of the diocese a beautiful Church was built. A son, James Hardin George, 3rd, was born Feb. 2, 1914. Now Mr. George, 1918, is a Chaplain in France.

ST. JAMES' CHURCH.

No record yet found gives the exact date of the building of St. James' Church, Zoar, which stood on the hill opposite the present Gray's Plain school house. As nearly as can be ascertained, it was about 1830, with Rev. Dr. Daniel Burhans, who had resigned the rectorship of Trinity parish, as first rector. In 1832, he resigned and went to Plymouth, Conn. No record is found of regular services for many years, but Rev. Mr. Stratton and Rev. Mr. Stocking, rectors of Trinity, gave occasional services. St. James is the little Church whose services, people and surroundings are so graphically and truthfully depicted in "Shiloh" by W. M. L. Jay. She was grand-daughter to Alfred Devine and Sarah Hard Curtis. Her husband, Rev. Curtis Woodruff, for many years City missionary at New York City, often officiated there.

Rev. H. V. Gardner had charge for several years in connection with St. Paul's, Huntington. He was followed by Rev. Mr. Davis (Rev. Mr. Taylor in "Shiloh") then by Rev. Collis I. Potter, residing in Huntington. Losses by death and removal so depleted the attendance that after the building of St. John's, Sandy Hook, the building was sold and removed.

ST. JOHN'S CHURCH.

St. John's Church, Sandy Hook, is the offspring of Trinity, Newtown. In the spring of 1864, Mrs. Susan Nichols Glover, direct descendant of Rev. John Beach, wife of William B. Glover, seeing the need of more personal local Sunday School work in the village, gathered the children in her home and taught them. The interest increased and after awhile the school was removed to the upper room of the old store building, which later became the Masonic hall (burned in 1905,) where services were held occasionally by Rev. George Davis who lived in Zoar and by Rev. Dr. Marble, until the present Church edifice was erected.

The first regular mission work by the Episcopal Church in this part of town was conducted by Rev. Wm. N. Ackley, assistant minister of Trinity parish and was continued by Rev Francis W. Barnett and other assistants of the mother Church.

The first organization of this movement in Sandy Hook was the Diocesan Missionary Association of St. John's Church, in the parish of Trinity Church, Newtown, Dec. 2, 1879. This organization was discontinued, on account of withdrawal of canonical consent of the rector of Trinity parish, Rev. T. W. Haskins, and St. John's parish was organized, June 1, 1880, the formal consent of Bishop Williams and the Standing Committee having been given, May 25, 1880. The original members were Minott Augur, James H. Warner, Smith P. Glover, Frederick Chambers, Ralph N. Betts, William E. Ackley, Isaac Percy Blackman, John L. Sanford, Charles M. Parsons, William B. Sniffen, Augustus W. Orgelman, Benjamin G. Curtis, Wm. G. Hard, James M. Blackman, Eli J. Morris, Martin

W. Lee, Wm. A. Sherman, James Turner, Charles H. Payne, Ammon Taylor, E. W. Wilson, M. B. Terrill, Chester Hard, Charles E. Minor, Alonzo Taylor, Wm. A. Bradley.

St. John's Guild was organized, June 1, 1880, at the house of S. P. Glover. This Guild had its beginning in the sewing society of the ladies of St. John's Church, organized, Sept. 30, 1876, under the administration of Rev. Thomas Mallaby, assistant to Rev. Dr. Marble of Trinity Church and has always been an important factor in the support and progress of the Church.

The present Church building was commenced in 1868, in accordance with the conditions of a bequest of $5,000 by the will of Wm. B. Glover, which was generously increased by his son, Smith P. Glover, who also purchased the land on which the Church stands for $1500 and gave it to the parish. The building was done by authority of Trinity parish, under the direction of a committee composed of Charles Morehouse, Smith P. Glover, James H. Warner, Fred'k Chambers and Eli J. Morris.

The corner stone was laid, Aug. 27, 1868. It was consecrated Oct. 12, 1869, by Bishop Williams. The first rector was Rev. H. L. Myrick, August, 1880. Until then it was a chapel of Trinity and served by assistants of Trinity. Mr. Myrick resigned in May, 1886, at which time Rev. A. P. Chapman took charge until April, 1891. Mr. Chapman was a faithful pastor and did good work in the place, conducting a private school in the parish hall. Rev. Otis Olney Wright became rector in May, 1891.

It was with keen regret that his people accepted his resignation to take effect in October, 1912. It was so true that "Mr. Wright's ministry extends beyond his parish and to the whole community. His efforts in establishing the Sandy Hook library and his interest and labors for the public schools cannot be forgotten, and through his articles in The Bee, a gratuitous, kindly service, he has had an audience of from 12,000 to 20,000 weekly."

He removed to Swansea, Mass, where he is leading a peaceful but busy life among a people whom he had served before going to Sandy Hook. His successor is Rev. Charles Tibbals, who became rector in February, 1913.

THE METHODIST CHURCH.

The first class meeting held by the Methodists was in 1800. The first preaching service was held in the house of Mrs. Phebe Peck, just above the village, with others afterward in the old town house. In 1805, a class was formed as a nucleus to forming a Church organization. Later a class was formed at Flat Swamp in 1828. Circuit preaching was had once in about four weeks, at school houses or at private dwellings. The first meeting house, dedicated in 1831, stood just north of Mrs. Marcus Hawley's residence.

In 1850, that building was sold, and a more commodious one built at Sandy Hook at a cost of $3,300.

The old building was removed near Newtown railroad station, and became the carriage-shop of C. H. Gay, and, later, was burned while the property of C. H. Bassett.

A Universalist Society, organized early in the nineteenth century, built

REV. OTIS OLNEY WRIGHT

See Page 94

ST. JOHN'S CHURCH
See Page 93

METHODIST EPISCOPAL CHURCH
See Page 94

ST. ROSE R. C. CHURCH
See Page 95

REV. JAMES McCARTAN

See Page 95

a commodious house of worship in the center of the village, but sold it to the Roman Catholics, who later sold it to the town and it is now the Newtown Town Hall.

THE FIRST BAPTIST CHURCH.

The First Baptist Church of which there is knowledge stood on the rocks by the Ezekiel Beers place, now owned by President Arthur T. Hadley of Yale College. It was a barn-like structure, not at all churchly in appearance.

About 1850, there was a revival among the Baptists, who built a neat little Church at the corner of Berkshire Cemetery. Death and removal of the members so weakened the Baptist society that no stated services were held for several years. The building was used for funerals and services were held occasionally by other Christian bodies.

In 1913, the cemetery wishing to enlarge the grounds, the building was sold and removed.

ST. ROSE CHURCH.

The first resident pastor of the Roman Catholic Church of Newtown was Rev. Francis Lenihan, who organized the parish, Aug. 1, 1859. Previous to his appointment, Newtown was served by a priest from Danbury. Father Lenihan purchased the first cemetery, but it was not blessed until the pastorate of Rev. James Daly, who came here in March, 1862, leaving in July, 1868. Rev. John Rogers became pastor, July 22, 1868, remaining until July, 1873. His successor was Rev. James McCartan, who came in August, 1873 and died, January, 1889. The present Church was erected during his pastorate, in 1882, and his grave is in the Churchyard.

The old Church, purchased by Rev. John Smith about 1858, had been a Universalist meeting house. It is now Newtown's Town Hall. Rev. Patrick Donahue succeeded Rev. James McCartan, remaining until 1891. Rev. Patrick Fox succeeded Rev. Patrick Donahue. Rev. George T. Sinnott succeeded Rev. Patrick Fox July 30, 1910. The new cemetery was bought, May 16, 1891. Ground was broken for the Church in 1881. Mass was first said in the completed Church, the first Sunday in August, 1883. It cost about $25,000, the old bell and organ being taken from the old Church. The body of the Church will seat 800, the galleries 300.

SANDEMANIAN CHURCH.

A Sandemanian society was organized in 1740. The building in which they held services stood midway between Mrs. Marcus Hawley's and the middle district school house. The Sandemanians disbanded in the early years of the last century

1717
NEWTOWN'S SCHOOL DISTRICTS

In the persistent efforts of the pioneers to provide school privileges for their children, the town was divided into school districts as the needs of different sections arose, but the districts were not recognized in law until about 1766 and had no corporate existence until 1794.

NORTH CENTER

Committees were chosen for the several districts at the annual town meeting and a tax laid on the rateable estates of the town to meet the expenses of the several schools, the length of the school year depending upon the amount of money raised for that purpose. All were under town management until the system of each district paying its own school expenses was adopted.

The first volume of Newtown Records shows when and how North Center and Middle districts came into existence, and tells of locating and building a school house for each district. The land that comprises the town of Newtown was bought from the Indians in 1705. Twelve years thereafter, Oct. 2, 1717, it was "voted by ye Inhabitants of ye town that a schoolhouse or town house shall forthwith or with all possible speed be erected of ye following dimensions: 25 foot square and 8 foot between joynts and whereas Joseph Grey and Peter Hubbell have undertaken to build ye said house (viz) to get, draw the timber, make ye frame, get all ye shingles and clapboards and lay them, ye town finding nails, it is agreed and voted to give ye workmen for said work 10 pounds money to be paid upon their accomplishing or compleating their work workmanlike.

Entered, Joseph Peck, Town Clerk."

Three months later, Jan. 8, 1718, a town meeting was held to fix the location of the town house when it was "voted, that the place for building ye schoolhouse or town house or house for holding town meetings in, and for teaching school in, shall be on ye main street or town street, near unto Abraham Kimberly's and John Lake's house, which is ye northeast corner of ye cross road yt leads to Pohtatuck brook."

The building served the two purposes until 1733, 18 years, when a larger town house was needed, and the town voted to give up the building to the town's children, the neighborhood moving it at their own expense. The location of the building was where the schoolhouse for what was the Middle district now stands, and is now used for the primary department of the consolidated district.

The agitation to build a second school-house was begun in 1727, when a town meeting of the inhabitants, Sept. 13, "voted, yt there shall be erected a school-house between ye date above sd and December next ensuing ye sd date, and ye charges arising in building sd schoolhouse shall be defrayed by ye town rate of ye inhabitants of sd town. Test, Joseph Peck, Town Clerk."

One month later, Oct. 19, 1727, it was voted that "Hugh Stillson, Ephraim Hawley and Jeremiah Northrop should be a committee in ye behalf of ye town to erect a school-house at ye place to be appointed, of 25 foot long and 18 foot wide, to be erected with all possible space and ye whole care of ye compleating ye sd house fit for service is left with ye above sd committee, the town ratifying and confirming what ye above sd committee shall do about ye premises above said. Joseph Peck, Town Clerk."

The building was finished in the early fall of 1728 and, at the annual town meeting in December of that year, the town "voted, that ye selectmen shall take care of ye school and are hereby authorized and empowered to hire a schoolmaster so long as ye overplus money in ye town rate will support it."

For three years, the records show that no definite time was set for the continuance of the school, but only as the money should hold out. At the annual meeting, Dec. 16, 1731 it was "voted, that a school for ye public service of ye town that may well answer ye end for promoting of common learning shall be kept this year for ye space of six months. To begin as soon as a sufficient schoolmaster may be obtained and to be a constant and continued school for six months and that it shall be supported and maintained, ye one half by ye sd town and ye other half by ye 'schoolers' in proportion to ye time which they attend ye school, and that John Golot, Moses Stillson and Ephraim Hawley are chosen and appointed to take ye whole care of ye school as above voted, the town ratifying and confirming what ye sd committee shall do in ye premises. Joseph Peck, Town Clerk."

Three years pass, and Dec. 19, 1734, the annual town meeting "voted, that Lieut Thomas Skidmore, Stephen Burwell and John Lake be a committee in ye behalf of ye sd town to take care of ye school, to lay out ye said 14 pounds as far as it shall go for ye maintaining of ye school to ye best advantage for ye support of ye school."

Although permission was given to build a school-house in 1733, no definite action was taken until Dec., 1737. There had been disagreement as to location that delayed action, and, Jan. 2, 1738, a new committee reported.

"We whose names are underwritten, being appointed a committee to fix ye spot or place for erecting a school-house at ye north end of ye town above sd, is westerly of ye spot where they, the sd north end, had dug for erecting sd school-house is as near ye common road as conveniency will allow, where we ye sd committee affixed stakes.

John Northrop, Moses Stillson, Joseph Botsford, Benjamin Hawley, Ephraim Prindle, committee."

In Dec. 1741, the town "voted, that Ensign John Glover and Abel Booth were chosen a committee for ye north school and to provide a sufficient school-master for sd work, and lay out half of ye money voted for ye school at ye south end.

March 1, 1769, voted, "that ye subscribers to a certain instrument for a school to be kept at ye Town house shall have liberty to use ye Town house for schooling ye six months coming, viz: Jonathan Booth, Doct. Lemuel Thomas, Abiel Botsford, and all their associates of sd school." This was the first private school held in Newtown. Voted, "Doctor Lemuel Thomas and Doctor Nathan Worshburn shall be committee for ye south school, Ebenezer Ford and Jonathan Booth for ye north school, Robert Summers, Amos Hard and Benjamin Curtis for ye Zoar school, Gamaliel French and Benjamin Burr for Huntingtown, Moses Wright, Ensign Joseph Prindle and Peter Nichols committee for Tinkerfield school, Jonah Sanford and Amos Merchant for Pohtatuck school, ye year ensuing."

Report of the committee appointed at the annual town meeting of Dec. 10, 1770, to look into the situation of the two schools in Newtown street: "To ye adjourned town meeting of Newtown inhabitants to meet on ye 17th day, instant. Whereas we ye subscribers being appointed a committee to take into consideration ye situation and circumstances of ye two schools in sd Newtown called ye north and ye south schools, in ye old society, we find yt ye list of ye north school is 3683 pounds, including ye list of Capt. Joseph Wheeler, and yt ye scholars are too numerous for one school, and yt ye northern parts, or Currituck so-called, should be set off for a district and begin north of ye house of Ensign James Blackman, then running westerly to New Milford road, leaving ye house of Thomas Chambers on ye north and keeping sd road until it strikes ye

Slut's Hill district then extending northward until it strikes ye Obtuse road to ye Lands End brook, and all other parts on districts already set off. The school called ye north school to extend northward to ye line already given, and to extend so far south as to include ye houses of Ebenezer Bristol and Widow Lake, and to be so understood yt ye two schools called ye north and ye south schools to enjoy all former privileges of subscriptions, donations, etc., as usual. The above district of Currituck voted exclusive of Thomas Chambers and Gideon Shepherd which are to remain to their former school." Jonathan Booth, Samuel Beers, Oliver Tousey, Ephraim Sherman, Joseph Wheeler, Committee.

Attest, Caleb Baldwin, town clerk."

In Dec., 1771, the town voted "that ye proprietors of ye north school shall have liberty to set up a school-house for their district at ye west end of ye meeting house about eight rods distance of ye meeting house." What friction caused that action we know not. Nothing further appears on record as to the matter, showing that the vote never materialized.

"Whereas, at a special Town meeting of the Town of Newtown held Saturday, January 5, 1878, at one o'clock p. m., it was voted that the school district lines be defined by the selectmen, and the Town clerk make copy of the same in a book kept for that purpose. Now, therefore, we the selectmen of the Town of Newtown for the time being have performed said duty with the assistance of Beach Nichols as surveyor and do hereby define and fix the lines of the following named districts in the words and figures here-in-after set down. Flat Swamp, Gray's Plain, Gregory's Orchard, Half Way River, Hanover, Head of the Meadow, Hopewell, Huntingtown, Lake George, Land's End, Middle, Middle Gate, North Center, Palestine, Potatuck, Sandy Hook, South Center, Taunton, Toddy Hill, Walnut Tree Hill, Walker's Farms, Wapping and Zoar. Said named districts twenty three in number being all of the districts into which said Town of Newtown is at present divided.

Newtown, April 1, 1878.

William N. Northrop, W. J. Sanford, William H. Hoy, selectmen.

Beach Nichols, surveyor.

Recorded by Charles Henry Peck, Town Clerk."

Survey of 1878

Beginning at a point on the highway on East Side of Taunton pond, 74 rods north of the east and west turnpike, thence southwesterly to the south east corner of Taunton pond, thence northwesterly along the east shore of sd pond to the north east corner, thence north six degrees west to the south line of Robert N. Hawley's Barnabas Hill land (so-called). Thence easterly in the south line of sd Hawley's land to the south east corner. Thence south easterly one and one half rods to the north west corner of Albert Turner's land. Thence easterly on the line between sd Turner and Edwin Camp to highway. Thence north 24 degrees 15 minutes, east 39.74 chains to west side of Bridgeport and Newtown turnpike. Thence same course 23.50 chains to danger signal post, at crossing of railroad and highway to Lake George, sd signal post being at the corner of Land's End, Lake George, Hanover and North Center districts. Thence south easterly along the Housatonic railroad to the crossing of highway and railroad near the old Brick Yard. Thence southeasterly a straight line to the intersection of the Green road with the road across Walnut Tree Hill. Thence Southerly on line of sd Highway to the Northeast Corner of James Turner's land (formerly Caleb Baldwin's) thence westerly on north line of sd Turner's land to the N. west corner near the Foundry pond. Thence s. 63 1-4 degrees west to the northwest corner of George C. Peck's homestead on West side of Island road, thence southerly on sd road to the southeast corner, thence westerly on line to southwest corner, thence northerly on west line to a point 2 3-4 rods south of sd Peck's northwest corner, thence south 63 1-4 degrees west to the southeast corner of Mrs. David H. Johnson's homestead on west side of Carcass lane, thence westerly on south line of sd Johnson's land to Newtown street, thence across sd street to the north-east corner of David B. Beers' homestead, thence westerly in north line of sd Beers land to land of L. B. Booth (formerly David H. Johnson), thence same course across sd Booth's land to highway at southwest corner, thence north 2 degrees west, 41 rods in line of Elmer W. Fairchild on the west and sd Booth and Norman B. Glover on the east to the N. W. corner of Norman B. Glover's land, thence on line of stone wall through land of sd Fairchild S. 71 degrees west 37 rods, thence on sd wall west 52 rods, thence on wall S. 16 degrees E. 5 rods, thence on wall north 88 degrees W. to place of beginning."

MIDDLE
First Town House. Built in 1718. Served Also for a School-house

Until the year 1733, at which time the two districts, North Center and Middle district were formed, and the town voted that the people of the north end of the town might build a school-house near the house of Abraham Bennitt, provided it be built at their own expense, and also voted at the same meeting that the south end of the town should have liberty to remove the town house (to make way for a new and larger town house) at their own expense to be their school-house, at such place as shall be thought most convenient for the neighborhood. It was done and the location of the building was where the school-house for the Middle District now stands. The school-house for North Center was long time in coming and during the interim all the children were being cared for at the school in Middle district.

Survey of 1878

"Beginning on the highway east of Taunton Pond seventy-four (74) rods North of the east and west turnpike, thence Southwesterly to the highway at the southwest corner of sd Pond, Thence Southerly by highway to East and West Turnpike, Thence Southerly by old abandoned road to angle in highway about 50 rods northeast of Mrs. Carroll's house, thence by highway easterly to the Norwalk turnpike, thence northeasterly by highway to the road leading to Palestine, thence southerly on sd Palestine road to Deep Brook. thence easterly by sd Deep Brook to the bridge on highway running past the cemetery, thence northeasterly by sd highway to the intersection of the road leading to Abel Stillson's house, thence north 75 degrees east to the southwest corner of Hermon H. Peck's home lot on East side of the Bridgeport and Newtown turnpike, thence on south line of sd home lot N. 66 degrees east to Deep Brook, thence down sd Brook to the South west corner of Roswell Turney's land about 15 rods upstream from the bridge on Turney's land, thence easterly on the south line of sd Turney's land, thence easterly on the south line of the sd Turney's land to the intersection of a straight line from Mile Hill Bridge to Mount Tom Brook bridge on Newtown and Sandy Hook road, thence northwesterly on sd line to Mt. Tom Brook bridge, thence easterly on sd Newtown and Sandy Hook road 24 rods, thence north 54 1-2 degrees east between the house and barn of James Turner (formerly William Glover) to highway leading to Walnut Tree Hill, thence by sd highway to the northeast corner of sd Turner's land (formerly Caleb Baldwin), thence westerly on the north line to the northwest corner near Foundry pond, thence south 63 1-4 degrees west to the northeast corner of George C. Peck's land on Island road, thence southerly on sd road to the southeast corner, thence westerly to southwest corner, thence northerly on line of stone fence to a point 2 3-4 rods south of sd Peck's northwest corner, thence south 63 1-4 west to southeast corner of Mrs. D. H. Johnson's homestead, on west side of Carcass lane, thence westerly along south line of sd Johnson's land to Newtown street, thence across sd street to the north line of D. B. Beers homestead, thence westerly on north line of sd Beers' homestead to land of L. B. Booth (formerly D. H. Johnson), thence same course across sd Booth's land to Highway at Southwest corner, thence north 2 degrees west 41 rods in line of Elmer W. Fairchild on the west and sd Booth and Norman B. Glover on the east to the northwest corner of Norman B. Glover's land, thence on line of stone wall through land of sd Fairchild south 71 degrees west 37 rods, thence on said wall west 52 rods, thence on wall south 16 degrees east 5 rods, thence on wall north 88 degrees west to place of beginning."

1738
TAUNTON

After town action on the several dates concerning the North Center and Middle districts, the first record of an out-lying district was for Taunton.

"December 3, 1738, voted and agreed that ye west farm called Taunton shall have liberty to build a school-house upon their own charge and to have their proportions of money voted for ye school from time to time according to their list of rateable estate provided they lay out ye money for ye school within ye year." District lines established in 1878:

"Taunton school district, beginning on the town line between Bethel and Newtown on the highest point of Jolley Hill at stone bounds near a high rock, thence S 85 degrees E to a stone bounds on highway leading southerly from Henry and George Fairchild's residence 4 1-2 rods south of William and Henry Fairchild's line, thence in a straight line Easterly to highway running northerly from Norman Northrop's residence at the line between said Northrop's and William Fairchild's, thence a straight line Easterly stone bounds near the sharp angle of old abandoned highway leading Southerly from Taunton Pond, thence Northerly by said old road and road west of said Pond to the South west corner of said Pond, thence Easterly a straight line to the South East corner, thence Northerly along the East shore to the North East corner, thence North 6 degrees West to Robert N. Hawley's Barnabas Hill land, thence Westerly in the south line of said Hawley's land to the South West corner, thence Westerly a straight line to Pond Brook Bridge near Shepaug Railroad crossing, thence down Pond Brook to Pokono Brook, thence up Pokono Brook North Branch to a rock in fence situated in a marsh the head of Pokono Brook, thence north 33 degrees West to the North West corner of the Town of Newtown, thence southerly along town line between Newtown and Bethel to place of beginning."

1745
ZOAR

January 20, 1745, the town voted that the eastward farms called Zoar shall have the same liberty to set up and carry on schooling among themselves as the farmers elsewhere have and to build their school-houses without any charge to the town and that Benjamin Curtis shall be a committee to provide a school master for Zoar. The limits of Zoar Easternmost school was established by vote in town meeting Dec. 5, 1768.

"The limits of Zoar Easternmost school shall extend from Zachariah Ferris's shop to the Great River at Peter Foot's, including Josiah Platt, and down the road to the Stratford line at Walker's Farm."

Zoar district originally took in the districts of Zoar, Grey's Plain, Half Way River and that portion of Newtown now included in the joint district with Southbury known as Wapping. Gray's Plain was set off in 1784 and Half Way River and Wapping in 1786. Zoar, as given by survey of 1878:

"Beginning at the mouth of Pole bridge brook on the Housatonic river, thence up said brook to a point directly in line with the southeasterly corner of Lawrence Mitchell's land on Housatonic river and the south east corner of Cornelia Curtis' land, thence southerly along said line of Cornelia Curtis' corner which is on highway leading from Berkshire to Bennett's bridge 24 1-2 rods northerly from a small stream crossing said road, thence in a straight line westerly to Mile Hill bridge on Pohtatuck brook, thence southerly by Pohtatuck Brook to its junction with Saw Mill Brook, thence southerly by sd Saw Mill brook west branch to the north abuttment of bridge over Saw Mill brook on highway leading from the north mouth of the old Lebbon road to the Toddy Hill road, near Captain Walter Bradley's residence, thence easterly a straight line to a pile of stones on the old Lebbon road near the south east corner of John Kane Jr's land, thence in a straight line N. 73 degrees E. to the bridge over a small stream crossing highway about 40 rods westerly of the High Rock road at Lockwood Shepherd house, thence easterly by highway to the mouth of the High Rock road, thence northerly to a point on highway 50 rods west of Frederick Chambers' dwelling house at corner of highway, thence easterly by said highway to Gelding Hill Brook between the dwelling houses of Thomas O. Chambers and Charles Johnson, thence northerly by said brook to the Housatonic river, thence northerly by said Housatonic river to Pole bridge brook, the place of beginning."

1745
LAND'S END
Wiskenear

At Newtown's town meeting Dec. 9, 1745, it was voted "that all ye northern inhabitants dwelling within ye township of Newtown, that is to say northward of ye Pond Brook and westward of a south line beginning at ye New Milford line so as to run 40 rods east of ye Dunnings and to be extended to ye above sd Pond Brook, shall have liberty to set up and carry on a school among themselves for ye well educating their children in reading and writing as ye law aims at, they not putting ye town to any charge to build their school-house and that they shall have power according to their list, to draw out their proportion for use aforesaid of ye money which this town hath this year voted for ye use of schooling, or shall be voted from years to years, so also their proportion of 40 shillings upon ye thousand in ye country, ordered by law for promoting of schooling whensoever ye country tax shall be levied on this town and collected. These bounds to include Jeremiah Turner as their most southern part and Lieutenant Smith was appointed to provide a teacher for Whiskenear and Jabez Hurd, collector of ye money." On the twenty-second day of Dec., 1779, the town in town meeting voted "that ye inhabitants of ye town living on ye main road leading from Newtown to Newbury, from Land's End brook to Newbury's south line, extending so far west as to include ye Widow Abigail Turner, shall be a district for a school." known by ye name of Land's End school, and so it is that the present district name dates back to the year 1779, a period of 134 years, in Dec. of this year, with the present district lines as established in 1878, which are as follows:

Beginning at a stone monument marked B. and N. on north east side of highway leading from Hawleyville Depot, to Danbury. Thence along the town line S. 41 degrees W. 34 rods six links to pile of stones on top of hill, 11 feet south of a big rock. Thence same coarse 54 rods to pile of stones a few feet west of a rock on the line of an old wall, running in a north and south direction, said pile of stones being on the corner of Newtown and Brookfield in the east line of Bethel. Thence S. 33 degrees, 51 minutes, E. 6.10 chains to a large rock in fence in a marsh, the head of Pokono Brook (North branch). Thence south easterly along said Pokono brook to bridge on Highway running south from James Green's residence. Thence down Pokono brook to Pond brook. Thence up Pond brook to bridge on highway near Shepaug railroad crossing. Thence easterly in a straight line to the south west corner of Robert N. Hawley's Barnabas Hill land (so-called). Thence in the southerly line to the south east corner. Thence south easterly one and one half rods to North West corner of Albert Turner's land. Thence easterly on line to the northeast corner on highway leading to Hawleyville from Newtown. Thence north 24 degrees, 15 minutes east 39.74 chains to west side of Newtown and Bridgeport turnpike. Thence same course 23.50 chains to danger signal at railroad crossing at Lake George, said signal being at the corner of Land's End, Hanover, Lake George and North Center districts. Thence N. 45 degrees west 238 rods to point on highway running easterly from R. N. Hawley's residence about 60 rods west of James Lake's house. Thence north 58 degrees, west 204 rods to Pond brook. Thence north 65 degrees west 20 rods Land's End mill on highway. Thence westerly by said highway to the intersection of road at Benjamin Hawley's old house. Thence northerly by highway to town line of Brookfield. Thence along said line south 41 degrees west to place of beginning."

1748
PALESTINE

At the annual town meeting Dec. 3, 1748, it was "voted that ye limits of ye farm called Palestine shall be northward of Mr. John Glover's house, so from there running easterly to include Noah Parmelee's house, and Ephraim Prindle's and Benjamin Stillson's house, and so on to Abraham Beers' house. It was also voted "that all parents or masters who send children to school shall find fire wood in proportion to ye scholars they shall send, and if any person fail of doing so it shall be in ye power of ye school committee to recover their proportion in money by an action of debt upon complaint made to ye Justice of ye Peace, who, upon recovery shall forthwith lay out sd money for procuring of wood for ye school or answering for ye wood procured before, by reason of ye aforesaid neglect." Voted "there shall be two pence upon ye pound of ye list of rateable estate of ye inhabitants for supporting of ye schools of ye several farms and shall stand good for ye year provided they shall keep a good school four months of ye year and render an account to ye selectmen that they have kept a good school as aforesaid." John Beers was appointed to be collector for ye Palestine school. Ye money arising out of ye town shall be expended according to their lists, two-thirds in Michalmas and winter season and the other third in spring and summer and ye parents, masters and mistresses of ye scholars shall add and pay one-third part so much money in cash of ye above mentioned seasons to ye support of ye respective schools in ye limits in which they dwell, that is to say one-third part of ye expenses shall be paid by ye scholars, and John Beers shall be collector for ye Palestine school.

Survey of 1878

Beginning on the Norwalk and Newtown Turnpike at the head of the Great Bogs, thence by the northeast side of the Great Bogs to the Southeast corner of W. D. B. Ferris' land, thence northerly in the east line of said Ferris' land to highway 32 rods south of the intersection of a road running northwesterly to W. D. B. Ferris' residence, thence northerly by highway to a point due west from the mouth of a road leading southerly from Mrs. Heman Northrop's house on Palestine road to Point of Rocks road, thence due west on said line to mouth of said road, thence southeasterly in a straight line to the north branch of Pohtatuck Brook or river at crossing of Orchard Hill road, to the Platt's Hill, thence westerly by said Platt's Hill road to its junction with the Hog Swamp road, thence southerly by the Hog Swamp road to the southeast corner of Mrs. Hermon Beers homestead, thence west and south in the line of said Beers land to brook, thence southerly by said brook to the road leading from Jerome H. Botsford's residence to Huntingtown, thence northwesterly by said highway to its junction with highway leading from J. H. Botsford's to Turney French's saw mill, thence northwesterly by highway to corner of highway at the residence of J. H. Botsford's, thence southwesterly by highway to the road leading from Hattertown to Dodgingtown, thence northerly by said highway to road leading easterly to heirs of Dr. Bronson's residence, thence westerly to old shut highway to an old cellar, once the house of Bill Wells and now owned by Jerome H. Botsford, thence northerly to a point on road leading from Dodgingtown to Hattertown about six rods south of Wanzer Platt's dwelling, thence northerly along said highway to the S. E. corner of Irving B. Goodsell's homestead (formerly Ezra Morgan's) thence northerly in the east line of said homestead to the Palestine road, thence easterly by said road to the southeast corner of said Goodsell's land, thence northerly to the southwest corner of the Great Bogs, thence northerly by the Great Bogs to Norwalk and Newtown turnpike at the foot of a hill, thence northeasterly by said turnpike to the place of beginning."

1755

HANOVER

Dec. 8, 1755, the town voted "that ye inhabitants of ye farms lying northerly of ye two mile brook, so-called in Newtown, shall have ye money that arises on their several lists for ye maintaining schooling and others that shall join with them providing sd money be laid out among them, and Ephraim Botsford was chosen committee-man to take ye care of ye schools.—John Northrop, town clerk."

The several schools did not always depend upon the amount apportioned them from the tax levied upon taxable property of the town, they at times added to their taxes by voluntary subscription, lengthening the school year. I have in my possession an original subscription paper drawn up in 1785, showing the spirit the handful of families in Hanover in those early days had which I have no doubt is a fair sample of the spirit existing throughout the whole community in their anxiety that their children be taught in at least the "three R's." "We, the subscribers whose names are under-written promise to pay the several sums annexed to our names for the purpose of hiring a schoolmaster for the time of five months. Dated at Hanover, this 10th day of October, 1785.

	℔	s
James Glover	1	11
Amos Terrill		11
Hezekiah Booth		16
Daniel Glover		16
Abraham Booth		6
Roger Terrill		4
Elijah Foote		6
Jonathan Sanford	1	
Solomon Sanford		14
Oliver Pulford		11
Jonas Sanford		17
Alexander Sperry		12
John Glover		12
Thomas Wheeler		4
Sum total	9	0

Jonathan Sanford was E. L. Johnson's maternal great-grandfather.

Survey of 1878

"Beginning at the danger signal at crossing of railroad and highway leading to Lake George, the corner of Hanover, Lake George, Land's End and North Center districts, thence north easterly to Simeon B. Peck's corner at Butterfield (so-called) on the Highway leading past Anthony McMahon's house, southerly to tunnel, thence N. easterly along the line of said Peck's land, to corner near Highway called the Butty Hill road, near the crossing of a small stream running northerly. Thence down small stream to Pond Brook. Thence up Pond Brook to the South west corner of Thomas Costello's land (formerly A. B. Terrill's). Thence northerly in the west line of said Costello's land to the northwest corner adjoining the Peter Lake Meadow (so-called) now owned by Michael Lillis. Thence in a straight line N. 14 degrees east 255 rods to the stone monument in the old saw mill road at the town line between Brookfield and Newtown. Thence on said Town line N. 41 degrees east to the Housatonic river. Thence down said river to the mouth of the first small stream north of the fording place. Thence up said stream a short distance to the old Union Bridge, now closed. Thence a straight line to the southeast corner of Thomas Cavanaugh's home lot. Thence S. 38 degrees west to an elbow in the road leading from Hanover across Walnut Tree Hill. Thence southerly by said road to the junction with the Walnut Tree Hill road. Thence north westerly by said road to the mouth of the Green road. Thence a straight line to the crossing of the railroad and highway near the old Brick yard. Thence northerly in line of railroad to danger signal, the place of beginning."

1761
SOUTH CENTER
KETTLETOWN

Jan. 30, 1761, Newtown voted in town meeting "that ye subscribers hereafter named, belonging to ye south end of ye town or south of Deep Brook according to their desire shall have ye liberty of setting up a school among themselves, and upon their keeping a school so long as may be found beneficial for learning their children to reade or wright, etc., that then they shall draw their part of ye money appropriated for ye use of schools in Newtown. The subscribers are Peter Nichols, John Peck, Ephraim Peck, George Terrill, Daniel Baldwin, Henry Peck, Gideon Peck, Aaron Peck, Thomas Stillson. Peter Nichols and George Terrill are to provide a suitable person to teach and instruct the children in learning and Ephraim Peck shall be the committee-man.—Attest, John Northrop, town clerk."

DEEP BROOK

Dec., 1767, the town voted "that all included in ye circle hereafter mentioned shall be a district for schooling known as Deep Brook school, viz: From Lieutenant Samuel Griffin to Eliphalet Hull, Noah Parmelee's, Jr., Benjamin Stillson, Gideon Northrop and Abraham Kimberly. Voted, William Birtch shall be exempted from ye above school. Voted, Ensign John Sheperd shall be committee."

The school-house for Deep Brook district stood on the triangular piece of ground, between three roads, now owned by A. P. Smith, editor of the Bee, and near his dwelling. It was called the Federal school-house. My authority was Abel B. Prindle and Town Clerk Charles Henry Peck.

At the annual town meeting Dec., 1791, Amos Sherman, Gen. John Chandler and John Beach were appointed committee to look into uniting the school at the south end of town with the school at Tinkerfield. The year following, this above committee reported as follows: "Whereas the town at their last meeting appointed a committee to examine into the circumstances of the South Center school district and Tinkerfield district and make report at this meeting which report is as follows: It is the opinion of the committee that the southerly center school and that of Tinkerfield district shall be united in one district and known as the South Center school district." The report was accepted and it was voted in town meeting December, 1792, "that the above two schools shall be united and known by the name of the South Center school district."

At the first called Kettletown, a few years later changed to

Tinkerfield, and in 1792 Deep Brook district, also known as South Center, was joined with Tinkerfield district and given the new name of South Center, which name it has since retained.

Survey of 1878

"Beginning at the Cold Spring culvert and running northeasterly by the Pootatuck brook to the Mile Hill bridge, thence northerly in a direct line with the Mount Tom brook bridge to the south line of Roswell Turney's land (formerly James Nichols'), thence westerly on said line to the southwest corner about 15 rods up stream from the bridge across Deep Brook on said Turney's land, thence up said Deep Brook to a point in line with the south line of Hermon Peck's home lot, thence S. 66 degrees W. crossing highway to said Peck's southeast corner of home lot on Bridgeport and Newtown turnpike, thence north 75 degrees west to the junction of the road leading to Abel Stillson's with the road leading past the cemetery, thence southwesterly along side of the road to Deep Brook, thence Southerly and Easterly by highway past William Stillson's to the mouth of the Point of Rocks road, thence southeasterly along said Point of Rocks road to its junction with a road leading southerly from Palestine road near heirs of Heman Northrop's dwelling, thence southeasterly in a straight line to the north branch of the Pootatuck Brook on Orchard Hill road, thence southeasterly along said brook to its junction with South branch, thence easterly along Pootatuck brook to Cold Spring culvert, the place of beginning."

SLUT'S HILL

In 1768 the town voted "that all included in ye circle hereafter mentioned shall be a district for schooling known by ye name of Slut's Hill school, viz: James Baldwin, Lemuel Sherman, Benjamin Hawley, Jeremiah Turner, Junr, and all ye rest within sd limits." The circle included the territory now known as Mount Pleasant as far west as Taunton pond (Quanneapague Lake) and toward Hawleyville on what is still known as the "Barnabas road." This district was discontinued later.

1768
LAKE GEORGE

In Jan. 1768, the town voted "that all whose names are hereafter mentioned shall be a district by ye name of Lake George school, viz: From Capt Joseph Wheeler to Newbury line, including all whose names are here annexed: Nehemiah Skidmore, Thomas Lake, Elnathan Skidmore, George Smith, Nathan Lake, Joseph Wheeler, Ezra Bryan. Voted, "that Nehemiah Skidmore shall be committee."

In my younger days I heard the district took its name from the combination of the names of two men who were foremost in bringing the matter about. The Christian name of one man was George and the surname of the other was Lake. The combination formed, "Lake George."

At the annual town meeting held in the following year, 1769, it was voted "that there shall be a tax of one farthing on ye pound for ye use of ye schools for ye year ensuing—and that ye rate may be paid in provisions." It was also voted "that wheat shall be rated at four shillings per bushel, rye at two shillings eight pence per bushel, flax six pence per pound, Indian corn two shillings six pence per bushel, and oats one shilling per bushel, for ye school rate of ye year ensuing, and also voted, "Ebenezer Bristol shall have thirty shillings as town treasurer for his services ye year ensuing."

Survey of 1878

Lake George District bounds: "Beginning at the danger signal at cross ing of railroad and highway leading to Lake George (the corner of Hanover, Lake George, Land's End and North Center districts), thence northeasterly to the northwest corner of Simeon B. Peck's land on highway leading past Anthony McMahan's southerly to Tunnel, thence northeasterly along the line of sd Peck's land to the corner near highway called Butty Hill road near the crossing of a small stream running northerly, thence down sd stream to Pond Brook, thence up Pond Brook to the southwest corner of Thomas Costello's land, thence northerly in the west line of said Costello's land to the northwest corner adjoining the Peter Lake meadow (so-called) now owned by Michael Lillis, thence in a straight line north 14 degrees east 255 rods to the stone monument on the old saw mill road at the town line between Brookfield and Newtown, thence on sd town line S. 41, W. to monument on highway running northerly from Benjamin Hawley's old house, thence southerly on highway to its junction with road running easterly, thence easterly along sd road to the Land's End Mill, thence S. 65 degrees E. 20 rods to Pond Brook, thence S. 58 degrees E. 204 rods to a point about 60 rods west of James Lake's house on road leading easterly from Bridgeport and Newtown Turnpike near Robert N. Hawley's residence, thence S. 45 degrees, E. 238 rods to the danger signal above described and the place of beginning."

1769
FLAT SWAMP

At the annual town meeting in Dec., 1769, it was voted, "that from Timothy Shepherd's to Agur Fairchild's and to Daniel Crowfoot's and Timothy Platt and Thomas Roberts and all within ye sd limits shall be a district for a school known by ye name of Flat Swamp school and that Daniel Crowfoot shall be school committee for ye year."

In 1878, these boundary lines were run: "Beginning on the Town line between Bethel and Newtown on the highest point of Jolly Hill so-called, at stone bounds near a high rock, thence southerly along the said Town line to the northeast corner bounds of Redding, thence due east to Shut Road south of Andrew Barnum's dwelling house, thence northerly by said highway to the Jangling Plain road to the old Fairfield County turnpike, thence due east to a point 6 rods south of Wanzer Platt's house on the Monroe turnpike, thence northerly by said turnpike to the southeast corner of Irving Goodsell's homestead (formerly Ezra Morgan's), thence northerly in the east line of said homestead to the Palestine road, thence by said road to the southeast corner of said Goodsell's homestead, thence in the east of said homestead to the southeast corner of the Great Bogs, thence Northerly by the Great Bogs to the Norwalk and Newtown turnpike at the foot of a hill, thence by said turnpike to Key Hole Rock, thence northerly to a point 60 rods east of bounds near the line between William and Henry Fairchild's on highway leading south from Henry and George Fairchild's residence and in line with aforesaid bounds and the corners of William Fairchild and Norman Northrop on highway east of said highway, thence westerly 60 rods along said line to aforesaid bounds 4 1-2 rods south along said line between William Fairchild, thence north 85 degrees west to place of beginning."

1779
SANDY HOOK
POHTATUCK BROOK

At the annual town meeting Dec. 22, 1779, it was voted, "that the inhabitants living or residing in the following limits, viz: Beginning at Josiah Curtis' and to extend easterly on the road to Woodbury to the Great River and northerly so far as to include Hezekiah Sanford, shall be a district for schooling and be known by the name of Pohtatuck Brook school."

That lay-out took in all the country from Tom brook on the west to the Great river on the east, and along the Great river northward to the southerly line of Hanover district, extending northwesterly to the line of beginning, Tom brook. The school-house for that large area was on the road to Woodbury, less than half a mile east of where Sandy Hook school-house stands, but on the opposite side of the highway. The writer's mother, born in Sandy Hook in 1804, attended school there until she was 15. The school-house was on what is now known as Gas street, not far in a southerly direction from the road that leads over the hill to St. Rose cemetery. There came a time, too, when, for residents on the plain land along the west bank of the Great river, after the Abijah Curtiss house (now James Cavanaugh's) was built, (a few others living in that vicinity and along toward Hanover), a small school-house was built near the edge of the highway that led to Hanover, near a house then know as the Dillazon Peck place. This school was kept open until 1854, when the children became so few in number, that it was given up and the children were received into Sandy Hook school. Patrons of the school had been paying teacher's salaries ranging from $1.50 a week in summer to from $10 to $12 a month with board for a man teacher in the winter.

"Pootatuck Brook School District," as established by vote of the town, in the year 1779, the greater part of which is now included in the Sandy Hook school district according to the survey of 1878 and the remainder of the same is now a portion of the two districts, Pootatuck and Walnut Tree Hill. The boundary lines of Sandy Hook district are as follows:

"Beginning at the southeasterly corner of Lawrence Mitchell's land (formerly Abijah B. Curtis') on the banks of the Housatonic river about 10 rods north of a ledge of rocks in river near the western bank, thence westerly in a straight line to a point on the west bank of the Pootatuck brook or river directly in the line with the said Mitchell's corner and the junction of the Union bridge and Pootatuck roads a little north of the upper rubber factory in Sandy Hook, thence up said Pootatuck to a small stream emptying into said Pootatuck near said upper rubber factory, thence westerly in a straight line to the northwest corner of Charles Parsons' land on Walnut Tree Hill road near house of Morris Leavey, thence southerly along said road to a point six rods north of the Sandy Hook and Newtown road, thence south 54 1-2 degrees west between the house and barn of James Turney (formerly William Glover) to Sandy Hook and Newtown road, thence westerly along said road to Mount Tom Brook, thence in a straight line southeasterly to the Mile Hill Bridge over the Pootatuck brook or river, thence easterly to the southeast corner of Cornelia Curtis' land (formerly Philo Curtis') 24 1-2 rods north of a small stream crossing the road from Berkshire to Bennett's Bridge, thence in a straight line northeasterly to Mitchell's corner, the place of beginning."

1779
POHTATUCK

The original school-house for Pohtatuck was close by the road in the brush, near a little stream near what was then known as the Dillazon Peck place, now the home of Mrs. Lester. In 1854, there were but seven children of school age, and they were allowed to attend school in Sandy Hook. There was no further school in Pohtatuck until the district area was increased and lines run as they now exist. At Ragged Corner, now Half Way River, the first school-house occupied ground on the highway nearer the

Housatonic river than now. When the main part of the present school-house in Sandy Hook was built in 1840, the site was changed from Gas Street, one-quarter of a mile beyond its present location. The name Pohtatuck Brook had been previously changed to Sandy Hook.

When lines were run for the present district of Pohtatuck in 1878, it took in that part of Pohtatuck Brook district along the west bank of the Great river, and also the Pohtatuck brook valley as far up the stream as the upper rubber factory. The present layout:

"Corner of Lawrence Mitchell's land (formerly Abijah B. Curtis) on the banks of the Housatonic river, about 10 rods north of a ledge of rocks in said river near the western bank. Thence westerly in a straight line to a point on the west bank of Pootatuck brook or river, directly in line with the aforesaid Mitchell's corner and the junction of the Union Bridge and Pootatuck roads, a little north of the Upper Rubber factory in Sandy Hook. Thence down said Pootatuck to Lawrence Mitchell's dam. Thence following said Mitchell's saw mill dam thence following said Mitchell's watering ditch to highway near said Mitchell's residence. Thence northerly and westerly in line of said highway to fording place on Housatonic river. Thence down said river to place of beginning."

1783
BEAR HILLS

Voted, 1783, "that ye limits hereinafter expressed shall be a district for schooling by themselves and known by ye name of Bear Hills district, viz: Beginning at a monument south of John Merritt at a place called Pine Swamp hill, thence running northwesterly betwixt Timothy Treadwell's and John Johnson's to Daniel Baldwin's east line of Platt's hill, thence running northerly a straight line to Little Boggs brook."

UNITING BEAR HILLS AND HUNTINGTOWN DISTRICTS.

At the annual town meeting in Dec., 1794, Capt. Moses Shepherd and Capt. Solomon Glover were appointed committee to examine into the circumstances and limits of the two school districts of Huntingtown and Bear Hills and make report at the next annual meeting. At the annual meeting in Dec., 1795, this committee reported as follows: "That the two above sd districts unite in one school for the term of three years, to be kept near the house of John Brisco on condition that the children of Justus Sherwood and William Nickerson Taylor shall not be taxed for fire wood and boarding the schoolmaster during that time. The report was accepted and voted in the affirmative. Caleb Baldwin, town clerk."

MIDDLE GATE

The experiment was carried out, but was not repeated. Before leaving these districts, we call attention to the spelling of the name Bear Hills, the writer believes it indicated, not the bareness of the hills, but a favorite home and haunt of bears.

The original name given Middle Gate district was Bear Hills, changed soon after the Newtown and Bridgeport turnpike was opened for traffic. There were three toll gates on the turnpike, one in Newtown near the Brookfield line and one on the line between Newtown and Monroe, which being midway between the upper and lower gate was called Middle Gate which changed the name of the school district from Bear Hills:

In time there came to be families living in a corner of Monroe so near to Middle Gate school, as to wish to be set off to that district. Selectmen of Newtown, acting with those of Monroe, changed the southwesterly line between Monroe and Newtown on the Guinea road to run eastwardly to bounds on Newtown turnpike opposite a chestnut tree called the "Five Mile tree," south of the Ambrose Beach place, thence in the same direction to the railroad crossing at the Pepper Street road near the old Burr place, thence in a northerly direction to the place of starting. The change was made under the administration of Aaron Sanford and Timothy Costello, selectmen of Newtown, and Eli B. Seeley, Elbert S. Olmstead and William R. Ferris, selectmen of Monroe, April 28, 1886.

"Beginning on the Town line between Monroe and Newtown at the crossing of highway leading from Monroe to Newtown, thence northwesterly along said Highway to its junction with the old Lebbon road. Thence northwesterly a straight line to the junction of Toddy Hill road with the Monroe road, thence northwesterly by said Monroe and Newtown road to Housatonic railroad, thence northerly by sd railroad to the Pootatuck Brook or river, thence by said brook southwesterly to Coger's mill, thence in a straight line to the northeast corner of Nathan Burr's dwelling house (formerly Peter Shepherd's), thence southerly in a straight line to the mouth of the Pine Swamp Hill road, thence southwesterly by said road to the Monroe and Newtown line, thence easterly on said line to highway, the place of beginning."

1784
GRAY'S PLAIN

Special town meeting, Feb. 7, 1784, voted, "that the people living at Gray's Plain, that is to say, from Benjamin Lattin's to the Widow Mallery's old house, thence to Stratford line by Ebenezer Lewises and all the people within said limits shall be a district for schooling and known by the name of Gray's Plain district and that Daniel Morris, Junr., shall be committee for the district."

In 1878, these lines were run: "Beginning at a point on highway 50 rods west of Frederick Chambers' dwelling house, thence easterly by said highway to Gelding Hill Brook between the dwellings of Thomas Chambers and Charles Johnson, thence northerly by Gelding Hill Brook to Housatonic river, thence southerly by said river to the road leading from the river at Wallace & Son's to Patrick Hartnett's residence, thence westerly by said road to highway leading from Half Way River to Berkshire at said Hartnett's, thence south 15 degrees east in the west line of Patrick Lynch's land to the southwest corner, thence due south crossing highway at bounds to a pile of stones at foot of Rock Oak in the east line of Alosia Porter's woodland about 30 feet west of a ledge of rocks, said bounds being the corner of Grey's Plain and Walker's Farms on the line of Half Way River district, thence north 66 degrees west to the top of Sandy Hill a point 40 rods north of Sandy Hill Brook on High Rock road, thence westerly to a rock 3-4 of a mile northerly from the road leading to Monroe on the Old Lebbon Road, thence northerly by said Old Lebbon Road to a pile of stones on west side near John Kane, Jr., land, thence north 73 degrees east to the bridge over a small stream crossing highway about 40 rods west of the mouth of High Rock road, thence easterly by highway to mouth of High Rock road, thence northerly to a point on highway 50 rods west of Frederick Chambers' dwelling to the place of beginning."

1784
HEAD OF MEADOW

Dec., 1784, voted, "that ye boundaries and limits hereinafter described shall be a district for schooling by themselves known by name of Head of Meadow district, viz: Beginning at a place called the causeway, thence running south so far as the top of the Mine hill, from thence eastward to the parting of the paths near Mr. William Northrop's house from thence northeast to the Crooked brook and from thence north to the place begun at. Petitioners for the above described district are Samuel Gillett, Gideon Northrop, David Shepherd, John Gillett, Nehemiah Birtch, George Shepard, Amos Shepard, Moses Gillett, George Northrop, Abraham Gillett."

Survey of 1878

"Beginning at Key Hole Rock, thence southerly by the Norwalk and Newtown turnpike to the head of the Great Bogs. Thence by the north east side of the Great Bogs to the south east corner of W. D. B. Ferris' land. Thence northerly in the east line of said Ferris' land to highway 32 rods south of the intersection of a road running north westerly to W. D. B. Ferris' residence. Thence northerly by highway to a point due west from the mouth of a road leading southerly from heirs of Heman Northrop's house on Palestine road to Point of Rock's road. Thence due east on said line to mouth of said road. Thence south easterly along said road to Point of Rock's road. Thence north easterly along said Point of Rock's road to mouth. Thence east and north past William Stillson's dwelling to Deep Brook Bridge, south of cemetery. Thence up Deep Brook to the Palestine road. Thence northerly on said road to Norwalk and Newtown turnpike. Thence westerly along said turnpike to a road leading to and past Arthur Peck's house. Thence by said road westerly to elbow in road about 50 rods N. E. of Mrs Carroll's house, the junction of an old abandoned road running northerly. Thence northerly by said old abandoned road to stone bounds on said old road near the sharp angle of said road. Thence westerly a straight line to the highway at the line between William Fairchild and Norman Northrop. Thence to a point directly in line and 60 rods east of stone bounds on west side of highway 4 1-2 rods south of Henry and William Fairchild's corners on road leading to Dodgingtown, from Henry and George Fairchild's residence. Thence southerly in a direct line to Key Hole Rock, the place of beginning."

1786
WAPPING

Dec., 1786, voted, "that the following petition be granted to the subscribers, that the limits herein mentioned be a district for schooling by themselves, viz: We the subscribers do petition to be set off a district by themselves for a school bounded as follows: Beginning at pole bridge and running from thence to Carlton bridge, so-called, and from thence to take in Nehemiah Knapps, from thence to cross to said bounds begun at. Abel Bennitt, Thomas Bennitt, James Bennitt, Richard Bennitt, David Rugg, Nehemiah Knapp, petitioners." Survey of 1878.

"Beginning at the mouth of the Pole bridge brook on the Housatonic river, thence northerly by said river to the south easterly corner of Lawrence Mitchell's land (formerly Abijah B. Curtis) on the bank of the Housatonic river about ten (10) rods north of a ledge of rocks near the western shore. Thence southerly in a straight line with the aforesaid Mitchell's corner and the south east corner of Cornelia Curtis land (formerly Philo Curtis) to the Pole bridge brook. Thence down said brook to its mouth, the place beginning."

This gives only that part of Wapping district on the Newtown side of Housatonic river, and when Newtown children attend the school in Wapping, Newtown has to pay Southbury its share of school expenses. The town of Southbury was incorporated in May, 1787. How long after its incorporation Wapping of Southbury and Wapping of Newtown became a joint district, Newtown records do not tell.

1788
GREGORY'S ORCHARD

1788, "We, the subscribers, inhabitants of part of Newtown included in the following bounds do desire to be set off as a district for keeping and maintaining a school. The bounds to be as follows: Beginning at a point on the line between Newtown and Redding which shall be due west from where the brook crosses the road north of Mr. Jarvis Platt's dwellinghouse, thence running east to the south side of where the sd brook crosses the road, from thence running easterly to where the Brook called Castle Meadow brook crosses the road above Gregories Orchard, so-called, thence southeast to the line between Newtown and Weston, thence westerly on the line between Newtown and Weston to Redding line, thence northerly on the line between Newtown and Redding to the place of beginning. Lazarus Beach, John Raymond, Jabez Rowland, Seth Gilbert, Jarvis Platt, petitioners. The above limits voted to be a district for schooling by themselves by the name of Gregories Orchard district.—Caleb Baldwin, town clerk."

In 1878, these lines were established:

"Beginning at the Monroe and Newtown turnpike at shut highway near Heirs of Dr. Bronson's spring. Thence westerly in said shut highway to old cellar formerly called Bill Wells', now owned by J. H. Botsford. Thence southerly in the lines of George R. Parmalee and Charles Short, Andrew Northrop, Ralph Benedict to David Somer's land. Thence southerly in said Somer's line to Gregory's Orchard and Reading Road, said line being nearly straight. Thence southeasterly by highway about 40 rods to the north west corner of Albert Edwards Meadow south east of the burying ground. Thence southerly in the west line of said meadow to the town line between Easton and Newtown. Thence easterly in the Town line between Monroe and Newtown to highway leading from Andrew Leavenworth's to Turney French's saw-mill. Thence northerly by said highway to the corner of highway at Jerome H. Botsford residence (leaving the homesteads of all persons on west side of the said road from Turney French's saw mill, south to Town line to be included in Huntingtown district). Thence south easterly by highway to Monroe and Newtown turnpike. Thence northerly by said turnpike to place of beginning."

1789
WALKER'S FARMS

The original Walker's Farms school district was made up of territory now lying in the town of Monroe.

Monroe was set off from Huntington, and held its first town meeting in June, 1823. The town of Huntington was incorporated in 1789.

In 1878, a survey was made of that part of Walker's Farms school district in the town of Newtown, which reads as follows:

"Walker's Farms District. Beginning on the old Lebbon Road at a rock 3-4 of a mile northerly from the junction of said road with the road leading from Monroe Centre to Botsford Depot. Thence easterly in a straight line to the top of Sandy Hill at bounds on the Road 40 rods Northerly from Sandy Hill Brook, Thence south 66 degrees east to stone bounds on west side of Highway east of the High Rock Road, Thence same course to the south west corner of Mrs. Alosia Porter's Woodland at the sharp angle of the road leading from Granville Latin's to Monroe Center, Thence same course to a pile of stones at the foot of a Rock Oak in the east line of Alosia Porter's woodland about 30 feet west of a ledge of rocks, said bounds being the corner of Gray's Plain and Walkers Farms on the line of Half Way River Districts, Thence due south to Half Way River, said course being directly in line with the church steeple at Monroe Centre, Thence westerly on said River (the town line between Monroe and Newtown) to highway leading from Monroe Center to Botsford's Depot. Thence north westerly along said Highway to junction of old Lebbon road, thence northerly along said road to rock the place of beginning."

"On the 23rd of March, 1886, the selectmen of Newtown and Monroe were called upon to change a southerly line that should put a few families into the Half Way River District. The line agreed upon was, that at the end of the Lebbon road the line should run in a straight line to the Railroad crossing on the Pepper street road near the old Burr place. Thence to a pile of stone on the north side of Highway on the first hill east of Lynson Beardsley's. Thence in a north easterly direction to a pile of stone on a rock on the west side of the old road leading north from Thompson Judson's house. Thence to a large rock on the south side of the road 42 rods west of Turkey Roost Bridge. Thence to a pile of stone on a rock on the east side of Paul's pond road, about 31 Rods north of Michael Curnance house to intersect the Eastern District line. Thence northerly following said Road to the first Bridge on the Josie Ring road. From thence to a pile of stone between land of George Ferris and the heirs of Stephen C. Whitlock on the bank of Half Way River.

Aaron Sanford
Timothy Costello
Samuel F. Tillson
Selectmen of Newtown.
Eli B. Seeley
Elbert Olmstead
William R. Ferris
Selectmen of Monroe.

Dated at Monroe, Conn., March 23, 1886.

Received for Record, April 28, 1886 and recorded by C. H. Peck, Town Clerk."

1789

TODDY HILL

Dec., 1789, voted "that the limits hereafter named, viz: Bounding westerly on Potatuck brook, northerly on Mileses brook, easterly on that branch of Mileses brook which runs through John Sherman's saw mill, southerly on the bare Hills towards Starlings, shall be a district for schooling and known as Toddy Hill district."

When Toddy Hill school disctrict was formed, it was made up of territory between the district of Zoar on the one side and that of Bear Hills on the other.

The layout as made in 1878: "Beginning at the junction of the old Lebbon road with the road leading from Monroe Center to Newtown, thence Northerly along the said Lebbon road to a pile of stones on the west side of road near the South East corner of John Keane, Jr's land, thence Westerly to the North abutment of the Bridge over the West Branch of Saw Mill Brook to its junction with the Pohtatuck Brook, thence Southwesterly by Pohtatuck Brook to the Housatonic Railroad, thence Southerly by said Railroad to the Monroe road leading to Newtown, thence South Easterly by said highway to Toddy Hill Road at its junction with the Monroe road, thence South Easterly a straight line to the old Lebbon Road as described above to the place of beginning."

1794

HUNTINGTOWN

The year in which the town gave Huntingtown people the privilege to put up a school house at their own expense does not appear on record, but the records do show that the annual town meeting held in Dec., 1794, Captain Moses Shepherd and Captain Solo-

mon Glover were appointed a committee to examine into the circumstances and limits of the two school districts of Huntingtown and Bear Hills and make report at the annual meeting in Dec., 1795. At that meeting the committee reports as follows: "That the two above said districts unite in one school for the space of three years, to be kept near the house of John Brisco, on condition that the children of Justus Sherwood and William Nickerson Taylor shall not be taxed for fire wood and boarding the schoolmaster during that time. The report was accepted and voted in the affirmative.
                                        Caleb Baldwin, Town Clerk."

The experiment was carried out though not repeated.

The lay out in 1878 was as follows: "Beginning at the junction of the North and South branches of Pootatuck brook or river and running north westerly by the said North branch to the highway called Orchard Hill road. Thence south westerly by said road to the Platt's Hill road. Thence westerly by said Platt's Hill road to its junction with the Hog Swamp road to the south east corner of Mrs Harmon Beers' homestead. Thence west and south in the line of said Beers land to Brook. Thence southerly by said brook to the road leading from J. H. Botsford's to Huntingtown. Thence north westerly by said Highway to its junction with the Huntingtown road at John Frank's. Thence southerly by last mentioned highway to Monroe and Newtown line including the homesteads of the inhabitants living on said road. Thence easterly by Monroe and Newtown line to the crossing of the Pine Hill road. Thence northerly on said road to its junction with road running east and west. Thence northerly in a straight line to the northeast corner of Nathan Burr's dwelling house. Thence in a straight line northerly to Coger's mill on south branch of Potatuck brook. Thence north easterly by said brook to its junction with its north branch the place of its beginning."

1866
WALNUT TREE HILL

The layout of Walnut Tree Hill school district was at a later date than that of any other and within the recollection of Newtown people who have not yet passed the meridian of life. It came about from the congestion of the schools in Sandy Hook and Pohtatuck, owing to an increased population. The district's history dates back to 1866. Dennis C. Gately, at that time superintendent of the New York Belting and Packing Co., located in Pohtatuck district, was the leading spirit in the movement of a new school district. He headed a petition calling the selectmen of the town to action and they, with other interested parties, looked over the ground and called a special town meeting to act upon the report the selectmen were to make. The warning read as follows: "The white male inhabitants of the town of Newtown, qualified to vote in town meeting are hereby warned to meet at the Town hall in Newtown on Monday, March 19, 1866, at two o'clock in the afternoon of said day for the purpose of forming and establishing a new school district out of Sandy Hook, Hanover and Pohtatuck districts.
                                        Zerah Fairman,
                                        David Sanford,
                                        William L. Terrill,
                                        David Somers,
                                            Selectmen."

The report of the selectmen: "Upon the application of Dennis C. Gately, George Botsford and others, residents of the town of Newtown, praying for the formation of a new school district to be composed mostly from Pohtatuck district and partly from the district of Sandy Hook and Hanover, the subscribers, after giving notice according to law to the several districts interested in said petition and having enquired into the facts set forth by the petitioners, do find that said petition should be granted and have therefore laid out a new school district to be called Walnut Tree Hill district."

By unanimous vote, the meeting accepted the report and also the layout as made by the selectmen, assisted by others.

The accepted layout of the district reads as follows:

"Beginning on the Walnut Tree Hill road at the north west corner of Charles Parsons' land near the house of Morris Leavey, thence easterly in a straight line to the mouth of a small stream emptying into the Pootatuck river opposite the upper rubber factory, thence down said Pootatuck river to Lawrence Mitchell's saw mill dam, thence following said Mitchell's watering ditch to highway near said Mitchell's house, thence northerly and easterly in line of said highway to fording place on Housatonic river, thence up said river to the first small stream emptying into said river the corner of Hanover district, thence up said stream a short distance to the old Union bridge road, now closed, thence a straight line to the southeast corner of Thomas Cavanaugh's house lot, thence S 38 degrees W to an elbow in the road leading from Hanover across Walnut Tree Hill, thence southerly and easterly by said highway to place of beginning."

In 1865, the year before the new district was laid out, the number of tax payers in Pohtatuck district was 48, not including the New York Belting and Packing Co., the valuation of whose property in the grand levy was $250,420 and the amount invested in business was $200,000. Walnut Tree Hill district first appears in the grand levy in 1866 with 699 acres of land, 21 houses, 30 resident tax payers and a taxable valuation of $29,783.

HOPEWELL

The names of the districts Hopewell, Half Way River and Pohtatuck of the early days do not appear in the list for the reason that no record shows when they were given special school privileges. Their situation reminds one familiar with the story "Uncle Tom's Cabin." where Miss Feely asks Topsy when she was born. Topsy replies, "Never was born—I 'spect I growd!" So we think the above three districts weren't born, only just growd!

Survey of 1878

"Beginning at an old cellar formerly called Bill Well's, now owned by Jerome H. Botsford. Thence southerly in the lines of George R. Parmalee and George Short, Andrew Northrop's and Ralph Benedict to David Somers' land. Thence in said Somer's line to Gregory's Orchard and Redding road, said line being nearly straight. Thence south easterly by highway about 40 rods to the north west corner of Albert Edward's Meadow south east of burying ground. Thence southerly in the west line of said meadow to the Town line between Easton and Newtown. Thence westerly to the south west corner of the Town of Newtown. Thence northerly along Town line to the north east corner of the Town of Redding. Thence due east to old shut road running past Andrew Barnum's residence. Thence northerly along said road to the Jangling Plain road. Thence easterly along said Jangling Plain road to the old Fairfield county turnpike. Thence due east to a point on Monroe turnpike 6 rods south of Wanzer Platt's dwelling house. Thence southerly to point of beginning."

1884
HALF WAY RIVER
Change of South Eastern Boundary in 1884

"Whereas the District of Half Way River having applied to the Selectmen of Newtown and Monroe to settle and define the south eastern boundary line of said district, do therefore by virtue of the powers vested in us, describe and establish the southeastern boundary line of said district as follows (viz.): Commencing at the mouth of Half Way River where it empties into the Housatonic following the said river to the north Point of Rocks at the great eddy, then running westerly to the north west corner of the great eddy where the second brook crosses the road leading to Polodore Stevens, then westerly to the stone bridge at the junction of road leading past Henry E. Plumb's and the old Monroe and Zoar bridge turnpike, then following the said road southerly to a place with a heap of stones at the Bassett's land on said turnpike, then westerly following the line of fence between Birdsey McEwen and Albert McEwen and that of land formerly owned by Orville McEwen and Walter Bradley to a point on Half Way River to meet the district line in Newtown.

Eli B. Seeley, Selectman of Monroe.
William L. Terrill, Selectman of Newtown.
Dated at Newtown, January 4, 1884. Received for record December 5, 1885.

C. H. Peck, Town Clerk."

"The above is a true copy of the original as recorded in Monroe Records, Vol. 8, page 767, as certified to by David A. Nichols, Town Clerk of Monroe. C. H. Peck, Town Clerk of Newtown."

The names of the districts Hopewell, Half Way River and Pohtatuck do not appear in the list for the reason that no record shows when they were given special school privileges, though we find on record that the first district name of Half Way River was "Ragged Corner."

Survey of 1878

"Beginning at an Oak tree opposite the Botsford bounds directly opposite Patrick Hartnett's residence on highway leading from Half Way River to Berkshire. Thence south 15 degrees east in the west line of Patrick Lynch's and to the S. W. corner. Thence due south to a pile of stones at the foot of a Rock oak in the east line of Alosia Porter's woodland about 30 feet west of a ledge of rocks, said bounds being the corner of Grey's Plain and Walker's Farms on the line of Half Way River district. Thence same course to Half Way River, said course being in a direct line with the church steeple at Monroe Center. Thence easterly by said river to the Housatonic river. Thence northerly by said Housatonic to highway leading from said Housatonic to highway at Patrick Hartnett's. Thence westerly along said highway to bounds at Hartnett's, the place of beginning."

THE SOUTHERLY HIGHWAY

"The Southerly Highway" was among the first highways laid out in the town after the lay-out of the four highways that radiated from the center of town, the easterly toward Woodbury, the westerly toward Danbury, the northerly toward New Milford and the southerly toward the Stratford line. A long time intervened in each case before the several lay-outs were passable except on foot or horseback, the only locomotion in these early days of the town's development, and for years thereafter.

The Southerly Highway is the road that intersects what has been known for the last 100 years as the Newtown turnpike, now a State road.

About two and one-half miles south of the flag-staff in Newtown Center, at a point just below the farm of H. N. Greenman, still remembered as the Jerome Northrop farm, the road running southwesterly through Huntingtown and on toward the Monroe line near Blanket Meadow is the Southerly highway. Any one familiar with the valley through which it runs cannot help recognizing the streams alluded to, but the names of settlers through whose land the lay-out ran vanished from the memory of man long years gone by. The only original names now known there are Gilbert and French. Lay-out of the Southerly highway from its intersection with the original lay-out of the road known as the road to the Stratford line to Castle Meadow brook.

Whereas, we are well sensible that through long delays, the publick, as well as particular persons have been greatly incommoded and damnified with respect to ye laying out of lands whereby necessary roads or highways are prevented being provided, we, moved with such consideration, with an aim, not only of ye good and necessity of particular persons, but of ye general and public good of ye town of Newtown aforesaid, have undertaken to lay-out, and have actually laid out, a highway within ye township of Newtown aforesaid, in manner following, (viz.) Beginning at ye northwesterly corner of ye three acre pitch belonging to ye heirs of John Treadwell at ye place it turns out of ye public road yt runs from Newtown to Stratford, thence running southardly down a narrow valley to ye northerly branch of ye Pootatuck brook and over it, thence running up ye hill southerly from ye brook in a narrow valley, thence southerly as marked trees direct until we come to Mr. Tousey's three score acre division on ye southard branch of Pototuck brook, thence running for a small space on ye northward side of yt three score acre division until we come to a small brook running eastward, thence running a few rods on ye northward side of sd brook eight or ten rods, more or less, where sd road enters John Golet's fifty acre division with his approbation. This road as above described is six rods in width, save all Pototuck brook and in ye low land adjacent to ye brook where it is ten rods in width from ye place aforesaid where it enters sd John Golet's land, running a few rods westerly, then southerly and within two rods eastward of a bunch of rocks and thence running southardly until it comes to a piece of springy land, running southwesterly through a leading valley until we come to ye northward side of John Griffin's fifty acre division, thence southardly to ye Elbo of a great brook where there is a great rock in sd Elbo on ye southwestward side of ye sd highway, thence southardly to Castle Meadow brook so-called, to ye place from above sd Mr. Toucey's sixty acres.

This road is to be followed according to ye direction of ye marked trees and from sd Golet's to Castle Meadow brook sd road is eight rods wide. At ye brook we finished our work, the road still to be extended.

Memorandum—that by agreement with aforesaid John Golet, in consideration of ye four rods in width that we have taken through sd Golet's fifty acres we agree to give to ye sd person three acres of land, two acres on ye west side of his fifty acres and so as to extend from above sd road to ye northwest corner of above fifty acres, and one acre on ye north end or side of sd division of land joining to sd end on ye piece of land on ye westward side of ye highway. Ye above work done on ye highway laid out this twentieth day of January, 1720, per us.

Thomas Bennitt,
Joseph Peck,
John Golet,
Selectmen.

Recorded February 3, 1720, Joseph Peck, Town Clerk.

The lay-out of the Southerly highway as given was accepted by the town according to this recorded vote: "At a lawful town meeting of the inhabitants of Newtown, holden January 25, 1720, ye southerly highway laid out by ye selectmen as appears of record Folio 1, page 86, from ye common road to Castle Meadow brook accepted of and established by ye vote of ye town and ordered to be recorded.

Test, Joseph Peck, Town Clerk.

Castle Meadow brook, mentioned as the line for the southern end of the lay-out for the Southerly highway, is a stream that has its source in the southwestern corner of Palestine district near what is still often spoken of as the "Doctor Bronson" place. Its course is southerly through Cranberry swamp and on down the valley until, in its winding course, it crosses the highway just below the school-house in Gregory's Orchard district, turning southeasterly. It starts as a very small stream but, with east and west tributaries swelling its volume as it flows down the valley, it becomes a large stream, spreading out into a broad sheet of water, known as Morgan's pond, whose surface is covered with the white blossoms of the pond lily in their season and whose waters breed and fatten myriads of fish of the carp and bullhead species. With nothing to impede the water's flow, it meanders on until, crossing the highway about a half mile below Huntingtown school-house near the home of John Frank, Sr., its waters empty into Pohtatuck brook.

We know not what the local colony numbered when they called for a highway, but it proved itself as prosperous as those in other parts of the town, shown by a petition to the town authorities "that they may build a school-house." The writer is glad to note among the names of the petitioners the name, not only of his great-grandfather, John Johnson, but also the name of his great-great-grandfather, Ichabod Johnson, whose homes were in that locality. The petition:

"We, the subscribers being destitute of a convenient school-house, have agreed to build a schoolhouse and our desire is to be set off by ye town as a party for schooling. The subscribers are as followeth: Joseph Griffin, John Tousey, Ichabod Johnson, Garshom Sumers, John Starling, John Johnson, Thomas Sharp, Junr., Samuel Griffin, John Bristol, Joseph Bristol, ye 3rd, Richard Nichols, Gamaliel French, Jr., Timothy Treadwell. The number of scholars that can attend upon the school is 32. At ye town meeting held December 24, 1764, the above written put to vote and allowed at said meeting. John Northrop, Clerk."

From 1720 to 1916 we count 196 years, nineteen decades of time have passed and what, for many, many years after the lay-out, was only a trail to be followed on foot or by horseback, became at last a highway, over which wagons, as they came into use, springless and fashionless though they were, served their purpose for convenience and usefulness until superseded by improved methods of transportation. A cosmopolitan people on work or pleasure bent are enjoying the fruits of those who did the foundation work there in their respective spheres in years long gone by.

THOSE WHO TOOK FREEMAN'S OATH
1742 TO 1796

The fourth volume of Newtown records gives the names of all who took the "Freeman's oath" from the 1742 to 1796, a period of 54 years. This volume being complete, there is every reason to believe that 1742 marks the time when the town's people became interested enough to want a representative in the affairs of the colony at the General Court that met alternately at New Haven and Hartford, semi-annually, in the months of May and October. Nothing shows that Newtown had a representative at the General Court until 1747, when the town was represented by Capt. Thomas Toucey and Mr. John Northrop. Up to the first town election for representation at the General Court, there had been two calls for making electors, the first in 1742, when 96 took the Freeman's oath; five years later, in 1747, 36 took the oath, making in all 132 up to 1747.

In that year the population of Newtown was 1100 and the list of polls and rateable estates returned to the General Court amounted to $56,700 in our currency. It was the first return made by the town to the General Court, and, in so doing, Newtown was entitled to representation. Names of Freemen of this corporation of Newtown, April, 1742—Mr. Elisha Kent, Job Sherman, Esq., Deacon John Botsford, Mr. Peter Hubbell, John Gillett, Henry Glover, Jeremiah Northrop, Sergeant John Glover, Captain Nathan Baldwin, Nathaniel Nickols, Lieut Thomas Skidmore, John Blackman, Benjamin Glover, John Sanford, Lieut. Obadiah Wheeler, John Shepard, Joseph Botsford, John Northrop, John Leavenworth, Captain Ebenezer Hubbell, Joseph Bristol, Abel Beers, Caleb Baldwin, Donald Grant, Moses Botsford, Peter Hubbell, Jr., Thomas Leavenworth, Freegrace Adams, John Hull, Joseph Bristol, Jr., Jeremiah Turner, Samuel Gillet, John Beers, Job Northrop, Moses Botsford, Gideon Botsford, Thomas Northrop, Enos Bristol, John Peck, Thomas Toucey, Esq., Moses Stilson, Alexander Briant, Samuel Beers, George Terrill, Abraham Bennitt, Daniel Booth, Thomas Bennitt, Abel Booth, Ephraim Bennitt, Daniel Beers, James Stillson, James Gifford, James Heard, Jr., Samuel Turner, Benoni Sherman, Jeremiah Burch, Heth Peck, Henry Botsford, Jr., Lemuel Camp, William Sharp, Nathaniel Peck, Benjamin Curtis, James Heard, Lieut. Joseph Smith, Benjamin Hawley, Captain Ephraim Peck, John Lake, Peter Ferris, Joseph Prindle, Joseph Heard, John Bristol, Nathaniel Brisco, Matthew Sherman, Edward Fairchild, Ensign Samuel Summers, Moses Stillson, Jr., Thomas Sharp, Ebenezer Bristol, Thomas Tousey, Esq., Doctor James Brisco, Nathan Foot, John Sherman, Jonathan Booth, Jr., Lieut Samuel Griffin, Stephen Burritt, Caleb Baldwin, Sr., Matthew Curtis, Abel Judson, James Brisco, Daniel Foot, Noah Parmalee, David Dunning, Joseph Botsford, Jr., Joseph Stilson.

1747, at the second meeting to make electors, 39 took the Freeman's oath. From that time to 1796 Freemen's meetings were held yearly and the names of all made electors are to be found recorded.

Electors made in 1747—Abner Heard, Nehemiah Skidmore, John Adams, Ebenezer Sanford, Moses Platt, Amos Marchant, James Baldwin, Benjamin Northrop, Abraham Johnson, Ichabod Johnson, Jonathan Fairchild, James Heard, ye third, Benjamin Stillson, Moses Peck, Jonathan Northrop, John Foot, James Fairchild, John Foot, Jr., Benjamin Dunning, Abel Botsford, Benjamin Burritt, Abel Dunning, Abraham Beers, Theophilus Nettleton, Josiah Daton, Moses Sanford, John Moger, John Blackman, Jr., Abraham Ferris, John Dunnings, Nathan Sherman, Thomas Chambers, Abraham Adams, Enos Beardslee, Nathan Hubbell, Jedediah Hubbell, Jeremiah Johnson, Ephraim Peck, Gideon Booth.

For 1747, we no doubt have the names of those who reached their majority after 1742 with perhaps a few hold overs when the first list was made in 1742. Meetings held in April of each year.

1748—Benjamin Mallory Ebenezer Booth, Richard Hubbell, Hezekiah Lyon, Abraham Kimberly, Andrew Wheeler, Ichabod Hubbell, Joseph Gunn; 1749—Joseph Peck Joshua Northrop; 1750—Richard Fairman, Dr. Timothy Shepherd, Agur Fairchild, Stephen Parmalee, John Lake, Jr., Ephraim Sherman; 1751—Nathan Lake, Nathan Burritt, George Terrill, John Skidmore, Abraham Bristol, William Burch, Samuel Summers, David Sherman, Ephraim Lake, Ephraim Blackman, Henry Peck; 1752—John Camp, Joseph Bristol, 3d, John Griffin, Daniel Winton, Nathan Baldwin, Abraham Hard, Joseph Wheeler, Benoni Hendrixson, Ephraim Adams, Nehemiah Curtis, Joel Sherman; 1753—Gideon Baldwin; 1754—Ebenezer Fairchild, Amos Northrop, Daniel Foot; 1755—Samuel Sanford, John Plat, Peter Nichols, Michael Dunning; 1756—Amos Heard, Obadiah Wheeler, Jr., James Blackman, Jonathan Terrill, John Febreque, Joseph Prindle, Cornelius Bristol, Aaron Peck, John Glover, Jr., 1757—Ebenezer Ford; 1758—none; 1759—Dr. Samuel Thomas, Caleb Baldwin, 3d, Jabez Baldwin, Stephen Pierson; 1760—none; 1761—Lieut Abel Prindle, Daniel Baldwin, Henry Glover, Jr.; 1762—Benjamin Curtis, Jr., Elijah Botsford, John Beach, Ezra Northrop, Thomas Roberts, Thomas Lake, Richard Smith, Samuel Burwell, William Hawley, Zadock Sherman, Abel Hurd, Jonathan Sherman, Amos Smith, Samuel Camp, Mr. John Beach, Obadiah Wheeler, Abijah Curtis, Joseph Blackman, Miel Peck, Jonathan Prindle, Joseph Smith, Arnold Glover, Lemuel Sherman, Jabez Botsford, Jehoshaphat Prindle, Thomas Ford, Jr., James Glover, Abraham Booth, Thomas Skidmur, Gershom Summers, Ezra Bryan, Thomas Tousey, Heth Peck, Jr., Abraham Bennett, Stillman Hubbell, Joel Camp, Zalmon Tousey, Benjamin Nichols, Oliver Tousey.

1763—Abel Botsford, Richard Nichols, Roger Terrill, Isaac Botsford, Joel Botsford, Elijah Stillson, Zadock Hard, Ruben Booth, Henry Peck.

1764—Joseph Griffin, Samuel Ferris, Theophilus Hard, Elijah Nichols, Abel Curtis, William Burwell, Ebenezer Peck, Abraham Kimberly, Job Bristoll, Seth Fairchild, Samuel French.

1765—Amos Botsford, Benjamin Stillson, Jr., Zachariah Clark, Abner Griffiin, Gamaliel French, Eliphalet Hull, Joel Prindle, Daniel Foot, Thomas Sanford.

1766—Nathan Woshburn, William Wright, Bailey Stillson, Ezra Peck, Nathan Peck, Jr., Robert Thompson, Neiram Hard, Abel Booth, Jr., Daniel Glover, Lemuel Wheeler.

1767—John Judson, Ebenezer Booth, Samuel Prindle, Peter Dunning, Nathaniel Northrop, Daniel Booth, Jr., Daniel Jackson, Joel Bassitt, Andrew Duning, John Shepherd, Jr., Neirum Curtiss, Daniel Peck, Benjamin Northrop, Jr.

1768—Ichabod Fairman, Abel Baldwin, Andrew Stilson, Josiah Lacey, Samuel Peck, Henry Peck, Esq., Eleazer Burritt, Jeptha Hubbell, Matthew Curtis, Eli Dunning, Richard Fairman, Matthew Curtis, Jr., Abraham Botsford, Jabez Botsford, Esq., Caleb Baldwin, Esq., Lieut. Amos Terrill, Joshua Hatch, Jared Dunning, Silas Hubbell, Asa Cogswell, Fitch Kimberly, Henry Wood, Oliver Fairchild, Captain Joseph Smith, Nathan Sherman.

1769—Samuel Sanford, Henry Fairman, Abel Bennitt, John Peck, Matthew Curtis, Jr., William Hall, Joseph Ferris, Jared Botsford, Nathaniel Towner.

1770—Asa Chambers, Abel Judson, Jr., Joseph Hatch, Abial Booth, Enos Northrop, Nathan Norton, Amos Burritt, Amos Peck, Elnathan Skidmur,

Peter Hatch, Isaiah Northrop, Cyrenus Hard, Zachariah Brown, Jonathan Bardslee, Theophilus Nichols, James Sanford.

1771—Moses Plat, Jr., John Hard, Asher Peck, David Peck.

1772—Zachariah Ferriss, Jabez Peck, Gershum Jackson, Ebenezer Johnson, Moses Botsford, Jr., Nathan Ferris, Nathan Prindle, John Beers, Jr., Noah Parmalee, Thomas Stilson.

From 1772 to 1777, there is no record of any having been made electors. The years between those dates marked the exciting period that culminated in the war of the Revolution.

THOSE WHO TOOK THE FREEMAN'S OATH IN 1776, ALSO THOSE WHO TOOK THE "OATH OF FIDELITY" FROM 1777 TO 1791.

"Freemen admitted and taking the Freeman's oath in the town of Newtown in the Independent State of Connecticut on September the 16th, 1777," the number was 48:

Deacon A. Bennett	Elijah Botsford,	Asa Cogswell
Lieutenant N. Brisco	Lieut. H. Fairman	Fitch Kimberly
Captain J. Northrop	Henry Peck, Esq.	Enos Northrop
Lieutenant J. Botsford	Eleazer Burritt	Silas Fairchild
George Terrill	Jeptha Hubbell	James Fairchild, Jr.
Joshua Northrop	Mr. Matthew Curtis	Jonathan Beardslee
Gideon Botsford	Eli Dunning	Henry Wood
Abraham Bennett, Jr.	Richard Fairman	Oliver Fairchild
Ezra Peck	Matthew Curtis, Jr.	Capt. Joseph Smith
Abel Baldwin	Abraham Botsford	Nathan Sherman
Captain J. Wheeler	Jabez Botsford, Jr.	Josiah Beardslee
James Fairchild	Caleb Baldwin	Ebenezer Fairchild
Samuel Brown	Lieut. Amos Terrill	Doctor James Sanford
Matthew Baldwin	Joshua Hatch	Ebenezer Smith
Lieut. B. Summers	Jared Dunning	Moses Platt
Capt. B. Dunning	Silas Hubbell	Josiah Platt

The same year, 1777, 73 Freemen came before a justice of the peace and took the oath of fidelity showing to the world, and posterity, that they were willing to sacrifice, in defence of principles set forth by the Declaration of Independence. November 11, 1913.

Mr. E. L. Johnson:

Dear Sir: Your articles on Newtown in the War of the Revolution interest me very much. I know that Newtown was a Tory town and that many if not the most of my ancestors were either pronounced Tories or luke-warm patriots. I would like to know whether any of those who bore the names of ——————— were sufficiently patriotic to come forward and take the oath of allegiance between 1776 and 1783. I thought it barely possible that my great-grand-father might have done so, as he had two sons in the Continental army, supposed to have lost their lives during the Ridgefield-Danbury troubles, as nothing was ever afterwards heard from them. I know that my great-grandfather, father of my mother's mother, was a noted or notorious Tory and for disloyal speech was obliged to sneak out of the State for one year to avoid arrest. It is possible there was some overt act of his in connection with others in striving to avoid assessment of taxes for war purposes, that his speech in an unguarded moment disclosed. I presume naturally many of the Tories in Newtown were members of the Church of England, hence their loyalty to the King. The writer is glad that the name of his paternal great-grandfather appears in the list of those who were first to take the oath in 1777. His son, Ezra, then a boy five years old, became in time grandfather of the writer. The great-grandfather's name was John Johnson.

The oath of fidelity to which freemen were obliged to subscribe before they could exercise the rights that accrued to them when they had taken the freeman's oath:

"You do swear by the ever-living God that you will truly and faithfully adhere to and maintain the government established in this state under the authority of the people, agreeable to the laws in force within the same, and that you believe in your conscience that the King of Great Britain hath not, nor of right ought to have any authority or dominion in or over this state, and that you do not hold yourself bound to yield any allegiance or obedience to him within the same, and that you will, to the unmost of your power, maintain and defend the freedom, independance and privileges of this state against all open enemies or traitorous conspiracies whatsoever, so help you God. And no person shall have authority to execute any of the offices aforesaid after the first day of January next, until he hath taken said oath, and all persons who hereafter shall be appointed to any of said offices shall take said oath before they enter upon the execution of their offices. And no freemen within this state shall be allowed to vote in the election of any of the officers of government until he hath taken the aforesaid oath in the open freemans' meeting in the town where he dwells."

"Names of those persons that have appeared to take the oath of fidelity prescribed by the General Assembly of this state at a General Assembly of the State of Connecticut holden at Hartford in said state on the second Thursday of May, A. D., 1777."

Newtown, Aug. 25, 1777, personally appeared and took the oath of fidelity:

Caleb Baldwin, Jr.
Jabez Botsford, Esq.
George Terrill
Lieut. B. Summers
Richard Fairman
James Fairchild, Jr.
Fitch Kimberly
Moses Shepherd
Elijah Botsford
Lieut. N. Brisco
John Botsford
Lieut. H. Fairman
Nathaniel Barnum
Eleazer Burritt
Nathan Curtis
Joshua Northrop
Josiah Beardslee
Abel Baldwin
Capt. J. Northrop
Amos Burritt
Elijah Foot
Eli Dunning
Henry Wood
David Baldwin
Gideon Botsford
Silas Hubbell
Oliver Fairchild
Abraham Baldwin
Capt. Richard Smith
Nirum Summers
Levy Bostwick
Ephraim Jackson
John Bunnill
Gershum Jackson
Samuel Hawley
David Jackson, Jr.
Ezra Birch
James Prindle
Ezra Dunning
Abraham Kimberly
Clement Botsford

Thomas Sharp
David Jackson
Joseph Gunn
John Keeler
Abel Smith
David Peck
Abraham Lewis
Abel Gunn
Isaac Hawley
Rev. Thomas Brooks
Nathan Burritt
Amos Northrop
Capt. Abel Botsford
Gamaliel French
Thomas Ford
John Skidmore
Nathan Washburn
James Glover
Eleazer Lacy
David Curtis
Daniel Sherman
Nathaniel Bunnill
Daniel Morris
Roger Hendrix
Col. John Chandler
Reuben Dunning
Reuben Taylor
Silas Hepburn
John Johnson
Abel Johnson
Joseph Botsford
Abel Foot
1778
Daniel Glover
Capt. Joseph Prindle
Lazarus Prindle
David Meeker
Cyrus Prindle
Jabez Baldwin
Abraham Baldwin
William Allen

John Smith
1779
Thomas Wheeler
Birdsey Glover
William Edmond
Theophilus Nichols
Liverius Peck
John Beach
Josiah Beardslee, Jr.
Zalmon Peck
John Hard
Andrew Stilson
Joshua Peck
David Hinman
Matthew Hall
1780
Nehemiah Strong
Lewis F. Sherman
John Hard
George Foot, Jr.
1781
Jotham Sherman
James Shepherd
Joel Prindle
Abiel Booth
1782
Amos Bennett
Abel Foot
Reuben Terrill
Hezekiah Dayton
John Summers
John Blackman, Jr.
Josiah Fairchild
Abel Skidmore
Amos Sherman
Nehemiah Curtiss
Abijah Curtiss
Stephen Crofoot
1783
John Fabrique
Jehosephat Prindle

THOSE WHO TOOK THE OATH OF FIDELITY

Ezra Sherman
George Sample
Hezekiah Booth
Capt. Peter Nichols
Capt. John Glover
Daniel Glover
Francis Pierce
Zalmon Booth
Cyrus Beers
Cyrennius Hard
Amos Hard
Nirum Hard
Reuben Booth
Solomon Glover
Ichabod Fairman
Joseph Foot
Henry Glover, Jr.
Elisha Wooster
Zalmon Tousey, Jr.
Salmon Curtiss
Stephen Burwell, Jr.
James Thomas
Ammon Hard
Levi Peck
John Crawford
John Beach, Jr.
Truman Blackman
Caleb Bennitt
Theophilus Botsford
Salmon Glover
Roger Terrill
Nathaniel Peck
Daniel Terrill
Elijah Peck
Alpheus Fairchild
Curtis Hard
Andrew Griffin
Abel Winton
Abraham Wheeler
Truman Sherman
Reuben Curtiss
James Foot
Elias Beardslee
Philo Parmalee
Timothy Treadwell
Eli Peck
Nirom Curtis
Abraham Booth
Nathaniel Judson
Amos Griffin
Isaac Tousey
Samuel Beers
Nathaniel Northrop
Daniel C. Sanford
Daniel Humphrey
Capt. E. Kimberly
William Hall
Josiah Blackman
Jonathan Booth
Capt. John Blackman
Capt. Henry Glover
James Bennett

Zachariah Clark
Isaac Trowbridge
Abel Ferris
Seth Griffin
Jonah Summers
Clark Baldwin
Ammon Hard
Daniel Baldwin
Zachariah Ferry
Lemuel Thomas
Abner Hard
Oliver Beers
Dr. Bennett Perry
Asher Peck
Enoch Peck
Joseph Bristol, Jr.
Moses Peck
Isaac Peck
Joseph Blackman
Gideon Peck
David Bristol
Reuben Adams
John Judson
Jacob Stilson
Abel Judson
Luke Lattin
Matthew Peck
Isaac Blackman
John Fairchild
Stephen Shepard
Truman Beers
1784
Samuel French
Amiel Peck
Samuel Peck
Benjamin Cook
Abel Booth
Peter Lake
Ephraim Lake
Joseph Bristol
Seth Fairchild
Philo Tousey
William Burwell
Philo Fairchild
Abraham Beers
Abel Prindle
Asa Chambers
Abel Tousey
John Walker
Jabez Peck
Philo Curtiss
Samuel Sanford
1785
Theophilus Hurd
John Beers, Jr.
Benjamin Stillson, Jr.
Elijah Nichols
Thomas Stilson
Philo Norton
George Peck
Enos Johnson
Obadiah Wheeler
Elias Beers

Joseph B. Wheeler
Moses Botsford
Curtis Wainwright
Nathaniel Brisco, Jr.
Peter Clark Hull
John Bostwick
Andrew Northrop
David Judson
Nathan Camp
David Botsford
Capt. Joseph Hepburn
Samuel Beardslee, Jr.
Elijah Hard
John Bassitt
Amos Shepherd
Dr. Preserve Wood
Abijah Hard
George Northrop
Eli Wheeler
Gideon Bostford, Jr.
Elijah Stillson
Joseph Hard
Birdsey Glover
Andrew Beers
Joseph Stillson
Gideon Dunning
George Shepherd
George Northrop
Josiah Hayes
1786
Elias Glover
William Northrop
Ebenezer Booth
Luther Harris
Wait Northrop
Drake Northrop
Benjamin Hawley
Noadiah Warner
1787
Daniel Baldwin
Robert Summers
Gold Curtiss
Zenas Washburn
Daniel Botsford
Vine Botsford
William Birch, Jr.
Eldad Tenney
James Hendrix
Jabez Beers
Samuel Trowbridge
1788
Donald Tousey
David Tousey
1789
Zadock Fairchild
Jonathan Fairchild
David Booth
1790
John W Chandler
Moses Kent Botsford
Clement Fairchild
Ezekiel Fairchild

Three hundred and nine in all with good old Anglo-Saxon names.

THOSE WHO TOOK THE FREEMAN'S OATH

1778
Capt. Richard Smith
Lieut. Amos Northrop
Amos Smith
Abel Gunn
David Peck
Ezra Birch
Mr. Joseph Gunn
Col. John Chandler
Reuben Taylor
David Curtis
Job Bunnill
Moses Shepherd

1779
Amos Burritt
Isaac Hawley
Joseph Botsford
James Glover
David Judson
Nathan Camp
John Johnson
Abel Johnson
Gershom Jackson

1780
John Botswick
Capt. Joseph Hepburn
Abraham Kimberly
Benjamin Burr
Dr. Preserve Wood

1781
David Baldwin

1782
Ephraim Sherman
Ephraim Jackson
Jabez Gerould
Gideon Dunning
George Shepherd
George Northrop
Josiah Hayes
Gideon Botsford, Jr.
Clement Botsford

1783
David Meeker
Hezekiah Booth
John Hard
Daniel Glover
Capt. Peter Nichols
Josiah Fairchild
Theophilus Nichols
Abraham Baldwin
George Foot, Jr.
John Summers
Abiel Booth
Mr. Nehemiah Strong
Mr. William Edmond
Capt. Abel Botsford
Thomas Ford
Capt. John Glover, Jr.
Amos Hard
Henry Glover, Jr.
Hezekiah Dayton
Zachariah Clark
John Hard

Zedekiah Morgan
Curtis Hard
Cyrenius Hard
Andrew Beers
John Beach
Josiah Beardslee
Thomas Bennitt
Solomon Glover
Abel Skidmore
Nirom Hard
Abijah Curtiss
Zalmon Peck
Ebenezer Beers
Capt. John Blackman
William Hall
John Peck
Abram Booth
Amos Skidmur
Zalmon Booth
John Blackman, Jr.
Jonathan Booth
Capt. Henry Glover
James Bennitt

1784
Zachariah Ferris
Liverius Peck
Amos Hard
Daniel Baldwin
Abel Booth
Nehemiah Curtis
Lewis Sherman
Samuel Peck
Clark Baldwin
David Beers
Auriel Peck
Ebenezer Sherman
James Foot
Capt. Joseph Prindle
Benjamin Curtis
Peter Lake
Dr. Bennitt Perry
John Smith
John Sanford, Jr.
Samuel Ferris
Seth Fairchild
Ephraim Lake
Joseph Bristol
John Fairchild
John Beach, Jr.
Abel Bennitt
Lemuel Nichols
Moses Peck
Cyrus Beers
Solomon Sanford
Salmon Glover
Salmon Curtis
Isaac Peck
Philo Tousey
Reuben Booth
Eli Wheeler
Philo Fairchild
Amos Sherman
Oliver Beers

Stephen Crofut
Truman Beers
William Burwell
Abraham Beers

1785
Elijah Nichols
David Hinman
Philo Norton
Thomas Stilson
Jotham Sherman
Amos Bennitt
George Peck
Reuben Curtis
Isaac Tousey
Lemuel Thomas
Cyrus Prindle
Theophilus Hard
Abel Tousey
Enos Peck
Isaac Trobridge
Enos Johnson
Joseph Foot
John Judson
Abel Judson
Elijah Hull
Nathaniel Northrop
Benjamin Stillson
Ezra Sherman
Asher Peck
Joseph B. Wheeler
Reuben Terill

1786
John Skidmur
Nathaniel Judson
Ezra Northrop
Richard Bennitt
Asa Chambers
Niron Curtis
John Beers, Junr.
Jonathan Prindle
Abel Hurd
Theophilus Hurd
Peter Fairchild
Zalmon Tousey, Junr.
Julius Camp
Josiah Blackman
Michael Parks
Isaac Baldwin
Ephraim Peck, Junr.
Ebenezer Sanford

1787
Noadiah Warner
Josiah Curtis
Moses Botsford
Rev. Zephaniah Smith
Asa Northrop
Wait Northrop
William Northrop
Niron Botsford
Luther Harris
Ebenezer Booth
Elias Glover
Drake Northrop

Ebenezer Mallery
Benjamin Hawley
Robert Summers
Abel Ferris
Daniel Croof
Gold Curtis
1788
Jacob Stilson
Donald Tousey
David Tousey
Daniel Baldwin
Lazarus Prindle
1789
Doctor Philo Perry
Captain Abijah Hard
Zadock Fairchild
Jonathan Fairchild
David Booth
1790
Mr Ephraim Sherman
John Winthrop
Moss Kent Botsford
Clement Fairchild
Ezekiel Fairchild
Joal Camp
Oliver Clark Hurd
Philo Curtis
Levi Peck
Sueton Baldwin
Josiah Tomlinson
Stephen Gilbert
Elias Glover
Lockwood Winton
1791
David Fabrique
Ezra Perry
Dr. Benjamin Curtis
Joal Booth
Beeman Peet Warner
Isaac Sanford
John Lott
Ziba Blakesly
1792
John Wooster Camp
John Curtis
Amon Skidmur
Caleb Bennitt
Abijah Birdsey Curtis
Lazarus Hard
Zachariah Clark, Junr.
Moses Beardslee
Stephen Taylor
Oliver Bancroft
Elias Beardslee
Joseph Blackman, Jr.
Daniel Blackman
Capt. Vine Botsford
1793
Simeon Glover
Daniel Clark Sanford
David Nichols
Ransford Baldwin
Daniel Prindle
Joseph Ferris
Hugh Murphe

Lewis Hubbell
Agur Beardslee
Andrew Wheeler
John Hubbell
Abel Curtis
James Clark
Truman Fairchild
1794
Peter Northrop
Alpheus Fairchild
Birdsey Glover
Job Nickerson
Austin Beers
Israel Botsford
Elnathan Skidmur
Philo Booth
Eli Beers
Ebenezer Ford Bennitt
Jotham Hawley
Lemuel Hawley
Roger Terrill
Silas Burton Judson
Patten Murry
Jacob Raymond
David Starling
John Mallery
Joseph Nichols
Isaac Wells
John Starling Beers
Leir Fairchild
Joseph Fairchild
Daniel Booth
Stephen Burwell
Cyrenius Peck
Andrew Hard
David Peck, Junr.
1795
Reuben Hull Booth
Ebenezer Turner
Lampson Birch
John Walker
David Curtis Deforest
Daniel Sherwood
Elias Beers
Joseph Wheeler, Junr.
David Curtis
1796
Elijah Judson
Gideon Baldwin
Enoch Peck
Daniel Sheperd
Caleb Baldwin, Junr.
Samuel Beers, Junr.
Amos Shepard
Philo Beardslee
Benony Hendryx
Red Wheeler
Henry Botsford
Richard Botsford
Daniel Perry
Gideon Peck
Mr Samuel Beers
Simeon Beers
Simeon Shepard, Junr.
Hermon Warner

Joel Prindle
Reuben Griffin
Collins Chapman
Benjamin Curtis, 3rd
Isaac Bennitt
Stephen Sanford
Peter Finch
Oliver Tousey, Junr.
William Nickerson
Abel Nichols
Webb Tomlinson, Esq.
Stephen Crofut, Junr.
1797
Amos Hard, Junr.
Gideon Lattin
Cyrus Hard
Cyrenius Hard, Junr.
Asa Chapman
Amon Beers
Philo Baldwin
Isaac Crofutt
Bailey Foot
Michael Baldwin, Esq.
1798
Jonathan Booth
Samuel C. Blackman
Charles Burroughs
Samuel Booth
Thomas B. Botsford
Isaac Wheeler
Jared Brace
Rufus Peck
Josiah Burroughs
David Lake
1799
Daniel Beers, Junr.
Beach Tomlinson
Daniel Botsford
Timothy Shepard
David Edmund
John Clark
William H. Fairchild
Lazarus Stilson
Richard Judson
David Summers
Wheeler Fairchild
Ezekiel Bennitt
Cyrenius Beers
Adonirum Fairchild
Ezra Curtis
Joseph Stevens Adams
Nathaniel F. King
Samuel Lane Judson
Samuel Northrop
Daniel Morris
Peter Stilson
Eli Crofut
Capt. Amos Morris
Dan Chapman
Nathanial Dikeman
Ezra Lake
John Turner
Zenas Stilson
Mark F. Hatch
Joseph Perry

1800

Edward Foot
Jacob Johnson
Alanson Northrop
Ezra H. Johnson
John Shepard
Lemuel Peck
Martin Botsford
James Peck
Andrew Peck, Junr.
Eden Birchard
Josiah Glover
James B. Stilson
Riverius Prindle
John Northrop, Junr.
Ebenezer Peck, Junr.
Nathan Peck, Junr.
Daniel Ferris
Dan Peck
Daniel Booth, Junr.
Daniel Nichols
David Booth, Junr.
Elihu Crofoot
Zalmon Taylor
Lemuel Foot
John Baldwin
Abel Prindle
Pattern M. Blackman
Eli Peck
Jarvis Platt
Seth Gilbert
Abel Beers, 3rd
John Turner
Eliakim Sharp
Micajah Nash
Benjamin Hard
Dennis Nash
Linus Sherman
Daniel Comstock
Daniel Hawley
John Skidmur
John Gillett
Philo Foot
Joseph Hawley
John Brisco
Andrew Griffin
Daniel Peck

1801

James Glover, Junr.
Amos N. Sanford
David Pulford
Ezra Glover
Joseph Sherman
Mathew Sherman
Ezra Sherman
Zardis Sherman
Lemuel Camp
Elnathan Peck
James Masters
Fldad Prindle
John Botsford
Elias Glover, Junr.
David Wheeler
David Edwards
Henry Glover

Elijah Jennings
Abner Judson
Jotham B. Sherman
Amos Peck

1802

Turney Peck
Justus Raymond
Gould St John

1803

John Hall, Junr.
Nathan Shepard
David Parmelee
Elisha Gilbert
George M. Shepard
Elijah Gilbert
Truman Peck
Jonathan Peck
Andrew Shepard, Junr.
Zalmon Beers
Samuel Trowbridge
Amos Smith
Hezekiah Northrop
John Botsford, Junr,
Richard D. Shepard
Aaron Beardslee
Abram B. Ferris
Billy Hall
Joshua Chapin
Abijah Merritt
Eli Hall
Isaac Tomlinson
Isaac Platt
Peter Foot, Junr.
Thomas Roberts
Amos Parmelee
Joseph Tousey
Jacob Beers
David S. Blackman
Ammon Shepard
Eliphalet B. Bradley
Isaac Skidmore
David Lyon
Jabez Hawley
John Raymond
Justus Platt
Ebenezer Crofut
Miles Johnson
Jabez Rowland
Aaron Wheeler
Ephraim Platt
Isaac Briscoe
John Crofut
Zalmon Roberts
Squire Knapp
Zalmon Lake
Samuel Peck, Junr.

1804

Moses Beardslee, Junr.
Abner Anson Nettleton
Hezekiah Rowland
Nathaniel Parmelee
Isaac Scudder
Joseph Wilkinson
Elias B. Crofut
Abram Botsford

Peter C. Hull
Marcus B. Parmelee
John Griffin
Ebenezer Griffin
Joseph Rowland
John Northrop
Thomas Botsford
Samuel Staples
Daniel Hard
Joseph Griffin
John Lake
Andrew Clark
Ichabod Johnson
Samuel Hubbell
Asahel Booth, Junr.
Timothy Jordan
John Peck, Junr.
Jonathan Goodsell
Lemuel Landers
Amos Terrill
Jeremiah Beers
Judson Peck
David Beers
Sherman Botsford
Philo Botsford
Abijah Bradley
Asa Dikeman
Albert Edwards
John Johnson, Junr.
John Underhill
James Terrill
Thomas Welch
David Platt
Joseph B. Barlow
Jared Bradley
Elihu Crofut. Junr.
Samuel Watkins
Lemuel Sheperd
Philo Sherman
Zalmon Sanford

1805

Nathan Turner
Thomas W. Peck
Jacob Camp
Nathan Platt
Zalmon Hall
Ethiel Starr
Samuel Blackman
Truman Blackman
Charles Prince
Agur Lewis
Samuel Camp
Ichabod Gilbert
Abel Beardsley
Cyrus Sherman
Jabez Sherman
Elijah Sherman
John Beardsley
Benjamin C. Glover
Edward Booth
Cyrus Fairchild
Nathan Lattin
Daniel Morris, Junr.
Andrew Crofut
Josiah Platt

THOSE WHO TOOK THE FREEMAN'S OATH

James Morris
Truman Sherman
John Bristoll
Isaiah Northrop
Lyman Edwards
Joseph Booth
Thomas Sanford
Moses Gillet
Isaac Peck, Junr.
Kiah B. Fairchild
Silas N. Glover
Hawley Stilson
Peter Shepard
Alfred D. Curtis
Nichols Curtis
David Judson
Silas Camp
Anson Judson
Philo Gilbert
Job S. Terrill
Philo Beardslee
Jonathan S. Fairchild
Ezra H. Jennings
Lemuel Fairchild
Roswell L. Sherwood
Ephraim Hubbell
James Mc Ray
Zalmon Northrop
1806
Job Lattin, Junr.
Zechariah Tomlinson
Joseph Burritt
John B. Wheeler
Nathaniel Brisco, Jr.
Moss K. Botsford, Jr.
Abner Beardslee
David Peck
James Thomas
Andrew Sherman
Nathaniel B. Nichols
James F. Beardslee
Obadiah N. Wheeler
Simeon S. Blackman
Gershom Summers
1807
Richard Peck
Ebenezer H. Fairchild
Eli Winton
Charles Hotchkiss
Arnold Foote
Sueton Shepard
Agur Blackman
1808
Amos H. Wheeler
Theophilus Botsford
John G. Tousey
Warren Wallace
Simeon Underhill
Rhesa Foot
Eli Bennitt
Josiah Sanford
Thomas Dibble
Zachariah Dunkum
1809
Elijah Sanford

Thomas Beers
William Botsford
Daniel Wells
Holbrook Curtis
Ebenezer Beers, Junr.
John Glover
Joseph Dick
David Jennings
1810
David C. Peck
Nehemiah Skidmore
Marcus Botsford
Ezra Gilbert
Clark Sherman
Eleazer Hawley
Heber Foot
David V. B. Baldwin
1811
Philo Baldwin
Abel S. Hawley
Ebenetus Curtis
David Clark
Joseph Bennitt
Stephen Nichols
Peter Nichols
James Wheeler
Ziba Fairchild
Ezra Fairchiild
Edmond B. Peck
1812
Thomas Blackman
Reuben Blackman
Daniel Morehouse
Amason Washburn
1813
Thaddeus Staples
Samuel Tousey
Amos Parker
Amos Wells
Philo Sherman, Junr.
Ezekial Peck
Levi Jackson
Abram Prindle
Lemuel Hawley
Cyrus B. Glover
Jabez B. Botsford
1814
Smith Wheeler
Andrew Northrop
Orman Sherman
Reuben Shepard
Martin Judson
Philo M. Jordan
Daniel Botsford, Junr.
Silas Fairchild, Junr.
Oliver Northrop
Ezra Jennings
Walter Northrop
Gould Curtis, Junr.
Henry Shepard
Squire Dibble
Ira Fairchild
James Staples
James Boyer

1815
Abiel K. Botsford
Zar Winton
Abraham Peck
Philo Beers, Junr.
Josiah Wetmore
Henry Beers
Peter Perry
Joseph Crofut
Jonah Sanford, Junr,
William Hubbell
Zachariah Prindle
Abner Beers
Ambrose Baldwin
James B. Fairchild
1816
Ziba Glover
Zerah Judson
Beera P. Summers
Solomon Timanus
Wooster Peck
Prosper A. Foot
John Hendricks
Villeroy Glover
Eli Platt
Benjamin F. Shelton
David Underhill
Nathan B. Sherman
Oliver Peck
Amos G. Peck
John Curtis, Junr.
Lue L. Sherman
Robert Middlebrook
Elisha Mills
John Hawley
1817
Philo Curtis, Junr.
Elisha Curtis
Hurlburt Cone
Clarke Fairchild
Gideon B. Ferris
Philo Northrop
David French
James Northrop
David Stilson
Abraham Bennitt
Samuel P. Glover
Levi E. Jordan
Cyrenus Northrop
Grandison Clark
Hiram Shepard
Ziba Perry
Eliel Crofut
Lucius Clark
Abel Bennitt, Junr.
Thomas Seely
Lawrenus Shepard
Calvin Hyde
William Platt
Samuel Staples, Junr.
Abner Blackman
Peter Lewis
Wheeler Bennitt
Henry Nichols
Philip A. Cannon

Bailey Beardslee
Amariah Beers
John Beers
David B. Botsford
Elijah Botsford
David Taylor
Squire V. Smith
Charles Shepard
Austin Booth
Tyrus Hawley
Israel Peck
Abner Peck
Russell Tousey
Philo Whitney
John Skidmore
Abraham Beardslee
James Bennitt, Junr.
Norman Northrop
Moses Beardslee, 3rd.
John Judson
Daniel Skidmore
Glover Skidmore
Zar Keeler
1818
Harry Glover
Winthrop Fairchild
Samuel N. Sanford
Eli Hard
Josiah Wheeler
Charles Botsford
Harry T. Hill
Wheeler Cable
Jabez Taylor
William B. Warner
Hezekiah Curtis
Ariellus Hamlin
Ephraim P. Wetmore
Josiah Fairchild, Junr.
Joseph Shepard
Philo Tousey, Junr.
Nathan J. Wilcoxon
Botsford Terrill
Hiram Curtis
Rufus L. Parmalee
Thomas S. Ferris
Cyrus Hyde
Henry Deane
David Sherman
Charles Sherman
Abijah Rowell
John Curtis, 3d.
Isaac Drew
Thomas O. Chambers
Nirom Shepard
Joseph Smith, 3d.
Philo Parmelee
Philo Sanford
John Sherman, Junr.
David A. Gilbert
Donald Baldwin
Andrew B. Glover
Theophilus Nichols
Philo Bennitt
1819
Abijah Beach Curtis

Simeon Nichols
Joel Bassett
Harry Sherman
Ezekiel Beers
Eli Hawley
Jeremiah Trowbridge
Walter Fairchild
Joseph D. Wheeler
John L. Hubbell
Eleazer Dibble
David M. Birch
Elam Crofut
Levi Parmelee
Levi Taylor
Beeman Fairchild
John Hawley
Isaac Underhill
Rufus Shepard
Everitt Clark
Philo M. Platt
Samuel Fairchild
Stephen L. Crofut
Nathaniel Mallory
Philo Lake
1820
Abiel B. Glover
David Curtis
Henry Peck
George Bradley
Abijah Bradley, Junr.
Lyman Lake
George Shepard, Junr.
Gideon S. Beers
Harry Platt
Hezekiah Platt
1821
Cyrenius H. Booth
Henry S. Hill
John Sanford, Junr.
David Nash
Anson Hubbell
Simeon Shepard
Jotham B. Hawley
Silas Jennings
Seth Prindle
Josiah Botsford
1822
Alexander Hall
Charles Chapman
Rufus Summers
Charles Glover
Austin N. Botsford
Marcus B. Summers
Levi Fairchild
Hiram Parmelee
Burtis Fairchild
Henry R. Lott
Philo Fairchild, Junr.
Daniel Curtis
Truman Sherman
1823
Seth Rogers
James E. Glover
Charles B. Booth
MacPherson Sherman

Gideon B. Botsford
Simeon N. Beers
Sylvester N. Beers
Sylvester Beers
Alben Hall
Nelson Tongue
Sylvanus Platt
Hart Shepard
Isaac Blackman
Hiram Fairchild
Cyrus D. Fairchild
Davis S. Sweet
1824
John Wetmore
William Hayes
Samuel B. Peck
Isaac Nichols
Daniel Baldwin
John Nash
Theodore B. Botsford
Norman Tuttle
Ezra Gray
Daniel Brisco
Joel T. Camp
Edwin Botsford
Levi Drew
George Benedict
Boyle Fairchild
John Wallace
Abel Whitney
Marcus Fairchild
Amos Curtis Sanford
Lemuel Beers
Edward Wheeler
John Lake, Junr.
Cyrus Camp
1825
Horace M. Shepard
Henry Dutton
William P. Edmonds
Charles Johnson
Walter Clark
Nathan Johnson
Lucius Peck
William Blakely
John B. Beers
Dibble Camp
Levi Peck
Solomon W. Stevens
Agur Perry
Beers Fairchild
Charles Clark
Ziba Blackman
Norman Beers
Hiram Baily
Hermon Fairchild
Russell D. Smith
Abel Dibble
William B. Taylor
Erastus Hull
Charles Peck
Ezra Platt
Asa B. Beardslee
Lewis S. Brisco

THOSE WHO TOOK THE FREEMANS OATH

Amos J. Hard
Jesse Beardslee
Thomas B. Barnum
Abel B. Terrill
Nichols B. Lake
John C. Wilkinson
Orrin Tongue
Lauriston Sherman
Jared Botsford, Junr.
Burton E. Clark
Ebenezer Dikeman
Charles T. Chafeen
Luther Camp
Charles Curtis
William M. Shepard
Walter Johnson
David W. Griffin
Rufus Skidmore

1826
Ives Glover
Joseph B. Curtis
Eli S. Lattin
Taylor Judd
Samuel B. Benedict
Hermon Parmelee
Daniel Shepard
Abram Winton
Luzon Crofut
George Botsford
Glover Hawley
Oliver Summers
Reuben Northrop

1827
Harson Twitchell
Wilton Beardslee
Charles Blakeslee
Elnathan Stillson
Hermon Hill
Stephen M. Downs
Joseph M. Hubbell
Abel Tousey
Turney French
William Baldwin
Robert Edmond
Moss Fairchild
David J. Glover
Hermon Beers
Wooster Taylor
Samuel Blakeslee
George Blackman
Charles Northrop
Stephen Merwin

1828
Beach Camp
Thomas D. Shepard
Seth Gilbert
Jotham Sherman
Joseph Perry
William G. Smith
Preston Durant
Jabez B. Peck
John B. Nichols

1829
David B. Beers
Isaac Stilson
Orrin Raymond
Joseph Nettleton
Joseph Sherman, Junr.
Medad Bradley
Roswell Lake
Abel B. Skidmore
William Stebbins
Albert Edwards, Jr.
Charles T. Hard
Joshua H. Taylor
Drusus Nichols
Starr Shepard
Auraunah Fairchild
Joseph Ferris, Junr.
Alfred Blackman
Daniel B. Hawley
David T. Taylor
Mark E. Leavenworth
William Beard

1830
Israel A. Beardslee
Philander Sharp
Thomas Ward
John C. Booth
Daniel S. Bulkley
Sherman J. Sharp
Delauzan Peck
Thomas Ward
Herman Peck
John L. Fairchild
Ezra Morgan
Isaac Blackman
Wheeler Shepard
Levan W. Merritt

1831
Isaiah S. Tomlinson
Herman S. Thorpe
Isaac Beers
Elias Johnson
Sidney Middlebrook
Orrin Shepard
Walter Glover
Granville S. Glover
John Glover
Russell Wheeler
Roswell Glover
Roswell Wheeler
Norman B. Glover
James A. Burritt
Hiram Camp
Joseph Blackman, Jr.
Warren Fairchild
James Foot
Charles C. Warner
Charles L. Stillson
Norman Tongue
Jacob Mayhew
John Beers
Anthony Mygatt
Ezra Patch
Alonzo German

James G. Blackman
Harry W. Tucker
Charles Brisco
Jotham Stilson
Walter Blackman
Abijah Hard
Carlos Shepard
David Taylor, Junr.
Charles Fairman
George C. Peck
Isaac B. Scudder
Samuel B. Blackman
Benjamin Hawley
John R. Skidmore
Samuel B. Hawley
Samuel P. Botsford
Charles C. Beers
William H. Peck
Abel F. Gillett
Jerome Middlebrook
Abram Jarvis
Amos Hard
Horace B. Dibble
Jacob Mayhew, Junr.

1832
Justus Thompson
Samuel M. Turney
Hanford Hull
Thomas B. Taylor
Alonzo Taylor
Lucius Middlebrook
Alva B. Beecher
Isaac F. Holtstander
Walter Lake
William B. Glover
Thaddeus H. Nichols
Sheldon Blackman
Ammon Smith
Albert Prindle
Elizur Northrop
Alonzo Johnson
Abel Stilson
Bronson Bulkley
Bennitt Platt
George Gilbert
Marcus H. Parmelee
John Johnson, Junr.
Judson Platt
Elizur W. Keeler
Lyman Smith
William B. Jennings
Reuben B. Burroughs
Hezekiah Peck
Eli Higgins
Zadock Sherman
Amos Foote
Simeon B. Peck
James Blackman
Charles Dikeman
Reuben N. Griffin
Isaac Lake
David Northrop
George M. Benedict
Charles Skidmore
Gershom Dimon

Sheldon Northrop	**1833**	Eli W. Blackman
Joel Thorp	Andrew Knapp	William Scudder
Charles Johnson, Junr.	Truman Perry	Isaac Hawley
Ammon Williams	Agur Clark	Joseph G. Ferris
Joseph B. Fairchild	Philo T. Platt	David Sanford
Oliver Evens	Elijah B. Terrill	Gideon B. Fairchild
Thomas H. Green	James A. Cargill	

NEWTOWN DURING THE REVOLUTION

We find no allusion in the town journal to the troubles brewing between Great Britain and her New England colonies until 1775, when, at an adjourned town meeting, March 6, 1775, at the meeting house, Mr. Daniel Botsford was chosen moderator and a memorial to the General Assembly of the Connecticut colony then in session at New Haven was laid before the meeting for consideration and action. No living soul of our beautiful town to-day can realize in the smallest degree with what dignity and solemnity that body of electors who represented the people of the town, that then had a population, according to the census of 1774, of 2,229 souls, met to express themselves upon the crisis they were soon to be called to meet. As yet no shot had been fired, no blood shed, though British troops were not so far away but that, on the 19th day of April following, the battle of Lexington was fought, when the shot was fired which was heard around the world. Paul Revere, a Boston patriot on the watch, placed two signal lanterns in the belfry of the old Boston North church steeple, and he himself (as the story goes) galloped through the country giving the alarm.

Memorial sent to the General Court at its session in New Haven, March 2, 1775, which shows a strong desire to settle the differences between the colonies and the mother country without war.

"To the Honorable, the General Assembly of ye Colony of Connecticut in New England to be holden at New Haven on the second day of March, 1775, the memorial of us ye inhabitants of Newtown in Fairfield County humbly showeth that your honor memorialists being very sensible and deeply affected with ye distrest estate of ye Colonies in general and this Colony in particular respecting ye unhappy differences that now subsists between ye parent state and her colonies and also being very apprehensive that ye late measures come into by ye late General Congress will not have ye desired effect of working an effectual union or reconciliation between said state and her colonies, your memorialists humbly pray your honors to take ye distrest estate of this Colony into your wise consideration and to adopt such measures as you shall think proper, and to prefer a petition to King and Parliament in ye name of ye Assembly who only are known to be ye representatives of ye people. We further remind your Honors that as General Congress or General Councils have always been extremely expensive so they have not always answered ye expectations of their constituents and further we have to observe to your Honors yt as our assemblies are ye only legal representatives of ye people they cannot substitute any persons to act in their stead and that if another Congress should take place and report yt we bind ourselves and our constituents it would be ye act and report, not of a committee but of Law makers, and again we are filled with amazement at ye dreadful consequences yt must take place if ye resolution of ye Congress carried into execution, two large towns or more besides ye many thousands, perhaps near one-half of this colony who are liege subjects of our Lord and King who have violated no law of ye realm, who are deeply affected with ye distrest state of ye Colonies, grieved with these acts of Parliament which affect ye interests of ye Colonies willing to take all reasonable or Constitutional measures to obtain redress of ye same, but differing from ye late Congress in mode of proceeding, only that we should be deprived of those privileges which ye law of God, of nature and of compact have give us, we are filled with amazement, your Honor petitioners beg leave once more to remind your Honors yt eleventh article of the Continental Congress come into and complied with, doth exclude ye Representatives of those towns from a seat in ye house of Representatives for as by ye best authority we can have ye town of New Haven on ye 27th day of February last, voted that they, nor inhabitants of Newtown or Ridgefield should have entertainment or subsistence within a town which doth as effectually exclude ye Representatives of those towns a seat there, as if ye General Assembly had passed it into a law of ye Colony, and again as ye Resolutions of General Congress in many of their resolves are repugnant to ye charter of this Colony, so ye late agreement of ye County Congress at Fairfield is directly in ye face of Magna Charter itself, where it stands enacted no freeman shall be taken or imprisoned or disseased of his freehold or liberties, or exiled, or any otherwise destroyed, and we will not pass sentence upon him, nor condemn him but by lawful judgment of his peers or by ye law of ye land. We will sell to no man, we will not deny or defer to any man either justice or right. We beg once more, leave to enquire where ye great difference lies between ye Honorable upper House and your Honor's petitioners. Your Honors have not proceeded to act in ye affair, and your Honors petitioners have only said they would not act at all. In ye course of our enquiries we further find yt ye very existence or being of Congress in matters of legislation is directly repugnant to English constitution, not only by ye concessions of ye Congress themselves, but by their own resolves, as in Page 8: 'Resolved, yt it is indisputably necessary to good government and rendered essential by ye English Constitution, yt ye constituent branches of ye Legislative, be independent of each other, yt therefore the exercise of legislative power in several Colonies by a council appointed during pleasure by ye Crown is unconstitutional dangerous and destructive to ye freedom of American legislation,' to which it may be answered, yt ye council or congress referred to is a council appointed by ye Crown and not by a neighboring Colony, which would be a position or construction so absurd, that no worshipper of a Congress but would blush to have it mentioned, and must then your petitioners with ye many thousands besides, who have long enjoyed peace and tranquility under auspicious reign of our Sovereign and under ye protection of this Assembly must we be compelled to quit our native country this once fair and pleasant Land with all our possessions, our friends, and all yt is near and dear to us and seek refuge in some gloomy corner of the earth darker than the grave, or must we adopt the doings of ye Congress or is it all a jest?

Voted, at said meeting, that the above memorial be presented to the Assembly now sitting at New Haven.
Newtown, March 6, 1775.

Jotham Sherman
Zadock Sherman
Thomas Skidmore
Jabez Baldwin
Selectmen.

Test, Caleb Baldwin, Town Clerk.

In the following year, 1776, the Declaration of Independence was signed. The public records of the colony of Connecticut, in its list of names of representatives from the several towns, has the name of Newtown with a blank. Whether the town did not elect, or, if elected, they refused to take the oath of office, history does not tell. The General Court met at New Haven in October, 1776, and the first resolution passed by the Assembly was:

"We approve of the Declaration of Independance published by said Congress, and that this Colony is and of right ought to be, a free and independent state, and the inhabitants thereof are absolved from all allegiance to the British Crown, and all political connections between them and the King of Great Britian is, and ought to totally dissolved."

At the session of the General Court at New Haven in May, 1775, was enacted what was known as the Tory Act, to guard the colony against Toryism. At the annual town meeting of Newtown, Dec. 5, 1775, the town voted "that a copy of the Tory Act shall be holden and continually kept in the Town Clerk's office and that the other Tory Act shall be kept at William Burwell's."

At the session of the General Court at New Haven in October, 1776, an act was passed prescribing and enjoining an oath of fidelity to the State, which reads: "Whereas, the King of Great Britain hath abdicated the government of this and the other United States of America, by putting them out of his protection, and unjustly levying war against them, and the said United States by their representatives in General Congress assembled by a Declaration bearing date the fourth day of July, one thousand seven hundred and seventy-six, for the reasons therein mentioned solemnly declared that the united Colonies of North America are, and of right ought to be, free and independent states and that they are absolved from all allegiance to the British Crown, and that all political connection between them and the state of Great Britain is, and ought to be, totally dissolved, which Declaration is approved by this Assembly, Therefore, it is expedient for the security of this state, that an oath of fidelity be taken by the freemen and officers thereof."

This preamble and resolve was followed by a copy of the oath of fidelity, that every freeman was obliged to take, before he could be received as an elector. The oath: "Be it enacted by the Governor, Council and Representatives in General Court assembled, and by the authority of the same, that all the members of the general Assembly, and other officers civil and military, and freemen within the state of Connecticut, shall take the following oath: 'You do swear by the ever-living God, that you will truly and faithfully adhere to, and maintain the government established in this state under the authority of the people, agreeable to the laws in force within the same, and that you believe in your conscience that the King of Great Britain hath not, nor of right ought to have, any authority or dominion in or over this state, and that you do not hold yourself bound to yield any allegiance or obedience to him within the same, and that you will, to the utmost of your power, maintain and defend the freedom, independence and privileges of this state against all open enemies of traitorous conspiracies whatsoever, so help you God.' And no person shall have authority to execute any of the offices aforesaid after the first day of January next until he hath taken said oath before they enter upon the execution of their offices. No freeman within this state shall be allowed to vote in the election of any officers of government until he hath taken the aforesaid oath in the open freeman's meeting in the town where he dwells, and the names of all the freemen who take said oath shall be enrolled by the town clerk in the records of the town, which oath shall be administered by a magistrate or justice of the peace."

This went into effect Jan. 1, 1777. That year, the General Court opened its sessions on the second Thursday of May and August 25, and between that year (1777) and 1782, 128 names are recorded as having taken the oath of fidelity. At a special meeting, Jan. 6, 1777, to consider assent to the articles of Confederation drawn up and sent by Congress to the several States, agreeable to a requisition of His Excellency, the Governor, it was voted, "that in consequence of the above notification and having particularly considered every Article by itself, unanimously approve of every article of Confederation as sent by Congress to the several States. Resolved, that the Representatives of this town transmit the votes of this meeting to the General Assembly of this state, approving of every article of Confederation of the United States in Congress as the sense of this town that the Delegates of this state be empowered by the Assembly to Ratify and confirm the same in Congress."

The freemen of Newtown were slow in conforming to the law,

and at the May session of the Legislature, Newtown was not represented in the General Court. From the time of the signing the Declaration of Independence to the close of the war, town meetings were held frequently, and information regarding the town's doings in helping carry on the war must be gathered from the town records At a special town meeting, April 7, 1777, it was "voted that Oliver Tousey, William Burwell and Jonathan Booth be appointed a committee to take care of the Excise money. Put to vote whether there shall be a committee appointed by this town to take care of such money as shall be remitted from time to time by any soldier in the Continental Army agreeble to the Governor and Council of Safety bearing date March 18, 1777, voted in the negative. Put to vote whether we will adhere to the Act of this State respecting regulating Trade, voted in the negative. Put to vote that the Town shall use their influence to prevent the spreading of small-pox by inoculation or some other way in this town, voted in the affirmative.

At a special town meeting, Oct. 6, 1777, Messrs Eli Dunning, Jabez Botsford, Esq., Mathew Curtis, Jr., and George Terrill, shall be committee to provide according to the Proclamation of the Governor and Council of Safety, September 12, 1777. Voted, that the Town Treasurer shall purchase wheat and deliver the same to those families belonging in the Continental Army, at the prices stated by law."

"Voted, that Capt. Jabez Botsford and Richard Fairman shall be a committee to take care of and provide necessaries of life for the families of those soldiers now in the Continental Army."

"Voted, that the salt belonging to this town purchased by the state shall be transported from Bedford in Boston state to this place at the expense of the town, and that in a manner that the selectmen shall think most expedient and safe either by land or water."

"Voted, that the selectmen shall take care of the pig iron allowed to this town by the state and that it be forwarded in the best manner to the most convenient forge."

August 25, 26 and 27, these freemen went before Jabez Botsford, justice of the peace and complied with the law: Jabez Botsford, Esq., George Terrill, Lieut. Benjamin Summers, Richard Fairman, James Fairchild, Jr., Fitch Kimberley, Moses Shepherd, Elijah Botsford, Lieut. Henry Fairman, Nathaniel Brisco, John Botsford, Nathaniel Barnum.—Caleb Baldwin, Jr., Town Clerk.

A noble example of 12 of Newtown's foremost men, who dared to become leaders and, with uplifted hand, swear before the ever-living God to uphold and defend, if need be with their lives, the cause espoused in the Declaration of Independence. From August 25, 1777, to 1791, 337 freemen took the oath of fidelity, when, with the war ended and peace restored, the observance of that law was no longer required.

At the annual town meeting, Dec. 7, 1777, the demands made upon the town by strenuous efforts in prosecution of the war, made an increase of the board of selectmen absolutely necessary and Caleb Baldwin, Jr., Col. John Chandler, Jabez Botsford, Esq., Mr. Nathan Bennett, Mr. Matthew Curtiss, Mr. Joshua Northrop, and Mr. Eli Dunning were chosen for selectmen.

"Voted, Mr. Job Burwell, Abel Baldwin, Josiah Beardslee, Capt, Jonathan Northrop, Jared Dunning, George Terrill, Jabez Botsford, Esq., James Glover and Mr. Matthew Curtis, shall be a committee of clothing for the soldiers for the year ensuing."

"Voted, Mr Isaac Hawley, Ebenezer Smith, Amos Terrill, Gideon Botsford, Jabez Botsford, Esq., and James Fairchild, be a committee to take the care of the families of the soldiers belonging to this town in the Continental Army."

In the year 1778, a loan office was established in the several colonies to receive such monies as might be offered for loan, and commissioners were appointed in each colony to receive loans, for which they were to deliver over to the lenders loan certificates bearing 4 per cent interest and payable in three years. Caleb Baldwin, Esq., was appointed commissioner for Newtown, and the loan money was to be used to help furnish the soldiers with things most needful. The loans made were 12: Aaron Gregory $70, Thomas Brooks £38 10s, Josiah Beardslee £100, Mary Judson $57 and two-thirds, Mary Judson and Thomas Brooks $300, Jonathan Fairchild $600, Sarah Baldwin $100, Caleb Baldwin $70, Thomas Brooks, Jr., and Mary Judson £38 10s, Caleb Baldwin, Jr., one Continental Loan Office certificate $300 also $33 and one-third, Elizabeth Robson $120, Capt. Abel Botsford $120.

That insubordination existed in Newtown in 1778 is shown by this Act passed by the General Assembly in that year:

Upon a representation made to this Assembly, that the three alarm companies formed within the limits of the first society of Newtown in the 16th Regiment having some time since made choice of persons inimical to this and the other United States of America, who for that reason were refused commissions, or wholly neglect and refuse to execute their offices whereby all the said companies are destitute of officers and by that means not in a condition to be called upon to perform military duty for the defence of the country, Resolved, by this Assembly, that the colonel or chief officer of said Regiment be directed and he is hereby ordered and directed to cause legal warning to be given said companies as soon as may be, to meet for the purpose of choosing commission officer and lead or order them to be led to such choice for their respective companies, and in case they neglect or refuse to elect such persons as are qualified according to the laws of this state, to execute such offices that then, the civil authority in, and selectmen of Newtown, with the advice of said Colonel or chief officer are hereby empowered and directed forthwith to nominate such officers as may be necessary, which choice or nomination shall, by said Colonel or chief officer be returned to this Assembly, or in the recess thereof, to his Excelency the Governor, who is desired to commissionate them accordingly, which officers shall immediately proceed to detach their quota of men for the Continental Army as soon as the field officers of said Regiment have proportioned them to the respective companies, which they are hereby directed to do."

The records show 1778 to have been more free from special town meetings than usual. There was routine work of looking after the needs of soldiers' families on the part of the committees having that duty to perform. Not until July of the following year, was there this call for a special town meeting:

"Advertisement—Notice is hereby given to Newtown inhabitants that there is to be a town meeting at the Town House in said town on Monday next at five o'clock in the afternoon, to adopt some measures to raise moneys to supply the family's of the officers and soldiers belonging to said town now in Continental service agreeable to a late resolve of the General Assembly and to do any other business necessary.

Jabez Botsford
Joshua Northrop
John Chandler
Eli Dunning
Selectmen."

Newtown, July 10, 1779.

Meeting met according to the warning. Henry Peck, Esq., appointed moderator: "Voted that the committee supplying the officers and soldiers' families now in Continental service agreeable to Resolve of the General Assembly, May 1779, make and adjust each man's proper proportion (obliged by law to pay rates in Newtown' of the sum of £108 reckoning the addition of 75 per cent on the prices of grain of the several kinds, and that they call on the inhabitants of said Town to return to them immediately or at a convenient season said dividend for the use of said families and that they make returns of the sum allowed by the Committee of the Pay-table once in six months to the Authority and selectmen that a settlement may be had agreeable to the minds of this or some future meeting."

A special town meeting was called for Monday, July 20, 1779, for the purpose of "raising a bounty for those who shall enlist into the Continental service agreeable to an act of the General Assembly calling for the same. Meeting was opened in accordance with the notification. Capt. George Terrill was chosen moderator and the meeting was adjourned with out an action being taken."

At a special town meeting, August 31, 1779, it was voted, "that there shall be one shilling on the pound on the list of 1775 paid into the town treasury to supply the committee for the supplying the families of the officers and soldiers belonging to this town in the Continental army. The meeting taking into consideration the circumstances of Nathan Turner and Calvin Turner, now returned from the enemy: Resolved, that the said Turner be not admitted to stay in this town." "Voted, that this meeting make known to the General Assembly of the State of Connecticut either by memorial or some other manner, the circumstances and true situation of this town in regard to those unfriendly persons in said town together with the reasons of the Friends to the Liberties of America in this town entering their protest against the Town Clerk's entering those unfriendly persons in the list of those that have taken oath of fidelity. Voted, that Jabez Botsford, Esq., Job Burrill and David Curtis shall be a committee of cloathing for the soldiers of the Continental army." Voted, "that the committee of clothing shall draw orders on the town treasury for such clothing as they shall procure for the soldiers and make return to the committee of the Pay-table and return such order as they shall obtain, into the town treasury."

A meeting of the Governor and Council of Safety at Hartford in October, 1779: Resolved, that the selectmen of Newtown receive from Joseph Hopkin, Esq., of Waterbury, ten fire-arms belonging to this state, also 150 pounds of gun-powder from the keeper of powder belonging to this state at Ripton, and also 300 flints of Captain George Smith of Hartford, they passing their receipts therefor, said selectmen to be responsible. Per order of Major Caleb Baldwin, also upon the memorial of Samuel Hazard, a refuge from the city of New York, now resident of the town of Newtown, showing that when he left New York, he left with some of his friends on Long Island considerable effects belonging to himself and family, and praying to have liberty to go onto said Island and bring off said effects. Resolved, that the said Samuel Hazard have liberty and liberty is hereby granted to him to go onto Long Island for the purpose of bringing away such effects, he conforming himself to the directions of Thaddeus Betts, Esq., of Norwalk, under whose care and inspection he is to conduct in the affair."

Voted, "that Capt. Jabez Botsford shall be collector of the provision tax." Voted, "that this meeting reconsider their former vote appointing Mr Ephraim Sherman, and appoint Capt. Jabez Botsford to collect and put up the whole both flour and meat, except that in the parish of Newberry." Voted, "that Mr Eli Dunning be collector of that part of the provision tax in the parish of Newbury."

By order of Newtown's selectmen, Richard Smith, Elijah Botsford, Eli Dunning, Abel Botsford, a special town meeting was held March 8, 1780, in compliance with a resolve of the General Assembly of the State, to appoint a board of Inspectors for better care in the inspection of food supplies furnished for Continental soldiers at the front. The meeting was held at the Center schoolhouse. Captain Henry Peck was chairman. "Voted that Lieutenant Amos Terrill, Mr. Josiah Beardslee, Joshua Hatch, Richard Fairman, Abel Baldwin, Captain George Ferris, Captain Elijah Botsford, Mr. Job Bunnill, Matthew Curtiss, Junr., Benjamin Burr, Asa Cogswell, Amos Northrop, Eli

Dunning, Captain Richard Smith, Moses Shepard, Joshua Northrop, Silas Fairchild, Captain Benjamin Summers, Mr. Nathan Sherman, shall be a committee of Inspectors of Provisions the year ensuing, agreeable to a Resolve of the General Assembly passed in January, 1780. Voted, that Mr. Abraham Bennitt shall be committee to supply the family of Lieutenant Ephraim Kimberley the year ensuing as a soldier in the Continental service." Also voted, "Lieutenant Amos Terrill shall be a committee to supply the family of Mr. Elijah Foot, a soldier in the Continental Army." Also voted, "in order to raise the eight men required for the years service to defend the Post at Horseneck, we proceed in the same manner as is directed for the Continental soldiers."

Another special town meeting, July 10, 1780, to raise a bounty for those who enlisted in the Continental service agreeable to the Act of the General Assembly. The meeting was regularly held at 6 p. m., July 10, 1780. Captain George Terrill was chosen moderator, and the meeting was dissolved without taking action.

A special town meeting, Nov. 13, 1780, to raise the quota of provisions of said town, agreeable to an act of the General Assembly in October, 1780, voted "that Mr. Ephraim Sherman and Mr. Eli Dunning be a committee for the purpose of putting up flour in this town for Continental use." Voted, "that Capt. Jabez Botsford and Mr Eli Dunning be a committee for the purpose of providing barrells and putting up beef and pork required by law for Continental Stores." Voted, "that this meeting has no objection to the wives and families of Ephraim Betts and Elias Skidmore repairing to Long Island there to tarry with their husbands, going under the direction of the authority and selectmen."

At the annual town meeting in December, 1780, it was voted "that the selectmen be a committee to ascertain the number of soldiers now in Continental service accounted for this town and make returns of their doings at the next meeting." At the adjourned meeting Dec. 25, 1780, it was voted "that Mr. Henry Wood, David Judson and Eli Dunning be a committee of clothing for the soldiers belonging to Newtown, and that Captain Abel Botsford and Ensign Clement Botsford be a committee to supply the soldiers' families with provisions for the year ensuing." Voted, "that this town will enable commanding officers of the several military companies, and the selectmen, to procure, by hireing at the town's cost if possible, the men now requested by peremptory detachment and all other peremptory detachments from the militia the year ensuing." Voted, "that Captain Elijah Botsford, Captain Jabez Botsford, Captain Abel Botsford, Captain Benjamin Somers, Captain George Terrill, Captain Richard Smith, Mr. Richard Fairman, Caleb Baldwin, Junr., and Joshua Northrop be a committee to class the inhabitants of the town for the puropse of filling the Continental army."

At a special town meeting, Jan. 22, 1781, it was voted that Jabez Botsford, Esq., shall be collector and receiver of Flour and Grain required of Newtown for the Continental Army, and that David Botsford be committee of Clothing for the army for the year. On February 14, 1781, another special meeting was held to receive returns of the several classes in the town, for recruits for the army, and it was voted that Major Caleb Baldwin, Colonel John Chandler, Mr. Richard Fairman and Mr. Amos Northrop be a committee to receive the returns of the several classes for recruits of Continental soldiers in Newtown by the 16th inst., and on failure of any class having hired, etc. Voted, that the committee be and they are hereby empowered forthwith on such report being made, or failure of said report by said day, to pray out a warrant against each and every such neglecting, lay for such sum or sums as shall be double the sum necessary to hire a man according to the statute and hire said man or see one be hired as soon as may be, provided nevertheless that said committee shall have it in their power to settle with any such neglecting class, so be it they save the town harmless as they shall think fit. Voted, that where any members of a class in this town already classed shall neglect to pay his or their proportion where a class shall hire a man, the committee above mentioned shall proceed immediately with such individual according to the statute in such case accordingly. Voted, this town will indemnify according to the above vote, and that they the said committee make report of their proceedings at the next town meeting. Voted, that said committee make returns of the said Recruits to His Excellency the Governor, at the next session of the General Assembly. Voted, that said committee double the classes already made in order to raise the eight men required for the year service to defend the Post at Horse Neck and proceed in the same manner to procure said men as is above directed for the Continental soldiers.

Special town meeting, April 9, 1781: Voted, that the selectmen forthwith call upon the eight classes made out of the sixteen classes, to raise their men for the state guards within six days and that the head of each deficent class make report to the said selectmen of the delinquents and that the selectmen proceed with them according to the statute respecting raising said men and hire, furnish and forward said men with the money they so collect so far as it be sufficient. In July, 1781, another special town meeting was held to agree upon some measures to raise 4 pence on the pound in beef cattle agreeable to an act of the General Assembly of this state and it was voted, that there be a rate of two pence on the pound on the list of 1780 in hard money or beef cattle by the first day of September next.

Voted that Mr. Richard Fairman and Mr. Eli Dunning be purchasers of said beef and that the collector pay over the money he shall collect on said rates, to the purchaser of said beef. Voted that the town of Newtown stand in the classes they now stand in for supplying the guards at Horse Neck. Voted, that the committee appointed to class the town for the Continental Recruits the present year adjust the classes for the state service the presennt year according to law.

Feb. 25, 1782, it was voted that the town stand in the classes as they now stand for supplying the guards at Horse Neck.

December, 1783, it was voted that a committee be appointed to examine into the matter of the last classing of the town to fill up the Continental Army and the state guards and make report at the next town meeting, and that Gen. John Chandler and Mr. Nehemiah Strong be the committee for that purpose.

In March, 1782, the town voted that the committee appointed to class the town for the Continental Recruits the present year shall adjust the classes for the state service according to law. The last classing of the town to fill up the Continental Army and the State Guards was in the Spring of 1783, when General John Chandler and Mr. Nehemiah Strong were appointed committee for that purpose.

With the surrender of Lord Cornwallis and his army after the battle of Yorktown in 1781, the war was practically ended, and no further doings of the town are to be found in the town journals concerning town care of its soldiers and their families.

This old pass was found among the papers of the late Mrs Sylvia E. Burr of Southbury, whose grandfather, Eliakim Sharp, was administrator on the estate of his brother, Thomas Sharp:

"To whom concerned permit the bearer Thomas Sharp of Newtown to pass unmolested to Stamford or Horse Neck and there joyn the Company Detached from Colol Bordleys Regt
     pr Jabez Botsford J of Peace Newtown, January ye 9 1781.

The name Bradley was often spelled Bordley as above. Col Bradley's regiment, the Fifth of the "Connecticut Line," Second Brigade, served from 1777 to 1781, was at White Plains, Valley Forge, Redding, Morristown and Horseneck.

Letter from Editor of Seymour Record—

                Seymour, Conn.,
                November 14, 1913.

Mr Ezra L. Johnson,
 Dear Sir: I have been much interested in the articles which you are furnishing The Bee regarding "Newtown's Place and Doings during the

Revolutionary War" and thinking you may be publishing later a list of those who went from Newtown to serve in the Revolutionary War, I enclose a copy of a pass given to my grandfather to return to his regiment at Horseneck in 1781. It was the late State Librarian, Mr. Hoadley, who told me that the name Bradley was frequently spelled Bordley in the old times, and Jabez Botsford 'J of Peace" who signed the pass is doubtless the same as is mentioned as Captain Jabez Botsford in your article in the Bee."

Arthur T. Nettleton loaned me, after the article in the Bee came out, a valuable relic of the past, though the hand that penned it had mingled with dust more than 100 years ago; the paper itself was as welcome to me as must have been the first olive branch that Noah's dove brought to the window of the Ark. This paper has a list of names of men in the army of the Revolution who enlisted from Newtown, for the preservation of which we are indebted to the painstaking care of Charles Henry Peck, who, not many years ago, was Newtown's town clerk, ever on the outlook to add to a growing cabinet of relics, whatever he could gather of things superseded by improved machinery or improved methods, old manuscripts and papers with names and doings of those efficient workers and helpers in our beautiful town, 100 and 200 years ago. Among the names is that of Peter Fairchild, ancestor of the wife of Charles Henry Peck, whose maiden name was Hannah Fairchild. We have living in town other descendants of Peter Fairchild, who bear the family name, Arthur Fairchild and his two sons, Arthur and Robert, also a daughter, Mary Hazen. All three of the children are graduates of the Newtown High School, still looking onward and upward. The sons are now with the Allies.

1778—1782—List of Continental soldiers now in service in the Continental Army, that answer for Newtown:

Captain Abel Botsford's company—
Serg'nt Abel Baldwin, Isaac Baldwin, Samuel Farwether, Nathan Hubbill, Bristol Ceaser, Levy Dcolph, Baiily Burritt, Thomas James, Jacob Parsons.

Captain Richard Smith's company—
Samuel Brooks, Thomas Brooks, Jacob Pason.

Captain Elijah Botsford's company—
Zalmon Prindle, Weight Lewis, Lemuel Hubbell, Josiah Terrill, Smith Tuttle, Eliphalet Allen, Eleazer Sherman, Nathan Ferriss, Abraham Gillette.

Captain George Terrill's company—
Nathaniel Osborn, Samuel Anderson, Benjamin Gregory, Abijah Prindle, Samuel Atwood.

Newberry Company—James Sanford, Samuel Lumnus.

Alarm Company—
Peter Fairchild, Jack Botsford, negro, John Kimberly, Mathew Marvin.

During the war, Newtown was free from all raids of the enemy. Many of its people were in sympathy with the Crown, and loath to take arms against it. The Probate records of Newtown of the early days show that in some instances property was confiscated and reverted to the colony. One man was hung in Newtown as a spy in June, 1777, by order of Brigadier-Gen. Samuel H. Parsons, who made his returns "that the execution had been duly performed."

The census, previous to 1800, was taken once in eight years, and the figures show the population of Newtown in 1774 2229, in 1782 2404, and 1790, 2764. In 1776, we had no representation in the General Assembly and none in town took the Freeman's oath. That was the year when the Declaration of Independence was signed.

PASSING OF FRENCH SOLDIERS THROUGH NEWTOWN.

Correspondence between the Commander-in-Chief of the Continental army, Gen. George Washington, and Count de Rochambeau, commander of the French forces who marched across country from Providence, R. I., to Bedford, N. Y., to join Gen. Washington's forces in his operations against Lord Cornwallis. When the army reached Hartford, Newtown was on the direct inland course from Hartford to Peekskill on the Hudson river.

Reaching Hartford, June 22, 1781, the Count wrote to the Commander-in-chief, June 23, 1781: "I arrived here (Hartford) yesterday with the first regiment, which has been followed this day by the second and will be so to-morrow by the third, and the day after by the fourth. I shall stay here this day and to-morrow to give time for our broken artillery carriages to be mended and our young artillery horses and oxen to refresh themselves. I shall set off the day after to-morrow with the first regiment for Newtown, the army to march in four divisions as before, and I shall probably arrive there on the 28th and stay the 29th and 30th to assemble the brigade and march in two divissions to the North River. The corps of Lauzun will march as far advanced as my first division through Middletown, Wallingford, North Haven, Ripton and North Stratford, in which last place it will be on the 28th. I have the honor, etc.

The Count de Rochambeau."

His Excellency,
    George Washington.
  General Washington replied:

                              Camps near Peekskill,
                                  27th of June, 1781.

Sir: I have the honor of receiving your Excellency's favor of the 23d instant from Hartford. It would have given me the greatest pleasure could I have made it convenient to meet you at Newtown, but independently of many arrangements which are necessary at the first taking of the field, I am detained by the hourly expectation of the Chevalier de la Lauzun. I am pleased to find that your idea of the position which will be proper for the troops under your command coincides with my own and I shall be happy in giving your quartermaster-general every assistance in reconnoitering and making out your camp. Lieutenant-Colonel Cobb one of my aids-de-camp will have the honor of delivering this letter and will return to me with any dispatch or message your Excellency may wish to communicate, or should you rather incline to come forward from Newtown before the army Col. Cobb will be proud to attend you. I shall be much obliged if your Excellency will present to Count de Barras by the next occassion my sincere thanks for the readiness with which he was pleased to accept the proposition I had the honor to make him, through his Excellency. I am, etc.,

                              George Washington.

The Count de Rochambeau.
    (Hartford.)

                                Headquarters, Peekskill,
                                      June 30, 1781.

Dear Sir: The enclosed letter to Count de Rochambeau is of very great importance and requires the utmost secrecy in its communication. This idea you will convey to the Count before its delivery, to affect which, you will first converse with the chevalier, Chastelleux, on the mode of its communication. Its object is to inform the Count that I have in contemplation a very sudden surprise of some part of the army which will be of great importance in our operations and which we have flattering expectations of obtaining, to cover and support which, if obtained we shall want the aid of the French army, in which case it will be necessary for the Count to push on his troops with greater haste than he at present intends, and by a different route from that now in view. The Duke de Lauzun's legion is to advance. The movements which I would wish to be made by the French army are particularized in my letter to the Count, which you will see. It will be for you to impress the gentlemen with the importance of their motions to support our operations, as it will be to little purpose for us to obtain advantages which we may not be able to maintain. As the Count with his troops is now in a very disaffected part of the country and the Tories will be desirous to give any information in their power, the most profound secrecy and dispatch must prove the soul of success to the enterprise. This idea you must impress with energy your best discretion in the mode. I am, etc., George Washington.

Lieut-col. David Cobb.
(Hartford.)

Reply.

Newtown, June 30, 1781.

Sir: I was at Count-de-Rochambeau's, this evening, when I recevied your Excellency's dispatches. General Chastellux was immediately sent for and the heads of departments consulted on the new intended route of the army. The Count inquired whether your Excellency was acquainted with the removal of the Yagers and some other troops from Long Island to New York. I assured his Excellency was perfectly acquainted with it and all the other movements of the enemy at New York and that your Excellency would never undertake a matter of this kind but upon certain intelligence and the surest ground of success. The Count was perfectly satisfied with the plan proposed and assured me that duty as well as inclination prompted him to comply with your Excellency's wishes.

Orders are accordingly given for the march of the first brigade in the morning, and the Duke's legion which is now at New Stratford, will undoubtedly march at the same time. It will be at the place of destination at the time proposed, 12 o'clock. The rest of the army will follow when the other division arrives, which comes up to-morrow. The Count in his letter wishes an answer from your Excellency by to-morrow night. It would be more agreeable if it came sooner.

I am, etc.,
David Cobb.

His Excellency
George Washington.

In the "History of the Catholic Church in the New England States" that fell into the writer's hands in Newtown's Bi-Centennial year, 1905, was the following statement: "In the campaign of 1781, Count Rochambeau marched his army from Providence, R. I., to Bedford, N. Y., in the month of June. He was on his way to join Gen. Washington in his operations against Lord Cornwallis. They encamped at Woodbury on the night of June 27, and reached Newtown on the 28th, and remained until Sunday, July 1, when they broke camp and, proceeding through Ridgebury, reached Bedford, N. Y., Monday, July 2; ready to join the army at Phillipsburg. They marched in regiments until reaching Newtown, following one another at intervals of a day's march, or at a distance of about 15 miles. There was no rest except what was imperatively necessary. The officers wore coats of white broadcloth trimmed with green, white underdress and hats with two corners instead of three like the cocked hats worn by the American officers, paid all their expenses in hard money, committed no depredations and treated the inhabitants with great civility and propriety."

The magazine of American History says that the army numbered 600 artillery, 600 cavalry, and 3600 infantry, 4800 men in all, and that when in Newtown five men deserted from the ranks. Their encampment was on the plain that stretches westward from the State road south of the Middle district school and along the side hill that slopes to the eastward from what is known as Ronald

MRS. MARY ANN BIRCH

100 Years of Age

She lived to be 102 years

See Page 141

Castle. Lamson Birch, who was born and always lived on that plain on the site of the house now owned by Michael Scanlon, was son of William and Catherine (Hubbell) Birch. They were married in September, 1750, and had a family of seven children. Lamson, the youngest, was born in September, 1771, and died in October, 1859, age 88 years. In 1781, when the French army encamped on the plains in front of and all about the home plot, Lamson was a boy of 10 years and so vividly was everything impressed upon his memory that in after years he was considered authority on matters that had been familiar to him at the time, to which reference is now made. His father was a Tory, and his family was regarded as a Tory family. The son used to tell in his later years how the father was compelled to keep his gun hidden in the brush or under his barn in order that the "suspicious and exasperated Whigs" might not find it, and steal it from him. He also held a Captain's commission in the British army. His son used to tell that he had seen it with the great red seal of King George the Third attached and, after the battle of Saratoga, he told his wife that the Whigs were going to be victorious, and the best thing for him to do would be to burn his commission at once, which he did, evidently, believing it would be policy for him to be quit of any of the belongings of royalty.

The writer, 27 years of age at the time of Lamson Birch's death in 1859, and 24 years when his own grandfather died in 1856 (who was born in 1772, nine years previous to the French encampment in Newtown) often heard the "back-log stories" told before the open fire place, in those days of long ago, and they come in these later years with vividness, in striking contrast to recollections of other stories, once listened to in wonderment and with much boyish delight.

The French army broke camp in Newtown, July 1 and proceeded westward to join Gen. Washington's army on July 6, at Phillipsburg, Westchester county, N. Y. There they met the American forces resting in two lines along the Hudson river. From there, the allied troops marched to King's Ferry and reconnoitered to learn the position of the British works about New York. The arrival of the French troops was a great help to the American commander, who was not slow in commending in the highest terms their rapid march from Providence across Connecticut to give him aid, in doing which, Newtown had so large a share.

Another person, born in Newtown in the period of the Revolution, lived to an extreme old age (102 years,) "Aunt Mary Ann" Birch, who was daughter of Solomon Glover. She married James Glover and lived in the district of Hanover, where they reared 12 children, all of whom became of age and nine lived to celebrate the mother's 90th birthday. Her husband died in 1836. She lived a widow for 16 years, then married Lamson Birch, to whom we have referred. Her father, too, was a Tory. He, with others of Tory proclivities, would hide in the woods, where they were accustomed to retreat when they expected to be molested, by their more patriotic neighbors. At one call of the Whigs at Mr Glover's house, they found him in bed and amused themselves by pricking him with bayonets. They also amused themselves by making free with a batch of pumpkin pies Mrs. Glover had just taken from the old brick oven. They threw a piece to the house dog, at which she told them to quit, as the pies were good enough for them, but not good enough for the dog. Mrs Mary Ann Birch's experience as a girl and her recollection of Revolutionary days were extremely interesting. When Lord Cornwallis surrendered in 1781, she was five years old, and distinctly remembered when the French army, returning from the war, marching to the coast to return to France, again passed through Newtown. Their encampment on the plain extended from the foot of Church hill eastward to where the railroad station is, and northward and southward for a half mile. She remembered the breaking up of the camp and the departure of the troops, their commander being no other than Gen. Lafayette. At that time, Gen Lafayette spent a night in Newtown with Col John Chandler, a Newtown lawyer, who then lived in a house on the site of the Grand Central hotel. He enlisted at the opening of the war and soon became Colonel of the 8th Regiment of Connecticut Continental troops In my boyhood, old people disputed whether Gen Washington once stayed in Newtown over night. That he passed though on his way from Rhode Island to the Hudson River, there can be but little doubt, but it must have been in advance of the French forces, as in his communication to the French commander previously quoted, he writes: "It would have given me the greatest pleasure could I have made it convenient to meet you in Newtown, but I am detained by the hourly expectation of the Chevalier de la Lauzun."

Correspondence that passed between officials in the service, when the writer's maternal grandfather, Jonathan Sanford, Jr., was drafted in 1779. His home was in Hanover school district, where he was born, Jan. 5, 1739, and at the time referred to was father of five children. A farmer by occupation, but not of robust health, he was rejected from the service, as the following physician's certificate shows:

"This may certify that Jonathan Sanford, Jr., of Newtown has been infirm for about nine or ten years past by reason of pleurisy, after which he fell into an ulcery state of his lungs which left him weak, which weakness he has never recovered from, nor never like to, so as to endure hardship and I really believe he is in a law sense freed from all military duty."

Dated this 30th day of September, 1779.

Test, Andrew Graham, physician.

Letter from Jabez Botsford, Newtown's First Selectman to Captain Yeats, stationed at Ripton:

Newtown, July ye 3rd, 1779.

Sir: I have injected into the state service in the room of Jonathan Sanford, Junr., a man that I have draughted in Newtown, the bearer William Woolcutt. I desire you will direct him in the matter and re-inlist him if you think proper.
From your Humble Servant.
Jabez Botsford.

To Captain Yeats at Ripton.

Captain Yeats' reply:

This may certify that I am willing to take the said Woolcutt into my company if he should fail to me.
John Yeats.

In meetinng demands sure to come upon its people during the Revolutionary war in money, in clothing, in provision and in men Newtown contributed all that was demanded of her people.

THE ROADSIDE TAVERN.

Not until the close of the Revolution did public travel so increase as to make it practicable to keep a house of entertainment for the traveling public. With lines of travel by stage in different directions and for what then were considered long distances, it seemed expedient to establish the wayside inn. Previous to the stagecoach, there was no means of reaching salt water save by pedestrianism, or private conveyance. Even mail was carried on horseback and delivered as best it could, and not until 1800 did the United States government appoint a postmaster for Newtown. The first postmaster was Caleb Baldwin, Jr., whose home was in Newtown Street where Charles F. Beardsley and family live. Stratford was our nearest sea-port on the southeast and Norwalk nearest on the southwest, the parish of Stratfield in the town of Stratford, to become in due time the town and later the city of Bridgeport, lying midway between; with Danbury nine miles to the westward, Woodbury nearly twice that distance eastward, Hartford 50 miles away, and all of Litchfield county northward. Newtown might well have been considered the central point for cross-country travel and, in 1790 or thereabouts, it came to pass that two men, in pleasant rivalry it may have been, decided to start a wayside inn. Caleb Baldwin was one and Czar Keeler the other. The infection spreading, it was not long after, that "Tom" Seely opened an inn on the premises now occupied by George Northrop near the North Center schoolhouse. "Uncle Tom" was a shoemaker by trade, a jolly good fellow, but, a better shoemaker than landlord, his inn was not of long duration. Czar Keeler and Caleb Baldwin were in the prime of life in the early days of the stagecoach, and both lived long enough, so that the writer remembers them as they were in their old age. They were "Uncle Czar" and "Uncle Kale" to all of us school children, and you can put it down as a sure thing when you hear children and "grown-ups" calling an old man or old woman "uncle" or "aunt," that everybody has a certain kind of love for them. The writer well remembers "Uncle Czar," for he lived to be past 90, as a jolly, genial man, and there was an honest heartiness about his laugh that made it positively catching. Keeler's Inn stood upon the open lot north of the W. J. Beecher residence, it was two stories in front, with a long sloping back roof, that came almost to the ground, with monstrous fireplaces in which blazing fires were always kept in winter and around the spacious hearth gathered friend and foe. It was the rendezvous on a winter evening for politicians and male gossips of the village. So cheerful was the room and so loath were the people to leave that it would sometimes be long after the ringing of the 9 o'clock bell of the old Episcopal church, which was the recognized signal for closing stores and for general retirement of all within hearing. Keeler's was called the "stage house" for all stage-coaches stopped there, and on that account it enjoyed a larger custom than either competitor. A large and suitable room for balls was on the second floor, and my mother was one of those who danced there in early days. From her lips I heard of the place and of those there who tripped "the light fantastic toe." May 29, 1820, Czar Keeler was appointed postmaster for Newtown and held the position until 1839. The appointment came to him while he was yet landlord of the Inn, and his public room contained the postoffice, a small upright fixture with a few pigeon-holes for letters and newspapers.

Caleb Baldwin's Inn had the reputation of being the pattern of neatness, homelike in all surroundings and it was also claimed that there could be had the best broiled chicken or sirloin steak to be found in Fairfield county. The motherly reputation of the hostess made it a much sought place for restfulness. The public duties of the host so often took him away from home that it became a divided service that he gave the inn. Appointed postmaster in 1800, he held it continuously until 1818. His father was town clerk from 1800 to 1843, and the son from 1843 to 1846.

The Bridgeport and Newtown turnpike, incorporated in 1801, so increased travel along the line from New Milford to Bridgeport, that the need of another inn within Newtown limits on the south led Robert Middlebrook of Trumbull to buy a 50 acre farm on which a large house had just been erected, that seemed just the building and the location for a wayside inn. A spacious front yard, well filled with young maple trees, added to its attractivenesss, and it was not long before the Middlebrook inn became as popular as any hostelry in Fairfield county. Within 17 miles of Bridgeport., belated travelers from either direction found it a matter of convenience to stop over. Uncle Robert was a good story teller, "Aunt Mary" was a splendid cook, the food was always of the best and the home-made cider brandy carried a bead that testified to its purity. The great open fireplace, with its blazing logs, never lacked for patronage and the treat was always on the one who was behind in the race of storytelling. Nothing pleased the guests more than to get a joke on the hostess, who was the best of cooks, and painfully neat and particular. One time she had a big mince pie on the table and going from the room for a moment, one of her guests raised the top crust, slipped a horse shoe in the pie and laid back the crust, just in the nick of time. Taking her knife to cut the pie and striking some hard substance, she uttered an exclamation of surprise and chagrin, but when the cause was ascertained and the guilty party known, the treat for the crowd was on the culprit. It was still an open house in my early days and I well recall that when six years old, I was sent there to get cigars, and, little-boy-like, I had the silver piece with which I was to pay, in my mouth, when a dog bouncing out, frightened me to "boo-hooing," and I swallowed the the silver piece. I was frightened. Aunt Mary comforted me as best she could and I ran home to my mother with the pitiful tale. The house is still standing and in all respects the same in architecture as when built, but the maple trees of more than a century's growth begin to show decay. The blacksmith shop that stood

CALEB BALDWIN INN

Now Residence of Charles F. Beardsley.

WILLIAM A. LEONARD

Proprietor for many years
of Newtown Inn
Formerly Dick's Hotel

See Page 146

opposite is gone and new forms and new faces pass along the streets.

Another inn of those early days was that opened by Dr Gideon Shepard during the later years of his life, when he had practically turned over his medical practice to Dr. Bennett Perry. Dr. Shepard's hostelry was on the grounds occupied by George Beers' house on the road to Sandy Hook, near Newtown Center. The house has still the old frame work, though remodelled, reconstructed and modernized. Jolly, bright, quick at repartee and a good story-teller, the latch string always out until the wee small hours, it was the resort for sleighing parties and balls in the winter season. Generous to a fault, he belonged to the class of whom it is said, "too honest to get rich." It was said of him that he once caught a poor man in his cellar stealing from the pork barrel and, as punishment, he made the man take home half there was left in the pork barrel. In vain the man pleaded to be let off, for the doctor told him that if he didn't take the pork home, he would prosecute him for theft. He took the pork and became a better man. The quaint words on the signboard that hung from the arm of a pole read on one side: "A plain tavern for plain folks, kept by a plain man." On the reverse, "Inn: Call and see. If not suited, the road opens both ways." The location of Dr Shepard's Inn, though a little off from the main street, was good, as it was on the main stage line from Hartford to New York.

We give a copy of an advertisement taken from the Hartford Courant of about 100 years ago.

"Hartford and New York; new line express stage. Fare only $6 through. Way passengers, six cents a mile. On the turnpike road through Farmington, Bristol, Watertown, Woodbury, Newtown, Danbury, Mt. Pleasant, down the North River to New York. Leaves Hartford every Monday, Wednesday and Friday at 4 o'clock a. m., without fail, and arrives at Mt. Pleasant same evening at 8 o'clock; lodge at Mt Pleasant; leave there every Tuesday, Thursday and Saturday at 3 o'clock a. m., and arrive at New York to dine the same day. Returning, leave New York every Monday, Wednesday and Friday at 11 o'clock a. m., and arrive at Hartford next day at 8 p. m. This line of stages connects at Mt. Pleasant, 36 miles from New York, with a packet expressly fitted up for the convenience and comfort of passengers and no steamboat on the river performs her trip with such punctuality. Passengers therefore will meet with no delay, but will find the best of horses, good carriages and careful drivers and punctuality in the arrival and departure of this stage not to be found in any line running at this time. Persons traveling through Hartford to New York will find this line the cheapest, most pleasant and expeditious, without the inconvenience of riding nights, of any out of this place."

Just think of it, you who take the 7 a. m., train out from Newtown, to have all of the day's business hours at your disposal in New York and home again inside of 12 hours; in striking contrast to 32 hours from Hartford to New York, including a sleep from 9 p. m. to 2.30 a. m., with a fresh relay of four horses at each of two points midway between the two places.

Dr Bennett Perry's residence was started as a hotel in 1819, changed ownership to Sallu Pell Barnum, then later became Dick's Hotel, still remembered by many. That hotel was burned at mid day in Sept. 1897 making way for the large and attractive Newtown Inn, which, to the present time, has been used more particularly as a summer resort. The Grand Central hotel is awaiting its golden opportunity to reopen as an all-the-year-round hotel. In the early 40s' the house where Miss Ann Blackman lives was built by Ziba Blackman for a hotel, but it was short-lived, owing in a measure to the opening of the Housatonic railroad about 1842.

CARE AND KEEP OF NEWTOWN'S DEPENDENTS.

In an annual report of the selectmen, we read:

"Those receiving aid from the town we seem to have with us always, and it seems hard to turn these unfortunates down and there will always be some entitled to sympathy." A statement as true now as it was years ago, that needs no argument to verify

Nothing appears in the earliest town journal to show that there was organized effort to place the unfortunates under the care and supervision of a system, other than that they were personally looked after and provided for, being placed in families where the town was willing to pay a nominal sum for board and when death came give a decent burial. That was the order of things in the town until 1809, when the matter was brought up at the annual meeting, resulting in a vote to farm them out at such place and in such way as directed by vote of the town. At the annual meeting, Dec. 10, 1810, it was voted that "the selectmen be authorized to contract for the keeping of the poor of this town with the overseer of the poor house belonging to the town of Weston and to transport the poor of Newtown whose expense is 75c a week or upwards, to the poor house at Weston.

For some unknown reason that plan was not adopted, and at the annual meeting Dec. 1842, it was "voted that Col. Timothy Shepherd, Capt. Daniel Meeker and Samuel Beers, Jr., be a committee to confer with a committee from the town of Danbury on the subject of a poor house." At an adjourned meeting, Dec. 28, 1812, it was "voted that the sum of six hundred dollars be appropriated to defray the expense of building a house for the accommodation of the poor of this town in connection with the town of Danbury and that the Newtown selectmen be a committee to carry the same into effect."

The house was located in the west part of town in Flat Swamp district and stood on the town line between Newtown and Danbury. Rules and by-laws were drawn and adopted by the selectmen of Newtown and Danbury, regulating the inmates.

Rules and by-laws regulating the Danbury and Newtown poor house:

1. That there be appointed by the selectmen of Danbury and Newtown three or more disinterested men as a visiting committee of the poor house, whose duty it shall be to see that the regulations relative to said poor house be carried into effect.

2. That it be the duty of the respective towns to see that there be some proper and discreet person employed as an overseer with necessary attendants to superintend the domestic affairs of said poor house, which overseer and attendants shall always be liable to be removed by said selectmen for just cause.

3. That it be the duty of the overseer to see that the victuals be well and seasonably dressed, that the rooms be washed once in each week in summer and as often in winter as occasion requires, bed linen changed and clean once in each fortnight, tables, table linen, dishes and other household untensils to be daily cleaned, beds and bedsteads to be often examined and kept free from vermin, that the poor be kept clean in their person and apparel, to have a change of linen weekly, that each person if practicable

be washed every morning, and if unable, to see that proper means be furnished for that purpose, that it be the duty of the overseer to see that no indelicate behavior be committed either by word or action, and that good and decent behavior be preserved among all, and that it be the duty of said oversseer for a breach by any of the poor, of this article, to punish the offender by a confinement in the dark room, to be kept on bread and water during a space not exceeding 24 hours, unless a further time be thought necessary by the visiting committee.

4. That it be the duty of the overseer personally to see all fires and lights extinguished, excepting what be absolutely required and those under proper and prudent care and also to see that not more than four persons lodge in one room, that distinct and separate rooms be appropriated for the lodging of males and females respectively, except in the case of husband and wife, unless absolute necessity require a different arrangement on particular occasions. Also that all persons removing any filthiness shall obey the directions of the overseer therein, whose duty it shall be to see the same so removed as not to offend or endanger the health of any person. Any person disobeying this order last mentioned shall be liable to the same penalty provided in the third article.

5. That the overseer do not permit any of the paupers or any other person confined, to beg money or any other thing of persons who may visit the poor house and should any person gratuitously give any thing for the use of the paupers or any one in particular the same shall be placed in the hands of the overseer to be reasonably applied to answer the purpose intended, except to those that commit a breach of this rule.

6. That no person be permitted the use of tobacco in anyway while in bed, or spit on the wall or partition, and after being furnished with spitting boxes, not to spit on the floor. Any person committing a breach of this article, he or she, shall be deprived of the use of tobacco for the space of one week, or until such person will better conform.

7. That it be the duty of the overseer to furnish at least two spitting boxes to each room, and keep in each a constant supply of sand.

8. That no person resident in the house shall go without the enclosure around the same, without liberty from the overseer, in which case he or she shall return decently and soberly at the time appointed on penalty of being denied going out for one week for the first offence, and one month for every succeeding offence.

9. That no article of household furniture or clothing belonging to the family of the overseer shall be used by the poor, unless with his approbation.

10. All those who are able to meet at meal times, shall come together at the time fixed, or when called on, where all shall observe regularity and decent behavior, during meal times, always giving sufficient opportunity for the religious exercises that may be performed on such occasions; and all those who are unable to attend, to be seasonably furnished in the most convenient manner practicable.

11. All persons resident in the house who labor under sickness shall occupy a room or rooms specially appropriated for that purpose.

12. That no person who is infected with a contagious disease of any kind, shall be permitted to reside as a pauper in the poor house, and if after being admitted, it shall be discovered that any one is infected with such disease, the overseer shall immediatly give notice to the selectmen of the town bringing such disordered person who shall remove him or her from the poor house, and otherwise provide for the same.

13. Upon notice given, such as are able to work shall repair to the several places appointed for that purpose, and then keep themselves diligently employed during the time and at such labor as shall be assigned by the overseer. For every breach of this article the same penalty is to be inflicted as is provided in the third article.

14. That any kind of wearing apparel, when worn out, or unfit for the use intended, the same shall be at the disposal of the overseer, for the benefit of the poor in such manner as he shall think proper.

15. That if any person shall attempt or commit actual violence on the overseer, his family or any resident paupers such person shall be restrained

of his liberty by being confined in the dark room and kept on bread and water during the space of 48 hours, and as much longer as the visiting committee shall deem necessary and in case of a second similar offence by those who are stubborn and perverse, such other reasonable chastisement under the direction of the visiting committee as in their opinion shall be judged expedient.

16. That a copy of the foregoing bylaws be handed to the selectmen of Danbury and Newtown respectively and also to the overseer of the poor house, whose duty it shall be to cause the same to be read to all the residents in said house at least once in three months, and also at the time of the entrance of each pauper into said house, the overseer shall cause him or her, to be made acquainted with said by-laws.

We the subscribers being appointed agents to make and enact such rules and regulations as are necessary for the well ordering of the poor house for Danbury and Newtown, have agreeable to our appointment on this 16th day of December, 1813, passed for the foregoing rules and by-laws to be observed by all concerned, and we do hereby order them to be complied with accordingly.

Samuel Phillips,	
Daniel Comstock,	Selectmen
Phineas Taylor,	of
Eliakim Benedict,	Danbury.
Eli Taylor.	
David Meeker,	Selectmen
Lamson Burch,	of
Zachariah Clark	Newtown.

At the annual meeting, Nov. 4, 1816, "voted, that a committee of two persons be appointed (Ebenezer Turner and Timothy Shepard, Esq.,) in behalf of the town to visit the poor house and take such measures as they judge proper to correct any abuse that may occur in said poor house."

Two years later, 1818, Abijah Merritt and Caleb Baldwin conferred with a committee from Danbury on the subject of the poor house, and Amos Shepard was appointed agent to take oversight of all the poor taken from Newtown to the poor house for the current year. The town also voted to take counsel on the charge of abuse of the contractors in supplying the poor of Newtown in the poor house and to institute a suit at law against them. The town made it optional with the selectmen, whether all who applied to the town for aid should be obliged to go to the copartnership house, or be farmed out with families. In some cases, it was the latter. The writer's maternal grandfather, Abijah Merritt, was one of Newtown's selectmen for 12 years at intervals, between the year 1819 and 1839 and to him in particular was given the oversight of the town poor. After his death in 1845, a large bundle of bills against the town for services rendered as selectman, accepted and paid during his administration, was found among his effects, that furnish material for occasional use in recalling events of the early days. From that source, we are able to give the joint expense of the poor for the two towns of Danbury and Newtown in 1819 and, with it, a copy of the expenses of two, among others, farmed out in families. Joint expenses of the poor of the two towns for 1819:

Whole expenses of the poor house for the year 1819,	$966.45
Deduct hide and tallaw,	62.77
	$903.68

Net expenses
weeks board:
Danbury   626
Newtown   411
State paupers   189
Expenses for town paupers $764.36
        For State paupers $139.32

                                                              $903.68

Received of the state $283.50

And it leaves for the towns $620.18
  Which is 59c and 8 mills a person per week.
  Allowing the same number for the last year as this, is a saving of $266.04, and two mills for both towns:
Amount for last year $999.19
Amount for this year $733.14.8

  In 1819, William Jones became a town charge and was cared for by Philo N. Platt of Hopewell, until his death in December, 1839. Under date of Dec. 9, 1819, this itemized bill was sent in:

Town of Newtown, to Philo N. Platt, Dr. To going to Redding after a physician, five miles, .33. Paid Philo Gilbert 20c for the use of his horse for the same, .25. Going to Redding after bark for tea for him, .16. Going same, .35. Going after watchers, going after medicine, going to Umpawaug after shirts for him, seven miles; paid Philo Gilbert 28c for his horse for the same, .50. A pint of rum for medicine for him and going to Redding, two miles and a half for the same, .25. By going to Taunton to notify the selectmen of his sickness, 4 miles, paid Eli Platt 16c for his horse to ride for the same, .25. Going to Redding after bark for tea for him, .46. Going to Taunton to notify selectmen of his death, paid 16c for use of horse for same, .25.

  Funeral charges:

To one quart rum for attendants at his burial and going after the same .33. To a white handkerchief, .33, Paid one dollar to Mrs. Olmstead for cleaning his bed, washing shirts and other clothes for him, 1.00. A winding sheet 2.25. Preparation for burial .25. For my trouble in watching and continual attendance from the first day of his sickness to his death, $15.00.

  Physician's bill:

Six visits, advice, attendance and medicine, $5.80. Philo Gilbert's bill for watching one night and assisting at the burial, .75. Ichabod Gilbert's bill for making coffin and assisting at the burial, $3.00. Philo N. Platt's bill $21.25 physician's bill, $5.80. Philo Gilbert's bill, .75. Total $30.80. To digging grave $1.50.

  March 15, 1820: Thirty dollars allowed on the above bill by us.

                                            Abijah Merritt,
                                            Clement Fairchild
                                                                 Selectmen.

Town of Newtown, to Thaddeus Bennett, Dr.
  To boarding Nancy Bennett, a child of Gideon Bennett, from the 10th of April, 1820, to the 6th of November, 1820, 30 weeks at 34c a week; 10 dollars and 20 cents.
                                                                           Thadeus Bennett.
        Abijah Merritt,
        Clement Fairchild, Selectmen.

  Here is another bill against the town for the care of Adam Clark's wife, who was farmed out to Jotham B. Sherman for the short term of three days:

Town of Newtown, Dr.
For clothing Adam Clark's wife:
  For one Petty coat, .75; For one skirt, .50; For one westcoat, .25; For one pair of stockings .50; For one handkerchief, .17; For three days board, .75; For cleaning Mrs. Clark from lice which was a great task, indeed $3.00.
Account against town of Newtown. $5.92.
  Paid   Abijah Merritt.

CARE OF NEWTOWN'S DEPENDENTS

We follow this with an appeal from New Fairfield to the town of Newtown to care for a Newtown charge who is sick in an adjoining town:

Selectmen of Newtown,

Gentlemen: Although it is painfull for me to wright, it may be so for you to read. It is disagreeable for us to hear of the misfortunes of our friends and sitisans, especially when they are so far from us that we cannot administer to their needs, but I must go on with my melloncholy story. Phidima Ann Elwood is taken sick and continues to be sick, so that she cannot perhaps safely be removed. We are informed she is an inhabitant of New Town and that she has property in the hands of the selectmen of sd town. She is at her brothers in New Fairfield and is poor and needs assistance and application has been made to the selectmen of the town of New Fairfield for her support. This is to notify you to pay the expence allready made and take your own way for her support for the future. Yours, etc.,

Samuel T. Barnum,
Nathan A. Hayes,
Selectmen.

Dated at New Fairfield, the 21st of December. 1820.

From 1818 until 1825, Newtown had its agents appointed from year to year to have the oversight of town poor in the co-partnership with Danbury. In 1826, a committee was appointed to meet a Danbury committtee to make rules in regard to the settlement of poor house accounts.

In 1827, the town voted to contract with any person for keeping the poor of the town for any number of years not exceeding five, at a price not exceeding $800 a year, and also voted to make sale of that part of the poor house and the land attached to it belonging to the town of Newtown. In December, 1828 the town voted to sell either at public auction or private sale that part of the poor house belonging to the town, together with the land belonging to it, if they think proper.

At a special town meeting, May 1, 1837, it was voted that the town approve the establishing of a county poor house, and that the selectmen for the time being be a committee to confer with the other towns in the county on the subject, and also a work house for the punishment of petty crimes in this county.

Many town meetings were called to consider the expediency of providing a permanent home for the town poor, but no definite action was ever taken. After the dissolution of the joint contract between Danbury and Newtown, which came about in 1850, the care of Newtown's poor was let to some responsible man for terms of five years. Daniel Botsford, a large land holder on Toddy Hill, was poor master for many years and he was succeeded by Eli J. Morris in Zoar. They two were the longest in the service and during their administration very few were farmed out in families. Joseph Moore in Huntingtown and Mrs. Lynch on Botsford Hill are best remembered by the generations of to-day as care-takers of the town's dependents. The consensus of opinion has long favored caring for them in private families, except such as for good cause should be cared for in State institutions. It is unnecessary to give statistics, for the town report for the year ending in September, 1912, gave a full and itemized report that was carefully distributed to the taxpayers of the town previous to the annual town meeting, always holden on the first Monday of October in each year.

BRIDGEPORT AND NEWTOWN TURNPIKE CO.

The Bridgeport and Newtown Turnpike Co., had a corporate existence of about 90 years, coming to a close in 1888.

When the early settlers of Newtown had prospered so that they were able to have farm produce to spare in exchange for the things they needed to help make home life more comfortable and thrifty, the nearest market on the south was Stratford on Long Island Sound southeasterly and Norwalk on the Sound southwesterly and nearer to New York. Between these two places lay the Housatonic valley, stretching northward through Fairfield and Litchfield counties on into Massachusetts.

On the shore lay the little seaport town of Bridgeport, beginning to send schooners and other smaller craft to open a trade with New York. Country roads were poorly developed and the idea was conceived of forming an incorporated company to build a turnpike that should connect the seaboard at Bridgeport with New Milford and eventually extend to the northerly boundary of Connecticut. The towns most directly interested at the start were Bridgeport, Huntington, Trumbull, Newtown, Brookfield and New Milford. In 1798 petitions were circulated through each of these towns which met with hearty response, excepting in Newtown, where the opposition to it was so strong at the outset that a petition was circulated for calling a town meeting to remonstrate against the General Assembly, that was soon to assemble in New Haven, granting a charter for the incorporation of a turnpike company.

The remonstrance April 7, 1800:

"Whereas the petition of Amos Hubbell, John S. Cannon and others was brought before the Honorable General Assembly at their session at New Haven in October, 1799, praying for a grant to enable the sd petitioners to repair the great road leading from Newfield through the towns of Trumbull, Huntington, Newtown and Brookfield to NewMilford with the privilege of a turnpike or turnpikes on said roads as per petition on file. Now we, the inhabitants of said Newtown, beg leave to represent to your honors that the said road passes through Newtown in its length about nine miles and that we are sensible of the necessity of thorough repairs on said road, that much the greater part of said road, within the limits of said Newtown can be made good and put into a state of complete repair without any great inconvenience and expense, and without the aid of turnpikes or tolls, and taking into our consideration the advantages of a free public road and from motives of pure public spiritedness and genuine liberality, we the inhabitants of said Newtown are determined, unless prevented by a grant in favor of said petition or the interference of the Honorable Assembly, to put said road in good, ample and every way sufficient repair at our own charge and expense, and the same keep and maintain in such repair free and clear from any tax toll or duty to be exacted or received from travelers on said road, and to effectuate this our laudable purpose we have in legal town meeting voted and granted the sum of four hundred and fifty dollars to be laid out and expended on the said road in repairs the present season at the rate or price of 75c for each day's labor for a man and a proportionate price for team, and also we have made a further provision of sixty days labor by voluntary subscriptions to be expended and done on said road, all of which we confidently assure ourselves will, if judiciously laid out, and expended, put the said road within the limits of our town in the most ample, complete and satisfactory repair. We, the said inhabitants therefore humbly remonstrate before your honors against the prayer of the petition aforesaid and pray your honors, that the same may not be granted and that our said road may not be obstructed by turnpikes and gates, and that we may enjoy the privilege of repairing and maintaining said road within the limits of said Newtown at our own expense and charge, free from toll or tax and we, with submission, as in duty bound will ever remonstrate and pray."—Dated at Newtown, April the 7th, A. D. 1800.

At a meeting of the inhabitants of Newtown legally warned and held in said Newtown on the 7th day of April, 1800: "Voted, that the foregoing remonstrance be offered and improved before the Honorable General Assembly of the State of Connecticut to be holden at Hartford in May, 1801, in behalf of this town, against the petition of Amos Hubbell, John S. Cannon and others, now pending before said Assembly."—Caleb Baldwin, Jr., chairman pro. temporary.

The matter did not come up at the May session in Hartford, 1801, but was carried over until the Oct. session of the same year, when it met in New Haven.

In the meantime better counsels had prevailed in Newtown. A special town meeting was held Oct. 19, 1801, to consult the interests of the town in regard to a turnpike road from Bridgeport to the New Milford line, when it was voted "that we will not remonstrate against the petition now pending before the General Assembly for the grant of a turnpike road between Bridgeport and New Milford."

On the second Thursday of Oct., 1801 the General Assembly met in New Haven and at that session it was voted "that said John Cannon and his associates and such persons as they shall associate with them, their heirs, assigns and successors, be, and they are hereby constituted a corporation by the name of the Bridgeport and Newtown Turnpike Company by which to sue and be sued in all courts of record, to appoint such officers, to ordain and establish such by-laws, ordinances and regulations as shall be necessary for the government of said Company and the raising such sum or sums of money as may be necessary and expedient to carry into effect the object of its institution, not contrary to law, subject however to be repealed by the Superior Court of this state. The Company is authorized to erect three turnpike gates on said road so established at such places as said County Court shall order. Provided always that the southmost gate shall not be erected south of the north side of the Old Post Road, socalled, Stratford to Fairfield, and further be it enacted that at each of said gates said Company shall be and they are hereby authorized to collect the following tolls, viz:

Every traveling four-wheeled pleasure carriage, driver and passenger, shall pay .25; Every two-wheeled pleasure carriage, passenger and driver, 0.12.5; Every loaded cart, team and the driver, 0.12.5; Every loaded wagon with two horses and driver, 0.08; Every man and horse, 0.04; Every stage including driver and passengers, 0.25; Every loaded sled, team and the driver, 0.10; Every sleigh with two horses and driver, 0.08; Every pleasure sleigh with one horse and driver, 0.06.3; Every other one horse sleigh and driver, 0.04; Every empty cart, wagon, sled sleigh and driver, 0.04; Every horse, cart and driver, 0.04; Horses, mules and neat cattle each, 0.01.

Provided, nevertheless, that persons traveling to attend public worship, funerals or society, town or freeman's meeting and persons obliged to do military duty traveling to attend trainings, persons going to or from grist mills and persons passing though said gates to attend or return from their ordinary farming business shall not be liable to the payment of said tolls. Said Company shall set up and maintain on the post of each gate or turnpike and in open view of the passengers an account written in capitals of all the fares allowed by this resolve and payable at such gate in the same manner as in by-law directed at the ferries within this state."

No change was made in toll rates until 1839 when pleasure wagons with springs began to come in use, and the corporation voted at their annual meeting, Dec. 3, "That the Directors direct the gate-keepers to take 10 cents toll for all one-horse wagons hung on springs of iron, steel or leather, and generally used as pleasure wagons."

It was ordered, too, by the General Assembly that "the first meeting of said Company shall be held at the house of Caleb Baldwin in said Newtown, on the third Tuesday in November next, and that the members of said company shall have as many votes as they hold shares in said company, provided always that said Company shall not be apportioned into a greater number than five hundred shares, nor into less number than two hundred and fifty shares, nor shall any member of said company whatever may be his number of shares be entitled to more than fifty votes."

The lay-out of the road was commenced in April, 1802, and finished in the early Fall of that year. It was laid out four and six rods in width, with roadbed 20 feet in width, extending from the south line of New Milford to the mouth of the Golden Hill road in the north line of the borough of Bridgeport. Oct. 2, 1802, it was reported that 500 shares had been subscribed. These shares were to be paid for in four equal instalments at such times as should be fixed by the directors, to be divided among 88 shareholders. The sum assessed in damages to individuals in consequence of laying out the turnpike from New Milford was $3,975.05. $857.70 being paid to land owners in Newtown.

Those remunerated and to what extent: Nathaniel Dikemen, $25.00; Daniel Hawley, $8.97; Jotham Hawley, $40.00; Joshua Hatch, $100.00; Jotham Hawley, $17.17; Joseph Hawley, $25.00; Jabez Hawley, $0.01; Gideon Botsford, $56.64; Clement Botsford, $4.00; Joseph Blackman, $0.50; Josiah Blackman, $40.88; Isaac Lewis, wife, $0.50; John Baldwin, $90.00; Moses Botsford, $58.50; Daniel Booth, $2.00; William Edmond, Esq., $11.25; Jabez Botsford's widow, $21.66; Samuel Peck, 63.67; Amos Peck's heirs, $13.00; Josiah Glover, $13.87; Ammon Hard, $3.00; Moses Peck, $40.00; Oliver Tousey, $9.00; Ashur Peck, $3.44; David Meeker, $32.44; David Sterling, $57.72; Phineas Taylor, $6.50; Phebe Summers, $12.80; Simeon Beers, $9.75; Zalmon Tousey $65.62; Lemuel Nichols, $0.75; Moses Peck, $11.87; Ebenezer Sherwood, $2.00; Stephen Taylor, $8.50.

March, 1804, it was voted "that the Directors make such contracts as they shall see fit with people living on the roads which meet the turnpike near Horse Tavern and also that the Directors be authorized to make one sleigh path by the side of the Turnpike road where they shall judge it necessary from Bridgeport to Nathaniel J. Burton's." It was also voted "that any persons living near any of the gates, the directors have liberty to contract with them to pass the gate to which they are contiguous, by the quarter of a year, or any toll less than the toll affixed by law, at their discretion." Also voted, "the Directors be authorized to open the Turnpike gate or any of them, when in their opinion the road is so bad as not to authorize the company to collect toll.

In 1813, it was voted that all persons passing directly from Bennett's Bridge to the Middle Gate and returning directly to said Bennett's Bridge, and all persons living on the road leading from the Middle Gate to said Bennett's Bridge and eastward of said road within the limits of said town of Newtown, and those who enter on said road at the north end of Toddy Hill, shall pass and re-pass said Middle Gate for half the customary toll. We do not know when the company began the taking of toll, but the first intimation comes from an order from the directors of the company Dec. 6, 1809, ordering Marcus Botsford, Esq., treasurer of the Bridgeport and Newtown Turnpike Co., to pay the stockholders a dividend of 50c a share out of the toll money for the 20th of Nov. 1809, David Baldwin, Elijah Nichols, directors.

It was decreed by the General Assembly that the turnpike should have three toll gates. When the road was opened for travel, the directors fixed the points where they should be located. The first gate was placed near the south line of the town of Trumbull about four miles north of Bridgeport city limits. The middle gate was located at the south line of Newtown, which was then the boundary line between Newtown and New Stratford, then part of the town of Huntington, but incorporated as a town in 1823 and named Monroe. The north gate was placed at the north part of Newtown, about one mile south of the Brookfield line.

The road was built in five mile sections. The contractors met in Newtown at the inn of Michael Parks, April 4, 1803.

At the annual meeting of the company, Dec. 4, 1804, Gen. David Baldwin, Samuel C. Blackman and Eliakim Walker were appointed a committee to see if the road had been built according to contract, and report defects, if any.

At the annual meeting of Dec. 3, 1806, it was voted "to farm out and let either by auction or otherwise the Bridgeport and Newtown Turnpike road, including bridges and sluices except Still River bridge near William Meeker's store, from the first of Feb., 1806, to the 10th of Oct. 1811, to keep and maintain the same in good repair during that period and that the undertakers shall be paid in equal half yearly instalments." It was also voted "to require of the toll gatherers that they be under some suitable oath for a faithful discharge of their duties." Voted "that the people living at Tashua and Chestnut Hill and those living the east side of the road in that quarter to pass the southern gate at half toll or less than full toll." It was also voted "that anything over four bushels weight of grain or salt be considered as a load for a cart or wagon."

It would be almost impossible to follow in detail the information from the records of the Bridgeport and Newtown Turnpike Co. pertaining to the construction of the turnpike and its operating expenses. Its written history from 1800 to 1888 would be replete with information concerning road building and maintaing roads.

With the Bridgeport and Newtown turnpike completed, New York city by way of Bridgeport and Long Island Sound seemed brought very near and though the harbor at Bridgeport had been little developed, the sloops, schooners and smaller craft could ply in and out of the harbor, opening traffic with the great metropolis. With the northern terminus of the turnpike at New Milford, an outlet was made for an extent of country east, west and north of New Milford by which either with their own teams, or by shipping through others, produce could be delivered at greater advantage than up to that time had been found possible, opening larger opportunities for increasing comfort, pleasure and profit. People from New Milford and adjoining territory would make Newtown the half-way resting place for a midday or a mid-night feed and rest, and the traffic all along the line made things lively.

It was a good three-days' work for those living in New Milford and towns adjacent to collect their freight, deliver it in Bridgeport and make their return. It was quite fortunate when teamsters could secure a load for both ways. A great deal of the merchants' trade was in barter, taking in farm produce, paying in trade and then turning it into money, as best they could. Much of the transportation was with oxen. My grandfather lived where I now live, so that I learned many facts from him as to how he did in the earlier years of his life. His motive power was an ox-team. He would aim to get his load together so that he could start in the middle of the day for Bridgeport, content if he reached Horse Tavern, as it was called, early enough to get his oxen fed and himself into bed by 11 o'clock. Horse Tavern stood on the beautiful spot where St. Vincent's hospital now stands. The north city line of Bridgeport was where Golden Hill street still is, near enough the city so that they could get in, in the early morning, dispose of their load, get together their return load, reaching Newtown on their return trip in the early morning of the second day out.

The first report of the receipts for toll at the gates begins under date of October, 1815, which, from that date until Nov. 5, 1816, was $2,192.67, from Nov., 1816 to Nov. 22, 1817, it was $2,408.75; from Nov. 22, 1817, to Dec. 1, 1818, $2,693.48; for 1819, $2,457.11.

The writer does not feel warranted in fixing the date of the opening of the road when toll began to be taken, but the record of the doings of the company indicate that the work, to what might be called its completion, extended over a period of at least six years. The books of the company further show that, from Nov. 20, 1819, when the first dividend was declared, to January, 1841, it paid the stockholders a quarterly dividend of 95c on a $50 share, skipping but four dividends during that time. From 1841 to 1864, the dividends were paid semi-annually in May and November. The approximate yearly average of toll receipts from 1830 to 1840 was $2,540.82. Out of that must be paid the cost of repairs on roads and salaries of gatekeepers, before a dividend was declared. The average yearly receipts for toll as nearly as can be ascertained from the year 1818 to the year 1840, was about $2,550 a year. With the completion of the Housatonic railroad in 1842, business along the turnpike began to drop off and in 1848 what was called the North gate, located near Brookfield line, was thrown open and no further toll collected at that point.

Although the North gate was abandoned in 1848, there was no lessening of the expenses to keep up the turnpike. A few still live who can recall that there were a goodly number of teams going over the road between New Milford and Newtown, destined for the Bridgeport market, and much that was forwarded from there to New York by water.

Of course, with diminishing receipts, and running expenses of the company somewhat on the increase, the dividends began to show a decided decline from what they were previous to 1860, but the company kept on its uniform course until 1880.

Dec. 2, 1873, at the annual meeting of the stockholders at the Central House in Newtown it was "voted that the stockholders meet one year from this day at this place and that the proprietor of the Central House furnish them with a good supper.—Attest, Henry Sanford, clerk."

Aproximate receipts for toll from 1860 to 1880 inclusive:

Year	Amount	Year	Amount	Year	Amount
1860	$ 960.57	1867	$1172.03	1874	$1252.03
1861	1055.67	1868	1290.86	1875	1064.11
1862	1084.95	1869	993.98	1876	957.41
1863	1077.94	1870	1111.43	1877	1072.32
1864	929.61	1871	1145.03	1878	1212.11
1865	1349.92	1872	1015.10	1879	1175.00
1866	1173.43	1873	1166.02	1880	1227.40

In the year 1882, it was voted to pay a dividend of 55c on each share of stock for the preceding year, and in 1883 to pay a dividend of 40c. At the annual meeting of the turnpike company at William J. Dick's hotel in Newtown, Dec. 2, 1884, it was voted that the company pay a dividend of 20c on a share of $50. At a special meeting at the same place, Jan. 19, 1886, it was voted to instruct the directors for the turnpike, to manage the affairs pertaining to its discontinuance to the best of their ability before the session of the General Assembly at Hartford for 1886.

Dec. 21, 1886, voted that the directors of the company appear before the committee appointed by the Superior Court for hearing said discontinuance. At a meeting at Leonard's hotel, formerly Dick's, Oct. 18, 1887, to hear and act upon the report of the doings of the directors and agents of the turnpike company in the proceedings to make its turnpike road a free public highway, to ratify the sale and disposition of the property of the company and divide the assets among the stockholders, after payment of its debt. Jan. 16, 1888, it was reported that the treasurer of the company had $99.60 in his hands for distribution and Charles Henry Peck, then treasurer of the company, was instructed to pay 20-100 dollars per share as the final dividend which was made on the 23d day of Jan. 1888, on which date the Bridgeport and Newtown Turnpike Co. became a thing of the past.

The toll received in 1841 was $1,009.30 from 1842 to 1843 it was $993.54, and in 1881 it was reported to be $17.07. Charles Henry Peck was its clerk when the books were closed and on the inside of the cover of the Bridgeport and Newtown Turnpike Co. records is written in a plain, bold hand this injunction: "I hope this book will be kept by some one, many years to come, as a souvenir.'—Charles Henry Peck, Ex-Clerk of sd Ex-Company.

Thus it is that, though being dead, he yet speaketh.

OLD DAYS OF THE STAGE COACH.
BEFORE THE COMING OF THE RAILROAD.

Facilities afforded in early days for carrying of passengers and speedy delivery of mails. In the Danbury Recorder, June 24, 1829, a one-sheet weekly then in the fourth year of its existence, and printed every Wednesday, several ads are found relating to the running of stages for 1829, intended more particularly for more important towns in Fairfield, New Haven and Litchfield counties:

"Summer arrangement for the Norwalk, Bridgeport, New Haven, Woodbury, Danbury and Litchfield stages:

New Haven and Norwalk stage: This stage will leave the General Stage office, New Haven, at 7o'clock in the morning (Sundays excepted) and arrive at Norwalk in season for the passengers to take the steamboat for New York. Fare through, $3.00. Returning will leave Norwalk daily on the arrival of the steamboat.

Woodbury and Norwalk stage: This stage will leave J. P. Marshall's stage house, Woodbury, on Mondays, Wednesday and Friday at 4 o'clock in the morning, and arrive at Norwalk by the way of Newtown and Bridgeport, in season for passengers to take the steamboat for New York. Fare through $3.50. Returning will leave Norwalk on Tuesday, Thursdays and Saturdays on the arrival of the steamboat. A stage from NewMilford regularly intersects this line at Newtown each way.

Litchfield, Newtown, Danbury and Norwalk accommodation and mail stage: This stage leaves Danbury daily at 7 o'clock in the morning. Leaves Litchfield on Tuesdays, Thursdays and Saturdays, at 4 o'clock in the afternoon on the arrival of the mail stage from Hartford, lodges at New Milford, leaves New Milford on Mondays, Wednesdays and Fridays at 4 o'clock in the morning, changes horses at Newtown and arrives at Norwalk in season for passengers to take the steamboat for New York. Fare $4.00. Returning leaves Norwalk for Danbury daily, for Newtown, New Milford and Litchfield Tuesdays, Thursdays and Saturdays on the arrival of the steamboat from New York."

S. Mott, E. Hayes, C. Patrick & Co., H. Barnes, proprietors.

May, 1829.

Danbury and Sing-Sing accomodation stage; Union Line: This line of stages commenced running from Danbury to Sing-Sing on Wednesday the 8th of April as follows: Leaving G. Nichols' hotel, Danbury every Monday, Wednesday and Friday at 7 o'clock a. m., arriving at Sing-Sing at 12 o'clock the same day, by the way of Mill-Plain, Sodom Corner and Summerstown. Returning leaves Sing-Sing immediately after the arrival of the steamboat Gen. Jackson, and arriving in Danbury at 6 o'clock p. m., Tuesdays, Thursdays and Saturdays. Baggage over 30 lbs, extra charge, and all baggage at the risk of the owner. Fare from Danbury to Summerstown, 75c; to Sing-Sing $1.50; to New York $2.00. This line of stages will intersect with Hartford, Litchfield, Newtown and New Haven stages, and is the quickest and shortest route from Danbury to New York, that can be traveled.

N. B. The proprietors of this line of stages will assure the public that they have the first rate horses and carriages, and they think honest and capable drivers, who will spare no pains in making the passage safe, agreeable and expeditious. Gentlemen and ladies of this and neighboring town please to patronize us with a fair trial on this route to New York, and if you should think it not for your interest and convenience to go this way, we will excuse you from a further trial and be your very humble obedient servants."

G. Nichols, Danbury, April 14, 1829.

Danbury and Poughkeepsie mail stage: The public are hereby informed that a stage for the accommodation of passengers will commence running on the 21st. of April, between the village of Danbury and Poughkeepsie, twice a week. Leaving Danbury every Tuesday and Friday mornings at 6 o'clock a. m., passing Southeast, Patterson, Stormville, Hopewell and Hackensack, arrives in Poughkeepsie in time for the steamboat, either for New York or Albany, on the same day. Returning, leaves Poughkeepsie every Wednesday and Saturday mornings at 7 o'clock a. m., and arrives in Danbury where it meets all the eastern and southern stages. This is the easiest and most direct route from Long Island Sound to the Hudson river and persons traveling to the West or North, will by this stage, reach Albany one day sooner than by any other conveyance and at much less expense. For seats apply to A. Seely's and G. Nichols' hotel (Danbury and at Jarvis' hotel and the steamboat house, Poughkeepsie. Fare $2.00. All baggage at the risk of the owner. Joel Stone, Danbury, April 6, 1829.

Those were times when the stage coach was in the height of its glory regarded as a rapid means of conveyance for carrying both passengers and mails. In the early 30s a line of stages was established between New Milford and Bridgeport, making daily trips and meeting at Czar Keeler's tavern, which stood just north of the Beecher residence.

Arriving at noon-time, dinner was promptly served and fresh horses provided for the rest of the journey. The writer, too young to remember the stirring events of those early days, vividly recalls stories told by his elders on long winter evenings before the blazing fires of the open fire-place. A cheering sight it must have been for the street folk when these stage-coaches, drawn by two pair of horses, went rattling through the streets, loaded down, as they sometimes were, outside and in, with passengers, with trunks and luggage piled on the top overhead, or tucked under the great leather boot covering in the rear. What an animated and busy life it must have given the village street thoroughfare for vehicles of all kinds plying between the upper towns and Bridgeport, while an occasional blast from the drivers horn apprized the whole town of the arrival and departure of the daily stage coach. With the completion of the Housatonic railroad in 1842, a quietus was given not only to the stage line but to the turnpike company itself. Newtown's "Traveler's Directory" and the time of arrival and departure of mails from the Newtown postoffice, as advertised in July, 1853.

Housatonic Railroad, Newtown Station.

Car go	North	South
Freight at	7.25 a. m.,	12.42 p. m.
Mail & pas'ger	11.10 a. m.,	12.42 p. m.
Special at	6.45 p. m.,	9.00 a. m.

Stages leave the Railroad Depot for Woodbury and Southbury daily at 12 m. For Southville Tuesdays, Thursdays and Saturdays, 1 p. m. Hawleyville Station, Danbury and Bethel stages arrive at 11 a. m., and 2.30 p. m.; leave at 11.40 a. m., and 3 p. m.

Newtown Postoffice mails arrive from the south, via railroad at 12.30 p. m.
From the North via Railroad 12.30 p. m.
From Woodbury and Southbury, via stage, daily at 12.30 p. m.
From Southville by stage on Tuesdays, Wednesdays and Saturdays, at 11.00 a. m.
  Mails close for the North, via railroad at 10.45 a. m.
For the South, via railroad, at 10.45 a .m
For Woodbury, Southbury, via stage daily at 10.45 a. m.
For Southville by stage on Tuesdays Thursdays and Saturdays at 10 45 a. m.
Post office open from 7 a. m. to 9 p. m. Sundays from 12m. to 1 p. m.

                                      Jerome Judson, P. M.

HIGHWAY RECONSTRUCTION—NEWTOWN STREET TO SANDY HOOK.—1834-1912.

The first reference we find to laying out a highway from Newtown village to Sandy Hook is under date of Nov. 18, 1715:

"We, that are the committee for to lay out highways, whose names are under written have this 18th day of November, 1715, laid out a highway or country road two miles from ye middle of ye town down by ye north side of ye old farm over Pohtatuck Brook and so toward ye single pine to a bunch of stones upon a rock which is two miles. The highway is 20 rods wide, according as common or undivided land will allow. We removed Daniel Foote's southwest corner of his four acre lot northwest six rods and we gave him seven rods at his east corner. Sd. Foot was present and consented to same. We lay out a road to go to Wodbury. We began it at ye first meadow in ye above sd road eastward of ye Pohtatuck Brook, turning of it more north till we come to some pines. We lay it 20 rods wide.

                                      Thomas Bennitt,
                                      John Glover
                                      Ebenezer Booth,
                                                          Committee.

Recorded, November 28, 1715.
                                              Joseph Peck, Clerk.

As there could have been naught but natural obstructions in the lay-out of the highway, we cannot account for its serpentine course unless, in the lay out, the Indian trail as it led from the Pohtatuck on the banks of the Housatonic river over the hills westward to Quanneapague lake and on to Danbury and the Hudson, river, was followed.

A century passed and the primitive way of working country roads continued. Men worked out their road tax with teams and shovels as best they could, content to share each with the others the privations and discomforts that fell to their lot.

As water power was more and more developed, travel and

business interests increased between the two villages and better roads were called for, but we learn nothing more until 1834, when, upon complaint to the County Court of Fairfield county, from tax payers living in the easterly and southeasterly part of the town in regard to the condition of the highway leading from the Newtown Church to Zoar Bridge, the following complaint was made:

Complaint for Ragged Corner Road.

To the selectmen of Newtown, Gentlemen: Complaint has been made to me that the road leading from the Newtown church to Zoar Bridge is in bad repair so much that it is unsafe to pass over it in carriages or wagons. This therefore is to request you to put said road in good and safe repair without delay and spare me the disagreeable necessity of bringing the subject before the County Court. The complaint is signed by 20 persons who represent the road to have been much neglected for a long time past. They are desirous that I should go immediately upon the road and view it. I have thought however that it would be reasonable that you should first be notified, that no unnecessary expense should be made to the town. I hope you will have the goodness to attend to this road soon and that no further proceeding on my part will be necessary. Very respectfully,

Your obedient servant,

A. D. Baldwin, Sheriff.

April 1834.

Early in Dec. 1834, a town meeting considered the question of a highway from Sandy Hook to connect with the Bridgeport and Newtown turnpike, at some point in South Center school district, near the house of Widow Lavina Burritt, to near the house of Elijah Sanford in Sandy Hook, and by vote of the tax payers it was left to the selectmen to look over the ground and report at an adjourned town meeting, Dec. 22, 1834. At that meeting, it was voted, "To accept the report of the selectmen so far as relates to the road from Sandy Hook to intersect the Bridgeport and Newtown turnpike near Widow Lavina Burritt's as reported by Silas Glover and others." It was also voted "that the selectmen be directed to lay out a highway beginning at or near the house of Widow Lavina Burritt to near the house of Elijah Sanford in Sandy Hook."

As the writer is perfectly familiar with the lay-out of that proposed highway, though never built, using it week in and week out, when in 1854-55 and '56 he was teaching the Sandy Hook school and boarding at his childhood home, we give the course it was decided it should take. Elijah Sanford's house is what is now known as the Gibson place. The road was to start in at the west of the house near the present gateway and taking a southwesterly course, follow along the easterly side of the ridge still covered by the beautiful line of white oaks, crossing Tom brook (that runs through the intervale down the open, to empty into the Pohtatuck not far from the pond near Sandy Hook bridge,) then up the slope and across the level where the railroad now runs, following on southwesterly along the north side of Deep brook, and on between the houses of Jerry Carey on the north and Miss Joanna Keating on the south, to connect with the road that passed by the house of Mrs. Ruth Prindle, now the home of Julia Prindle, then to turn to the bend and follow the highway as it led to the house of Widow Lavina Burritt, which is still standing. There the new highway was to connect with the turnpike.

Does the reader wonder why Sandy Hook and Bennett's Bridge territory should clamor for such road, that would turn so much travel from Newtown Street? The turnpike was an assured thing and in successful operation. The new lay-out would be an easy grade the whole distance, not much different in measurement than the road from Sandy Hook to Newtown Street and that all the way up hill.

Although the lay-out of the road was accepted, yet, for some reason, not on record, the project was abandoned. It did not do away with further effort to connect Sandy Hook with the Bridgeport turnpike at some point below the village of Newtown. For in 1837, another special town meeting was called for the express purpose of considering the same matter.

Warning is hereby given to the inhabitants of the Town of Newtown qualified to vote in town meeting that a town meeting will be held at the Town hall in said Newtown on Saturday, the 17th inst., June, at 2 o'clock in the afternoon for the purpose of taking into consideration the propriety of repairing the middle turnpike road or such parts of the same, as said meeting may think advisable, or to survey and lay out a new road from the Episcopal church to the village of Sandy Hook in the most feasible place and also the necessity of laying an additional highway tax and to do other business if necessary.

Abijah Merritt,
James B. Fairman
Israel A. Beardsley,
Newtown, June 10, 1837.
Selectmen.

For some reason the meeting called for June 10, 1837, went by default and an indignant contingent of tax payers quietly bided their time until Nov., 1838, when this petition was circulated. This petition was signed by 20 tax payers and reads:

To James B. Fairman, Abijah Merritt and Isreal A. Beardsley, the honorable selectmen of the Town of Newtown, We, the petitioners resident electors of the Town of Newtown represent to your body that whereas the road known as the road running from the bridge situated at Sandy Hook to the Episcopal church, situated in Newtown Center is entirely out of repair, dangerous to travel and ridiculously inconvenient to a very large proportion of the inhabitants of said town. We therefore, petition your body to call a meeting to take into consideration the necessity and expediency of repairing said road, or laying out a new road on or near the line of said road, and we further petition that said meeting be called within two weeks from date of this petition or as soon as legal.

Newtown, November 5, 1838.
John Dick, Charles Blakeslee, A. B. Beecher, William Clark, Stiles H. Judson, George Curtis, Samuel B. Peck, David J. Glover, J. S. Tomlinson, H. W. Tucker, Abijah B. Curtiss, Charles L. Dick, S. N. Beers, Warren Sherman, David Sanford, Royal O. Gurley, Moses Parsons, Ezra Patch, Josiah Sanford, Joseph Dick.

In response to this petition, the selectmen called a special town meeting, Nov. 28, 1838:

Warning: Whereas a petition of a number of inhabitants of said town for a special town meeting to be warned forthwith for the purpose of taking the subject into consideration of the expediency of repairing the old road leading from the Episcopal church in said Newtown to Sandy Hook bridge or the laying out of a new road from the Episcopal church to said Sandy Hook bridge.

James B. Fairman.
Abijah Mirritt,
Isreal A. Beardsley,
Newtown, November 16, 1838.
Selectmen.

At this town meeting, Nov. 28, the selectmen were ordered to repair the road from the Episcopal church to Sandy Hook bridge and no new lay-out for a road was tolerated.

At the town meeting, Nov. 28, 1838, the opposition to building a new highway from Newtown Street to Sandy Hook was so strong that no further effort was made along that line.

In 1838, the Housatonic railroad was commenced, survey for which had been completed. The location for the railroad station had been decided and so decided as to satisfy the people of the two villages of Newtown and Sandy Hook. All the more care was given to the upkeep of the highway between the two villages, although the idea of Sandy Hook having an outlet to the Newtown and Bridgeport turnpike at some point in a southwesterly direction, a mile or two below Newtown village, had not all that time been given up and was held in abeyance until 1872. In the early part of January of that year, a petition having the requisite number of signers was placed in the hands of Newtown's selectmen, asking for a special town meeting, held Jan. 27, 1872:

Warning is hereby given that a special town meeting will be held for the purpose of taking into consideration the propriety and necessity of surveying and laying out a new highway commencing near the watering trough and residence of Mrs Samuel B. Peck, running southwesterly and terminating on the old highway near the dwelling house of John McNamara (the house where Thomas Carey lives.)

The meeting voted that the selectmen be instructed to survey and estimate the cost of said road and report at an adjourned meeting. At the adjourned meeting, the selectmen's report was read and a resolution passed instructing the selectmen to lay out and construct a new highway over the route proposed. The vote was by ballot and carried by a majority of three. Yes 129, no 126. Excitement ran high. Another special meeting was held to rescind the vote. Feb. 17, 1872. A motion by Dr. Erastus Erwin to rescind passed at the special meeting, Jan. 17, voted upon by ballot. A large number of those who favored it lived in the south part of town and worked in the rubber factory, in Sandy Hook. There were 381 ballots, yes 186, no 195, and the motion was lost. Another special meeting, Saturday, May 25, 1872, to lay out a highway over practically the same route, to run under the Housatonic railroad near the dwelling of Martin Keating, and terminating on the old highway a few rods south of the dwelling of John McNamara. A vote passed without discussion that the meeting adjourn without date, and attention was again directed to the improvement of the Middle turnpike, as it was called, from Newtown to Sandy Hook. A special town meeting called for May 10, 1872, voted that the road from Sandy Hook bridge to Newtown Street be graded and gravelled and a committee of three appointed to contract and superintend the same provided that the amount expended do not exceed $3,000. The committee were instructed to contract for the grading and gravelling and to borrow the money in the name of the town, if there were not sufficient funds in the treasury to defray the expense. An amendment was carried that, in the place of $3,000, $2900 should be substituted; carried by acclamation.

William J. Dick, Jabez Botsford and Henry L. Wheeler were appointed committee to contract and superintend the work of grading and gravelling the road from Sandy Hook bridge to Newtown street and to pay for the same. A special meeting, Aug. 23,

1873, voted an additional tax of one mill to defray in part the gravelling of Sandy Hook and Newtown road.

Between 1850 and 1870 public sentiment seems to have settled to its normal condition. Then came another wave of dissatisfaction in regard to the road from Newtown Street to Sandy Hook. Special town meetings were called galore, many of which have been referred to, but further consideration of another effort to get a highway to connect Sandy Hook and points adjacent with the Bridgeport turnpike southwesterly was agitated, until it resulted in a call for a town meeting in November, 1874.

The meeting, Nov. 28, 1874, voted that the lay-out of a highway to Martin Keating's house be indefinitely postponed. A special town meeting Dec. 26, 1874, to act upon the petition of Martin Keating and others for a road and two bridges from the house of Martin Keating, meeting and connecting with the public road near the dwelling of Widow Keating (now Mrs James Corbett's) referring to his old right of way, the same right of way to continue thereafter a road fit for public travel. The special meeting Dec. 26, 1874, voted: That the selectmen lay out and construct a highway from Martin Keating's first house to the highway on the west side of said road, provided that Martin Keating and Widow Keating will deed all their right of way to the town for public use.

The road was built and is now in use.

In 1885 a sidewalk from Newtown to the Sandy Hook bridge was agitated and at a special town meeting, March 13, 1886, the selectmen were instructed to lay a plank or tar walk on the north side of the road from Newtown Street to Sandy Hook, near the Niantic mills, should a tar walk be laid, plank might be substituted where tar was impracticable. The petition had more than 20 names. A resolution offered by William C. Wile that the selectmen be instructed to lay a tar walk on the north side of the highway four feet, six inches wide, not to cost over $2,000 was passed.

At a special town meeting, March 20, 1883, by petition to consider the vote passed at the special meeting of March 13, 1883, the selectmen were instructed by resolution to commence work as soon as practicable. As the walk was never built, we consider that the selectmen never found a time when they thought it practicable.

Upon petition, a town meeting was warned for the 15th of March, 1890, to macadamize or gravel the highway leading from Newtown Street to Sandy Hook bridge and to provide means for the work. Voted that a committee of five be authorized to expend a sum not exceeding $4,000 in macadamizing the road from Samuel C. Glover's house in Newtown Street to the Newtown depot of the Housatonic railroad, said road not to be less than 12 feet wide, and to expend a sum not to exceed $500 in gravelling or macadamizing the road from the depot to Sandy Hook bridge, and that the selectmen be three of that committee and L. B. Booth and D. G. Beers the other two. The committee were empowered to borrow not to exceed $4500. Another special meeting, March 29, 1890, voted to confirm and ratify the doings of the last town meeting.

At a special meeting Feb. 28, 1891, it was voted that the whole matter of building a sidewalk from Newtown to Sandy Hook be indefinitely postponed.

At a special town meeting, Aug. 13, 1892, to take action regarding the macadamized road from the head of Newtown Street to the Housatonic railroad, and the construction of a road without side ditches from the South Center schoolhouse to the intersection of the macadamized road in Newtown, it was voted that the selectmen make such repairs as they thought necessary on the macadamized road from Newtown Street to the Housatonic railroad. A special meeting, April 24, 1893, considered buying a stone crusher and engine plant complete for said town and to make a proper side walk between Newtown Street and Sandy Hook. A resolution to purchase a stone crusher and engine complete the cost not to exceed $1800, was lost 99 to 58.

Two hundred years have passed since the lay-out of the road was made and the long steep grade of Church hill had not varied much in all that time. With the completion of the State road from Newtown Street to the Monroe line and with the road to Sandy Hook included in the State work, drastic measures have been taken to eliminate the grade of Church hill to a great degree, and with the improvements along the line to the railroad station, it would seem that the permanency of the work is assured for many years to come. When further improvements on the same line from the station to Sandy Hook eliminated the abrupt curve of the road by Tom Brook and widened the bridge that spans that stream, no stretch of road will be found in the state that will be better. The work is a credit to Highway Commissioner McDonald, as well as to C. M. Crosby, foreman, in charge of the work; to the contractors, the B. D. Pierce Co. of Bridgeport and Newtown's First Selectman William C. Johnson, inspector for the state. The most drastic part of the work was cutting down and grading Church hill. From the summit of the hill and for about half of its length a cut was made averaging in depth from four to five feet, with the deepest cut about seven feet. From the point where the cut runs out to the watering trough, a heavy fill was made, the deepest part of which may measure from five to seven feet. The road bed the length of the hill was laid out 26 feet in width. The hill is extremely wet and springy and a rubble stone drain three feet wide and three feet deep was dug in the center of the roadbed from the top of the hill for 300 feet, to carry the water that would accumulate by seepage to an open ditch at the bottom of the hill. For surface drainage, cobble gutters on either side of the road extended half the length of the hill, carrying the water into catch basins, that empty into 12-inch drain tile that carry the water to the outlets at the foot of the hill. In front of all driveways 12-inch tile have been laid. The entire road has been crowned with gravel to the depth of 10 inches and has been thoroughly rolled by a heavy steam roller. On top of the gravel, several hundred tons of crushed rock have been carted upon the road and that, too, has been rolled down with the steam roller. In front of the High School property, the plank bridge has been replaced with 24-inch tile which extends along the whole front of the school grounds, which will insure an unbroken front of lawn almost to the wheel track. At the junction of the Queen street road with the State highway, a double 15-inch tiling takes the place of the plank bridge.

BUILDING, EQUIPMENT, RUNNING EXPENSES AND NET PROCEEDS IN THE EARLIEST DAYS OF THE HOUSATONIC RAILROAD 1835-1843.

I have a report of the directors of the Housatonic Railroad Co. made to the stockholders at the annual meeting, Nov. 22, 1842, and report of the investigating committee made at the same time.

At the beginning of the work of building the road I was a babe in the cradle and but 10 years when the trains began running on schedule time. My father was one of those interested in the project of building the road. When the report for 1842 came out, he with others received a copy. This report was handed down from father to son, and has been carefully kept for more than 50 years.

As early as 1835, the question of connecting the seaboard at Bridgeport with Albany by railroad began to be agitated along the Housatonic valley, which, in due time, resulted in a stock company; stock was subscribed to the amount of $869,500. So sanguine were the projectors of the ultimate success of the scheme, they did not wait until the whole amount of stock required for building this entire line was guaranteed before breaking ground at Bridgeport, with New Milford as the first objective point. When the preliminary work of survey, purchasing right of way, etc., had been completed, construction was soon under way. Commencing at Bridgeport and working slowly up the valley, it was watched with much curious interest and statements were freely made that it would never be completed and would be the cause of bankrupting every one who put money into it. The work progressed but slowly, for it was all done with hand shovels, hand picks, hand blasting tools, wheelbarrows and one-horse dump carts. The steam shovel had not taken the place of the wheelbarrow, the steam drill had not taken the place of sledge hammers, swung by sturdy arms of men who working in triplets, by alternate blows upon a drill held and manipulated by a third person slowly bored the way into solid rock nor had the lightning been harnessed to take the place of the boy depended on to carry "hurry messages" from one stand point to another. As the work pushed on though Stepney, Botsford, Newtown, and Hawleyville, reaching the latter place through a tunnel, whose construction was the wonder of all the people far and near, continuing its tortuous winding way along the valley to New Milford, people became less incredulous and an impetus was given to the sale of stock. The completion of the roadbed to New Milford had more than kept pace with the selling of stock, and it was decided to call a halt in work on the road-bed further on, for the time being, and complete track-laying from tide-water to New Milford, so that they could begin running trains. In laying the track, first was laid what were called mud-sills: timbers hewed from large white oak and chestnut trees 8 inches thick and from 12 to 16 feet in length, imbedded in the earth, laid parallel with the road-bed, on which were laid cross-ties flattened on one side to lie firmly on the mud-sills. The ties had niches cut at either end, eight inches wide and six inches deep, to receive the Southern pine timbers on which were spiked the long strips of iron on which the wheels of the engines and cars were run. These strips were three inches wide and an inch thick, fastened on the wooden rails by iron spikes, the heads of which were countersunk into the strip. It was soon found that the oscillations of the engine and cars caused the ends of the straps to spring up, making what came to be called "snake heads," which would at times be caught up by the wheels of the car and thrust through the floor, endangering the lives of passengers. In course of time, that track gave way to the all-iron rail, to be discarded at a later period for the heavy steel rails in use to-day, with which all are familiar.

The first through passenger train on the Housatonic railroad from New Milford to Bridgeport was on St. Valentine's day, 1840. That does not mean that no train was seen anywhere on the line until that date, for, as track-laying extended north of Bridgeport, a work train would naturally follow with rails and other supplies as the work advanced, so that there was daily expectancy of seeing the locomotive. It was in the early winter of 1839-1840, when the writer, having just passed his seventh birthday, was sitting on the little bench at the schoolhouse, close to the box-stove, looking at the big boys and girls on the outside benches craning their necks in great expectancy. Some one shouted, "The locomotive is coming," whereupon all the children, without a permit from the teacher, went helter-skelter out the door and on to the stone walls where all stood in mute amazement to see the first of these work trains as it passed.

Domestic animals were more excited than were human beings. My grandfather had a five-year-old colt in his barnyard never broken to harness, that scaled an eight-board fence, and, from all reports, did not stop until it reached Zoar Bridge, where it was found a few days later. Ever after the horse went by the name of Gabriel. The Housatonic was the first railroad built in Connecticut. It was looked upon with great interest, not only as a business proposition, but also as likely to revolutionize modes and speed of travel.

The first engines were small affairs, wood burners, with no protection from the weather, either for engineer or fireman. The coaches were on four wheeled trucks; also the freight cars, which for the most part were openly exposed to all kinds of weather. By the report of the directors to the stockholders at the annual meeting in Oct. 1838, it appears that a contract had been made for the construction of the entire road from Bridgeport to the Massachusetts State line for $936,000. The report further says: "Under that contract the road was made from Bridgeport to New Milford, and the cars of the company commenced running upon it, between those places, in 1840." Running of the first train from New Milford to Bridgeport told me in my younger days: On the 14th day of Feb. 1840, an excursion train was run to celebrate the completion of the road as far as New Milford. The train reached Newtown from New Milford about noon, where it was greeted by an outpour-

TYPE OF FIRST ENGINES AND CARS USED ON
HOUSATONIC RAILROAD
See Page 166

ing of people from all parts of town, a few of whom boarded the train for the eventful trip, among whom were Legrand Fairchild, (Botsford Fairchild's father) and Zalmon S. Peck, Newtown's long known and well-remembered postmaster of later years. The run was made to Bridgeport without accident. The end of the road was at the foot of Beaver Street, now Fairfield avenue, with a short branch over which to shunt cars to the steamboat dock, where freight destined for New York was transferred to the boat. On the dock was a big pile of wood. The cars were cut off to allow them to run down to the landing. Hand brakes at first were only stout planks thrust through openings in the floor of the car and held against the wheels by the brakemen. The momentum of the train was too great for the power applied and the cars smashed into the pile of wood at the end of the track. Among those badly injured was Zalmon S. Peck of Newtown, whose right thigh was caught by the platform of the car and badly broken. He was taken to a hotel, corner of Wall and Water streets, where he remained until sometime in April, when he had so far recovered as to be taken home. There were four others injured at the same time, and in the settlement with the railroad, the company paid Mr. Peck $614.11. He was a sufferer from that accident the rest of his life.

In Dec., 1840, a settlement was made with the contractors by the directors. The sum of $459,153.13, was allowed for the work done. and the contract was abandoned, the company reserving to itself all claims which it might have upon the contractors for defect of plan, construction or materials of the bridges over the Housatonic and Still river, subject to future adjustment. In the autumn of 1840 a new contract was made with Alfred Bishop, of Bridgeport for the construction of the northern division of the road from New Milford to the Massachusetts line for $500,000. This division of the road was completed and opened to North Canaan, about a mile and a quarter from the Massachusetts line, on the 27th of December, 1841, For work done under this contract, Mr. Bishop was paid in March, 1842, $492,405.05 and was released from his contract and the unfininshed part was completed at the expense of the company. With the Massachusetts State line once reached, the directors made the Berkshire railroad a perpetual lease to keep it in repair and pay for its use a rent of 7 per cent per annum upon its cost, not exceeding $250,000. Its track, of the same width as that of the Housatonic and of the same material, could be used in connection with the Housatonic as one entire road, forming a connecting link with what was called the western railroad, leading from Boston to Albany and the West, which then meant as far as Syracuse, where passengers could change to the "Canal Packet-boat, for Buffalo." The annual report goes on to say:

"The Board of Directors have at last the pleasure to announce the final completion of an unbroken communication from Bridgeport to Albany. That consummation of our efforts during five years of constant struggling with embarrassments and difficulties of no ordinary character, is at length accomplished, and we are now to learn whether our anticipations of the value of the improvement to the community, and its productiveness, as an investment to the stockholders, are to be realized or disappointed. In conclusion we would offer to the stockholders our congratulations upon the completion of the great project undertaken by them, and express the opinion, that, provided some measure shall be adopted during the coming winter to provide for the payment of a portion of the indebtedness of the company, we may see it relieved from its embarrassments and hereafter doing a successful business and conferring upon the community important benefits"

From the report of the directors of the Housatonic Railroad Co. made to the stockholders at the annual meeting in Bridgeport, Conn., Nov. 23, 1842, statistics concerning cost of "right of way," equipment, earnings of the road, expenses of the road, expenses of transportation department, etc:

Right of way	$ 56,659.15	Freights	$61,719.14
Grading and superstructure	968,542.48	Passengers	42,541.91
Turn-rounds	1,182.89	Transporting mails	1,612.94
Depots and engine houses	13,632.45		
Engineering	24,407.23		$105,873.99
		From April 16 to October 1, 1842:	
Total cost of Road	$1,064,424.20	Freights	$21,556.51
Cost of Rolling Stock:		Passengers	15,065.22
5 Engines	$32,500.00	Transporting mails	1,375.73
10 Cars for passengers	15,200.00		
69 Freight cars	19,900.00		$37,997.46
9 hand cars	660.00		
		Amount of earnings	$143,870.72
	$68,260.00	Expenses	76,899.55
Earnings, from opening of the Road		Net proceeds	$66,971.17
to 16th of April, 1842:		Add wood on hand	1,500.00
			$68,471.17

Salaries of employees of the roads, depot agents, engineers, conductors, track men, and day laborers:

Depot agents, Bridgeport: R. B. Lacey, per month, $50.00, C. A. Kirkland $41.65, A. W. Fox, $30.00, E. F. Sherwood, $28.00, four laborers, rate of $26.00, Stepney—A. Northrop, $12.50, Botsford—E. Botsford, $6.00, Newtown—Henry May, $10.42, Hawleyville—D. B. Hawley, $25.00, Brookfield—$10.42, New Milford—D. Marsh, $33.34, Gaylords' Bridge—J. J. Graves, $25.00, Kent, R. H. Platt, $20.00, Cornwall—$10.42, Cornwall Bridge—F. W. Pease, $25.00, West Cornwall—C. Pratt, $20.00, Falls Village—D. H. Hunt, $25.00, North Canaan— J. R. Fuller, $33.34, Sheffield—E. F. Ensign, $25.00, Great Barrington—C. W. Hopkins, $33.34, West Stockbridge, W. Jones, $41.66.

Engineers: E. F. Moore, $83.33, R. Benjamin, $45.00, P. Tait, $50.00, H. Kimball, $50.00, J. B. Hawley, $50.00, W. Sterling, $40.00.

Nine others are employed in engine department with pay from $22 to $30 per month.

Conductors: T. P. Prentice, $41.66, A. D. Smith, $60.00, H. Edwards, $35.00, J. Bostwick, $35.00.
Five others are employed on the cars, with pay from $24 to $26 per month.

Expenses paid at the transportation department from the opening of the road until Oct. 1, 1842: Bridgeport, $7,319.41, Botsford, $123.25, Stepney, $571.83, Newtown, $789.31, Hawleyville, $881.04, Brookfield, $387.25, New Milford, $2,867, Gaylord's Bridge, $377.92, Kent, $423.58, Cornwall Bridge, $283.87, West Cornwall $212.95, Falls Village, $251.83, North Canaan, $1,076.60.

In the smith shop: B. Hotchkiss $39.50, S. Hull $32.50, H. Zabonlinski $26.00, G. B. Smith, carpenter, $30.00, E. Hogan, Watchman $24.00.

27 men, including track walkers and spike men, are employed in repairing the road; pay from $20 to $37.75 per month.

Nine laborers at the several depots, employed in sawing wood, etc. pay, from $20 to $26 per month.

The company employs 90 persons besides its officers. In the foregoing list of engineers, conductors, mechanics and day laborers, we have what may be called the working force of the Housatonic, 90 persons in all, besides its officers, as given in the annual report of the company for 1842.

Up to the 18th of April, 1842, the business done upon the road had been much less than anticipated, amounting only to $9,723.64, one reason given for which was that navigation of the Hudson river, by reason of the unusual mildness of the weather, continued most of the winter unobstructed, diverting traffic from the railroad to the river boats. Earnings and expenses of the road from the first of December, 1841, to April 16, 1842, a net income of $882.41, per day, for 118 days:

Earnings,—Freight		$18,667.24
	Passengers	10,579.56
	Mail	875.00
Gross earnings		$30,121.80
Equal to $225.26 per day. 118 running days.		
Expenses		20,398.16
Net proceeds		9,723.64
Equal to $82.41 per day		

Expenses, including depot expenses and all expenses of transportation department, salaries of officers, repairs of road, etc., $20,398.16. Equal to $172.86 per day.

With 1843, R. B. Mason, superintendent of the Housatonic, issued an order that on and after Jan. 16, there should be one passenger and one freight train each way, daily excepting Sunday, between Bridgeport and West Stockbridge, and that passengers should be at the depots 15 minutes before time for the cars to leave. The train for the north should leave Newtown at 1:25 p.m. and, going south, should leave Newtown at 4.50 p.m. schedule time between Newtown and Bridgeport, one hour and 15 minutes.

Leave	Passenger	Freight
Bridgeport	12.15 a. m.	6.30 a. m.
Newtown	1.25 p. m.	8.25 a. m.
Hawleyville	1.45 p. m.	9.00 a. m.
New Milford	2.30 p. m.	10.15 a. m.
Kent	3.30 p. m.	11.15 a. m.
West Corwall	4.20 p. m.	12.10 p. m.
North Canaan	5.15 p. m.	1.05 p. m.
Great Barrington	6.00 p. m.	2.15 p. m.
West Stockbridge	6.45 p. m.	3.15 p. m.

Passenger and freight trains going south:

Leave	Passenger	Freight
West Stockbridge	11.30 a. m.	5.00 a. m.
Great Barrington	12.15 p. m	6.00 a. m.
North Canaan	1.05 p. m.	7.00 a. m.
West Corwall	1.45 p. m.	8.00 a. m.
Kent	2.35 p. m.	9.00 a. m.
New Milford	3.35 p. m.	10.15 a. m.
Hawleyville	4.30 p. m.	11.15 a. m.
Newtown	4.50 p. m.	11.50 p. m.
Bridgeport	6.00 p. m.	1.50 p. m.

The Postmaster at Bridgeport also gave this notice.

Post Office Bridgeport
Jan. 24, 1843

A mail agent has been appointed by the Postmaster General on the line from Bridgeport to West Stockbridge to accommodate and to take charge of the mails from the postoffice in Bridgeport to the postoffice at West Stockbridge and from the postoffice at West Stockbridge to the postoffice at Bridgeport. He is also directed to act as mail messenger and in that capacity to receive letters written after the mail is closed, and way letters and other mailable matter, to note on them where received, if on the route, if not into the office at the end of the route at which they should be mailed, and also to the person addressed when desired and practicable. He is instructed to receive postage on prepaid letters, and collect it on letters not prepaid when delivered him. The above arrangement will commence this day, January, 24, 1843.

J. Sherman, Jr., P. M.

For the accommodation of the towns of Danbury, Bethel and the south part of Brookfield, it was decided that the third station in Newtown was to be near the extreme northerly part of town, and, one inducement to have it located at Hawleyville, Glover Hawley, then a resident, gave land for depot buildings, and also gave the right of way of over a quarter of a mile through his farm. His home was the brick house at Hawleyville and, when a postoffice was established there, Glover Hawley was first postmaster. In return, the station was named Hawleyville for him and the numerous Hawleys in that vicinity.

NEWTOWN'S POSTOFFICES AND POSTMASTERS 1800—1912.

Names of postmasters, date of appointment and time of service of each official from the first incumbent down to 1912.

The writer obtained the information from the postoffice department at Washington, through the First Assistant Postmaster General. Down to 1843, there was but one postoffice in town, which was, as a matter of course, located in the village. The first appointment was dated, Oct. 1, 1800, Caleb Baldwin, postmaster, and the office became permanently established, Jan. 1, 1801. Caleb Baldwin was one of the town's leading business men: town clerk, from 1800 to 1840; the records remain as a lasting monument to his memory. Newtown's second postmaster was Czar Keeler, appointed, May 29, 1820, holding office 17 years. March 8, 1837, Thomas Blackman was appointed and held office for four years. May 28, 1841, D V. B. Baldwin's appointment was announced, and he held the office about two years. This brings us down to 1843, when trains began running on the Housatonic railroad, one mail each week-day, being carried each way. Henry May the company's agent at Newtown, obtained the appointment of postmaster, and tried the experiment of having the postoffice removed to the depot, to make it more convenient for people living east of the railroad, more especially for the convenience of people living in Sandy Hook. The change did not work and the department at Washington ordered its removal back to Newtown street. Henry May served as postmaster, for a little more than three years. Charles B. Curtis was appointed, serving less than two years, when David H. Johnson, merchant, trading in a store just north of Trinity Rectory, was appointed. His was a short term, his successor, Nathan W. Keeler, being appointed. Keeler was son of Czar Keeler, Newtown's second postmaster. He was a merchant tailor, and ran the office in connection with his trade for three years, when his successor, A. S. Treat, was appointed. Treat was a young lawyer, not of Newtown birth, and received the appointment of postmaster under Millard Fillmore, who had succeeded to the presidency by the death of Zachary Taylor. His tenure of office was brief, for in March, 1843, Franklin Pierce was inaugurated President, and as "to the victor belong the

WILSON M. REYNOLDS

spoils," Jerome Judson, a born Democrat was appointed postmaster which office he held for a little more than eight years. In 1861, Abraham Lincoln was inaugurated President, and Zalmon S. Peck was appointed Newtown's postmaster, April 27, 1861. From that time to the present, the names we are to deal with are those well known to those who have reached or passed middle life. In April, 1867, an assassin's bullet killed the President and Andrew Johnson became his successor. He made radical changes in office, some for and others without cause, and, March 27, 1867, Charles Henry Peck was appointed postmaster, holding office until April, 1869, when, under Grant's administration, Zalmon S. Peck was reappointed, holding office until the incoming of Cleveland, in 1885. Postmaster Z. S. Peck's record is for a longer period than that of any back to the beginning, covering approximately 24 years, less two intervening, when Charles Henry Peck was in the office under Andrew Johnson.

When Grover Cleveland assumed the presidential office, he appointed L. B. Booth postmaster, one of Newtown's later merchants, Nov. 17, 1883. Three of the next four are Newtown born, while the last named has, with his family, been ours by adoption many, many years. John B. Wheeler received appointment, April 20, 1889, serving a four-year term. John J. Northrop's appointment came June 22, 1893, one term under Cleveland's second administration. George F. Duncombe's appointment came May 21, 1897, covering a little more than eight consecutive years. Wilson M. Reynolds, received appointment Oct. 13, 1905, under the Roosevelt administration.

Newtown's postmasters, as given by the First Assistant Postmaster General, Oct. 19, 1912:

Caleb Baldwin, Jan. 1, 1801; Czar Keeler, May 29, 1820; Thomas Blackman, March 8, 1837; D. V. B. Baldwin, May 28, 1841; Henry May, August 15, 1843; Charles B. Curtis, October 23, 1846; David H. Johnson, Jan. 14, 1848; Nathan W. Keeler, Feb. 28, 1850; Amos S. Treat, Jan. 10, 1853; Jerome Judson, June 2, 1853; Zalmon S. Peck, April 27, 1861; Charles H. Peck, March 27, 1867; Zalmon S. Peck, April 26, 1869; Levi B. Booth, Nov. 17, 1885; John B. Wheeler, April 20, 1889; John J. Northrop, June 22, 1893; George F. Duncombe, May 21, 1897; Wilson M. Reynolds, Oct. 13, 1905; Robert Bradley, June 1, 1914.

When the Housatonic railroad was finished so that trains began to run on schedule time, it was plain that new conditions called for two more postoffices in Newtown, one at Cold Spring, the other at Hawleyville. The stage coach must give way to steam. The postoffice department was appealed to and Nov. 10, 1843, one was established at Cold Spring. Edwin Botsford was first postmaster, and held office for six years. His son, Oliver S. Botsford, was his successor in 1849, and held office until the fall of 1883, Austin B. Blakeman being appointed Sept. 28, of that year and holding the office until his successor, Lawrence Taylor, was appointed Nov. 3, 1910. The name Cold Spring was changed to Botsford in the spring of 1883. In 69 years up to Nov. 10, 1912, the office at Botsford had four postmasters:

Edwin Botsford, November 10, 1843; Oliver S. Botsford, January 19, 1849; A. B. Blakeman, September 28, 1883; Lawrence Taylor, November 3, 1910.

The postoffice at Hawleyville was established, March 27, 1844, with Glover Hawley as postmaster, for two years. Levi C. Morris, running a store for dry goods, groceries, etc., was appointed, April 6, 1846, the office was kept open until July 16, 1846, about 100 days, then discontinued and re-established, July 3, 1847, when Josiah B. Fairchild held the office until succeeded by Asa N. Hawley, appointed August 16, 1848, holding office for six years. Daniel Booth Hawley was appointed March 31, 1854, and held office until January, 1880, 26 consecutive years. Robert Millious, appointed Dec. 9, held office until succeeded by F. C. Sanford, appointed Jan. 5, 1883, he was succeeded by Samuel C. Blackman, Sept. 28, 1885, and he by Mary E. Lancaster, appointed July 10, 1889, continuing in office until April 21, 1890. F. C. Sanford was re-appointed, April 21, 1890, to be replaced by Andrew B. Fancher. May 13, 1890, he was succeeded by Edmond C. Platt, Sept. 27, 1901, who still holds the office, 1917.

The last of Newtown postoffices in order of establishment was that for Sandy Hook, April 8, 1862. William Hall was first postmaster, Henry L. Wheeler second appointee, June 14, 1865. He held office until April 16, 1867, when John Judson was appointed, holding office for two years, Ezra Patch, appointed April 29, 1869. His was a four-year term, succeeded by William B. Sniffen, Sept. 3, 1883, but only for two years, supplanted by George Winton, Nov. 23, 1885, under the administration of President Grover Cleveland. He served a four-year term, succeeded by W. B. Sniffen, who was re-appointed April 3, 1889. Thomas J. Bradley succeeded him, June 27, 1893. He was succeeded by the appointment for the third time of W. B. Sniffen, April 6, 1897, who held the office until his death in 1907. Edgar C. Page was appointed postmaster, Feb. 25, 1907, to fill the vacancy caused by death.

Sandy Hook postmasters:

William Hall, April 8, 1862; Henry L. Wheeler, June 14, 1865; John Judson, April 16, 1867; Ezra Patch, April 29, 1869; William B. Sniffen, September 3, 1883; George Winton, November 23, 1885; William B. Sniffen, April 3, 1889; Thomas J. Bradley, June 27, 1893; William B. Sniffen, April 6, 1897; Edgar C. Page, February 25, 1907; Frederick Reiner January, 1916.

Postal Laws and Salaries, 1800—1912.

It is a far-off cry from the stage driver and mail coach, to the mail train and postman of to-day. With a daily mail delivery to every city, town and village in Connecticut and a house-to-house distribution daily (Sundays excepted) to every family in town, where, 100 years ago people counted themselves lucky to have the mail delivered once a week, it is hardly possible to realize the difference between then and now. We need to go back only 100 years to find that Hartford, Norwich, Middletown, New Haven, Litchfield, Danbury and Bridgeport were central points radiating to different points of surrounding country.

From musty files of papers of a century or more ago, there came by patient research information that can be gained in no other way. From a Hartford Courant of a century or so ago, we can show how a net work of mail routes were laid out, so that, before the coming of mail roads, the people throughout the State of Connecticut could feel quite sure of a weekly mail, and a mail once a week was considered reasonable. Sixty-nine hours were allowed for carrying mails between Hartford and New York, 48 hours from Hartford to New London, and in like proportion between other points within the state, no traveling being allowed on Sunday. Gideon Granger, a Connecticut statesman, graduate of Yale in the class of 1787, was appointed by President Jefferson, Postmaster General in 1801, and re-appointed by President Madison in 1809. He made these stipulations for carrying mails for 1809 and 1810:

The Postmaster General may expedite the mails and alter the times of arrival and departure at any time during the continuance of the contracts, he stipulating what he considers to be an adequate compensation for any extra expense that may be occasioned thereby.

Fifteen minutes shall be allowed for opening and closing the mails at all offices where no particular time is specified.

For every thirty minutes delay, unavoidable accidents excepted, in arriving after the time prescribed in any contract, the contractor shall forfeit one dollar and if the delay continues until the departure of any depending mail whereby the mails destined for such depending mail lose a trip, an additional forfeiture of five dollars shall be incurred. And whenever a lost trip ensues from whatever circumstances, the amount to be paid to the contractor for a regular trip is to be deducted from his pay.

Newspapers, as well as letters, are to be sent in the mail and if any person making proposals desires to carry newspapers other than those conveyed in the mail for his own emolument, he must state in his proposals for what sum he will carry with the emolument and for what sum without that emolument.

Should any person making proposals desire an alteration of the times of arrival and departure above specified, he must state in his proposals the alteration desired and the difference they will make in the terms of the contract. Persons making proposals are desired to state their prices by the year. Those who contract will receive their pay quarterly in the months of August, November, February and May, in one month after the expiration of each quarter. No other than a free white person shall be employed to carry the mail. Where the proposer intends to carry the mail in the body of a stage or carriage, he is desired to state it in his proposals.

The Postmaster General reserves to himself the right of declaring any contract at an end whenever one failure happens which amounts to the loss of a trip.

The contract for the above routes are to be in operation on the first day of April next, and are to continue in force for two years.—[Gideon Granger, Postmaster General].

General Postoffice, Washington City, October 31, 1808.

Some of the principal mail routes and schedules in Connecticut in 1809:

From Hartford by Farmington, Harwinton, Litchfield, Washington, New Milford, Danbury, Ridgefield, Salem and Bedford to New York once a week. Leave Hartford every Tuesday at 2 p. m., arrive at Litchfield on Wednesday by 9 a. m. and at New York on Friday by 11 a. m. Returning leave New York every Friday at 6 p. m., arrive at Danbury on Saturday at 8 p. m., at New Milford on Monday by 9 a. m., at Litchfield by 6 p. m., and at Hartford by 10 a. m. on Tuesday.

From Litchfield by Cornwall and Sharon to Poughkeepsie once a week. Leave Litchfield every Wednesday at 2 p. m., arrive at Sharon by 7 p. m., and at Poughkeepsie on Thursday by 2 p. m. Leave Poughkeepsie on Thursday at 5 p. m. and arrive at Litchfield on Saturday by noon.

From Middletown by Middle Haddam, East Haddam and Haddam to Saybrook, once a week. Leave Middletown every Friday at 4 a. m. and arrive at Saybrook by 5 p. m. Leave Saybrook every Saturday at 4 a. m., and arrive at Middletown by 6 p. m.

From New Haven by Woodbridge, Waterbury and Watertown to Litchfield once a week. Leave Litchfield every Friday at 6 a. m. and arrive at

New Haven by 3 p.m. Leave New Haven every Friday at 5 p.m. and arrive at Litchfield on Saturday by 3 p.m.

From Danbury by South East, Franklin, Pawling, Dover, Kent, Sharon, Salisbury, Sheffield, Great Barrington, Stockbrige, Lenox, Pittsfield, Lanesboro, Williamstown and Pownal to Bennington once a week. Leave Danbury every Saturday at 9 p.m. and arrive at Pittsfield on Monday at 7 p.m. and arrive at Bennington the next Tuesday by 7 p.m. Leave Bennington on Monday at 5 a.m and arrive at Pittsfield by 8 p.m. Leave Pittsfield on Tuesday at 5 a.m and arrive at Danbury the next Wednesday by 7 p.m.

From Bridgeport by Trumbull, Huntington, Newtown, Brookfield to New Milford once a week. Leave Bridgeport every Tuesday at 2 p.m. and arrive at New Milford every Wednesday at 6 a.m. and arrive at Bridgeport on Thursday by 10 a.m.

Enough has been given to show the carrying out of mail delivery among the cities and towns of a State, a method that remained intact until the coming of the railroads and transportation of mail by steam.

Mrs Johnson's maternal grandfather, Rhesa Foote, born in Newtown in 1781, had as one of his boy companions, Lewis Peck. In school and out of school, they were boon companions and as they grew to man's estate they were to each other as Damon and Pythias, almost inseparable. In seeking their life work, they became separated, one going to North Carolina, the other remaining in Newtown. A long correspondence was kept up and we have many letters that passed between them, bearing dates of 1801, 1802, 1803, letters written on fool's-cap paper, bearing with the address, in large figures of red chalk, the numbers, "25 cts." "50 cts.," as the size of the package might be, one sheet 25c, two sheets, 50c postage. Postage paid by the receiver of the letter.

We will give the rates of postage established by Congress in 1806. There were two rates, one for letters and newspapers carried by land and the other for the same rate of postage when carried by packet boat, property of the United States and two cents extra when carried by private vessels.

For letters conveyed by land, single, double and triple, not exceeding 40 miles, 8c; over 40 miles and not exceeding 90, 10c; over 90 and not exceeding 150, 12 1-2c; over 150 and not exceeding 300, 17c; over 300 and not exceeding 500, 20c; over 500 miles, 25c. Double letters are double, and triple letters triple, these rates. A packet of the weight of one ounce, at the rate of four single letters and in like proportion for one of greater weight. No allowance being made for intermediate mails. Single letters passing by sea in packet boats, the property of the United States, 8c each; double letters 16c and triple letters, 24c. All letters or packets by private vessels at two cents each with the addition of postage, if destined to any other place than where the vessel may arrive. No vessel can be permitted to report, make entry or break bulk, until the master has delivered to the postmater all the letters brought in his vessel, except those for the owner or consignee.

Postage on Newspapers: Each paper carried not over 100 miles, one cent, and over 100 miles, one and one-half cent; but if carried to any postoffice in the state in which it is printed, whatever be the distance, the postage is only one cent. Magazines and pamphlets are rated by the sheet; any distance not exceeding 50 miles, one cent; over 50 and not exceeding 100 miles, two cents."

No trouble in making change for the half-cent, for half-cents were coined in those days. Some will be interested in being told the source from which the writer found the rates of postage in force when the postoffice was established, which has its proper place in this article. The writer has in his possession a file of Almanacs, in their completeness from the year 1762 to the year 1884. From the year 1800 to the year 1884, every change made in in the postal laws is sure to be found in the almanacs in use under date of the year in which a change came, and so it is that the copy issued in the year 1806 contains the postage laws as they were first issued.

The writer gives information from a group of pamphlets that had the beginning of growth with his maternal ancestors, 150 year ago.

Rates of postage established by Acts of Congress passed March 3, 1825: "For a single letter, composed of one piece of paper for any distance not exceeding 30 miles, 6c; over 30 miles and not exceeding 80 miles, 10c; over 80 and not exceeding 150 miles 12 1-2c; over 150 and not exceeding 400 miles 18 3-4 cents; over 400 miles 25c. Double letters, double rates; triple letters, triple those rates. Letters composed of four pieces of paper, quadruple those rates. The net amount of postage from the postoffices in Connecticut for the year ending March 31, 1827, under the above rates as reported in the state register for the year 1829 was $30,160.13.—[Gideon Granger, Postmaster-General. Washington.]

Net amount of postage received from the Newtown postoffice for the year ending March 31, 1827, was $60.80.

By act of Congress in 1852, rates of postage were changed, on letters not exceeding a half ounce to 5 cents for 500 miles and to 10 cents on letters over half and not exceeding an ounce. In 1858, rates of postage on single letters weighing not over half an ounce for not exceeding 3000 miles, 3 cents, prepaid by stamps. Over 3000 miles 6c. Double weight, double postage. Postmasters' compensation by law of 1854, on any sum not exceeding $100, 60 per cent, and, in offices where the mails arrive regularly between 9 o'clock at night and 5 in the morning, 70 per cent on the first $100. On any sum over $100 and not exceeding $400, 50 per cent; over $400 and not exceeding $2,400, 40 per cent; and on all sums over $2,400, 15 per cent. In 1864 the rate of postage on letters of a half ounce was changed to three cents any distance within the United States prepaid with stamps, to take effect, July 1, 1865. In 1884 postage on one-half ounce letters was made two cents and still remains so.* When salary was based on percentage of receipts, salaries paid at different offices in Newtown, gathered by the writer from a personal study of public documents in the Connecticut State Library at Hartford.

Salaries of postmasters in Newtown Street:
1816 $35.01, 1822 $53.52, 1824, $61.57, 1828 $65.17, 1830 62.71, 1832 $78.75, 1835 $132.73, 1838 $160.90, 1841 $169.77, 1845 $190.84, 1849 $279.69, 1851 $419.96, 1855 $448.26, 1859 $437.89, 1863 $444.90, 1865 $447.65, 1879 $580.87, 1881 $609.40, 1883 625.71, 1887 $756.17, 1889 $892.92, 1893 $979.69, 1895 $959.82, 1897 $922.43, 1899 $934.86, 1901 $1000.00, 1903 $979.69, 1905 $1000.00.

Business at the postoffice in Newtown Street so increased that the postmaster's salary is $1300 and the salary of each of the two rural carriers $990.

The postoffice in Sandy Hook is a salaried office of $1000 and sends out two rural delivery clerks, $990 each.

Hawleyville postoffice has increased its business, so that, from a salary of $16.95 per year in 1845, its receipts at the present time warrant a salary of about $800, and it sends out a rural delivery clerk on a salary of $1100.

*NOTE: Since the Government has increased letter postage to three cents.

RESTRICTIONS TO DOMESTIC ANIMALS RUNNING UPON COMMON LANDS AND MANNER OF DISPOSAL WHEN UNCLAIMED.

The first 100 years of the town life, horses, cattle, sheep and swine were allowed to run at large on the common or undivided land, owners being held for all damage where they broke into enclosures properly fenced. Each owner must have an ear mark for cattle, sheep and swine, by which he could know his own when found in a mixed herd. To mark horses in that way would be disfigurement of beauty, so a branding iron was used and some letter or mark branded on the shoulder or body of the horse.

A few recorded ear marks from the first volume of Newtown's records, date of 1715. It was necessary that they should be recorded, for so disputes as to ownership could be easily adjusted.

Daniel Foote's ear mark for his creatures is a half penny on ye near side of ye upper side of ye near ear and a nick in ye same between ye half penny and ye top of ye ear.

Joseph Peck's ear mark for his cattle and other creatures is a half penny on ye under side of ye near ear.

Caleb Dayton's ear mark for his creatures is two half pennies upon ye for side of each ear.

Joseph Peck's ear mark for his cattle is two half pennies cut out under ye near ear.

Ebenezer Booth's mark for his creatures is one half penny cut out of ye fore side of right ear.

John Burn's ear mark for his creatures is two slits down ye loop of ye left ear.

Jeremiah Northrop's ear mark for his creatures is a crop off ye right ear and a half penny the fore side of ye same.

Ebenezer Johnson's ear mark for his chattils and other creatures is a crop off ye ear and two slits in ye crop.

Stephen Parmaley's ear mark for his creatures is three nicks cut in ye under side of ye off ear.

John Seeley's ear mark for his creatures is a short slit in ye fore ear, a slit ye under side of ye near ear and a half penny on ye fore side ye same.

James Hard's ear mark for his creatures is two slits in ye near ear and a hole in ye far ear.

Abraham Kimberly was chosen brander of horses and it was voted, that the brander's shop or yard, in which to brand or mark the animals of "horse kind of any sort" should be on his premises. Kimberly's lot was the sixth lot south of the cross highway, on the easterly side of the street. As those lots were laid out 16 rods wide. lot No. 6 was 96 rods south of the road leading toward Sandy Hook, and that highway was laid out to be ten rods wide, each lot being laid out 40 rods in length and 16 rods wide. Swine running at large were most troublesome of all domestic animals and frequent resolutions were passed at town meetings.

Resolution passed at the annual meeting in Dec., 1715:

"At ye aforesaid meeting agreed upon and voted by ye inhabitants that swine shall be at large on ye commons ye years ensuing, that is without yoaking and ringing and if any damage is done by such swine threw ye insufficientness of fence that shall not be judged according to law by ye fence viewers, the owners of such fence are to bare ye damage, but if any swine are taken damage feazent when ye fence is sufficient then ye owners of all such unruly swine shall pay ye pondage and damage according to the law.—Recorded Dec. 27, 1715. Joseph Peck, Clerk."

Dec. 8, 1736, upon ye petition of ye farmers belonging to ye farmers belonging to ye farm called Zoar that they might have liberty to build a pound to impound creatures belonging to other towns that should do them damage in their inclosures. It was voted to grant ye farmers liberty to build themselves a pound upon their own charges for ye end above sd provided ye aforesd farmers impound none of ye creatures belonging to ye inhabitants of Newtown, in their pound.

At a meeting, Dec. 19, 1737, voted ye swine belonging to inhabitants of Newtown shall be free commoners so long as they do no damage and ye owners of ye swine to pay damage where ye fence is good and according to law, and where fence is not good ye owners of such fence are not to recover any damage or poundage, and if such swine be not sufficiently yoked after ye first time they do damage then ye owners to pay all damages after ye first time they do damage.

By sufficiently yoking to be understood nine inches above ye neck, four inches below ye neck, six inches long on each side of ye neck is a grown swine, and proportionally for lesser swine. Swine so yoked not to be deemed damage feazant. This act to continue for two years.

At a town meeting at the south schoolhouse, April 16, 1756: "Voted—Whereas ye law cuts off swine from running at large as free commoners unless ye town shall agree otherwise and finding that ye swine do dig up commons so that it is great demage to ye flock of sheep feeding on sd commons, which to prevent it is further enacted and voted at ye sd meeting that all ye swine belonging to ye inhabitants of Newtown from 10 weeks old and upwards shall be singed of running at large on ye commons by ye tenth day of May next or shall be liable to be pounded according to the law, nothing in this vote or act to be construed otherwise than, that if swine do damage in any man's inclosure ye owner thereof shall be liable to pay all damages.

John Northrop, Town Clerk."

When stray cattle, sheep, swine or horses, were impounded (there were no local newspapers in those days), the town crier went the round to cry or announce the fact. After a space of six months and no one appearing to claim the animal or animals, they were appraised and sold at public auction; if they sold for more than expense incurred, the over-plus went into the treasury of the town.

Newtown, Feb. 23, 1755. On account of ye charges arising upon a mare yt was sold at public vandue at ye sign post. Sold for 20 pounds old tener, ye above sd mare was posted at several neighboring towns as ye law directs and sold per me. Joseph Bristol, constable of Newtown at ye sum above sd.

For crying sd mare, £5; for keeping sd mare, £2 2s 6d; for damage £1; for prizing damage, 15s; for pounding, 6s 8d; for recording, 3s 4d; for silling, 10s; one quart of rum, 12s; clerk's fee for entry, 6s.

Newtown, Nov. 2, 1756, then taken up damages feasant and impounded by Lieutenant Nathaniel Brisco, a brown bayish mare, with a star in her forehead, branded with this figure, (9) on ye right and left shoulder, her right hind foot white, ye above described mare was posted at ye several neighboring towns as ye law directs and sold at public vandue at one pound and six pence per me, William Birtch, constable, ye charge as follows:

Damage, 1s 2d; my fee for travel and vandure, 14s 7d; keeping of mare, 3s; to drummer and poundage, 1s 2d; prizing damage, 4d; clerk's fee, 6d. Total £1 9d.

Newtown, June 7th, 1757, then taken up by James Hard, a gray mare and impounded in Newtown pound, branded on ye right shoulder with a figure 7. No ear mark to be found. The above sd mare was posted at ye several towns as ye law directs and sold at a public vandue at £3, 7s, lawful money per me, William Bristol, Newtown constable.

My fee for travel and posting and selling, 8s; charge for vendue, 2s 1d; poundage and pasture, 5s 11d; drummer's fee for beating ye drum, 9d; ye clerk's fee, 6d; apprisal, £3, 7d; expenses, 17s 3d; overplus, £2, 9s 1d;

Ye mare was sold at ye post, June 27, 1757.

Newtown, July ye 12th, 1757, then taken up by jeremiah Turner, one grey mare about two or three years old and impunded in Newtown pound. No brand mark to be found on her. A small streak of white in ye forehead and a few gray hairs down ye nose. The above sd mare was posted in ye several towns as ye law directs and sold at a public vandue at 3 pounds, 19 shillings lawful money. Sold ye first day of August, 1757, by me William Birtsch, Newtown constable.

My fee for travel, posting and selling sd mare, 9s 5d 2far.; charge of vandue, 2s 4d; poundage and damage, 4s 2d; keeping mare, prizers and administering oath, 2s 8d; to ye drummer for fee for beating ye drum, 9 far. clerk's fee for recording sd mare, £6, 19s, 10d, 2 far.

Newtown, August 17, 1762. Then taken damage feasant by Arnold Glover of Newtown, one grayish mare and impunded in ye Newtown pound, about two or three year old, with a white streak down its face, branded with these letters, II, on ye left shoulder.

Ye above said mare was posted in ye several towns as ye law directs and sold at apublic vandue to George Lemon of Stratford, for £2, 6s, 6d, lawful money per me, William Birtch, Newtown constable.

	£	s	d
The constable's fee for posting and selling	0	10	6
Damage	0	15	0
Poundage and keeping sd mare	0	4	8
For viewing the fence and prizing the damage.	0	5	0
Ye justice's fee for administering oath to prizers	0	0	8
Ye drummers fee and charge of vandue,	0	3	3
Ye Town clerk's fee for recording,	0	0	9
	1	19	8

Ye above sd mare was sold on ye 6th of September, 1762.

Mare sold for	2	6	6
Expense,	1	19	8
Overplus,	0	6	10

Found in ye woods near Gray's Plain in Newtown a two year old steer, reddish, pied on ye back, marked with a swallow fork on ye off ear and one happenny on ye foreside of ye near ear. Sd steer died and was skinned by Ebenezer Peck and recorded, June ye 19th, A. D. 1769, per me, Caleb Baldwin, 3rd, Town Clerk, on ye 20th day of December, 1769. I appointed Jonathan Prindle and Ebenezer Johnson to apprize sd skins and they were sworn by me, Henry Glover, Justice of ye Peace, and they apprized sd skins at 14 shillings lawful money, and ye sd Ebenezer Peck is allowed for his trouble and cost about sd steer ye sum of seven shillings per me, Henry Glover, Justice of ye Peace.

	£	s	d
Ebenezer Peck	0	7	0
Justice fees	0	1	0
Appraisers fees,	0	1	6
Clerk's Fees,	0	1	6
	0	11	0

RESTRICTIONS TO DOMESTIC ANIMALS

Value of sd hide,	0 14 0
Cost,	0 11 0
Overplus	0 3 0

Recorded per me, Caleb Baldwin, ye srd Town Clerk.

Newtown, May ye 21st, 1756. Taken up by Lieut. Joseph Smith of ye parish of Newberry in ye county road from Newtown to New Milford, a leather pouch with thirty shillings of silver and six coppers in sd leather pouch. Entered by me, John Northrop, Town clerk, May ye 28th, 1756. The owners appeared February 4th, 1757, for ye above sd money and received ye same at ye hand of Lieut. Joseph Smith before me, John Northrop, town clerk. Received by Ebenezer Mills and John Mills, sons of law to ye man that lost sd money."

"Newtown, June 19th, 1754, fund in ye highway by Dina Nichols, daughter to Nathaniel Nichols a gold ring without seal to it, with a posey to it, etc. Ye owner appeared for sd ring."

Newtown, May ye 14th, 1767, then found by a child near ye house of Aaron Peck, a spanish mill dollar. The owner may have ye same by laying claim to it as may be thought reasonable.

Aaron Peck.

Received for record, July 10, 1767. Caleb Baldwin, Town Clerk.

Taken upon ye road that leads from Sanford's mill to Zoar near Hard's meadow lot, a square silver shoe buckle with iron fluke and tongue. Sd buckle somewhat worn. Taken up by Lieut. Samuel Griffin, and is in his custody, recorded July 4, 1768, per me, Caleb Baldwin, 3rd Town Clerk. On ye 13th day of January, 1769, I appointed William Burwell and Jabez Baldwin to appraise sd buckle and they were sworn according to law. Sd Burwell and Baldwin appraised sd buckle and set ye value of sd buckle at £0, s3, d1. Sd Griffin is allowed for his trouble 8d.

	£	s	d
Cost Griffin for his trouble,	0	0	8
Justice's fees,	0	0	6
Appraiser's fees,	0	0	8
Clerk's fees,	0	1	0
Total cost,	0	2	10

Taken up as lost goods by Zadock Hard on ye 26th day of April, 1769, a small side of leather about three or four soles cutout of ye but of it, sd leather supposed to be tanned with black oak bark.

Recorded, May ye 8th, 1769, per me Caleb Baldwin, Register.

On ye 8th of November, 1769, I appointed William Burwell and Ephriam Sherman to appraise sd side of leather. Sd Sherman and Burwell were put under oath as ye law directs per me, Caleb Baldwin, Justice of ye Pece and they caled sd leather s5, d, lawful money. The sd Hard is allowed for his trouble about sd leather one shilling.

	£	s	d
Justice's fee,	0	1	0
Two appraisers' fees,	0	0	4
Clerk's fee,	0	1	3
	0	2	7
Value of leather,	0	5	5
Cost,	0	2	7
Overplus	0	2	10

NEWTOWN'S SHEEP INDUSTRY.

An abstract of the work of the assessors in making up the town's grand levy for the year ending Oct. 1, 1911, stated "that in the returns made of taxable property, no sheep were returned as being owned in town."

Although the writer has been conscious of a gradual decline in that source of the farmer's income, he had not thought to live to see the time when there would be no ownership of sheep in Newtown. On the other hand, the report of our town treasurer for the year ending Sept. 1, 1911, showed that for that year, 407 dogs were registered, by which the income of the town was increased by $478. When we have a State law compelling owners of dogs to keep them confined or chained from sundown to sunrise, their havoc among sheep will be less than now. For with dogs, as with lawless bipeds, the great part of their villainous and deadly work is done under cover of darkness. Whether sheep came into town along with horses and cows, we have no way of knowing. It is natural to suppose that at the start all the upland in its virgin loveliness was covered with timber and underbrush, and swamp land would be no ground for sheep. The inference is that, previous to 1800, sheep were kept as one common flock, tended by a shepherd chosen by the town, each owner to pay towards the expense of tending through the season, according to the number owned. The season lasted from early in May, to late in October.

The records are silent in regard to sheep until 1800. Nothing is found on the records showing that they were taxed with live stock, nor were they allowed to go on the commons except under the care of a duly appointed shepherd. At a town meeting held in April, 1732, it was voted "That the Commons should be cleared for the benefit of the flock of sheep where it shall be thought to be most needful by those who are appointed by law to take care of that work." Swine were by vote of the town free commoners when they were "ringed or yoked," and "the selectmen of ye town shall decide whether sd swine are sufficiently yoked or not well yoked." Swine were the most troublesome of all pests to the well-doing of sheep, were much in evidence at the annual town meeting. In 1752. "Voted: Whereas the law cuts off swine from running at large free commons unless the town shall agree otherwise and finding that the swine do dig up the commons so that it is a great damage to the flock of sheep feeding on sd commons destroying much of the grass growing thereon, which to prevent it is further enacted and voted that all the swine belonging to the inhabitants of the town of Newtown, from ten weeks old and upward shall be ringed if running at large on the commons by the tenth of May next, or shall be liable to be pounded according to law."— John Northrop, clerk.

The year following the town appointed Vincent Stillson, Abiel Botsford, Josiah Bardslee, and Silas Camp, they or either of them to impound all swine above two months old that they find on the commons after the 28th day of March, except they be well ringed, giving notice to the owner of the swine, within twelve hours of their being impounded, said vote being for better protection of the sheep. In spite of all precautions, sheep would occasionally stray from the flock and some time might elapse before they would be restored to the owner. The laws of the colony provided for such a contingency and, when stray sheep were brought in, they were duly advertised and held for a specified time. After having been duly appraised, if no owner appeared, they were sold at the sign post, and what the sheep brought, less expenses of keeping, advertising and officers' fees went into the town treasury. If expenses exceeded receipts, the town was so much out. The process of appraisal, of procedure and disposal:

Notice—Taken damage feasant by Thomas Skidmore, Junr., of Newtown, on ye 25th of Dec., 1758, and impounded in Newtown pound, four sheep. One black sheep, marked with a crop on ye near ear and a hole in ye off ear. Two white sheep with a crop on ye off ear and a half-penny under ye seide of ye same ear. One white sheep with a slanting crop on ye near ear and a hole in ye off ear, and I cried ye same in ye several towns as ye law directs and sold them one ye second day of January, 1759, at four of ye clock, afternoon, at ye sign post in Newtown, for four shillings each, sixteen shillings for all four by me, William Birch, constable of Newtown.

Constables fee for crying and selling and all his trouble is 10 shillings; poundage and damage, 4 shillings; the prizer's fee and oath, 1 shilling and 10 pence; charges for keeping sheep, 4 shillings; paid the drummer, 9 pence; cost of vandue, 2 shillings; clerk's fee for recording, 6 pence. Total expense, £1, 3 shillings, 1 pence. Amount from sale of sheep, 16 shillings.

Expenses exceeded the amount for which the sheep sold by seven shillings and one penny.

We do not know how many sheep were numbered in the town in any year previous to 1800.

From 1800 to the present time, sheep appear upon the levy with other domestic animals liable to taxation, so that we find for 1803 the number of sheep listed in Newtown was 4010. The industry continued to be as remunerative as any that farmers could turn their hand to for at least 30 years. In 90 preceding years, the common land had been much improved, highways had been cleaned to some extent and the practice introduced at the outset, of having a common flock tended by a shepherd hired by the season, was kept up as far down as 1830, so that farmers, in addition to sheep kept on their farms, would avail themselves of turning some sheep into the common flock, the number any one man could put in being limited to 30. Shearing time came the latter part of May and at that time the early lambs could be turned off, so that the starting of the common flock came early in June, and the season lasted until the latter part of September, when there came the breaking up of the flock and the return of the sheep to individual owners.

We have no dates to follow previous to 1823. At the opening of each season, a sheep master was appointed, who was expected to hire a shepherd for the season, see to collecting the sheep from the various school districts into one flock, make choice of the most desirable of the common lands for feeding grounds, and make arrangements for yarding the sheep over night where they could have an enclosed field for their night's rest; wherever they stopped. Saturday nights, there they remained over Sunday. Farmers paid for the privilege of keeping the flock over nights and over Sunday, the privilege going to the highest bidder, which was expected to pay the expenses of tending the flock, including the hiring of a shepherd and a boy as a helper. Farmers thought the droppings from the sheep well worth the price paid in securing them to keep, as the droppings made excellent fertilizer for grain crops and especially for rye and wheat. Stopping places were arranged closely enough together to be easily reached in a 10-hour feeding drift.

The late Charles H. Peck, at one time Newtown's town clerk gave much spare time to making a careful study of Newtown's early history. Among the treasures of the early days was an old book called the Sheep Company's record book, which contained the recorded doings of the company's work for 1823, 1824, 1825, 1826 and 1827. Entries have been made from the sheep book, kindly loaned to the writer by its present owner, Arthur T. Nettleton.

A sheep company was organized in June 1823, and continued effective for five succeeding years. The call of the first meeting:

"Warning is hereby given that a meeting of the owners of sheep in the town of Newtown will be held at Mr. Caleb Baldwin's house in said Newtown on Monday, the 9th day of June, 1823, at 6 o'clock in the afternoon, for the purpose of raising a public flock for the ensuing year, appointing officers for said meeting and of doing any business proper to be done at said meeting. Dated at Newtown, June 2, 1823. Moss K. Botsford, sheep-master."

The meeting was duly held and it was voted "That Mr. Benjamin Hard, Esq., should be moderator, Judge Samuel C. Blackman clerk, and that a public flock should be raised for the benefit of owners of sheep, and that Moss K. Botsford should be sheep-master, and that the shepherd should begin to collect the flock on Monday, June 17." It was also voted "that the articles and by laws which were adopted by the proprietors of the flock the last year be adopted as the rules and regulations for the ensuing year." going to show that the existence of the common flock dates back of 1823. They were also to pursue the same route in collecting the flock as the shepherd did the last year, and no person should turn into the flock more than 20 sheep. There were 83 sheep owners who furnished sheep and the flock numbered in its completeness 938. The route laid out for collecting the flock was from Chestnut Tree Hill through Zoar to Ebenezer Beers, thence through Toddy Hill to Caesar's (the old darky) thence through Taunton, Palestine, Land's End and Hanover to Wapping, and thence through Sandy Hook to Newtown Street, which point it was expected could be reached inside of eight days. Of course the flock must feed along the route, as they were drifting toward their round-up, must also lie by for rest over Sunday, besides being delayed more or less by those who not living on the direct line of the drift, did not reach a station on time. The flock once formed, the shepherd, under the supervision of the sheepmaster, was ready to start out on the season's tour. A boy accompanied the shepherd and they had their keep over night and Sundays wherever the flock was yarded. In figuring expenses of the flock, it was expected that farmers would pay enough for the privilege of having the flock yarded on some plot on which they wanted to raise rye or wheat, the following season, that the amount received would not only pay all flock expenses, but return a small dividend for the owners. The records give the names of sheep owners, the expenses of tending the flock during the season, the money paid by farmers for the privilege of keeping the sheep nights and over Sunday, and the net returns, if any, to owners of the sheep. Also a tabulated account of the nightly and over-Sunday receipts, with the names of those who were highest bidders for the chance of securing the sheep when out on the drift.

Number of sheep put into the flock by each individual, June 1823:
Caleb Baldwin 9, Philo Baldwin 10 Samuel C. Blackman 20, Alfred Blackman 1, Thomas B. Botsford 10, Moss K. Botsford 19, Henry Botsford 7, Clement Botsford 10, Jabez B. Botsford 13, Moses Botsford 20, Daniel Botsford, Jr., 20, Israel C. Botsford 20, Theophilus Botsford 20, William Botsford 3, Ebenezer Beers Jr. 9, Abel Beers 20, Ester Beers 4, Joseph Booth 6, James G. Blackman 5, Joseph Blackman 20, Daniel Blackman 9, Daniel Baldwin 7, **Thaddeous Bennitt 5,** James Bennitt 14, Harry Glover 2, David and Henry Glover 27, Benjamin Hard 16, Cyrus Hard 10, Abijah Hard 5, Abner Judson Jr. 6, Peter Lewis 18, James Nichols & Co. 29, Abner A. Nettleton 12, Oliver Northrop 14, Andrew Northrop 9, David C. Peck 20, Isaac Peck 10, Dan Peck 10, Enos and Wooster Peck 12, Samuel Peck 9, Ephraim Platt, 15, Marcus H. Parmalee 6, Abel Stilson 9, Richard D. Shepherd 8, Ammon Shepherd 5, David Shipman 17, Wooster Sherman 5, Truman Sherman 8, Brace Smith 6, Joseph Tousey 9, Abel Bennitt 7, James W. Bennitt 7, Simon M. Beers 15, Abijah B. Curtis 20, Elihue S. Curtis 20, Epinetus Curtis 20, Gould Curtis 11, Zachariah Clark Jr. 20, James Clark 14, Stephen Crofut 10, Squire Dibble 13, Eleazer Dibble 6, Kiah B. Fairchild 9, Hawley Fairchild 6, Ezra Fairchild 9, Levi Fairchild 7, Philo Fairchild 9, Clement Fairchild 11, Adoniram Fairchild 13, Josiah Fairchild 9, Joseph Fairchiild 7, Josiah Glover 17, Abiel B. Glover 17, Andrew Wheeler 6, Herman Warner 12, Amos Wells 3, Ephraim P. Wetmore 4, Jerod Botsford 12, Ezra Sherman 8, James Nichols 10. Whole number of sheep in the flock, 1823, 938.

The privilege of keeping the flock over night and over Sunday was sold at auction by the sheepmaster to the highest bidder. Names of those in the bidding; the demand for the sheep's keep was so popular that, in some instances, the same farmer secured several chances:

1823		Price each night.	To whom keep of sheep was sold.
June	18, Wednesday,	$1.07	Abel Stillson.
	19, Thursday,	1.12	Daniel Botsford, Jr.
	20, Friday,	1.21	Abel Stillson.
	21, Saturday,		Adoniram Fairchild.
	22, Sunday,	1.60	" "
	23, Monday,	1.38	Henry Glover.
	24, Tuesday,	1.10	Zachariah Clark, Esq.
	25, Wednesday,	1.20	Henry Botsford.
	26, Thursday,	1.54	Daniel Blackman, Esq.
	27, Friday,	1.28	Zachariah Clark, Jr., Esq.
	28, Saturday,		Zachariah Clark, Jr., Esq.
	29, Sunday,	2.25	Zachariah Clark, Jr., Esq.
	30, Monday	1.77	Joseph Fairchild.
July	1, Tuesday,	1.83	Henry Glover.
	2, Wednesday,	1.77	Henry Botsford.
	3, Thursday,	1.77	Israel C. Botsford.
	4, Friday,	1.75	Capt. Henry Glover.
	5, Saturday,		Capt. Henry Glover.
	6, Sunday,	2.77	Henry Botsford.
	7, Monday,	1.82	Daniel Botsford, Jr.
	8, Tuesday,	1.76	Daniel Blackman, Esq.
	9, Wednesday,	1.79	Joseph Booth.
	10, Thursday,	1.84	Daniel Botsford, Jr.
	11, Friday,	1.83	Capt. Philo Baldwin.
	12, Saturday.		Capt. Philo Baldwin.
	13, Sunday,	2.74	James Nichols.
	14, Monday,	1.80	Wooster Peck.
	15, Tuesday,	1.90	Ziba Glover.
	16, Wednesday,	1.91	Wooster Peck.
	17, Thursday,	1.92	Moss K. Botsford.
	18, Friday,	1.91	James G. Blackman.
	19, Saturday,		James G. Blackman.
	20, Sunday,	2.93	Isaac Peck, Jr.
	21, Monday,	1.92	Theophilus Botsford.
	22, Tuesday,	1.76	James G. Blackman.
	23, Wednesday,	1.75	Benjamin Hard, Esq.

	24, Thursday,	1.73	Abel Stillson.
	25, Friday,	1.63	Abel Stillson.
	26, Saturday,		Abel Stillson.
	27, Sunday,	2.31	Cyrus Hard.
	28, Monday,	1.52	Cyrus Hard.
	29, Tuesday,	1.18	Zachariah Clark, Jr., Esq.
	30, Wednesday,	1.18	Zachariah Clark, Jr., Esq.
	31, Thursday,	1.30	Charles Botsford.
Aug.	1, Friday,	1.29	Zachariah Clark, Jr., Esq.
	2, Saturday,		Zachariah Clark, Jr., Esq.
	3, Sunday,	1.85	Zachariah Clark, Jr., Esq.
	4, Monday,	1.31	Daniel Blackman, Esq.
	5, Tuesday,	1.34	Joseph Toucey.
	6, Wednesday,	1.33	Joseph Toucey.
	7, Thursday,	1.33	Cyrus Hard.
	8, Friday,	1.35	Zachariah Clark, Jr., Esq.
	9, Saturday,		Israel C. Botsford.
	10, Sunday,	2.25	Israel C. Botsford.
	11, Monday,	1.40	James G. Blackman.
	12, Tuesday,	1.38	Cyrus Hard.
	13, Wednesday,	1.43	John Beers.
	14, Thursday,	1.44	Jabez B. Botsford.
	15, Friday,	1.45	Abel Stillson.
	16, Saturday,		Theophilus Botsford.
	17, Sunday,	2.26	Theophilus Botsford.
	18, Monday,	1.49	Moss K. Botsford.
	19, Tuesday,	1.55	James Clark.
Aug.	20, Wednesday	1.58	James Clark.
	21, Thursday,	1.60	Philo Fairchild.
	22, Friday,	1.61	Dan Peck.
	23, Saturday,		Israel C. Botsford.
	24, Sunday,	2.50	Israel C. Botsford.
	25, Monday,	1.61	Abel Stillson.
	26, Tuesday,	1.94	Amariah Beers
	27, Wednesday,	2.00	James Nichols.
	28, Thursday,	2.01	James Bennitt.
	29, Friday,	2.04	Capt. James Nichols.
	20, Saturday,		Theophilus Botsford.
	31, Sunday,	3.03	Theophilus Botsford.
Sept.	1, Monday,	2.00	Philo Fairchild.
	2, Tuesday,	2.01	Daniel Botsford, Jr.
	3, Wednesday,	2.00	Capt. James Nichols.
	4, Thursday,	1.97	Jabez B. Botsford.
	5, Friday,	1.95	Capt. James Nichols.
	6, Saturday,		Isaac Peck, Jr.
	7, Sunday,	2.88	Isaac Peck, Jr.
	8, Monday,	1.97	Joseph Booth.
	9, Tuesday,	1.93	Abel Stillson.
	10, Wednesday,	2.06	Joseph Tousey.
	11, Thursday,	2.00	Joseph Tousey.
	12, Friday,	1.99	Joseph Booth.
	13, Saturday,		Capt. Henry Glover.
	14, Sunday,	2.76	Capt. Henry Glover.
	15, Monday,	1.89	David C Peck.
	16, Tuesday,	1.36	Abel Stillson.
	17, Wednesday,	1.39	Capt. James Nichols.
	18, Thursday,	1.35	Andrew Northrop.
	19, Friday,	1.40	Andrew Northrop.
	20, Saturday,		Andrew Northrop.
	21, Sunday,	2.42	Andrew Northrop.
	22, Monday,	1.46	Abel Stillson.
	23, Tuesday,	1.58	David C. Peck.
	24, Wednesday,	1.61	Joseph Turney.
	25, Thursday,	1.80	Israel C. Botsford.

Weekly amounts received from farmers for the privilege of yarding the sheep nights and Sundays for 1823:

June 23,	$6.38
June 30,	9.34
July 7,	11.71
July 14,	11.76
July 21,	12.49
July 28,	10.70
August 4,	8.00
August 11,	9.00
August 18,	9.45
August 25,	10.45
September 1,	12.98
September 8,	12.78
September 15,	12.63
September 22,	9.38
September 25,	4.99
	$152.15

Expenses of keeping the flock.

Baldwin & Beers, bill for salt,	$ 4.41
Caleb Baldwin's bill for salt,	4.93
Caleb Baldwin, for three dinners,	.75
Shepherd's bill for himself and boy, 3 months and 7 days,	48.75
Sheep-master's bill for services,	6.00
Clerk's fees,	3.75
Inspecting committee, 50c each,	1.50
Auditing committee, 2 shillings each,	1.00
Peter Lewis' bill,	1.29
Committee's expenses,	.50
Clerk's fee, making out dividend,	.36
	$75.24

Amount paid by farmers for the privilege of yarding sheep.	$152.15
Deduct expenses	75.24
	$ 76.91
No. of sheep	938
Overplus	$76.91

Dividend per head per season .082 each

In compliance with the by-laws of the organization, Capt. Moss K. Botsford was ordered to pay a dividend on sheep entered in the public flock, conformable to the by-laws of said flock and awarded by a committee appointed for that purpose, when the flock of 1823 was disbanded.

For 1824, Daniel Blackman was chosen sheepmaster and any sheep owner was allowed to put in any number of sheep, not exceeding 30, all other regulations were to be followed as for the year previous. The sheepmaster was to employ Caesar to tend the sheep, at $12 a month, if not to be had at lower price. It was voted, that every school district have their sheep collected with the following:

James Clark, Philo Beers, Daniel Botsford, Jr., Nathan Johnson, Jacob Beers, Hezekiah Northrop, Zachariah Clark, for the first night: Nirom Fairchild, Esq., Zadock Fairchild, Baldwin Botsford, Henry Beers, David C. Peck, Theophilus Botsford, for the second night; and finish the third night with Curtis Glover, Abijah B. Curtis, Philo Curtis. Then to start from Chestnut Tree Hill, on Wednesday morning through Zoar to Ebenezer Beers, thence through Toddy Hill to Caesar's thence through Mile Hill to Dan Peck's thence through Huntingtown, Palestine, Flat Swamp, thence through Taunton, Currituck, Land's End and Hanover to Wapping, thence through Sandy Hook to the Street, Friday night. The season lasted from June 18, to Sept. 26. At the season's close, the finanical standing of the flock was looked into and found to be

Bills allowed by the auditing committee, Sept. 23, 1824	
Caleb Baldwin's bill,	$ 6.89
Baldwin & Beers, for salt,	.25
A. B. Glover, for salt,	2.54
Ceasar's bill as shepherd, for 3 months and 8 days,	29.25
Thomas Lakes' son assistant,	9.75
Extra pay, Zera Blackman,	1.67
Inspecting committee,	1.50
Auditing committee,	1.33
Clerk's bill,	3.75
Sheep-master's bill,	4.75
Cash collected,	1.58
	$73.26
Received from farmers for yarding the sheep,	$96.73
Expenses of flock,	73.26
	$23.47

Divided per head on 620 sheep for the season 3c, 5mills.

For 1825, Daniel Blackman was appointed sheepmaster. Ned Booth was hired as shepherd at $10 a month and a shepherd's boy for $3.00 a month. Owners were allowed 30 sheep in the flock under the same rules and regulations as in the previous year. The flock numbered 497.

Received from farmers for yarding sheep, $72.05, expense of caring for flock, $55.73, balance due sheep owners, $16.32.

Dividend per head on 497 sheep, 3c and 2 mills, which Daniel Blackman, sheepmaster, is ordered to pay to the sheep owners of the flock of 1825.

In 1826, Daniel Blackman was again chosen sheepmaster, and the route for collecting the flock was changed. It was to commence in Newtown Street, thence through Slut's Hill and Taunton and to Esquire Clark's and through the lower part of the town and around through Mile Hill to Daniel Botsford's Jr., thence through Zoar, Wapping, Sandy Hook and by Major Curtis' and through Hanover to Theophilus Botsford's. Thomas Green was hired for shepherd at $10 a month, and a Shepherd's boy for $4 a month. Received from farmers for yarding, $73.37, expenses of the flock for the season, $67.53, balance due sheep owners $5.84.

The flock numbered 740, and a dividend of seven mills per head was declared at the end of the season.

For 1827, David Blackman was chosen sheepmaster and Thomas Green was hired as shepherd at $16 a month and furnish himself with a boy helper. It was also voted that the person who should keep the flock over Saturday night and Sunday should furnish a sufficient quantity of salt, not exceeding 12 quarts. Expense of the flock for season of 1827, was $70.34, amount received from farmers for yarding, $70.34. Expenses and receipts balanced and there were no dividends to declare.

There is every reason to presume that the year 1827 marked the disbanding of the common flocks, as the record book contains no further entries.

It was the duty of the sheepmaster to have the managing of the flock. It was the shepherd's part to take care of the flock from its formation to the close of the season, and until the flock should be disbanded. In forming the flock, each sheep owner had some distinctive mark by which he could identify his own, when the time for disbanding came. The usual way for marking sheep and cattle, was by slits, notches or holes cut in or out of the ears. Almost an endless variety of changes could be made in making the markings of one sheep to differ from those of any other.

When orders went out from the sheepmaster for disbanding the flock, the shepherd's orders were to make the final round-up at Caleb Baldwin's in Newtown Street, for, as the city of Boston is still looked upon as the Hub of the universe, Caleb Baldwin's place was looked upon as the central point around which revolved the little Newtown world, with its eight miles square.

The tavern with its ample surroundings, was kept open as a public house, where north and southbound and east and westbound stages stopped for horses to rest, and passengers for mid-day meals. It was also the central point for the stopping of drovers with cattle, horses and sheep, on cross-country trips and brought much trade and exchange along those lines. So it came about that Caleb Baldwin's tavern was made the gathering of sheep owners for the breaking up on the season's flock. The house, in all its old-time beauty, is now the home of Charles F. Beardsley and family.

After 1800, sheep went on the grand levy at a valuation of 75c per head. Though sheep were included with other stock when lists were handed in, the sheep tax was abated, no doubt to encourage farmers to raise more sheep. Up to within 60 years, dogs were very little trouble to sheep, nor were dogs half as plenty as now.

Our town clerk, says that no sheep have been entered on Newtown's grand levy since 1900, and from that fact we assume that the demise of Newtown's sheep industry dates from that year. The rapid decline in the number of sheep began about 1860. That was about the time that the satinet factory, run first by Beecher & Tucker, and later by Alva B. Beecher alone, closed out the business and spoiled the home market for wool. There can be no doubt but what that and the increasing destructiveness of dogs among sheep had much to do with the discontinuance of Newtown's sheep industry.

Our good town clerk, Oscar Pitzschler, courteously made it possible for me to have access to the grand levies from 1802 to 1900, a period of 98 years; most surprising it is that, for that long stretch of time, so few of the grand levies are missing.

Number of sheep returned to the board of assessors yearly from 1802 to 1900: years not filled out being because levies for those years have not been found:

Year	Sheep	Year	Sheep	Year	Sheep
1802	3800	1835	2469	1868	757
1803	4016	1836	2683	1869	481
1804	3386	1837	2584	1870	290
1805	3264	1838	2500	1871	255
1806	3591	1839	2558	1872	312
1807	3452	1840	2790	1873	376
1808	3458	1841	2825	1874	397
1809	3977	1842	2816	1875	423
1810	4145	1843		1876	417
1811	3803	1844	2215	1877	453
1812	3998	1845	2102	1878	541
1813	3871	1846	1933	1879	530
1814		1847	1384	1880	663
1815		1848	1510	1881	650
1816	2905	1849	1361	1882	500
1817	2834	1850	1419	1883	450
1818	3162	1851	1560	1884	436
1819		1852	1659	1885	465
1820		1853	1504	1886	383
1821		1854	1525	1887	349
1822	3300	1855	1634	1888	201
1823	3250	1856	1400	1889	264
1824	3400	1857	1290	1890	230
1825	3550	1858	1158	1891	228
1826	3684	1859	1103	1892	189
1827	3576	1860	820	1893	162
1828	3104	1861	731	1894	153
1829	2551	1862	658	1895	170
1830	2379	1863	810	1896	116
1831	2489	1864	845	1897	116
1832	2685	1865	840	1898	89
1833	2376	1866	830	1899	117
1834		1867	835	1900	50

GOD'S ACRE

In our town are 13 cemeteries, all, except one or two, still in use, and may be spoken of as well kept. The oldest of all is that part of the village cemetery known as the "town plot" at the southerly end, containing one and a half acres, which was set apart March 24, 1711, by a vote of the townsmen as a place in which to bury their dead. It lay in its virgin condition until the following year, when by action of the town, Dec. 9, 1712, it was voted that "Stephen Parmely shall have the use of one acre and a half of land which is the burying place for our dead, provided he clear the land of brush and sow it with English grass seed." The plot lay open to the commons until March, 1769, when the town voted that "Mr. John Chandler shall have the liberty to fence the burying ground for pasture so long as he will keep it in good fence.

The plot alluded to is the south part of the village cemetery. In "the old plot" the dust of ancestors of some of us has lain undisturbed for nearly 200 years. As we wander among the graves of those removed, long years gone by, from life's tempestuous sea, we instinctively step lightly and walk softly among the old headstones, or tread on turf that covers scores of unmarked graves, wherein, with brain no longer busy and hands that long since rested from labor, they lie unmindful of the tide of human life that ebbs and flows about them.

The many inscriptions to be found are interesting, not only in device, but in composition and expression. Newtown's first physician lies buried here. Lemuel Thomas, "a skillful and useful practioner of surgery and physics, who departed this life September 30, A. D. 1775, aged 48 years." The four ministers who officiated in Newtown during the first century of the town's history lie buried near each other. Each was a graduate of Yale college and with each, Newtown was their first and only charge. First was Rev. Thomas Toucey, born in Wethersfield in 1688, resigning his charge in 1724 and died in 1761. Rev. John Beach, immediate successor of Rev. Mr. Toucey, was born in 1700, was in charge of the Presbyterian body until 1732, then resigned and was admitted to Holy Orders in the Church of England, appointed missionary at Newtown and Redding, and was such until in 1782 he died. Rev. John Beach's colaborer in Newtown from 1743 to 1776, was Rev. David Judson, minister over the Presbyterian body. He was born in 1715, served the people until September, 1776, and in that month he died. Rev.

Philo Perry, successor of Rev. John Beach, was born in Woodbury in 1752, settled over Trinity in 1787; died in 1798 and was also buried in the old plot. These four men, who served in the office of the sacred ministry during the first century of the town's history, were all buried among those whom they loved and served so well.

Though surrounded in God's Acre by scores of graves containing the dust of those to whom they ministered, there is a bit of pathos to think that none of their kindred are buried beside them, save in the case of Rev. Mr. Judson where a little headstone marks the grave of his son David, who died in 1749, age one year, six months and 20 days and a little daughter, Mary, age seven years and 20 days. Newtown's first physician and its first four ministers were from among the early graduates of Yale college and must have been men of more than ordinary ability. We have spoken of the "old plot." A few words of the village cemetery as it is to-day. The old plot served its purpose for about 130 years; then came enlargement on the north and later two other accessions of land by purchase. A cemetery association was formed, under whose faithful services, gratuitously rendered, its well kept grounds will compare favorably with those of any country town.

In 1748 the people in the north part of the town petitioned to have a plot of ground laid out for a burying ground and the town voted, "that the people living in ye northwest part of ye township of Newtown, upon their desire should have 60 rods of land for a burying place to bury their dead in, at a place northerly or from Benjamin Hawley's dwelling house, first bounds is heap of stones in the line of Caleb Baldwin's land, then run southerly six rods to a heap of stones, then westerly 11 rods, joing to the main highway thenr un northerly five rods to first bounds laid out by us.—Joseph Bristol Lemuel Camp, committee."

In that burying place, Land's End, stands a headstone that marks the grave of Jeremiah Turner, the first white child born in Newtown, says the inscription. With this cemetery, as with all in constant use, the grounds have been enlarged and in the care everything is done with excellent taste.

Next in order to the cemetery at Land's End came that at "Zoar Farm" so called. "On May 6, 1767, Samuel Adams of Newtown sold a half acre of land for one pound, sixteen shillings and nine pence to Benjamin Curtis. Zachariah Clark, John Adams, Moses Platt, Abel Botsford, Abner Hard, Theophilus Nettleton, John Beach, Benjamin Curtis, Jr., Nehemiah Curtis, Henry Glover, Ja., Nathaniel Mallory, John Sherman, Josiah Platt, Abijah Curtis and Josiah Beardsley, for a burying place in the farm called Zoar." In 1770, the town of Newtown generously voted, in town meeting assembled, "that the farm called Zoar, shall have the old burying cloth, and that the town shall proceed to procure a new one for the use of the town, and the selectmen shall procure a new burying cloth as they shall have opportunity."

The cemetery has been twice enlarged and in neatness and artistic adornment shows well for the loving care of those whose loved ones are there. (Now called Berkshire)

In 1787 the people at Taunton farms wanted one for their neighborhood and the town records show that on "November 24, 1787, Joseph Foote sold 24 square rods of ground, which with the 40 square rods sold two days previously by Hezekiah Daton to the same parties for 30 shillings formed the nucleus for Taunton Cemetery."

Dec. 28, 1787, Joseph Griffin sold to Samuel Griffin, Gamaliel French and others 48 square rods of ground "for the sole purpose of a burying ground so long as it should be used for that purpose." and that is the Huntingtown cemetery, since twice enlarged.

The land for the Sandy Hook cemetery was sold by Abijah Merritt to David Meeker, Abijah B. Curtis and Marcus Botsford, selectmen of Newtown, for $60.00, containing a half acre, more or less, and be used as a public burying ground and for no other purpose.

There are two cemetery plots in Flat Swamp district, near the school house. One on an open knoll was given by Philo Toucey abuot 1800. He lived nearby and intended it for a family burying ground, and it so remained for a term of years. Later, the bodies were removed to our village cemetery. A few head stones still remain, but there is now but one body which bore the Toucey name. The older plot nearby, on a triangular piece of ground between three roads, dates back of 1800, but we gather no facts as to its history and it is no longer in use.

In Half Way River district, there is what is known as the Bradleyville cemetery.

In Hopewell is a cemetery, an acre or so in extent, that joins the Redding line.

A small cemetery, too, in Palestine, near Morgan's Four Corners, for the family of Platt of which there were many in the early days.

There used to be a few graves marked by headstones beside the highway on a cross road leading from Hopewell to Gregory's Orchard, but, while on a prospecting tour along that way, I found that brush had been cut, a stone wall built, the headstones had all disappeared, and I was told they had been put in the renovated stone wall. It came at once to my mind, "Cursed be he that removeth his neighbor's landmark and all the people shall say Amen."

The burying ground at Cold Spring was enclosed about 1825, by Capt. Henry Botsford for family use, the first burial in which was his own son, who died in 1829. Later, by free will of Capt. Botsford it was opened for a public burial place.

In the order of organization of the several cemeteries in Newtown, St. Rose's cemetery comes last. In September, 1860, Peter Nash sold to Rev. Frances J. Lenihan two acres of land in Pootatuck district for $200. It was at once consecrated for use. In 1892 soon after the coming of Rev. Patrick Fox, another purchase was made by St. Rose by which the ground has been much enlarged. It is beautifully located in the Glen, the part of town most noted for scenic beauty and grandeur, where mountain, river, hill and valley blend in one harmonious whole, and where the evergreen in its profusion speaks of immortality and the never-ending life. In the cemetery is a marble slab that marks the burial place of Mary Cain, who died Sept. 7, 1860, and on the back of the slab is inscribed "she was the first one buried in this cemetery." The location of the cemetery is fine and its natural surroundings most beautiful.

We anticipate the question, "What was the burying cloth and what was its use?" In my early childhood, it was the custom in the several towns to depend upon some one person skilled in handicraft, to make coffins. No stock of coffins was kept, but as deaths occurred, dimensions were obtained and the coffin made. Lumber obtained from our native woods was used. Willow, poplar or chestnut was preferred. In shape, tapering at each end, but wider at the proper place to accommodate the elbows, stained and varnished, the initials of the name and years of age, made with round headed brass tacks. The maker of the coffin was expected to attend at the burial. Before the advent of the hearse the coffin was carried in a straight box farm wagon, with the "burying cloth" of black broadcloth, furnished by the town, spread over the coffin. No handles were used at the time, and, from the entrance to the cemetery, the coffin was carried to the grave on a hand bier. No box for coffins had then come in use. The coffin was lowered into the grave, a bundle of straw spread over it and the earth then shoveled upon it. The expenses for burial, including coffin and everything, would be from $3 to $15.

INSCRIPTIONS AND EPITAPHS
From Old Headstones on the "Town Plot of Newtown Cemetery.

Some effort has been made to make choice of particular cases, and to take inscriptions from those that date up to 1800. It is a matter of surprise that the number of headstones that date back of 1800 is comparatively small, and that none have as yet been found that date back of 1741, as the plot was set apart for a burying ground in 1711. Some of the earliest burials might have been at Milford, Derby or Stratford, places from which the settlers came, and some graves might not have had headstones, yet for all that it does seem though there might have been a number that would date back of 1741. One dislikes to believe it due to vandalism, although from the writer's personal knowledge, there was time when a certain stone mason (now dead) was caught leveling up a foundation for a monument, by taking an old headstone from its place and breaking it up. Caught in the act, he was told that if ever caught at it again he would be prosecuted. Being one to whom a penny seemed as large as a cart wheel, we presume the threat had the desired effect. Those moss-covered headstones, standing, as most of them have, for more than 150 years, are still a silent reminder of those who long since preceded us and, as we are doing, generations now unborn will pause at your headstone and mine. and wander still farther among these same old headstones with the quaint inscriptions that interest us so much to-day.

Beneath, the dust
of Sueton Grant
who died October 7, 1760,
aged 15 years, 10 months and 13 days,
the son of Donald Grant
of the parish of Duthel in the
County of Inverness in Scotland
and of Arminal his wife.

"Loud speaks the Grave
My Goal unnerves the Strong,
My shades deform the gay,
the Fair, the Young
Ye Youth, awaken. Catch the
shortlived day
Improve your Time and Talents
while ye may."

INSCRIPTIONS AND EPITAPHS

Here lies the body of
Elizabeth Grant, daughter
of Mr. Donald Grant
of the Parish of Duthel,
in ye County of Inverness
in Scotland,
and Mrs Arminal, his wife,
died May ye 5, 1762,
Aged 16 years
and 12 days.

Here lies the body of
Mr. Donald Grant
of the Parish of Duthel
in ye County of Inverness,
in Scotland
Died January 10, 1763,
in ye 55th year
of his age

Beneath, the Dust of
Donald Grant. who Died
October 18, 1767, aged 20 years,
1 month and 3 days,
son of Donald Grant of the
Parish of Duthel,
in the County of Inverness,
Scotland, and
Arminal, his wife.

Here lies buried
the body of
Caleb Baldwin, Esq.,
who departed this life
March 9, A. D. 1771, in ye
70th year of his age.

In memory of
Mrs Mehitable, wife of
Caleb Baldwin, Esq.
She died
Sept. ye 28, A. D. 1758,
aged 61 years.

Mrs. Betty Baldwin
late widow of
Col. Caleb Baldwin
departed this life
June 8, 1787
aged 56 years,
This monument is erected in
remembrance of an affectionate
mother, by her youngest son.

Sacred to the
memory of Mr.
Lemuel Thomas
for many years a skilled
and useful practioner of
surgery and physics
who departed this
Life September 30, A. D.
1775. AE 48.

In memory of
Rev'd Mr. David Judson,
pastor of the First
Church of Christ in
Newtown, who departed
this life Sept. ye 24,
A. D. 1776, in ye 61
year of his life.

Here lies ye body
of Mary Judson
Daughter of the Rev.
David Judson and his
wife Mary who died
July the 23, 17—
Aged 7 years and 20 days

David, son of Rev. Mr.
David Judson and Mary Judson
Died Dec. 11, 1749, Aged 1 year 6
Months and 20 days.

Here lyeth interred
the earthly remains of
the Rev'd John Beach,
A.M., late missionary
from the
venerable society for
the propagation of the
Gospel in foreign parts,
who exchanged this life
for mortality
on the 19th day of March,
1782,
in the 52nd year of his
ministry.
"The sweet remembrance of the just
Shall flourish when he sleeps in dust."
Reader let this tablet abide.

In memory of
Rev. Philo Perry,
Pastor of the Episcopal
Society in Newtown,
Who died Oct. 26, 1798,
in the 46th year of his age,
and the thirteenth of his ministry.
"I heard a voice from heaven
saying unto me, write
From henceforth blessed are the
dead who die in the Lord."

Here lies interred the Body of
Thomas Tousey Esq.
who Died March 14, 1761
in the 74th Year of his age.
Down to an impartial Grave's
devouring shade
Sink Human Honors and the
Hoary Head
Protract your years acquire
what mortals can
Here see with deep Concern the
End of Man.

Here Lyes ye Body of
Mrs. Johannah Wheeler
wife to Capt. Obadiah Wheeler
Who Died Febu'ry ye 15
A. D. 1758 in ye 62
Year of her Age.

Here lies buried
the Body of Capt.
Obadiah Wheeler
Who departed this Life
February ye 24, A. D. 1770
in ye 76 year of
his age.

The once well respected
Mr. ~~David~~ [Daniel] Booth
Here rested from the hurry
of life the 8th of April, A. D. 1777,
aged LXXIII,

"Could a virtuous, honest and
  amiable character, could blessings of the poor echoing from
  his gate,
Could ye sympathetick
  Grief of an aged partner or the
Soft'ning tears of a numerous offspring
  Disarm the King of Terrors,
He had not died. What is Life?
  to answer Life's great aim,
From Earth's low prison from this
  vale of tears
with age incumbered and oppres-
  sed with fears
Death set him free, his Christ had
  made his peace
Let grief be dumb; let pious sorrows cease."

To the memory of
Mr. Lemuel Camp,
Who, on the 30th Day of Jan'ry,
1784, in obedience to Nature's law
With Meekness and Christian
Fortitude resigned his Life to the
    Almighty Giver,
  and quietly fell asleep,
This monument is inscribed.
"The marble monument may yield
    To time; Time to Eternity,
But the remembrance of the just
    shall flourish
  When Time shall cease
And Death is swallowed up with
    Victory."

Here Lyes ye body of
Mrs. Betty Ferris wife to Mr.
Abraham Ferris, who died
August ye 28th, 1759, in ye 36
Year of her age

Here lies burried ye body of Ezra
son of Obadiah Wheeler who
departed this life Maye ye 10th
A. D. 1768 in ye 12 Year of his age.

To the memory of
Alice Camp,
widow of
Lemuel Camp,
Who died Dec. 5, 1796
in the 87th year
of her age.

"The sweet remembrance of the
    just
Shall flourish when they sleep in
    dust."
"Why do we mourn departing
    friends
  Or shake at Death's alarms?
'Tis but the voice that Jesus sends
  To call them to his arms."

In memory of
Miss Currence Camp
who departed this life
with Christian fortitude
April 30, 1799,
A. E. 22.
"As I am so you must be
Lean on Christ and follow me."

Here lies ye Body of Mrs.
Ann Peck, wife of Mr.
Henry Peck who died
April ye— 1741, in ye—
Year of her age.

Here lies buried
the Body of Mrs Mercy
Peck, wife of Mr. Henry Peck
who died April ye 17th
1751, in ye 27th
year of her age.

In memory of
Mr. Henry Peck
who departed this life
March 20th 1796
in the 77th Year
of his age.

Here lies interred, the
body of Mrs. Jane, the
dear wife of Richard
Fairman, Esq., who dw
elt together in the mar
ried state 30 ye
ars, wanting 23 days,
And was in his opinion a
woman of the best sense and
judgement that he was e
ver acquainted with, a
nd he believes truly pious,
who dep'r'd this life in the
58th yr of her age, May 16,
1775.

INSCRIPTIONS AND EPITAPHS

In memory of
Richard Fairman, Esq.,
who departed this life
Sept. the 22, A. D. 1775,
in the 64th year
of his age

Here lies the
remains of
Mrs Rebekah Nichols
The amiable and
virtuous consort
of Captain Peter Nichols
who departed this life
October 12, 1793.
In ye 61st yr. of her age.

In memory of
Mr. Abraham Ferris
who died April ye 4th A. D. 1789
in ye 68th year of his age
"No Gift of Nature, Art or Grace
Exempted from ye Burying Place.
All must obey death's solemn call
Before that tyrant all must fall."

Lies intome'd the
Remains of Mrs. Zilpha
wife to Zalmon Peck who
departed this life Dec.
the 31st A. D. and we deposited on New Year's day
1797 in the 40th year of her age
"Farewell, my loving sons, my friends.
Bear well in mind death is your ends
For God has called you when he pleased.
Happy are they whose hopes rely
On Israel's God who built the sky

In memory of
Mr. Epphriam Bennitt
who died
of a cancer in his breast
October 7, 1779
In the 65 year
of his life.
"Many are the afflictions
Alloted in this life
And few have endured trial
More severe."

In memory of
Mr. Vincent Stillson
Who died Jany 2, 1797
In ye 73rd Year of his age
also of
Mrs. Sarah Stillson
Who died Jan. 3, 1797
In ye 35th year of her age
They are both inter'd
in one Grave.

To the memory of
Mr. David Curtis,
the agreeable companion & the
generous friend who was
suddenly arrested by remorseless
Death, July 29th, A. D. 1783
in the 42nd year of his age,
this monument is inscribed:
"Of this man may it with propriety be said
His friends were many, his enemies few,
The partial friend may virtues magnify,
The flattering marble may record a lye,
But God, who judgeth righteously and just
Will raise his children from the sleeping dust
Proclaim their worth in Earth, in air and heaven
Their pardon seal'd and write their sins forgiven."

Safely inter'd here lies
the remains of Mrs. Mary,
the amiable consort
of Mr. Jabs. Baldwine,
who made her exit January ye 1770, in the
36th year of her age leaving behind her, 5 children.
"When a fond mother's care
has nursed her
Babes to manly size, she
Must with us'ry pay
the grave."

In memory of
Mrs Sally Cooke
2nd wife of Daniel B. Cook
who departed this Life
December 12 A. D. 1794
Aged 20 Years
this stone is erected.
"Could the Piety which adorns
or Benevolence which endears
human nature
Could tenderest friendship
or the Purest Love
Disarme the King of terrors
She had not died."

In Memory of
Reuben H. Booth
who was drowned
Nov. 24, 1814
aged 43 years.
"How in an instant he was called
Eternity to view
Not time to regulate his house
Nor bid ye world adieu."

In memory of Mr. Jonathan Booth. He died February ye 8, A. D. 1755, aged 73 years.

Here Lies ye Body of Lieut. John Griffin who departed this Life May 5 A. D. 1777 in ye 51 Year of his age "Who has Gone to Rest For Immortality."

In memory of Mrs Jerusha ye Amiable Consort of Zalmon Tousey who departed this life February 11, 1785

In memory of Gideon Botsford who died Sept. 22, 1791, Aged 70 years 4 months.

In memory of Mrs Meriam, widow and relict to Mr. Gideon Botsford, Dic'st. She died Nev. 16, 1795 Aged 66 years. the grave."

In Memory of Mr. James Baldwin Junr., who departed this Life June the 9th A. D. 1773 in the 56th Year of his age.

Here Lies ye Body of Mrs Thankful Baldwin wife to Mr Nathan Baldwin Died October ye 25 1741 In ye 79 year of her age.

In memory of Mr. Abraham Botsford, who departed this life March ye 25th, A. D. 1791, in ye 64th year of his age.

In memory of Mrs Nancy Botsford relict of Abraham Botsford. who died Oct. 24, 1795 in ye 64th year of her age.

In memory of Oliver Tousey, Esq'r who departed this life Jan. 27, 1799. in ye 73rd year of his Age "Stop, reader, shed a mournful tear Upon the dust that slumbers here And while you read the fate of me Think on the glass that runs for thee."

To the memory of Mrs Deborah Tousey late Consort of Oliver Tousey Esq'r who departed this life March 15 1801 in the 70th year of her age

In memory of Isaac Tousey who departed this life Dec. 5th, 1794 aged 39 years 11 mos. and 10 days

In memory of Zalmon Tousey who died June 26, 1810 In ye 7—year of his age.

In memory of Gideon Bennitt son Gideon and Pulchrea Botsford Who Died December the 18 A. D. 1774 Aged 4 months 12 days.

Here lyes ye body of Mr John Glover He died in ye faith and communion of ye church of England June ye 2, A. D. 1752 and in ye 78th year of his age. in the 40th year of Her Age. "Man is dom'd to die A sentence of ye Judge on high No ransom can give but in ye ransom paid, he yet shall live."

David Son of Mr. Jonathan and Mrs. Pheobe Booth. Died Sept. ye 22nd, 1753, aged 4 years, and 11 days.

Joseph, son of
Mr. Jonathan
and Mrs Pheobe
Booth. Died
August ye 11, 1751,
Aged 3 years & 1 month.

This monument is
Erected in Memory of
Capt'n Peter Nichols
Who exchanged this Life
for Immortality June 15,
1799 in ye 67 Year of his
Age.

Here lies the body
of Sarah Booth.
dau. of Mr. Jonathan
& Mrs. Pheobe Booth.
Died Febry 15, 1759,
in the 15th year
of her age.

Here lies ye
body of
Hester, wife of
Jonathan Booth.

In Memory of
Moses Wheeler
son to Mr Abiel and Mary
Booth. He died Feby 15
A. D. 1770 in ye 7
Year of his age.

In memory of
Andrew Booth
son of
Mr. Abel and Mary Booth
Who died Jan. 17, 1775,
Aged 14 years.

In memory of
Moses Wheeler Booth
second son of Mr
Abiel and Mary Booth
Who died Jan. 21, 1795

Here lies ye Body of
Mr. Samuel Starling son of
Mr. John Starling
who departed this Life June ye 6th
1764 in ye 27 Year
of His age

To the memory of Mrs.
Elizabeth Jennings Edmond,
eldest daughter of the late
Hon John Chandler and Mrs Mary
Chandler, who departed this
life February 17, 1795, aged 29 years
8 months and 17 days
this monument is erected by her
sorrowing husband
William Edmond.

Here lies ye body of
Mr John Starling son of
Mr John Starling and Mrs
Sarah Starling
Who Departed this Life August
ye 6th 1767 in ye 25th Year
of his Age

Here lies buried the Body of
Mr John Sterling
who departed this Life
July ye 19th 1780 in ye 72nd
Year of his age.

In Memory of
Mr. Jacob Starling
who departed this Life
October 9, 1796
in ye 57th Year of His Life.

In memory of Mrs. Sarah
Starling Relict of
Mr. John Starling
who departed this Life
Dec. 13th 1797
In ye 87th year
of her Age

Here Lyes buried ye
Body of Mrs Bethiah
Botsford, wife to Mr.
Gideon Botsford, who
died November ye 26,
1754, about 38 years
of her age.

NEWTOWN'S LAWYERS

Judge William Edmond was born Sept. 28, 1755, in Woodbury, Conn. He was graduated from Yale College in 1777; took part in an engagement with the British in Ridgefield, was severely wounded in the leg, April 27, 1777, and lay on the field over night. He never recovered from the effects of that wound. In May, 1782, he established himself in the practice of law in Newtown and there resided until his death, Aug. 1, 1858, aged 83. In 1797, he was elected a member of Congress, serving 4 years. He was appointed judge of the Superior Court in 1805, which office he held until 1819. He was a remarkable man, plain and unassuming in manners, mild and amiable in deportment, just and honest in dealing, honorable and magnanimous in feeling.

It is told that a man went to engage him in a suit against a neighbor who had borrowed a wash-tub and had allowed it, through neglect, to fall to pieces. After hearing the story, the Judge asked how much the tub was worth. Being told "about a dollar," the Judge gave the man a dollar and told him to go home and live in peace with his neighbor.

He married, Nov. 30, 1784, Elizabeth J., daughter of Col. John and Mary Chandler. She died Feb. 17, 1795, and he married, Feb. 14, 1796, Elizabeth, daughter of Benjamin Payne of Hartford. His children: Mary E., born 1785; Elizabeth P., 1798; Sarah, June 24, 1800, (married Dr. Cyrenius Booth in 1820); William P., 1802; Ann, 1804; Robert 1805.

Samuel Curtis Blackman, born in Monroe, Conn., March 22, 1768, graduated from Yale in 1793, continued in practice more than 50 years. When the Probate district was established, he was chosen Judge and held the office for 17 years, until, at 70 years, the law rendered him ineligible.

He was for many years a school-visitor. His late home was the first house south of the Congregational Church, now the Grand Central, where he died, Nov. 17, 1858, in his 91st year. He married Sarah Toucey of Newtown, born, April 23, 1777, who died, Dec. 6, 1835. Their children: Caroline, Sarah, George, Alfred, William and Samuel.

Asa Chapman, born at Saybrook, Sept. 2, 1770, graduated at Yale in 1792; admitted to the bar in 1795; settled in practice in Newtown, "was repeatedly elected the representative of that town to the General Assembly of the State and, in 1817, was elected member of the Governor's Council, comprising at that time 12 members;" elected Judge of Superior Court and Court of Errors in 1818, holding this office until his death in New Haven, Sept. 25, 1825.

He married at Newtown, Mary daughter of Bennett Perry, M. D. Had five children, the eldest Charles.

Holbrook Curtis, born in Newtown, July 14, 1787, studied with Dr. Burhans and with Judge Asa Chapman; graduated from Yale 1807; admitted to Fairfield County bar in 1809, was in Newtown the next 4 years. Later moved to Watertown, Conn., elected Judge of Probate in Watertown and was judge of the County Court for Litchfield County.

GOVERNOR ISAAC TOUCEY

See Page 199

In 1821, was sent to the General Assembly and returned in 1822, '33, '37, '39, '43, and '45. He married a daughter of Hon. William Edmond of Newtown. Died, Feb. 21, 1858.

Reuben Booth, born in Newtown, Nov. 26, 1794, graduated at Yale. 1816; entered the law-office of David S. Boardman at New Milford, for about a year, then moved to Danbury and continued his studies with Moses Hatch; was instructor in Danbury Academy; admitted to the bar in 1818. In 1822, he represented Danbury in the General Assembly and, the same year, was Judge of Probate for Danbury; held probate office till 1835. Elected State Senator in 1830; was Lieutenant-Governor of this State in 1844—5. Died in Danbury, Aug. 14, 1848.

Henry Dutton, born Feb. 12, 1796, grduated at Yale with honor in 1818; tutor in the college from 1821 to 1823; attorney and counselor-at law in Newtown, Bridgeport and New Haven; author of Dutton's Conn. Digest; commissioner for the revision of the State Statutes and of Swifts Digest; Professor of law in Yale; member, clerk and Speaker of Connecticut House of Representatives; State Senator; Governor of Connecticut in 1854 and Judge of the Superior Court of Errors, 1861. In 1847, he became Kent professor of law in Yale Law School. For a year he acted as Judge of the New Haven County Court. Was married to Eliza Elliott Joy of Fairfield County. He died April 26, 1869.

Hon. Isaac Toucey, born in Newtown, Nov. 5, 1796,, studied law with Hon. Asa Chapman of Newtown; Admitted to the bar in 1818, settled in practice at Hartford; was State's Attorney for Hartford county from 1822 to 1835. when he was elected representative in Congress and continued there four years; elected Governor of State, 1846. During latter part of President Polk's term ,Governor Toucey was Attorney general of the United States. In 1850, he was in the Connecticut Senate; elected to the United States Senate in 1851, for the term of six years; was in President Buchanan's Cabinet as Secretary of the Navy. He was offered a seat on the bench of the Supreme Court, but declined it.

He was a devout member of the Episcopal Church and, in his will left Trinity College, Hartford, a sum whose interest is to pay for the education of a candidate for the ministry in the Episcopal Church.

He married Catharine Burrill, but left no children. His last years were spent in retirement at his pleasant home in Hartford where he died, July 30, 1869.

David Hull Belden, born in 1798, was son of Rev. David Belden of Wilton, Conn. He early located in Newtown, and most of his life was spent there. At his death, May 7, 1872, was the eldest member of the Fairfield County Bar, having been associated with it for more than 50 years. He was a successful lawyer and served as State's Attorney. In 1829, he represented the town in the Legislature and was one of the founders of Newtown Academy. Oct. 20, 1824 he married Cornelia, eldest daughter of John and Clarissa Peck Johnson, who died in 1828. He later married her sister, Susan Jane, who died in 1835, leaving Cornelia, Clarissa, David and

John. His third wife was Miss Ann Clarke, who died in 1862, leaving four children: Mary, who died in 1862; Fred, who died a few years later; Howard and Reuben. There were no children by the fourth wife, Miss Sarah J. Peck.

Charles Chapman, born in Newtown, June 21, 1799 son of Asa Chapman judge of the Supreme Court of Connecticut. He commenced his law studies with his father, later studied at Litchfield Law School and completed them with the late Chief Justice Williams in Hartford. He was admitted to the bar in 1820, began practice in New Haven and in 1832 removed to Hartford, where he spent the rest of his life. Six times he represented Hartford in the State Legislature; was elected to Congress in 1851 by the Whigs; was also U. S. Attorney for the district of Connecticut, from the Spring of 1841 to the close of 1844. Had a very large practice, especially in criminal cases. He died in Hartford in 1870.

David B. Beers, born in Newtown, Feb. 18, 1805, studied law at Litchfield Law School; practiced law to some extent; resided in Newtown most of his life, dying July 28, 1885 in the same house in which he was born. April 12, 1835, he married Margaret Pray Of their four children, Emma E. died young; George in 1859, aged 17; Emma S. several years later; John Samuel, born April, 1836, was for many years a successful business man in Bridgeport, studied for the ministry, was ordained in 1871 and became a very useful clergyman in the Episcopal Church. Died at Natick, Mass., Nov. 20, 1886.

A grandson, George Emerson Beers, graduate of Yale, also of Yale Law School, is professor of Law, also Compensation Commissioner at Yale University.

Isaac M. Sturges, born at Wilton, July 6, 1807, admitted to the bar in January 8, 1837 and at once commenced practice in Newtown removing to Bridgeport in 1848. Elected Representative from Wilton in 1837, from Newtown in 1844, and again in Wilton in 1876. Was Judge of Probate for Newtown in 1844 and judge of Bridgeport City Court in 1860-1. He died at Wilton, Oct. 30, 1877.

Alfred Blackman, son of Judge Samual Curtis Blackman, born at Newtown, Dec. 28, 1807, graduated at Yale in 1828; admitted to the bar in 1830; practiced law in Seymour until 1842, when he moved to Waterbury and, a year later, to New Haven, where he spent the rest of his life. In 1842, elected to the State Senate from the 5th Senatorial district. In 1855, represented New Haven in the General Assembly. Was Judge of Probate, Judge of the County Court, Mayor of the city and Clerk of the U. S. District Court from 1853 to 1868. He died in New Haven, April 20, 1880.

Hon. Amos Sherman Treat, born Feb. 5, 1816, in Bridgewater, Conn, prepared for college at Hudson, Ohio, and entered Yale in the in the class of 1838 remaining only two years; was admitted to Litchfield County bar in 1843; practiced in Newtown for 10 years, where he was postmaster and member of the Board of Education; also judge of Probate. In July, 1854, he removed to Bridgeport; was Clerk of Fairfield County Court from 1854 to 1859, member of the Peace Congress in 1862, and one of the managers of the Sani-

tary Commission during the Rebellion; was member of the Conn. legislature from Bridgeport in 1858, '62, '69, and '79, and from Woodbridge from 1871 to 1873; was Speaker of the House in 1872; was connected with various business enterprises relating to the growth of the city.

Lineal descendant of Robert Treat, former Governor of the State. He died, April 24, 1886.

Judge Daniel Blackman, son of Col. Reuben Blackman, was born in Newtown, Dec. 31, 1822, where his elementary education was received. Taught in Newtown Academy, then went to Southbury, where he studied law under Joel Hinman and taught school. Was admitted to the bar in Fairfield when quite young and located in Danbury, where he remained seven years. From there, he went to Cassopolis, Mich., where he edited the Cassopolis Democrat for two years. He was elected Circuit Judge, later went to Chicago and practiced law until his death, Jan. 11, 1896.

Julius B. Curtis, born at Newtown, Dec. 10, 1825, son of Nichols and Sarah A. Curtis, descendant of Capt. Wm. Curtis, one of the early settlers of Stratford. He was educated in the public schools and in Newtown Academy; read law with Hon. Edward Hinman of Southbury, with Isaac N. Sturges, and Amos S. Treat, of Newtown and further studied at the State and National Law School at Ballston Springs, N. Y.; was admitted to the bar at Fairfield, Dec, 27. 1850; member of State Senate from 12th district in 1858 and 1860; judge of Court of Probate for Stamford in 1867, '68, '69, and Judge of City Court of Stamford from 1889 to 1893. Commenced law practice at Greenwich in 1851 and removed to Stamford in November, 1864.

Luzon B. Morris, son of Eli Gould and Lydia Bennett Morris, was born at Newtown, April 16, 1827. Attended Conn. Literary Institute at Suffield; was graduated at Yale College, 1854; studied law at Yale Law School, also in private office work; admitted to bar in 1856. Began practice in Seymour, but afterward moved to New Haven. Represented town of Seymour in General Assembly two sessions, 1855-6. Judge of Probate for New Haven District for six successive terms, 1857-'63. In 1870, '76, '80 and '81, represented New Haven in General Assembly, and, in 1874, was member of State Senate. Was member of committee formed in 1880 to settle controversy over boundary line between New York and Connecticut. In 1884, was chairman of committee to revise Probate laws of Conn. Candidate for Governor in 1888, elected Governor in 1892; took office January, 1893. In 1856, married Miss Eugenia Tuttle of Seymour. Their children: Charles G. Morris and Mrs Arthur Hadley of New Haven, Dr. Robert T. Morris and Roy Morris of New York, Mrs. Charles Pratt of Brooklyn, New York.

Richard Botsford, son of Austin N. and Volucia Glover Botsford, born in Newtown, Oct. 28, 1830, attended district school and private school of Harry Peck in Taunton; studied at Hobart Academy, Hobart, N. Y. for three years; studied at State Normal School, New Britian; taught school at St. Charles. Ill, also in Wisconsin and Missouri. While teaching he read law, and in 1856 entered a law office at Black Rock Falls, Wisconsin, was admitted to the bar in 1857 and began practicing his profession at Elgin, Ill., was Attorney for Illinois Central R. R. more than 25 years to the time of his death, April 5, 1908, at Elgin, Ill. He was Judge of King County Court, four years. He had two children.

James Nichols, born in Newtown, Dec. 25, 1830, admitted to bar of Hartford County, 1854; settled in practice in Hartford, was at one time Assistant Clerk of Superior Court. In 1861, was elected Judge of Probate for Hartford. In 1867, he abandoned law and, later, became president of the National Fire Insurance Co. Died in Hartford in 1916. Married Miss Isabella Starkweather.

Hon. Charles H. Brisco, son of Charles and Mary Brisco, was born in Newtown, Dec. 20, 1831; studied law with Amos S. Treat; admitted to the bar in 1854; began practice in Enfield in 1854. In 1868, he moved his office to Hartford, practiced alone until 1877, when he associated with J. M. Maltbie until about October, 1881. Represented Enfield in the General Assembly in 1857, '64 and '78, the latter year Speaker of the House. Member of State Senate, 1861, serving as chairman of Committee on Military Affairs. Was first judge of the Court of Common Pleas for Hartford County serving from 1869 to 1875. Was married in 1855 to Anna J. Travers of Newark, N. J., who died in 1875. Second marriage to Alice E. Bradley of Newtown, 1878. Children by first marriage, Willis A., AnnieT. and Alice A.

Judge David Belden, son of David H. and Susan Johnson Belden, was born in Newtown, Aug. 14, 1832. As a boy, worked with Hiram Parmalee of Hattertown to learn carpenter's trade. In 1853, went to California and studied law. Began practice at Nevada City in 1855; elected County Judge of Nevada County in 1858; sent to State Senate in 1864; was Judge of 20th judicial district of California from 1871 to 1880 and of Superior Court of Santa Clara County from 1880 to his death, May 14, 1888, at San Jose, California. Married Miss. Elizabeth Farrell in 1861. "Newtown was honored to have been the birthplace of such a man."

Austin N. Botsford, son of Austin N. and Volucia Glover Botsford born at Newtown, April 21, 1842; attended district school and Newtown Academy; graduated from Yale Law School and went to Fort Dodge, Iowa, whrere he still resides; has retired from active law practice, but still has a few retainers. He has three children.

Johnson Tuttle Platt, son of Philo Toucey and Jeanette Tuttle Platt, born at Newtown, Jan. 12, 1844; graduated from Harvard Law School, 1865; admitted to bar in Boston same year; commenced pratice at Pittsfield, Mass. but soon removed to New Haven, became instructor in Yale Law School in 1869; full professor in 1872; member of Court of Common Council many years, and, in 1874, was made Corporation Council. For a number of years was Master of Chancery for State of Connecticut, and, at time of death, Jan. 23, 1890, was serving as United States Commossioner.

"During nearly a quarter of a century at the bar and 20 years at Yale Law School, he had been honorably known as a learned lawyer, an independent thinker, a public-spirited citizen, and a kind-

WILLIAM J. BEECHER

See Page 203

FREDERICK P. MARBLE

See Page 203

hearted and high-minded man."

Julius C. Cable, born at Newtown, Oct. 11. 1849, son of Nathaniel J. and Phebe Cable; studied in Newtown and at Cornell University; graduated from Yale Law School in 1873; admitted to bar at New Haven, June, 1873; member of Common Council of New Haven, Clerk of City Court and, from 1883 to 1887, City Attorney of New Haven. In 1893 appointed Judge of City Courts.

William J. Beecher was born in Bridgeport, Conn., March 5, 1859. His parents removed to Easton, where he was educated at the district school and Staples Academy; graduated from Yale Law School in 1880. In July of that year was admitted to bar at New Haven to practice in all the Courts of the State and, in August of that year, opened an office in Bridgeport, removing to Newtown in 1881. In November, 1886, was elected Judge of Probate for the District of Newtown and served four years. In 1894, he again opened an office in Bridgeport with Frank M. Canfield as partner, retaining his office at Newtown. In 1901, he was chosen director of Newtown Savings bank; was also attorney for the Bank, the last two years serving on loaning committee; was again elected Judge of Probate in 1906, which office he retained until his death, Dec. 3, 1915. Two daughters, the Misses Florence Glover and Marguerite Katharine Beecher, survive him.

Charles N. Northrop, son of William and Julia Lamberton Northrop, born, Nov. 21, 1859. Attended Newtown Academy and entered Yale, but did not graduate owing to ill-health; later studied law and was graduated from Yale Law School, 1880; commenced practice in Lincoln, Neb., returning soon to Newtown. In 1882 was Secretary of Board of School Visitors; in 1885 was again elected, but declined when re-nominated in 1888. In 1887 was chosen Town Clerk and about that time was elected secretary of Newtown Savings Bank; in 1891, was elected Town Treasurer, which office he held until his death in May, 1908. In 1887, he married Mary Grace Hammond. Their children are Eleanor Louise and Nelson William Northrop.

Frederick Parker Marble, lawyer. Born Newtown Conn., July 14, 1859, son of Rev. Newton E. Marble, D. D. and Mary Gillis Marble. Great, great grandson of Gen. John Stark. Educated at Newtown Academy and Trinity College, Hartford. Left college at the end of sophomore year and tutored for year in the Bermuda Islands. Studied law with the Hon. George Stevens, Ex-District Attorney, at Lowell, Mass., and was admitted to the Massachusetts Bar in 1882, and to practice in the U. S. Courts in 1888. Married Fannie Isabelle Talbot of Lowell, Mass., April 17, 1894. Practice has been largely concerned with banking and trust estates. Director and Counsel for Union National Bank of Lowell, President of the Lyon Carpet Company of Lowell, formerly director of the Talbot Mills, North Billerica, Mass., and of the First National Bank of Lowell, President of the Lowell Humane Society, member of the American and Massachusetts Bar Associations, member of the Sons of the Revolution, member of Kilwining Lodge, F. & A. M. of Lowell, Republican, Vestryman of St. Anne's Church, Lowell,

President of the Vesper-Country Club, Tyngsborough, Mass., member of the Yorick Club, Lowell and of the Engineers' Club, Boston. Home, 15 Fairview Street, Lowell. Office, Sun Building, Lowell, Mass.

Nichols Curtis Downs, son of Monroe D. and Charlotte N. Downs born in Newtown, Dec. 12, 1861; educated in public schools and Newtown Academy; studied law with Julius B. Curtis of Stamford, admitted to the bar in Fairfield County, May 15, 1884; was deputy judge of Borough Court of Stamford 1887-93, judge of City Court of Stamford from 1893. Borough Attorney 1887-91 and in 1895 was Corporation Counsel for City of Stamford.

James M. Betts, son of Dr. Ralph N. and Mary Hough Betts was born at Sandy Hook, April 9, 1878. Attended private school of Mrs. Emily Bennett, Sandy Hook, school at St. Johnsbury, Vt. Bridgeport High School, and the last year of the class of 1902 at Newtown Academy. Took a course at Yale, graduating in 1906; took three years course in two years at Yale Law School, for Connecticut courts, passing six months later for practice in New York Courts. Is associated with Armitage and Douglas in Woolworth Building, New York.

NEWTOWN'S DOCTORS OF THE OLD SCHOOL

All who have given thought to the matter, will agree with the writer that there are no two classes of professional men who come into so close touch with individual and family life as clergymen and physicians—the one who comes when there may be greatest suffering of mind, the other when the body is racked with pain or burning with fever. Then, too, if they are men actuated by pure motives and by high Christian principle they can be a great power for good in any community.

The first disciple of Esculapius Newtown ever had, who commenced practice in Newtown in 1756, was Dr. Lemuel Thomas. From whence he came and where he received his education, we know not. Newtown records show that he was born in 1727 and was married by Rev. David Judson, the Presbyterian minister in Newtown, to Mary Foote, Sept. 15, 1756. Three children were born to them, Lucy, born July 17, 1757; James, born Jan. 29, 1759; Lemuel, born Jan. 5, 1767. The records also show that his announcement to settle in Newtown for practice was well received by landed proprietors, for, at a town meeting held at the north schoolhouse six months after his marriage, it was "voted that Dr. Lemuel Thomas may have liberty to take up two acres and a half of land in ye town street for a horse pasture between ye school house at ye south end of ye town and Mr. Fabrique's house leaving an eight rod highway on ye east side thereof and sd Dr. Thomas shall possess sd two acres and a half of land and improve ye same so long as he shall continue in this town and practice doctering among us and if he should lay aside doctering as aforesaid or remove out of ye town ye sd land to return to ye town again, he taking away ye fence."

Dr. Thomas practiced "doctering" in Newtown until his death. At the extreme south end of Newtown cemetery (old part) is a slab of red sandstone that marks the grave where his remains were buried and on it this inscription:

"Sacred to the memory of Mr. Lemuel Thomas, for many years a skillful practitioner of surgery and physic who departed this life, September 30, A. D. 1775, aged 45 years. He is said to have been a self educated physician and possessed of considerable ability."

Dr. Gideon Shepherd, who was born in Newtown and had studied medicine with Dr. Thomas, his professional predecessor, became, at Dr. Thomas' death, his immediate successor, and was practising physician in Newtown for over 40 years.

It seems no more than just and right to lay before this generation the estimate of one who knew Dr. Shepherd's worth as a physician and citizen. The occasional finding of choice bit of biography seems to him who delves in lonely surroundings as a voice from the almost forgotten past.

Dr. Rufus Blakeman, who was born in Monroe in 1795 and practiced medicine in Greenfield Hill from 1822 to his death in 1870, says of Dr. Shepherd in an address delivered before the State Medical Society in 1853, that:

"His professional coevals in neighboring towns generally conceded to him a precedence as a consulting physician and that he was one of the most prominent of the originators and supporters of the Fairfield County Medical Society and the records show him to have been one of the most active and frequent members." Of Dr. Shepherd's personal character Dr. Blakeman further says: "He was eccentric, but social, instructive and agreeable in his intercourse with society. He ever sustained a reputation of great moral purity and while he was highly esteemed by his friends, his enemies or traducers were rarely found. What few physicians can boast he was the father of 17 children, thereby refuting the charge that while enjoying the profits of a special branch of his profession as a prompt accessory in the accumlation of responsiblites on his friends, he was cautious in the assumption of similar burdens on himself. In his religious sentiments he was a zealous Sandemanian." Right here we will pick a few plums from Dr. Shepherd's genealogical tree.

Dr. Gideon Shephard, married Sarah Watkins, March 20, 1776. Their first Mary, born Feb. 25, 1777; Abijah, born Nov. 28, 1778; Lucy, born Oct. 23, 1780 Betsy, born Feb. 11, 1782; Silas Munson, born Oct. 27, 1783; Sarah Ann, born Sept. 3, 1786; Eunice, born Jan., 1790; Maria, born March 10, 1794.

The above named Eunice, my 7th child, departed this life, Oct. 16, 1793.

The above said Sarah, my wife, departed this life, March 10, 1794, at birth of ?th child

Dr. Gideon Shephard and Lucinda Peck joined in marriage covenant, November 6, 1794.

Fanny Shephard, born Feb. 19, 1797; Maria Shepard, Aug. 23, 1798; William Peck, Feb. 16, 1800; Sally, April 6, 1802; Thomas Darwin Shepard, April 30, 1804; Charles Sydenham and Harriett Shepard, twins, born March 2, 1806; Lewis Parsons Shepard, Dec. 14, 1807; Harriet Shephard, born Oct. 20, 1809; Martin Hebrinden Shepard, born Jan. 17, 1814.

The following vote from the records of Fairfield Medical Society sufficiently evinces the estimation in which he was held by his brethern:

"Voted, that Dr. Gideon Shepherd receive the patronage of this society in consumption and chronic cases of disease and that it be the duty of all members of this society to recommend him when counsel is deemed expedient, etc., and that it be his duty to report all cases of that description to which he may be called to attend, with their particular symptoms, the particular medicines and the constitution of the several patients together with the predisposition of their ancestry." Then Dr. Blakeman goes on to say: "Although the existing generation of physicians may smile at such blending of professional opinion with popular belief, regarding excellence of the skill of individuals in special classes of disease, yet the fact is undoubted that such were professional concessions as late as the close of the last and commencement of the present century. His mode of treatment of consumption, as I learn from his statement of cases left on the records of the society was not peculiar, being in general mildly antiphlogistic and similar to the present treament of phthisis. To meet occurring symptoms, local bleeding counterirritants with anodyne and demulcent expectorants were his general prescriptions. His devotion to the science of medicine and its observant application to the diseases which he treated was strongly developed. My early impressions of the doctor are that he devoted greater attention to the occurring improvements in medical science than most of his contemporary brethren

Although not endowed with extraordinary intellectual powers, his talents were respectable and of a character calculated for usefulness rather than display or striking originality. If he did not attain eminence as a professional scholar he was diligent in his efforts to acquire such portions of existing medical literature as were more immediately adapted to the emergencies of practice ordinarily presented to the notice of physicians. To the juniors in the profession his counsels were parental and he took the preference as a consulting physician."

Though a disinterested reader may tire of this long sketch given one long since dead, is it any more than is due to the memory of him who was Newtown's family physician for more than 40 years, when testimony of one who spoke of what he knew can be found, to be reiterated after a lapse of more than 50 years, to remind the children's children what he was to those who were ever glad to welcome him to their homes in hours of joy or sorrow.

I have heard said by those who were intimately aquainted with Dr. Shepherd that when asked to sit at the table when calling at meal time his reply would often come, "No no, I never eat poor folkses victuals." He was full to overflowing with quaint retorts. and beaming with stories and jokes. In Taunton in his day the name Fairchild predominated and at times when meeting some man on the road his salutation would be, "Good morning, Mister Nirum Fairchild, sah! if 'taint you it must be your brother, sah! and if it aint your brother sah I ask your pardon, sah!"

When he became incapacitated by age for practice, he removed to Hunter, N.Y., where he resided with one of his daughters until he died at the advanced age of 89.

Two bills copied from originals in my possession that Dr. Shepherd sent in against the town of Newtown for attendance upon persons who were town charges show the customary charges for medical services in the earliest years of the town life.

Newtown to Dr. Gideon Shepherd attending Henry Murry:

May 11, 1818, to one visit and tincture of digitilis and vial	0	3	4
May 12, one visit and blister salve,	0	2	3
May 14, one visit and cream tartar,	0	3	0
May 15, three visits and spirits niter,	0	6	3
May, 16, juniper senica root, vial and visit	0	3	4
May 19, three visits,	0	7	3
May 22, one visit, elixier vitnol, one vial,	0	2	11
May 23, to two visits,	0	5	0
May 26, part of a visit, spirits nitre,	0	2	8
May, 27, part of a visit and medicine,	0	2	11
May 28, part of a visit and pills,	0	2	0
May 29, part of a visit,	0	1	9
	£2	0	8

In dollars $6.78.
Thirteen visits and four half visits
1820, Newtown, to Dr. Gideon Shepherd Dr.

Feb. 2, To one visit, 5 medicines, 10, for Daniel Prindle.			
March 20, To 1 visit, medicines for Daniel Prindle,	0	10	0
April 5, To visit, 2.6, bittres for Hannah Parmalee,	0	4	0
May 24, one visit to the poor house,	0	0	7
May 25, one visit in part, for negro girl named Mary,	0	4	0
June 12, delivering a black girl at Dick's called Sook,	0	18	0
On the 20th of May, 1 visit to see Polly Ann Foot,	0	3	0

Dr. Gideon Shepherd stood by when the writer's father and mother first saw light and looked after them in their younger days here. So beloved was he by everyone that his name was a household word for long years after his death. He was one of those men looked up to as father. He was was of an extremely charitable disposition and indulgent in his pecuniary claims upon poorer patients. This with the necessary demands for the support of his numerous family, kept him poor, though not indigent as to respectable living.

Bennett Perry was a contemporary of Dr. Gideon Shepherd, practicing with him and thus a relief but no hindrance to him who was beginning to bend and totter under the weight of years.

Dr. Perry was son of Dr. Nathaniel Perry of Woodbury. He studied medicine with his father and located in Newtown, where he practiced medicine until his death, in 1821, at the age of 66. His home was what in later years was known as Dick's hotel, where Newtown Inn now stands. His reputation was that of a physician of superior talents, well developed by education. His medical practice covered a period of over 40 years.

Dr. Perry belonged to Hiram lodge, A. F. and A. M., previous to the year 1797; the lodge room was in his own dwelling, from 1797 to 1818. Unfortunately, we can find no record as to his history and his ability as a physician. The young people of his day were the town's maturer people of the writer's early manhood and he well remembers that the name of Dr. Perry, too, was a household word in every family life. What were his political affiliations, the writer knows not, but he served on the board of Newtown's selectmen in 1793. That he had some of the medical practice townwise, the following bill, copied from the original in the writer's possession, goes to show:

Town of Newtown to Dr. Bennett Perry, Dr.

February, 1819, For Molly Brisco to 2 visits, medicine and directions.	0	6	0
March 7, 4 visits and medicine, for a child of Sherwood Peck	0	15	0
April, To 23 visits, medicine and directions for Mr. Daniel Baldwin	4	5	6
May, To a visit, medicine and directions in consultation to Mr. Downs at Ragged Corner, so-called,	0	15	0
September, To 4 visits and part of a visit, medicine and directions Seth Hill's child,	2	5	0
To medicine for Pihlo Parmalee's wife and directions,	0	1	6
November, To a visit, medicine and directions,	0	9	0
	£8	17	0

The Town of Newtown to Bennett Perry, Dr.

Jan., 1820, to visit and medicine and directions for Ebenezer Sherwood at the Poor House,	$1.50
To advice, medicine and dirtceions for Parmalee's wife,	0.34
To advice and medicine for Mr. Bradley and Mrs. Bradley,	0.50
To advice for Sherwood Peck's wife,	0.50
	$2.84
November, 1820, to visits ad medicines for Ammon Prindle,	$9.00
Polly Ann Prindle, daughter of Ammon, to 24 visits and directions,	6.00
Morgan Banks, a visit and directions,	1.00
	$16.00
	2.84
Newtown, November 23, 1829. Same allowed,	$18.84

My mother, born in 1804, was fifteen at the time of the incident I am about to relate, and used to tell me the story, which made a lasting impression on my memory. Dr. Perry had a daughter who married Elisha Mills, a lawyer who practiced in the town of Huntington. In the Spring of 1819, he decided to remove with his family to Illinois which only the year before, had been admitted into the Union. The journey was to be made by horses with a large covered wagon, loaded down with luggage and household effects generally, and particularly such necessities for domestic use as could not possibly be procured en route. There were eight persons in all, Mr. Mills, his young wife, two little boys, the youngest not six years, a nephew, two helpers and a hired girl. The young wife and mother bravely yielded to the husband's judgment without a murmur. Kind-hearted friends and neighbors from far and near gathered at Dr. Perry's to see them start on their long journey and watched them as the heavy vehicle made its slow descent of the hill to the plain below, when it turned to the westward and disappeared in the distance. After a journey of 55 days, they reached a place called Shawneetown, near where Cairo stands. The noble wife, whose powers of endurance had been severely overtaxed, attacked with malarial fever, soon breathed her last and was buried in a land of strangers, leaving the bereaved husband and two motherless children to continue their journey to the new home, now to be made desolate without her. In this illustration is embodied trials and privations to which the early ancestors were subjected, when they left their comfortable Connecticut homes to build for themselves homes in the new and wild West.

Doctor Oliver Bancroft, was a physician in Newtown with Dr. Perry. The house in which he lived stood on ground just north of what is still known as the Belden house. When the house now owned by William Homer Hubbell was built, the Bancroft lot was bought, the house torn away and the lot became part of the enlarged grounds of David H. Johnson's building lot.

Bill of Dr. Oliver Bancroft against the State of Connecticut, as copied from the original:

The State of Connecticut to Oliver Bancroft, Dr., for William Maerabe, 1819.

February 19, to visit and medicine,	$1.25
February 19, to laudanum,	.17
	1.42
For Elizabeth Manse:	
October 22, to calling and medicine,	$0.34
October 23, To visit and medicines,	.67
October 25, To visit and medicine,	0.60
October 26, To visit and medicine,	.62
October 28, To visit and medicine,	.75
November 3, to laudanum,	.25
Nov. 12, to one ounce laudanum,	.25
	3.48
For Bettsy Brennan:	
October 25, to directions and medicine,	0.50
December 23, To directions and medicine,	.25
	0.75
Amount,	$5.65

Dr. Rufus Skidmore, son of Dr. James and Polly Sherman Skidmore was born in Newtown, 1793, was graduated from medical department of University of Vermont in 1817, and soon after went west, settling in Kentucky. Here he formed the acquaintance of Henry Clay in the early period of his brilliant political career and a warm friendship grew up between them. When Dr. Skidmore decided to go to Havana, Cuba, with the desire to make a study of yellow fever, Clay tried to dissuade him from going, but failing in that, presented him with a gold ring as a parting remembrance. This ring came into the possession of the oldest daughter, Mrs,

Jane A. Burr, who presented it to the Bridgeport Historical Society in whose possession it now remains.

Dr. Skidmore contracted the disease he went to study and combat, but recovered and returned to Newtown, married Jerusha Ferris, grand-daughter of Joseph Ferris of Palestine district, and practiced his profession until his death in 1828. The widow with the three daughters, lived on the Ferris-Skidmore homestead in Palestine until after the marriage of the daughters, Jane A. to Barak Burr, of Easton, Marietta to Alanson Lyon of Redding and Martha Elizabeth to James Johnson of Bridgeport. The old house was burned while the property of Oliver Turney Northrop.

Dr. John Judson was born in Newtown, Feb. 11, 1789. He studied medicine at Yale college, receiving a diploma and was licensed to practice medicine in October, 1812, at the age of 23. In 1814, he located in Newtown and became famous as the leading physician of his section. The advantage he had of being in touch with the mature minds of Dr. Shepherd and Dr. Bennett Perry, must have been of great assistance to him in his extensive practice. He died in July, 1839. He was one of a family of 15 children.

Dr. Cyrenius H. Booth was born in Newtown, May, 25, 1797. He studied medicine under Dr. Bennett Perry, and attended a long course of medical lectures delivered by Dr. Hosack of New York, who then stood at the head of his profession. About 1820, he commenced practice in his native town, which he followed until his death in September, 1871. His wife, Sarah Edmond, was daughter of Hon. Judge William Edmond. For a half a century practically, the doctor was a familiar figure, driving over the hills and along the valleys in answer to the beck and call of his town's people, his saddle bags filled with pills and nostrums for ills to which flesh is heir. The writer remembers him as a man of infinite mirth, a famous story teller and a great favorite with children and young people.

Copy of an original bill of Dr. Booth, showing rate of charges by him:

Newtown, November 27, 1820.

Amon Prindle to Cyrenus H. Booth, Dr.
To 18 visits, attendance and medicine and directions, $14. Paid.
To 18 visits, attendance and medicine and directons, $14. Paid. Polly Ann
Polly Ann Prindle to C. H. Booth, Dr., November 27, 1820,
To attendance, medicine and directions and 23 visits, $10, Paid.

Dr. Booth had one son, William Edmond Booth, born April., 1821. A graduate of Yale, who at a very early age began the practice of medicine in Danbury, where he continued until his death in Feb., 1859, aged 37 years and 10 months.

In the interim between 1830 and 1848, while Drs. George Judson, Cyrenius H. Booth, Erastus Erwin and Monroe Judson were the medical practitioners of Newtown, Dr. Thomas Dutton came in from the outside world. He was well received and lived in the house remodeled, by H. N. Tiemann. He was a stranger to the people, his coming into Newtown to practice being due to the fact that he was a younger brother of Henry Dutton, attorney at law, who commenced the practice of law in Newtown and later went from Newtown and became Governor of Connecticut. Dr. Dutton built up a good practice, but, with four well established practioners

DR. MONROE JUDSON

See Page 211

in the home field, with the fact that a great grief came into the home life, he withdrew to a new field. In the extreme northeast corner of the old part of Newtown village cemetery, now so deeply shaded by evergreens that no ray of sunshine can penetrate, stands a headstone that marks the grave where the fond mother's hopes were buried long years ago. The inscription reads:

>Sacred to the Memory
>of Eliza Maria,
>Daughter of Thomas and Lucinda Dutton
>Who died September 28, 1846,
>Aged 15 years and 10 months
>My faith looks up to Thee
>Thou Lamb of Calvary
>Saviour Divine.

Dr. Russell B. Botsford was born at Newtown, May 7, 1794, and commenced the study of medicine with Dr. Gideon Shepherd during two years of his medical course. In New Haven, he was in Dr. Gilberts office. He received his diploma, Sept., 1816. In the Spring of 1817, he commenced the pratice of medicine in Danbury. In 1820 he was married. Being of a very depressed temperament and dyspeptic habit, from too intense application to study, and a very laborious practice, in 1832, he was afflicted with a rush of blood to the head, which resulted in attacks of an epileptic character, which continued with more or less frequency and severity until Dec. 20, 1855, they terminated his life at the age of sixty-two.

Dr. George Judson was son of Dr. John Judson and was born in Newtown in 1814. He commenced the study of medicine with his father, attended a course of lectures at Bellevue Medical College in New York, graduating in 1837, and was a successful physician in his native town until his death in 1853. Dr. Monroe Judson, brother of Doctor George Judson was born in Newtown in January, 1820, and he, too, commenced his studies with his father, after whose death, continuing his studies with his brother, he entered Yale Medical College in 1841, graduated in 1843, and followed the practice of medicine until 1888. His death occurred ten years later, in 1898.

Erastus Erwin, M. D., was born in Roxbury, Conn., in 1805. He was graduated from Yale college in the class with Dr. Jewett and Knight of New Haven. For a short time, he practiced in New Jersey, but finally settled in Sandy Hook, Newtown. He moved from Sandy Hook to Newtown Street in 1841, where for 35 years he had a large practice in Newtown and towns adjoining. He was a contemporary with Dr. Cyrenius H. Booth, outliving him two years dying in Oct., 1873. A man of strong and positive convictions, he made bitter enemies. but he also made hosts of warm and true friends.

Dr. Moses Botsford Beers, son of Ebenezer and Phebe Botsford Beers, was born Jan. 7, 1819 in Newtown. He left Newtown in early life studied for his profession in some western town, probably in Michigan, as he lived in Portland, Mich, later removing to Hersey, Mich. where he died July 9, 1877. He married Loraine Curtis and had one daughter who married J. Selwyn Newland. She died in 1870, leaving a son Albert Newland.

Dr. Henry Hawley Foote son of Rhesa and Polly Hawley Foote, was born in Newtown, Jan. 6, 1823; was educated in the public schools and Newtown Academy. Studied medicine at Durham, Greene Co. N. Y., graduated from Yale Medical College. Practiced medicine at Bradford, N. Y. and at Roxbury, Conn; died Dec. 24, 1859, at the house of his sister, Mrs. Beach Camp, Newtown, Conn.

William Camp son of Beach and Catharine Foote Camp was born at Newtown, May 23, 1832; received his education at public school, Newtown Academy, school of Rev. Geo. L. Foote at Roxbury, Conn. and of F. W. Foote, Elizabeth N. J. Was assistant to J. Homer French at Newtown Academy, 1853. While teaching, studied medicine with Dr. Erastus Erwin, completing his medical studies at Yale. Was assistant resident physician at Hartford Insane Retreat, in 1855, practiced at Kent, Conn., from 1857 to 1863 when he went to Minnesota in search of health, coming the same year to his childhood home where he died, March 20, 1864. He married Ophelia, daughter of Legrand and Delia Beers Randall. Their only son William H. was many years druggist at Canaan, Conn.

Dr. James W. Gordon, son of John and Margaret Colgan Gordon, was born in St. Louis, Mo. Dec. 22, 1862. His mother brought him to Newtown when very young. He attended the public school until 16 years of age. He entered St. Charles College, Ellicot City, Md. 1877. After a three years course he enterd St. John's College, Fordham, N. Y. He studied medicine in the office of Dr. Robert Hubbard, Bridgeport, Conn., and in medical department of University of New York, where he attended lectures three winters, spending his vacations in study with Dr. Hubbard. Graduated in 1888. Became first assistant on staff of physicians attached to Asylums of N. Y. City. Later opened an office in Bridgeport. July 15, 1895, he came to Sandy Hook, where he built up a large practice. He was member of the Board of Education, member of Bridgeport Medical Society, Fairfield County Medical Society and State Medical Society. In 1890 he married Miss. Louise Telgman of Kingston, Ontario. One daughter, Margaret Doretta Leonardi blessed the union. He died Jan. 26, 1904.

Ralph N. Betts Jr. son of Ralph N. and Anna Plowman Betts was born in Woodbury Sept. 25, 1841; received his education in the public schools and the Academy, studied for the practice of dentistry with his uncle at Mount Kisco, N. Y. At the completion of his studies he located in Sandy Hook, where he practiced his profession for thirty years.

His death Oct. 19th, 1906, brought keen sorrow to the members of St. John's Church Sandy Hook of which he had been for many years an honored member.

DR. CHARLES H. PECK

See Page 213
See Genealogical Section Page 118

Dr. Andrew Egan son of Andrew and Mary Clark Egan, born in Newtown, June 7, 1856, was educated in public schools, Newtown Academy and by private tutors. Taught in Sandy Hook school three years, and one term in Middle district. Attended one term at Yale, then entered University of New York, and graduated from Medical department, 1879. Just before graduation, by competitive examination was appointed Assistant physician in Hospital for Insane on Ward's Island N. Y. remaining four years; the last year occupying position of Assistant Medical Superintendant. Early in 1883, was promoted to be Medical Superintendent of the Hart's Island Hospital and Work House Hospital on Hart's Island, N. Y. Occupied that position ten years, when he resigned to accept position in Health Department of N. Y. City and to engage in private practice. For the last twenty years practiced as a specialist.

Dr. Charles H. Peck son of Captain Albert and Louisa Booth Peck was born in Newtown, Conn. June 18, 1870. He received his preliminary education at the Newtown Academy, and entered the College of Physicians and Surgeons, The Medical Dept. of Columbia University, in 1889, graduating in 1892, at the head of his class, being awarded the first Harsen Prize of $500. He was appointed on the House Staff of the New York Hospital in July 1892, serving through both the medical and surgical services, two complete periods of 18 months each, a term of three years in all. On leaving the Hospital, he commenced private practice, July 1895 and has continued in New York City to the present time. He was appointed Assistant Surgeon to the Hudson Hospital, Out Patient Dep't., in July 1895 and served in this capacity for three years. He was appointed Surgeon to the French Hospital in Jan. 1897, serving until Dec. 1909, a period of 12 years; during the latter 8 years of this time he was President of the Medical Board.

Since his resignation, he has been consulting surgeon to the French Hospital, and in addition has held the position of consulting Surgeon to many other hospitals, viz; The General Memorial Hospital, N. Y. City; Hospital for Ruptured and Crippled, N. Y. City; Stamford Hospital, Stamford, Conn.; United Hospital of Portchester and Rye, N. Y.; White Plains Hospital, White Plains, N. Y.; The Hackensack Hospital, Hackensack, N. J.; The Greenwich Hospital, Greenwich, Conn.; Vassar Brothers Hospital, Poughkeepsie, N. Y., and the Nyack Hospital, Nyack, N. Y., all of which positions he holds at the present time.

In Jan., 1904 he was appointed Assistant Surgeon to the Roosevelt Hospital, advanced to the position of Junior Surgeon two years later, and Senior Surgeon in 1909, continuing as Senior Surgeon to the present time; this latter position is one of the most important in New York City.

He has held teaching positions in the Medical Dep't. of Columbia University, first as an assistant instructor of Operative Surgery from 1900 to 1904; as Instructor in Surgery from 1904 to 1909; as Professor of Clinical Surgery from 1909 to the present time. He was decorated by the French Government in 1909, with the Order of Officer of Public Instruction.

He has made many important contributions to Medical Literature. and is a member of many Medical Societies. The N. Y. Academy of Medicine, of which he has been Secretary and Chairman of the Surgical Section; of the N. Y. Surgical Society, having held the positions of Secretary and Vice President, and of which he is at present the President being elected in 1917. He has been 2nd Vice President and at present First Vice President to the N. Y. County Medical Society. A member of the American Medical Association since 1903, and Chairman of its Surgical Section in 1915, at the San Francisco meeting at the time of the Exposition. He was elected a member of the Society of Clinical Surgery in 1909; a Fellow of the American College of Surgeons in 1913; a member of the American Surgical Association, and is now Treasurer; Elected member of Southern Surgical Association in of 1917. A member of the Medical Advisory Board of Council of National Defense, being appointed by Secretary of War on April 3, 1917. Chairman of Auxillary Committee of National Defense of N. Y. City, appointed by the Council of National Defense in Feb. 1917.

*He was appointed Director of Base Hospital No. 15 (The Mackay Unit) of the Roosevelt Hospital on March 16, 1917, by the Surgeon General of the U. S. Army and received his commission as Major on May 9, 1917. The Hospital Unit was ordered for active duty to be sent to France early in June, 1917. Accompanied by his oldest son, Charles Howard Jr. a medical student, and his youngest brother Albert W. Jr.

Dr. Earle Peck, son of Elliot M. and Annie Curtis Peck was born at Newtown Aug. 22, 1891. He attended public school at home, graduated from Newtown High School in class of 1910, graduated from Jefferson Medical College in 1914; was six months in Municipal Hospital and fifteen months at Germantown Hospital. Was appointed first assistant Resident Physician at Municipal Hospital July, 1916. During the Infantile Paralysis epidemic he devoted himself with indefatigable zeal to those committed to his care, contracted the disease and died Sept. 5, 1916.

NEWTOWN'S GRAND LEVY FOR 1739.
Listers, John Beers, Alexander Bryan, John Peck.

Taxpayers in the town as far back as 1739, 28 years only since the incorporation of the town in 1711. On the desk before me lies a homemade book, 12 inches long and five inches wide, made from eight sheets of foolscap paper, imported from England. It is the grand levy of Newtown for 1739, dating farther back than any levy yet found. One hundred and seventy years have passed. It shows the impress of time, but the ink is not faded, the penmanship is clear, though the orthography differs somewhat from that of today. At that early day, in the valuation the house went in, with three acres of land, at £3 invariably, no discrimination being made in houses. Horses, cattle and swine were included, but no sheep. Land was designated as meadow, boggy meadow, pasture land, brush pasture, plow land, good pasture, improved land. Man or women owning real estate was assessed for one poll, £18,. A valuation was also placed upon a man's trade.

*Since the foregoing was written Dr. Peck has returned from France commissioned as Lieut. Col. with headquarters at Washington, D. C. The body of the son who gave his life for his country, now rests on the soil of France.

GRAND LEVY FOR 1739

We copy five individual assessments as they stand recorded, and for the balance we give the names of the property holders and the total of his assessments:

Lemuel Camp, his list:

	£	s	d
2 heads—2 horse kind	42	0	0
12 year old. 5 cows	17	0	0
3 three year old 4 oxen	25	0	0
1 two year old-3 one year old	5	0	0
3 swine—3 acres hum lot	8	0	0
3 acres plow land	1	10	0
8 acres of meadow	5	04	0
44 acres of pasture land	5	12	0
30 acres of brush pasture	3	0	0
His mill and trade	23	0	0
	138	6	0

Thomas Northrop, his list:

	£	s	d
1 Head	18	0	0
Trade	18	0	0
	36	0	0

Widdo Mary Bennitt, her list:

	£	s	d
1 Head	18	0	0
3 acres hum lot	3	0	0
2 horses, 3 oxen, 6 cows	36	0	0
2 one year old, 7 swine	9	0	0
6 acres and half of meadow	2	12	0
1 horse more	3	0	0
10 acres and a half of pasture	4	4	0
16 acres of plow land	8	0	0
30 acres of brush pasture	3	0	0
4 acres of boggy meadow	1	0	0
Trade	12	4	0
	100	0	0

Samuel Sherman, his list:

	£	s	d
One head	18	0	0
Three acres hum lot	3	0	0
10 acres good pature	4	0	0
6 acres brushy pasture	0	12	0
2 acres meddo	0	16	0
2 oxen, 2 cows, 1 horse	17	0	0
1 sow	1	0	0
Trade for selling brooms	30	0	0
	74	8	0

Widdo Sarah Beers, her list:

	£	s	d
3 acres house lot	3	0	0
13 acres good pasture	5	14	0
10 acres improved land	5	0	0
4 acres boggy medow	1	0	0
7 acres good meddo	2	25	0
8 acres brush pasture	0	16	0
4 oxen, 5 cows	31	0	0
4 two year olds	8	0	0
3 one year olds	3	0	0
4 horses, 6 swine	18	0	0
For her trade	10	0	0
	142	16	0

	£
Jeremiah Northrop	109
John Botsford, Sen.,	101
Eleazer Hubbell	79
Andrew Wheeler	55
George Terrill	95
Mathew Sherman	60
Benjamin Hawley	86
Benjamin Dunning	64
John Glover	143
Job Sherman	130
Thomas Skidmore	104
Abraham Bennett	94
Amos Botsford	54
Stephen Burrill	116
Benjamin Glover	86
Robert Seeley	27
Robert Seeley, Jr.	29
Capt. Nathan Baldwin	132
Henry Botsford, Jr.	45
Jeremiah Johnson	39
Samuel Moger	25
James Baldwin	119
Josiah Burritt	73
Henry Botsford	107
Moses Botsford	52
Caleb Baldwin	87
Edward Fairchild	109
Moses Lyon	77
Samuel Sherman	91
Benjamin Burritt	57
John Foote, Jr.,	30
David Fairchild	21
Mary Bennitt	100
John Blackman	126
Peter Hubbell	159
Joseph Stilson	48
John Fabrique	49
David Dunning	35
Peter Hubbell, Jr.,	43
Ezra Hubell	21
Stephen Burral	32
Benjamin Northrop	59
Lemuel Camp	138
John Botsford, Jr.,	64
Daniel Foot	93
Josiah Daton	58
Samuel Turner	37
Alexander Bryan	64
Donald Grant	52
Jeremiah Seeley	31
Thommus Northrop	30
Samuel Bailey	24
Samuel Stillson	32
Benjamin Stillson	46

	£		£
John Platt, Jr.,	43	John Hull	65
Benjamin Curtis	82	Nathaniel Brisco	57
Joseph Hard	25	Joseph Bristoll, Jr.,	31
Joseph Prindle	48	Abner Booth	44
Moses Stillson	94	Widow Mary Booth	41
James Stillson	35	Ebenezer Johnson	77
John Foot	70	Jeremiah Turner	40
Wilmont Turner	33	Samuel Ferris	108
John Shepard	89	Stephen Hawley	128
John Bristol	44	Jonathan Booth	43
Stephen Parmaly	42	John Adams	42
Samuel Griffin	74	Elizabeth Dunning	37
William Sharp	33	Mr. Jonathan Booth	85
Moses Stillson	91	Daniel Booth	150
Jonathan Stillson	43	Ebenezer Sanford	46
Noah Parmaly	89	John Platt	132
Joseph Botsford	132	Job Northrop	46
Peter Ferris	44	Henry Glover	64
John Lake	96	James Brisco	18
Francis Harrison	30	Abel Booth	84
David Henrixson	22	Nathaniel Nickols	127
Samuel Henrixson,	30	Jonathan Hubbell	61
Benoni Henrixson,	27	Ebenezer Platt	69
Buckland Williams	38	James Fordes	73
Jehoshaphat Prindle	51	Job Sanford	60
Ephriam Peck	145	Thomas Leavenworth	57
Samuel Sherman	74	Thomas Bennitt	64
John Gillette	72	William Lyon	30
John Beers	49	Thomas Sharp	44
Sarah Beers, widow,	142	John Leavenworth	58
Joseph Bristol	86	Rubin Adams	29
Timothy Shepherd	19	James Hard	107
Jedediah Parmelee	25	Obadiah Wheeler	163
John Ferris	21	Deacon Joseph Peck	168
Nathaniel Parmelee	27	Joseph Peck	78
Samuel Parmelee	30	Capt. Thomas Tousey	142
Lieut Johnson		Ephraim Prindle	32
Lieut. John Northrop	111	·irgant Eherman	47
Moses Johnson	33	Daniel Sherman	25
Samuel Sanford	51	·nuel Johnson	21
Abiel Beers	64	John Reed	5
Samuel Brown	10	Nathaniel Lyons	4
Abraham Kimberley	66	James Brisco	60
Freegrace Adams	164	Peter Hubbell	159

The last person on the list is Peter Hubbell, Newtown's first town clerk, and on the second page of the first volume of Newtown records we find that he appropriated space for his family record, which, for precise diction and complete detail, we copy.

With the increase of worldly possessions, he and his good wife were duly mindful of the Bible injunction to increase and multiply upon the earth. In addittion to Peter Hubbell's official duties, he was a tiller of the soil and, with the good wife and mother, became possessed of a small farm, so that in 1739, we find that their worldly goods liable to taxation had a valuation of £159 and distributed as follows:

	£	s	d		£	s	d
3 heads, 4 oxen, 4 cows,	82	0	0	61 acres of plow land	30	10	0
3 one year olds, 5 horses kind	18	0	0	4 acres of pasture land	1	12	0
23 swine	23	0	0	3 acres of meadow	1	04	0
3 acres of home lot	3	0	0	Sum total	159	06	0

Peter Hubbell was marryed to Katherine Wheeler his wife, by the Rev. Mr. Charles Chauncey, minister in Stratfield, both of Stratfield, on January ye 19th, 1709.

Ephraim Hubbell, his eldest son, was born in Newtown on December ye ye 21, 1711.

Peter Hubbell, son of Peter Hubbell by Katherine his wife, born April ye 5th, 1715.

Ezra Hubbell, son of Peter Hubbell, by Katherine his wife, was born February ye 28th, Anno Domini 1717.

Sarah Hubbell, daughter of Peter Hubbell by Katherine his wife, was born in Newtown, February 27, 1719, being ye fifth year of ye reign of our most Greatious Sovereign Lord King George which began August ye first, 1714.

Jedediah Hubbell, son of Peter Hubbell by Katherine his wife, was born in Newtown, August ye 22, 1720.

Matthew Hubbell, son of Peter Hubbell by Katherine his wife, was born in Newtown, September ye 5th, A. D. 1723.

Gideon Hubbell, son of Peter Hubbell by Catherine his wife, was born in Newtown, April ye 28, 1726.

Newtown, November ye 10th, 1729, about 2 of ye clock afternoon, Comfort Hubbell, son of Peter Hubbell was born of Katherine his wife.

Enock Hubbell, son to Peter Hubbell, born of Katherine his wife, in Newtown, August ye 10th, 1735, about five of ye clock in the afternoon.

The number of property holders in the town in 1739, was 152 and the amount of taxable property laid down by the listers or assessors was £9,289 sterling. At the annual town meeting in December, 1739, it was voted that the town rate for defraying the town charges the year past should be two pence half penny on the pound, to be levied on the list of polls and rateable estate of the inhabitants, and that one penny on the pound should be levied for the schools and be laid out in the winter season and be gathered with the town rate and be taken out of the town treasury for the schools, known as the North and South schools, and that John Lake and Nathaniel Nickols shall be school committee for the south school and Ensign John Glover and Abel Booth Committee for the north school. Back in 1739, our schools were under town management.

GRAND LEVY OF 1767

In any staid old agricultural town, the number of taxpayers would correspond nearly to the number of families, upon whom devolved the duty of meeting the current town expenses, and also their share of the expenses of the Common wealth. The grand levy of 1739, showed the names of 147 tax-payers for that year. The grand levy for 1767, shows the number of tax-payers to have increased to 341. It is interesting to note the great increase in those of the same family name, and to see how great an increase had been made in 28 years. There were 457 tax-payers in 1786.

There is one word "Faculty" between some names that, to some, needs explanation. The word is used as representing some trade or profession, which was included with other property at an estimated valuation and upon which a tax was laid. Some assessments ran as high as £30, and from that down to £3. If the writer has been correctly informed, the three of the surname of "Nichols," Nathaniel, assessed £30 for "faculty," Peter assessed £10, Richard £16, 10s, each follow wool carding in the southerly part of town.

A list of the Polls and Rateable Estate of the inhabitants of Newtown for the year 1767, as possessed for the 20th of August:

Adams, John	109	18	0	Bristol, Ebenezer	51	17	6
Adams, Ephraim	28	14	6	Faculty	10	8	0
Adams, Samuel	48	2	0	Bryan, Ezra	36	0	0
Baldwin, Caleb, Esq.,	138	7	6	Faculty	12	0	0
Faculty	10	0	0	Beardslee, Josiah	187	5	0
Baldwin, Caleb, Capt.	10	0	0	Beardslee, Isreal	80	15	0
Baldwin, Caleb, Sec	94	16	0	Faculty	8	0	0
Baldwin, Nathan, Capt.	33	14	3	Beardslee, James	21	0	0
Baldwin, Nathan, Jr.	64	15	0	Brisco, Nathaniel, Lieut.	154	5	0
Baldwin, Daniel	126	14	6	Brisco, James	25	0	0
Baldwin, James	107	08	0	Beach, John	78	2	6
Baldwin, Gideon	90	10	0	Burwell, Stephen	47	17	0
Baldwin, Jabez	91	15	6	Burwell, William	24	2	0
Booth, Daniel	424	1	0	Faculty	18	0	0
Faculty	15	0	0	Burwell, Rebecca, Widow	7	0	0
Booth, Abel	176	9	0	Burritt. Benjamin	69	0	3
Booth, Jonathan	189	0	0	Burritt, Eleazer	60	2	6
Faculty	25	0	0	Burritt, Nathan	68	6	6
Booth, Abraham	91	0	0	Bulkly Jabez	26	0	0
Booth, Hezekiah	76	14	6	Barnum, Francis	3	0	0
Booth, Reuben	54	14	0	Barnum, Nathaniel	18	0	0
Booth, Ebenezer	78	12	6	Brinsmade, Zechariah	26	0	0
Faculty	18	0	0	Burr, James	3	8	0
Bassit, Thomas	30	0	0	Camp, Joel	71	0	0
Bassit, John	30	2	9	Camp, Lemuel	145	0	0
Bassit, Joel	49	18	6	Camp, Samuel	62	14	0
Bennitt, Abraham	126	13	0	Camp, Silas	82	5	6
Bennitt Ephraim	75	15	0	Cadey, Nathaniel	24	0	0
Beers, Daniel	100	5	6	Coggswell, Asa	52	18	1
Beers, John	146	15	0	Clark, Zerchariah, Jr	59	18	0
Beers, Samuel	134	5	6	Clark, James	1	8	0
Birtch, Jeremiah	29	1	4	Curtiss, Benjamin	106	13	6
Birtch, Wiliam	67	17	6	Curtiss, Matthew	94	8	6
Faculty	9	0	0	Curtis, Benjamin, Jr.	90	2	6
Botsford, Amos, Jr.,	20	0	0	Curtiss, Nehemiah	84	4	0
Faculty	50	0	0	Curtiss, Abijah	74	7	0
Botsford, Abel	72	12	0	Curtis, Nirom	27	4	0
Botsford, Abel Jr.,	58	10	0	Chambers, Thomas	41	0	0
Faculty	10	0	0	Chambers, Asa	21	0	0
Botsford, Abraham	67	10	0	Crowfoot, Daniel	77	5	0
Botsford, Gideon	141	5	0	Dunning, Benjamin Capt.	79	6	0
Botsford, Jabez	37	18	0	Dunning, Peter	1	0	0
Botsford, John	87	1	0	Dunning, David	86	6	0
Faculty	10	0	0	Dunning, David, Jr.	45	6	0
Botsford, Moses	95	10	0	Dunning, Eli	68	16	0
Botsford, Joseph	24	5	6	Faculty	10	0	0
Botsford, Elijah	60	5	0	Dunning, Ezra	40	14	0
Botsford, Henry	24	16	0	Dunning, Abijah	26	4	0
Botsford, Isaac	23	10	0	Dunning, Andrew	21	0	0
Botsford, Ezra	34	0	0	Dunning, Jared	50	6	6
Botsford, Jared	18	0	0	Dibble, John	1	5	0
Birtch, George	36	15	0	Dibble, Eleazer	1	0	0
Faculty	6	0	0	Fairman, Richard, Esq.,	126	10	0
Blackman, John, Capt.	142	10	0	Faculty	25	0	0
Blackman, James	67	0	0	Fairchild, Agur	76	3	6
Blackman, Joseph	82	11	6	Fairchild, Jonathan	120	15	0
Blackman, Ebenezer	84	15	0	Fairchild, Ebenezer	43	18	1½
Blackman, Nathaniel	30	11	6	Fairchild, James	129	17	6
Bristol, Joseph, 2nd	58	13	0	Faculty	8	0	0
Bristol. Joseph	3	0	0	Fairchild, Seth	57	16	0
Bristol, Job	39	10	2	Fairchild, David	34	3	6
Bristoll, Enos	11	12	0	Fairchild, John	24	0	0

GRAND LEVY FOR 1767

Name	£	s	d
Fairchild, Oliver	57	13	6
Ford, Ebenezer	131	6	6
Ford, Thomas	60	5	0
Fabrique, John	19	5	0
Fabrique, John, Jr.,	29	0	0
Ferris, Abraham	95	2	6
Ferris, Peter	76	5	0
Ferris, Samuel, Jr.	56	5	6
Foot, Daniell	21	10	0
Foot, Daniel (Taunton)	28	6	0
Foot, George	28	12	0
Foot, Peter	24	5	0
French, Gamaliel	53	14	0
French, Samuel	28	10	0
Glover, John, Capt.	127	5	0
Glover, Henry, Capt.	154	11	0
Glover, Henry, Jr.	65	14	6
Glover, John, Jr.	127	14	6
Glover, James	100	10	6
Glover, Daniel	54	4	6
Glover, Arnold	44	8	6
Grant, Arminel	45	9	9
Faculty	30	0	0
Griffin, Samuel, Lieut.	37	14	0
Griffin, John Lieut.	45	10	0
Griffin, Joseph	61	6	6
Griffin, Samuel, Jr.	58	16	6
Griffin, Abner	36	6	0
Gray, James	24	10	0
Gillett, Samuel	108	12	0
Gunn, Joseph	52	0	0
Gunn, Joseph, Jr.	107	13	0
Hall, William	43	0	0
Faculty	4	0	0
Hall, Asa	39	0	0
Harris, Jabez	34	13	6
Hard, Abner	139	15	0
Hard, Amos	141	14	2
Hard, Ammon	18	0	0
Hard, Joseph	21	0	0
Hard, Hannah, Widow	7	15	6
Hard, Nirom	54	15	6
Hard, Zadok	75	6	6
Hawley, Abel	60	16	6
Faculty	6	0	0
Hawley, William	89	5	6
Hawley, Benjamin	77	8	0
Hawley, Benjamin, Esq.	71	0	0
Hatch, Joshua	40	3	0
Hatch, Peter	46	4	0
Hendricks, Roger	22	0	0
Hendricks, Zadock	18	0	0
Hull, John	45	15	0
Hull, Eliphalet	57	5	0
Hull, Elijah	64	9	6
Hubbell, Peter	54	0	0
Hubbell, Enoch	38	2	6
Hubbell, Jeptha	36	10	0
Hyde, Joseph	34	0	0
Hurd, Abel	73	12	0
Hurd, Theophilus	39	5	0
Faculty	15	0	0
Faculty	3	0	0
Jackson, David	69	0	0
Jackson, David, Jr.	18	0	0
Jackson, Daniel	43	1	0
Jackson, Ephraim	24	0	0
Jackson, Gershom	23	0	0
Johnson, Ichabod	69	1	6
Johnson, John	52	10	0
Johnson, Ebenezer	18	0	0
Judson, Abel, Lieut.	144	10	0
Judson, John	40	5	6
Kimberley, Abraham	61	12	0
Kimberley, Abraham, Jr.,	51	14	0
Kimberley, Fitch	21	0	0
Lake, John	27	8	6
Lake, John, Jr.,	35	10	0
Lake, Nathan	58	14	0
Lake, Ephraim	52	0	9
Lake, Thomas	69	0	6
Lattin, Benjamin	18	0	0
Lattin, Job	27	0	0
Lattin, Jacob	18	0	0
Lane, James	52	0	0
Merchant, Amos	53	15	0
Faculty	15	0	0
Mallory, Nathaniel	20	8	0
More, John	27	0	0
Morehouse, Abel	15	0	0
Morehouse, Stephen	2	10	0
Morehouse, Daniel	8	14	0
Nichols, Nathaniel	210	5	0
Faculty	30	0	0
Nichols, Peter	112	1	6
Faculty	10	0	0
Nichols, Richmond	87	19	0
Faculty	16	8	0
Northrop, Amos	95	18	0
Northrop, Joshua	79	3	0
Northrop, Jeremiah, Jr	1	8	0
Northrop, Ezra	42	10	0
Northrop, John	140	0	0
Nichols, Caleb	52	0	0
Northrop, William	18	4	0
Northrop, William, Jr	57	19	0
Northrop, Wait	81	3	0
Northrop, Nehemiah	39	16	0
Faculty	9	0	0
Northrop, Abel	14	7	6
Northrop, Isiah	4	17	0
Northrop, Benjamin	82	16	0
Northrop, Benjamin, Jr.,	44	19	6
Northrop, Enos	69	7	0
Northrop, Jonathan, C'p.	118	19	0
Northrop, Gideon	35	11	0
Nettleton, Theophilus	72	10	0
Ogden, Ebenezer	45	11	3
Faculty	20	0	0
Parmelee, Jedediah	47	10	0
Parmalee, Noah	56	4	6
Parmalee, Noah, Jr.,	33	6	0
Peck, Henry	73	0	0
Peck, Henry, Jr.,	84	15	6
Peck, Heth	111	6	0
Peck, Heth, Jr.,	60	12	6
Peck, Benajah	18	0	0
Peck, Ameiel	56	17	0

Name	£	s	d	Name	£	s	d
Faculty	5	0	0	Stilson, Benjamin, Jr.,	48	5	9
Peck, Daniel	68	7	6	Stilson, Israel	37	0	0
Peck, John,	148	9	0	Stilson, Elijah	47	13	6
Peck, Jabez	51	16	0	Stilson, Jonathan	37	0	0
Peck, Nathaniel	51	18	6	Stilson, Jacob			
Peck, Nathaniel, Jr.,	37	11	0	Stilson, Daniel	18	0	0
Peck, Ebenezer	83	8	0	Stilson, Bailey	30	4	0
Peck, Ezra	41	1	0	Stilson, Thomas	49	12	0
Peck, Joseph	75	8	6	Skidmore, Thomas	67	13	6
Peck, Ephraim	104	8	0	Skidmore, John	63	18	6
Peck, Samuel	24	0	0	Skidmore, Nehemiah	100	17	0
Peck, Aaron	29	4	0	Smith, Amos	80	7	0
Peck, Gideon	73	5	0	Smith, George	83	6	0
Peck, Moss	113	7	0	Smith, Joseph, Dea	52	13	6
Peck, Enoch	31	12	0	Smith, Joseph, Lieut.	75	4	0
Peck, Elihu	19	15	0	Smith, Richard	102	15	0
Peck, John, Jr.,	28	8	0	Faculty	10	0	0
Prindle, Joseph	5	0	0	Starling, John	156	5	0
Prindle, Joseph, Jr.,	91	12	0	Summers, Gershom	57	10	0
Faculty	15	0	0	Summers, Samuel	74	10	0
Prindle, Jonathan	69	7	6	Summers, Robert	49	11	6
Faculty	5	0	0	Summers, Benjamin	32	12	0
Prindle, Abel, Lieut.	28	7	6	Summers, Ebenezer	28	8	6
Prindle, Jehoshaphat	26	12	0	Shepherd, John Jr.	48	11	0
Prindle, William	34	15	0	Shepherd, John	63	3	0
Prindle, Abijah	18	0	0	Faculty	3	0	0
Prindle, James	36	0	0	Shepherd, Abraham	27	13	6
Prindle, Eliadah	23	0	0	Shepherd, Timothy	161	3	0
Prindle, Joel	29	4	6	Shepherd, Simeon	62	11	6
Prindle, Ephraim	34	13	6	Seeley, Nehemiah	46	0	0
Platt, Moses	152	12	6	Seeley, Robert	27	3	0
Platt, Josiah	53	12	6	Seeley, Ottmiel	40	4	0
Pearce, Francis	18	0	0	Sherwood, John	56	6	0
Rugg, Oliver	18	0	0	Sherwood, John Parrick	58	6	6
Roberts, Joel	20	0	0	Taylor, Abner	11	19	3
Roberts, Thomas	25	16	0	Taylor, Ebenezer	63	18	6
Sanford, Jonathan	169	10	0	Thomas, Lemuel, Dr.	40	6	0
Sanford, Jonas	57	5	0	Faculty	10	0	0
Sanford, John	41	9	0	Turrell, George	50	9	6
Faculty	10	0	0	Faculty	3	0	0
Sanford, Hezekiah	50	0	6	Turrell, Roger	66	2	0
Sanford, James	32	7	6	Turrell, Amos, Lieut.	80	4	6
Sanford, Thomas	62	14	0	Turrell, Jared	31	14	0
Sanford, Thomas	62	14	0	Turner, Jeremiah	145	5	0
Sanford, Hannah, Widdo	17	0	0	Tousey, John	148	10	0
Sanford, Samuel	59	15	0	Turner, Jeremiah, Jr	59	12	6
Faculty	8	0	0	Tousey, Oliver	110	10	0
Sanford, Nathaniel	19	13	0	Tousey, Zalmon	84	9	0
Sanford, Ebenezer	63	18	6	Thompson, Robert	18	0	0
Faculty	5	0	0	Treadwell, Timothy	23	0	0
Sherman, Zadock	74	6	6	Turner, Miller	46	18	6
Sherman, Nathan	41	1	9	Wheeler, Joseph, Capt.	82	2	0
Sherman, David,	81	19	6	Wheeler, Obadiah, Jr.	74	13	6
Sherman, Lemuel	87	15	0	Wheeler, Andrew	57	12	6
Sherman, Jotham	81	7	6	Wheeler, Josiah	70	2	6
Faculty	10	0	0	Wheeler, Lemuel	54	16	6
Sherman John	79	4	0	Wheeler, Thomas	90	6	0
Sherman, Ephraim	62	14	0	Winton, Daniel	68	4	0
Sharp, Thomas	18	0	0	Wright, William	45	12	0
Stilson, Andrew	90	11	6	Washburn, Nathan, Dr.	24	0	0
Stilson, Vincent	58	6	0	Wheeler, Obadiah, Capt	29	2	6

To the Honorable General Assembly the foregoing is a true list of the polls and rateable estates of the inhabitants of Newtown as possessed the 20th day of August, A. D. 1767.

Certified by us,
Abel Booth,
Amos Northrop,
Bailey Stillson,
John Fabrique,
Henry Glover, Jr.
Zadock Sherman,
Jonathan Prindle
Listers.

The above persons were sworn to a faithful discharge of their office as listers before me,

Caleb Baldwin, Town Clerk.

RATABLE ESTATES FOR 1809.

The statute laws of the State of Connecticut make it obligatory upon its citizens to prepare a list of taxable property, that shall be handed into the Board of Assessors on or before the first of November of each year, the law leaving it to the Assessors to fix the valuation subject to the approval of the Board of Relief.

An act was passed by the Connecticut Legislature at its annual session in 1808, by which printed forms were sent out showing what kinds of property were liable to taxation and also placing a sum at which the property should be valued, and on which the tax should be levied. It was my good fortune to have come into my possession from my grandfather, 60 years ago or more, a printed copy of a list of ratable estates, showing what property must be listed for that year and what valuation must be placed upon it.

Copy of the perfected list for 1809, compiled in compliance with the act passed by the Assembly at its session in 1808:

Poll, from 21-70 years of age	$60.00
Poll, from 18-21 years of age	30.00
Oxen and bulls, 4 years old and upward	10.00
Cows, steers and heifers, with bulls of 3 years old	7.00
Heifers, steers or bulls, of 2 years old	3.34
Stallion or seed horse, more than 3 years old	67.00
Horse kind, 3 years old, and upward	10.00
Horse kind, of 2 years old	7.00
Horse kind, of 1 years old	3.34
Mules of 3 years old and upward	10.00
Mules of 2 years old	7.00
Mules of 1 year old	3.34
Acres of rough land	1.67
Acres of upland, meadow and clear pasture	1.34
Acres of boggy meadow, mowed	0.84
Acres of Boggy meadow, not mowed	0.34
Acres of other meadow	1.25
Acres of bush pasture	0.34
Acres of uninclosed land, 1st rate	0.34
Acres of uninclosed land, 2d. rate	0.17
Acres of uninclosed land, 3d rate	0.09
Coach	168.00
Chariot	134.00
Phaeton	100.00
Coachee	75.00
Carricole	68.00
Chaise, riding chair or sulky	00.00
Other four-wheel carriage, on springs	30.00
Lumber box wagon and no springs	00.00
Gold Watch	34.00
Silver or other watch	10.00
Steel or brass-wheeled clock or timepiece	20.00
Wooden-wheeled clock or time-piece	7.00
Ounces of silver plate	00.00
Money at interest	0.00
House fire-places, whether used or not	5.00
House fire-places, depreciated one-quarter, used or not	3.75
House fire-places, depreciated one-half, used or not	2.50

House fire-places, depreciated three quarters, used or not	1.25	or not, two stories	20.00
Store or ware-house, whether part of a dwelling house or not, one story	10.00	Store or warehouse, whether part of a dwelling house or not, three stories	30.00
Store or warehouse, whether part of a dwelling house		Bank stock	00.00
		Sheep one year old	00.00

The listers desire to have the above list filled up. Each person is required to insert the name of the religious society to which he belongs, and return the list, completed, on or before the 10th day of September, next.

August 20, 1808

Particular attention is called to the segregation by which land was entered, and also to the varying prices per acre, according to quality, also the varying prices of stock according to age, of fire-places according to usage, and of vehicles according to style.

During all the years preceding and down to this time, no dwelling house had appeared on a levy.

NEWTOWN BOROUGH.

Proceedings of the General Assembly of our State, by which, at its May session, 1824, the Borough of Newtown was incorporated. The borough, still intact, numbers yet a few of the second, third and fourth generation of families of those days. With the domain very much enlarged, with its scenic beauty much improved; with its wide main street, its beautiful, well-kept lawns; its commodious sanitary public buildings, its abundant spring water supply from a lake not more than a half mile away, a Beach Memorial Library of volumes in the thousands; a trunk line of State highway from Newtown to Bridgeport, in the near future to run from Newtown to the Berkshire Hills; the Berkshire division of the New York, New Haven and Hartford railroad with three stations in Newtown, the main station within 10 minutes walk of Newtown Village, with the Federal express to and from Boston and Washington, D. C., daily; a township 48 square miles in extent, with 400 miles of highways and by-ways that one can travel enough to cause pleasure seekers to increase in numbers as time goes on. It will not do to close without including Sandy Hook, a village by itself in Newtown, and the scenic beauty of Mt. Pisgah, with its base washed by the sparkling waters of the Pootatuck as it leaps and dashes along through the Glen, one of the Switzerlands of America, for their rightful share of admiration. To know all that there is to know about the scenic beauty of Newtown, one needs to come and dwell among us.

An act incorporating the Borough of Newtown, passed by the General Assembly of Connecticut, at its May session, 1824:

Section 1. Resolved by this Assembly, that all the electors of this state, inhabitants of the town of Newtown, in the County of Fairfield, being within the following bounds, to wit, beginning at the foot of Newtown Street at the road leading to Redding and running easterly to Queen Street so called, thence northerly through the center of said Queen Street to the east and west turnpike, thence westerly on said turnpike to Carcass Lane, so-called, thence northerly the whole length of said lane to the road leading to Walnut Tree Hill so-called, thence northerly in a direct line from said lane to the junction of Hall Lane so-called, and the road leading to Hawley's Bridge, thence westerly through the center of said Hall Lane to the Bridgeport and Newtown turnpike, thence westerly in a direct line from said lane 50 rods from the west side of said turnpike, thence southerly in a line parallel with said turnpike and the aforesaid Newtown street to the center of the aforesaid road leading to Redding near Daniel Beers' dwelling house, thence easterly to the place began at, be, and the same are hereby ordained, constituted and declared to be, from time to time and forever hereafter, one body corporate and politic, in fact and in name, by the name of "The Warden, Burgesses, and Freemen of the Borough of Newtown," and by that name they and their successors, forever, shall have perpetual succession, and shall be persons in law, capable of sueing and being sued, pleading and being impleaded, in all suits of what nature soever, and also to purchase, hold and convey any estate real or personal, and may have a common seal, and may change and alter the same at pleasure, and shall be freemen of said Borough.

Section 2. And for the better government of said Borough, be it further resolved that there shall be a meeting of said Bourough, holden annually in the month of May, at such time and place as by the by-laws of said Borough shall be directed, for the purpose of choosing all the officers of said Borough, and the officers chosen at such meeting shall continue in office for and during the term of one year from said annual meeting, unless others shall be sooner chosen and qualified in their stead.

Section 3. And said borough of Newtown shall have all the powers and privileges conferred on other inland Boroughs with this State, and be subject to the same restrictions and liabilities to which said other inland Boroughs are by law subjected. And all the officers of said Borough shall be qualified in the same manner, and have the same powers, as the officers of other inland boroughs so far as the local situation thereof will permit.

Section 4. The first meeting of said Borough shall be holden at the house of Czar Keeler in said Borough, on the second Monday of June, A. D. 1824, at one o'clock in the afternoon of said day, for the choice of a warden, burgesses, clerk, treasurer and bailiff, and to transact such other business as shall be necessary, which may be, from time to time adjourned, and a copy of this paragraph of this resolve, certified under the hand of the Secretary of this State, and posted upon the public sign-post in said Borough at least three days before said second Monday of June, shall be legal warning to the freemen of said borough to attend said first meeting, and the officers chosen at such meeting shall continue in office until the expiration of the annual meeting in the month of May, A. D. 1825, unless others are sooner chosen and qualified in their stead, and that said Borough shall at such meetings first choose a clerk of said Borough, who shall immediately be sworn, and shall forthwith make a record of his being chosen and sworn, and the record thus by him made, in such case, shall be good and effectual in law. Such records may be made by clerks thereafter, and shall be valid, anything in this resolve notwithstanding. And said Borough shall thereupon proceed to choose a warden and other officers of said Borough mentioned in this paragraph of this resolve, and that Benjamin F. Shelton shall have as to the first election of the warden, burgesses, clerk, treasurer and bailiff of said Borough, the same powers and proceed in the same manner, as the warden, burgesses and bailiff of said Borough are by this resolve to have and proceed in at the future elections in said Borough, and shall be moderator of said meeting, till a warden be chosen and qualified according to this resolve.

Said Borough shall at first said meeting, appoint a time and place for holding said meeting of said warden and burgesses, which meeting shall have power to adjourn from time to time, always provided that anything in this resolve notwithstanding, the inhabitants living within the limits of said Borough, shall to all intents and purposes, be and remain a part of the town of Newtown, entitled to all its privileges and subject to all its burdens, as if this resolve had not been passed. Provided, nevertheless, that if this resolve, or any provision therein contained, shall be found inconvenient, or in any way inadequate, the same may be repealed, altered or revoked, by the General Assembly.

Section 5. All charges and expenses that shall have been and may be incurred in consequence of this act of incorporation shall be borne and defrayed by said Borough, by taxes on the polls and rateable estate of said Borough within said limits.

NEWTOWN'S FIRE COMPANIES, 1803—1913.

Dodgingtown is the name of a hamlet in Flat Swamp school district about mid-way between the village of Newtown and that of Bethel, made up for the most part of families living on their own farms, and a few mechanics busied with their several trades. A little community within itself, with many social qualities and interests in common. Among other things, they have a well-organized fire department of about 40 members and, although they have no fire engine as yet, so well equipped otherwise and so systematic in drill that, when they take part in an out-of-town drill, the lookers-on sit up and take notice. They took part in a firemen's parade in West Haven, where, in competition with 64 other companies, they were awarded a silver cup, as best in drill of any company on the grounds. The village of Newtown also has a fire company of about 45 members that has been an organized company for 25 years. They, too, have no fire engine, but in other respects and appliances are well up to date and have done valient work in many cases of fire in the past in Newtown, in Sandy Hook and near-by vicinities. Both companies are voluntary, independent companies, never having been aided by town appropriations.

The building that furnishes accommodation for appliances necessary for the demand of a hook and ladder company is a neatly constructed, commodious structure on town property, near the town hall, which, with the town hall, adds much to the attractiveness of the borough, as well as to that of the beautiful village street, with its well-kept lawns, beautiful shade trees and residential buildings. The town hall and fire company building, under the care and supervision of the janitor, Patrick Gannon, speak well for the janitor and the town officials responsible for its care.

Turning now to the town records we find that, in the matter of town protection from fire, in 1803, a special town meeting was called by petition to determine what the town should do to guard against the ravages of an outbreak of fire.

At a lawful town meeting Dec. 19, 1803, the first movement was made to provide the town with protection from fire, when a vote was passed "that the town treasurer be directed to pay to William Edmond, Esq., one hundred dollars toward purchasing a fire engine for the use of the town," On the 6th day of Feb., following, a special meeting, called by petition to reconsider the vote appropriating $100, for a fire engine, the vote of the previous meeting was rescinded, and Elijah Nichols was appointed chimney viewer instead.

No future doings, townwise, in regard to fire engines until 1807. In the meantime, while the matter had been held in abeyance, a subscription paper had been circulated and $450 subscribed toward the expense of a fire engine, and a house in which to store it.

Another petition, drawn by Hon. William Edmond, a citizen of Newtown, a lawyer of high repute and member of Congress at a time when the office sought the man and not the man the office, was circulated, Nov. 21, 1807, and on the 23d, of Nov. they were able to report $450 subscribed. At the annual town meeting, on the 7th day of December, 1807, the petition was read in open town meeting:

"To the inhabitants of Newtown in legal Town meeting convened: The inhabitants of sd town street and its vicinity beg leave to represent that seriously alarmed at a recent event which threatened for a time to lay their dwellings in ashes, to unhouse their families, to sweep away their public buildings and produce a scene of destruction and distress awful to contemplate and too painful to describe, they met at the house of Caleb Baldwin on the 21st of Nov., 1807, to take into consideration their exposed and dangerous situation, and to devise the best practicable means of guarding themselves in future against destruction by fire. At this meeting the opinion was unanimous that it was the duty of the house-holders to see that their chimneys were swept or cleaned by burning without loss of time and to provide themselves with ladders as expeditiously as possible. It was also thought advisable to procure a fire engine if possible as the best instrument properly served with which to contend against so unruly and dangerous an element and indeed as the only one in which any just confidence of success might be placed in the hour of danger. To effect this so desirable an object a subscription was immediately opened and a committee appointed to wait upon the inhabitants in the street (not then present) and the meeting was adjourned to the 23d of Nov. to receive the report of the committee that the sum of $450 had been subscribed for the purpose with a liberality evincive of a strong sense of danger and of the expediency and necessity of the measure. Having proceeded thus far and accomplished so much by their individual exertions, it was thought advisable by the meeting to state their proceedings to the town at their annual meeting and to solicit that aid without which all their efforts to accomplish so important an object must prove ineffectual, especially as it appeared from the best information to be procured that the probable expense of a good and effectual engine delivered at Newtown with the cost of a house to shelter it would amount to about $700, that about $200 would be needed in addition to the subscription to carry the object of it into effect and without which their utmost exertion must prove fruitless. Thus circumstanced they came before the Town to solicit their approbation and encouragement confiding in their wisdom, their justice and their generosity and trusting that their enlightened and liberal fellow citizens on a subject interesting to all will be ready to discard a narrow policy, to sacrifice the pride of opinion, and the spirit of party to the general good and viewing the subject in the same light with the petitioners will cheerfully grant from the Town a sum equal to the deficiency of the subscription or in such way as their wisdom shall desire to enable the petitioners to accomplish the proposed object, and the petitioners as in duty bound will ever pray. William Edmond for and in behalf of the petitioners."

After the reading of the petition, the meeting voted that the petition of the inhabitants of Newtown Street and vicinity for a grant of money from the town towards purchasing a fire engine be recorded. Caleb Baldwin, Town clerk.

At the conclusion of the reading of the petition, the town voted:

That the selectmen of Newtown be, and they are hereby authorized, empowered and directed to draw orders in favor of Joseph Nichols, upon the Town treasurer of Newtown for the sum of $200 to be applied to the purchase of a fire engine and a house to shelter the same, provided that nothing in this vote shall be construed to subject the town hereafter to the payment of any other or further sum than is herein before granted either for said fire engine, a house to shelter it, or for cisterns, ladders, fire hooks, ropes, buckets, working the engine, or any expense whatever, respecting the same, but said town shall be exempted therefrom in the same manner as though this vote had not been passed." "Voted that the petition of the inhabitants of the town street and its vicinity for a grant of money from the town towards purchasing fire engine be recorded. Attest, Caleb Baldwin, town clerk.

No further records are to be found in regard to subsequent action on the part of the town, though for years, among offices provided for at the annual town meeting, was that of chimney viewer, given Elijah Nichols, for which no pay was given.

NEWTOWN ACADEMY.

The following letter was written by Mr. George L. Foote, eldest son of Rhesa and Polly Foote, a short time before his graduation from Washington (now Trinity) College, Hartford, Conn.

Washington College, Hartford, Conn.
Jan. 24, 1837.

To Messrs. Henry Beers, Samuel C. Blackman,
   Henry Dutton, D. H. Belden and David V. B. Baldwin.

Sirs:

The subject upon which I am about to address you at this time may be one in which you feel no concern and about which you would not like to be troubled. If so, pardon the trouble this may give you. But should you feel any interest in the subject, I ask of you a careful examination of my plans and a frank communication of your opinion. The subject of public education has for a long time occupied my attention and, in examining the various means presented for usefulness, this stands among the most prominent in my estimation. I have accordingly concluded to direct my attention to the subject and use my exertions for the promotion of this object for two or three years after I shall finish my studies, and, thinking of my native town, I have concluded to propose to you a plan that I have formed and ask your advice and co-operation. I wish to establish somewhere an Academy in which boys and girls may pursue their studies after leaving the primary schools and be fitted either for business, for teachers or for college. I wish such a school to be select—that is, to have certain qualifications requisite for admission; to have not "all branches" taught in it, but such as shall be most useful, and to have such taught on a thorough plan; and to have the school established on the principles of the Bible, believing that the best class-book for every institution, though I would not have any **sectarian** principles inculcated, nor would I hesitate to declare my preference for the church of my affections and the nursery of my childhood and youth. I would have it **emphatically a Christian** school, such a school as every well-wisher of his country would desire to see established in every town. In examining the various situations for the location of such a school, my preference has been given to Newtown for various reasons: It is my **native** town and there are attachments that bind me there, which I find nowhere else. It is a quiet place and very free from evil influence calculated to draw off boys who might be boarding from home. There is no school of this kind established there, though I have felt the need of such a one for many years. There are many boys and girls who, I think, would attend such a school, living in the town. My mother lives there, with whom I could board and receive boarders and be at home, and I could then be in a situation to assist the younger members of the family. And lastly, I should have some pride, whether censurable or not, to see such a school started in my native town, and started by my exertions. These are some of the reasons that have led me to select that as the place of location, and of the weight of these reasons you can each judge.

Now, gentlemen, do you think such a school would succeed in Newtown? Are there moneyed men who would feel interested in such a plan, enough to put a building in some eligible situation and, after fitting it to my mind, rent at a reasonable per cent so that I could make it an object worthy of my employment? Do you think pupils enough could be obtained, and would you give me your influence in obtaining pupils? Knowing, as you do, the circumstances in which I am placed; the character of the inhabitants of Newtown; the proverb that "a prophet hath no honor in his own country," your own feeling on the subject and the situation of Miss Sarah Blackman's school, would you advise me to persevere in this plan or to relinquish it altogether?

My object in writing at this time is, that having obtained your opinion, I may make some calculation on the subject the coming Spring, and have everything ready to begin in the fall when I shall have finished my studies in this place. It is, gentlemen, with some experimental knowledge of your character and good feelings that I make this communication, and I earnestly hope that you will do me the favor of answering me immediately, if you think the subject worthy of an answer.

I am, gentlemen, with great esteem for you,
Your friend and humble servant,
George L. Foote.

This communication evidently met with the hearty approval of the gentlemen to whom it was addressed, who immediately went to work to create a public interest in its favor, which resulted in calling an informal meeting at Mr. Caleb Baldwin's, Feb. 8, 1837, "to form an association for the purpose of purchasing a location, and building a suitable house in the borough of Newtown to be occupied as an Academy for the education of the young in the various branches of science, and to raise a sum of money sufficient for said purpose."

The subscription was to be binding, provided the sum of $1000, should be raised; $1475 was pledged at once.

The original list of subscribers may be interesting to their children and grand children:

Harry Beers	$100	Joseph Dick	$25	Jabez B. Peck	$25
David H. Belden	100	Charles C. Warner	25	Lemuel Beers	25
Rev. Samuel C. Stratton	100	Abel B. Skidmore	25	Charles Blakeslee	25
		Boyle Fairchild	25	Botsford Terrill	25
Josiah Glover	50	Josiah B. Fairchild	25	Samuel Fairchild	25
John Judson	25	Amariah Beers	25	James Nichols	25
Ebenezer Turner	25	Wooster Peck	25	John Johnson	25
Thomas Blackman	25	Caleb Baldwin	50	Charles B. Booth	25
Wm. Blakeslee	25	Charles Brisco	25	Simeon N. Beers	25
Charles Fairman	25	Charles Noble	25	Gould Curtis	25
Henry Dutton	25	Daniel Skidmore	25	Robert S. Peck	25
Moses Parsons	25	David V. B. Baldwin	50	George M. Benedict	25
David Curtis	25	Amos G. Peck	25	Charles Johnson	25
Charles Clark	25	Jabez B. Botsford	25	Philo Clarke	25
Samuel A. Peck	25	Abel Botsford	25	Beach Camp	25
Josiah Sanford	25			Thomas O. Chambers	25

A sufficient amount being subscribed, a constitution and articles of association were adopted, March 2, 1837. The officers appointed: Rev. Samuel C. Stratton, David V. B. Baldwin, David H. Belden, Josiah Sanford, Samuel Beers, trustees; Charles Clark, secretary; David V. B. Baldwin, Charles Brisco, Samuel Fairchild, building committee. The building committee were instructed to erect a building not to exceed 36 x 26 feet. It was completed during the summer, and in the fall of 1837 the school was opened in charge of Mr. George L. Foote, who, fresh from college with his heart full of love for the work, entered upon his duties with all the enthusiasm, energy and self-devotion with which he was possessed, and which he exhibited to such a remarkable degree through his ministerial life. He was ably assisted in both male and female departments, two of his assistants being his sisters, Misses Mary and Harriet Foote. At the May session of the Legislature, 1838, the Association petitioned for an act of incorporation and a resolution granting it passed the General Assembly.

The year 1839 was a prosperous one for the institution. The number of pupils ranged from 100 to 150. Mr. Foote continued principal of the Academy until the Spring of 1840. He resigned, much to the regret of a host of patrons, to enter upon the work of the ministry in Roxbury, Conn., where he remained ten years, removing to the diocese of New York where he died at Morris, Otsego Co., Oct., 1863.

In the Spring of 1840, Rev. Levi Corson succeeded as principal. He also supplied the pulpit of Trinity Church. Miss Mary Foote was teacher of the female department. He was principal only one year, being succeeded by Rev. Thomas T. Guion. He also, though an excellent and devoted teacher, was in charge only one year, being succeeded, the spring of 1842, by Mr. Charles W. Wooster, who was in charge only a year. Amos S. Treat was a good teacher, but his preference was for the law, and he left teaching to devote himself to the practice of his profession.

Mr. Elizur Keeler was next in charge. He was Newtown born and had experience in some of the public schools of the town. He taught several years, maintaining a well-deserved popularity, both as boarding and day school, and was much beloved by his pupils. When he left Newtown for a position with a Waterbury firm, Newtown lost a good teacher, a valued citizen, and the Congregational Church a consistent member.

In 1852, after a lapse of two years, during which the building was closed, the trustees secured Mr. J. Homer French, who came from Clyde, N. Y. He was an excellent disciplinarian, a superior teacher, and excelled as a mathematician. He was associate author of Adam's series of arithmetics, and, later, author of French's Arithmetic, which was used in the Academy in later years.

Before the close of the first year, the building was repaired, the old time benches giving way to revolving chairs and modern desks. An able corps of assistants helped make the school popular, a large number of pupils coming from other towns. In Jan., 1853, the Academician, a monthly paper printed in Bridgeport and conducted by the pupils, was started. It was popular, but a failure financially and did not finish the second year. Mr. French resigned during the summer of 1855.

Names of teachers and pupils, who made up the coterie at Newtown Academy, 60 years ago, helping make things lively on the village street and looking forward to the time when, in maturer life, they might become a part of the great army of home and nation builders, to take up and carry on the work as their ancestors should lay it down.

The names that follow were copied from the pupils' paper, the Academician:

Instructors: J. Homer French, principal; Rev. William L. Bostwick, teacher of classics; Miss Cornelia L. Hubbard, preceptress; Miss Fanny Easton, assistant; Mrs Mary E. French, teacher of French; Mrs. Mary E. Sanford, teacher of music.

Female Department:
Jane Banks,	Newtown	Delia Fairchild,	Newtown
Sarah E. Beecher,	Sandy Hook	Sarah Grace Blakeslee,	Newtown
Ann S. Beers,	Newtown	Alosia S. Botsford,	Newtown
Charlotte B. Beers,	Newtown	Emma J. Boroughs,	Newtown
Harriet B. Blackman,	Newtown	Elizabeth Clarke,	Newtown
Julia Esther Blackman,	Newtown	Lydia Jane Camp,	Newtown
Mary J. Blakeslee,	Newtown	Jane Eliza Camp,	Newtown
Catherine E. Fairchild	Newtown	Juliette Curtis,	Newtown
		Martha Dikeman,	Newtown

Harriet F. Fairchild,	Bethel	F. Mortimer Fairchild,	Newtown
Lucy A. Fairchild,	Newtown	Daniel B. Fairman,	Newtown
Susan A Fairchild,	Newtown	Martin V. B. Glover,	Newtown
Mary Jane Foote,	Hobart, N. Y.	William Henry Glover,	Newtown
Betsey Glover,	Newtown	Andrew W. Grey, Jr.,	Newtown
Esther A. Hawley,	Newtown	Edson N. Hawley,	Newtown
Harriette M. Lake,	Sandy Hook	Nathan Harrison,	North Branford
Wihlelmina B. Norman,	Bridgeport	William G. Hard,	Newtown
Sarah M. Prindle,	Newtown	Elmer B. Hawley,	Newtown
Augusta Sanford,	Newtown	William G. Hawley,	Newtown
Mary Jane Sherman	Newtown	William B. Hurd,	Jersey City
Mary Caroline Skidmore,	Newtown	D. Jackson Lake,	Newtown
		Walter Baldwin Lake,	Newtown

Male Department:

David Banks,	Newtown	Frederick H. Lyon,	Redding Ridge
Booth G. Beers,	Newtown	Charles S. Midldebrook,	Bridgeport
Daniel G. Beers,	Newtown	Franklin Middlebrook,	Sandy Hook
George Beers,	Newtown	George Arthur Mott,	Bridgeport
Isaac Beach Beers,	Newtown	Joseph G. Munson,	Sandy Hook
John Hobart Beers,	Newtown	Henry Nichols,	Newtown
Julius A. Beers,	Newtown	Albert W. Peck,	Newtown
Silas N. Beers,	Newtown	Edward B. Peck,	Newtown
Benjamin C. Benedict,	Newtown	George B. Peck,	Sandy Hook
George B. Blakeslee,	Newtown	Henry S. Peck,	Newtown
William Blakeslee,	Newtown	Nelson J. Peck,	Newtown
Daniel Theodore Booth,	Newtown Milford	William Arthur Porter,	Bridgeport
George A. Bradley,	Newtown	Elias F. Sanford,	Sandy Hook
John Huntington Brewster,	Newtown	Edward M. Sherman,	Newtown
		Edwin M. Sherman,	Newtown
George Bulkley,	Newtown	Norris Sherman,	Sandy Hook
Edward Burroughs,	Trumbull	Philo B. Sherman,	Newtown
George B. Camp,	Newtown	Eugene R. Silliman,	Bridgeport
Hobart B. Camp,	Newtown	Robert R. Skidmore,	Newtown
Frederick Chambers,	Newtown	Charles E. Smith,	Newtown
Lemuel B. Clark,	Danbury	Frederick B. Terrill,	Newtown
George Clark,	Newtown	Franklin W. Tucker,	Sandy Hook
David Curtis,	Newtown	Augustus Warner,	Newtown
Frederick L. Curtis,	Bridgeport	James Wheeler,	Newtown
		John B. Wheeler,	Newtown
		John Henry Woolsey,	Bridgeport

More than three-score years have passed since that happy band of pupils gathered as a school and, at the morning roll call, answered "Here!" As we call the roll to-day, the silent ones are in the majority. Here and there is one remaining, but each beyond the allotted time of life, three score and ten, and, as those who have gone before have done, will soon answer the roll call for the last time.

September, 1855, Mr. J. E. Goodhue, native of New Hampshire and a Yale graduate, succeeded Mr. French. Though the attendance was less than during Mr. French's administration, the time was one of marked prosperity for the school, and Mr. Goodhue won the good-will of his pupils and the lasting regard of his patrons.

When, at the end of three years, he resigned to enter Berkeley Divinity School, in preparation for the ministry in the Episcopal Church, it was with real regret that his resignation was accepted. From 1858 to 1874, the changes were frequent. Miss Susan Walker, who had been Mr. Goodhue's assistant, continued in charge, with Miss Mary J. Sherman as associate principal. When Miss Walker retired to work among the freedmen at Washington, D. C., Miss Martha J. Morris, sister of ex-Gov. Luzon B. Morris, a talented teacher and congenial friend of Miss Sherman, took her place. The school prospered under their guidance, until Miss Morris accepted a position at Westville, Conn., and Miss Sherman became the wife of Franklin Fairman of Chicago, one of Newtown's sons.

Henry K. Lever, Sidney B. Frost, J. R. Fairman and John Betts each had short terms. Beach Hill, a superior teacher, opened a private school in Bridgeport, of which he remained principal until his death. Henry Beard became a Congregational minister and removed to Minnesota. His popular assistant was Miss Arabella Fitch, who became the wife of Daniel G. Beers.

Miss Frances Marble was a successful teacher, but found greater scope for her abilities in Bridgeport High School, and, later, as founder of the Courtland School, of which she was the beloved principal until her death. Miss Alice Bradley, became the wife of Hon. Charles Brisco, of Enfield, Conn.

In the Autumn of 1874, Rev, J. P. Hoyt, pastor of the Congregational Church, took charge. As a teacher of the classics he excelled and so thorough was his teaching, that his pupils became his assistants in different branches. John M. Otis, George Judd, J. Frank Gillette, among the young men, and Misses Adella Botsford, Esther Camp, Carrie Lake, Nellie Judson and Effie Glover, acted as assistants. At the close of the Spring term of 1880, Mr. Hoyt tendered his resignation, at which time he made the statement that "the school commenced with 12 pupils; the number increased to 63; 200 pupils have been connected with the Academy from 9 different towns; 100 have finished a course of study; 11 have entered college or are nearly prepared, and 40 have become teachers." The trustees prevailed upon him to re-consider his resignation, and he remained another year, having as associate, Mr. George H. Cummings, who continued in charge the following year. In March, 1882, Mr. D. B. Plummer became principal. He was succeeded by Miss Effie Glover, who remained in charge until the old building was sold to L. B. Booth and moved to its present position and became the Post Office.

Prof. Francis M. Wilson became principal, Oct. 1, 1885, teaching in the old ball-room in Miss Ann Blackman's house, until the new building on Sunset Hill was completed, the summer of 1886. He remained in charge until the close of the school-year, 1886-87, assisted by Miss Florence Keep. Prof. Schultz was principal in 1888 and until the coming of Prof. E. Pennington Cliff in 1891. In 1892, the building was moved from Sunset Hill nearly a mile and a quarter across the fields to its present position. Prof. Cliff, opened school in September, in St. Patrick's Hall, pending the moving and repairing of the building, with Miss Sarah Beers in charge of intermediate department, Mrs. M. C. Rogers, the primary, Mrs. Charles S. Platt teacher of music and Miss Mary Bacon of drawing and painting. Prof. Cliff remained in charge until the close of 1894-5 having as assistants at different periods Miss Lillian French, Miss Grace Goodsell, Miss Jessie Sanford, and Miss Sample. Prof. W. H. Hoyt, became principal in 1895, Miss Mabel Cummings assistant, remaining until 1898, when it was announced that the sixty-

MISS SUSAN J. SCUDDER
First Woman to be Elected on
School Board

MRS. EDITH G. MITCHELL

Second Woman to be Elected on
School Board

second year of Newtown Academy would be opened by Prof. H. B. Mac Farland, with Mrs. Mac Farland, assistant. Miss Jennie Briscoe assisted one term with Prof. Mac Farland in 1898, continuing during his term of service until 1901, when he was succeeded by Prof. Gardner, with Miss Briscoe as assistant. Prof. Gardner remained until the town made it a Free High School.

Miss Briscoe in upper room as a private school in 1902. Prof. Tibbetts first High School Principal.

In closing this record of Newtown Academy, it should be stated that owing to the difficulty in obtaining correct information some names may have been unintentionally omitted.

Newtown Academy with its principal, five assistants and 88 pupils with a reputation that drew from cities, as well as from adjoining towns, was well patronized, although the whole expense of keeping it up came upon those who patronized it, each pupil obliged to furnish books and stationery for individual use. Now, with expenses paid by a tax levied on the taxable property of the town, every incentive is placed before our children to make the best improvement of present-day advantages. In numbers enrolled, the school of 60 years ago compares favorably with the number enrolled in our High School.

The High School building, originally the Newtown Academy, built on Sunset Hill in 1886, was moved in 1892, to its present position. In 1902 it was sold to the town for a free High School.

Its Principals
Prof. A. M. Tibbetts, 1902-03
" Ross Jewell 1903-07
" Curtis Cook 1907-10
" W. L. Carpenter 1910-12
" Leonard Johnson 1912-16
" Leo Hickson 1916 to date

Assistant Teachers
Miss Elizabeth Goodwin 1903-05
Miss Daisy Kemble 1905-06
Miss Blanche Welch 1905-07
Miss Edith Ganong 1906-07
Miss Marguerite Lawton 1907-08
Miss Ruth Snow 1907-08
Miss Lula Roberts 1908-10
Miss Bessie Mitchell 1909-11
Miss Sue Short 1910-13
Miss Dorothy Curtis 1911-12
Miss Bessie Olson 1912-13
Miss Ethel Salmon 1913-14
Miss Irene Warren 1914-16
Miss Helen Houlihan 1913-
Miss Doris Downs 1916-

Sub Freshmen Teachers
Private School
Miss Jennie Briscoe 1902-03
Mrs. Ross Jewell 1903-06
Mrs. Charles H. Northrop 1907-08
Miss Mary Lester 1909-10
Miss Lillian Troy 1910-to date

HIGH SCHOOL GRADUATES

High School opened, 1902. First class graduated, 1905.

F. Loretta Houlihan
Mary Hoyt
Eleanore L. Northrop
Pearl F. Parsons
Ethel M. Peck
Harley T. Peck

Class of 1906
Anna May Betts
Edward J. Egan
Katherine Honan
Anna V. Keane
Margaret L. Keane
Jennie M. Ruffles
Elizabeth Egan

Class of 1907
Harold E. Botsford
Augusta Campbell
Francis J. Carmody
Eleanor S. Cavanaugh
May J. Egan
Helen F. Hawley
Daniel C. Honan
John G. Houlihan
Margaret L. Keating
Ada J. Lake
Mary M. Lester
May F. McNamara
Catherine Murphy
Carlton S. Smith
Lillian M. Troy
Alma L. Williams
Randolph B. Williams

Class of 1908
Lottie M. Behn
Helen M. Blakeman
Nonie A. Brennan
Marguerite Cavanaugh
Elsie C. Ferris
Annie Murphy
Crossley Wallace
Vivian R. Wetmore

Class of 1909
Florence G. Beecher
Helen F. Houlihan
M. May Houlihan
Thomas F. Lynch
Earle Taber
Benj. D. Smith
Anna H. Ruffles
Lena Blake
Gertrude Bradley
Anna L. Keane
Mary T. Kelly
C. Agnes Lynch
Mary Lynch

Class of 1910
Nora C. Blake
Ruth E. Ruffles
Clarice E. Botsford
Mary Hazen Fairchild
Mary W. Lynch
Catherine V. Lynch
Percy C. Platt
Earle Peck
Rychie E. Veness
Jennie L. Lynch
Catherine F. Farrell
Anna M. Houlihan
Catherine A. James

Class of 1911
Lillian M. Beers
Mayla A. Botsford
Anna L. Carlson
William E. Driscoll
Arthur W. Fairchild
Herbert C. Ferris
Lucie F. Wright
Mary A. Northrop

Class of 1912
Jesse M. Bailey
Marguerite K. Beecher
Michael J. Blake
George M. Ferris
Helen M. Keane
Catherine A. Lester
Joseph D. Keane
L. Phillips Morris
Annie G. Murphy
Edith N. Northrop
James A. Peck
S. Bessie Ruffles
Horace A. Smith

Class of 1913
Elizabeth H. Blake
Charles W. Botsford
Annie C. Brenner
George G. Canfield
Robert D. Fairchild
Gordon J. Gale
C. Frances Griffin
Frank L. Johnson
Helen A. Kilbride
Mary C. Kilbride
Viola P. Kutscher

Class of 1914
H. Sanford Beers
Sarah A. Beers
Mildred Christopher
G. Herbert Beers
Jessie M. Beers
Arthur J. Ferris
Florence N. Gaffney
Israel Goldstein
Thomas F. Keane
Catherine C. Mayers
Evelyn B. Read
Alice C. Smith
E. Marion Summers
F. Leonard Wright
Charlesina E. Driscoll
Jennie R. Honan

Class of 1915
Amy M. Bantle
Esther M. Beck
Marion N. Curtis
Walter L. Glover
Mary V. Houlihan
Wilbur E. Olmstead
Francis H. Platt
Grace E. Ruffles
George M. Stuart
Russell H. Wheeler

Class of 1916
Bertha Summers
Maude Summers
Hazel Hopkins
Herman Oppe
Earle Wentsch
Anna Corbett
Mary Keane
Catherine Scanlon
Dorothy Harris
Mollie Goldstein
Mae Jordan
Frank Corbett
Charles Ferris
John Kelly
Charles Platt
Paul Cavanaugh
Philo Botsford

Class of 1917
Daniel Christopher
Charles Olmstead
Harold Ray
Anna Lang
Mary Murphy
Blanche Gilbert
Ruth Tilson
Mildred Stevens
Clarence Skiff
Mae Fairchild
Dora Strisik
Agnes Leavy
Aileen Houlihan

THE JOHN BEACH MEMORIAL LIBRARY.

About 1874, it was made known that a contribution of 100 volumes would be made by some one to form the foundation of a town library, provided other books should be purchased and a library association organized within a year from the date of the gift. The donor proved to be Mrs Caleb Baldwin, whose home was the house now owned by Charles F. Beardsley. Sufficient money was obtained to purchase a suitable book-case and the few other things necessary, and the Newtown Library Association was organized, Dec. 11, 1875, in the post office building, north of the store of R. H. Beers & Co.

Its history up to July 23, 1900, was given by Mrs Charles S. Platt, at the laying of the corner stone of the John Beach Memorial Library:

"It was organized by a little band of men who must have felt and known what good reading means to a place like this. These men, Ezra L. Johnson, Abel Stilson, Douglas Fairchild, Edwin Clarke, Zalmon S. Peck, Edgar F. Hawley, Charles Fairman and Elmer Fairchild. The charter was received and recorded by Charles H. Peck, town clerk, Jan. 15, 1877; also recorded in the secretary's office at Hartford, Jan. 16, 1877. It was soon removed to the residence of Theophilus Nichols. It started with 100 books and Miss Charlotte Nichols librarian.

The Dramatic Club gave the proceeds of one of their entertainments and books were added from time to time in small numbers. In 1885, the Association was in a critical condition. A few, realizing this, called a meeting and elected new officers. Prof. Charles S. Platt was made president, a room was hired in the Brick building and the books removed. Prof. Platt and wife commenced a series of entertainments, their efforts were abetted by a few faithful workers, the public responded and, at the end of his term of office, $1360.00 had been raised by entertainments alone, and the books numbered over 3000. Again the life of the Association seemed threatened. The few who had labored so hard to supply the funds of the institution were discouraged. The town demanded rent for the small room in which it existed. What could a library do without a home in which to exist? It was then put into the heart of Rebecca D. Beach to furnish the beautiful home for which we are now assembled to lay the corner-stone, which will commemorate the good her ancestors labored so nobly to impart in our midst, and aid in carrying on this institution of which we may justly be proud."

The following have at this time, 1900, been officially connected with the Association:

Presidents—Ezra L. Johnson, Daniel G. Beers, Marcus C. Hawley, Rev. J. A. Crockett, Charles S. Platt, Arthur S. Hawley, Samuel J. Botsford, Rev. George T. Linsley.

Vice-presidents—Charles M. Beresford, Rev. G. M. Wilkins, Edgar F. Hawley, Reuben H. Smith, William A. Leonard, Rev. George T. Linsley, Rev. O. W. Barker

Secretaries—Mary F. Peck, J. F. Gillette, Mary E. Beers, Effie M. Glover, Emma F. Terrill, Ella E. Platt.

Librarians—Charlotte E. Nichols, Mrs. John Gay, Miss Abbie L. Peck.

Treasurers—Miss. Mary C. Morgan, C. H. Northrop, Arthur T. Nettleton.

Trustees—Abel Stilson, Marcus C. Hawley, E. F. Hawley, D. G. Beers, A. F. Clark, Charles M. Beresford, Charles H. Gay, George P. Sanford, C. F. Beardsley, Prof. Shultz, Rev. O. W. Barker.

The corner-stone was laid by John Francis Beach, seventh in descent from Rev. John Beach, assisted by John Kimberly Beach, sixth in descent. The box deposited in the corner-stone contained

Newtown Bee, July 13, 1900; eight clippings from copies of the Bee relating to the library; the Newtown Courier published by R. H. Beers & Co; the New York Times, July 23, 1900; Pathfinder, June 10, 1850; catalogue of Newtown Library; historical sketch of library by Mrs. C. S. Platt; list of present officers; autographs of present officers; list of present subscribers and honorary members; autograph of Miss Rebecca D. Beach, John Francis Beach and John Kimberly Beach; Columbian half-dollar from Rev. George T. Linsley; minor coins of years 1899 and 1900 from Arthur T.

Nettleton; paper stating that box was sealed by Daniel Camp, July 23 1900; paper stating that corner-stone was laid by John Francis Beach, assisted by John Kimberly Beach; copy of Ulster County Gazette, Jan. 4, 1800; Newtown Academician, April, 1874.

The corner-stone was formally laid by John Francis Beach, who said: "I lay the corner-stone of this Library to the memory of John Beach.'" He was assisted by his uncle, John Kimberly Beach.

The building was completed and formally opened, Dec. 11, 1900, at which time it was presented to the Library Association by Miss Rebecca Beach. Ladies assisting at the reception: Mrs G. T. Linsley, Mrs G. P. Sanford, Mrs L. C. Morris, Mrs. W. J. Beecher, Mrs. O. W. Barker, Mrs. Grace Glover. In 1903, the Association failed in its attempt to have the town make it a free library. In 1907, the library was catalogued by High School pupils under the direction of Prof. Ross Jewell. The Dewey Decimal Classification and Cutter's Order mark was used, and index was made upon a typewriter.

Officers since the opening of the new library: President, Rev. George T. Linsley, 1899-1901; Vice-president, Rev. Otis W. Barker. President, 1902-05; Rev. James H. George (Vice-president). President 1905 until his decease, January 1, 1917; Dr. F. J. Gale, (Vice-president,) now acting President. Treasurer, Mr. A. T. Nettleton, 1900-1908. Mr. A. J. Smith, 1909-1917.

Secretaries—Mrs. Chas. S. Platt, Mrs. William S. Hawley, Mrs. Austin B. Blakeman.

Trustees—A. P. Smith, C. F. Beardsley. Librarian—Miss Abbie Peck.

MEMORIALS GIVEN SINCE 1900:

Memorial shelf in memory of Herbert Skidmore, by Mrs. Estella Skidmore Beard, 1900.

Memorial shelf in memory of Henry Botsford Dikeman, by Mrs. Oscar Dikeman, 1901.

Memorial shelf in memory of Mrs. Helen M. Laflin, by Mrs. Grace Allen, 1903.

Memorial shelf in memory of Henry Glover Beecher, by W. J. Beecher and family, 1904.

Memorial shelf in memory of Mary Carter Booth, by Rev. Robert C. Booth, 1904.

Memorial shelf in memory of Mrs. Elizabeth D. Gardner, by Mrs. Wm. Gardner, 1907.

Memorial shelf in memory of Prof. Charles S Platt, by Mrs Ella E. Platt, 1909.

Memorial shelf in memory of Abel French Clarke, by Mrs. Abel F. Clarke, 1914.

$300 from Mr. and Mrs Austin B. Blakeman for the Helen Mac Gregor Blakeman fund for books for girls, 1910.

$500 from estate of Abel French Clarke, 1914.

Mrs. Julia Chase who died at Sharon, Conn., Sept. 13, 1904, presented to Newtown Library through her executor Dr. Wm. W. Knight, a cup and saucer belonging to a set used in the family of her great, great grandfather, Rev. John Beach; also one of his sermons and a Masonic apron of her grandfather's, Isaac Beach, son of Lazarus Beach, born May 19, 1773, died July 20, 1822, aged 49 years and 2 months, 1 day.

PROF. CHARLES L. PLATT

See Pages 88 and 232

MAIN STREET LOOKING SOUTH

Residence Mrs. S. G. Glover
Opposite Beach Memorial Library

See Page 232

BEACH MEMORIAL LIBRARY

See Page 233

A sword presented to Capt. Julius Sanford in October 1862, by Newtown friends, taken from him when prisoner in 1863, was returned to his daughters, Mrs. Sherwood Thompson and Mrs. Gertrude Bolmer of New Haven, in 1910, and by the mpresented to Newtown Library.

The sword presented by Newtown friends bears this inscription:

"Capt. Julius Sanford, Co. C, 23rd Regt. C. V.   Presented Oct. 1862, by many friends of Newtown, Conn., as a token of respect."

Capt. Sanford was a prisoner at Camp Ford, Tyler, Texas, for 14 months and died November 1, 1879, as a result of this imprisonment, leaving a widow and two daughters, Mrs. Sherwood S. Thompson and Mrs. Clarence B. Bolmar. Through the postmasters of Newtown, Conn., and Leadbetter, Texas, Mrs. Thompson was placed in communication with Dan Hensley of Leadbetter, Texas, who had the sword in his possession. In his letter he says, "My brother, Mount Hensley, was a Confederate soldier in Co. 2, Texas Cavalry, Queen's Brigade, and was stationed in Louisiana in 1863. My brother while scouting took some Federal soldiers prisoners, among them, Capt. Sanford. Shortly after he came home on furlough, and brought the sword with him. My brother was killed in March, 1864. The sword has been hanging in our house nearly 47 years, and is a bad specimen of its former beauty."

The sword is placed in a handsome case and hangs in the Newtown Library.

The sword was taken from Capt. Sanford when he was taken prisoner in Bayou Beouz La., June 24, 1863.

SANDY HOOK FREE PUBLIC LIBRARY.

The Sandy Hook Free Public Library Association was incorporated June 25, 1906, on application of Otis Olney Wright, Smith P. Glover, George F. Taylor, Daniel J. Keane, Albert W. Bassett, and H. Birdsey Sniffen. It is located in the Glover Block in a room generously donated by S. P. Glover. Rev. O. O. Wright was the first chairman of the board of directors and served continuously until his removal from Sandy Hook in 1912. The organization of the library and its maintainence during those years was in large measure due to his efforts. The library was incorporated as a free library and it has always been so maintained. It is open to all inhabitants of the town, free of charge, and money for its support is raised entirely by voluntary subscription and public entertainments. The present number of books in circulation is 2458 and the number of takers of books 149.

Miss May McNamara, now the librarian, receives no salary, and those who have served in this capacity are Mrs. Arthur Kennedy, Mrs. W. H. Stevens and Mrs. H. Birdsey Sniffen.

Contributed by Mrs. Edith W. Mitchell, Secretary.

NEWTOWN SAVINGS BANK.

The Newtown Savings Bank was incorporated in June, 1855, by the Legislature of Connecticut. The incorporators were Henry Beers, Henry Beers Glover, Edward Starr, Theophilus Nichols, Henry Sanford, Samuel Curtis, S. P. Barnum, Henry Baldwin, D. B. Beers, Jerome Judson, Monroe Judson, Moses Parsons, James B. Blakeslee, Charles F. Blakeslee, Alva B. Beecher, Samuel B. Peck, William Beard, Zerah Fairman, David H. Johnson and Walter Clarke.

None of these corporators are now living, the last one Charles F. Blakeslee, died in Franklin, Pa. July 8, 1913.

In a pass-book issued by the bank in September, 1855, the depositor was informed that the bank had "been established for the purpose of affording a secure investment to persons who have not the facilities of safely putting their income otherwise to use." That this principle has been maintained is borne out by the steady growth and financial strength of this excellent institution.

Sixty-four years ago, the favored spot in which we now dwell was the same as it is to-day, in this one respect; it possessed men who believed in uprightness and moral integrity, and they also believed that it was a good thing to plant in this neighborhood an institution that should stand for these principles, and, at the same time, afford to men and women of humble means an opportunity to lay by little by little, such sums as they could spare from their necessary expenses, as might, in the future, be of help to them in procuring a home or enabling them to provide for themselves, or those depending upon them, some substantial support, which stress of circumstances that might overtake them should demand.

The early incorporators of the Newtown Savings Bank were men of sterling worth and, whether they builded better than they knew or not, they builded well, and the principles they laid down in the original by-laws, and in the first books they issued to depositors, show wisdom and foresightedness.

Pursuant to notice given by Henry Beers Glover, committee appointed by the Legislature, the first meeting to organize the Newtown Savings Bank was held at the office of David B. Beers in Newtown, July 14, 1855.

After hearing the charter read, the meeting adjourned to August 25, 1855, to meet at the same place. At this meeting, the by-laws proposed by Mr. Glover were adopted and officers elected as follows:

President, Henry Beers. Vice-presidents, David H. Johnson, Edward Starr and Samuel B. Peck. Secretary and Treasurer Henry Beers Glover.

Trustees, Walter Clarke, Henry Beers Glover, David B. Beers, Theophilus Nichols, Jerome Judson, Henry Baldwin, Alva B. Beecher, Henry Sanford, Moses Parsons, Zerah Fairman, Samuel Curtis, James B. Blakeslee, Sallu P. Barnum, Monroe Judson, Charles F. Blakeslee and William Beard.

The bank commenced business, September 15, 1855, in the office of Henry Beers Glover. The first depositors that day were Mr. Glover, Charles Henry Peck and his wife, Hannah D. F. Peck.

NEWTOWN SAVINGS BANK
See Page 236

SIMEON B. PECK
See Page 237

November 15, 1858, Theophilus Nichols was elected president for the ensuing year. November 5, 1859, Charles Warner was elected secretary and treasurer. October 20, 1860, Henry Beers was again elected president and Henry Beers Glover, secretary and treasurer. On this day, it was voted "that the president, vice-president and secretary be a committee to procure a safe for this bank at not exceeding $100." At this time the bank had $6,825.06 loaned on real-estate in other States, $3,500 of this amount being loaned in Milwaukee at 10 per cent. March 18, 1865, David H. Johnson was unanimously elected president in place of Henry Beers, deceased. In this year, more than one-half of the bank's deposits were invested in United States bonds. At a special meeting, March 30, 1870, Henry T. Nichols was elected secretary and treasurer, to fill the vacancy caused by the death of Henry Beers Glover. In this year, the bank was moved from the residence of Mr. Glover to the home of Mr. Nichols, now the annex to Newtown Inn. November 5, 1870, Ezra Morgan was elected president. October 31, 1871, Simeon B. Peck was elected president. October 23, 1883, he having declined a re-election, Philo Clarke was elected president.

At a special meeting, Aug. 6, 1887, Charles H. Northrop was elected secretary and treasurer, to succeed Henry T. Nichols, deceased. August 31, 1887, the bank was moved from the residence of the late Mr. Nichols to an office in the Henry Sanford building. October 23, 1897, John B. Peck was elected president in place of Philo Clarke, deceased. October 25, 1898, he was succeeded by Aaron Sanford and Arthur T. Nettleton was elected secretary and treasurer. February 25, 1902, David C. Peck was elected president, filling the vacancy caused by the death of Mr. Sanford.

December 8, 1906, the old Academy lot, so called, between the Congregational parsonage and the residence formerly owned by David B. Beers, was purchased by the bank from Mrs. Emma S. Beers, of Natick, Mass. It has a frontage of 60 feet and a depth of 120 feet.

At a meeting of the trustees, December 15, 1906, it was voted that Arthur T. Nettleton, David C. Peck and Cornelius B. Taylor be a building committee to have plans and specifications prepared for the erection of a bank building on said lot. March 8, 1907, after hearing the report of said building committee, it was voted to proceed with the erection of a new bank building on the lot recently purchased for the purpose. It was further voted that said building committee be authorized and empowered to make such contracts as they deemed proper and sufficient for the erection of said building and to have the supervision and direction of the work specified in contracts. The bids were opened in the spring of 1907, but were high and unsatisfactory and it was decided to defer building for a time. The matter was taken up again the latter part of 1908; contracts were let in March, 1909 and ground was first broken March 15, 1909, by the treasurer, Arthur T. Nettleton.

Joseph McArthur Vance of Pittsfield, Mass was the architect of the building and E. H. Shaw of Great Barrington, Mass, the contractor. The Barrington Building Co. had the sub-contract from

Mr. Shaw for the interior work. M. G. Keane of Bridgeport, Conn., furnished the granite and lime stone and E. J. Hall of Sandy Hook, Conn., the contract for the heating and plumbing.

The vaults of the bank were built by the York Safe and Lock Co. of York, Pa., and are of massive construction. The building is of the modified French Renaissance type of architecture, 30 by 50 feet, and is constructed of Pompeian brick, trimmed with Indiana limestone and terra-cotta.

May 5, 1910, the bank formally opened its doors for business in its new home.

The first annual report of the bank, Oct. 1, 1855, showed deposits of $17,165.43. Oct. 1, 1918, the deposits were $1,391,942.79 and the surplus and undivided earnings on book and par value of securities were $121,639.50. The present officers and trustees of the bank are:

President, David C. Peck; Vice-Presidents, Cornelius B. Taylor, John B. Wheeler and Theron E. Platt. Secretary and Treasurer, Arthur T. Nettleton. Trustees, David C. Peck, John B. Wheeler, Theron E. Platt, Cornelius B. Taylor, Henry G. Curtis, Hobart, H. Curtis, Frank Wright, Arthur T. Nettleton, Edward S. Lovell, Robert C. Mitchell, Eli B. Beers, William B. Glover, William T. Cole, H. Carlton Hubbell, Arthur J. Smith and Thomas M. Holian.

David C. Peck was first elected trustee, Oct. 23, 1883, and president, Feb., 25, 1902. Cornelius B. Taylor was elected trustee, Oct. 23, 1897, and vice-president, Oct. 25, 1902. John B. Wheeler, Oct. 20, 1888, and a vice-president, Oct. 25, 1913; Theron E. Platt, Oct. 18, 1890, and a vice-president, Oct. 25, 1913.

In this brief history of the Newtown Savings Bank, space does not permit biographies of the officers and trustees from 1855 to 1919. Within this long period of time 59 have passed away. From this large number who have departed in the last few years are Wm. Homer Hubbell, trustee from Feb. 25, 1902, to Sept. 16, 1912; Daniel Glover Beers, trustee from Oct. 26, 1878, to Feb. 12, 1913; and a vice-president from Oct. 26, 1895, to Feb. 12, 1913; Austin B. Blakeman, trustee from Oct. 25, 1913, to Oct. 19, 1915; Judge William J. Beecher, attorney for the bank and trustee from Oct. 26, 1901, to Dec. 3, 1915, and William A. Leonard, trustee from Oct .25, 1902, to April 13, 1918.

The following is a list of the Presidents, Treasurers and Trustees, with their terms of service, from incorporation of the bank to January 1, 1919.

PRESIDENTS.

Henry Beers, from August 25th, 1855, to November 15, 1858.
Theophilus Nichols, Nov. 15, 1858, to October 20, 1860.
Henry Beers, October, 20, 1860, to November 19, 1864.
David H. Johnson, March 18, 1865, to November 5, 1870.
Ezra Morgan, Nov. 5, 1870, to October 31st, 1871.
Simeon B. Peck, October 31, 1871, to October 23, 1883.
Philo Clarke, October 23, 1883, to March 3, 1897.
John B. Peck, October 23, 1897, to October 25, 1898.
Aaron Sanford, October 25, 1898, to February 10, 1902.
David C. Peck, February 25, 1902, to date (Jan. 1, 1919.)

PHILO CLARKE

See Page 238

DAVID C. PECK

See Page 238

NEWTOWN SAVINGS BANK

TREASURERS.

Henry Beers Glover, August 25, 1855, to November 5, 1859.
Charles C. Warner, November 5, 1859, to October 20, 1860.
Henry Beers Glover, October 20, 1860 to March 26, 1870.
Henry T. Nichols, March 30, 1870, to August 1, 1887.
Charles H. Northrop, August 6, 1887, to October 25, 1898.
Arthur Treat Nettleton, October 25, 1898, to date (Jan. 1, 1919.)

TRUSTEES.

Baldwin, Henry	Aug. 25, 1855, to Oct. 28, 1865. Oct. 31, 1866, to Oct. 29, 1870.
Barnum, S. P.	Aug. 25, 1855, to Nov. 14, 1857. Nov. 5, 1859, to 1861.
Blakeslee, Chas. F.	Aug. 25, 1855, to Nov. 15, 1858.
Blakeslee, James B.	Aug. 25, 1855, to Nov. 5, 1859. Oct. 26, 1861, to Oct. 26, 1863.
Blackman, Bennet	Oct. 31, 1866, to Oct. 19, 1870.
Blackman, Joseph	Oct. 31, 1866, to 1877.
Blakeman, Austin B.	Oct. 25, 1913, to Oct. 19, 1915.
Beecher, Alva B.	Aug. 25, 1855, to Nov. 5, 1859. (Vice-President, 1860.) Oct. 26, 1861, to Oct. 25, 1867.
Beecher, William J.	Oct. 26, 1901, to Dec. 3, 1915.
Beers, Henry	Nov. 14, 1857, to November 19, 1864.
Beers, Daniel G.	Oct. 26, 1878, to Feb. 12, 1913. Also one of the Vice-Presidents from Oct. 26, 1895, to Feb. 12, 1913.
Beers, Eli B.	Oct. 24, 1903, to date (Jan. 1, 1919).
Beers, David B.	August 25, 1855 to Oct. 27, 1866.
Beard William.	Aug. 25, 1855, to July 29th, 1857.
Booth, Lewis.	Nov. 14, 1857, to Oct. 20, 1860. Oct. 21, 1861, to 1867.
Booth, C. H.	Oct. 20, 1860, to Oct. 21, 1861. Oct. 22, 1864 to 1866.
Botsford, William	Oct. 22, 1879, to Nov. 2nd 1898.
Clarke, Walter.	Aug. 25, 1855, to Nov. 14, 1857.
Clarke, Philo.	Oct. 20, 1860, to March 3, 1897.
Clarke, Edwin.	Oct. 30, 1875, to Oct. 26, 1878.
Curtis, Samuel.	Aug. 25, 1855, to Nov. 5, 1859. Oct. 31, 1863, to Oct. 27, 1866. Oct. 31, 1871, to Oct. 31, 1872.
Curtis, Henry G.	Oct. 25, 1882, to Oct. 23, 1883. Oct. 23, 1897, to date.
Curtis, Hobart H.	Oct. 25, 1898, to date. (Jan. 1, 1919.)
Cole, William T.	Oct. 24, 1914, to date. (Jan. 1, 1919.)
Erwin, Erastus.	Oct. 28, 1865, to Oct. 29, 1870.
Fairman, Zerah	Aug. 25, 1855, to Oct. 20, 1860. Oct. 26, 1881, to Mar. 21, 1875.
Fairchild, Herman	Oct. 29, 1870, to May 29, 1874.
Glover, Henry Beers	Aug. 25, 1855, to March 26, 1870.
Glover, Smith P.	Oct. 30, 1875, to Oct. 26, 1878.
Glover, Walter H.	Oct. 28, 1899, to Jan. 16, 1901.
Glover, William B.	Oct. 26, 1912, to date. (Jan. 1, 1919.)
Hawley, Asa N.	Oct. 26, 1887, to 1889.
Hawley, Robert S.	Oct. 28, 1885, to Oct. 27, 1887.
Hubbell, Wm. Homer	Feb. 25, 1902, to Sept. 16, 1912.
Hubbell, H. Carlton	Oct. 30, 1917, to date. (Jan. 1, 1919.)
Holian, Thomas M.	Oct. 28, 1918, to date. (Jan. 1, 1919.)
Judson, Monroe.	Aug. 25, 1855, to Nov. 15, 1858. Oct. 20, 1860, to Oct. 26, 1861. Oct. 27, 1866, to Oct. 29, 1870. Oct. 21, 1873, to March 28, 1898.
Judson, Jerome	Aug. 25, 1855, to Nov. 15, 1858. Oct. 21, 1881, to May 15, 1891.
Judson, John.	Oct. 21, 1873, to Feb. 27, 1881.

Johnson, David H. Oct. 20, 1860, to Oct. 26, 1861. (one of the Vice-Presidents, 1861, 1862, 1863, 1864.) Re-elected Trustee Oct. 27, 1862. Continued to Oct. 28, 1865, when he was elected President. Trustee Oct. 25, 1867, to Oct. 29,1870.
Lovell, Edward S. Oct. 28, 1899, to date. (Jan. 1, 1919.)
Leonard, William A. Oct. 25, 1902, to April 13, 1918.
Mitchell, Robert C. Oct. 20, 1900, to date. (Jan. 1, 1919.)
Nichols, Theophilus Aug. 25, 1855, to Oct. 27, 1862.
Nichols, Henry T. March 30, 1870, to Oct. 26, 1878.
Nichols, Philo. Oct. 23, 1883, to Oct. 24, 1914.
Nortrop, Wm. N. Oct. 31, 1874, to Oct. 28, 1899.
Northrop, Hosea B. Oct. 26, 1878, to Oct. 25, 1902.
Northrop, Charles H. Oct. 28, 1885, to Oct. 28, 1899.
Northrop, John J. Oct. 21, 1891, to Oct. 25, 1898.
Nettleton, Arthur T. Nov. 17, 1898, to date. (Jan. 1, 1919.)
Parsons, Moses. Aug. 25, 1855, to Nov. 14, 1857. (Elected one of the Vice-Presidents, Nov. 14, 1857. Served one year. Vice-President from 1860 to 1868.) Trustee from Nov. 15, 1858 to Oct. 31, 1874.
Peck, Simeon B. Nov. 15, 1858, to June 6 ,1885.
Peck, Hezekiah. Oct. 30, 1862, to Oct. 31, 1866. Oct. 30, 1869, to 1881.
Peck, Amos G. Oct. 28, 1865, to Oct. 31, 1871.
Peck, Charles Henry Oct. 29, 1870, to Oct. 26, 1878.
Peck, Elliott M. Oct. 26, 1878, to Dec. 1, 1886.
Peck, David C. Oct. 23, 1883, to date. (Jan. 1, 1919.)
Peck, John B. Oct. 27, 1887, to Dec. 2, 1899.
Prindle, Abel B. Oct. 31, 1872, to Oct. 21, 1873. Oct. 27, 1887, to Oct. 20, 1888.
Platt, Theron E. Oct. 18, 1890, to date. (Jan. 1, 1919.)
Sanford, Henry. Aug. 25, 1855, to Nov. 19, 1882.
Sanford, Frederick. Nov. 14, 1857, to Nov. 15, 1858. Nov. 5, 1859, to Oct. 26, 1861.
Sanford, Aaron. Oct. 31, 1871, to Feb. 10, 1902.
Starr, Edward. Nov. 15, 1858, to Nov. 5, 1859. Oct. 27, 1862, to Oct. 22, 1864.
Skidmore, Philo H. Oct. 29, 1870, to Oct. 26, 1878.
Stilson, Abel. Oct. 31, 1874. to 1886.
Sherman, Cyrus B. Oct. 26, 1878, to Sept. 16, 1903.
Smith, Arthur J. Oct. 30, 1917, to date. (Jan. 1, 1919.)
Terrill, Botsford. Nov. 14, 1857, to Oct. 26, 1861.
Terrill, A. B. Nov. 15, 1858, to Nov. 5, 1859. Oct. 26, 1861 to Oct. 30, 1875.
Terrill, Wm. L. Oct. 28, 1865, to June 11, 1897.
Taylor, Cornelius B. Oct. 23, 1897, to date. (Jan. 1, 1919.)
Warner, Charles C. Oct. 20, 1860, to Oct. 27, 1862. Oct. 29, 1870, to 1884.
Warner, James H. Oct. 26, 1878, to Oct. 22, 1879.
Wheeler, John B. Oct. 20, 1888, to date (Jan. 1, 1919).
Wright, Frank Oct. 25, 1898, to date. (Jan. 1, 1919.)

FREE MASONRY IN NEWTOWN.

The history of Hiram Lodge, No. 18. A. F. and A. M., is divided into two parts:

The first period of its records begins with the order for the institution of the lodge, dated at New Haven, Jan. 6th, 1791, and extends to April 15th, 1848. Its charter was revoked in 1851 and restored in 1866; accordingly, the second period of its active existence dates from its revival in 1866 and continues until this present

ARTHUR T. NETTLETON

See Page 240

CORNELIUS B. TAYLOR

See Page 241

time. There are 57 years of ancient records and 51 years of modern, with a dormant space of 25 years between; the charter is, therefore, 126 years old, 1917.

The order for the consecration of Hiram Lodge, No. 18:

"New Town A. D. 1791, 5791, January 17th, Monday.

Hiram's Lodge Consecrated and the Worshipful Master Installed in due form by Right Worshipful Master Nathan Preston by virtue of a warrant from The Most Worshipful Grand Master of Connecticut, in the following words, i. e.—

To the Right Worshipful Nathan Preston, Master of King Solomon's Lodge in Woodbury:

Pierpont Edwards, Grand Master of the State of Connecticut, sendeth Greetings:

Whereas the Grand Lodge of sd (State) have constituted a lodge in Newtown (by the) name of Hiram Lodge and have (appointed) Brother Peter Nichols of said Newtown (to be Master) of said Hiram Lodge and said (brethren) have requested that the (said) Lodge should be (consecrated.)

[Words in parenthesis ( ) doubtful.]

I do therefore request and authorize to repair to said New Town on the third Monday inst. January and at such time and place in sd Newtown as said brother Nichols shall appoint to Install him in the presence of the said Lodge, first Master thereof, giving him the charges accustomed on such occasions and in particular that he regard the ancient land marks and great principles of the noble and blessed institution of Masonry—

Given under my hand in New Haven the sixth day of January A. L. 5791—

Pierpont Edwards,
Gd. Master."

The original charter of this lodge, under which we are now working, bears the date of January 19th, 1791, and reads as follows:—

"To all and every one, Right Worshipful and loving brethren, Free and Accepted Masons, now residing, or that may hereafter reside in New Town in the county of Fairfield, and state of Connecticut. The right Worshipful Pierpont Edwards Esquire Grand Master of the Ancient and honorable society of Free and Accepted Masons in the State of Connecticut.

Sendeth Greeting.

Whereas, Application hath been made unto us by Peter Nichols, sundry other brethren, of the ancient and honorable Society of Free and Accepted Masons now residing in New Town aforesaid, that we would be pleased to constitute them into a regular Lodge and appoint their worthy brother Peter Nichols their first Master, and that also we would appoint Bennett Perry their first Senior Warden and Jonathan Prindle their first Junior Warden, with full power granted to them and their Successors, to rule govern and regulate the same that Masonry may increase & flourish in these parts.

Now Know Ye, That we trusting and relying on the fidelity, resolution and good conduct, and putting in them as special trust, have nominated, ordained, constituted and appointed Mr. Peter Nichols our right Worshipful & well beloved brother, to be the first Master of Hiram Lodge in Newtown aforesaid, and that our beloved brother Mr. Bennett Perry to the first Senior Warden, & our beloved brother Mr. Jonathan Prindle the first Junior Warden of said Lodge and we do hereby impower him the said Master to congregate the brethren together, and form them into a regular Lodge, he taking Especial care in choosing the necessary officers for the due regulation thereof for one year, at the end thereof the Lodge shall have full power to choose and appoint their Master, & other officers and so annually: The Master and Wardens for the time being taking especial care that all and every Member admitted into sd Lodge from time to time have been or shall be made Regular Masons, and they the said

Master, Wardens and brethren of said Lodge and their successors forever, are hereby required strictly to observe and obey such ordinances, and regulations as shall from time to time be communicated to them from this Grand Lodge, agreeable to the Constitution thereof, and that they do annually send an account in writing to the Grand Lodge of the names of the Members that shall be made, passed, raised, or admitted in said Lodge, and their places of abode, & the day and place of making, with any other that they think proper to communicate for the benefit of their Lodge, and lastly that they do regularly communicate with the Grand Lodge by attending with their Master & Wardens or by sending to the half yearly Communications such Charities as their Lodge shall think fit, (for the) ————for the relief of poor brethren.————

Given under our hands and seal at New Haven this 19th day of January Anno Lucis five thousand seven hundred ninety one.————

Elias Shipman, Grand Sec'ry.
Pierpont Edwards."

Dated Newtown

May 10th A. L. 5791—"

In this connection, and before proceeding with the direct history of Hiram Lodge, No. 18, I will insert here a copy of what appears to be an official communication from the Master of the original Hiram Mark Lodge to the first Master of this Lodge. It is interesting and valuable as showing to what extent the spirit of Freemasonry was abroad in this part of the country, and as marking the beginning of Royal Arch Masonry in Connecticut, in the institution of Hiram Chapter, No. 1:

"Bro. Nichols, you are requested to Inform the Grand Lodge that Holland Mark Lodge in New York have granted a Dispensation & Installed Officers for a Hiram Mark Lodge in New Town—and all so that the Holland Chapter of Royal Arch Masons in New York have granted their dispensation & Charter to certain Royal Arch Masons in Newtown & Installed them in the several offices of the Chapter of Royal Arch Masons in Newtown—& that the sd Mark Lodge & Royal Arch Chapter are at present unable to open their Chapter in so decent a manner as may be necessary & therefore we hope the Grand Lodge will not exact the accustomed dues from Hiram Lodge—but assist the sd Mark Lodge & Chapter of Royal Arch with part of the dues from Hiram Lodge—

David Baldwin, Master."

The earliest records of this Lodge, and of Hiram Chapter are of great interest and value, and they should be preserved with care, and without delay. In the nature of the case they supplement and illustrate the history of each other, the Lodge and the Chapter, and may serve to throw light upon many subjects of personal and family life.

The members of the Chapter were largely from the roll of Hiram Lodge; and the places of meeting have probably been the same, without exception. At first, as we have seen, the communications were held in Bro. Bennett Perry's house, at Newtown—in Newtown street, as we would say, or as we should say, perhaps, now the Borough; where it continued to meet until October 5, 1821, when it began to assemble at Bro. Czar Keeler's Lodge room, and apparently was located there, in a private house which stood just north of Mrs. W. J. Beecher's residence, until Nov. 5, 1823, when it was removed to Wm. Blakesley's Lodge room, which was probably the ball room in the Blakesley house at the head of the street.

It may be said in authority, I think, that Bennett Perry's house was that later known as Dick's Hotel, the site of which is now occupied by the Newtown Inn.

And so in the records of Hiram Chapter, No. 1, we find it meeting

MASONIC TEMPLE

See Page 242

in "Bennett Perry's Lodge Room," 1797-1818, and later it is called "Bennett Perry's Chapter Room." The Chapter also met in Czar Keeler's Room, and Dec. 12, 1823, "At the Chapter Room at Wm. Blakesley's."

It is worthy of note at this point, that Mrs. Sarah Grace Glover, daughter of William Blakesley, found in the attic of the Blakesley house what is probably the original altar of Hiram Lodge, and a few years ago presented it to us, and it is here, in this hall.

The oil painting of the Trestle Board hanging in the East, was also discovered some years ago stowed away in a barn, and fortunately brought to light, retouched and saved to us as a relic, and a token of the zeal and enthusiasm of our ancient brethren of Newtown.

October 14, 1824, there was a movement made to build a Masonic Hall. "Voted, that the Master Lodge agree to build a Masonic Hall provided that the Chapter will defray one-half of the expense." Later it was "Voted that Brothers Theophilus Nichols, Henry Dutton & Alexander Hall be a committee to act with the committee appointed to contract and build the Masonic Hall the above Committee, to meet and confer with the committee appointed by the Chapter for the above purpose." And June 1, 1825, "Voted that this Lodge be adjourned to the Saturday previous to St. John's at 3 o'clock P. M.; and Voted that Brothers Tousey, John Nash & Macpherson Sherman be a committee to move the furniture of the Lodge to the new hall."

I have seen no mention of any dedication, but it is interesting to think that about this time 82 years ago, this Lodge was making itself a new home very much as it is this day.

The Lodge was incorporated by special act of the General Assembly the first Wednesday in May, 1825; and June 7, 1826, it was voted to get the Hall insured for $500.

This Hall was sold by vote of the Lodge, April 15, 1848, to D. H. Belden, Esq., for one hundred dollars, and all the personal property was disposed of. Our town historian, Mr. E. L. Johnson, holds the opinion that this building became what is now the dwelling house belonging to the Misses Julia and Lillian Dikeman.

The men who founded this Lodge were real enthusiastic Masons. They were trying to be men. There was an earnestness and dignity in their proceeding which indicate a deep sense of obligation to each other, and a genuine reverence for the science of morality; they made some effort to be of use to one another. "Brotherly love, relief and truth" were not mere high sounding words to them. To use their oft repeated form of speech: Masonry was an "Antient, Noble and Royal Art." And they expected and required true masonic conduct and character in the brethren.

They aimed at real self improvement by having lectures, orations, and other addresses. They met to listen to sermons on the anniversary of St. John Baptist, and on St. John Evangelist's Day, November 23, 1791, it was "Voted that we invite the Lodges of Danbury, Woodbury, Huntington, Stratford & Newfield to attend with this Lodge at the celebration of St. John on the 27th of December next." And a committee was appointed "to confer with the Rev. Philo Perry to preach a sermon on sd day." The Rev. Philo Perry was the rector of Trinity Parish, and a member of Hiram Chapter, No. 1, R. A. M.

It should be noted that some of the most prominent citizens of Newtown were members of this ancient Lodge. Of the founders we know very little. Peter Nichols, the first Master, was born in 1732, died in 1799, and was the great-grandfather of Philo Nichols, formerly an active member. His name appears in the History of the Grand Lodge as a delegate from the Stratford Lodge to a conference of Lodges, April, 1783, to consider the organization of the Grand Lodge of Connecticut.

Bennett Perry was a doctor of medicine, and Jonathan Prindle, the grandfather of the late Abel Prindle, was a tailor by trade.

Nichols and Prindle and Sanford and Glover and Blackman are names that have come down through the century of our history, and are with us to-day. The first Junior Warden was Prindle, and the present Junior Warden is Prindle, 'though not of the same family.

David Baldwin, who spent his whole life in Newtown, 1758-1811, and was very active in Masonic circles, is described in the Fairfield County Record as "A merchant; a prominent and leading man; a militia general and popularly known as 'General.' "

Judge Samuel C. Blackman was a notable man in his day; attorney David H. Belden was another. The Rev. Daniel Burhans, 31 years rector of Trinity church, was an active Mason.

Asa Chapman, a Newtown man, was Master of this Lodge in 1800, and attended the session of the Grand Lodge. He was the head of the Chapman Law school, and judge of the Supreme Court of this State; and his son, Charles Chapman, a distinguished lawyer, was a member of Congress and district attorney; and Henry Dutton, Master of this Lodge in 1827, was judge of the Supreme Court of Connecticut, and the governor of the State.

As to the causes of the revival of this ancient Lodge I can do no more, nor better, than to quote from the preface of the second book of Records: "It was a long time before Masonry revived in Newtown—not until the years 1860-6, when a decided reaction took place. Perhaps one of the great incentives to this was the war, which was about to be and was fought during those years.

"Two new Lodges had been organized, one at Bethel and one at Monroe, to which members were added from Newtown."

It was through Eureka, No. 83, that the Charter was restored. Quoting from the Historical sketch of that Lodge—which has ever been a good brother to us: "April 3, 1866, a motion was passed to recommend the brethren of Newtown to the Grand Lodge, for granting them a dispensation, charter or warrant, empowering them to work as a regular Lodge."

"This petition was granted by the Grand Lodge at its annual communication, May, 1866, at New Haven."

CAPT. JULIUS SANFORD
First Master Hiram Chapter
See Page 245

LOUIS T. BRISCOE
Past Master of Hiram Lodge No. 18
High Priest of Hiram Chapter No. 1

Bro. Julius Sanford was first Master, Bro. Wm. L. Horr the first S. W., Bro. George Woffenden, first J. W.

The first place of meeting was fitted up by Bro. Julius Sanford, in his building by the roadside, near the Foundry pond, in which the first installation of officers was held June 25, 1866.

In 1873 the Lodge was removed to the Hall owned by Bro. Smith P. Glover, where it continued until the building was destroyed by fire May 31, 1905, when it found temporary accommodations in Minott Augur's Hall, over the Sandy Hook Market.

June 21, 1906, it was voted to build a new Masonic Hall, provided the money could be raised. The money was raised, and Brothers A. M. Brisco, L. C. Morris, C. P. Northrop, S. A. Blackman and G. A. Northrop served as the building committee.

The amount of the contract was $2,949.50.

The Hall being completed, or nearly so, the Lodge moved into it Nov. 21, 1906. It is paid for and has been dedicated as the permanent home of Hiram Lodge, No. 18, Hiram Chapter, No. 1, R. A. M. and Jephtha Chapter, No. 51, Order of the Eastern Star.

In the "Guide to the Royal Arch Chapter," by John Sheville, P. G. H.P. of New Jersey, and James L. Gould, P. G. H. P. of Connecticut, it is stated that, 'At what time or by whom Royal Arch Masonry as a separate rite was introduced into the United States has never yet been settled.'

'Prior to the organization of any Grand Chapters there existed in the City of New York two Chapters, one known as the Old Chapter and the other called Washington Chapter, the origin or early history of which has never been published. The latter body, Washington Chapter, issued charters to a number of subordinate Chapters, in which charters it styled itself 'The Mother Chapter.' From this body originated the first Chapters of Rhode Island and Connecticut. The first Chapter in Connecticut was called Hiram Chapter, No. 1, and located at Newtown in Fairfield County.

"Five other Chapters were instituted in Connecticut under the authority of this Washington Chapter: Franklin Chapter, No. 2, New Haven; Washington, No. 3, Middletown; Franklin, No. 4, Norwich; Solomon, No. 5, Derby, and Vanden Broeck, No. 5, at Colchester.

"The first convention of Chapters in Connecticut was held on the first Wednesday of July, 1796, at Hartford, in which all the Chapters above named were represented by delegates, except Franklin Chapter, at New Haven. A regular organization was perfected and articles of agreement were entered into for the government of the several Chapters in this State. Another convention was held October 20, 1796. at New Haven, of which David Baldwin (of Newtown) was chairman."

The same writer says: "So far as I can learn, this was the first governing body in Royal Arch Masonry organized in the United States."

THE CHARTER OF HIRAM MARK LODGE.

"At a meeting of Holland Mark Lodge held in Holland Lodge Room in the city of New York on Thursday the twenty-eighth day of April A. L. 5791. Present, the Worshipful Master and other officers of the Lodge. Whereas, our Brother Andrew Beers, in behalf of himself and sundry other brethern, did, on the 11th day of February last, present a Memorial to this Lodge praying to withdraw themselves as members thereof with an intention to hold a Lodge of Master Mark Masons at Newtown, in the County of Fairfield, and state of Connecticut, and the prayer of the said memorial having been granted.

"Now Be It Known, that by virtue of the power regularly committed to us, we have in ample form constituted these our well beloved brethren into a regular Lodge of Master Mark Masons by the name and stile of Hiram Mark Lodge and installed the several officers into their respective stations in the manner we have received it, to wit:

"The Worshipful Brother Andrew Beers, Master; Brother David Baldwin, Sen. Warden, and by proxy, Brother Nathan Douglass, Junior Warden of the said Lodge.

"In witness whereof, we the three presiding officers of Holland Mark Lodge have hereunto set our hands, and caused the seal of Holland Lodge to be hereunto affixed.

"John Pintard, Master,
"John Abrams, Senr., Warden,
"Attest, I. Tivorback, Secretary."
"Samuel Low, Junr., Warden.
—Hiram Mark Lodge.—

The first presiding officers were appointed by Holland Mark Lodge, viz:

Andrew Beers, W. M.
David Baldwin, S. W.
Nathan Douglass, J. W.

CHARTER

Copy of the Original Charter of Hiram Chapter, No. 1, Royal Arch Masons, Newtown, Connecticut.

At a Washington Chapter of Royal Arch Masons, held in Holland Lodge Room in the City of N. York, on Friday, the twenty-ninth day of April, A. L. 5791.

Whereas our Brother Andrew Beers, in behalf of himself and sundry other brethren, residing in the State of Connecticut, did on the nineteenth day of March last, present a Memorial to this Chapter, praying to withdraw themselves as Members thereof, with an intention to hold a chapter of the Royal Arch in Newtown, in the County of Fairfield, in the State of Connecticut, aforesaid; and the prayer of the said Memorial having been granted:

Now be it known that by virtue of the power regularly committed to us, we have in ample form, constituted these our well-beloved Brethren into a regular Chapter of Royal Arch Masons, and installed the several Officers into their respective stations, in the manner we have received it, to wit:

The Most Worshipful Brother Andrew Beers, H. P., the Right Worshipful Brother David Baldwin, K. g., and the Right Worshipful Brother Oliver Peck S——

In witness whereof we the three Presiding Officers of Washington

Chapter have hereunto set our hands and caused the Seal of the said Chapter to be affixed.   Jos. Ogden Hoffman, H.P.W.C.R.A.M.
George Anthon, K. W. C. R. A. M.
Attest: Asher (?) Collins, Sec'y.   Martin Hoffman, S. W. C. R. A. M.

Andrew Beers, whose name appears in the Charter of Hiram Mark Lodge, and in the Charter of Hiram Chapter, No. 1, was made in New York. He was the first Master of Hiram Mark Lodge and continued as such until after June 31, 1793. He was the first H. P. of this Chapter, by appointment, but his name does not appear on the records, such as we have, after the signing of the By-Laws, March 3d, 1792.

David Baldwin, 1758-1811, who was made in New York and belonged to Holland Mark Lodge, and was a member of Washington Chapter, and was one of the petitioners for a Mark Lodge, and Royal Arch Chapter in Newtown, was the first S. W. of Hiram Mark Lodge and the first King of Hiram Chapter, No. 1—was H. P. "for a series of years successively," to use his own language, until the election of officers Sept. 6, 1810. He was many years W. M. of Hiram Mark Lodge, and of Hiram Lodge, No. 18. And as has already been stated, represented this Chapter at the organization of the Grand Chapter of Connecticut, of which he was Grand Scribe, 1807; Grand King, 1808; and Deputy Grand High Priest in 1809.

Samuel C. Blackman, who was Master of Hiram Lodge, No. 18, 1803-1808, was several times Master of Hiram Mark Lodge; many times High Priest of this Chapter; Grand Secretary 1806, 1807 and 1808; Grand Scribe 1809, 1810 and 1811; and Deputy Grand High Priest, 1812 and 1813.

"Hiram Chapter, No. 1, continued prosperously until the year 1835, which is the date of the last record, when the officers were duly elected, and for several years after was represented at the annual convocations of the Grand Chapter, but eventually was obliged to give up its charter. At the May Session in 1870 this Chapter was revived, and a new charter issued, under the name of Hiram Chapter, No. 1, the old Charter having been lost, since which time it has continued comparatively prosperous."

It should be said here that the Original Charter which was lost, was found, and is now in the safe-keeping of the Chapter; and that photographic copies of the same have been made.

Contributed by Rev. O. O. Wright.

Order of the Eastern Star.

Jephthah Chapter, No. 51, Order of the Eastern Star, was instituted on the evening of Oct. 5, 1899, and constituted, Dec. 7, 1899, at Sandy Hook, in the rooms occupied by Hiram Lodge, No. 18, A. F. and A. M.

Monthly meetings were held there until the morning of May 31, 1905, when a fire destroyed the entire building. Temporary accommodations were found in the old G. A. R. Hall, until Dec. 14, 1906, when the Chapter held regular meetings in a new building erected by Hiram Lodge, No. 18, until April 9, 1910, when the Chapter surrendered its charter to the Grand Chapter of Connecticut, owing to the loss of many members by death and removal.

Contributed by Miss Jennie Briscoe.

THE RUBBER INDUSTRY.

The beginning of this industry in Sandy Hook, was in a building now in the rear of Corbett and Crowe's store, where Nelson Goodyear and Henry Alden made rubber coats in 1841-42. Later, they moved into Dick and Sanford's satinet factory by the bridge.

Josiah Tomlinson, whose wife was sister of Charles Goodyear, owner of the rubber patents of that day, then commenced work in the Glen. Charles Goodyear was born in New Haven, but spent much time in Sandy Hook, experimenting, in connection with his discovery in 1839 of the vulcanization of rubber. Tomlinson failed and Wm. B. Glover, who underwrote him, lost heavily, but paid dollar for dollar.

He was succeeded by Frame and Grecian, then in 1846 by the N. Y. Belting and Packing Co. Its history is inseparable from that of the rubber industry. The company was founded at a time when little was known of vulcanized rubber beyond the crude result of the experiments of Charles Goodyear and the development of the industry, as it pertains to goods for mechanical purposes almost from its inception to its present enormous proportions, has devolved largely upon this company.

The accidental discovery of vulcanization by Charles Goodyear, and his subsequent experiments, gave a wonderful impetus to its development. Rubber at once became an essential in the sciences, in manufacturing and in domestic life, and now forms one of the great industries of modern times.

Dr. Werner Esch, said in 1912, in a "Hand Book of India Rubber." "The discovery of the process of vulcanization by Charles Goodyear in 1839 was not, as is often said, a matter of chance, but the outcome of years of investigation. Goodyear, like many other inventors, kept on dabbling with rubber, in spite of numerous failures, and tried mixing all sorts of substances with rubber. It always was his intention to make an invention and, as a result of the experience gained by experiments, he knew, when observing the effect of heat on a mixture of rubber and sulphur, that the heating was the essential factor in the process. It is a matter for admiration to see how this man, overwhelmed with ideas and hard-pressed, pursued working out his invention. The way in which he worked it out is clearly demonstrated by his first publication on his method for the metallisation of rubber, in which he gave sufficient instructions for the technical preparation of perfect rubber goods. And these instructions for the manufacture of soft rubber have, even up to the present time, lost no essential part of their technical importance in any of those methods of vulcanization devised by Goodyear's inventions." By the discovery, Charles Goodyear enriched the world, but he himself lived and died poor.

In 1856, the factory was destroyed by fire, but was immediately re-built. The same year, Mr. Dennis C. Gately was made superintendent. He had had an experience of several years with the Boston Belting Co. and had been associated with Mr. Cheever,

FABRIC FIRE HOSE COMPANY
Formerly
N. Y. Belting and Packing Co.

DENNIS C. GATELY
See Page 248

WILLIAM T. COLE

See Page 248

treasurer of the N. Y. Belting and Packing Co. Under his supervision, the business increased rapidly to large proportions. A year in his younger days with a noted chemist had given him sufficient knowledge of chemistry to aid his inventive genius, and he made valuable inventions. The products manufactured included, besides the largest belts in the world for machinery, the smallest sizes for use; hose for fire-engines, gardening and various other uses; wagon and car springs; solid vulcanite emery-wheels; corrugated matting and mats; etc., a full list of which would make a formidable catalogue.

Too much emphasis cannot be placed upon the influence of Mr. Gately and that of his family for good upon the community. The enlarging of the business meant the influx of a large number of families, who were helped to obtain homes in the vicinity. Walnut Tree Hill became populated to such an extent that school privileges were necessary. Pohtatuck school-house, though enlarged, was not sufficient. Through the influence of Mr. Gately, the town voted to form a new district, and for many years a flourishing school was kept in the new Walnut Tree Hill district. Many young men and women have filled places of responsibility in different communities whose start in life beyond the home was in Walnut Tree Hill school.

There were many sad hearts when, in 1884, Mr. Gately left the beautiful home in the Glen for the new home at Mamaroneck, N. Y.

Universal sorrow was expressed when, in 1900, it was announced that N. Y. Belting and Packing Co. was to move its business to Passaic, N. J. Many families went with them, while some, who had made for themselves pleasant homes, remained, hoping that some other industry would take the plant. Mr. I. Percy Blackman, a Newtown boy who commenced work with them in 1876, went with them and is now their superintendent, with a force of 1200 hands. In 1916, they turned out over 12,000,000 pounds of rubber goods. Thanks are due to Mr. I. Percy Blackman for some of this information, also to Mr. Anthony Patch, oldest resident of Sandy Hook.

By the courtesy of Mr. W. T. Cole, president of the Fabric Fire Hose Co., the following information is given as a sequel to the removal of the N. Y. Belting Co. to Passaic N. J.

"The Fabric Fire Hose Co., formerly of Warwick, N. Y. by virtue of its affiliations with the United States Rubber Co., of which parent organization the New York Belting and Packing Co., was also a subsidiary, acquired the Sandy Hook property, formerly occupied by the New York Belting and Packing Co., and the entire plant of machinery operated by the Fabric Fire Hose Co., of Warwick since 1880 was transferred to the so-called lower mill at Sandy Hook in the spring of 1901. The company also brought with its plant a number of its old employees."

The upper mill, or "Dutch Shop," was operated for several years as a rubber reclaiming plant, which was discontinued in 1915 and succeeded by the Premier Mfg. Co., Charles S. Cole and George A. Gauthier, Proprietors; manufacturers of high class machine tools; and for the first time in history the Dutch Shop parted from its identity with rubber.

THE NEWTOWN BEE.

The Bee owes its origin to John T. Pearse of Bethel, Conn.

Started as an experiment, it quickly gained a hold upon the Newtown public and was enlarged, though always known to printers as a "patent outside"—which means that two of its four pages were printed by a New York firm that supplied the same reading matter to local publishers in different places. Mr. Pearse had a "nose for news," as Samuel Bowles of the Springfield Republican used to say, but was not fitted for a publisher, as he was non-resident, living at Bethel; was eccentric, now suspending the Bee's issue, then transferring the paper to another and again taking it to his own hands. The Newtown Chronicle was meanwhile started by James E. Madigan, and the Winter of 1880-81 found the Bee apparently driven from the field for good, as its 300 or more subscribers looked in vain for the paper, and its effects in the room over Daniel Camp's plumbing shop were heavily mortgaged to Henry Sanford, the village merchant. Reuben Hazen Smith, formerly editor of the Waterbury American, was then exchange editor on the Springfield Republican, to which duty had been added that of telegraph editor on the Sunday edition, just begun. Chafing under enforced violation of the 4th commandment, he was looking about for a loophole of escape. His brother, Henry called attention to the Bee, which ended in its purchase and the removal of the Smith family to the Fairchild place in South Center. It was no easy task mastering the old Washington hand press and the second-hand type white with lye, and the first revived issue in April of 1881 was hardly legible, but was kindly wrapped for the mail in the hospitable dining room of E. Levan Johnson. How much the Bee owes the generous hand, active brain and fertile pen of that prince among men only Heaven can reveal.

Grit and spunk, aided by Charles B. Johnson, Frank Wright, Robert D. Smith (the Bee Man's loyal brother), Robert C. Mallette, two other brothers, Allison P. Smith and Arthur J. Smith, finally won out. Rev. Charles H. Smith came for a little in the early struggle and proved what personal canvass could do to add funds and make subscribers friends, and that able financier, Arthur J. Smith, later laid the bed-rock of paying advertising. At one time, the Bee Man knew every subscriber, excepting those on the distant mail list, personally, and he closed one year with all but three or four subscriptions paid in advance and those three or four assured.

This personal work, involving miles of walk and early and late hours, was what turned the Bee from a loss into a valuable asset, finally capitalized at $500 in the incorporated Bee Publishing Co. Another financial spur was the early purchase of the Chronicle for $300, giving the Bee an advertising grip that it has never lost, though the rates were raised when subscriptions topped 1000 and

REUBEN H. SMITH

See Page 250

ALLISON P. SMITH

See Page 250

ARTHUR J. SMITH

See Page 251

NEWTOWN BEE

See Page 250

again when they passed the 2000 mark. The policy of the Bee Man was simply that of Burns—"A man's a man for a' that," with its irresistible resultant that whatever concerned him and his, no matter how trivial, was of interest to that circle and neighborhood. So the Bee, without flourish or literary effort, banned gossip, grudges, hate and scandal as far as possible and spread from district to district, from town to town, George F. Duncombe being finally called in to aid in the canvass. The Bee Man claimed absolute and fearless action personally and so temporarily angered Republican friends by being an independent Republican in Cleveland's day and dared to be the only man to vote no license in his precinct. At the floodtide of success, the failure of the health and heart of Mrs. Smith, whose loyal support made success a double joy, led the Bee Man to drop it all in October of 1892 and flee to California with his family. Newtown gained two things with the Bee Man's help, its Grange and eventually, the wiping out of its house of ill-fame on Taunton Lake. The latter, assaulted by Rev. J. P. Hoyt, could only be banished, it seemed, by buying the property and turning it into a home, C. B. Taylor, Levi C. Morris, Charles Nichols and other friends of righteousness and pure living endorsing the note on which the Newtown bank advanced the funds. The Bee shared its owner's prosperity, a new Campbell press and new type making the paper easier to issue and more readable when issued, when it moved to the quarters over the post-office, then owned by Town Clerk and Merchant L. B. Booth. A gasoline engine also took the place of the hard labor of John Griggs, beloved sexton of the Congregational Church and of Frederick Andrews.

The controlling interest in the Bee Publishing Co. property and business was sold by Reuben H. Smith to his brothers, Allison P. Smith and Arthur J. Smith, in October, 1892. A. P. Smith became president and editor, and A. J. Smith, treasurer and general manager. Six years later, Henry M. Smith of Hartford, another brother, entered the employ of the Bee Publishing Co., as general agent. A year later he was sold an interest in the business, and was made vice-president and general agent. As a result of the united effort of the three brothers, the circulation of the Bee was increased from about 2200 to something over 4000. In October, 1903, the present building occupied by The Bee Publishing Co. was erected. Some years later a new press and linotype machines were installed. Owing to ill health, Henry M. Smith was forced to retire from the business about four years ago, to the sincere regret of his associates.

It will be observed from the above that the Messrs. A. P. and A. J. Smith have about completed 25 years of service on the Bee. During that period they have seen almost every newspaper property in Western and Southern Connecticut change hands from one to six times.

Contributed by Reuben Hazen Smith and Allison P. Smith.

POHTATUCK GRANGE.

Pohtatuck Grange, No. 129, P. of H., was organized, March 9, 1892, by State Deputy J. H. Blakeman of Housatonic Grange, Stratford. There were 19 charter members:

Mr. and Mrs. Zalmon S. Peck, Mr. and Mrs. S. J. Botsford, Mr. and Mrs. W. C. Johnson, Mr. and Mrs. Reuben H. Smith, Lemuel Glover, W. H. Glover, J. J. Schermerhorn, H. C. Beers, A. O. Bierce, C. B. Johnson, L. M. Johnson, Fred Chambers, E. S. Lovell and two others not mentioned in the record. The following officers were chosen:

Master, Z. S. Peck; Overseer, S. J. Botsford; Lecturer, R. H. Smith; Steward, H. C. Beers; Asst. Steward, A. O. Bierce; Chaplain, W. C. Johnson; Treasurer, W. H. Glover; Secretary, J. J. Schermerhorn; Gate Keeper, E. S. Lovell; Ceres, Mrs. Z. S. Peck; Pomona, Mrs. S. J. Botsford; Flora, Mrs. R. H. Smith; L. A. Steward, Mrs. W. C. Johnson.

The meeting for organization was held in Fireman's Hall, which was over the Savings Bank in the Sanford Building. As this room was not suited to the needs of the Grange, a committee was appointed to look up a hall.

The officers elected at this meeting were installed by Deputy Blakeman, assisted by S. C. Lewis, Asst. Steward of the Conn. State Grange.

The Grange was held at houses of different members until a room over L. C. Morris's store was leased and was occupied for over 20 years, being twice enlarged to meet the needs of the rapidly growing Grange.

The first class initiated:

Mr. and Mrs. C. E. Beers, Geo. A. Northrop, E. F. Northrop, Homer W. Baldwin, Mrs. J. J. Schermerhorn, C. M. Parsons, Mrs. Walter Glover, Letty J. Stoddard and Mrs. E. L. Johnson joined later.

It evidently made some attempt at co-operative buying, for we find that for some time a purchasing agent was elected annually. The order was also on very fraternal relations with the neighboring granges, for frequent mention is made of visits paid to and received from Harmony Grange, No. 92, of Monroe; Housatonic Grange, No. 99, Stratford, and others. Fairfield Co. Pomona Grange was first entertained by Pohtatuck Grange, Oct. 28, 1896. Nor has it been selfish in its activities, but has done much for its home community, and we believe Newtown is the better because this Grange has existed in its midst for 25 years.

In 1894, a Fourth of July celebration was held under its auspices. Oct. 10, of the same year, a Grange Fair was held in the Town Hall. There were exhibits of farm products, a ladies' industrial department, exhibits by merchants and manufacturers, also of cattle and horses. This Fair was such a success that one was held annually until it became merged into the Newtown Agricultural Fair, at which the Grange offered premiums. The Farmers Institute was an annual event. Many plays and entertainments have been held under its auspices, which have been a benefit to the community as well as of financial aid to the Grange.

At one time the order numbered about 80 members, but in later years the membership was depleted by death, by removal from

ZALMON S. PECK

First Master of Pohtatuck Grange
See Pages 171 and 252

town and other causes. In 1914, the hall, with all its contents, was destroyed by fire, and it was with some difficulty that a new home was found and the lost property replaced. At present it meets in Firemen's Hall where it was at first organized. The members now number about fifty, many of whom are young people deeply interested in its work.

THE LIST OF PAST MASTERS

Z. S. Peck, S. J. Botsford, W. H. Glover, C. B. Johnson, Edgar Northrop, K. L. Coleman, C. M. Beresford, Mrs. F. W. Mitchell, J. J. Northrop, A. P. Smith, W. B. Glover, Austin Botsford, W. N. Mitchell and Mrs W. N. Mitchell.

Contributed by Mrs. W. N. Mitchell.

THE DOMESTIC ECONOMY OF OUR MOTHERS

This article was written about twenty years ago, by Mrs. E. L. Johnson, by request of the Lecturer of Pomona Grange, and read by her at a meeting of the Grange in Stratford, Conn. Discrepancy in dates is due to partial revision by the writer, who will be, April 6, 1919, 82 years old.

I am asked to give a reminiscence of our mothers' housekeeping arrangements, and of the conditions under which they worked; how they preserved and what they preserved; how their dealings with the butcher, the baker and the candle as well as the candlestick maker differed from ours; how their kitchen conveniences compared with ours, etc.

Nothing more fascinating to me could have been assigned as subject of a paper, and yet, I undertake it with the feeling that it must necessarily be so closely connected with my own home experiences during childhood, as to seem to many, perhaps intensely egotistical.

The house which comes most vividly to my mind's eye, and with whose household arrangements I was most intimately acquainted, because it was for many years my home, was of a type common then, though seldom seen now. The roof on one side reached to within five or six feet of the ground. A space under this low roof half the length of the house, and five or six feet in width, was an open porch or "shed" as it was then called, where were kept the wash-bench, a table or bench for the family wash-basin, in summer, and in summer also, the cheese press and various household farming utensils. There when it was not too severely cold, the washing was done. The remaining room under this low roof was used sometimes as a bedroom, sometimes as a store-room. The chimney was of stone to the top, and occupied space sufficient for a room of moderate dimensions, and had fire-places on three of its sides. The narrow kitchen extended the entire length of the house, and the fire-place in that was immense, large enough for a fire of huge logs. It contained the brick oven, the always present dye-pot, and sufficient space besides for seats for the little ones. The fire-place in the large square room adjoining the long, narrow kitchen was also very large, while that on a third side of the chimney, in the bed-room, was much smaller. There were also fire-places in two bed-rooms on the second floor, and the stairs to the garret were built of stone into the chimney on a third side. The only other room on the ground floor was the milk-room. On the second floor, besides the two rooms containing fire-places, was the space over the kitchen under the rafters. It was approached by the stairway at one end of the kitchen and contained at one end, bins for rye, oats and buckwheat, while at the other was always a bed for the wayfarer, or for some of the children, if crowded from their rooms by extra guests.

There was never hired help for the house and only occasional days for the farm from some one in the neighborhood.

The long kitchen was dining-room as well during the warm weather, except when there was company; then the square room, always the family sitting-room, did duty as dining-room. In the winter, however, the cooking-stove was moved into the sitting-room and all ordinary work was done there; the washing, work connected with the butchering, and all extraordinary work being done in the kitchen, with a big fire on the hearth.

The expression, "Have you come for fire?" is still used occasionally, but in these days when friction matches are in every home and in some pocket of almost every man, it is likely that many have no idea of the origin of the question. Every woman expected to keep coals enough buried in some fire-place to start fire when needed. It was a sorry time when they and the tinder-box failed. My grandmother once went nearly a half mile for coals when she lost fire.

Although my recollection extends over considerably more than three quarters of a century, I can never remember when it was the custom to cook exclusively by the fire on the hearth. Stoves were found in most houses seventy-five years ago, but few of them had ovens that could be used for general baking; consequently every house-wife heated her brick-oven twice or three times each week in summer and once or twice in winter.

The furnishing of the oven-wood was a subject of really vital importance for, if too light or flashy, or if it was green, the heat would not hold long enough to bake the food. The wood must burn freely, yet not too rapidly, and must be of a kind, a part of it at least, to leave coals that could remain after the blaze was gone.

Mr. A. and Mr. B., who lived not far from my home, were discussing the question of oven-wood, each trying to convince the other that his wife was the more particular, when Mr. B., who had listened to the description of the kind Mr. A. had to furnish, stuttered, "W-w-well, my w-w-wife has to have hers t-t-turned and b-b-brass f-f-ferrules put on it."

The house-wife must have needed to have her wits about her, to have bread, cake and pies ready to go into the oven at the same time and when the heat was just right, the bread light enough, yet not too light; the cake mixed so that it need not stand too long, and the pies "set up" all in good time.

Apple, berry or mince pies could be baked with bread and cake, but not many custard or pumpkin pies, because the steam arising from them would cause the bread and cake to be heavy.

It was considered as much of a disgrace to be without pie, if a guest dropped in for dinner or supper, as without bread; and it was a common practice to bake, after the weather became cool enough so that they would keep two or three days, ten or twelve pumpkin pies at one baking. In that case, the crusts were set up and the pumpkin mixed, while the first food was baking; then some lighter wood than was used at the first heating, was burned for a shorter time, and the pies baked by themselves. Our mothers certainly needed the same kind of "faculty," on baking days, with which Mrs. Harriet Beecher Stowe, invests Mrs. Katy Scudder in "The Minister's Wooing."

The stove most used in our neighborhood, during my childhood, was the Rotary. It revolved upon a track by means of a crank which turned a wheel, the cogs of which fitted into corresponding cogs on the outer edge of the circular top. There were five lids of graduated sizes for different sized cooking utensils.

If it could have had a good oven, I am sure none could be better and I often wish, when I must lift a heavy kettle from one part of the stove to the other, that I had my mother's old rotary.

Rye flour was the staple for bread; few families used wheat, except for cakes, pie-crust and company biscuit. Some even made pie-crust of rye. Corn was used much more than now. Hasty-pudding was almost a daily food in some form at some seasons of the year, and it was expected that every miller know the best way to crack corn for samp. In many families, the kettle of samp must be boiled every Saturday during the Spring and Summer to be eaten with milk for the Sunday evening meal. In cooking it, there was need of close watching and frequent stirring to prevent scorching. Boiled Indian pudding was a common dish, almost never seen now. Every house-wife had the pudding-bag, made of stout linen tightly woven.

When used, it was wet, turned wrong side out, and dusted with flour, to prevent the batter from leaking, turned again and the batter poured in, leaving space, when tied, for its swelling; then it was immersed in the liquor in the huge pot containing the beef, pork, potatoes, turnips and any other vegetables for the dinner. They called the meat and vegetables "pot luck." In those days, the pudding was always served first, no doubt because, if it was left until the last, it would become sodden.

Almost as soon as the buckwheat was harvested and threshed, griddle cakes made their appearance upon the breakfast table, and regularly appeared until Spring. In my own home Sunday morning was the exception, because fresh bread was baked on Saturday and because nothing was to be done on Sunday to add to the work. I may add incidentally, that the steel knives and forks, always scoured twice, and often three times each week-day, were never scoured on Sunday.

The custom of having baked beans always Saturday night and Sunday morning did not prevail as extensively in our vicinity as in Massachusetts; yet the pan of beans was apt to be ready for the oven on Saturday, when other things came out, and often made the late Sunday dinner in hot weather, when a fire was uncomfortable. At any season, whatever was to be eaten Sunday was prepared on Saturday, as far as possible.

During the Summer, the list from which our mothers chose meats to place upon the table, consisted of salt pork, salt beef, ham and dried beef, with now and then a fowl from the barn-yard. Salt pork was cooked with almost everything. Of fish, there was codfish, salted mackerel, Housatonic River shad (of which most farmers laid in a supply in the Spring), with now and then a mess of pan fish from the brooks. Almost all farmers kept a few or a great many sheep, and it is quite within my recollection that the only fresh meat, apart from one's flock of fowls, was by some farmer killing a lamb or calf and lending to his neighbors what he did not himself need. When it became possible to get regularly, once each week in Summer, a piece of meat from a butcher's cart, it was considered a wonderful thing.

The only refrigerator our mothers had was the well, and happy was the woman whose well was deep and cold and never-failing. Two or three or more pails or baskets were almost always hung in it. She depended on it to cool her cream for churning, and to keep the butter solid for the table, as well as to preserve a little longer any fresh bit she was fortunate enough to have.

That woman was to be congratulated in that she did not have to wait for the ice-man.

In winter the conditions were more favorable for fresh meat. Farmers took turns in butchering their pork and beef, and loaned to each other. It was desirable, however, to choose a very cold time for butchering, else the task of chopping the sausage meat was very great. If quite cold and the meat could be frozen by spreading in a cold room by an open window, the task of chopping was much easier.

Our mothers knew nothing of creameries, or separators or cheese factories; but every woman made butter and cheese from her own dairy, often milking the cows also.

Once a week in summer, a market wagon went the rounds of the neighborhood, collecting butter, cheese, eggs and chickens. The chickens were carried in a coop swung from the rear axle. The produce was taken to Bridgeport or New Haven, the returns for one week being made the next, and the house-wife whose butter cleared a York shilling thought herself well off. If more than that was realized, the price was considered extra good.

In many homes it was considered economy to spin and weave linen for some uses, even after cotton cloth became comparatively cheap. The spinning and weaving were to be done in the Spring before soap-making, and house-cleaning, so that the lye not needed for soap could be used for whitening the cloth and the thread. A section of the ash-crib, as it was called, in which the ashes were leached, was like a V, the bottom of the V resting in a grooved plank slightly inclined, to form a trough. As the ashes were filled into the crib, they were wetted enough to dampen them, but not enough to cause the lye to run until the day for the soap-making, when they were thoroughly soaked. A certain quantity of lye that would float an egg must be poured into a certain quantity of heated grease. Some of our mothers understood enough of chemistry, although they did not call it that, to know what conditions were necessary to "bring" the soap, and were almost always successful; others boiled and boiled and spent a great deal of time, and strength, and patience, with very indifferent results.

Seventy years ago, neither you nor I had seen a kerosene lamp. Lard oil and sperm oil were used by some, but were considered not greatly superior to the tallow dip, the only light many of our mothers had ever known. Candles must be made every Spring and Autumn, and the evening before the dipping the whole family was set to work helping put the wicks upon the candle-rods. These rods were of hickory, a little larger than an ordinary lead pencil, made very smooth, and about two feet long. The wicking was wound around a book or a board whose length would make a wick, when cut and doubled, the desired length for the candle. Every separate thread of the wicking must be drawn out because a loosely twisted wick would burn better than one tightly twisted. Seven or eight of these wicks, each composed of seven or eight threads, were put double upon the rods, and twisted just enough to keep them in place. Early in the morning, the big brass kettle was hung upon the crane in the fire-place, and sufficient tallow for the candles to be made put into it to melt. A little alum was usually pounded and added, to harden the tallow, and, if bees-wax was abundant, the addition of a certain proportion made the candles much nicer. Water was also added to prevent the tallow from scorching. While this was melting, the ends of two long poles or ribs were put upon two "horses" or chairs, and the candle-rods with their wicks, put upon them a little distance apart. As soon as the tallow was melted and somewhat heated, the kettle was placed near the candle-rods, then filled with water to within an inch or less of the top, and the process of dipping commenced. At first the wicks on three or four rods could be dipped at once, but after a few dippings they became heavy. A kettle of water must be kept constantly hot, and a little added occasionally, both to keep the tallow warm and to raise it in the kettle as it was dipped off. Great care must be taken that it be made not too hot, or what had cooled on the wicks would be melted off, rather than added to. My mother used to say that she never dipped candles that she did not have unexpected company, for it was work she could not put aside and must be done in a cold room. The introduction of molds was considered a wonderful improvement.

It is a little less than forty years since we commenced using glass jars and canning our fruit. Our mothers, before that invention, must keep their fruit in crocks and jars, and it must be made very rich, that it spoil not by fermentation. They had no porcelain or granite ware, and their preserving kettles were usually of brass, which must be made as bright as gold, cleaned first with salt and vinegar, then with rotten stone or brick dust, then with soap and water.

The currant worm was not, years ago, the pest that it now is and the crop was usually abundant, so that currants were preserved in as large quantities as the ability to furnish sugar would allow. Raisins to the amount of about a quarter of their weight were used by many; sugar was used pound for pound and the preserve cooked until it was a rich, clear mass. An incident will show that sugar was sometimes and in some places scarce in those days. About eighty years ago, my mother went with one of her babies to spend the day with an acquaintance. She took with her milk for her baby, but did not think it necessary to take sugar. When she wanted to feed the baby, she asked for sugar. The woman went to a chest and, reaching to the bottom, brought out a box with the remark, "John bought a couple of pounds about a year ago, and I guess it isn't all gone yet."

Gooseberries were much more abundant than now and no collection of preserves was complete without them, both in preserve and in jam. Jellies were not made as much as now. Sometimes jam was made of blackberries, but they were oftener dried for pies, either in the sun without sugar, or scalded with a little sugar, spread upon plates and put into the brick oven, when the food was drawn out.

Pies made from berries dried in that way were delicious, and often the oven was slightly heated for the purpose of saving the berries by drying.

Plums of several sorts were then, as now, considered the best of fruits for preserving. Peaches were abundant, and every housewife expected to have a good supply. They were pared, the stones taken out and the sugar added to them at night. In the morning, a syrup had formed, and in that the peaches were cooked until clear, then skimmed out, and the syrup boiled until somewhat thick, the peaches added again, and scalded in the syrup for a few minutes, then placed in crocks for the winter. If cooked sufficiently, there was rarely any trouble about keeping them.

Grapes were preserved then as I suppose most of us do them now, except that we do not make them so rich. Quinces must be boiled first to make them tender, but even then the quince preserve of years ago was apt to be hard, unless one was very skillful in the making.

One of the duties of every housekeeper was to examine very often her stock of preserves, and she who did not now and then have to check incipient fermentation by scalding was indeed very fortunate.

As soon as apples began to drop, when in any degree near maturity, our thrifty mothers commenced drying them, spreading them on cloths laid on roofs, or on platforms made for the purpose. Perhaps an earlier way was to string the quarters and hang them around the kitchen or in the sun out of doors.

The old time garden contained no tomatoes, consequently our mothers knew nothing of chili sauce, green tomato pickle, or chow-chow. Cucumber pickles, usually put in brine, were the stand-by, the cucumbers being taken from the brine and soaked from time to time as needed.

I must not forget to speak of another accompaniment to almost every meal during the winter in many families—cider apple sauce.

Something like it is now called apple butter. The cider was taken sweet from the press, and boiled until nearly as thick as molasses. Some of this was always saved to use with mince pies in the winter.

Half sweet and half sour apples were used, and sometimes a few quinces. There was always a busy company preparing the apples the evening before the apple sauce was to be made. The big brass kettle was scoured in the same way and just as bright as the small preserving kettle, and in the morning early it was hung upon the crane with the boiled cider in it, and the apples added only as fast as those before got to cooking. The mass needed constant care through almost the whole day. The making of it was considered of so much consequence that, when the teacher who boarded around the district, sent to see if he could go to some place, the reply sometimes came, "Mother can't have you next week, she hain't made apple sass."

Our mothers had no sewing machines, and I well remember when my mother brought home, from a visit to the American Institute at New York, a sample that she said she saw sewed on a sewing machine, and every one was amazed that it was possible. As they could not sit down at the machine and sew, they took their sewing or their knitting and went, uninvited, to visit neighbors. Sometimes the result was rather embarrassing to the one visited, as was the case with old Mrs. Blank, when several of her neighbors went to spend the afternoon with her. She and her husband, "Uncle Thoph" to every one, lived alone. When it was time to get tea, she announced to her visitors, "La! me! I thought I had enough for Thoph and me a week, but I hain't got enough for tea."

As has been stated, most farmers kept a flock of sheep which were sheared in June, the wool taken to some factory where it was "scoured" and carded into rolls about three quarters of an inch in diameter and two feet long. The rolls were spun at home for household use.

The yarn needed for stockings for the men and boys was usually cleaned at home, dyed indigo blue in the dye-pot before mentioned, mixed with white wool and carded into grey rolls.

Homespun dresses of wool were worn in winter. The yarn for these was spun white and dyed at home. My mother dyed indigo blue in different shades. Cochineal red, and used butternut bark for shades of brown. From these colors in warp and woof a pretty plaid was planned, the cloth woven in some home loom, then taken to the factory to be pressed.

Many houses had looms for weaving the wool and linen for household use and rag carpets.

It was one of my chief delights to wind for the weaver on a "quill-wheel," the little paper tubes or "quills" that were slipped on a wire in the shuttle when weaving woolen or linen goods.

I would like once more to hear the musical whizzing of the old wool wheel, as it sounded when I was a child, and my mother kept time to its music in the long narrow kitchen of the old house at home, but I am thankful that the women of to-day need not tread in all the foot-steps of our mothers.

BERKSHIRE

For the past one hundred years the history of Berkshire has been largely bound up in the history of the Curtis family

The first of the family to come from Stratford was Matthew Curtis, who settled on Mile Hill and his son, Gold Curtis, who married Elizabeth, daughter of Abraham Gold, also lived there.

Gould, the eldest son of Gold, married Joanna Peck and made his home in Berkshire. Being a captain in the militia, he was called "Captain Gould."

He built the white homestead at the end of the village towards Bennett's bridge. This was probably about 100 years old. He was a farmer, owning about 200 acres of land lying on the hill back of the house along the "Pole bridge road and in the Zoar district."

He had five children: Mary, who married Cyrenius Beers, a native of Newtown, but a pioneer of Chicago; Samuel; Elizabeth, second wife of Robert S. Peck, also second wife of Simeon B. Peck; a child who died in infancy; and Sarah, who married Dr. Monroe Judson. Samuel, born in 1818, developed into a rather remarkable business man for his day and generation. He first went into the comb and button business with his uncle David Curtis, in the factory near the bridge at Sandy Hook, (later the Beecher and Tucker satinet factory, then the Niantic Mills, now, 1917, the Harris Wire Mills.) They dissolved partnership a year or so later, and David Curtis moved "Out West," so called, to Painted Post, about 300 miles out into New York state.

Samuel Curtis returned to Berkshire, married Mary, daughter of Henry and Sarah Blackman Nichols, and of this union two children were born: Henry Gould, who married Annie, daughter of George and Sarah Peck Beers, and Julia, who married Henry S. Hawley.

In 1845 "The Berkshire Co." was formed. The partners were Samuel Curtis, Amos Hard, Julius and John Curtis. They built the first factory (which was destroyed by fire 1852) and established the water power. The factory was re-built the same year. The business was the making of combs and buttons.

When that partnership was dissolved a year or so later, John Warner, a cousin of Mr. Curtis became his partner. This partnership under the name of Curtis and Warner lasted about ten years, when Mr. Warner moved to New Haven, and for a short time Matthew Fairchild was Mr. Curtis' partner. About 1870 Mr. Curtis owned the whole business. When his son Henry Gould attained his majority, the firm became S. Curtis & Son. The firm name is still the same. Until 1901, the business was exclusively the manufacture of combs and buttons. Since then the business carried on in the same factory built in 1852, is the manufacture of paper boxes, and is under the ownership, and management of William R. Curtis, younger son of Henry G. Curtis. The older son, Harry Beers

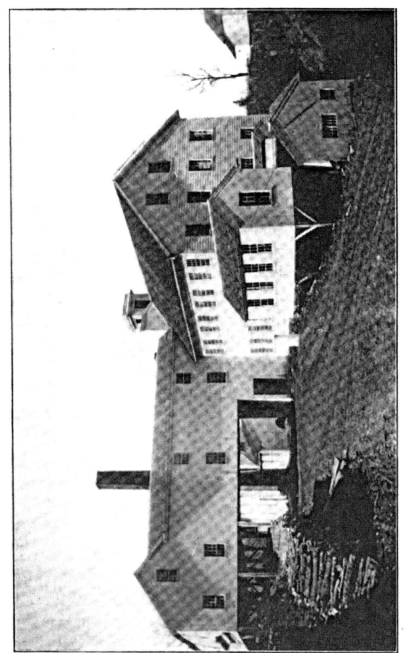

FACTORY OF S. CURTIS & SON

Curtis, is a member of the Bridgeport Hardware Manufacturing Corporation.

Mr. Samuel Curtis owned nearly all of Berkshire in 1870 and in his day it was called the "White Village," all houses being white with green blinds and all fences white. From 1874 he employed a carpenter for seven years. Mr. Henry Curtis' house was built in 1875, the year of his marriage.

Mrs. Julia Hawley has two children, Curtis, who is unmarried, and Mary, the wife of Hobart G. Warner, of the firm of Taylor, Curtis & Co. of Sandy Hook. Her home, an attractive residence adjoining her brother's on the west, is also the home of Mr. and Mrs. Warner and their three sturdy boys, Hobart, Austin and Henry Hawley.

Just beyond his father's on the site of the grandfather's home, William R. Curtis has a fine modern residence, built in 1906. His wife is Bertha Niles George, second daughter of Rev. James H. George, deceased rector of Trinity Church. Two wide awake boys, Gould and Nelson bid fair to help keep Berkshire for some time to come a home of the Curtis family as it has been "for the last hundred years."

There were two or three other small concerns in Berkshire in the fifties. One was a hat factory where wool hats were manufactured.

This was owned by Rufus Somers, who lived where Mr. Charles Minor's house stands, the factory being quite near it.

Another business concern was a tannery located across the way from the house of Mr. Samuel Curtis. The little brook was dammed for water power for grinding the bark. Mr. John Curtis owned the tannery which was given up in the early sixties and the factory converted into a dwelling house which was removed a few years ago.

A Baptist Church stood at the top of the hill near the cemetery overlooking the village. Mr. Henry Curtis remembers that when he was a boy there were large congregations every Sunday, and Berkshire pond was used for the baptism. Losses by death and removal so depleted the numbers of the members that regular services were given up, and in 1913 the building was sold and torn down and the ground it occupied added to the cemetery.

THE MEN'S CLUB.

The Men's Literary and Social Club of Newtown Street, usually spoken of as The Men's Club, was organized in 1894 according to the following extract from the Minutes:—

At a meeting held at the study of Rev. G. T. Linsley it was voted to organize a men's literary club.

The following officers were elected: President, Rev. G. T. Linsley; Vice-president, Dr. E. M. Smith; Secretary-Treasurer, Allison P. Smith.

It was voted that these officers constitute an executive committee. It was voted that the first meeting should be held on Tuesday evening, May 1st, at the residence of A. P. Smith. Prof. P. E. Cliff was appointed essayist.

The President, Rev. O. W. Barker and Frank Wright, were appointed a committee on Constitution and By-laws.

May meeting. (First meeting.)

The May meeting of The Men's Literary & Social Club was held on Tuesday, May 1st. at the residence of A. P. Smith. Prof. P. E. Cliff was the essayist, his subject being, "Evolution and the Faith."

The following gentlemen were present and were constituted members of the club: Charles H. Northrop, John J. Northrop, Robert H. Beers, E. F. Hawley, Frank Wright, P. E. Cliff, Rev. G. T. Linsley, Rev. Otis W. Barker, Dr. E. M. Smith, M. J. Houlihan, C. M. Penny, G. F. Duncombe, Arthur S. Hawley, A. J. Smith and A. P. Smith.

At this meeting the Committee on Constitution and By-laws presented a Constitution and By-laws were adopted and in force until March 2nd. 1909, when a new one drawn up by a committee consisting of Rev. James H. George, Hermann N. Tiemann, Sr., Rev. Alexander Steele, Frank J. Gale, M. D., was presented and adopted.

From the above it will be seen that The Men's Club has existed for more than twenty-three years and has been of the greatest benefit to the town, as well as to its members. It has virtually formed the Board of Trade, Civic Federation and Village Improvement Society of the town and has been instrumental in advocating and establishing a large number of reforms and improvements.

Its membership is limited to twenty active members and they are representative men drawn from the different sections of the town.

Besides helping the town as above mentioned, the literary papers have formed a prominent feature of its meetings, which have tended in no small measure to broaden and educate its members.

The past membership has included such representative men as Daniel G. Beers, E. Levan Johnson and Prof. C. S. Platt.

The present membership is as follows:

President, L. M. Johnson; Vice-president, Alfred Walker; Secretary and Treasurer, H. N. Tiemann. Sr.

Chas. F. Beardsley, Robt. H. Beers, Chas. S. Cole, Wm. R. Curtis, Frank J. Gale, M. D., Chas. B. Johnson, Wm. C. Johnson, Walter H. Kiernan, M. D., Rev. T. J. Lee, Patrick H. McCarthy, Dr. W. J. McLoughlin, John J. Northrop, Chas. G. Peck, David C. Peck, Rev. George T. Sinnott, Allison P. Smith.

Honorary members: Rev. F. W. Barnett, Carlos D. Stillson.

Contributed by Hermann N. Tiemann Sr.

Former Presidents:

Rev. George T. Linsley, 1894-1895; 1895-1896; 1896-1897; Dr. Edwards M. Smith, 1897-1898; Rev. Otis W. Barker, 1898-1899; Daniel G. Beers, 1899-1900; Allison Parrish Smith, 1900-1901; Robert H. Beers, 1901-1902; Ezra L. Johnson, 1902-1903; David C. Peck, 1903-1904; Rev. James H. George, 1904-1905; John J. Northrop, 1905-1906; Prof. C. S. Platt, 1906-1907; P. H. McCarthy, 1907-1908; Charles F. Beardsley, 1908-1909; Carlos D. Stillson, 1909-1910; Frank J. Gale, M. D., 1910-1911; William C. Johnson, 1911-1912; Rev. Alexander Steele, 1912; Austin B. Blakeman, 1912-1913; Charles B. Johnson 1913-1914; Rev. F. W. Barnett, 1914-1915; Rev. G. T. Sinnott, 1915-1916; Rev. T. J. Lee, 1916-1917.

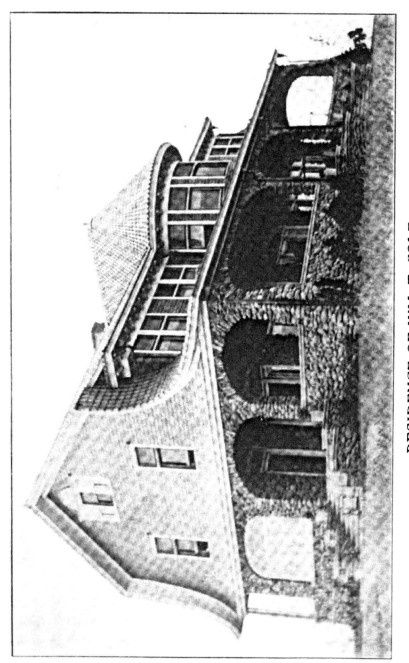

RESIDENCE OF WM. T. COLE

THE COUNTRY CLUB

THE NEWTOWN WATER CO.

This company, which supplies the borough of Newtown and adjacent territory with water, is a joint stock company organized in May, 1906, by special charter, with a capital of $50,000. Stock isued, $25,000. Officers, 1906-07: C. B. Taylor, President; D. C. Peck, Vice-President; W. A. Leonard, Secretary; L. C. Morris, Treasurer; W. B. Glover, Superintendent. Directors: C. B. Taylor, D. C. Peck, L. C. Morris, A. J. Smith, W. A. Leonard, W. J. Beecher, and W. H. Hubbell.

The reservoir is situated on Reservoir Hill, the highest point on Mt. Pleasant, 750 feet above tide-water, 180 feet higher than the flag-pole, 240 feet at the residence of L. C. Morris, and about 300 feet at Newtown R. R. Station. Upon the highest point of this hill, the company has constructed a reservoir of concrete, 32 x 52 feet, 14 feet deep. Its source of supply is beautiful Taunton Lake, 2200 feet distant, at an elevation of 235 feet, with capacity of about 175,000 gallons, with 25 H. P. gasoline engines directly connected to 8¼ x 10 inch, Triplex Pump, which has a capacity of 300 gallons per minute. There are two of these outfits. The water runs from the reservoir to different branches, supplying water to an estimated population of 600 people, with 38 public hydrants for the fire protection. The system has about 5½ miles of 8, 6, 4, and 2-inch pipe, serving Mt. Pleasant as far north as J. Albert Blackman's, south to the Country Club, east to the R. R. station, west to Alfred Walker's. The company has acquired land sufficient to build a reservoir of more than double the present size and with view to further expansion; a pipe and gate through the south wall has been provided for, the present south wall to form one side of the new reservoir, when built. The pipe lines are of a size to provide for a large future growth.

Officers for 1917: C. B. Taylor, President; D. C. Peck, Vice-President; W. A. Leonard, Secretary; L. C. Morris, Treasurer; W. B. Glover, Superintendent. Directors: C. B. Taylor, D. C. Peck, L. C. Morris, A. J. Smith, W. A. Leonard, Wm. B. Glover, F. J. Gale.

THE COUNTRY CLUB.

The Newtown Country Club, Inc., was started in Dec., 1915. The first officers were W. T. Cole, President; Dr. Charles H. Peck, Vice-President; Wm. A. Leonard, Treasurer; and H. C. Hubbell, Secretary.

The property of D. C. Bacon, one mile south of the village, was purchased for Club purposes, and during the year 1916, this, with adjoining land was laid out in a 9-hole golf course, tennis courts, etc.

At the present time, 1917, the Club has a membership of about one hundred.

The Officers are the same as in 1915, except that Rodney P. Shepard has taken the place of W. A. Leonard, as Treasurer.

A 40 YEAR LEASE OF MOUNTAIN LAND IN SANDY HOOK.

Soon after Newtown was purchased from the Indians, prospectors began to turn their attention to the Sandy Hook mountain, whose Indian name, whatever it might have been, had been transformed to that of Pisgah. The southerly part of the range in particular, and more especially that part lying back of the grist mill, extending along the stream unto what is now known as the Black bridge, seemed to the crude prospectors the most likely part in which to begin search for minerals, in which, they felt sure, the range abounded.

In 1764, John Staley Blackwell of the "Province and City of New York" leased for a term of 40 years a certain tract of mountain land in which to carry on mining. Of how much prominence Blackwell might have been in the "Province and City of New York," we cannot ascertain. We would hardly think him a timid adventurer for a few pages further on in the same "Book of Land Records" we find it recorded at a later date that Jeremiah Northrop of Newtown, in the Colony of Connecticut, leased to the said Blackwell "a tract of land lying in the northerly part of Newtown, in the Parish of Newbury, on the east side of the road that leads from Newtown to New Milford."

The lease was a "40 year" interest in ore mines, minerals, fossils of all sorts and kinds discovered or to be discovered throughout the full term of 40 years, "and, if need be, to dig to the center of the earth." Aside from Blackwell's making such ventures for mining purposes, the results of his ventures are as a sealed book to us of the present day, and there is nothing to be found on the mountain side that goes to show that the work of excavation was even once begun. Death may have intervened and removed the lessee.

Know all men by these presents that we, Nathan Curtiss, Hannah Sanford, Widow Thomas Sanford, Hezekiah Sanford, Samuel Sanford, Josiah Plat, Sarah Plat, wife of said Plat, and Louis Sanford, all of Newtown in the County of Fairfield, and Colony of Connecticut, and Amos Sanford of Sharon in the County of Litchfield and Colony aforesaid—for and on account of the consideration, hereafter in this instrument to be set forth,—for ourselves and heirs, executors and administrators, for the full term of forty years from the date hereof, do let and lease out unto John Staley Blackwell of the city and province of New York, his heirs and assigns for the above term, all our rights, title and interest in ore mines and minerals of every sort and kind, now discovered or to be found or discovered throughout the full term of forty years, in a certain tract of land within the township of Newtown and bounded as follows:

Beginning at two Black oak spiers marked in the south line of the land of Asa Cogswell, which was formerly Benjamin Mallory's land and on the easterly side of the highway that goes to Mr. Hubbell's ferry, then running south five degrees east bounding part on highway, and part on land of Peter Hubbell 80 rods to a heap of stones, then east 30 degrees, south about 20 rods in the line of the land of Nathaniel Cady Blackman to a spruce tree marked, and stones to it on a ledge of rocks on the westerly side of Pototuck brook, then bounding on said ledge of rocks, as they run to said corner of the above said land that was formerly the above said Mallory's, then west five degrees, south 98 rods to the first mentioned bounds began at. And for further confirmation this very land was conveyed by Peter Hubbell to his son, Jedediah, as will more fully appear by the Public Records of Newtown, Book 5, folio 357.

Now it is to be understood that the right of the above named Hannah Sanford, Thomas Sanford, Hezekiah Sanford, Samuel Sanford, Louis Sanford, Josiah Platt and his wife, is only in 13 acres of the above lands and lies in the southerly part of said land and bounded north upon the land of Ebenezer Ford, which he bought of Amos Sanford, and for further confirmation of the above, 13 acres may be seen by the records of the Probate Court for the district of Danbury. Now we, the above granters, do give to the above grantee, his heirs and assigns full power and authority to break ground, dig and use all proper means and measures, in quest of mines and minerals, and also to fell and cut wood or timber of all sorts except chestnut, and also to build houses for said business in and through said tract of land and if need be to dig to the center of the earth with free liberty to pass and repass andof transportation of all necessaries that may be needful for the carrying on of said work or mineral business without let, hindrance or molestation whatsoever, all to the best advantage of him, the said grantee.

The consideration of the above said lease or grant is as follows: That the above named John Staley Blackwell, the said grantee, or his heirs and assigns, in and throughout said term, shall, once every month render, or cause to be rendered, to the above said grantors, one thirteenth part of all the ore according to quantity and quality that shall be gotten upon the said tract of land above described, well ordered and fit for market, and that above ground at the mouth of the pits or shafts where the same is dug or gotten and according to their respective rights, which rights are as follows: (viz.) the above said Matthew Curtiss one fourth, and the above said Hannah Sanford, the other three fourths during the term of her natural life, and after her death or decease, to her heirs (viz.) to Thomas Sanford, Hezekiah Sanford, Samuel Sanford, Amos Sanford, Sarah Platt, Louis Sanford, it is to be equally divided. And whereas it may so happen that the above said grantee or his heirs, assigns or administrators may neglect to pursue the business or search of the said ore or mine and by that means the grantors may be disappointed of the true meaning and intent of the above lease, by his, the said grantee or his heirs, or executor or administrator shall neglect to dig or search after said mine, ore or minerals and the grantors by that means be debarred of having any trial made which to prevent it is to be understood that if the above named grantee or his heirs or executors shall neglect to dig or search or make trial for said mine within the term of one year, then, and in this case it shall be taken and deemed his, the grantee's neglect and sufficient to make the foregoing instrument void and of none effect. But, in case it so happens that the grantee or his assigns shall be obliged to desist or stop from the business or laboring by reason of water or other impediments that shall or may obstruct the way of his or their working for want of proper implements or engines, then and in this case, it shall not be taken as his or their neglect until that after a proper time has been allowed for him, the said grantee, to furnish himself with necessary engines that be absolutely necessary for carrying on the work or mineral business to effect which, shall not exceed three years time. Then and in this case, that is to say after a sufficient time, or not exceeding three years as aforesaid. He, the said grantee, or his heirs or assigns, do not furnish him or themselves with proper engines, then in this case, the foregoing to be null and void.

But on the other hand, if the said grantee or his assigns shall use his or their best endeavors and all proper means in quest of said ore or mines, then the above instrument shall be good and valid in law to all intents and purposes, and in witness, the grantors as conveying and the grantee as concurring, have set to their hand and seals this eight day of September, Anno Domini, 1764, and in the fourth year of the reign of our Most Sovereign Lord, George the Third of Great Britain, etc., King. Signed, Sealed and delivered in presence of John Camp and Caleb Baldwin, witnesses.

Hannah Sanford	(Seal)
Matthew Curtiss	(Seal)
Samuel Sanford	(Seal)
Josiah Plat	(Seal)
Louis Sanford	(Seal)
Hezekiah Sanford	(Seal)
John Staley Blackwell	(Seal)

Signers and sealers of the above written instrument personally appeared in Newtown on ye day and date mentioned and acknowledged ye same to be their own free act and deed. Before me,
Caleb Baldwin, Justice of ye Peace.

On ye 21st day of September, A. D., 1764, personally appeared Capt. John Staley Blackwell, signer and sealer of ye above written instrument, in Newtown and acknowledged ye same to be his own free act and deed before me, Caleb Baldwin, Justice of ye Peace.

The above and foregoing instrument recorded September 26th, A. D. 1764, per me,
John Northrop, Town Clerk.

In the execution of the lease, one of the interested parties, Thomas Sanford, refused to sign his name, necessitating further negotiations and Matthew Curtiss, one of the lessees, goes bonds in the sum of 5000 pounds to protect the said leasor, John Staley Blackwell, from all hindrance in the execution of said lease. A copy of the indenture, copy or deed, immediately follows the copy of the lease and may be found on Page 206, of Volume 8, Newtown Land Records, and reads as follows, viz:

This indenture witnesseth that Matthew Curtiss of Newtown in the County of Fairfield, Colony of Connecticut of the one part and John Staley Blackwell of the Province and City of New York of the other part, viz: Whereas, I the said Matthew Curtiss together with Hannah Sanford, Hezekiah Sanford, Samuel Sanford, Josiah Plat, Sarah Plat, the wife of said Plat, and Louis Sanford, all of said Newtown, did execute one certain lease dated September the eight, Anno Domini, 1764, all our right, title and interest in ore, mines, minerals and fossil bodies of every sort or kind now discovered or to be discovered in a certain tract of land as described by said lease.

Now, said lease having been executed by the above grantors to the said grantee and there being Thomas Sanford of said town heir to the said Hannah Sanford, which the said Thomas has not set his hand nor executed his part of the lease and especially as said Thomas Sanford does as yet refuse to set to his hand to said lease so that if possibly to hinder or obstruct the other above named proprietors of settling or leasing their respective right or of having any proper trial made to effect in quest of said mine or mineral according to the will and intention of the majority of the other proprietors, therefore, I the said Matthew Curtiss, do hereby bind myself and heirs, administrators, firmly by this indenture in the penal sum of five thousand pounds good and lawful money, to secure and defend the above said John Staley Blackwell, his heirs, administrators and assigns against all let or hindrance or molestation, by or from him, them or either of them, the said Thomas Sanford, his heirs, administrators, executors and assigns, shall comply with the afore said grantors of the above named lease, and set to his or they, their hands unto the above mentioned lease, to ratify and confirm the same, then the above named penal sum to be null and void and of none effect. But in case it so happens that the above said Thomas, his heirs, or assigns do not set his, or they their hands, but at any time within the aforesaid term of 40 years, shall pay according to his right, his equal part of all the cost or charge that the said John Staley Blackwell, his heirs or assigns shall have been at in quest of, and laboring for said ore or mine, which share or right is, by the afore said lease, referred to the records of the court of Probate for the district of Danbury, then, and in case the above said penal sum against the aforesaid Curtiss, his heirs, etc., to be null and void, and of none effect, otherwise to stand in full force and virtue in law. Now on the part of the above named John Staley Blackwell, is this: Whereas, in the above named lease in that part of it giving liberty of cutting wood and timber is not meant in the whole tract of land described in said lease, but only in the 13 acres which is described to the said Hannah Sanford and her heirs as in the consideration in the above said lease is to render one 13th part of all the ore or mines that is gotten on said tract of land and that according to their respective rights, of which the said Curtiss is one fourth part. Now on the account of him the said Curtiss giving this instrument, I bind myself and heirs, executors and administrators, notwithstanding the consideration in the above said lease, to render him, his heirs, etc., one tenth instead of one-thirteenth of all the ore or mines that shall be gotten upon the whole described lands mentioned in said lease and that according to quantity and quality according to his right which is one-fourth part of said mine or else forfeit the said right and it shall return to the said Curtiss, his heirs, etc., and in confirmation of the above, the parties have interchangeably set their hands and seals, this 21st day of September, Anno Domini, 1764, and in the fourth year of His Majesties' reign. Signed, sealed and delivered in presence of

Caleb Baldwin,
John Camp,
Matthew Curtiss,
John Staley Blackwell.

Matthew Curtiss and John Staley Blackwell indenture recorded September 27, A. D. 1764.

On the day and date of the written instrument personally appeared Mr. Matthew Curtiss and Captain John Staley Blackwell in Newtown and acknowledged the instrument which they had signed and sealed to be their own free act and deed. Before me

Caleb Baldwin, Justice of ye Peace.

Per John Northrop, Town Clerk.

THE CONSERVATION OF TIMBER.

It may be a surprise to some that the conservation of timber was a matter that the settlers felt of vital importance and was frequently discussed and as frequently acted upon at proprietors' meetings. Stringent measures were devised to meet emergencies as they arose.

In April, 1738, it was "voted that no person shall cut or fall any oak or walnut tree under 12 inches over at ye stub, nor any chesnut tree under 18 inches over at ye stub within ye sequesterment for ye space of three years from ye date above. This act to hold three years and no longer.

Voted, Job Sherman, Seargant James Botsford, Lemuel Camp, Henry Glover, Searg'nt Benjamin Dunning were chosen and appointed agents in ye behalf of ye town to prosecute those that shall cut any oaks or walnuts or chesnuts contrary to ye above sd acts.

Voted also at sd meeting, Thomas Skidmore, Joseph Bristol, John Blackman, Nathan Baldwin, Sr., agents in ye town's behalf to prosecute those that shall or have done harm in ye destruction of ye young timber in ye sequesterment.

Joseph Peck, Town Clerk."

Copy of petition for calling a proprietors' meeting, Dec. 29, 1748:

"We the subscribers, desire that ye clerk of ye proprietors of ye common and undivided land in Newtown in ye county of Fairfield that he give notis that there is to be a proprietors meeting in Newtown for several reasons. First place, to make choice of a committee to inspect any persons that have inclosed of incroached ye said proprietors common and undivided lands and such committee be empowered to prosecute. Secondly to take some measures to order such way as may be most for ye advantage of ye proprietors to secure and preserve ye timber yt is grone or groing on ye common land, formerly supposed to be sequestered so that ye said timber might not be destroyed. Third, to consider and see if it is not reasonable to vote that ye proprietors shall have the overplush money and over and above what is necessary to maintain sd flock. Fourthly, that the proprietors might take a thought whether there may not be some of ye common land afore mentioned of sd proprietors taken up and not damnify the flock. Fifthly, to think what a distinction there was made in sd sequesterment by cutting and destroying ye young timber in times past, whether it be not reasonable that some satisfaction should be made to some proprietors by destroying ye young timber in the dog hunt. Sixthly, for ye town to have ye liberty or privileges of ye proprietors of laying ye land accruing to Job Sanford's right within ye sequesterment.

Benoni Henry desires to take up a small peace of land where his home stands.

Also to take sum speedy care to settel ye line from Danbury S. E. corner to ye head of Fairfield bounds and to prevent ye incroachment Danbury people are making overbounds and also to pay ye proprietors clerk for his past service.

Recorded by Job Sherman, proprietors' clerk.

NEWTOWN'S MILITARY RECORD
1777-1919

List of Newtown Men in the Continental Army, 1777-1782

Allen, Eliphalet
Anderson, Samuel
Atwood, Samuel

Baldwin, Serg't. Abel
Baldwin, Major Caleb
Baldwin, Capt. Isaac,
Bennett, Ezekiel
Botsford, Capt. Abel
Botsford, Capt. Elijah
Botsford, Jack (negro)
Brooks, Samuel
Brooks, Thomas
Bristol, Caesar
Burritt Bailey

Chandler, Col. John

Deolph, Levy
Dunning, Jared

Edmond, William

Fairchild, Peter
Fairweather, Corp. Samuel
Ferris, Nathan

Gillette, Abraham
Gregory, Benjamin

Hubbell, Lemuel
Hubbell, Nathan

James, Thomas

Kimberly, Lieut. Abraham
Kimberly, Capt. Ephraim
Kimberly, Fitch
Kimberly, John

Lewis, Dwight
Lumnus, Samuel

Marvin, Matthew
Meeker, Richard

Northrop, Joshua

Osborne, Nathaniel

Parsons, Jacob
Pason, Jacob
Prindle, Abigail
Prindle, Peter
Prindle, Samuel
Prindle, Zalmon

Sanford, James
Seeley, James
Shaw, Thomas
Sherman, Eleazer
Smith, Capt. Joseph
Smith, Capt. Richard

Terrill, Capt. George
Terrill, Josiah
Tuttle, Smith

Whiteley, William

The following were of Newtown's quota to see service at New London in the War of 1812. *See Page 293*

Camp, Samuel

Glover, Ebenezer Booth
Glover, Corp. Villeroy
Glover, Ziba

Nichols, Henry

Prindle, Joseph
Stillson, Abel, Jr.
Winton, Czar

WRITTEN FOR MEMORIAL DAY.

By Ezra L. Johnson, May, 1913.

"Glory guards with solemn round the resting places of our nation's dead," and Memorial Day should lose none of its interest or meaning as the years go by. A custom established by act of Congress many years ago will probably be observed by the people of our great nation so long as our government shall hold its name among the nations of the earth. By individuals, by families, by the children of our common schools, by organized societies, by great corporations of business and in every possible way by which it can be brought about, this day will be socially and religiously observed while the earth itself lavishly contributes of its abundance in flowers and evergreen to deck the graves of the nations dead.

Memorial Day stirs anew in the hearts of all in whose bosom the love of country dwells, tender and loving thoughts of those who were once of us, but no longer with us. Not new thoughts, but thoughts long since born in us, that may have lain dormant during the time that has intervened between the year that had gone and the coming of the last. Memory recalls names and dates that are seldom spoken in the common round of everyday life and we are led to recall as best we can, when and where and how, did our brave ones do and dare and die, in order that our nation might live, or if spared to return to their homes still to live among us, we regard them with more than an indifferent consideration.

The bombardment of Fort Sumter, which was the Bunker Hill of the Civil War, commenced at 4.30 a. m., April 12, 1861. On Monday, April 15, 1861, President Lincoln issued a call for three month's service of 75,000 volunteers. The first response to that call, from Newtown, came on April 24, 1861, when three men, David O'Brien, Thomas O'Brien and Edward Carley, enlisted and were mustered into the government service May 11, 1861, serving three months, and were mustered out August 11, 1861. David O'Brien re-enlisted was mustered into the Ninth Regiment, Sept. 27, 1861, and served until Nov. 27, 1862, when he was discharged for disability. Thomas O'Brien re-enlisted in the Ninth Connecticut Regiment, was mustered in Sept. 26, 1861, and died in service, Nov. 16, 1862. Edward Carley re-enlisted in the Twelfth Connecticut Regiment, was mustered in Nov. 20, 1861, promoted to sergeant Jan. 23, 1863, and was killed May 27, 1863, at Port Hudson, La.

Catalogue of Newtown volunteers in the War of the Rebellion:

3rd Conn. Vols.
Enlisted
Corp. David O'Brien, April 24, 1861
Sergt. Edward Carley April 24, 1861
 Killed at Fort Hudson, La. May 27, 1863.
Thomas O'Brien   April 24, 1861
 Died Nov. 16, 1862.

1st Conn. Cavalry
Sergt. Louis L. Stuart Oct. 16, 1861
George Bulkley   Dec. 4, 1861
Henry W. Fairchild Oct. 18, 1861
Charles J. Merritt, Nov. 14, 1861
James Kelly,   Jan. 5, 1864
 Died Sept. 3, 1864, Andersonville, Ga.
George Rankins   Jan. 5, 1864

2nd Conn. Light Battery
Martin Lillis   Feb. 19, 1864
James Nichols,   Feb. 16, 1864

1st Regt. Heavy Artillery
Thomas Wade,   Aug. 27, 1864
Edward A. Dunning, Jan. 1, 1864
Charles H. Burritt, May 23, 1861
Daniel Davis,   May 23, 1861
James P. Hall,   May 23, 1861
John P. Hubbell, May 23, 1861
Charles S. Shepard, May 23, 1861
Sergt. Henry Nichols, Mar. 5, 1862
George S. Coley, Jan. 20, 1862

2nd Regt. Heavy Artillery
Edward A. Banks, Dec. 29, 1863
Charles T. Conger, Dec. 26, 1863
Sergt. James Sheridan, Jan. 4, 1864
William Connell, Jan. 4, 1864
Peter Flood,   Jan. 4, 1864
Patrick Lynch,   Dec. 31, 1863
Martin Blake,   Dec. 31, 1863
William W. Foster, Jan. 4, 1864
Hawley Reed,   Jan. 2, 1864
Andrew H. Sanford, Jan. 5, 1864
Patrick Kaine,   Jan. 2, 1864
 Killed June 1, 1864 at Cold Harbor.
Edward Reicker,   Dec. 31, 1863
Nathan H. Root,   Aug. 11, 1862
Barney Casey,   Jan. 28, 1864
2nd Lieut. Senaca Edgett, Feb. 5, '64
Robert Clark,   Jan. 5, 1864
Michael Farrel,   Feb. 10, 1864
Corp. Starr L. Booth, Sept. 5, 1864
Andrew Flanagan, Feb. 10, 1864
Charles E. Gilbert, Feb. 13, 1864

5th Regt. Conn. Vols.
Sergt. Major John H. Brewster,
                  June 21, 1861
Patrick Quinn,   Aug. 27, 1864
Corp. Henry J. Glover, June 21, 1861

Enlisted
William Conley,   June 21, 1861
George D. Squires, June 21, 1861
John H. Faulkner, June 21, 1861
George Briscoe,   June 26, 1861

6th Regt. Conn. Vols.
Hall Shepard,   Aug. 29, 1863
Frederick Elwood, Aug. 29, 1863
Benj. W. Matthews, Aug. 29, 1863
Corp. James Sullivan, Jan. 5, 1865

7th Retg. Conn. Vols.
Israel C. Botsford, Sept. 7, 1861
Charles Butcher, Aug. 24, 1861
Jeremiah Brown,   Sept. 7, 1861
Levi H. Edwards, Sept. 7, 1861

8th Regt. Conn. Vols.
Theodore Smith,   Jan. 5, 1864
Thomas Bradley,   Nov. 18, 1864
Charles E. Hawley, Feb. 15, 1864
David B. Hawley, Oct. 14, 1864
Allen B. Clark,   Dec. 17, 1863
William Davis,   Dec. 17, 1863
William Gleason, Nov. 18, 1864
Charles M. Parsons, Feb. 11, 1864
Charles R. Sherwood, Dec. 17, 1863
Frederick E. Smith, Dec. 17, 1863
Frederick Wenzel, Feb. 11, 1864
John Cunningham, July 27, 1864
Charles H. Payne, Dec. 17, 1863
 Killed at Cold Harbor, Va.
Capt. Henry C. Hall, Sept. 14, 1861
Sergt. John D. Seeley, Sept. 14, 1861
Sergt. Joseph B. Weed, Sept. 21, '61
George W. Brown, Sept. 21, 1861
George A. Evarts, Sept. 21, 1861
Horace Gilbert,   Sept. 30, 1861
George Hawley,   Sept. 27, 1861
James Riley,   Sept. 27, 1861
Robert Tappan,   Sept. 21, 1861
Hanford Tongue,   Sept. 21, 1861

9th Regt. Conn. Vols.
James Hawley,   Sept. 14, 1861
John G. Foote,   Sept. 20, 1861
Michael Ney,   Jan. 27, 1865

10th Regt. Conn. Vols.
George W. Ramsey, Sept. 15, 1861
Charles May,   Sept. 9, 1861
William L. McArthur, Sept. 26, 1861
James D. Hull,   Oct. 9, 1861
George Taylor,   Oct. 29, 1861
Thomas Johnson,   Jan. 10, 1865

11th Regt. Conn. Vols.
Sergt. David Andress, Spt. 18, 1861
Henry Bissell,   Feb. 25, 1864
Sergt. Geo. S. Hubbell, Oct. 18, 1861
Fritz Meyer,   Jan. 27, 1865
Sergt. G. W. Williams, Oct. 26, 1861

	Enlisted
Levi E. Stuart,	Oct. 26, 1861
Corp. Wm. A. Smith,	Oct. 18, 1861
Jerome L. Stanley,	Nov. 16, 1864
Wagoner J.W. Greene,	Oct. 18, 1861
David S. Payne,	Nov. 1, 1861
Lewis Fairchild,	Nov. 3, 1861
George McLean,	Nov. 28, 1861
Elijah B. Nichols,	Nov. 1, 1861
Lewis Fairchild,	Mar. 29, 1864
Harmos L. Nichols,	Mar. 1, 1864
Elijah S. Pete,	Nov. 1, 1864
Joseph White,	Nov. 29, 1864

12th Regt. Conn. Vols.

	Enlisted
1st. Sgt. Smith Downs,	Oct. 23, 1861
Edward Carley,	Oct. 5, 1861
Munroe D. Downs,	Jan. 2, 1861
Arthur Fairman,	Oct. 8, 1861
Gideon Botsford,	Oct. 9, 1861
Charles Jones,	Oct. 18, 1861
Cyrus W. Wheeler,	Feb. 25, 1861
Corp. John Tappan,	Oct. 9, 1861
Joseph Curtis,	Sept. 27, 1861
Patrick Flannery,	Jan. 20, 1865
Jacob Johnson,	Jan. 13, 1865
Carl Peterson,	Jan. 6, 1865

13th Regt. Conn. Vols.

	Enlisted
Sergt. John Kane,	Jan. 1, 1862
Sergt. F. S. Twitchell,	Nov. 18, 1861
Corp. Roswell Taylor,	Dec. 14, 1861
William Ellwood,	Feb. 11, 1862
Corp. R. A. Fairchild,	Dec. 27, 1861
John W. Farrell,	Dec. 2, 1861
Ezra M. Hull,	Oct. 23, 1861
George Dimelow,	Nov. 21, 1861
Charles Monson,	Nov. 14, 1861
Stephen Tyrrell,	Dec. 2, 1861
Charles L. Briscoe,	Feb. 5, 1862
Chester D. Peck,	Jan. 27, 1861

14th Regt. Conn. Vols.

	Enlisted
Gottlieb Spitzer,	Sept. 30, 1863
Corp. Chas. Spring,	Sept. 28, 1863

15th Regt. Conn. Vols

	Enlisted
Paul Groever,	Aug. 23, 1864
Christian Wieble,	Sept. 15, 1864
Arlan Peterson,	Aug. 23, 1864

17th Regt. Conn. Vols.

	Enlisted
Hos. Steward. George H. Spencer,	Aug. 14, 1862
Corp. Chas. G. Curtis,	July 11, 1862
William Curtis,	Aug. 9, 1862
William A. Gordon,	Aug. 12, 1862
Alpheus B. Fairchild,	July 12, 1862
Ira Sherman,	July 22, 1862
Andrew C. Hull,	Jan. 27, 1865
Charles Wooster,	July 22, 1862
Milton C. Taylor,	Aug. 12, 1862
Henry J. Jackson	Dec. 31, 1863
Corp. Dennis Hayes,	Aug. 13, 1862
Martin V. B. Glover,	Aug. 14, 1862

	Enlisted
James Gordon,	Aug. 11, 1862
Killed July 1, 1863, at Gettysburg.	
James Kane,	Sept. 10, 1862
Charles C. Chapman,	Aug. 11, 1862
Henry B. Bigelow,	Aug. 11, 1862
Thomas Bradley,	Aug. 11, 1862
Corp. Al. Northrop,	Aug. 12, 1862
Matthew Colgan,	Aug. 14, 1862
Oliver Downs,	Aug. 9, 1862
John Hickey,	Aug. 9, 1862
Michael T. Holloran,	July 11, 1862
James Eagan,	Aug. 5, 1862
Michael T. Halloran,	July 11, 1862
Henry A. S. Peet,	Aug. 14, 1862
Michael Ryan,	Aug. 9, 1862
Andrew Schriver,	Aug. 13, 1862
Lawrence Shaughness,	Aug. 13, 1862
Pearl Smith,	Aug. 13, 1862
John Walsh,	Aug. 12, 1862

20th. Regt. Conn. Vols.

	Enlisted
Sergt. H. T. Manley,	July 28, 1863
Sergt. Chas. Shepherd,	Aug. 14, 1863
Sergt. I. C. Tomlinson,	Aug. 5, 1863
Corp. Fred. G. Alldis,	July 28, 1863
Corp. H. W. Benedict,	Aug. 12, 1863
Corp. Charles L. Dick,	Aug. 10, 1863
Corp. David W. Jones,	Aug. 11, 1863
Killed May 3, 1863, at Chancellorsville, Va.	
Corp. C. H. Roberts,	Aug. 12, 1863
Wounded July 3, 1863, at Gettysburg; died, July 23, 1863	
Corp. Geo. H. Sherman,	Aug. 3, 1863
Wag. Chas. W. Dayton,	Aug. 4, 1863
Lemuel Botsford,	Aug. 11, 1863
John S. Knapp,	July 28, 1863
John A. Lattin,	Aug. 5, 1863
George H. Lewis,	Aug. 11, 1863

23rd Regt. Conn. Vols.

	Enlisted
Julius Sanford, Captain of Company C,	Sept. 10, 1862
1st. Lieut. John Peck,	Aug. 24, 1862
Sergt. Cyr. N. Squires,	Aug. 25, 1862
Corp. R. A. Fairchild,	Sept. 12, 1862
Corp. John Griffin,	Sept. 10, 1862
Corp. Beach Nichols,	Sept. 11, 1863
Corp. Austin L. Peck,	Aug. 24, 1862
Corp. Nelson J. Peck,	Aug. 24, 1862
Mus. Geo. P. Blakeslee,	Aug. 24, 1862
Charles Booth, Jr.,	Aug. 29, 1862
Corp. Starr L. Booth,	Aug. 24, 1862
Corp. Edwin Benedict,	Sept. 7, 1862
George B. Camp,	Aug. 24, 1862
Henry B. Coger,	Aug. 23, 1862
Truman Guernsey,	Aug. 25, 1862
Wag. Elam M. Tongue,	Sep. 10, 1862
James M. Beers,	Sept. 11, 1862
Gustavus Briscoe,	Sept. 11, 1862
Charles Briscoe,	Sept. 11, 1862
Newell Clark,	Sept. 11, 1862
Michael Corbett,	Sept. 8, 1862

NEWTOWN'S MILITARY RECORD

	Enlisted
Arthur Dimon,	Sept. 8, 1862
Theodore B. Fairchild,	Sept. 23, 1862
David R. French,	Sept. 10, 1862
David A. Gillette,	Sept. 10, 1862
Henry Johnson,	Sept 14, 1862
Michael Keenan,	Sept. 8, 1862
John Lillis,	Sept. 13, 1862
Patrick McDaniels,	Sept. 11, 1862
David M. Peck,	Sept. 10, 1862
Benajah Peet,	Sept. 5, 1862
Ammon Taylor,	Sept. 10, 1862
Daniel B. Weed,	Sept. 10, 1862
Hawley Beers,	Sept 2, 1862
Henry A. Gilbert,	Sept. 2, 1862
Peter D. Olmstead,	Sept. 2, 1862
Peter M. Oakley,	Oct. 27, 1862
Martin Lillis,	Nov. 5, 1862
George R. Gage,	Nov. 12, 1862
John McGrath,	Nov. 10, 1862
Smith B. Wood,	Nov. 11, 1862

24th Regt. Conn. Vols.

	Enlisted
Sergt. Hugh Dunn,	Aug. 13, 1862
John H. Bumford,	Sept. 20, 1862
Bernard Kelly,	Sept. 10, 1862

29th (Colored) Regt. Conn. Vols.

John Jones,	Dec. 1, 1863
Sergt. James Evans,	Dec. 21, 1863
Sergt. James Parker,	Jan. 5, 1864
Matthew Rigby,	Jan. 5, 1864
Corp. Allen Banks,	Jan. 5, 1864
James Adams,	Jan. 4, 1864
Jerome Brown,	Jan. 4, 1864
Hiram Cornell,	Jan. 4, 1864

31st (Colored) Regt. Conn. Vols.

Asa Franklin,	Dec. 22, 1863

An incomplete list of the names of soldiers buried in Newtown:

In St. Rose's Cemetery: G. P. Lillis Dennis Hayes, Andrew Eagan, Bernard Casey, Martin Lillis, —— Colgan, Bernard Kelly.

In Sandy Hook Cemetery: Frederick Wentzel, Charles Roberts, —— Benedict, Charles Sherman, 1812, —— Curtis, John E. Glover, Lyman B. Somers.

In Newtown Cemetery: George Blakeslee, Capt. Julius Sanford, Nelson Peck, Capt. Leonard J. Wright, Marion Wheeler, Daniel Camp, Herson Hawley, Peter Keeler, David Shepherd, Benjamin Matthews, Gustavus Briscoe, Charles Briscoe.

In Land's End Cemetery: William G. Hawley, Lemuel Wilkinson, David Peck, Andrew C. Hull, Henry Hoyt, Ely Seeley; in the Spanish-American War, Willis Hawley.

In Taunton Cemetery: Edwin Benedict, Charles Butcher, Daniel Gregory, William Maynard, George B. Camp, Edward Taylor, George Taylor, Gustavus Briscoe.

In Huntington Cemetery: William Fischer, Horace Gilbert, Ziba Glover in War of 1812, Arthur Dimon, Lemuel Botsford.

In Cold Spring Cemetery: Elijah Nichols, George A. Bradley, Caleb Davis.

In Zoar Cemetery: Charles Dayton and Martin Hook.

The following "Newtown Boys" enlisted from some other place than their home town:

3rd Heavy Artillery
Edwin A. Banks, Norwalk, Jan. 2, 1864.
George Clinton, Jan. 5, 1864

3rd Light Battery
Michael Carmody, Oxford, Sept. 15, 1864.
Jasper L. Curtis, Seymour, Sept. 13, 1864.
William E. Curtis, Seymour, Sept. 15, 1864.
Edward Troy, Naugatuck, Sept. 9, 1864.

5th Infantry
Ephraim D. Briscoe, Hartford, Feb. 27, 1864.

12th Infantry
Wagoner, Orlando N. Platt, Oxford, Aug. 9, 1862.

15th Infantry
Sergeant Daniel Camp, Naugatuck, Aug. 9, 1862.

17th Infantry
George Lake, Roxbury, Dec. 30, 1863.
1st Lieutenant, Albert W. Peck, Bridgeport, July, 23, 1862.

23rd Infantry
Sergeant Robert B. Fairchild, Bridgeport, Sept. 30, 1862.

Brooklyn Zouaves
Adelbert Nash.

CUSTER POST, No. 46, G. A. R.,

Was mustered in at Sanford's Hall, Aug. 15, 1878. The records show that the ceremonies were performed by Senior Vice and Acting Department Commander Charles E. Fowler of New Haven, assisted by Comrades from Bridgeport, Danbury, New Haven and Hartford.

The following named comrades were duly initiated and instructed in the secret work of the order: William C. Wile, Chas. Rinisland, A. W. Peck, G. P. Lillis, Edward Troy, Chas. W. Dayton, Daniel Camp, James Taylor, L. W. Williams, William Sniffen, Patrick McMahon, Chas. Hawley, Frederick Wentzel, George W. Graham, Chas. Riebold, Alpheus Northrop, Matthew Colligan, Chas. F. Hubbell, John Ferris, Henry Orgleman, Benjamin Horton, Levi M. Williams, George Blakeslee, Andrew Hamlin, James Smith, L. J. Wright, Bernard Casey, Henry Johnson, and Michael McMahon.

At the conclusion of the muster-in ceremonies, the Post formed in line and escorted the visiting officers and comrades to Sandy Hook where a public installation was held on the grounds of Hobart Warner, (the E. T. H. Gibson place,) Commander Fowler acting as mustering officer. The following were the officers installed;— Commander, Wm. C. Wile; S. V. Commander, Chas. Rinisland, J. V. Commander, A. W. Peck; Adjutant, Griffin P. Lillis; Quartermaster, Edward Troy; Officer of the Day, Chas. W. Dayton; Chaplain, James Taylor; Surgeon, L. W. William; O. Guard, Daniel Camp; Sergt. Major, Wm. Sniffen; Q. M. Sergt. P. McMahon; Sentinel, Chas. Hawley; Sentinel, Fred Wentzel;

Of those mentioned in connection with the mustering-in of the Post, all except Edward Troy and Chas. E. Hawley have answered the final roll call. The present members of the Post, Nov. 1918, are, Commander Edward Troy; Sen. Vice Commander, Henry B. Coger; Jun. Vice Commander Chas. G. Blakeman; Adjutant, Ephraim D. Briscoe; Quarter Master, Chas. E. Hawley; Chaplain, Ammon Taylor; Officer of the Day, Patrick Lynch. These with Beach Nichols, now at a Soldier's Home, Dayton, Ohio and Charles M. Parsons of New Haven, are the remaining members of the roll of Custer Post. Only nine left of the seventy-seven.

"On Fame's eternal camping ground
Their silent tents are spread
And Nature guards with solemn round
The bivouac of the dead"

Note: Charles E. Hawley passed away Jan. 5, 1919.
Patrick Lynch passed away April 2, 1919.

DR. WILLIAM C. WILE
First Commander of Custer Post
See Page 274

EDWARD TROY
Last Commander of Custer Post
See Page 274

The following is the Roll of Members of Custer Post, No. 46, G. A. R. as appears from the records:

Albertin, E. T.
Ashmead, George

Ball, Chas. H.
Benedict, Ephraim
Blakeman, Chas. G.
Blakeslee, George B.
Bradley, George A.
Briscoe, Chas L.
Briscoe, Ephraim D.
Butcher, Chas.

Camp, Daniel
Camp, George B.
Casey, Barney
Clark, Lemuel B.
Coger, Henry B.
Colgan, Matthew
Conger, Chas. T.
Costello, Michael
Crofut, Horace S.
Curtis, Charles G.

Dayton, Chas. W.

Ferris, John

Gilbert, Chas. E.
Gilbert, Horace Jr.
Graham, George W.
Gray George B.

Hamblin, Andrew E.
Hawley, Chas. E.
Hooper, Wm. L.
Horton, Benjamin
Hotchkiss, Hubbard A.
Hotchkiss, Levi H.

Johnson, Henry
Jorey, Peter

Keating, Patrick

Lillis, Griffin P.
Lillis, Martin

Lockwood, Eli
Lynch, Patrick

Mason, Louis S.
McGuire, Chas. A.
McMahon, Michael
McMahon, P.
Morey, Lewis
Murphy, Thomas O.

Nash, Adelbert
Nichols, Beach
Northrop, Alpheus

Orgelman, H.

Parsons, Chas. M.
Peck, Albert W.

Reibold, Chas.
Rinisland, Chas.
Roswell, E. J.

Smalley, Garret E.
Smith, Chas. L.
Smith, James
Sniffen, Wm. B.
Squires, John C.
Stowe, Wm. D.

Taft, Frederick B.
Taylor, James
Taylor, Milton C.
Tongue Elam
Troy, Edward

Wayland, John B.
Weed, Daniel
Wentz, George
Wentzel, Frederick
Wile, Wm. C.
Williams, George
Williams, Levi
Williams, Lewis W.
Wilson, James A.
Wright, Leonard

Only two from Newtown were in the Spanish-American war. Willis Hawley, who died in Hospital at Philadelphia, Pa., of typhoid fever. Charles G. Morris, enlisted in the Navy June 15th, 1898; was rated coxswain, acting first class boatswain's mate. Discharged Aug. 22, 1898.

CONNECTICUT HOME GUARD.

Following the declaration by Congress of a "State of war" between this country and Germany, the State Legislature in March, 1917 passed a law, approved March 9, 1917, authorizing the Governor to appoint a board composed of three members to be known as The Military Emergency Board to "take proper action to perfect and maintain a body of armed troops for constabulary duty within the state of Connecticut to be known as the Home Guard."

Following the appointment of this Board, recruiting officers were appointed in the various cities, towns and villages of the state and our town was so fortunate as to have as recruiting officer, Captain Seaman M. Mead, an officer of experience and a long time member of the Coast Artillery Corps, C. N. G., then on the retired list.

Captain Mead at once issued a call for a meeting to be held in the Brick Building, Newtown, on Monday evening, March 26th, for the purpose of organizing a Home Guard company for this town.

The meeting was largely attended, in fact the crowd was so large that the room was too small and an adjournment was made to the dining-room of The Newtown Inn, which was kindly placed at his disposal.

Captain Mead briefly stated the purpose and scope of the organization and called for enlistments. The response was so enthusiastic that Capt. Mead asked Messrs. Harry M. Greenman, Jesse B. Woodhull and Hermann N. Tiemann, Sr., to assist in making out the papers.

At that meeting the following men enlisted:—Edward B. Allen, Robert H. Beers, J. Robert Beecher, Frank E. Banks, Louis T. Briscoe, John C. Beers, Adolph Carlson, Henry G. Carlson, Willis E. Carter, Harry M. Greenman, Walter L. Glover, Frank C. Goodsell, Villeroy G. Hard Jr., John Hendriksen, William E. Honan, Charles L. Jackson, William A. Leonard, Edward S. Lovell, L. Phillips Morris, Levi C. Morris, Patrick H. McCarthy, Arthur A. McDonald, George A. Northrop, Charles G. Peck, Oscar G. Pitzschler, Edward S. Pitzschler, Robert W. Tiemann, Hermann N. Tiemann Sr., George M. Stuart, Rodney P. Shepard, Allison P. Smith, Jesse B. Woodhull and Hervey W. Wheeler.

Another meeting was held in Sandy Hook the following Saturday, March 31st., and the following enlisted:—Harold I. Bishop, George L. Clark, Martin L. Conger, Thomas J. Corbett, William H. Hanlon, Carl A. Johnson. Charles B. Johnson, Michael Kilbride, James E. Lynch, Charles G. Meeker, W. John Murphy, George V. Pearsall, Matthew Rhomoser, Patrick M. Shea, Anson B. Trimble and Edward W. Troy.

A number of the above were rejected on their physical examination, but recruits kept coming in until sixty-one had enlisted and a company was formed with Seaman M. Mead as Captain. He immediately started drills, the drills being held alternately in the Town Hall, Newtown and St. Rose's Hall, Sandy Hook, and he had Hermann N. Tiemann Sr., and Harry M. Greenman appointed First and Second Lieutenants respectively.

At the start great difficulty was experienced in getting uniforms and equipment, owing to the tremendous demand for such things to equip the Regulars, the National Guard and the large number of military organizations which were being formed; and before we were uniformed, Captain Mead was ordered to the Reserve Officers Training Camp at Madison Barracks, N. Y.

The company then held a meeting and elected Hermann N.

Tiemann Sr. Captain, Harry M. Greenman 1st. Lieutenant and Henry G. Carlson 2nd. Lieutenant. It also elected the following civil officers:

Pres. H. W. Wheeler.
Vice-Pres. R. P. Shepard.
Sec'y P. H. McCarthy.
Treas. E. C. Platt.

The subject of drills then came up and it was found almost impossible to agree as to when they should be held, as open air drills were needed, the Town Hall and St. Rose's Hall being too small to use, except for squad drills. However that matter was finally settled, and the drills went on.

Meanwhile the Co. was still trying to get uniforms and equipment. Finally, after much correspondence and a trip to Hartford to see the Chief Quartermaster, it was told it could have its rifles if it would send for them. Mr. Edmund C. Platt of Hawleyville kindly offered his motor truck for that purpose and on May 30th Corporal R. W. Tiemann with a detail went to Hartford and got the rifles. Pvt. Charles L. Jackson drove.

All this time the various National Guard units were preparing to be mustered into the Federal service and all kinds of rumors were rife as to disposition of the Home Guard, from being sent to the Texan border to being sent to France, but the drills went steadily forward and the men began to show considerable proficiency when a General Order was received from Home Guard Headquarters by which the Newtown company was reduced to one Active, or First Line, platoon, the second platoon being held as a Reserve. Capt. Tiemann, whose commission as captain had not been issued altho he had been officially addressed by that title from Headquarters, was told to take command of the Active platoon with the rank of 1st Lieutenant, Lieutenants Greenman and Carlson were returned to the ranks and the number of non-coms was materially reduced.

However, the drills kept up and the platoon was invited to participate, with the other units of the District, in the Fourth of July parade in Bridgeport.

On receiving this invitation the Chief Quartermaster was gotten in touch with and asked about uniforms. He said he could furnish them if they were sent for and on Sunday July 1st Sergt. John Hendriksen and Corpl. Frank C. Goodsell volunteered to go to Hartford with their autos and get the uniforms which enabled the platoon to take part in the parade.

Courtesy of Lieut. Hermann N. Tiemann, Sr.

NEWTOWN'S HONOR ROLL

Names of men from Newtown in U. S. Service 1917—1919:—

Anderson, Fred, 1917—Co. E. 102nd Inf. A. E. F.

Bailey, Jesse M., D. C. M. 1917—San. Detachment 103 M. G. Bat. A. E. F.
Bailey, John F., 1918—Motor Co. Camp Greenleaf, Georgia.
Barnett, Lieut. William Edward, 1917—Co. B. 104th Inf. A. E. F.
    Was with U. S. Cavalry on the Mexican border in 1916.
Barnett, Capt. Rev. Francis B., 1917—A. E. F.
    Rector Christ Church, Ridley Park, Phila., Pa.
Barnett, Rev. Joseph N., 1917—Co. A. 303rd M. G. Bat. A. E. F.
    Was Curate at St. George's Church, New York.
Bale, Thomas, 1918—26th Reg. 3rd Amb. Corp. A. E. F.
*Beehler, Lieut. Charles H., 1917—Aviation. Killed in action Nov. 1918 A.E.F.
Beehler, Robert M., 1917—Navy
Beers, Wagoner George Herbert, 1917—Cited for bravery 102nd Amb. Co. 26th Div. A. E. F.
Beers, H. Sanford, 1918—Naval Training Station, Boston Harbor.
Behn, W. L., 1918—Co. C. 301st Engineers A. E. F.
Blake, Lieut. James E., 1917—26th Eng. Co. C, A. E. F.
Blake, Michael J., 1918—321 Aero Service Squad, A. E. F.

Carey H. F., 1918—U. S. A. A. S. with French Army, France.
Carey, T. P. 1918—Fort Story, Virginia.
Carmody, Lieut. Richard, 1917—C. C. A. 1st Bat. 56th. Reg. San. Dept. A. E. F.
Carr, William E. 1917—Quartermasters Corps. Finance Branch A. E. F.
Cavanaugh, Corp. Paul V., 1918—S. A. T. C. Columbia University, N. Y.
Coholon, Lieut. Philip, 1918—Discharged
Cole, Charles H., 1917—Mobile Veterinary, A. E. F.
Conger, Martin L., 1918.
Conger, William R. 1917—168 Aerial Squadron, A. E. F.
Crick, Corp. James W., 1918—Motor Truck Co. 465 Motor Supply Train, A. E. F.

Davidson, George I., 1917—103rd Co. F. Artillery, A. E. F.
Donlon, Michael J., 1918—3rd Div. B. N. Co. I. Camp Upton, L. I.
Driscoll, William E., 1917—102nd San. Train, Field Hos. 27th Div., A. E. F.
Dubret, Albert, 1917—504 Engineers Bat. Co. D., A. E. F.
Dutcher, Richard H., 1918—U. S. Naval Training Station, Pelham Bay, N. Y.

Edwards, Charles L., 1917—Co. F. 328th Inf. Camp Gordon, Atlanta, Ga.
Elko, Andrew Jr., 1918—Co. K. 5th Inf. U. S. Army, Panama.
Fairchild, Sergt. Arthur W., 1917—103rd Machine Gun Bat. San Detach.
Fairchild, Robert D., 1917—Mobile Veterinary, Sec. 2—2nd Div., A. E. F.
Ferris, Capt. George M., 1917—Washington D. C.
    Was Candidate for Holy Orders, Trinity Ch., Newtown, Conn.

Gale, Gordon J., 1918—S. A. T. C. Wesleyan University, Conn.
Galyas, John, 1918.
George, Lieut. James Hardin, 1918—Y. M. C. A., B. E. F., France.
Rev. James Hardin George, Rector of Calvary Ch., Columbia, Missouri.
Glover, Walter H., 1918—Fire Island, N. Y.
Goldstein, Corp. Israel, 1917—Bat. F. 103rd Reg. F. A., A. E. F.
Goodsell, Sergt. Frank C., 1917—Co. L. 56th Inft., A E. F.
Gracco, Nicholas, 1918.

Hanlon, Edgar,—Annile Transport Dept., A. E. F.
Hanlon, Richard—21 Co. 20th Eng. A. P. O. 738, A. E. F.
Hawley, Maj. James N., 1917.
Hawley, Robert, 1918.
*Hawley, Philo, 1918—Died in the service.
Hicock, Ely P., 1918—Motor Amb. Co. 44, A. E. F.

Hicock, Sergt. Henry, 1918—Co. C. 504th Engineering Brigade, A. E. F.
Hillhouse, Henry, 1917—Portsmouth, Virginia.
Hillhouse Julian, 1917—Discharged.
Honan, Miss. Kathryn A.,1918—Nurse, U. S. Hospital No. 9, Lakewood, N. J.
Honan, Michael J., 1918—16th Co. 4th Reg. Motor Mechanic D. M. A.,A. E. F.
Hurd, Charles, 1918—Camp Devens, Mass.

James, Herbert T., 1918—U. S. N. Air Station, Killingholme, N. Y.
James, Jesse Loderick, 1917—3rd Amb. Corps., 101st San. Div. A. E. F.

Keane, John J., 1918—Co. F., 316th U. S. Infantry, A. E. F.
Keane, Joseph D., 1917—U. S. S. Leviathan.
Kelly, Francis D., 1917—3rd Balloon Squad, Aviation Sec. Signal Corp, A.E.F.
Kelly, John R., 1918—S. A. T. C., Columbia University, N. Y.
Kiniry, Frank J., 1918—Co. F. 316th Regular Inf., A. E. F.
Klingler, Arnold, 1918
Klinger, Werner, 1918—2nd Bat. Edgewood Arsenal, Maryland
Kraeplin, Edward, 1918—3rd Co. U. S. Naval Training Sta. Gulfport, Miss.

Lang, Alonzo, 1918—10th Co. Fort Story, Virginia.
Larner, Patrick, 1918—Co. B. 7th Bat. U. S. N. G., Conn.
Liefield, Clemence A., 1918—Co. C. Evac. Hos. Camp Greenleaf, Chickamauga Park, Ga.
Lillis, John, 1918—152nd Depot Brigade Camp Upton, N. Y.
Lovejoy, Leroy J., 1918.
Lynch, James E., Cook, 1917—Bat. A. 319th Heavy Artillery, A. E. F.
Lynch, John G., 1918—Co. 57, Med. Replacement Unit, A. E. F.
Lynch, Thomas F., 1918—114th Inf. M. G. Co., A. E. F.

Maynard, Benjamin S., 1918—U. S. Naval Aviation Forces in France, A. E. F.
McMahon, Alfred, 1918—Battery B. 12th Field Artillery, A. E. F.
Mead, 1st Lieut. Seaman M., 1918—Selfridge Field, Aviation, Mount Clemens, Michigan. Lieut. Mead enlisted for the Spanish American War with a Stamford Co.
Meeker, Clarence G., 1917—Co. A. 102nd Reg. U. S. Inf. A. E. F.
Morris, Sergt. Levi Phillips, 1917—Central Records Office, A. G. O. Dept., A. E. F.

Nichols, George E., 1918—U. S. S. Agamemnon.

O'Dea, Earl T., 1917—Engineering Co., A. E. F.

Peck, Lieut. Albert W., 1917—Base Hospital No. 15, Qu'tmaster Medical Co. A. E. F.
Peck, Lieut. Col. Charles H., 1917—Asst. Director of General Surgery, A.E.F. Returned to U. S. for service.
*Peck, Segt. C. Howard, Jr., 1917—Base Hospital No. 15. Died March 7th, 1918, A. E. F.
Perkins, Corp. Frank E., 1918—Adm. Labor Co. 50, A. E. F.
Peterson, Otto, 1917—Co. H. 1st Conn. Inf. Camp Yale, New Haven, Conn.
Peterson, Walter, 1918—Camp Wheeler, Georgia.
Pippines, Nicholas, 1918.
Pitzchler, Corp. Edward S., 1917, 10th Co. 3rd Bat. Depot Brigade, Camp Devens, Fitchburg, Mass.
Platt, Charles, 1918—S. A. T. C. Columbia University, N. Y.
Platt, Percival C., 1917—H'dq't's Surgical Directors, A. E. F.

Rasmussen, John L., 1917—Co. F. 56th Eng., A. E. F.
Ray, Ryder, 1918—Co. E. 367th Reg., A. E. F.
Read, Fred. W. B., 1918, H'dq't's. No. 1. Hos. Group Camp Greenleaf, Chickamauga, Ga.
Reynolds, Sergt. Lester J., 1918—Camp Polk, North Carolina.
Roemer, Sergt. Otto, 1917—34th Co. 9th Bat. 151st Depot Brig., Camp Devens Fitchburg, Mass.

Ruffels,Clarence, 1917.

Scanlon, John J., 1917—Base Hospital, No. 18, A. E. F.

*Slater, Carl H., 1918—316th Infantry Supply. Died in service, A. E. F.
St. John, Earl G., 1918.

Terrill, Herbert W., 1918—Co. D., 113th Inf., A. E. F.
Tiemann, Corp. Robert W., 1918—Co. D., 316th Inf., A. E. F.
Tilson, Frank S., 1918—Prov. Unit C., Q. M. C. Register Service, A. E. F.
Tilson, Josiah, 1918—Co. 16Tr. Bu. Replacement group. Camp Greenleaf, Chickamauga, Ga.
Tobias, David C., 1917—Ordnance Dept. 110th Am. Train, A. E. F.
Troy, Francis J., 1918—Fitting-out Sec. Naval Dis. Base, New London, Conn.
Troy, John Joseph, 1918—Co. F. 74th Inf. Camp Devens, Mass.
Troy, Corp. John P., 1918—Adm. Labor, Co. 14, A. E. F.

Valenti, Peter J., 1917—U. S. Armed Guard, Camp Sims, Phila. Naval Yard.
Valentine, George J., 1917—111 Machine Gun Co. U. S. Inf., A. E. F.

Wetmore, Corp. Fred, 1917—Co. C. 33rd Inf. Gatun Canal Zone.
Wetmore, Corp. Jesse, 1917—Co. C. 33rd Inf. Gatun Canal Zone.
Wheeler, Russell, 1918—Naval Training Station, Pelham Bay, N. Y.
Wirtes, Stephen, 1917—Remount Depot. Camp Devens, Mass.
Woodhull, Jesse B., 1917—O. E. C. Nat. Army Chief Ordnance, A. E. F.
Wulff, Theodore L., 1917—Bat. C. 3rd Field Art., A. E. F.
Yawman, James W., 1918—Base Vet. Hos. No. 1., A. E. F.

UNITED STATES GOVERNMENT WAR LOANS..

During the war with Germany, our Government issued four war loans, or Liberty Loans, as they are called, two in 1917 and two in 1918.

The people of Newtown subscribed over $500,000 for these bonds and the entire amount was paid the Government to help carry on and win the war. The Newtown Savings Bank received the subscriptions, collected the money and forwarded it to the Federal Reserve Bank of New York.

In the Third Liberty Loan campaign, Honor Flags were presented to towns and communities attaining their quota. The quota assigned to Newtown was quickly oversubscribed and Newtown was the first town in the State to be awarded an Honor Flag; the first town in the State to receive and fly the flag and win the first Gold star on the Honor Roll Board at the State Capitol, Hartford. For having trebled its quota two blue stars were also awarded this town and were sewed on the flag. W. G. McAdoo, Secretary of the United States Treasury, telegraphed his congratulations to the people of Newtown for the renewed evidence of their loyalty and patriotism.

In the Fourth Liberty Loan campaign there was another Honor Flag contest. The campaign started Saturday, Sept. 28, 1918. Newtown's quota was $92,300 and before 9 o'clock Monday morning over $121,000 had been subscribed. The Honor Flag was awarded that day and at 8 o'clock Tuesday morning, October 1, 1918, it was flying from the Newtown Savings Bank building. Newtown had again won high honors. There was no other town in the State ahead of it for "first honors" and it was undoubtedly the only town in the State at that time having two Honor Flags in its possession. The total subscriptions to the Fourth Loan were over $192,000, two blue stars being won, as in the Third contest.

The people of Newtown have helped to keep alight the torch of Liberty and uphold justice and democracy throughout the world.

In a letter received from Governor Marcus H. Holcomb, dated October 14, 1918, he congratulated the town and said, "the record which Newtown has made is one of which it may well be proud and one which will be a source of pride to its citizens in the future."

NOTE—The credit of the prompt raising of these Liberty Loans, is due largely to the indefatigable effort of the Treasurer of Newtown Savings Bank, Arthur T. Nettleton.

THE RED CROSS WORK

Newtown's Military Record will be incomplete unless it includes some account of the Red Cross work.

Although much interest was manifested in the work and through the leadership of Mrs. James W. Gordon, entertainments were given, money raised and deposited in the Savings Bank for the purpose of purchasing a Ford Ambulance to be sent to France as Newtown's gift to the soldiers, no organization was effected until March 11th, 1917, when twenty ladies met in the Guild room of Trinity Church and elected officers; but because of an epidemic in mild form of small pox, work was not started until May 15th, 1917.

The organization is an Auxiliary of Bridgeport. Its officers, from May 15th, 1917, to Oct., 1918 were; Chairman, Mrs. E. B. Allen; Treasurer, Mrs. F. H. Mitchell; Secretary, Miss Charlotte C. Minor; Chairman of Surgical Dressings, Mrs. A. J. Smith; Knitting, Mrs. H. N. Tiemann; Garments and Hospital Supplies, Miss C. C. Minor.

The meetings were held in the Guild room of Trinity Church until the Autumn of 1917, since which time they have been held in the parlor of the Congregational Church, Tuesdays from 10 A. M. to 5 P. M. coffee being served at noon, each lady taking her own lunch.

Miss Dorothy Allen one of the prime movers in the organization, did good work soliciting funds and with her car brought material for all branches and returned the finished work to Bridgeport headquarters. Milton C. Hull of Danbury a returned soldier, captured her in August 1918.

The officers elected Oct., 1918, for the year were, Chairman, Mrs. F. H. Mitchell; Treasurer, Mrs. L. C. Morris; Secretary, Mrs. A. B. Blakeman; Chairman of Surgical Dressings, Mrs. A. J. Smith; Knitting, Miss B. Frances Honan; Garments and Hospital Supplies, Miss Charlotte C. Minor. The branches of the Newtown Auxiliary are, Sandy Hook, meeting Tuesdays with Mrs. T. F. Brew, Chairman; Botsford, meeting Wednesdays, at the home of some member. Mrs. Herbert T. Coger, Chairman; Dodgingtown, meeting Thursdays at the home of some member, Mrs. R. D. Smith, Chairman.

Christmas, 1917, 55 Christmas boxes were shipped to the boys in France and U. S. Camps. Easter 1918, 20 boxes were shipped to France. As no Christmas boxes could be shipped to France in 1918, to each boy was sent a special Christmas Card, which was a poem by Mrs. A. B. Blakeman, printed by Mr. Frank Wright of the Newtown

Bee. Christmas boxes were sent to all boys in Camps in this country.

About 60 boys were completely outfitted with sweater, two pairs socks, helmet, wristlets and comfort kit.

The town's people gave, in Feb., 1918, a War Supper, to raise money to buy clothing for refugee children. Sufficient money was raised for material for 419 garments, which were sent to Col. Chas. H. Peck, who distributed them in a home for refugee children in Liefra-Aube, France, in the Somme section.

In April another War Supper was given; the money to be added to the Ambulance fund, but finding that no more Ford ambulances would be accepted by the Government, a "Kitchen-trailer" was purchased and sent to the 102nd Ambulance Co.

In July, 1918, Mrs. C. O. Kraeplin gave the use of "Sophie's Tea Room" and grounds to the ladies of the Botsford branch for a Red Cross sale of fancy articles, food, etc.

The net receipts were more than $300, for the Red Cross treasury.

A quilt made by Mrs. Alfred Osborn, containing 2,288 pieces given for the sale, sold by ticket for more than $50.00 and a beautiful doily of embroidery and crochet made by Mrs. Levi C. Gilbert, sold by ticket for about $40.00.

From May 1917 to Dec. 31st, 1917, 3004 hospital garments and bandages were completed; from Dec. 31st, 1917 to Dec. 31st, 1918. 8526 hospital garments and 676 refugee garments were completed, making a total of 9202 garments. Of knitted garments, including sweaters, socks, helmets and mufflers, 2064 were completed.

The making of Surgical Dressings was commenced in July, 1918 and continued until Dec., during which time 13710 were folded.

Great credit is due the officers of all the branches and their faithful workers for punctual attendance at the meetings and interest manifested in doing the required work, not only during the war but since the signing of the armistice, in the making of hospital and refugee garments.

It is worthy of note that a group of Hawleyville Red Cross workers have almost invariably been met at the R. R. Station by Mr. Cornelius B. Taylor, been taken to the Red Cross rooms, and taken to the Station for their return. Donations from him of fresh fruit during the summer were frequently enjoyed during the lunch hour.

In addition to the work reported by the different branches, a Junior Auxiliary composed of 68 pupils of the High School, under the supervision of Miss Houlihan, contributed the making of 150 Property bags by the girls and 100 splints by the boys.

Over $123.00 has been handed in as the pledge made by students at High School, to personally earn and donate to the United War Work Campaign.

Pupils from some of the public schools and the parochial school have met each Saturday P. M. with Mrs. T. F. Brew and under her instructions have knitted six blankets for Belgian babies. More blankets have been knitted by the children in other districts under the instruction of their teachers.

In the expectation of the home-coming of the Soldiers and Sailors, a beautiful "Welcome Home" flag has been designed and made by Mrs. Levi C. Morris, and donated to the town by the Red Cross.

It is hung between the Congregational Church and the store of R. H. Beers.

The Red Cross also furnished one for the R. R. Station and one for Sandy Hook.

As the last pages of this Record go to press a movement is on foot to erect by the town, as a Soldiers' and Sailors' Testimonial, a new High School building.

By the courtesy of State Librarian, Geo. S. Godard the following list has been received

NEWTOWN MEN IN THE WAR OF 1812

Record of Conn. Militia in the War of 1812

Camp Samuel   place of service not shown.

Curtis, Abijah, capt. service at New London, under Lieut.-col. T. Shepard, Aug. 3, 1813 to Sept. 16, 1813.

" Abijah B. capt. service at New Haven under Col. Elihu Sanford, Sept. 8, 1814 to Oct. 20, 1814.

Fairchild, Kiah B. serg't. place of service not shown, under command of Arnold Foot, Oct. 24, 1814 to Nov. 15, 1814.

Glover, Ebeneizer B., priv. place of service not shown, under command of Ransom C. Canfield, Aug. 3, 1813 to Sept. 16, 1813.

" Villeroy, corp. place of service, New London, under command of Abijah B. Curtis, Aug. 3, 1813 to Sept. 16, 1813.

" " " place of service not shown under command of Abijah B. Curtis, Sept. 8, 1814 to Oct. 20, 1814.

" Ziba   place of service not shown.

Nichols, Henry, priv. place of service New London, under command of Abijah B. Curtis, Aug. 3, 1813 to Sept. 16, 1813 also

" " " place of service not shown, under command of Abijah B. Curtis, Sept. 8, 1814 to Oct. 20, 1814.

Prindle, Joseph, " place of service not shown, under command of Seth Comstock, Sept. 16, 1813 to Nov. 1, 1813.

Sherman, Charles, maj. place of service not shown, commander not shown, June 11 1813 to June 13, 1813.
" " " place of service New Haven, under command of Col. Elihu Sanford, Sept. 8, 1814 to Oct. 21, 1814.
" " priv. place of service, New London, under command of Charles French, June 1, 1813 to June 16, 1814.
" " " place of service not shown, under command of Charles French, Aug. 9, 1814 to Aug. 16, 1814.
" " musc. place of service, Ne wLondon, under command of Abijah B. Curtis, Aug. 3, 1814 to Sept. 16, 1813.
" " " place of service not shown, under command of Abijah B. Curtis, Sept 8, 1814 to Oct. 20, 1814.
Stilson, Abel, jr. priv. place of service not shown, under command of Arnold Foot, Oct. 24, 1814 to Nov. 15, 1814.
Winton, Czar, priv. place of service not shown, under command of Arnold Foot, Oct. 24, 1814 to Nov. 15, 1814.

Abijah B. Curtis was commissioned Major at the close of the war. His sword, presented by his grand-daughter, Mrs. H. C. Miles of Milford, Conn., to the Connecticut Society of Daughters of 1812, is placed in the State Library at Hartford in a beautiful case which has been presented to the Society.

Enlisting orders for the military corps to be formed for the defence of the state.

Roll of enlistments in 2d Co. 1st reg't infantry, Newtown, Feb. 10, 1813.

Elihu S. Curtis
Zachariah Prindle
Ithamar Merwin
Chancy Tibbell, for 45 days
Philer H. Dibble for the present tower of duty
Leveret————(Heath?) for the present tower of duty
Harry Blakeley for the present tower of duty
Lyman Beecher for the present tower of duty
Asahel Harington, 18th Sept. 1814 for the present tower of duty
Charles Wheeler, 18th Sept. 1814 for the present tower of duty
Samuel Addison, 18th Sept. 1814 for 14 days
Bennitt Prindle for 1 month from the 18th of Sept. 1814
Eathiel Whitney for this tower of duty
Ira Keeler, Oct. 8th to the end of this tower of service
Abijah B. Curtis

INDUSTRIES OF NEWTOWN IN 1852—1853

For the matter that makes up the greater part of this we are indebted to the Newtown Academician, a monthly paper issued by the pupils of Newtown Academy in 1852 and 1853. The pupils of the school builded better than they knew, when they scurried about town and got together so many "ads", showing the great variety of business enterprises successfully carried on in our town, not by any means confined in location to the business centers of the town.

From no other source can any one form the faintest idea of conditions as then existing, so far as relates to industries, other than that of farming. An interesting bit of history this that comes down from a former generation and we do well to give due credit to the source from which our information comes. Though the Academician was short lived, it was useful in its day and generation.

Business cards of professional men and ads of various Newtown industries copied from the Newtown Acadamician of 1852 and 1853:

NEWTOWN STREET

DAVID H. BELDEN—Attorney and Counsellor at Law; office at his residence, second door north of Trinity church.
DAVID B. BEERS—Attorney and Counsellor at law; office first door south of Academy.
AMOS S. TREAT—Attorney and Counsellor at Law; office first door south of Postoffice.
C. H. BOOTH, M. D.—Physician and Surgeon; office at his residence, third door south of the Hotel.
ERASTUS ERWIN—Physician and Surgeon; office opposite the Hotel.
GEORGE JUDSON—Physician and Surgeon; office at his residence, north end of the street.
MONROE JUDSON, M. D.—Physician and Surgeon; office at his residence nearly opposite Charles Fairman's shoe store.
MISS MARIA FAIRMAN—Milliner; head of the Main Street, keeps constantly on hand an assortment of millinery goods, bonnets, ribbons, silks, flowers, etc.
HENRY SANFORD—Dealer in dry goods, groceries, crockery, produce, drugs and medicines, etc.
EDWARD STARR—Dealer in dry goods, groceries, crockery, produce, boots and shoes, ready made clothing, drugs, medicines. etc.
DAVID H. JOHNSON—Dealer in dry goods, groceries, crockery, hardware, produce, drugs, and medicines, etc.
WILLIAM BLAKESLEE—Gold and Silversmith; watches, clocks and jewelry repaired to order; shop at head of the street.
GLOVER & ALLEN—Joiners and House Builders; shop west of Congregational church.
CHARLES FAIRMAN—Boot and Shoemaker; store above D. H. Johnson's store.
PIKE & BROTHER—Boot and Shoemakers; opposite the Hotel.
GEORGE PECK—Custom Boot and Shoemaker; shop near the foot of Church Hill.
BURR HAWLEY—Tailor; shop next door above D. H. Johnson's store.
NEWTOWN HOTEL—S. P. Barnum, Proprietor.
ISAAC BRISCOE'S MEAT MARKET—Near the head of the Street.
THEOPHILUS NICHOLS—Agent for the best Fire, Life and Health Insurance Company.
ISAAC BEERS—Manufacturer of every variety of Horn Combs; factory in rear of Trinity church.
GEORGE LAWRENCE—Manufacturer of Horn Combs; factory first door south of the Hotel.
CHAS. FAIRMAN'S LIVERY STABLE—In the rear of his Shoe Store.

INDUSTRIES OF NEWTOWN IN 1852—1853

SANDY HOOK

WILLIAM B. GLOVER—Dealer in Dry Goods, Crockery, Hardware, Farming Implements, Produce, Drugs, Medicines, etc. Near the Bridge.

LEVI MORRIS—Dealer in Dry Goods, Groceries, Crockery, Hardware, Farming Implements, Produce, Drugs, Medicines, etc. West of the Bridge.

CHARLES TWITCHELL—Blacksmith and Carriage Ironer; Custom work done to order. Shop east of the Bridge, north of W. B. Glover's Store.

MISS M. E. KINDERGON—Milliner and Dress Maker; over Morris' Store.

MISS H. S. A. STILLSON—Dressmaker; shop two doors north of L. Morris' store.

NATHAN R. COUCH, TAILOR—Cutting done to order at short notice and warranted to fit if properly made up. Shop next store of Samuel B. Peck.

NATHAN SHEPARD—Custom Boot and Shoemaker. Repairing done with neatness and dispatch.

DAVID GLOVER—Carriage Maker; shop at the saw mill. Custom work done to order.

SANDY HOOK HOTEL—B. Gregory, Proprietor.

DUDLEY SQUIRE'S OYSTER AND DINING SALOON—Oysters served up in every style. Next door north of Glover's Store.

J. B. & C. F. BLAKESLEE—Iron and Brass Founders and Machinists.

A. B. BEECHER—Manufacturer of Satinets. Factory west side of Bridge.

HENRY L. WHEELER—Tinsmith and Dealer in Tin, Copper, Sheet Iron Wares, Stoves, etc.

SANDY HOOK FLOURING AND CUSTOM MILL—Saw Mill and Plaster Mill. David Sanford, Proprietor.

JOHN DICK & CO.—Manufacturers of American Rivets, Factory on the Pohtatuck below the Flouring Mill.

DANIEL HALL—Manufacturer of every variety of Horn Buttons. In Dick's Machine Shop.

MOSES PARSONS & SONS—Manufacturers; Corner of Main and Mountain Road.

AMMON SHEPARD—Wool Hat Maker; factory between Sandy Hook and Housatonic Railroad Depot.

H. H. TAYLOR—Physician and Surgeon; Sandy Hook.

TOWN

WARNER & CURTIS—Manufacturers of every variety of Horn Combs. Factory in Berkshire, one and a half miles east and south of Sandy Hook.

RUFUS SOMERS—Manufacturer of Wool Hats; Berkshire.

ISAAC J. WELLS—Custom Boot and Shoe Maker, Berkshire.

ROYAL O. CLARK'S MEAT MARKET—Two and a half miles east of Sandy Hook. Customers supplied at their houses.

DAVID JONES—Manufacturer of Horn Combs. Shop at Dick's Rivet Factory; half a mile below Sandy Hook.

BURTON E. CLARK—Tanner and Currier. One and a half miles South of the street on the turnpike. Cash paid for hides.

LEVI PECK—Tanner and Currier. Two miles South of the Street on the Turnpike. Cash paid for hides and bark.

DAVID CURTIS—Tanner and Currier. Calculate to manufacture leather to the best advantage. Bark and mill driven by water power. Factory in Berkshire.

WILLIAM J. DICK & CO.—Manufacturers of American Rivets. Factory a few rods below Sandy Hook.

GEORGE WHEELER—Wool Hat Manufacturer. One and a half miles north of the Street on the Turnpike.

MRS. GEORGE ANDREWS—Milliner and Dressmaker. Third door east of the Railroad Depot.

EZRA MORGAN—Dealer in Dry Goods, Groceries, Crockery, Produce, etc. at Morgan's Four Corners in the south west part of town.

WILLIAM PLATT, JR.—Manufacturers of Horn Combs near Ezra Morgan's store.

INDUSTRIES OF NEWTOWN IN 1852—1853

MARTIN REED—Manufacturer of every variety of Horn Combs. Factory at the old Cotton Factory, half a mile below Sandy Hook.

GRECIAN & CO.—Manufacturers. Factory near the Housatonic R. R. Depot.

L. L. PLATT & CO.—Manufacturers of every variety of Horn Buttons. Factory at the Housatonic R. R. Depot.

BLACKMAN & SKIDMORE—Horn Comb manufacturers. Four miles north of the Street on the Brookfield road.

LEROY TAYLOR—Manufacturer of every variety of Horn Combs. Two miles west of the Street at the outlet of Taunton Pond.

WILLIAM PLATT—Horn Button Manufacturer. One mile west of Botsford Station.

ALFRED N. SHARP—Dealer in Dry Goods, Groceries, Crockery, etc. Four miles west of the Street.

GEORGE MOREHOUSE—Dealer in Dry Goods, Groceries, Crockery, etc., in the southwest part of the town—Gregory's Orchard.

WILLIAM B. PRINDLE—Manufacturer of chairs, cabinet ware and coffins. One mile south of Newtown Street near the Turnpike. He has a good Grist Mill connected with said establishment. All work done to order.

IVES GLOVER, BLACKSMITH—One and a half miles south of Newtown Street, near the Turnpike. All work in his line done to order and at short notice.

CHARLES BEERS—Manufacturer of Horn Combs. One mile below Newtown Street; near the cemetery.

PECK & CLARK—Manufacturers of Horn Combs on the Turnpike one mile south of Newtown village.

EBEN BEACH—General Blacksmithing; on the Turnpike in South Center District.

DAVID D. LOPER—House and Decorative Painter, Newtown.

PETER M. NASH—House and Decorative Painter, Newtown.

CHARLES B. NICHOLS—Manufacturer of Woolen Stocking Yarn. Four miles south of Newtown Street on the Turnpike. Wool carded to order. Take wool for pay.

JOHN WARNER—Dealer in Dry Goods, Groceries, Crockery, Hardware, etc. Store a few rods south of St. James Church in Zoar district.

ALONZO SHERMAN—Blacksmith, one half mile west of St. James Church. Custom work done to order.

JULIUS ROBERTS—Carriage and Sleigh Maker. Next door to Alonzo Sherman's Blacksmith Shop.

WILLIAM A. BRADLEY—Dealer in Dry Goods, Groceries, Crockery, etc. Bradleyville, Zoar.

ABIJAH BRADLEY—Manufacturer of cabinet ware and churns.

MATTHEW FAIRCHILD—Manufacturer of Horn Combs. Factory a few rods east of the Street.

S. T. ALLING—Physician and Surgeon. A few rods south of the Bridge in Sandy Hook.

DENNIS W. NASH—Carpenter and Joiner, one mile southwest of the Street in Head of Meadow District.

HORACE GILBERT—Dealer in Groceries and Yankee notions. Huntingtown.

BRADLEY & SHERMAN—Blacksmiths and Horseshoers. Shop west of Congregational Church.

SIMEON NICHOLS—Satinet manufactory; three miles south of Newtown on Newtown and Bridgeport Turnpike.

JOHN GRIFFIN'S STEAM PLASTER MILL—At Botsford Depot.

GLOVER HAWLEY—Hawleyville; dealer in Spruce and Hemlock Lumber, and timber for building purposes.

BRONSON BULKLEY—An expert workman in wood craft, builds ox-carts, cart tongues, ox-sleds, stone boats, wagon axles, etc. Work done with neatness and dispatch. Shop at upper end of Newtown Street

UNCLE BILL PECK—An expert hog butcher, pork packer and smoker of hams and shoulders. Season lasts from first of November to the first of April. Office one door north of the blacksmith's shop, head of Newtown Street on road to Danbury.

BILL JOHNSON—(Colored.) Day laborer, at all seasons of the year regardless of weather. Call at old red house west of the meeting house. Can be found there when at home.

TO COMB MAKERS—20,000 Buenos Ayres horns, low for cash or short approval credit; also exchange for tips at a fair price. Elam Shepard, Newtown, Aug. 30, 1825.

FURNITURE WAREHOUSE—William G. Smith informs his customers and the public in general that he keeps on hand an elegant assortment of furniture, not inferior to any in this country. The articles which he manufactures are Sofas, Secretaries, Book Cases, Lockers, Bureaus, Pillar and Claw Tables, Mahogany and Cherry Tea Tables, Common Tables, Bedsteads, Chairs, etc., of every description; together with Venetian Window Blinds made to order as cheap as can be bought in New York. All kinds of lumber taken in exchange for the above articles. Mahogany and pine lumber kept constantly on hand and for Sale. Newtown, June 14, 1829.

NOTE—The cabinet shop stood on the ground north of Charles F. Beardsley's house, where Arthur T. Nettleton's house now is.

REVISED LIST, 1918

David H. Belden	Residence of P. E. Abbott.
D. B. Beers	Summer Residence of Miss Louise Bigelow.
Amos S. Treat	In block now R. H. Beers' store.
C. H. Booth, M. D.	Residence of Mrs. Marcus Hawley.
Erastus Erwin M. D.	Summer home of Dwight C. Wheeler.
George Judson, M. D.	Residence of George A. Northrop.
Monroe Judson, M. D.	Residence of Mrs. A. B. Blackman.
Miss Maria Fairman	Residence of Michael Crowe.
Henry Sanford	Store of R. H. Beers.
Edward Starr	Was between Trinity Church Rec. and Miss Louise Bigelow.
David M. Johnson	Morris & Shepard.
William Blakeslee	Residence of Mrs. Lucy Cavanaugh.
Charles Fairman	Next above present Town Hall.

Norman Glover bought the place and Chas. Fairman moved to house now owned and occupied by Patrick McCarthy.

Pike & Brother	Little Shop where brick building stands.
George Peck	Home of Miss Abbie Peck and Sister.
Burr Hawley	Where Post Office now stands.
Newtown Hotel	Newtown Inn.
Isaac Briscoe	In rear of home of Michael Crowe.
Theophilus Nichols	Former home of M. C. Skidmore, deceased.
Isaac Beers	Trinity Church sheds near that location.
George Lawrence	Location not known.
Charles Fairman,s Livery Stable,	In rear of Mrs. S. F. Schermerhorn's house.
Wm. B. Glover	Where Sandy Hook Post Office now stands.
Levi Morris	Corbett & Crowe, Drugs and Groceries.
Charles Twichell	H. C. Bassett.
Nathan R. Couch	Patrick Campbell's Saloon.
Nathan Shepard	Home of Arthur Baird.
David Glover	Shop adjoining Flour Mill.
Sandy Hook Hotel	Edward Troy's Hotel.
Dudley Squires	Brick store on same location.
J. B. & C. F. Blakeslee	Between Gibson Place & Mrs. Minott Augur.

Charles Blakesley, who lived in the house where Mrs. Minott Augur now lives built a brass foundry on the lot back of the house, where he cast brass door keys. These were finished in what is now the Harris Wire Mill.

REVISED LIST, 1918

A. B. Beecher — Harris Wire Mill.
Henry L. Wheeler — John Haugh, Hardware Store.
Sandy Hook Flouring Mill — Patrick Campbell
John Dick & Co. — Shop destroyed.

Josiah Sanford and Joseph Dick erected a satinet factory north of the flouring mill, and very near the Dayton Street bridge. Later, William J. Dick and Charles Dick went into business with their father, Joseph Dick and engaged in the manufacture of rivets and wooden screws. The first gimlet pointed screws were also made in this factory, under a patent taken out by Lorenzo Bidwell. The manufacture of horn combs and buttons was also carried on here by Ambrose Stillson.

Daniel Hall — Shop destroyed.
Moses Parsons & Sons — House rebuilt by Wm. S. Stevens, cor. Dayton Street.
Ammon Shepard — Opposite Richard's Store
Warner & Curtis — S. Curtis & Son, Berkshire.
Rufus Somers — Home of C. E. Miner, Berkshire.
Isaac J. Wells — Shop demolished, Berkshire.
Royal O. Clarke — Home of Arthur Page, Berkshire.
Burton E. Clarke — Home of George A. Benwell on State Road.
Levi Peck — On estate of E. L. Johnson, House and shop burned.
David Curtis — Opposite H. G. Curtis Factory, removed.
Wm. J. Dick & Co. — See John Dick & Co.
George Wheeler — Next to John B. Wheeler, on Brookfield turnpike.

George Wheeler's hat factory was located right back of house formerly owned by Michael Dugan, north of residence of John B. Wheeler. Mr. Wheeler remembers very distinctly, of running in there as a boy, to watch the process of hat making.

Mrs. George Andrews — Residence of Miss Margaret Carmody and Mrs. John Houlihan.
Ezra Morgan — Home of Irving Goodsell.
Martin Reed

The old Cotton factory stood where the New Primier Mf'g. Co., Dutch Rubber was. The cotton factory was built by David Sanford for the purpose of manufacturing wool filling and cotton warp for satinet.

Grecian & Co. — Location not known.
L. L. Platt & Co. — Factory removed.
William Platt — The Crowe Keane Button Co.
Alfred N. Sharp — Home of Eleazer A. E. Bevans, Dodging town.
George Morehouse — Location unknown.
William B. Prindle — Wetmore's Mill.
Ives Glover — Home of David Glover.
Charles Beers — Moved to Ohio, House burned.
Peck & Clark — Home of Hermon H. Peck.
Eben Beach — Home of William H. Prindle.
David Loper — Old house on Reservoir Hill, (destroyed).
Peter N. Nash — Built house the home of Miss Anna McCartan.
Charles B. Nichols — Residence of O. Howard Hall.
John Warner — Near Gray's Plain School house.
Matthew Fairchild — Home of George B. Beers.

It was Dr. Gideon Shepard's Inn; later owned by Matthew Fairchild, then by Botsford Terrill, then by William Terrill.

Dennis W. Nash — Home of Arthur L. Peck.
Horace Gilbert — Owned by Schimelman Bros.
Simeon Nichols — Owned by Bridgeport Hydraulic Co.
John Griffin — Estate of Nathan C. Herz, deceased. Home of Marcus Busker.

Glover Hawley   Hawleyville, property R. R. Co.
                                     Home of Wm. Sturges.
Bronson Buckley   Home of Mrs. Cora Pierce.

Josiah Tomlinson and Charles Goodyear had a shop on Dayton Street near the Methodist Church where they cast pewter spoons. They conceived the idea of re-inforcing the spoons by means of a steel wire running the length of the handle. The wire being laid in the mold, and the moulten metal then poured in. The spoons were buffed and finished at what is now the Harris Wire Mill.

Augurs old meat market building was used as a machine shop, and a man by the name of Gurley together with young Charles Blakesley carried on brass business.

A shop was built by Daniel Conly on Dayton Street just north of the Methodist Church, for the manufacturing of hats, the hats being taken to Dicks machine or rivet shop, for finishing. Conly married a daughter of Squire Clark, who was father of Mr. Philo Clark.

THE CROWE-KEANE BUTTON COMPANY.

The button industry is an old established business in this town, their manufacture having been first begun in 1844, in a small factory near the Housatonic R. R. Station under the management of Grffin, Platt and Summers. Later this Company dissolved each going into business for himself.

Part of the present factory of The Crowe-Keane Button Co. was moved from Botsford R. R. Station where an old factory was located by William Platt.

The machinery was brought here from Waterbury by Lorin Platt, a brother of William Platt. He (Wm. Platt), continued in the business until 1870 when it was sold to Patrick Keane & Son, who enlarged and improved the business. When Mr. Keane died in 1896, P. F. Crowe succeeded him in the management of the business until June 8th, 1909, when the present stock company was formed.

This industry is the only manufacturing in the lower part of the town, and employs from 20 to 25 girls and 10 to 15 men. Horn and hoof buttons are made in all sizes.

An interesting bit of Newtown history in connection with the work now being done by the "Connecticut Light and Power Co."

Reader! Did you ever hear it said that nearly one hundred years ago the question was being agitated of building a canal along side of the Housatonic river, from tidewater to the northern boundary of the state of Connecticut, expecting by so doing to furnish transportation facilities for getting farm produce from the up-country towns in Fairfield and Litchfield counties to the seaboard and thus find a more ready market? The matter was to be brought up for action at the General Assembly that would convene in May, 1822, and the town appointed a committee to represent it on that matter. We give the recorded doings of the meeting as they are to be found in the Town Journal, Vol. 5, page 175, which go to show the town in favor of the proposed project. The measure did not meet with general approval, although it helped to make an interesting chapter to be added to Newtown history and reads as follows: "At a special town meeting of the inhabitants of Newtown, legally warned and held at the old church on the 9th day of April, 1822, at 4 o'clock, for the purpose of taking into consideration the subject of the proposed canal along the Housatonic river, it was voted that Smith Booth be made moderator."

"Voted that whereas it has been represented to the meeting that a petition will be brought to the next General Assembly to incorporate a company for the purpose of establishing a navigation by the Housatonic river by means of a canal near its bank or by improving the bed of the river as far as the state line, and whereas said operations are in part to be done within the limits of this town, therefore voted that this town approve the object of said petition and hereby consent that said canal may be laid through the town and the contemplated operations in the river be made and this town waive all objections the said petition on the ground that said petition shall not be regularly served upon this town and the Representatives from this town are hereby instructed by all proper means to forward the object of said petition, provided that nothing herein contained is to be construed to subject this town to expense of purchasing the land over which said canal may pass."

Voted to adjourn without delay.

Caleb Baldwin, Town Clerk

VERSES COMPOSED ON THE DEATH OF ONE, BENJAMIN GLOVER.

Composed by Benjamin Glover's Wife on the death of her husband.
Hail, all ye dead men, I am come to lodge along with you,
  Edge close and give me room to rot, I claim it as my due.
I bring no bags of cash to let, nor interest to be cast,
  For I was rid of all these things before I breathed my last.
I four score years and seven have lived in trouble and distress,
  And seventeen years of it was blind as was poor Bartimeus.
I naked came into this world and naked go I out,
  And not one farthing do I leave behind for heoirs to snarl about.
When I was young I did design with riches to be crowned,
  But soon I found out my mistake, for want did me surround.
Loss followed loss till in short time of all I was bereft,
  I made my will and thus disposed of all that I had left.
I will my soul to God on high who gave it to me first,
  I will my body to the grave to moulder with the dust.
  To his brother:
When you paid natures debt your sires did quietly submit,
  Because you left great store of wealth they had their share in it.
It was other motives that moved mine to yeild that I should die,
  Because a great deliverance then they should receive thereby.
And what's the odds between us now, you are dead and so am I;
  Now I sleep as much as you, as quietly I lie.
Here rich and poor together meet, the Lord hath made them all,
  Then Let us all in quiet sleep till Christ for us doth call.

Extract from a letter written by Franklin Fairman of Chicago, Ill, in 1913.

Ichabod Fairman, son of one of the old settlers of Newtown, married Rebecca Glover, daughter of Benjamin and Mary Burwell Glover.

She must have been a daughter of the lady who wrote the verses quoted. Mrs. Glover seems to have been a rather striking character. One of her sayings was, "The more you oppose 'em the more they'll 'tarnally marry", showing that opposition to the marriage of children was a burning question. On looking up the records I find that Ichabod Fairman was of the mature age of 20, and that two of his brothers and one sister were married at about the same age.

I find that Mrs. Mary Glover was my gt. gt. grandmother. I therefore am thankful for resurrecting this specimen of her composition.

Franklin Fairman

INDEX

A

Abrams, John, 246
Ackley, Rev. Wm. N., 88, 93.
" Wm. E., 93.
Adams, Abraham, 120
" Ephraim, 120, 218
" Freegrace, 27, 30, 33, 52, 59, 70, 119, 216, 218
" John, 119, 190, 216, 218
" Joseph S., 125
" Reuben, 123
" Samuel, 190, 218
" William, 53
Alden, Henry, 248
Allen, Mrs. Grace, 234
" William, 122
Allyn, John, 1
Andrews, Frederick, 251
Anthon, George, 247
Arms, Rev. Wm. M., 78
Atwater, Rev. Jason, 42, 78
Augur, Minott, 93, 245

B

Bacon, Mary, 230
Bailey, Hiram, 128
" Jesse M., 232
" Samuel, 215
Baisley, Jonathan, 73
Baldwin, Abel, 73, 120, 133, 135, 160
" A. D., 160
" Betty, 193
" Caleb, 37, 43, 44, 47, 49, 65, 70, 71, 73, 111, 113, 119, 120, 133, 136, 143, 145, 149, 170, 171, 215, 218.
" Maj. Caleb Jr., 65, 82, 98, 99, 108, 133, 134, 135, 136, 137, 143, 145, 149, 190, 193, 218, 265, 266, 267
" Caleb, 3rd, 120, 178, 179, 182, 183, 184, 185, 186, 187, 218, 221, 225, 227.
" Mrs. Caleb, 233.
" Daniel, 33, 104, 108, 120, 183, 208, 218.
" Capt. David, 83, 155, 242, 245, 246, 247.
" David V. B., 170, 171, 226, 227.
" Gideon, 120, 218.
" Henry, 77, 236, 239.
" Homer W., 252.
" Jabez, 120, 131, 179, 195.
" James, 64, 105, 119, 215, 218.
" Jerusha, 73.
" John, 154.
" Mary, 195.
" Mehitable, 193.
" Capt. Nathan, 27, 28, 57, 60, 61, 65, 67, 70, 71, 72, 119,, 120, 215, 218, 267.
" Philo, 75, 183.
" Richard, 21.
" Sarah, 134.
" Theophilus, 46.
" Thomas, 21.
" Timothy, 20.
" Widow Anna, 73.
Bancroft, Oliver, 128, 209.

Banks, David, 229.
" Jane, 228.
Bantle, Amy M., 232.
Bardslee, John, 27, 28.
Barker, Rev. Otis W., 79, 233, 234, 262.
Barlow, Joseph B., 126.
Barnes, H., 158.
" Lucas, 76.
Barnett, Rev. Francis W., 10, 88, 93, 262.
" Rev. Francis B., 88.
" Lieut Rev. Joseph N. 88.
" Mary P., 88.
" Lieut Wm. Edward, 88.
Barnum, Andrew, 106, 114.
" Francis, 218.
" Sallu Pell, 77, 145, 236, 239.
" Samuel T., 151.
" Thomas B., 129.
Bassett, Albert, 235.
" Charles H., 94.
" Joel, 75, 120, 128, 218.
" John, 123, 218.
" Thomas, 218.
Beach, Ambrose, 109.
" Eben, 76, 77.
" Isaac, 234.
" Rev. John, 11, 57, 63, 65, 82, 85, 190, 193, 218, 233, 234.
" John Francis, 233, 234.
" John Kimberly, 233, 234.
" Lazarus, 111, 234.
" Rebecca D., 233, 234.
" Reuben, 76, 77.
Beard, Henry, 230.
" Mrs. Estella, 234.
" William, 76, 236, 239.
Beardsley, Aaron, 126.
" Abner, 127.
" Abraham, 128.
" Agur, 125.
" Bailey, 128.
" Charles F., 143, 187, 233, 234, 262.
" Elias, 123.
" Enos, 120.
" Israel A., 161, 218.
" James F., 127, 218.
" Jesse, 129.
" Josiah, 73, 122, 124, 133, 134, 135, 180, 190, 218.
" Josiah Jr., 122.
" Lyman, 111.
" Moses, 75, 125.
" Moses Jr., 126.
" Moses 3rd, 128.
" Philo, 75, 125, 127.
" Rev. E. Edwards, 81.
" Samuel, 75.
" Wilton, 129.
Beck, Esther M., 232
Beebe, James, 25
Beecher, Alva B., 76, 161, 187, 236, 239.
" Florence Glover, 203, 232.
" Henry Glover, 234.
" Marguerite Katherine 203, 232.
" Sarah, 228.
" William J., 203, 234, 238, 239, 242, 263.
Beers, Abel, 119.
" Abel S., 126, 183.
" Abiel, 216.

Beers, Abner, 77, 127.
" Abraham, 102, 120, 124
" Amariah, 128, 184, 227.
" Andrew, 83, 124, 246.
" Anna, 260.
" Anna S., 228.
" Arabella Fitch, 81, 92.
" Austin, 125.
" Booth G., 229.
" Charles C., 129.
" Charles E., 252.
" Mrs. Charles E., 252.
" Charles H., 77.
" Charlotte, 228.
" Cyrenius, 125, 260.
" Cyrus, 123, 124.
" Daniel, 119, 218, 223.
" Daniel G., 87, 92, 163, 229, 230, 233, 234, 238, 239, 262.
" David B., 83, 99, 129, 200, 236, 239.
" David, 126.
" Ebenezer, 83, 124, 212.
" Ebenezer Jr., 127, 182, 183, 185.
" Eleazer, 73.
" Eli, 125.
" Eli B., 238, 239.
" Elias, 123, 125.
" Elizabeth L., 92.
" Emma S., 200, 237.
" Ester, 183, 185.
" Ezekiel, 95, 128.
" Florence, 11.
" Frederick H., 11.
" George, 145, 200, 229, 260.
" George B.
" George Emerson, 200.
" Gideon, 128.
" Harry, 226, 227, 236, 237, 239.
" Harry Croswell, 252.
" Henry, 127, 185.
" G. Herbert, 232.
" Hermon, 129.
" H. Sanford, 232.
" Isaac, 85.
" Isaac Beach, 229.
" Jabez, 123.
" Jacob, 126, 185.
" James
" Jane Fitch, 87.
" Jeremiah, 126.
" Jessie M., 232.
" John, 102, 119, 128, 129, 184, 214, 218.
" John B., 128.
" John Hobart, 229.
" Julius A., 229.
" Lemuel, 128, 227.
" Lillian, 232.
" Mrs. Lucy, 78.
" Lyman, 76, 77.
" Mary E., 233, 234.
" Dr. Moses B., 212.
" Norman, 128.
" Oliver, 124.
" Phebe B., 212.
" Philo Jr., 127, 185.
" Robert H., 40, 44, 233, 262.
" Samuel, 123, 125, 218.
" Sarah A., 232.
" Sarah M., 230.
" Sarah Nichols, 92.
" Sarah Peck, 260.
" Silas Norman, 85, 92, 229.
" Simeon, 125, 154.

INDEX

Beers, Simeon N., 128, 161, 183, 227.
" Susan Lynne, 92.
" Sylvester, 128.
" Thomas, 127.
" Truman, 123.
" Widow Sarah, 216.
" Zalmon, 75.
Benedict, Benjamin C., 229.
" Eliakim, 149.
" George, 128.
" George M., 129, 227.
" Gideon, 64.
" Capt. John, 46.
" Joseph, 64.
" Joseph Jr., 64.
" Ralph, 111.
" Samuel B., 129.
Benjamin, R. 168.
Bennett
  or
Bennitt, Abel, 110, 120, 124, 183.
" Abel Jr., 129.
" Abram, 37, 64, 71, 75.
" Abram Jr., 73.
" Abraham, 119, 120, 127, 136, 215, 218.
" Amos, 122, 124.
" Caleb, 41, 75, 123, 125.
" Deacon, 36.
" Ebenezer F., 125.
" Eli, 27, 177.
" Emily, 204.
" Ephraim, 119, 195, 218.
" Ezekiel, 125.
" Gideon, 150.
" Isaac, 125.
" James, 110, 123, 124, 184.
" James Jr., 128, 183, 184.
" Job, 133, 135.
" Joseph, 127.
" Legrand, 76.
" Nancy, 150.
" Nathan, 133, 150.
" Richard, 110, 124.
" Thaddeus, 150, 183.
" Thomas, (Justice of Peace), 14, 15, 22, 27, 28, 30, 35, 45, 52, 53, 55, 56, 59, 61, 73, 110, 117, 119, 159, 216.
" Wheeler, 127.
" Widow Mary, 215.
Beresford, Charles M., 233, 252.
Betts, Anna May, 231.
" Anna Plowman, 204.
" Ephraim, 136.
" James M., 204.
" John, 230.
" Thaddeus, 135.
" Mary Hough, 204.
" Dr. Ralph N. Jr., 212.
" Dr. Ralph N., 93, 204.
" Ralph N. Jr., 212.
Bierce, A. O., 252.
Birch, David M., 128.
" Ezra, 122, 124.
" George, 218.
" Jeremiah, 119, 218.
" Lamson, 41, 75, 125, 141, 149.
" Mary Ann, 141, 142.
" Nehemiah, 110.
" William, 104, 120, 177, 178, 181, 218.
" William Jr., 123.
Birchard, Eden, 126.
Bishop, Alfred, 167, 198, 200.
Blackman, Abner, 127.
  or
Blakeman, Ada M., 234.
" Agur, 127.
" Alfred, 183.
" Ann, 146, 230.

Blakeman, Austin B. 171, 234, 238, 239, 262.
" Bennett, 239.
" Caroline, 198.
" Daniel, 125, 183, 184, 185, 186.
" David S., 126.
" Ebenezer, 46, 218.
" Eli W., 130.
" Ephraim, 120.
" George, 129, 198.
" Harriet B., 228.
" Helen M., 232, 234.
" Isaac Percy, 93, 249.
" Isaac, 123.
" James, 97, 120, 218.
" James G., 129, 183, 184.
" James H., 252.
" James M., 93.
" J. Albert, 263.
" Capt. John, 28, 65, 75, 119, 123, 215, 218, 267.
" John Jr., 120, 122.
" Joseph, 38, 77, 120, 123, 154, 183, 218, 239.
" Josiah, 103, 154.
" Julia E., 228.
" Mary F., 88.
" Nathaniel, 218.
" Pattern M., 126.
" Reuben, 127.
" Dr. Rufus, 205, 206.
" Samuel, 126, 198.
" Samuel A., 172, 245.
" Samuel B., 129.
" Samuel C., 41, 76, 77, 79, 125, 155, 182, 183, 198, 226, 247.
" Miss Sarah, 79, 198.
" Sheldon, 129.
" Simeon S., 127.
" Thomas, 127, 170, 171, 227.
" Truman, 126.
" Zerah, 186.
" Ziba, 128, 145.
Blake, Elizabeth, 232.
" Lena, 232.
" Michael J., 232.
" Nora C., 232.
Blackwell, John Staley, 264, 265, 266, 267.
Blakeslee, Charles, 129, 161, 227, 236, 239.
" George B., 229.
" Mary J., 228.
" James B., 236, 239.
" Sarah Grace, 228.
" William, 77, 128, 227, 242, 243.
" William Z., 229.
" Ziba, 41, 75, 125.
Boardman, David S., 199.
Bolmer, Mrs. Gertrude, 234, 235.
Booth, Abel, 37, 40, 65, 71, 97, 119, 123, 197, 216, 218, 221.
" Abel Jr., 120.
" Abiel, 75, 120.
" Abner, 216.
" Abraham, 83, 85, 103, 120, 218.
" Andrew, 197.
" Asahel Jr., 75, 126.
" Austin, 128.
" Charles B., 128, 227.
" Dr. Cyrenius H., 198, 210, 211, 239.
" Daniel, 47, 48, 64, 83, 119, 125, 194, 216, 218.
" Daniel Jr., 120, 126.
" Daniel T., 229.
" David, 123, 154, 196.
" David Jr., 126.
" Eben, 28.
" Ebenezer, 27, 33, 52, 53, 57, 59, 120, 123, 124, 159, 176, 218.
Booth, Edward, 126.
" Ezra, 83.
" Gideon, 120.
" Hesler, 197.
" Hezekiah, 103, 127, 124, 218.
" Joel, 125.
" John C., 129.
" Jonathan, 26, 27, 28, 33, 43, 60, 70, 73, 9, 123, 124, 133, 196.
" Jonathan Jr., 119, 216, 218.
" Joseph, 27, 183, 184, 196, 197.
" Levi B., 99, 163, 171, 230, 251.
" Mary, 197.
" Mary Carter, 234.
" Moses W., 197.
" Naomi, 77.
" Pheobe, 77, 196.
" Reuben H., 120, 123, 124, 125, 195, 199, 218.
" Rev. Robert C., 234.
" Samuel, 125.
" Sarah, 197, 226.
" Dr. Wm. Edmond, 210.
" Widow Mary, 216.
Bostwick, Gershom, 46.
" John, 123, 124, 168.
" Levy, 122.
" Rev. William L., 228.
Botsford, Capt. Abel, 37, 40, 73, 75, 76, 77, 120, 122, 124, 135, 136, 190, 218, 227.
" Abel Jr., 64, 73, 218.
" Abiel, 97, 180.
" Abraham, 73, 75, 129, 196, 218.
" Abram, 126.
" Adella, 230.
" Alosia, 228.
" Capt. Amos, 37, 38, 44, 72, 73, 120, 215, 218.
" Austin, 201, 202.
" Austin Nichols, 251.
" Mrs. Bethia, 197.
" Chas. 128.
" Chas W., 232.
" Chauncey, 41.
" Clarice E., 232.
" Ensign Clement, 122, 124, 136, 154, 183.
" Daniel, 75, 123, 125, 151.
" Daniel Jr., 127, 183, 184, 185, 186.
" David, 136, 186.
" Edwin, 168, 171.
" Capt. Elijah, 40, 120, 121, 122, 133, 135, 136, 218.
" Ephraim, 103.
" Ezra, 218.
" George, 113.
" 121, 122, 124, 133, 154.
" Gideon, 37, 72, 73, 89, 121, 122, 124, 133, 154, 196, 218.
" Gideon Jr., 73, 123, 124, 196.
" Harold E., 231.
" Capt. Henry, 64, 125, 183, 191, 215, 218.
" Isaac, 120, 218.
" Israel, 125, 183, 184.
" Capt. Jabez, 38, 40, 73, 120, 122, 127, 133, 134, 135, 136, 137, 138, 142, 154, 162, 218.
" Sergt. James, 267.
" Jared, 73, 120, 183, 218.

INDEX

Botsford, Jerome, 102, ,111, 113, 114.
" Joel, 120.
" Dea. John, 61, 62, 67, 73, 119, 122, 126, 133, 215, 218.
" John Jr., 126, 133, 215.
" Joseph, 119, 122, 216, 218.
" Lieut. J., 121.
" Marcus, 127, 154, 191.
" Mayla, 232.
" Martin, 126.
" Mrs. Meriam, 196.
" Moses, 65, 73, 119, 121, 123, 154, 183, 215, 218.
" Moses Jr., 121.
" Moss K., 127.
" Mrs. Nancy, 196.
" Niram, 124.
" Oliver, 171.
" Philo, 75, 126, 232.
" Pulcrea F., 89.
" Richard, 125, 201.
" Dr. Russell B., 211.
" Samuel J., 233, 234, 252, 253.
" Sherman, 126.
" Theophilus, 123, 183, 184, 185, 186.
" Thomas, 126, 183.
" Capt. Vine, 123, 125.
" Volucia G., 201, 202.
" William, 127, 183, 239.
Bowles, Samuel, 250.
Braase, Thomas, 28, 33.
Bradley, Abijah, 126.
" Abijah Jr., 128.
" Alice E., 202, 230.
" Eliphalet, 126.
" George, 128, 229.
" Gertrude, 232.
" Jared, 126.
" Medad, 129.
" Robert, 171.
" Thomas J., 172.
" Capt. Walter, 101, 115.
" William A., 94.
Brennan, Nonie A., 232.
Brenner, Annie C., 232.
Brewster, John Huntington, 229.
" Rt. Rev. Chauncey B., 87.
Brinsmade, Zachariah, 218.
Briscoe, Alfred M., 245.
" Alice A., 202.
" Anna T., 202.
" Charles, 129, 202, 227.
" Hon. Chas. H., 202, 230, 231.
" Daniel, 128.
" Isaac, 126.
" James, 28, 64, 119, 216, 218.
" Jennie, 231, 247.
" John, 108, 113, 126.
" Lewis S., 128.
" Mary, 202.
" Molly, 208.
" Lieut. Nathaniel, 37, 38, 64, 69, 72, 119, 122, 133, 177, 216, 218.
" Nathaniel Jr., 127.
" Willis A., 202.
Bristol, Abraham, 120.
" Caesar, 182, 185.
" Cornelius, 120.
" David, 123.
" Ebenezer, 98, 105, 119, 218.
" Enos, 119, 218.
" Job, 120, 218.
" John, 33, 117, 119, 127, 216.
" Joseph, 33, 60, 65, 60, 123, 177, 190, 216, 267.

Bristol, Joseph Jr., 117, 119, 123, 124, 216, 218.
" Joseph, 3rd., 120.
" William, 178.
Bronson, Dr. William, 103, 111, 117.
Brooks, Rev. Thomas, 49, 50, 134.
Brown, Samuel, 121, 216.
Brownell, Rt. Rev. Thomas, 89.
Bryan, Alexander, 71, 119, 214.
" Alice, 27, 28.
" Ezra, 105, 120, 213.
" Richard, 3.
" Samuel, 50.
Buck, Rev. George H., 10.
Bulkley, Bronson, 129.
" Daniel, 129.
" Jabez, 218.
Bunnill, Job, 124, 135.
" John, 122.
" Nathaniel, 123.
Burhans, Rev. Daniel, 84, 86, 93, 244.
Burns, John, 176.
Burr, Barak, 210.
" Benjamin, 124, 135.
" James, 218.
" Jane A., 210.
" John, 25, 27, 33, 34.
" Nathan, 109, 113.
" Sylvia E., 137.
Burrill, Catharine, 199.
" Stephen, 215.
Burritt, Amos, 120, 122, 124.
" Benjamin, 120, 21), 218.
" Eleazer, 120, 121, 122, 218.
" James S., 129.
" Joseph, 127.
" Josiah, 27, 28, 33, 55, 60, 215.
" Nathan, 73, 120, 122, 218.
" Widow Lavina, 160.
Burross, John, 19.
Burroughs, Charles, 75.
" Edward, 229.
" Emana J., 228.
Burrows, Reuben, 76.
Burton, Nathaniel, 154.
Burrill, Catharine, 199.
Burwell, Job, 133, 135.
" Samuel, 120.
" Stephen, 97, 125, 215, 218.
" Stephen Jr., 123.
" William, 122, 124, 132, 133, 179, 218.
" William Jr., 120.
" Widow Rebecca, 218.
Bush, Justus, 13.

C

Cable, Julius C., 203.
" Nathaniel J., 203.
" Phebe, 203.
" Wheeler, 128.
Cadey, Nathaniel, 248.
Cain, Mary, 191.
Camp, Alice, 194.
" Beach, 10, 84, 129, 212, 227.
" Catharine Foote, 10, 212.
" Currence, 194.
" Cyrus, 128.
" Daniel, 234, 250.
" Dibble, 128.
" Edwin, 98.
" Father, 230.
" Hiram, 129.

Camp, George B., 229.
" Hobart B., 229.
" Jacob, 126.
" Jane Eliza, 10, 228.
" Joel, 120, 125, 218.
" Joel T., 128.
" John W., 125, 265, 267.
" Julius, 124.
" Lemuel, 60, 65, 119, 126, 190, 194, 215, 218, 267.
" Lydia J., 228.
" Samuel, 120, 126, 218.
" Silas, 127, 180, 218.
" William, 212.
" William H., 212.
Campbell, Augusta, 231.
" Patrick, 24.
Canfield, George C., 232.
" Col. Samuel, 50.
Cannon, John S., 152, 153.
" Philip A., 127.
Carey, Jerry, 160.
" Thomas, 162.
Cargill, James A., 130.
Carlson, Anna, 232.
Carpenter, W. L., 231.
Carmichael, Rev. Wm. N., 84.
Carmody, Francis J., 231.
Carroll, Mrs., 99, 110.
Cavanaugh, Eleanor S., 231.
" James, 107.
" Marguerite, 232.
" Paul, 232.
" Thomas, 104, 114.
Chambers, Asa, 120, 123, 124, 218.
" Frederick, 85, 93, 94, 101, 109, 229, 252.
" Thomas O., 97, 101, 109, 128, 218, 227.
Chandler, Elizabeth J., 198.
" Col. John, 133, 134, 136, 137, 142, 189, 197, 198.
" Mrs. Mary, 197, 198.
Chapman, Asa, 198, 200, 244.
" Charles, 200, 244.
Chase, Mrs. Julia, 234.
Chastelleaux, Chevalier, 139.
Chauncey, Rev. Thomas, 54.
Cheever, 248.
Christopher, David, 232.
" Mildred, 232.
Clarke, Abel F., 234.
" Mrs. Abel F., 234.
" Adam, 150.
" Agur, 130.
" Andrew, 126.
" Charles, 128, 227.
" David, 127.
" Edwin, 233, 239.
" Elizabeth, 229.
" Everett, 128.
" George, 229.
" Grandison, 127.
" Hannah, 58.
" James, 125, 184, 218.
" Rev. Jehu, 41, 75.
" Jennie, 10.
" John, 73, 125.
" Lemuel B., 229.
" Lucius, 127.
" Philo, 227, 237, 238, 239.
" Rev. Sylvester, 90.
" Walter, 128, 236.
" William, 161.
" Zechariah, 120, 123, 124, 149, 184, 190, 218.
Clay, Henry, 209.
Cleveland, Pres. Grover, 71, 172.
Cliff, E. Pennington, 230, 262.
Cobb, Lieut. David, 140.

Coe, Charles W., 76.
Coger, Eli, 109.
Cogswell, Asa, 38, 73, 120, 135, 218, 264.
Colburn, Daniel, 73.
Cole, Charles S., 262.
" William T., 238, 239, 249, 262, 263.
Coleman, K. Lester, 252.
Comstock, Daniel, 126.
" David, 149.
Cone, Hurlburt, 127.
Cooke, Benjamin, 123.
" Curtis, 231.
" David B., 195. 3
" Mrs. Sally, 195.
Corbett, Anna, 232.
" James, 163.
" Frank, 232.
" & Crowe, 248.
Cornwallis, Lord, 137, 139, 140, 141.
Corson, Rev. Levi, 228.
Costello, Thomas, 104, 106.
" Timothy, 109, 112.
Courtney, Bishop, 87.
Cravner, Rev. Wm. C., 262.
Crawford, John, 123.
Crockett, Rev. J. Addison, 86, 234.
Crofut
or
Crofoot, Andrew, 126.
" Daniel, 106, 218.
" Ebenezer, 126.
" Elam, 128.
" Eli, 125.
" Elias, 126.
" Eliel, 127.
" Elihu, 126.
" Elihu Jr., 126.
" Isaac, 125.
" John, 125.
" Joseph, 127.
" Luzon, 129.
" Stephen, 122, 124, 183.
" Stephen Jr., 125.
" Stephen L., 128.
Croof, Daniel, 125.
Crosby, C. M., 164.
" George H., 230.
Cummings, Mabel, 230.
Currence, Michael, 112.
Curtis, Abel, 125.
" Abijah, 83, 122, 124, 190, 218.
" Maj. Abijah B., 107, 108, 110, 120, 125, 161, 183, 191.
" Abijah Beach, 128.
" Alfred Devine, 93, 127.
" Alfred, 127.
" Benjamin, 47, 73, 119, 120, 190, 194, 216, 218.
" Dr. Benjamin, 124, 125, 190, 218.
" Benjamin 3rd, 125.
" Benjamin G., 93, 97.
" Burton E., 129.
" Charles B., 170, 171.
" Cornelia, 101, 107, 110.
" Daniel, 128.
" David, 125, 128, 135, 227, 260.
" David 2nd, 229.
" Dorothy, 231.
" Elisha, 127, 183.
" Elizabeth, 260.
" Epenitus, 127, 183.
" Ezra, 127.
" Frederick L., 229.
" George, 161.
" Capt. Gold, 33, 123, 125, 260.
" Gould Jr., 127, 183, 227, 260.
" Gould 3rd, 261.

Curtis, Harry Beers, 261.
" Henry G., 238, 239, 260, 261.
" Hezekiah, 128.
" Hiram, 128.
" Hobart H., 238, 239.
" Holbrook, 127, 198.
" John, 125, 260.
" John Jr., 127.
" John 3rd, 128.
" Joseph, 31, 73.
" Josiah, 27, 28, 40, 106, 124, 125.
" Julia N., 260.
" Julius B., 201, 204, 260.
" Marion N., 232.
" Mary, 260.
" Matthew, 73, 119, 218, 260.
" Matthew Jr., 120, 133, 135, 265, 266, 267.
" Molly, 73.
" Nathan, 122, 264.
" Nehemiah, 120, 122, 124, 190, 218.
" Nelson George, 261.
" Nichols, 127, 201.
" Niram, 120, 123, 124, 218.
" Philo, 107, 110, 123, 125.
" Reuben, 123, 124.
" Salmon, 123, 124.
" Samuel, 236, 239, 260, 261.
" Sarah, 260.
" Sarah A., 201.
" William R., 87, 260, 261, 262.
" Capt. William, 201.

D

Daly, Rev. James, 95.
" Robert, 62.
Danforth, Rev. Ralph, 79.
Davis, Rev. George, 93.
Dayton, Caleb, 176.
" Hezekiah, 191.
" Josiah, 120, 215.
Deane, Henry, 128.
Delzell, Rev. Samuel, 79.
Denslow, Mrs. Emily H., 64.
Dibble, Eleazer, 128, 183, 218.
" Horace B., 129.
" Squire John, 41, 127, 183, 218.
" Thomas, 127.
Dick, Charles, 76, 161.
" John, 161.
" Joseph, 127, 161, 227.
" William J., 156, 162.
" & Sanford, 248.
Dikeman, Asa, 126.
" Ebenezer, 129.
" Henry B., 234.
" Julia, 243.
" Lillian, 243.
" Martha, 228.
" Nathaniel, 125, 154.
" Mrs. Oscar, 234.
Donahue, Rev. Patrick, 95.
Douglas, Nathan, 246.
Downs, Charlotte N., 204.
" Doris, 231.
" Monroe, 204.
" Nichols C., 204.
" Stephen, 129.
Drew, Isaac, 128.
" Levi, 128.
Driscoll, Charlesina, 232.
" William, 232.
Dudley, Joseph, 25, 28.
Duncomb, George F., 171,

251, 262.
Dunen, John, 28.
Dunkum, Zechariah, 127.
Dunning, Abel, 120.
" Abijah, 218.
" Andrew, 120, 218.
" Capt. Benjamin, 26, 27, 28, 33, 60, 65, 120, 121, 215, 218, 267.
" David, 119, 120, 215, 218.
" Eli, 121, 122, 133, 135, 136, 137, 218.
" Elizabeth, 216.
" Ezra, 122, 218.
" Gideon, 123, 124.
" Jared, 121, 133, 218.
" John, 120.
" Michael, 120.
" Peter, 120, 218.
Dutton, Eliza Maria, 211.
" Gov. Henry, 128, 199, 210, 227, 243, 244.
" Lucinda, 211.
" Dr. Thomas, 76, 210.
Durant, Preston, 129.

E

Easton, Fanny, 228.
Edmond, Ann, 198.
" David, 125.
" Elizabeth J., 197, 198.
" Mary E., 198.
" Robert, 129.
" Sarah, 198, 210.
" Wm. P., 122, 128, 154, 198.
" Hon. Wm., 41, 75, 124, 154, 197, 198, 210, 224.
Edwards, Albert, 114, 111, 126.
" H., 168.
" David, 126.
" Pierpont, 241, 242.
Egan, Andrew, 213.
" Dr. Andrew, 213.
" Edward, 91.
" Rev. Edward, 91.
" Edward J., 231.
" Eliza Gordon, 91.
" Elizabeth, 231.
" Mary Clark, 213.
" May J., 231.
Elwood, Phidema Ann, 151.
Ensign, E. F., 168.
Erwin, Dr. Erastus, 76, 162, 211, 212, 239.
Esch, Dr. Werner, 248.
Evans, Oliver, 130.

F

Fabrique, David, 83, 205.
" John, 62, 120, 215, 219, 221.
" John Jr., 219.
Fairchild, Adelia, 228.
" Adeline J., 78.
" Adoniram, 75, 125.
" Agur, 120, 118.
" Alpheus, 123, 125.
" Arthur W., 138, 232.
" Araunah, 129.
" Beeman, 128.
" Beers, 128.
" Botsford, 167.
" Boyle, 128, 227.
" Burtis, 128.
" Catharine, 228.
" Clarke, 127.
" Clement, 75, 123, 150.
" Cyrus, 126.
" Cyrus Dibble, 128.
" David, 215, 218.

INDEX

Fairchild, Ebenezer H., 121, 127, 218.
" Edward, 27, 28, 33, 65, 119, 215.
" Elizabeth, 78.
" Elmer, 99, 100, 233.
" Ezekiel, 123, 125.
" Ezra, 127.
" George, 100, 106, 110.
" Gideon B., 130.
" Hannah, 138.
" Harriet, 229.
" Henry, 77, 100, 106, 110.
" Hermon, 128, 239.
" Hezekiah B., 77.
" Hiram, 128.
" Ira, 127.
" James, 121, 218.
" James Jr., 121, 122, 133, 136.
" James B., 127.
" John, 123, 124, 218.
" John L., 129.
" Jonathan S., 123, 125, 127, 134, 218.
" Joseph, 75, 125.
" Joseph B., 130.
" Josiah, 122, 124, 172, 227.
" Josiah Jr., 128.
" Kiah B., 127, 183.
" Le Grand, 85, 167.
" Lemuel, 127.
" Levi, 128.
" Lucy A., 229.
" Marcus, 128.
" Mary Hazen, 138, 232.
" Matthew, 260.
" Mortimer, 229.
" Moss, 129.
" Oliver, 121, 122, 219.
" Peter, 124, 138.
" Philo, 41, 75, 123, 124.
" Philo Jr., 128.
" Robert D., 138, 232.
" Samuel, 128, 227.
" Seth, 123, 124, 218.
" Capt. Silas, 38, 41, 73, 75, 121, 136.
" Silas B., 76.
" Silas Jr., 127, 136.
" Susan A., 229.
" Truman, 75, 125.
" Walter, 128.
" Warren, 129.
" Wheeler, 125.
" William, 100, 106, 110.
" William H., 75, 76, 77, 125.
" Winthrop, 128.
" Zadoc, 122, 123, 125.
" Ziba, 127.
Fairman, Amos B., 75.
" Benjamin, 75.
" Charles, 77, 227, 233
" Daniel B., 229.
" Franklin, 230.
" Lieut. Henry, 73, 120, 133.
" Ichabod, 73, 120.
" James B., 161.
" Jabez, 75.
" Mrs. Jane, 194.
" Richard, 47, 72, 97, 120, 133, 135, 136, 137, 194, 218.
" Zerah, 113, 236, 239.
Fancher, Andrew B., 172.
Farnam, J. B., 230.
Farrell, Catherine F., 232.
" Elizabeth, 202.
Ferris, Abel, 123, 125.
" Abraham, 120, 194, 195, 219.
" Abram B., 126.
" Arthur, 232.

Ferris, Betty, 194.
" Daniel, 126.
" Elsie C., 232.
" Esther, 76.
" Capt. George, 112, 135.
" George M., 232.
" Gideon B., 127.
" Herbert, 232.
" Jerusha, 210.
" John, 216.
" Joseph, 83, 120, 124, 125, 210.
" Joseph Jr., 129.
" Joseph G., 130.
" Peter, 119, 216, 219.
" Samuel, 27, 33, 52, 83, 120, 125, 216, 219.
" Thomas S., 128.
" Wm. D. B., 102, 109, 110.
" William R., 112.
" Zachariah, 100, 124.
Ferry, Zachariah, 123.
Fillmore, Pres. Millard, 170.
Finch, Peter, 125.
Fitch, Arabella, 230.
Fisk, Phineas, 27, 53, 54.
Foote, Abel, 122.
" Amos, 129.
" Arnold, 41, 75, 127.
" Daniel, 21, 26, 27, 33, 61, 63, 64, 119, 120, 159, 176, 215, 219.
" Edward, 126.
" Elijah, 103, 122, 136.
" Frederick W., 212.
" Rev. George L., 89, 212, 226, 227.
" Rev. George W., 90.
" George Jr., 122, 124, 219.
" Harriet, 227.
" Heber, 127.
" Rev. Henry L., 90.
" Dr. Henry H., 212.
" Hepsa, 17.
" James, 123, 124, 129.
" John, 120, 216.
" John Jr., 120, 215.
" Joseph, 123, 124, 191.
" Lemuel, 126.
" Mary, 227, 228.
" Mary Jane, 229.
" Philo, 126.
" Polly Hawley, 212, 226.
" Prosper A., 127.
" Rhesa, 127, 174, 212, 226.
Ford, Ebenezer, 37, 43, 72, 97, 120, 219.
" Thomas, 122, 124, 219.
" Thomas Jr., 120.
Fox, A. W., 168.
" Rev. Daniel W., 78.
" Rev. Patrick, 95, 191
Frame, & Grecian, 248.
Frank, John, 113, 117.
French, Gamaliel, 97, 117, 120, 191, 219.
" J. Homer, 212, 228.
" Lillian, 232.
" Mrs. Mary, 228.
" Samuel, 120, 219.
" Turney, 102, 111, 129.
Frost, Sidney B., 230.
Fuller, J. R., 168.

G

Gaffney, Florence U., 232.
Gale, Dr. Frank, 234, 262, 263.
" Gordon, 232.
Ganung, Edith, 231.

Gannon, Patrick, 224.
Gardner, Elizabeth D., 234.
" Rev. Henry V., 93.
" Mrs. Wm. D., 234.
" Prof. W. H., 231.
Gately, Dennis C., 113, 248, 249.
Gauthier, George A., 249.
Gay, Chas. H., 94, 233.
" Mrs. John, 234.
Geeler, James P., 77, 94.
George, Bertha Niles, 87, 261.
" Caroline, 87.
" Rev. James Hardin, 10, 86, 234, 262.
" Mrs. James Hardin, 86.
" Rev. James Hardin, Jr., 87, 92.
" Marilla, 87.
" Theodora, 87.
Gerould, Jabez, 124.
Gifford, James, 119.
Gilbert, Blanche, 232.
" David A., 128.
" Elijah, 126.
" Ezra, 127.
" George, 129.
" Ichabod, 126, 150.
" Philo, 127, 150.
" Seth, 126, 129.
" Stephen, 125.
Gillette, Abel, 129.
" Abraham, 110.
" Frank, 232, 233.
" John, 60, 73, 110, 119, 126, 216.
" Moses, 73, 110, 127.
" Samuel, 110, 119, 219.
Gillis, Miss Mary, 84.
Glover, Abiel B., 128, 183.
" Andrew B., 128.
" Arnold, 120, 178, 219.
" Benjamin C., 62, 119, 126, 215.
" Betsey, 229.
" Birdsey, 122, 123, 125.
" Charles, 128.
" Charlotte, 77.
" Cyrus B., 127.
" Daniel, 103, 123, 124, 219.
" David J., 129, 161, 184.
" Effie, 230, 233.
" Elias, 123, 125.
" Elias Jr., 126.
" Ezra, 126.
" Mrs. Grace, 234.
" Granville, 129.
" Harry, 128, 184, 191.
" Capt. Henry, 47, 62, 83, 49, 123, 124, 126, 178, 184, 216, 219, 267.
" Henry Jr., 123, 124, 219, 221.
" Henry B., 77, 85, 236, 237, 239.
" Ives, 129.
" James, 27, 103, 122, 124, 133, 141, 219.
" James F., 128.
" John (Town Clerk), 15, 17, 25, 27, 33, 35, 47, 52, 54, 55, 57, 59, 62, 76, 83.
" Capt. John, 119, 123, 127, 129, 159, 196, 215, 219.
" Josiah, 126, 154, 183, 227.
" Lemuel, 252.
" Martin V. B., 229.
" Norman B., 44, 99, 100, 129.
" Rebecca, 75.
" Roswell, 129.

INDEX

Glover, Salmon, 123, 124.
" Samuel C., 163.
" Mrs. Sarah Grace, 243.
" Silas N., 127, 160.
" Simeon, 125.
" Capt. Solomon, 43, 81, 83, 108, 113, 123, 124, 141.
" Smith P., 93, 94, 235, 239, 245.
" Stanley, 25.
" Susan Nichols, 93.
" Villeroy, 127.
" Walter, 129.
" Walter H., 239, 252.
" Mrs. Walter H., 252.
" Walter L., 232.
" Wm. B., 93, 94, 99, 248.
" Wm. Benj., 238, 239, 263.
" Wm. H., 229.
" Ziba, 127, 183.
Gold, Abraham, 260.
" Elizabeth, 260.
Goldstein, Irael, 232.
" Mollie, 232.
Golot, John, 33, 64, 116, 117.
Goodhue, Rev. J. E., 84, 229.
Goodsell, Grace, 230.
" Irving, 106.
" Jonathan, 126.
Goodwin, Elizabeth, 231.
Goodyear, Charles, 248.
" Nelson, 248.
Gordon, Dr. James W., 212.
" John, 212.
" Margaret Colgan, 212.
" Margaret Doretta, 212.
Gould, James L., 245.
Graham, Rev. M., 71.
Granger, Gideon, 173.
Grant, Arminal, 192, 219.
" Donald, 36, 71, 119, 192, 193, 215.
" Elizabeth, 193.
" Sueton, 192.
" Pres U. S., 171.
Gray, Andrew Jr., 229.
" James, 219.
" Joseph, 23, 24, 26, 27, 28, 33, 39, 60, 96.
Graves, J. J., 168.
Green, James, 101.
" Thomas, 186.
Greenman, H. M., 116.
Gregory, Aaron, 134.
Griffin, Abner, 219.
" C. Frances, 232.
" Lieut. John, 191, 219.
" Joseph, 191, 219.
" Lieut. Samuel, 76.
" Samuel Jr., 191, 216, 219.
Griggs, John, 251.
Griswold, Zalmon, 76.
Gunn, Abel 122.
" Joseph, 120, 122, 219.
" Joseph Jr., 219.
Guion, Rev. Thomas T.
Gurley, Royal, O., 76, 161.

H

Hadley, Arthur T., 95.
" Mrs. Arthur T., 201.
Hall, Albin, 128.
" Alexander, 77, 128, 243.
" Asa, 219.
" Billy, 75.
" Eli, 126.
" Ezra J., 238.
" John Jr., 126.
" Matthew, 122.
" William, 123, 172, 219.
Halley, Capt., 28.
Hammond, Mary Grace, 203.
Hard Abel, 124.
" Capt. Abijah, 123.
" Abner, 119, 123, 190, 219.
" Abraham, 120.
" Amos, 97, 126, 123, 124, 129, 260.
" Ammon, 123, 154, 219.
" Benjamin, 126, 132, 182.
" Charles T., 129.
" Chester, 94.
" Curtis 122, 124.
" Cyrenius, 83, 121, 123, 124.
" Cyrus, 184.
" Daniel, 126.
" Eli, 128.
" Hannah, Widow, 219.
" James, 24, 28, 33, 35, 47, 59, 62, 63, 80, 119, 176, 177, 216.
" James Jr., 119.
" James 3rd, 119.
" John, 121, 124.
" Joseph, 123, 216, 219.
" Josiah Jr., 62.
" Lazarus, 125.
" Lucius M., 77.
" Niram, 120, 123, 124, 219.
" Theophilus, 120, 123.
" William G., 93, 219.
" Zadoc, 120, 179, 219.
Hare, Bishop Wm. Hobart, 87.
Harris, Dorothy, 232.
" Jabez, 219.
" Luther, 75, 123, 124.
Harrison, Francis, 216.
Hartnett, Patrick, 109, 115.
Haskins, Rev. Thomas W., 85, 93.
Hatch, Joseph, 120.
" Joshua, 135, 154, 219.
" Mark F., 125.
" Moses, 199.
" Peter, 219.
Hawley, Abel S., 127, 219.
" Arthur S., 233, 234, 262.
" Asa N., 172, 239.
" Benjamin, 97, 102, 105, 106, 119, 122, 123, 129, 190, 215, 218.
" Daniel B., 76, 154, 168, 172.
" Edgar F., 234, 262.
" Edson N., 229.
" Eleazer, 127.
" Elmer B., 229.
" Ephraim, 64, 96.
" Esther A., 229.
" Glover, 129, 170, 172.
" Helen, 231.
" Henry S., 260.
" Isaac N., 77, 122, 130, 133.
" Jabez, 126, 154.
" Jehiel, 64.
" Capt. John, 25.
" John, 127, 128.
" Joseph, 126, 154.
" Jotham B., 128, 154, 168.
" Julia Nichols, 260.
" Lemuel, 125, 127.
" Marcus C., 234.
" Mrs. Marcus C., 94, 95.
" Mary, 261.
" Robert N., 77, 98, 100, 101, 102, 106.
" Robert S., 239.
" Samuel, 62, 129.
" Stephen, 65, 216.
Hawley, Tyrus, 127.
" William, 120, 219.
" Wm. G., 229.
" Mrs. Wm. S., 234.
Hayes, E., 158.
" Josiah, 123, 124.
" Nathan A., 151.
Hazard, Samuel, 135.
Hecock, Capt. Ebenezer, 46.
Hendrix, James, 123.
" Roger, 122, 219.
" Zadoc, 219.
Hendrixson, Benoni, 120, 216.
" David, 216.
" Samuel, 216.
Henry, Benoni, 268.
" Nathaniel, 61.
" Samuel, 57, 59, 61.
Hensley, Dan, 235.
" Mount, 235.
Hepburn, Capt. Joseph, 123, 124.
" Silas, 122.
Hickson, Leo, 231.
Hill, Beach, 230.
" Harry T., 128.
" Henry S., 128.
" Hermon, 129.
Hills, Rev. Horace H., 84.
Hinman, David, 124.
" Joel, 201.
Hinsdale, Rev., 63.
Hoffman, Jos. Ogden, 247.
Hogan, E., 168.
Holian, Thomas, 238, 239.
Holly, Capt. John, 27, 33.
Holstander, Isaac F., 129.
Honan, Daniel C., 231.
" Jennie R., 232.
" Katherine, 231.
Hopkins, Hazel, 232.
" Joseph, 135.
Horr, Wm. L., 245.
Hosack, Dr., 210.
Hotchkiss, B., 168.
" Charles, 127.
Houlihan, Aileen, 232.
" Anna M., 232.
" F. Loretta, 231.
" Helen, 232.
" John G., 231.
" Mary V., 232.
" Michael J., 262.
Hoy, Wm. H., 98.
Hoyt, Rev. James P., 79, 230, 251.
" Jesse, 76.
" Mary, 231.
" Meeker, 76.
" Norman, 76.
Hubbard, Cornelia, 228.
" Dr. Robert, 212.
Hubbell, Amos, 152, 153.
" Anson, 128.
" Ebenezer, 119.
" Ephraim, 127.
" Eleazer, 215.
" Enoch, 219.
" Ezra Jr., 219.
" H. Carlton, 239, 263.
" Ichabod, 120.
" Jedediah, 120, 264.
" Jeptha, 120, 121, 219.
" John, 18, 125.
" John L., 128.
" Jonathan, 27, 28, 33, 51, 60, 64, 216.
" Joseph M., 129.
" Josiah, 18, 19.
" Lewis, 125.
" Nathan, 120.

INDEX

Hubbell, Peter, Town Clerk;
  15, 23, 26, 27, 33, 39,
  53, 56, 60, 65, 215, 219,
  264.
" Peter Jr., 119.
" Richard, 19.
" Samuel Jr., 19.
" Silas, 120, 121, 123.
" Stillman, 120.
" William, 127.
" William Homer, 209.
  238, 239, 263.
Hull, Elijah, 124, 219.
" Eliphalet, 104, 120, 219.
" Erastus, 128.
" Hanford, 129.
" John, 65, 119, 216, 219.
" Peter Clark, 123, 126.
" S., 168.
Hurd, Abel, 120, 219.
" Graham, 76.
" Jabez, 101.
" Oliver Clark, 125.
" Theophilus, 219.
" William B., 229.
Humphrey, Daniel, 123.
Hunt, D. H., 168.
Hyde, Cyrus, 138.
" Joseph, 219.

I

Innis, Albert C., 10.

J

Jackson, Daniel, 27, 28, 33, 57.
" David, 122, 219.
" David, Jr., 122, 219.
" Ephraim, 122, 124, 219.
" Gershom, 122, 124, 219.
" Levi, 127.
" Lewis, 41.
Jagger, Bishop Thomas A. 87
James, Catherine A., 232.
Jardine, George, 86.
Jarvis, Abraham, 129.
Jefferson, Pres. Thomas, 173.
Jennings, David, 127.
" Elijah, 75, 126.
" Ezra H., 127.
" Wm. B., 129.
Jewell, Ross, 231, 234.
" Mrs. Ross, 21.
Johnson, Abel, 75
" Abraham, 119.
" Alonzo, 129.
" Pres. Andrew, 171.
" Charles, 41, 76, 77, 101, 109, 128, 130, 227.
" Charles Beach, 10, 252, 253, 262.
" Clarrissa, 199.
" Cornelia, 199.
" David H., 85, 99, 170, 171, 209, 236, 238, 240.
" Mrs. David H., 98.
" Ebenezer, 14, 19, 33, 52, 64, 176, 178, 219.
" Elias, 129.
" Enos, 123.
" Ezra H., 9, 41, 75, 77, 126.
" Ezra Levan, 3, 91, 234, 243, 262.
" Mrs. Ezra L., 84, 91, 252.
" Frank L., 232.
" Frederick Foote, 10, 87, 91.
" Frederick F. Jr., 92.
" Ichabod, 9, 117, 119, 126, 219.
" Jacob, 75, 126.
" James, 210.
" Jeremiah, 64, 120.

Johnson, John, 117, 122, 124, 199, 219, 227.
" John Jr., 126.
" Julia Merritt, 10, 252.
" Levan Merritt, 10.
" Miles, 75, 126.
" Moses, 33, 64.
" Nathan, 128.
" Percy L., 10.
" Philo, 75.
" Susan Jane, 199.
" Walter, 129.
" William Camp, 10, 164, 252, 262.
" Mrs. Wm. C., 252.
Jones, David W., 76.
" William, 150, 168.
Jordan, Levi E., 127.
" Mae, 232.
" Philo M., 127.
" Timothy, 126.
Joy, Eliza Elliot, 199.
Judd, George, 230.
" Phineas, 46, 71.
" Taylor, 129.
Judson, Lieut. Abel, 119, 123, 124, 219.
" Abel Jr., 120.
" Abner, 76, 126, 183.
" Andrew, 171.
" Anson, 127.
" Rev. David, 36, 69, 70, 73, 81, 189, 190, 205.
" Ch. of Rev. David, 74.
" David & Mary, 190, 193.
" David, 123, 124, 136.
" Elijah, 125.
" Dr. George, 76, 211.
" Jerome, 159, 171, 236, 239.
" Dr. John, 120, 123, 124, 128, 210, 211, 219, 227.
" John, 172, 239.
" Joseph, 31.
" Martin, 127.
" Mary, 134.
" Dr. Monroe, 211, 236, 239, 260.
" Nathaniel, 123.
" Nellie, 230.
" Richard, 125.
" Samuel Lane, 125.
" Silas Burton, 125.
" Stiles H., 161.
" Thompson, 113.
" Zerah, 127.

K

Kane, Elisha Kent,
" John Jr., 109, 112.
Keane, Anna L., 232.
" Anna V., 231.
" Daniel J., 235.
" Helen M., 232.
" Joseph D., 232.
" Margaret L., 231.
" Mary, 232.
" M. G., 238.
" Thomas F., 232.
Keating, Joanna, 160.
" Margaret, 232.
" Martin, 162, 163, 164.
Keeler, Czar, 41, 143, 144, 158, 170, 171, 223, 242.
" Elizur W., 76.
" John C., 10.
" Mrs. John C., 10.
" Nathan W., 170, 171.
Keep, Florence, 230.
Kelly, John, 232.
" Mary T., 232.
Kemble, Daisy, 231.
Kennedy, Mrs. Arthur, 235.

Kent, Abigail, 69.
" Rev. Elisha, 69.
" Ch. of Rev. Elisha, 69.
" James, 69.
" Josiah, 69.
" Moss, 69.
" Samuel, 69.
" Thomas, 69.
" Thomas Jr., 69.
Kiernan, Dr. Walter H., 262.
Kilbride, Helen A., 232.
" Mary C., 232.
Kimball, H., 168.
Kimberly, Abraham, 21, 22, 26, 33, 43, 54, 55, 57, 96, 104, 120, 122, 176, 216, 219.
" Abraham Jr., 219.
" Eleazer, 14.
" Capt. E., 123.
" Ephraim, 136.
" Lieut. Ephraim, 136.
" Fitch, 122, 133, 138, 219.
Kirkland, C. A., 168.
Knapp, Nehemiah, 110.
Knight Dr. Wm. W., 234.
Kutscher, Viola P., 232.

L

Lacy, Eleazer, 122.
" Josiah, 120.
" R. B., 168.
Laflin, Mrs. Helen M., 234.
Lake, Ada J., 231.
" Carrie, 230.
" David, 125
" Ephraim, 120, 123, 124, 219.
" Ezra, 125.
" Harriet, 229.
" Jackson, 229.
" James, 102, 106.
" John, 27, 28, 33, 43, 60, 64, 96, 97, 119, 216, 219.
" John Jr., 120, 128, 219.
" Nathan, 105, 120, 219.
" Nichols B., 129.
" Peter, 104, 106, 123, 124.
" Philo, 128.
" Roswell, 129.
" Thomas, 219.
" Walter, 129.
" Walter B., 229.
" Widow, 96.
Lane, James, 219.
Lancaster, Mary F., 172.
Landers, Lemuel, 126.
Lang, Anna, 232.
Lattin, Benjamin, 109, 219.
" Eli S., 129.
" Gideon, 125.
" Granville, 111.
" Jacob, 127, 219.
" Luke, 123.
" Nathan, 126.
Lauzan, Chevalier de la, 139, 140, 141.
Law, Jonathan, 21.
Lawton, Marguerite, 231.
Leadbetter, Rev. Alexander, 75, 76.
Leavenworth, Andrew, 111.
" John, 22, 31, 45, 60, 61, 63, 65, 216.
" Mark E., 129.
" Thomas, 119, 216.
Leavy, Agnes, 232.
" Morris, 109, 114.
Lee, Martin, 94.
" Rev. Timothy J., 79, 262.

Lemon, George, 178.
Leonard, Wm. A., 157, 233, 238, 240, 263.
Lenihan, Rev. Francis, 191.
Lester, Catharine, 232.
" Mary, 231.
" Mrs., 107.
Lever, Henry K., 230.
Lewis, Abraham, 122.
" Agur, 126.
" Ebenezer, 109.
" Edmund, 31, 80.
" Isaac, 154.
" Israel, 154.
" James, 31.
" Peter, 183.
Lillis, Michael, 104, 106.
Lincoln, Abraham, 171.
Lines, Bishop Edwin S., 87.
Linsley, Rev. Geo. T., 10, 86, 234, 261, 262.
" Martha, 86.
" Mrs. Mary Chauncey 86, 234.
Lovell, Edward S., 240, 252.
Low, Samuel Jr., 246.
Lum, Edwin A., 76.
Lynch, C. Agnes, 232.
" Catherine V., 232.
" Jennie L., 232.
" Mary, 232.
" Mary W., 232.
" Mrs., 151.
" Patrick, 109, 115.
" Thomas F., 232.
Lyon, Alanson, 210.
" David, 126.
" Frederick, 229.
" Hezekiah, 120.
" Moses, 25, 59, 62.
" Nathaniel, 216.
" William, 216.

M

Madigan, James E., 250.
Madison, President, 173.
Mallaby, Rev. Thomas, 88, 94.
Mallette, Robert C., 250.
Mallory, Benjamin, 120, 264.
" Ebenezer, 125.
" John, 125.
" Nathaniel, 128, 190, 219.
" Widow, 109.
Maltbie, J. M., 202.
Marble, Rev. Dr. Newton F., 84, 203.
" Frances A., 230.
" Frederick P., 84, 203.
" Mary Gillis, 84, 203.
Marsh, Philo J., 77.
" Daniel, 168.
Marshall, Abigail, 77.
" Isaac, 77.
Mason, R. B., 169.
Martin, Dr. W. A., 92.
Masters, James, 126.
Mayers, Catherine, 232.
Mayhew, Jacob, 129.
" Jacob Jr., 129.
May, Henry, 168, 170, 171.
McCartan, Rev. James, 95.
McCarthy, Patrick H., 262.
McDonald, 164.
McEwen, Birdsey, 115.
MacFarland, Prof. H. B., 231.
" Mrs. H. B., 231.
McLaughlin, Dr. W. J., 262.
McMahon, Anthony, 103, 106.
McNamara, John, 162.
" Mary F., 231, 235.
Meeker, Capt. David, 122, 147, 149, 154, 191.

Merchant, Amos, 97, 119, 219.
Merritt, Abijah, 126, 149, 150, 161, 191.
" John, 108.
" Levan W., 129.
Merwin, John, 20.
" Stephen, 129.
Middlebrook, Charles H., 229.
" Franklin, 229.
" Jerome, 129.
" Robert, 127, 144.
" Sidney, 76, 129.
Miles, Joseph, 27, 28.
Millous, Robert, 172.
Mills, Ebenezer, 179.
" Elisha, 127, 208.
" John, 179.
" Jonathan, 28.
Minor, Chas. E., 94, 261.
" John, 19.
Mitchell, Bessie, 231.
" Edith W., 235.
" Frank W., 253.
" Mrs. F. W., 253.
" Lawrence, 100, 107, 108, 110, 114.
" Robert C., 238, 240.
" Wallace N., 253.
" Mrs. Wallace N., 253.
Moger, John, 120.
" Samuel, 215.
Moore, E. F., 168.
" Joseph, 151.
" Rev. Wm., 26, 78, 93.
More, John, 219.
Morehouse, Abel, 219.
" Daniel, 41, 127, 219.
" Stephen, 219.
Morgan, Daniel N., 85.
" Ezra, 103, 106, 129, 237, 238.
" Mary C., 234.
" Nathaniel, 48.
" Zedekiah, 121.
Morris, Adonijah, 60.
" Amos, 125.
" Charles G., 201.
" Daniel Jr., 109, 126.
" Daniel, 122, 125.
" Eleazer, 38.
" Eli Gould, 201.
" Eli J., 93, 94, 151.
" James, 127.
" John, 28.
" Levi C. Sr., 172.
" Levi C. 2nd, 245, 251, 252, 263.
" Mrs. L. C., 234.
" Levi Phillips, 232.
" Luzon B., 201, 229.
" Martha J., 229, 230.
" Dr. Robert, 201.
" Roy, 201.
Moss, Abigail, 69.
" Rev. Joseph, 69.
Munson, Joseph O., 229.
Mott, Arthur, 229.
" S., 158.
Murphy, Annie, 232.
" Catherine, 231.
" Hugh, 125.
" Mary, 232.
Murray, Joseph, 64.
Murry, Patten, 125.

N

Nash, David, 128.
" Dennis, 126.
" John, 128, 243.
" Micajah, 126.
" Peter, 191.
Nettleton, Abner Anson, 126, 183, 237, 238, 239, 240.
" Arthur T., 138, 182.
233, 234.
Nettleton, Joseph, 129.
" Theophilus, 120, 190, 219.
Newland, Albert, 212.
" J. Selwyn, 212.
Nichols, Rev. Abel, 89, 125.
" Beach, 98.
" Benjamin, 20, 120.
" Caleb, 219.
" Charles, 251.
" Charlotte, 233.
" David H., 115, 125.
" Daniel, 126.
" Dina, 179.
" Drusus, 129.
" Elijah, 120, 123, 124, 154, 224.
" Gideon, 219.
" Henry, 260.
" Henry T., 229, 237, 239, 240.
" Isaac, 77, 128.
" Capt. James, 77, 89.
" Capt. Jonathan, 219.
" Joseph, 125, 225.
" Lemuel, 124, 154.
" Lucy Beach, 89.
" Mary, 260.
" Nathaniel, 119, 127, 179, 216, 219.
" Capt. Peter, 97, 104, 120, 123, 124, 127, 195, 197, 219, 241, 242, 244.
" Philo, 240, 244.
" Mrs. Rebekah, 195.
" Richard, 19, 83, 117, 120.
" Richmond, 219.
" Sarah Blackman, 260.
" Simeon, 128.
" Stephen, 127.
" Thaddeus H., 129.
" Theophilus, 121, 122, 124, 128, 233, 236, 237, 238, 240, 243.
Nickerson, Job, 125.
Noble, Charles, 227.
Norman, Wilhelmina, 229.
Northrop, Abel, 219.
" Alanson, 126.
" Lieut. Amos, 120, 122, 124, 135, 136, 219, 221.
" Andrew, 111, 114, 123, 168, 184.
" Asa, 124.
" Benjamin, 44, 60, 64, 119, 215, 219.
" Benjamin Jr., 120, 219.
" Charles, 129.
" Chas. H., 203, 233, 237, 239, 240, 262.
" Mrs. Chas. H., 231.
" C. P., 245.
" Cyrenin, 127.
" David, 129.
" Deacon, 73.
" Drake, 123, 124.
" Edgar F., 255.
" Edith N., 232.
" Eleanor L., 203, 231.
" Elizur, 129.
" Enos, 120, 121, 219.
" Ezra, 120, 124, 219.
" George, 110, 123, 124, 143.
" George A., 245, 252.
" Gideon, 104, 110.
" Heman, 102, 105, 110.
" Hezekiah, 126.
" Hosea B., 240.
" Isaiah, 121, 127, 219.
" James, 127.
" Jeremiah, 119, 176, 215, 219.
" Jerome, 116.
" Job, 119, 121, 122, 216.
" Capt. John, (Town Clerk), 45, 48, 59, 61,

INDEX

63, 64, 65, 67, 69, 70. 80, 103, 117, 119, 121. 122, 216, 219, 266, 267.
Northrop, John Jr., 126, 179, 180.
" John J., 171, 240, 253, 262.
" Jonathan, 73, 120, 133.
" Joshua, 133, 134, 136, 219.
" Julia L., 203.
" Mary A., 232.
" Nathan, 123.
" Nathaniel, 120.
" Nehemiah, 219.
" Nelson W., 203.
" Norman, 110, 128.
" Oliver, 127, 183.
" Oliver T., 210.
" Peter, 125.
" Reuben, 129.
" Samuel, 75, 125.
" Sheldon, 129.
" Thomas, 64, 119, 215.
" Wait, 123, 124, 219.
" Walter, 127.
" William N., 123, 124, 203, 219, 240.
" William Jr., 219.
" Zalmon, 127.
Norton, Philo, 83, 124.
" Nathan, 120.

O

Ogden, Ebenezer, 219.
Olmstead, Charles, 232.
" Elbert, 112, 150.
" Wilbur E., 232.
Olson, Bessie, 231.
Oppe, Herman, 232.
Orgleman, Augustus W., 93.
Osborne, Ephraim, 33.
" Joseph, 28.
Otis, John M., 230.

P

Page, Edgar C., 172.
Palmer, Carrie Mason, 92.
Parmalee, Amos, 126.
" David, 126.
" George, 111.
" Grandison, 76.
" Hermon, 129.
" Hiram, 76, 77, 102, 104, 128, 202.
" Jedidiah, 216, 219.
" Levi, 128.
" Marcus H., 126, 129, 183.
" Nathaniel, 126, 216.
" Noah, 119, 121, 216, 219.
" Philo, 128.
" Rufus, 76, 128.
" Samuel, 64, 216.
" Stephen, 27, 33, 37, 52, 59, 64, 120, 176, 189, 216.
Parks, Michael, 41, 75, 155.
Parsons, Rev. Arthur, 91.
" Charles M., 93, 107, 113, 252.
" Mary E., 76.
" Moses, 161, 221, 236, 240.
" Pearl F., 230.
Patch, Anthony, 249.
" Ezra, 161, 172.
Patrick, Brig. Gen. Samuel H., 138.
Payne, Charles H., 94.
Pearce, Samuel, 64.
" Thomas, 64.
" John T., 250.

Pease, F. W., 168.
Peck, Aaron, 104, 120, 179, 220.
" Abbie L., 233, 234.
" Abel T., 77.
" Abner,
" Abraham, 127.
" Capt. Albert W., 213. 229.
" Albert W. Jr., 213.
" Amiel, 123, 219.
" Amos G., 77, 126, 154, 227, 240.
" Andrew Jr., 126.
" Annie Curtis, 214.
" Mrs. Ann E., 77, 194.
" Arthur, 110.
" Asher, 123, 154.
" Benajah, 219.
" Charles Henry, 98.
" Charles, 128, 112, 115, 138, 157, 171, 182, 233, 236, 240.
" Charles G., 262.
" Lieut. Col. Charles Howard 213, 263.
" Charles Howard Jr. 213.
" Dan, 126, 183.
" Daniel, 75, 120, 126, 220
" David, 41, 75, 122, 124, 184.
" David C., 237, 238, 240 262, 263.
" Dillazon, 107, 129.
" Dr. Earle, 214, 230.
" Ebenezer, 120, 126, 178 220.
" Edmond B., 127.
" Eli, 123, 126.
" Elihu, 220.
" Elijah, 123.
" Elliott M., 77, 214, 240
" Elnathan, 126.
" Enoch, 123, 220.
" Enos, 183.
" Ephraim, 31, 33, 57, 59, 67, 72, 119, 120, 216, 220.
" Ethel, 120.
" Ezekiel, 127, 129.
" Ezra, 73, 120, 220.
" George B., 76, 123, 124
" George B., 229.
" George C., 76, 98, 99.
" Gideon, 72, 123, 125, 220
" Hannah D. F., 234.
" Harley, 76.
" Harry, 90, 104, 201.
" Capt. Henry, 120, 134, 135, 194, 219.
" Henry S., 229.
" Hermon, 129.
" Hermon H., 99, 105.
" Heth, 36, 47, 66, 70, 71, 119, 219.
" Heth Jr., 120, 219.
" Hezekiah, 129, 240.
" Isaac, 123, 124, 184.
" Israel, 128.
" Jabez B., 77, 104, 121, 123, 129, 220, 227.
" James, 36, 120.
" James A., 232.
" John, 119, 120, 124, 117, 220.
" John B., 237, 238, 240.
" Jonathan 126.
" Joseph, (Town Clerk) 14, 16, 20, 22, 28, 33, 35, 52, 55, 64, 96, 120, 159, 176, 177, 267.
" Joseph Jr., 64, 73, 117, 216, 220.
" Joshua, 122.
" Judson, 126.
" Lemuel, 126.
" Lewis, 174.

Peck, Levi, 77, 123, 128.
" Liverius, 122, 124.
" Lucius, 128.
" Mary F., 233.
" Mrs. Mary, 194.
" Matthew, 123.
" Miel, 120.
" Moses 120, 123, 124, 154, 220.
" Nathan, 120, 126.
" Nathaniel, 72, 119, 123 220.
" Nelson J., 229.
" Oliver, 77, 127, 246.
" Mrs. Phebe, 94.
" Richard, 127.
" Robert S., 227, 260.
" Rufus, 125.
" Samuel, 123, 154, 220, 227.
" Samuel B., 128, 161, 162, 183, 236.
" Sherwood, 208.
" Simeon B., 103, 106, 129, 237, 238, 240, 260.
" Theodosia, 76.
" Truman, 126.
" William M., 129.
" Wooster, 76, 77, 184, 227.
" Zalmon S., 122, 124, 167, 171, 195, 233, 252, 253.
" Mrs. Zalmon S., 252.
" Mrs. Zilpha, 195.
Penny, Dr. C. M., 262.
Perry, Agur, 128.
" Dr. Bennett, 123, 145, 198, 208, 210, 241, 242, 243, 244.
" Daniel, 125.
" Joseph, 125, 129.
" Mary, 198.
" Dr. Nathaniel, 208.
" Peter, 127.
" Rev. Philo, 83, 86, 190, 193, 244.
" Truman, 130.
Phillips, Samuel, 149.
Pierce, B. D. Co., 164.
" Francis, 123, 220.
" President Franklin, 170.
Pierson, Stephen, 120.
Pintard, John, 246.
Pitzchler, Oscar, 187.
Platt, Bennett, 129.
" Charles, 232.
" Charles S., 88, 233, 234, 262.
" Ebenezer, 64, 216.
" Eli, 150.
" Edmund C., 172.
" Ella E., 230, 233, 234.
" Ephraim, 126, 183.
" Francis H., 232.
" Isaac, 126.
" Jarvis, 111, 126.
" Jennette Tuttle, 202.
" John, 25, 28, 33, 44, 54, 60, 64, 120, 216.
" Johnson T., 202.
" Joseph, 73.
" Josiah & wife, 100, 121, 126, 190, 220, 264, 265, 266.
" Judson, 129.
" Justus, 126.
" Moses, 73, 119, 121, 190, 220.
" Nathan, 126.
" Percival C., 232.
" Philo N., 150.
" Philo T., 130, 202.
" R. H., 168.
" Sylvanus, 129.
" Theron E., 238, 240.
" Timothy, 106.

Platt, Wanzer, 114.
" William,
Plummer, D. B., 230.
Polk, President James K., 199.
Porter, Mrs. Alosia, 109, 111, 115.
" Wm. Arthur, 229.
Potter, Rev. Collis P., 93.
Pratt, C., 168.
" Mrs. Charles M., 201.
Pray, Margaret, 200.
Prentice, T. P., 168.
Preston, Nathan, 241.
Prime, James, 46.
Prindle, Lieut. Abel, 120, 123, 124, 220, 244.
" Abel B., 240.
" Abijah, 220.
" Abram, 127.
" Albert, 129.
" Ammon, 208.
" Cyrus, 122, 124.
" Daniel, 125, 207.
" Ebenezer, 21, 26, 27, 28, 33, 54, 55, 59, 65.
" Eldad, 126.
" Eliadah, 220.
" Ephraim, 65, 97, 102, 216, 220.
" James, 122, 220.
" Jedidiah, 64.
" Jehoshaphat, 65, 120, 122, 216, 220.
" Joel, 122, 125, 220.
" Jonathan, 120, 124, 178, 220, 221, 241, 244.
" Capt. Joseph, 65, 97, 119, 120, 122, 124, 216, 220.
" Julia, 160.
" Lazarus, 122, 125.
" Nathan, 121.
" Riverius, 75, 126.
" Mrs. Ruth, 160.
" Samuel, 33, 53, 120.
" Sarah M., 229.
" Seth, 128.
" William, 220.
" Zachariah, 127.
Pulford, Oliver, 103.

R

Randall, Delia Beers, 212.
" Legrand, 212.
" Ophelia, 212.
Raymond, Jacob, 125.
" John, 111, 126.
" Orrin, 129.
Ray, Harold, 232.
Read, Evelyn B., 232.
" John, 33.
Reiner, Frederick, 172.
Revere, Paul, 130.
Reynolds, Willson M., 171.
Roberts, Joel, 220.
" Thomas, 106, 120, 126, 220.
" Lula, 231.
Robson, Elizabeth, 134.
Rochambeau, Count de, 139, 140.
Rogers, Rev. John, 95.
" Mrs. M. C., 230.
Rood, M., 27, 28, 51.
Roosevelt, Theodore, 171.
Rowland, Hezekiah, 126.
" Jabez, 111.
" Joseph, 126.
Ruffels, Anna, 232.
" Bessie D., 232.
" Grace, 232.
" Jennie M., 232.
" Ruth, 232.
Rugg, David, 110.
" Oliver, 220.

S

Salmon, Ethel, 231.
Sample, George, 123.
" Miss, 230.
Sanford, Aaron, 84, 109, 112, 237, 238, 240.
" Amos C., 128, 264, 265.
" Amos N., 126.
" Augusta, 229.
" Daniel C., 123, 125.
" David, 24, 113, 126, 130, 161.
" Ebenezer, 119, 124, 216, 220.
" Elias F., 229.
" Elijah, 23, 160.
" Emily A., 76.
" Frederick, 240.
" Frederick C., 172.
" George P., 233, 234.
" Hannah (Widow), 220, 264, 265.
" Harriet Emma, 92.
" Henry, 84, 156, 236, 237, 240, 250.
" Hezekiah, 106, 220, 264, 265, 266.
" Isaac, 125.
" James, 121, 220.
" Jeanie, 78.
" Jessie, 230.
" Job, 216.
" John, 119, 220.
" John Jr., 124.
" John L., 93.
" Jonah Jr., 97, 127, 220.
" Jonathan, 44, 103, 142, 220.
" Josiah, 127, 161, 227.
" Capt. Julius, 235, 245.
" Louis, 264, 265, 266.
" Mrs. Mary, 228.
" Moses, 120.
" Nathaniel, 220.
" Samuel, 21, 22, 26, 27, 33, 54, 65, 120, 123, 128, 216, 220, 264, 265, 266.
" Solomon, 103, 124.
" Squire John, 23.
" Stephen, 125.
" Thomas, 120, 127, 220, 264, 265, 266.
" Wm. Atwater, 23.
" W. J., 98.
" Zalmon, 126.
Scatacooks, 51.
Scanlon, Catharine, 232.
" Michael, 141.
Schermerhorn, John J., 252.
" Mrs. John J., 252.
" Mrs. Sarah F., 44.
Schultz, Prof., 230.
Scott, George, 76, 77.
Scudder, Isaac, 41, 126.
" Susan, 78.
" William, 130.
Seabury, Bishop, 83.
Sears, James, 75.
Seeley, A., 158.
" Eli B., 109, 112, 115.
" Jeremiah, 215.
" Sergt. John, 24, 27, 28, 33, 57, 176.
" Nehemiah, 220.
" Ottmiel, 220.
" Robert, 57, 59, 62, 215, 220.
" Robert Jr., 215.
" Tom, 143.
Sharp, Eliakim, 126, 137.
" Thomas, 26, 33, 59, 60, 117, 119, 122, 137, 216, 220.
" Widow, 27, 59.
" 119, 216.
Shaw, E. H., 237.

Shelton, Benjamin F., 127, 223.
Shepard Abraham, 73, 220.
or
Shepherd, Ammon, 76, 126, 149, 183.
" Amos, 110, 123, 149.
" Andrew Jr., 126.
" Charles, 128.
" Daniel, 125.
" David, 110.
" George, 110, 127.
" George Jr., 126, 128.
" Dr. Gideon, 145, 205, 206, 207, 211.
" Dr. Gideon's Children 206.
" Hannah, 76.
" Hart,
" Henry, 127.
" Horace, 41.
" James, 123.
" John, 68, 104, 119, 120, 126, 216, 220.
" Joseph, 128.
" Lemuel, 126.
" Capt. Moses, 40, 75, 108, 112, 122, 126, 133, 136.
" Nathan, 126.
" Niram, 128.
" Peter, 128.
" Reuben, 127.
" Richard D., 126, 183.
" Rufus, 128.
" Simeon, 125, 128, 220.
" Stephen, 123.
" Sueton, 127.
" Dr. Timothy, 41, 73, 105, 120, 125, 147, 149, 216, 220.
Sherman, Amos, 122, 123, 124.
" Andrew, 127.
" Benjamin, 21, 25, 27.
" Benoni, 119.
" Charles, 128.
" Clark, 127.
" Cyrus, 126.
" Cyrus B., 240.
" Daniel, 122, 216.
" David, 120, 128, 220.
" Ebenezer, 124.
" Edward M., 229.
" Edwin M., 229.
" Elijah, 126.
" Ephraim, 120, 124, 135, 136, 179, 220.
" Ezra, 123, 127, 183.
" Henry, 128.
" Jabez, 126.
" Job, 27, 28, 33, 65, 66, 67, 69, 70, 71, 119, 220, 263, 267.
" Joel, 120.
" John, 38, 112, 119, 128, 190, 220.
" Jonathan, 75, 120.
" Joseph, 126.
" Joseph Jr., 129, 170.
" Jotham, 122, 126, 129, 131, 150, 220.
" Lauriston, 129.
" Lemuel, 105, 120, 220.
" Lewis F., 122, 124.
" Linus, 126.
" Lue L., 127.
" Mary J., 229, 230.
" Matthew, 126, 215.
" McPherson, 128, 247.
" Nathan, 120, 121, 127, 136, 220.
" Norris, 229.
" Ornan, 127.
" Philo, 126.
" Philo Jr., 127.
" Philo B., 229.
" Rev. Samuel, 62, 63, 215.

INDEX

Sherman, Truman, 123, 127, 128, 183.
" Warren, 161.
" William, 76.
" William A., 94.
" Wooster, 183.
" Zadoc, 120, 129, 131, 220.
" Zardis, 126.
Sherwood, Daniel, 125.
" Ebenezer, 154.
" E. F., 168.
" John, 73.
" John P., 220.
" Justus, 108, 113.
" Roswell L., 127.
" Thomas, 19.
Sheville, John, 245.
Shipman, David, 183.
" Elias, 242.
Short, Sue, 231.
Shultz, Prof., 233.
Silliman, Eugene R., 229.
Sinnott, Rev. George, 95, 262.
Skidmore, Abel, 121, 124.
" Abel B., 129, 227.
" Ammon, 125.
" Amos, 124.
" Daniel, 77, 128, 227.
" Elias, 136.
" Elnathan, 105, 120, 125.
" Glover, 128.
" Herbert, 234.
" Isaac, 126.
" Dr. James, 209.
" Jane A., 210.
" John, 75, 120, 126, 128, 220.
" John R., 129.
" Marietta, 210.
" Martha E., 210.
" Mary Caroline, 229.
" Nehemiah, 105, 119, 127, 220.
" Philo N., 240.
" Polly Sherman, 209.
" Lieut. Thomas, 35, 60, 65, 80, 97, 119, 120, 131, 181, 215, 220, 267.
" Robert R., 229.
" Dr. Rufus, 209.
" William, 229.
Skiff, Clarence, 232.
Smith, Abel, 122.
" A. D., 168.
" Alice C., 232.
" Allison P., 234, 250, 251, 262.
" Ammon, 129.
" Amos, 120, 124, 126, 220.
" Arthur J., 231, 234, 240, 250, 262, 263.
" Benjamin D., 232.
" Brace, 183.
" Carlton S., 231.
" Charles E., 229.
" Rev. Charles H., 250.
" Ebenezer, 24, 27, 35, 52, 53, 54, 55, 135.
" Edwards M., 262.
" Capt. George, 105, 135, 220.
" G. B., 168.
" Rev. Henry Bagg, 78.
" Henry M., 250.
" Horace A., 232.
" John, 122, 124.
" Lieut. Joseph, 48, 67, 119, 120, 121, 179, 220.
" Dea. Joseph 3rd, 128, 220.
" Lyman, 129.
" Reuben Hazen, 234, 250, 251, 252.

Smith, Mrs. R. H., 251, 252.
" Capt. Richard, 49, 120, 122, 124, 135, 136, 220.
" Robert D., 250, 251.
" Russell D., 128.
" Squire Van, 128.
" Rev. Zephaniah, 124.
Sniffen, Rev. Charles, 10.
" H. Birdsey, 235.
" Mrs. H. Birdsey, 235.
" William B., 93, 172.
Sperry Alexander, 103.
Stanley, Caleb, 25.
Staples, Samuel, 126.
" Samuel J., 127.
Stark, Maj. Gen. John, 84, 203.
Starling, Jacob, 197.
" John, 197, 220.
" Samuel, 197.
" Sarah, 197.
Starkweather, Isabella, 210.
Starr, Edward, 236, 240.
" Etheil, 126.
Stebbins, William, 129.
Steele, Rev. Alexander, 79, 262.
Sterling, David, 75, 125, 154.
" John, 73, 115.
" Wm., 168.
Stevens, Hon. George, 203.
" Mildred, 232.
" Polodore, 115.
" Solomon W., 128.
" Mrs. Wm. H., 235.
Stilson, Abel, 99, 105, 129, 184, 233, 240.
" Ambrose, 76, 77.
" Andrew, 120, 122, 220.
" Bailey, 120, 220, 221.
" Benjamin, 102, 104, 120, 124, 215.
" Benjamin Jr. 120, 123, 220.
" Carlos D., 262.
" Charles L., 129.
" David, 127, 220.
" Elijah, 120, 123, 220.
" Elnathan, 129.
" Hawley, 127.
" Hugh, 60, 63, 96.
" Isaac, 129, 220.
" Jacob, 123, 125, 220.
" James B., 119, 126, 215
" Jonathan, 216, 220.
" Joseph, 119, 123, 215.
" Jotham, 129.
" Lazarus, 125.
" Moses, 60, 69, 97, 119, 126.
" Moses, Jr., 119.
" Peter, 125.
" Samuel, 215.
" Sarah, 195.
" Thomas, 104, 121, 124, 220.
" Vincent, 180, 195, 220.
" William, 105, 110.
" Zenas, 125.
Stocking, Rev. S. S., 84, 93.
Stoddard, Letty J., 252.
Stone, Rev. Benj. W., 84.
" Joel, 158.
Storo, Abram, 28.
Stratton, Rev. Samuel, 84, 93, 227.
St. John, Gould, 75.
Strisik, Dora, 232.
Strong, Nehemiah, 122, 124, 137.
Stuart, George M., 232.
Sturges, Isaac M., 200.
Summers, Beera P., 127.
or
Somers, Lieut. B., 121, 122, 133, 136, 220.
" Bertha, 232.
" David, 125.

Summers, Ebenezer, 220.
" Gershom, 117, 120, 127, 220.
" John, 122, 214.
" Jonah, 123.
" Marcus B., 128.
" Marion E., 232.
" Maude, 232.
" Niram, 122.
" Oliver, 129.
" Phebe, 154.
" Robert, 87, 125, 220.
" Rufus, 128, 261.
" Ensign Samuel, 65, 119, 120, 220.

T

Taber, Earl, 232.
Tait, P., 168.
Talbot, Fannie Isabella, 203.
Taylor, Abner 220.
" Alonzo, 94, 129.
" Ammon 94.
" Cornelius B., 237, 238, 240, 251, 263.
" David, 128, 129.
" David, J., 129.
" Ebenezer, 220.
" Eli, 149.
" George F., 235.
" Jabez, 128.
" Joshua H., 129.
" Lawrence, 171.
" Levi, 128.
" Phineas, 149, 154.
" Reuben, 122.
" Stephen, 125, 154.
" Thomas, 23, 129.
" William A., 108.
" William B., 128.
" Wooster, 129.
" Pres. Zachary, 170.
" Zalmon, 126.
Teglman, Louise, 212.
Tenney, Eldad, 123.
Terrill Abel B., 129, 240.
or
Turrill, Lieut. Amos, 38, 75, 103, 121, 126, 133, 135, 136, 220.
" Botsford, 128, 227, 240.
" Daniel, 123, 128.
" Elijah B., 130.
" Emma F., 234.
" Frederick B., 229.
" Capt. George, 38, 121, 122, 133, 136, 215, 220.
" James, 41, 75, 126.
" Jared, 220.
" Job S., 75, 127.
" Jonathan, 120.
" Reuben, 75, 122.
" Roger, 40, 73, 75, 103, 123, 125, 220.
" William L., 240.
Thomas, James, 75, 123.
" Dr. Lemuel, 97, 123, 189, 193, 205, 220.
" Dr. Lemuel, ch. of, 205.
Thompson, Robert, 220.
" Mrs. Sherwood, 235.
Thorpe, Herman S., 129.
" Joel, 136.
Tiemann, Hermann N. Sr., 210, 262.
Tibbals, Rev. Charles, 94.
Tilson, Ruth, 232.
Timanus, Solomon, 127.
Tivorback, I., 246.
Tomlinson, Beach, 125.
" Isaac, 126.
" Isaiah, 129.
" Josiah, 125, 161, 248.
" Mary, 76.
" Webb, 125.
" Zachariah, 127.

INDEX

Tongue, Nelson, 128.
" Norman, 129.
" Orrin, 129.
Toucey, Abel, 123, 124.
or
Tousey, "Brother", 243.
" David, 125.
" Deborah, 196.
" Donald, 123.
" Hon. Isaac, 123, 124, 199.
" Mrs. Jerusha 196.
" John, 220.
" Joseph, 126, 184.
" Oliver, 43, 49.
" Oliver Jr., 125, 133, 154, 196, 220.
" Philo, 123, 191.
" Philo Jr., 128.
" Russell, 128.
" Sarah, 198.
" Sinclair, 77.
" Rev. Thomas, 33, 33, 36, 45, 46, 54, 55, 57, 58, 63, 65, 72, 120, 189, 193, 216.
" Ch. of Rev. Thomas, 58.
" Zalmon, 154, 196, 220.
Towner, Nathaniel, 120.
Travers, Anna J., 202.
Treadwell, John, 33.
" Timothy, 123, 220.
Treat, Amos, S. 77, 170, 171, 200, 202, 228.
" Robert, 201.
Troy, Lillian, 231.
Trowbridge, Isaac, 123, 124.
" Jeremiah T., 128.
" Samuel, 123, 126.
Tucker, Franklin W., 229.
" Harry W. 129, 161.
Turner, Abigail, 101.
" Albert, 98, 102.
" Ebenezer, 41, 125, 149.
" James, 94, 98.
" Jeremiah, 21, 24, 27, 33, 36, 101, 178, 216, 220.
" John, 125.
" Nathan, 126.
" Samuel, 215.
" Wilmont, 216.
Tuttle Eugenia, 201.
Twitchell, Harrison, 129.
" Isaac, 128.

U

Urmston, Rev. N. M., 75.

V

Vance, Joseph McArthur, 237.
Veness, Rychie E., 232.

Vinton, Rt. Rev. Alexander 87.

W

Wainwright, Curtis, 123.
Walker, Abigail, 77.
" Alfred, 262, 263.
" Eliakim, 155.
" John, 123.
" Susan, 229.
Wallace, Crossley, 232.
" John, 123.
Ward, Thomas, 129.
Warner, Augustus, 229.
" Austin, 262.
" Beeman P. 125.
" Charles C., 129, 227, 237, 239, 240.
" Henry Hawley, 262.
" Hermon, 125, 183.
" Hobart G., 261.
" Hobart G. Jr., 261.
" James H. 93, 94, 240.
" John, 260.
" Noadiah, 124.
" William B., 128.
Warren, Irene, 231.
Washburn, Amason, 127.
" Dr. Nathan 87, 120, 122, 220.
" Zenas 123.
Washington, Gen. George, 139, 140, 141.
Watkins, Samuel, 126.
Weed, Rev. Joseph, 54.
Welch, Blanche, 232.
" Thomas, 126.
Wells, David, 127.
" Isaac 125.
" Josiah, 183.
Wetmore, Ephraim P., 128, 183.
" John 128.
" Josiah, 127.
" Vivian, 232.
Wheeler, Aaron, 127.
" Abraham, 123.
" Amos H., 127.
" Andrew, 60, 73, 125, 183, 215, 220.
" David, 126.
" Edward, 128.
" Eli, 123, 124.
" Ezra, 194.
" George, 108.
" Henry L. 162, 172.
" Isaac, 125.
" James, 127 229.
" Johannah, 194.
" John B., 77, 127, 171, 172, 229, 238 240.
" Capt. Joseph, 38, 73, 75, 76, 77, 97, 105, 124, 220.
" Joseph Jr., 125.

Wheeler, Joseph, 128, 220.
" Lemuel, 120, 220.
" Lieut. Obadiah, 66, 67, 68, 70, 75, 119, 120, 194, 215, 220.
" Obadiah Jr., 120, 123, 220.
" Russell, 76.
" Roswell, 129.
" Thomas, 220.
Whitaker, Rt. Rev. Ozias, 87
White, Rt. Rev. John H., 92.
" Mrs. Sarah K., 90.
Whitlock, David Jr., 19.
" Stephen C., 112.
Whitney, Abel, 128.
" Philo 128.
Whittingham, Rev. Richard, 89.
Wilcoxen, John, 31.
" Nathan J., 128.
Wile, Dr. Wm. C., 163.
Wilkins, Rev. G. Morris, 86, 234.
Williams, Rt. Rev. John, 86, 90, 94.
" Alma, 231.
" Ammon, 130.
" Buckland, 216.
" Chief Justice, 231.
" Randolph, 231.
Wilson, E. W. 99.
" Prof. Francis M., 230.
Winton, Abel, 123.
" Abram, 129.
" Czar, 127.
" Daniel, 220.
" George, 172.
" Lockwood, 125.
Woffenden, George 245.
Wolcott, William, 142.
Wood, Henry, 73, 120, 121, 122, 136.
Woodruff, Rev. Curtis, 93.
Woolsey, John H. 229.
Wooster, Charles W. 228.
Wright, Frank, 238, 240, 250, 262.
" Leonard F., 232.
" Lucie, 232.
" Moses 97.
" Rev. Otis Olney, 94, 235, 262.
" William, 120, 220.

Y

Yeats, Captain, 142.

Z

Zabonlinski H. 168.

INDEX TO NEWTOWN'S MILITARY RECORD 1776—1918

A

Adams, James	273
Albertin, E. T.	275
Alldis, Frederick	272
Allen, Dorothy	281
Allen, Dorothy	281
Allen Edward B.	276
Allen, Mrs. Edw. B.	281
Allen, Eliphalet	269
Anderson, Fred	278
Anderson, Samuel	269
Andrews, David	271
Ashmead, George	275
Atwood, Samuel	269

B

Bailey, Jesse M.	278
Bailey, John F.	278
Baldwin, Abel	269
Baldwin, Caleb	269
Baldwin, Isaac	269
Bale, Thomas	278
Ball, Chas. H.	275
Banks, Allen	273
Banks, Edward	271
Banks, Edwin	273
Barnett, Rev. Francis B.	278
Barnett, Rev. Joseph N.	278
Barnett, Wm. Edw.	278
Beehler, Chas. H.	278
Beehler, Robert M.	278
Beers, Geo. Herbert	278
Beers, Hawley	273
Beers, H. Sanford	278
Beers, James M.	272
Behn, W. L.	278
Benedict, Edwin	272
Benedict, Ephraim	275
Benedict, Henry W.	272
Bennett, Ezekiel	269
Bigelow, Henry B.	272
Bissel, Henry	271
Blake, James E.	278
Blake, Martin	271
Blake, Michael	278
Blakeman, Chas. G.	275
Blakeman, Mrs Austin B.	281
Booth, Charles, Jr.	272
Booth, Starr	272
Botsford, Abel	269
Botsford, Elijah	269
Botsford Gideon B.	272
Botsford, Israel	271
Botsford, Jack	269
Botsford, Lemuel	272
Bradley, George A.	275
Bradley, Thomas	272
Brew, Mrs. Thomas F.	281
Brewster, John H.	271
Briscoe, Charles L.	272
Briscoe, Ephraim D.	275
Briscoe George	271
Briscoe Gustavus	272
Bristol, Caesar	269
Brooks, Samuel	269
Brooks, Thomas	269
Brown, George W.	271
Brown, Jeremiah	271
Brown, Jerome	273
Bulkley, George	271
Bumford, John H.	273
Burritt, Chas. H.	271
Burritt, Bailey	269
Butcher, Charles	275

C

Camp, Daniel	275
Camp, George B.	275
Camp, Samuel	269
Carey, H. F.	278
Carey, T. P.	278
Carley, Edward	271
Carley, Michael	275
Carmody, Richard	278
Carr, Wm. E.	278
Casey, Bernard	275
Cavenaugh, Paul	278
Chandler, John	269
Chapman, Chas.	272
Chipman, Chas. C.	272
Clark, Allen B.	271
Clark, Lemuel B.	275
Clark, Newell	272
Clark, Robert	271
Clinton, George	273
Coger, Henry B.	275
Coger, Mrs. Herbert T.	281
Coholan, Philip	278
Cole, Chas.	278
Coley, George S.	271
Colgan, Matthew	275
Conger, Chas. T.	275
Conger, Martin L.	278
Conger, Wm. R.	278
Conley, William	271
Connell, Wm.	271
Corbett, Michael	272
Cornell, Hiram	273
Costello, Michael	275
Crick, James W.	278
Crofutt, Horace S.	275
Cunningham, John	271
Curtis, Abijah B.	269
Curtis, Chas. G.	275
Curtis, Jasper L.	273
Curtis Joseph	272
Curtis, Wm. E.	272

D

Davidson, George T.	278
Davis, Caleb	273
Davis, Daniel	271
Davis, William	271
Dayton, Chas. W.	275
Deolph, Levy	269
Dick, Chas. L.	272
Dimelow, George	272
Dimon, Arthur	273
Donlon, Michael J.	278
Downs, Monroe D.	272
Downs, Oliver	272
Downs, Smith	272
Driscoll, Wm. E.	278
Dubret, Albert	278
Dunn, Hugh	273
Dunning, Edward A.	271
Dunning, Jared	269
Dutcher, Richard H.	278

E

Eagen, Andrew	273
Eagen, James	272
Edgett, Seneca	271
Edmond, William	269
Edwards, Chas. L.	278
Edwards, Levi, H.	271
Elko, Andrew, Jr.	278
Elwood, Frederick	271
Elwood, William	272
Evans, James	273
Evarts, George A.	271

F

Fairchild, Alpheus B.	272
Fairchild, Arthur W.	278
Fairchild, Henry W.	271
Fairchild, Kiah B.	269
Fairchild, Lewis H.	272
Fairchild, Peter W.	269
Fairchild, Reuben A.	272
Fairchild, Robert B.	274
Fairchild, Robert D.	278
Fairchild, Theodore	
Fairman, Arthur	272
Fairweather, Sam'l	269
Farrell, John W.	272
Farrell, Michael	271
Faulkner, John H.	271
Ferris, George	278
Ferris, John	275
Ferris, Nathan	269
Fischer, William	273
Flannagan, Andrew	271
Flannery, Patrick	272
Flood, Peter	271
Foote, John G.	271
Foster, Wm. W.	271
Franklin, Asa	273
French, David R.	273
Freedman, Benjamin	

G

Gage, George R. 273
Gale, Gordon J. 278
Galyas, John 278
George, J. Hardin 278
Gilbert, Chas. E. 271
Gilbert, Henry A. 273
Gilbert, Horace 271
Gilbert, Horace, Jr. 275
Gilbert, Mrs. Levi C. 281
Gillette, Abraham 269
Gillette, David, A. 273
Gleason, William 271
Glover, Ebenezer B. 269
Glover, Henry J. 271
Glover, John E. 273
Glover, Martin V. B. 272
Glover, Villeroy 269
Glover, Walter H. 278
Glover, Ziba 269
Goldstein, Israel 278
Goodsell, Frank C. 278
Gordon, James 272
Gordon, Mrs. James 281
Gordon, William 272
Gracco, Nicholas 278
Graham, George W. 275
Gray, George B. 275
Greene, John W. 272
Gregory, Benj. 269
Griffin, John 272
Groever, Paul 272
Guernsey, Truman 272

H

Hall, Henry C. 271
Hall, James P. 275
Hamblin, Andrew S. 271
Hanlon, Edgar 278
Hanlon, Richard 278
Hawley, Chas E. 275
Hawley, David B. 271
Hawley, George 271
Hawley Harrison 273
Hawley, Maj. James Nichols 278
Hawley, Philo 278
Hawley, Robert 278
Hawley, Willis 273
Hawley, William G. 273
Hayes, Dennis 273
Hicock, Ely 278
Hicock, Henry 279
Hickey, John 272
Hillhouse, Henry 279
Hillhouse, Julian 279
Holcomb, Gov. Marcus 281
Honan, Kathryn 279
Honan, Michael J. 279
Honan, Miss B. Frances 281
Hook, Martin 273
Hooper, Wm. L. 275
Horton, Benjamin 275
Hotchkiss, Hubbard A. 275
Hotchkiss Levi H. 275
Houlihan, Miss Helen 281
Hoyt, Henry 273
Hubbell, George S. 271
Hubbell, John P. 271
Hubbell, Lemuel 269
Hubbell, Matthew 269
Hull, Andrew C. 272
Hull, Ezra M. 272
Hull, James D. 271
Hull, Milton 281
Hurd, Charles 279

J

Jackson, Henry J. 272
James, Herbert T. 279
James Jesse Loderick 279
James, Thomas 269
Johnson, Henry 275
Johnson, Jacob 272
Johnson, Thomas 271
Jones, Chas. 272
Jones, David W. 272
Jorey, Peter 275

K

Kaine, Patrick 271
Kane, James 272
Kane, John 272
Keane, John J. 279
Keane, Joseph D. 279
Keating, Patrick 275
Keeler, Peter 273
Keenan, Michael 273
Kelly, Bernard 273
Kelly, Francis D. 279
Kelly, James 271
Kelly, John R. 279
Kimberly, Abraham 269
Kimberly, Ephraim 269
Kimberly, Fitch 269
Kimberly, John 269
Kiniry, Frank J. 279
Klingler, Arnold 279
Klingler, Werner 279
Knapp, John S. 272
Kraeplin, Edward 279
Kraeplin, Mrs. C. O. 281

L

Lake, George 274
Lang, Alonzo 279
Larner, Patrick 279
Lattin, John A. 272
Lewis, Dwight 269
Lewis, George H. 272
Liefield, Clemence A. 279
Lillis, Griffin B. 275
Lillis, John 279
Lillis, Martin 275
Lockwood, Eli 275
Lovejoy, Leroy J. 279
Lumnus, Samuel 269
Lynch, James E. 279
Lynch, John G. 279
Lynch, Patrick 275
Lynch, Thomas 279

M

Manley, Henry A. 272
Marvin Matthew 269
Mason, Louis S. 275
Matthews, Benj. W. 271
May, Chas. 271
Maynard, Benjamin 279
Maynard, William 273
Mead, Seaman M. 279
Meeker, Clarence G 274
Meeker, Richard 269
Merritt, Chas. J. 271
Meyer, Fritz 271
McAdoo, Wm. G. 280
MacArthur, Wm. 271
McDaniels, Patrick 273
McGrath, John 273
McGuire, Chas. A. 275
McLean, George 272
McMahon, Alfred 279
McMahon, Michael 275
McMahon, P. 275
Minor, Miss Charlotte C. 281
Monson, Chas. 272
Morey, Lewis 275
Morris, L. Phillips 279
Morris, Mrs. Levi C. 281
Murphy, Thomas O. 275

N

Nash, Adelbert 275
Nettleton, Arthur T. 281
Ney, Michael 271
Nichols, Beach 275
Nichols, Elijah B. 272
Nichols, George F. 275
Nichols, Harmos 272
Nichols, Henry E. 271

INDEX TO NEWTOWN'S MILITARY RECORD 1776—1918

Nichols, James 271
Northrop, Alpheus 275
Northrop, Joshua 269

O

Oakley, Peter M. 273
O'Brien, David 271
O'Brien, Thomas 271
O'Day, Earl T. 279
O'Halloran Michael T. 272
Olmstead, Peter D. 273
Osborne, Mrs. Alfred 281
Osborne Nathaniel 269
Orgelman, Harry 275

P

Parker, James 273
Parsons, Chas. M. 275
Parsons, Jacob 269
Pason, Jacob 269
Payne, Chas. H. 271
Payne David S. 272
Peck, Capt. Albert W. 275
Peck, Lieut. Albert W. Jr. 279
Peck, Austin, L. 272
Peck, Col. Charles H. 279-281
Peck, Sergt. C. Howard Jr. 279
Peck, Chester D. 272
Peck, David M. 273
Peck, John F. 272
Peck, Nelson J. 272
Peet, Benajah 273
Peet, Elijah B. 272
Peet, Henry A. S. 272
Perkins, Frank E. 279
Peterson, Arlan 272
Peterson, Carl 272
Peterson, Otto 279
Peterson, Walter 279
Pippines, Nicholas 279
Pitzchler, Edward S. 279
Platt, Chas. 279
Platt, Orlando 273
Platt, Percival C. 279
Prindle, Abijah 269
Prindle Joseph 269
Prindle, Peter 269
Prindle, Samuel 269
Prindle Zalmon 269

Q

Quinn, Patrick 271

R

Ramsay, George W. 271
Rankins, George 271
Rasmussen, John L. 279
Ray, Ryder 279
Read, Fred W. B. 279
Reed, Hawley 271
Reibold, Chas. 275
Reicker, Edward 271
Reynolds, Lester J. 279
Rigby, Matthew 273
Riley, James 271
Rinisland, Chas. 275
Roberts, Chas. 273
Roemer, Otto 279
Root, Nathan H. 271
Roswell, E. J. 275
Ruffels, Clarence 279
Ryan, Michael 272

S

Sanford, Andrew H. 271
Sanford, James 269
Sanford, Capt. Julius 272
Scanlon, John J. 279
Schriner, Andrew 272
Seeley, Eli 273
Seeley, James 269
Seeley, John D. 271
Shaughness, Lawrence 272
Shaw, Thomas 269
Shepard, Chas. S. 271
Shepard, Hall 271
Sherman, Chas. 272
Sherman, Eleazer 269
Sherman, George 272
Sherman, Ira 272
Sherwood, Chas R. 271
Slater, Carl H. 280
Smalley, Garrett E. 275
Smith, Mrs. Arthur J. 281
Smith, Chas. L. 275
Smith, Frederick E. 271
Smith, James 275
Smith, Joseph 269
Smith Pearl, 272
Smith, Richard 269
Smith, Mrs. Robert D. 281
Smith, Theodore 271
Smith, Wm. A. 272
Sniffen, Wm. B. 275
Spencer, George H. 272
Spitzer, Gottlieb 272
Spring, Chas. 272
Squires, Cyrenius N. 272

Squires, George D. 271
Squires, John C. 275
Stanley, Jerome L. 272
Stilson, Abel Jr. 269
Stowe, Wm. D. 275
Stuart, Levi E. 272
Stuart, Louis D. 271
St. John, Earl G. 280
Sullivan, James 271

T

Taft, Frederick B. 275
Tappan, John 272
Tappan, Robert 271
Taylor, Ammon 273
Taylor, Cornelius B. 281
Taylor, George 271
Taylor, James 275
Taylor, Roswell 272
Terrill, Capt. George 269
Terrill, Herbert W. 280
Terrill, Josiah 269
Tiemann, Mrs. Hermann N. 281
Tiemann, Robert N. 280
Tilson, Frank S. 280
Tilson, Josiah 280
Tobias, David C. 280
Tomlinson, Isaac C. 272
Tongue, Elam 275
Tongue, Hanford 271
Troy, Edward 275
Troy, Francis 280
Troy, John Joseph 280
Troy, John P. 280
Tuttle, Smith 269
Twitchell, Franklin S. 272
Tyrell, Stephen 272

V

Valenti, Peter J. 280
Valentine, George J. 280

W

Wade, Thomas 271
Walsh, John 272
Wayland, John B. 275
Weed, Daniel 275
Weed, Joseph 271
Wentz, George 275
Wentzel, Frederick 271
Wetmore, Fred 280
Wetmore, Jesse 280
Wheeler, Cyrus W. 272
Wheeler, Marion 273

Wheeler, Russell 280
White, Joseph 272
Whiteley, Wm. 269
Weible, Christian 272
Wile, Wm. C. 275
Wilkinson, Lemuel 273
Williams, George W. 275
Williams, Levi 275
Williams, Lewis 275
Wilson, James A. 275
Winton, Czar 269
Wirtes, Stephen 280
Wood, Smith B. 273
Woodhull, Jesse B. 280
Wooster, Chas. 272
Wright, Frank 281
Wright, Leonard W. 275
Wulff, Theodore L. 280

Y

Yawrman, James W. 280

Preface to Genealogical Section

When in 1916 a card was issued for the purpose of deciding whether or not it would be best to place in permanent form the papers dug from the early records by Ezra L. Johnson, the intention was to use only those papers.

After commencing the work in the winter of 1916-17 my busy brain during the sleepless hours of many nights conceived the idea that a genealogical section that should contain the names of many of the descendants of the early settlers could give added interest to the volume.

It has proved far more puzzling than it was expected it would be; has involved an immense amount of correspondence often with fruitless results. The names of many men prominent in the records of the early years do not appear because there was no interest in furnishing information, yet in spite of many omissions the work has grown to immense proportions as can easily be seen.

It does not pretend to be a complete genealogy even of Newtown's earliest citizens.

It has been impossible to prepare an Index except of the original family names without more delay and expense than was warranted.

Trusting that the effort may prove of interest to some of the descendants of the early settlers of old Newtown and with thanks to the very many friends who have assisted in giving information, I drop my pen with a heart full of thanksgiving to the Heavenly Father who has given health and strength to complete the work.

Jane E. Johnson

INDEX

Family Names of the Early Settlers.

	Page		Page
Adams	1	Kimberly	95-96
Baldwin	1-2	Lake	96-100
Beach	2-8	Merritt	100-101
Beardsley	8-9	Morgan	101-102
Beers	9-17	Morris	102-103
Birch	17-18	Nichols	103-108
Blackman		Northrop	108-111
or		Parmelee	111-113
Blakeman	18-25	Peck	113-120
Blakeslee	25-26	Perry	120-121
Booth	27-32	Platt	121-123
Botsford	32-39	Prindle	124-126
Briscoe	40-41	Sanford	126-128
Camp	41-44	Scudder	128-129
Clarke	44-47	Shepard	
Coburn	47	or	
Curtis	48-52	Shepherd	129-130
Dikeman	55	Sherman	130-134
Edmond	55	Skidmore	134-138
Fairchild	56-65	Stilson	138-140
Fairman	66-67	Summers	140-141
Ferris	67-69	Taylor	141-142
Foote	69-72	Terrill	142
Glover	72-78	Toucey	143-145
Hall	78-80	Tyrrill	145
Hard	80-81	Warner	145-146
Hawley	81-84	Wetmore	147
Hubbell	84-86	Wheeler	147-149
Johnson	86-95	Whitney	149

DESCENDANTS
OF SOME OF NEWTOWN'S EARLIEST SETTLERS

ADAMS

1 Freegrace Adams		m.	Mary Galpin in 1700 Settled in Newtown in 1711.
2 *Abraham	"	"	Hannah Warner
3 *Eli	"	"	Anna Baldwin
4 *Truman	"	"	Minerva Porter

Anna Baldwin, mother of Truman Adams was noted alike for her profound knowledge of the Bible and for her dainty handiwork.

Minerva Porter, wife of Truman Adams, died where she had lived the last twenty-five years with her daughter, Nancy Adams Clarke, near the home of her grandson, Robert Adams Clarke in Hawleyville, Conn. She died Aug. 28, 1883, aged 96 years, 10 months.

6 *Robert Adams Clarke   ch.   Nancy Adams   Newtown, Conn.
                                                    &
                                                    William Clarke   "   "

7 Ellen Lucy   "
7 Julia E.   "
7 *William Blackman "   ch.   *Emeline Blackman   Hawleyville, Conn.
7 Herbert   "   &
                                      Robert A. Clarke   "   "

8 Edna Clarke   Terrill
8 Helen Julia   "
8 Mortimer Clarke   Ellen Lucy Clarke   Ansonia   "
8 Grace Fairchild   "   ch.   &
8 Herbert William   "   Mortimer Terrill   "   "
       In U. S. service
8 Robert Leslie   "

9 Seelye Clarke Vial   Howard Vial   "   "
9 Doris Jeannette "   ch.   &
                               Helen J. Terrill,   Montpelier, Vt.

8 Mortimer C. Terrill   m. Ellen Mommers, South Manchester, Conn.

                                    Julia E. Clarke,   Danbury, Conn.
8 Elise Sherman Brush   ch.   &
                                    Chester H. Brush

     Graduated from Vassar 1908, A. B. degree.
                              m. David Alexander Bliss, South Norwalk, Ct.
                                    Grace Judson,   Brooklyn, N. Y.
8 Robert Judson Clarke,   ch.   &
                                      Herbert Clarke

BALDWIN

1 Caleb Baldwin first of the name in Newtown, was baptized in Milford in 1702. m. Mehitabel—1st. Jerusha Daton, 2nd. wife.

                                  Mehitabel   Newtown, Conn.
2 Lieut. Caleb Baldwin   ch.   &
                                  Caleb Baldwin

He was prominent in town affairs serving as Town Clerk from 1765 to 1799

3 Gen. David Baldwin,   ch.   Naomi Hurd, 1st wife,   Newtown, Conn.
                                &
                                Lieut. Caleb Baldwin 2nd.

3 Caleb   "   ch.   Betsey Betts 2nd wife   "   "
                                &
                                Lieut. Caleb Baldwin 2nd.

4 David Van Brooks   ch.   Hannah Brooks   Brookfield, Conn.
                                &
                                Gen. David Baldwin,   Newtown, Conn.

m. Nancy——1st wife. Betsey Platt Curtis 2nd wife, widow of Joseph Curtis.

3 Caleb Baldwin was Town Clerk from 1799 to 1843. His name appears in other offices of public trust in the early records, also as a popular Inn keeper.

His second wife Sarah Prindle Baldwin was the donor of the books that formed the nucleus of the Newtown Library.

4 Henry Baldwin   ch.   Caleb Baldwin 3rd.
4 Elizabeth   "   &
                                Betsey Beers 1st wife   Newtown, Conn.

5 Anna M. Booth   ch.   Elizabeth Baldwin,   New Milford, Conn.
                                &
                                Lewis Booth

6 Harry Booth Brownson   Huntington, Conn.
6 Marie Louise   "   Anna M. Booth
6 *Edythe Elizabeth "   ch.   &
6 Anna Gertrude   "   Henry Israel Brownson

7 Sheldon Thomas "   ch.   Gertrude Buckingham,   Huntington, Conn.
                                &
                                Harry B. Brownson

6 Marie Louise   "   m.   William W. Watson,   Endicott, N. Y.
                         ch. died in infancy

7 Edythe Brownson Bowles ch.   Anna G. Brownson,   Huntington, Conn
7 Ralph Henry   "   &
                                Harry L. Bowles.

BEACH

1 Rev. John Beach, First Rector Trinity Church m. Sarah Beach 1st wife.
            m. Abigail Holbrook 2nd

Ch. by 1st. marriage

2 Phoebe Beach   m. Capt. Daniel Hill   Redding Ridge, Conn.
2 John   "   Jr.   " Phebe Curtis   Newtown, Conn
2 Lazarus   "   " Lydia Sanford   Redding, Conn.
2 Lucy   "   " Rev. Epenetus Townsend   Salem N. Y.

   ch. John Beach Jr. and Phebe Curtis,   Newtown, Conn.
3 John B.   "   m. Mabel Beers   "   "
3 Phebe   "   " Zalmon Glover   "   "
3 Hannah   "   " John Curtis   "   "
3 Sarah   "   " Joel Booth   "   "
3 Mary   "   " Abel Beers   "   "

GENEALOGICAL SECTION

```
    Ch. John Beach 3rd, and Mabel Beers           Newtown, Conn.
4 Lucy         "       m. Capt. James Nichols,        "      "
                                (See Nichols)
4 Matthew      "       b. 1763, d. 1766
4 Ann          "       m. Dr. Elisha Sheldon      Litchfield   "
4 Boyle        "       "  Elizabeth Staats     New Baltimore, N. Y.
4 Phoebe       "       "  Barent Houghtaling      "      "    "   "
4 John         "       "  Marcia Curtis           Newtown, Conn.
4 Charlotte    "       "  Epenetus Wead no desc.  Kirkwood, Mo.
4 Ann Beach, 3rd dau. of Mabel Beers, and 3 John Beach. m. Elisha
Sheldon.
```

```
5 Elizabeth Sheldon         4Ann Beach          Newtown, Conn.
5 Mary          "     ch.         &
                            Dr. Elisha Sheldon    Sheldon, Vt.

6 Mary Helena Peck         Elizabeth Sheldon   New Haven, Conn.
6 Phebe Warren   "    ch.         &
m. Birdsey C. Lake         Henry Edward Peck     "      "     "

5 John Staats Beach                             New Baltimore N. Y.
5 Isaac        "           Elizabeth Staats      "      "    "   "
5 Matthew      "    ch.           &
5 Anne S.      "           Boyle Beach           "      "    "   "
5 Jane Elizabeth "

6 *Alexander Hamilton Beach    *Angeline Dickenson   Cleveland N. Y.
6 Mary Elizabeth    "    ch.          &
6 Charlotte Ann     "          John Staats Beach      "        "  "

7 John Arthur       "                                 "        "  "
7 Mabel Beers       "          Elizabeth Tufts        "        "  "
7 Mary Elizabeth    "    ch.          &               "        "  "
7 Ella May          "          Alexander H. Beach     "        "  "

7 Rev. John Arthur          Charlotte A. Beach    Waterloo, N. Y.
7 Muriel        "     ch.          &
7 Alfred Huntington"        Rev. John Arthur D. D.  Glen Ellyn, Ill

                            Muriel Arthur         Cedar Rapids, Iowa
8 Martha Trewin       ch.          &
                            Harold R. Trewin          "      "    "

6 Reginald Heber Lear
6 *William Frederick "         Anne Sheldon Beach
6 *Ellen Elizabeth   "  ch.           &
6 *Clara Ellen       "         Charles Briggs Lear    Naples, Ill.

7 Ethel Adeline       "                              Kirkwood, Mo.
7 Mary Baldwin        "                                 "       "
7 Reginald Heber Jr.  "        Carrie May Baldwin       "       "
7 Olive Beach         "  ch.          &                 "       "
7 Irene Axtell        "        Reginald Heber Lear      "       "
7 Eugene Sawyer       "                                 "       "
```

3 Phoebe Beach, eldest daughter of John Beach Jr. m. Zalmon Glover.
                                            (See Glover.)
4 Lucy Ann Glover, eldest daughter of Phebe Beach and Zalmon Glover.
                   m. Abner Anson Nettleton

```
                            Lucy Ann Glover       Newtown, Conn.
5 *Joseph Nettleton   ch.          &
                            Abner Anson Nettleton    "      "

6 *Edgar Anson Nettleton    Phoebe Curtis            "      "
6 *Charles Pulaski    "  ch.          &
6 *Joseph Foster      "     Joseph Nettleton         "      "
```

GENEALOGICAL SECTION

```
7 *Joseph Hinman Nettleton                              Brooklyn, N. Y.
7  Flora Curtis              "         Ann Eliza Atwood    Branford, Conn.
7  Phebe Beach               "   ch.         &
7  Frederick H.              "         Edgar A. Nettleton    "        "
7  Mabel Branford            "                             West Haven, Conn.

8 Alexander Edgar Nettleton
8 Joseph Foster              "         Harriet Levine
8 Flora Roberta              "   ch.         &
8 Clara Levine               "         Joseph H. Nettleton   Brooklyn, N. Y.
8 *Harriet Frances           "   m.    Walter Kraft

                                       Flora Curtis Nettleton
8 Bertha Jane Libby              ch.         &
                                       Locke Austin Libby

                                       Bertha Jane Libby
9 Jane Wolcott Welles            ch.         &
9 Judith Beach             "           Clayton Wolcott Wells  Wethersfield, Ct.

8 Marjorie Nettleton Thompson
8 Curtis Keith               "         Mabel Branford Nettleton, West Haven, "
8 Eleanor Lois               "   ch.         &
8 Katherine                  "         Andrew Keith Thompson

7 Charles Sumner Nettleton m. Emily Estelle Brotherton  Shelton, Conn.
7 Albert Israel              "                          Montpelier, Iowa
7 Ernest Clifton             "         Frances Ann Halleck  Shelton, Conn.
7 *Rebecca H.                "   ch.         &
7 *Rose A.                   "         Charles P. Nettleton   "      "
7 Francis Irving, M.D.       "                                "      "
7 *Ruth E.                   "                                "      "

                                       Anna Margaret Johnson, 1st wife
8 Howard Albee               "   ch.         &
8 Clyde Harrison             "         Albert I. Nettleton   Montpelier, Iowa
                                       Clara Marguerite Hartman, 2nd. wife.
                                                             Gilbert Iowa

9 Clarence Wayne             "         Nellie Genes Wunder
9 Elsie May                  "   ch.         &
9 Roy P.                     "         Howard A. Nettleton    Mohall, N. Dakota

                                       Ellen Edith Franklin
9 Evelyn Idel                "   ch.         &
                                       Clyde H. Nettleton    Montpelier, Iowa

                                       Amzetta Barker         Redlands, Calif.
7 Lucy Beach                 "   ch.         &
                                       *Joseph F. Nettleton

                                       Jean Mairs Mitchell    Shelton, Conn.
8 Francis Irving, Jr.        "   ch.         &
                                       Dr. Francis I. Nettleton

4 John Beach, third son 3 John Beach and Mabel Beers  Newtown, Conn.

5 *John Sheldon Beach                  Marcia Curtis         New Haven, Conn.
5 *Daniel Beers              "   ch.         &
5 *Ann Eliza                 "         John Beach 4th            "       "
```

Rebecca Donaldson Beach was the donor of the John Beach Memorial Library.

```
6 *Rebecca Donaldson "
6  Rodman Vernon     "
6  John Kimberly     "                 Rebecca Gibbons        New Haven, Conn.
6  Donaldson         "   ch.                 &
6 *Francis Gibbons   "                 John Sheldon Beach L L.D.  "      "
```

GENEALOGICAL SECTION

7 John Francis Beach
7 John Francis " ch.

Elizabeth Charnley Wells, New Haven, Ct.
&
Francis Gibbons Beach

5 Mary Beach 5th dau. John Beach Jr. m. Abel Beers Newtown, Conn. See Beers.
2 Lazarus Beach, m. Lydia Sanford.
3 Sarah Beach, 2nd dau. Lazarus, m. James Sanford
4 Lemuel Sanford, m. Charlotte Platt.
5 Betsey Sanford 4th dau. Lemuel Sanford, m. George Barnum.

6 *Charlotte Augusta Barnum
6 *Hannah Sanford "
6 Sarah E. "
6 George W. " ch.
6 Henry Taylor "
6 Charles Lemuel "

Betsey Sanford,   Redding, Conn.
&
George Barnum   Bethel "

7 *Cora Barnum Osborne
7 Bessie Louise " ch.

Charlotte A. Barnum   Danbury, Conn.
&
David Osborne, Jr.

7 *Alida E. Benedict
7 Jeannette B. " ch.

Hannah S. Barnum,   Bethel Conn.
&
Lewis B. Benedict   " "

7 George Whitfield Norvell   Was Rhodes Scholar and went to Oxford, England, now Supt. School in Colo.
7 Grace Edith "
7 Philip David " ch.
7 Julia Sanford "

Sarah E. Barnum   Centerville, S. Dakota
&
Rev. Joseph E. Norvell " "
Member Dakota M. E. Conference

7 Addie Belle Barnum
7 Sarah Elizabeth " ch.
7 Bertrand Andrew "

Nora B. Koons   Centerville, S. Dakota
&
George W. Barnum " "

7 Luella Maud "
7 George Koons "
7 Royal Charles " ch.
7 Fred Clifford "
7 Kenneth Henry "

Nora Koons Barnum " "
&
Henry Taylor Barnum " "

7 Sheldon Charles " ch.

Helen Sitgreave   Delaware, S. Dakota
&
Charles L. Barnum   Lead City "

8 Ethel Celeste Morgan ch.

Jeannette B. Benedict   Bethel, Conn.
&
Clifford B. Morgan " "

8 Bessie Louise Schmidt
8 Robert T. Jr. " ch.

Bessie L. Osborne   Danbury "
&
Robert T. Schmidt " "

1 Rev. John Beach, 2Lazarus, 3Sarah, m. James Sanford, 4Lemuel m. Charlotte Platt, 5Rev. David Platt Sanford.

6 *Grace Hyde Sanford
6 *Alice " ch.

Caroline Hamlin, 1st wife
&
Rev. David P. Sanford

6 Caroline Hamlin "
6 *Harriett Emma "
6 Rev. David Lewis "
6 Rev. Edgar Lewis " ch.
6 Amelia "
6 Frederick Harriman "

Deaconess Sanford

Emma Bartow Lewis, 2nd wife
&
Rev. David P. Sanford

GENEALOGICAL SECTION

7 Theodora George
7 David Sanford "
7 Bertha Niles " ch.
7 Caroline Anna "

7 Rev. James Hardin Jr.

*Harriett E. Sanford
&
Rev. James H. George d. at Newtown, Conn., Jan., 1917.
U. S. Service in France.

8 Henry Gould Curtis ch.
8 Nelson George "

Bertha Niles George, Newtown, Conn.
&
William R. Curtis " "

8 James Hardin George 2nd

Carrie Mason Palmer, Columbia, Mo.
ch. &
Rev. James H. George Jr.

7 Helen Traver Sanford
7 *Alice Amelia "
7 Charles Briscoe "
7 Edgar Lewis " ch.
7 John Beach "
7 Arthur Hall "
7 David Platt "

Anna Traver Briscoe
&
Rev. David L. Sanford, Morrisville, Pa.

8 Wm. Richard Brown, Jr. ch.

Helen Traver Sanford
&
Wm. Richard Brown, M.D. Phil. Pa.

8 Charles Briscoe Sanford, Jr. ch.

Katherine Uri Thompsonville, Conn.
&
Charles B. Sanford

8 Anna Winslow Truax
ch.
8 Albert Winslow "

*Alice Amelia Sanford
&
Albert Truax Hartford, Conn.

7 Vera Sanford
7 Eva Matthews " ch.
7 Anna Munson "

Eugenia Munson
&
Rev. Edgar L. Sanford HoneyBrook, Pa.

7 Joseph Bates " ch.

Eva Starr Bates, 1st wife
&
Frederick H. Sanford Brooklyn, N. Y.

7 Edith Harmonie " ch.

Natalie Drake 2nd wife
&
Frederick H. Sanford

2 Lazarus Beach, 4th son, Rev. John Beach, m. Lydia Sanford
3 Lazarus " Jr. m. Polly Thompson Hall
4 Fanny " dau, Polly Hall and Lazarus Beach Jr. Redding, Conn.

5 William Whitehead Ladd
5 Caroline Medora "
5 Ellen Louise " ch.
5 Catherine "

Fanny Beach Brooklyn, N. Y.
&
James Ladd Throggs Neck, N. Y.

6 William Whitehead Jr. "
6 Walter G. "
6 Rev. Henry M. " ch.
6 James B. "

Sarah Hannan Phillips
&
William W. Ladd, Throgg's Neck, N. Y.

7 Elizabeth Ladd ch.

Elizabeth Adelaide Rowe
&
Wm. Whitehead Ladd Jr. New York, N. Y.

6 Walter G. " m. Kate Everit Macy, New York, N. Y.

7 Coit "
7 Henry M. Jr. " ch.
7 William W. 2nd. "

Martha Williams Coit
&
Rev. Henry M. Ladd Rutherford, N. J.

GENEALOGICAL SECTION

7 Frances Serrill   Ladd   Rebecca Serrill
7 Frances Serrill   " ch.   &
    James B. Ladd   Baltimore, Md.

6 Fanny Gilfillan   *Caroline Medora Ladd 1st.
6 Wm. Whitehead Gilfillan ch.   &
    *Dr. Wm. Gilfillan   Brooklyn, N. Y.
    m.
    Catherine Ladd 2nd. wife   "   "

7 *Katherine Ladd Van Wyck   Fanny Gilfillan   "   "
7 Samuel Beach   " ch.   &
    Albert Van Wyck   "   "

6 Henry Wallace M.D.   Ellen Louise Ladd   "   "
6 William Wallace, Jr.   ch.   &
    William Wallace M. D.   "   "

    Carrie Louise Bostwick   "   "
7 Ellen Louise "   ch.   &
    Henry Wallace M. D.   "   "

8 Kathleen Evelina von Gontard   Elizabeth Ladd
8 Elsa   " "   ch.   &
    Alexander C. F. von Gontard

7 Frances Serrill Ladd   m.   Merrill Kercher   Baltimore, Md.

3 Sarah Beach, 2nd dau. 2Lazarus Beach.
    Sarah Beach m. James Sanford.

4 James Sanford Jr.   m.   Eliza French

5 Turney Sanford
5 James 3rd. "
5 Sarah   "   Eliza French   Redding, Conn.
5 Stephen "   ch.   &
5 Betsey   "   James Sanford, Jr.   "   "
5 Charles "

    Mary Roe
6 George Turney "   ch.   &
    Turney Sanford

    Florence Hill   Redding, Conn.
7 Beulah   "   ch.   &
    George T. Sanford   "   "

    Sarah Meeker   "   "
6 William C. "   ch.   &
    James Sanford 3rd   "   "

    Edith Cole   "   "
7 James Harold "   ch.   &
    Wm. Clinton Sanford   "   "

6 David S. Duncomb   Sarah Fairchild 1st wife   "   "
6 George F. "   ch.   &
    Wm. Edgar Duncomb   "   "

6 Emma Eliza   "   Sarah Sanford 2nd wife
    m.   ch.   &
    George B. Beers   Wm. E. Duncomb   Easton, Conn.

7 William M. Duncomb   New York, N. Y.
7 Frederick How Duncomb   Lydia Lane Lockwood
7 Raynor Sanford "   ch.   &
7 David Sanford "   David S. Duncomb   Mount Vernon, N. Y.

    Mabel Taylor   Newtown, Conn.
8 Frederick Taylor "   ch.   &
8 Raynor Lockwood "   Frederick H. Duncomb   "   "

7 Julia Beers Duncomb	m.	Rev. Walter Aiken	Torrington, Conn.
6 Emory Perkins Sanford	ch.	Mary Sophia Banks & Stephen Sanford	Redding, Conn
6 Stephen Ernest "			" "
7 Jesse "	ch.	Olivia Sanford & Emory Perkins Sanford	" "
7 Stephen "			" "
7 *Margery Beers "	ch.	Alice Beers & S. Ernest Sanford	
7 Marvin "			Bridgeport, Conn.
6 James Arthur Sherwood	ch.	Betsey Sanford & George B. Sherwood	Easton, Conn.
7 Hazel Elaine "	ch.	Eva Whitehead & James Arthur Sherwood	
6 Elsie Sanford	ch.	Hannah Sherwood & Charles Sanford	Redding, Conn.
6 Lucy "			
7 Raymond Platt	ch.	Elsie Sanford & Philo T. Platt	Newtown, Conn.

BEARDSLEY

All records agree that the Newtown Beardsleys, some of whom settled in Newtown early in 1700, were descended from William, called 'Goodman Beardsley." "It is claimed on very good authority that William Beardsley gave Stratford its name in 1643."

4Israel, 3Thomas, 2Joseph, 1William.
Israel, m. Elizabeth Blazze.

5 Jared Beardsley	m.	Grace Perry	Newtown, Conn.
6 Israel Abner "	"	Esther Toucey	" "
6 Asa Blazze "	"	Flora Toucey	" "

Ch. Israel Abner and Esther Toucey

7 *Philo Shelton "	m.	Harriet Beach	" "
7 *Flora Jane "	m.	Aaron Sanford	" "
8 Mary Elizabeth Sanford	ch.	Flora Jane Beardsley & Aaron Sanford	" "
8 William Henry "			" "
9 Mary E. Sanford	m.	Harley T. Proctor	Cincinnati, Ohio

Their Ch.

10 William Proctor	m.	Emily Pearson Bodstein	New York City
10 Lillian Sanford "	"	Wilhelm Hoeninghaus	
10 Rodney "	"	Beatrice Stirling	

Ch. Asa Blazze Beardsley and Flora Toucey   Newtown, Conn.

7 Emily Esther "	unm.		
7 Mary Elizabeth "	m.	William J. Dick (d. Jan. 1918, age 88 yrs.)	
7 Philo Toucey "	unm.		Newtown, Conn.
7 Julius Theodore "	unm.		" "
7 John Mark "	unm.		" "
7 Frances Josephine	unm.		" "
7 Henriette "	unm.		" "

4 Jesse, 3William, 2Daniel, 1William
5 William Beardsley, b. 1777 m. Molly Sanford 1st wife
                              " 2nd Mrs. Esther M. Taylor

GENEALOGICAL SECTION

Their ch.

6 Lois	Beardsley	m.	Eliel Crofut	Newtown, Conn.
6 Lydia	"	"	Jeremiah Turner	" "
6 Jesse	"		unm.	
6 Polly Ann	"	"	Benjamin Beers	" "
6 Ruth	"	"	Ziba Morse	" "
6 William Sanford	"	"	Nancy J. Nichols	Bridgeport, Conn.
6 Aaron Thomas	"	"	1st Mary Curtis, 2nd Frances Hamlin	"
6 Caroline	"	"	Albert Booth	Newtown, Conn.
6 Anna	"	"	Hawley Nichols	" "
6 Sally Maria	"	"	1st Henry Lewis, 2nd Abraham Lyon	"

6 Emily and 6Eliza by 2nd wife unm.
5 Jonathan, 4Josiah, 3Josiah, 2Joseph, 1William

6 Abel Beardsley	m.	Eunice Rowell	Newtown, Conn.
7 Abel Ferris "	"	Hannah Gray	" "

Their ch.

8 Henry S.	"	d. young	
8 John B.	"	unm.	
8 Emma L.	"	unm.	
8 Charles F.	"	m. Mary Josephine Lake	
8 Lester W.	"	unm.	
8 Martha A.	"	" Harry Blake	Waltham, Mass.
8 Edward	"	unm.	
8 Ida M.	"	unm.	
8 Nellie B.	"	" George Crosby	Worcester, Mass.
8 Frederick	"	unm.	

9 Clarence Lake "		Mary Josephine Lake	Newtown, Conn.
9 Paul J. "	ch.	&	
		Charles F. Beardsley	New York City
9 Clarence L. "	m.	Viola May Gamsby	New Haven, Conn.

BEERS

1 Samuel Beers only son of "John of Stratford" born 1679. Married Sarah Sherman in 1706, and settled in Newtown.

Their sons from whom the various Beers families are descended were,
2 John, Samuel, Daniel, Abraham, Nathan.
John born 1710; married Mary Seeley,   Newtown, Conn.

Their Ch.

3 Cynthia Beers	m.	1st. Thomas Skidmore	" "
	m.	2nd Jotham Sherman, 3rd wife	" "
3 Anna "	m.	John Fabrique	" "
	m.	2nd. Caleb Baldwin	" "
3 Amy "	"	Jotham Sherman 2nd wife	" "
3 Phebe "	"	1st Samuel Ferris	" "
	"	2nd Benjamin Curtis	" "
3 Naomi "	"	John Jackson	" "
3 John "	"	Sarah Sterling	" "
3 Sarah "	"	Eliada Prindle	" "
3 Andrew "	"	Sarah Gunn	" "
3 Oliver "	"	Catherine Hubbell	" "
3 Mary "	"	Phineas Taylor	" "

3 John Beers b. 1745	m.	Sarah Sterling	" "

Their Ch.

4 *Jeremiah "	"	Polly Peck 1st. wife	" "
4 *Jacob "	"	Laura Toucey no ch.	
4 *Hannah "	"	Isaac Bennett	

GENEALOGICAL SECTION

Ch. of Jeremiah Beers and Polly Peck 1st wife.

5 *Marcia	Beers	m. Levi Peck	Newtown, Conn.	
5 *Delia	"	" Le Grand Randall	Roxbury,	"
5 *Anna	"	" Araunah Fairchild no ch.	Newtown, Conn.	
5 *Julia	"	" Elias Beers, Jr. (see Elias)	"	"
5 *Polly	"	" John Purdy (no desc. located)		

5 *John "   Flora Sherwood 2nd wife
5 *Julius " ch. &
              Jeremiah Beers

6 *Cornelia Peck   Marcia Beers
                ch. &
                    Levi Peck

7 Anna Cornelia Judson   Cornelia Peck.
m. *Henry Tucker   ch. &
                          John Judson

Ch. Delia and LeGrand Randall   Roxbury, Conn.

6 *Charles Randall		m. Maria Ferry	New Milford, Conn.	
6 *Helen	"	" Philip Wells no ch.	Roxbury	"
6 *Henry	"	" Sarah E. Prindle	"	"
6 *Ophelia	"	" Dr. Wm. Camp, (See Camp)	Newtown, Ct.	"
6 Celia	"	" Leverett Castle no ch.	Roxbury	"

7 Le Grand   "   Salt Lake City, Utah
7 Clark   "   Maria Ferry   Bethel Conn.
7 *Le Roy   "   ch.   &
7 Orris Ferry "   Charles Randall New Milford, *
7 *Charlotte "
7 *Sarah   "

8 Alice Couch "   *Alice Couch 1st. wife Norwalk, Conn.
m. George Allen   ch.   &
                      *Le Roy Randall   New Milford "

8 Mary Ethel Randall   Mary Potter 2nd wife   "   "
8 Lee   "   ch.   &
8 Mary Ethel   "   Le Roy Randall   "   "
m. Russell Noble

                        4 Hannah Beers
5 *Jacob Beers Bennett ch.   &
                        Isaac Bennett   Medina, N. Y.

                        *Jane Turner   New York, N. Y.
6 Alice Bennett   ch.
                        *Jacob Beers Bennett

2 Samuel Beers, born 1712, married Abigail Blackman.

Their Ch.

3 Abel	"	Died unmarried	Newtown, Conn.	
3 Simeon	"	m. Phedima Nichols	"	"
3 Abigail	"	" Ezra Booth	"	"

Ch. Simeon "   and Phedima Nichols   "   "

4 Abel	"	m. Mary Beach	"	"
4 Samuel	"	" Rissa Hard	"	"
4 Esther	"	unm.	"	"
4 Rebecca	"	" David C. Peck	"	"
4 Abner	"	unm.		

GENEALOGICAL SECTION

Ch. 4 Abel Beers "Maj. Abe" m. Mary Beach
5 Sylvia   "   m. Sinclair Toucey (see Toucey)B'klyn, N. Y.
5 John Beach   "   " Eliza Dunn   Council Bluffs, Iowa
5 Isaac   "   " 1st. Maria Nichols Glover, Newtown, Conn.
                              2nd Eliza Bostwick   Monroe,   "
5 *Charles Curtis"   " Harriet Peck   Newtown, Conn.
5 *Mary   "   unm.
5 *Esther   "   " David H. Johnson 1st. wife "   "
5 *Phebe   "   unm.   "   "
5 *Rebecca   "   " David H. Johnson 2nd wife (no desc.) "

6 Sarah Beach Beers   ch. Eliza Dunn   Council Bluffs, Iowa
                              &
                              John B. Beers   "   "   "

7 *John Beach Beers Rohrer   Sarah B. Beers   "   "   "
7 Isaac Beers   "   ch. &
7 Carrie Test   "   Millard Fillmore Rohrer "   "   "

6 *Sarah Esther Beers   Harriet Peck   Newtown, Conn.
                         ch. &
6 *John Beach   "   Charles C. Beers   "   "

2 Daniel Beers, born 1714, married Mabel Booth. Their Ch.
3 Cyrus, Jerusha, Amos, Daniel, Ann, Mabel, Esther and Austin.
3 Mabel Beers married John Beach 3rd. (See Beach record.)
2 Abraham Beers born 1716; married Sarah——?   Newtown, Conn.
  Their Ch.
3 James, Philo, Truman, Abraham, Jr., (Eli and Elias) twins.
3 Desc. through Eli.
  Ch. Eli Beers and Rebecca Toucey 1st. wife.
4 Daniel
4 Alonzo   "   m. Flora Glover   Brookfield, Conn.

  Ch. Eli   "   & Phedima Peck 2nd wife.

4 Sylvester   "   m. Sally Morris   Newtown, Conn.
4 Lemuel   "   m. Eliza Shepard   "   "
4 Hermon   "   m. Phebe Sherman   "   "
4 Dimah Ann   "   m. Walter Clarke (See Clarke) "   "
4 Alonzo Beers married Flora Glover   Brookfield,   "
  Their Ch.
5 Daniel G. Beers   m. Harriet Starr   "   "
5 Rebecca   "   " Benjamin Jones   "   "
5 Sarah Minerva "   " Philo Clarke (See Clarke record)
5 Eli Starr   "   unm.
5 Joseph Toucey "   " Wealthy Ward   "   "
5 Harriet Sophia "   " Edwin Smith Hoyt   Waterbury, Conn.
5 George Alonzo "   " Jennie Burge   Brookfield,   "

                              Sally Morris   Newtown, Conn.
5 *Daniel Morris "   ch. &
m *Caroline Terrill   Sylvester Beers   "   "

  Desc. of Eli through Lemuel
  Ch. Eliza Shepard and Lemuel Beers   "   "
5 *George   Beers   m. Sarah Peck   Newtown, Conn.
5 *Caroline   "   " Cyrus Beers Sherman, (no ch.) "   "
5 *Susan J.   "   " James Blakeslee (See Blakeslee record)
5 *Ann E.   "   unm.   "   "
5 Fannie S.   "   unm.
5 *Marietta   "   " *John C. Beers
5 Henry L.   "   " *Julia Glover 1st wife
                              Florence K. Frill 2nd wife

5 Eli B.   "   " *Sophronia Sherman Warner, Newtown, Ct.

Ch. George Beers and Sarah E. Peck.

6 Anna	"	m.	Henry G. Curtis, (See Curtis)	
6 George B.	"	"	Grace Blakeman	Newtown, Conn.
6 Robert H.	"	"	Sarah Sanford	

Ch. George B. Beers and Grace Blakeman

7 Lillian	Beers	m.	Herman Tiemann, Jr.	Bridgeport, Conn.
7 George Herbert	"		In U. S. service in France	" "
7 Jessie Martha	"	m.	Kurtz P. Wilson, Jr.	Baltimore, Md.
7 Sarah Alice	"	m.	Henry Cook Mitchell	Hartford, Conn.

8 Herman Newell Tiemann 3   Lillian Beers   "   "
8 Grace Louise " ch. &
8 George Herbert "   Herman N. Tiemann, Jr.   Bridgeport, Conn.

7 Henry Sanford Beers   Sarah Sanford   Newtown, Conn.
7 Robert Edmond "   ch. &
     Robert H. Beers

6 James L. "   *Marietta Beers   Brooklyn, N. Y.
6 Carrie F. " ch. &
6 Ella L. "   *John C. Beers   " "

7 Mildred Otis   ch.   Carrie F. Beers   Bridgeport, Conn.
    &
    John M. Otis

8 Robert Lewis Jr.   Mildred Otis
8 Elizabeth " (twins) ch. &
8 Marshall "   Robert Lewis

6 Nellie Gilbert Beers   ch.   Julia F. Glover 1st. wife
    &
    Henry L. Beers

6 Harry Sherman "   Florence K. Frill 2nd. wife
6 Florence Susan " ch. &
    Henry L. Beers

6 Fannie May "
6 Alice Sherman "   Sophronia Sherman Warner   Newtown, Ct.
6 Eli Burton " ch. &
6 John Cyrus "   Eli B. Beers   " "

7 *Margery Beers Sanford ch.   Alice Sherman Beers   " "
7 Marvin " "   &
    Ernest Sanford   Bridgeport, Conn.

6 Fannie May Beers   m.   Louis Edwards   " "

Desc. of Eli through Hermon   Newtown, Conn.

5 Harriet	Beers	m.	*Rev. Charles Husband	
5 *John Hobart	"	"	Keturah Sharp	Chicago, Ill.
5 Flora Jane	"	"	*James Hobart Warner (See Warner)	
5 Sarah M.	"		unm.	Newtown, Conn.
5 *Wm. Hermon	"	"	Caroline R. Gately	" "

6 *Charles Howard Husband ch.   Harriet Beers
    &
    Rev. Chas. Husband

6 *Anna Sharp Beers   Keturah Sharp   Chicago, Ill.
6 Keturah Sherman "   ch. &
    John H. Beers   " "

7 Julianna Holmes   ch.   Keturah S. Beers   " "
    &
    Woodward Holmes

GENEALOGICAL SECTION

6 William Hermon Beers
   Capt. in U. S. service   ch.
6 Eloise Gately   "
            Caroline R. Gately   Mamaroneck, N. Y.
            &
            William Hermon Beers

7 Alice Barrett Farley   New York, N. Y.
7 Caroline Johnson "   Eloise Gately Beers
7 Katherine Cheney "   ch.   &
7 Frank Cheney "   Frank Cheney Farley

Desc. through Elias Beers

4 Zenas   ch.   Mary Abiah Peck 1st wife   Newtown, Conn
4 Smith   "   &
                         Elias Beers

4 Norman   "   Betty Botsford 2nd wife
4 Elias Jr.   "   ch.   &
                      Elias Beers

5 George   "   Julia Brown 1st wife
5 Mary   "   ch.   &
                      Zenas Beers

5 William H.   "   Amelia Hendrickson, 2nd wife
5 John   "   ch.   &
5 Alfred H.   "   Zenas Beers

6 Ella   "   ch.   Harriet Ayton
                      &
                      George Beers

7 John H. Crawford Jr.   ch.   Ella Beers
                            &
                            John H. Crawford   Orange, N. J.

6 Samuel Wells   ch.   Mary Beers
                      &
                      William Wells   Rutherford, N. J.

6 Ellen A. Beers   *Susan A. Smith   Brooklyn, N. Y.
6 Florence E. "   ch.   &
                      William H. Beers

7 Douglas McGowan   ch.   Ellen A. Beers
                           &
                           Arthur J. McGowan   New York City

6 Mildred Beers   Lavinia Cronk
6 Lottie   "   ch.   &
                    John Beers

7 Robert Mason Jr.   ch.   Mildred Beers
                       &
                       Robert Mason   Buffalo, N. Y.

7 Evelyn Klune   Lottie Beers
7 Mildred   "   ch.   &
                     William Klune

6 Eugene F. Beers   Ozemma Smith
6 Bessie   "   ch.   &
                      Alfred H. Beers   Huntington, N. Y.

7 Ruth Beers   Constance Lewis
7 Marjorie "   ch.   &
                   Eugene F. Beers
6 Bessie   "   m.   Edward Carman

5 Julia Elizabeth Beers   Betsey Dikeman   Newtown, Conn.
5 Sylvia Maria "   ch.   &
5 Charles Elias "   Norman Beers   "   "

GENEALOGICAL SECTION

6 Grace Elizabeth Lake   Sylvia M. Beers, 2nd wife   Passaic, N. J.
6 Florence Amelia "   ch. & " "
       Lamson B. Lake

5 Charles E. Beers   m. Florence Burritt (no ch.) Newtown, Conn.

5 *Mary Frances Beers   Julia Beers   Newtown, Conn.
5 *Edgar "   ch. &
5 *Cornelia "   Elias Beers Jr.

2 Nathan son of Samuel born 1718 married Lydia Hawley
3 Nathan Jr., Ebenezer, Ezekiel their sons.
4 Ebenezer Beers   m. Phebe Botsford 1st wife
   Their sons
5 *John "   " Roxy Ann Glover
5 *James B. "   " Huldah Clarke
5 *Charles H. "   " Mary E. Glover   Newtown, Conn.
5 *David H. "   " Lucy Fairchild " "
5 *Dr. Moses B. "   " Loraine Curtis " "
5 *Horace "   " Emily Terrill " "

   Ch. of John Beers and Roxy Ann Glover: " "

6 *Mary Jane Beers   m. Charles E. Blakeman " "
6 *Sarah Maria "   " Lamson B. Lake " "
6 Angeline Eliza " twins   " William H. Beers " "
6 *Caroline Eliza " twins   " Robert Wilberforce Burritt " "
6 *James Morris "   " Emily Beach, 1st wife " "
       Cornelia Twitchell, 2nd. " "

7 *Austin B. Blakeman " "
7 *Julia E. " unm.   Mary J. Beers " "
7 *Ida A. " unm. ch. &
7 Charlotte E. "   Charles E. Blakeman " "

       Ada Mac Gregor " "
8 *Marjorie "   ch. &
8 *Helen Mac Gregor "   Austin B. Blakeman " "

       Charlotte E. Blakeman " "
8 Maud E. Ives   ch. &
       Frank H. Ives " "
" "   m. Tracy Peck " "

   Ch. Sarah M. Beers, 1st wife, and Lamson Lake

7 Carrie Louise Lake   m. Frank A. Mallett (no ch.) Monroe "
7 *Frederick Beers "   died in young manhood " "
7 Katherine Augusta "   m. William C. Johnson (no ch.) Newtown, Ct.

7 Sarah E. Beers   Angeline E. Beers " "
7 Robert W. "   ch. &
7 John M. "   William H. Beers " "

8 *Ruth Botsford "   Sarah E. Beers   Bridgeport "
8 Ada "   ch. &
       Morris Botsford " "

7 Minnie E. Burritt   Bridgeport, Conn.
7 Ina L. "   Caroline E. Beers " "
7 *Wilson J. "   ch. &
7 Robert W. "   Robert Wilberforce Burritt " "
7 Ida May " " "

       Esther Smith 1st wife
8 Darthia "   ch. &
       Robert W. Burritt
       *Janet Paton 2nd. wife

7	*Emily F. Beers		Emily Beach 1st wife	New Haven, Conn.
7	*Ernest Beach "	ch.	&	
			James M. Beers	" "
			Cornelia Twitchell 2nd wife	" "

8	Virginia Beers		Georgiana Isbell,	" "
8	Allyn "	ch.	&	
	In U. S. Service.		Ernest B. Beers	" "

5 Ch. James B. Beers and Huldah Clarke   Brooklyn, N. Y.

6	*John C. Beers		See Lemuel Beers record	" "
6	*Albert "	Unm.	Huldah Clarke	" "
6	Frederick W. "	ch.	&	
6	*Ann Eliza "	Unm.	James B. Beers	" "

Ch. of Frederick W. Beers and Angeline Hawley

7	Rev. Clarence H. Beers	m.	Ada M. Winterburne	Bethlehem, Conn
7	*Charles A. "			
7	*Harriet E. "	m.	Ralph W. Murdock	
7	Howard F. "			Brooklyn, N. Y.
7	Robert A. "	m.	Mabel Baker	Bridgeport, Conn.
7	*William L. "			
7	*Herbert N. "			
7	Helen M. "			

8	John Frederick "			
8	Amy Marie "		Ada M. Winterburn	Bethlehem, Conn.
8	Emily Huldah "	ch.	&	
8	Anna "		Rev. Clarence Beers	" "

ch. Charles H. Beers and Mary E. Glover

6	*Silas Norman Beers	m.	Sarah Nichols	Newtown, Conn.
6	*Daniel Glover "	"	Arabella Fitch	" "
6	*Mary Elizabeth "	m.	Frederick Beehler	" "

7	*Susan Lynne "	ch.	Sarah Nichols	" "
			&	
			Silas N. Beers	" "

8 Frederick F. Johnson Jr. ch.	Susan Lynne Beers	Redlands, Calif.
	&	
	Rt. Rev. Frederick F. Johnson, St. Louis Mo.

Ch. of Daniel G. Beers and Arabella Fitch:

7	Jane Fitch Beers	m.	Rev. James H. George	Newtown, Conn
7	*Helen "	d.	unm.	" "
7	Harry Croswell "	m.	Mabel Grace Smith	" "
7	Elizabeth Louise "	m.	2nd wife Bishop F. F. Johnson, St. Louis Mo.

8	Sherman Johnson "		Mabel Grace Smith	New Haven, Conn.
8	Jeannette Elizabeth "	ch.	&	
			Harry C. Beers	Lanesboro, Mass..

Ch. Mary E. Beers and Frederick Beehler

7	Ella Beehler	m.	Walter Bounty	Stamford, Conn.
7	*Alice "	d.	in childhood	" "
7	Gertrude "	m.	Clarence Wm. Vail	
7	*Charles "		In Aviation Corps, killed Dec. 19, 1918
7	Robert Morris "		In Naval Reserve	
7	Arthur Leslie "	d.	in infancy.	
7	*Leonard Frederick "	d.	in infancy	

8 Dorothy Elizabeth Vail	ch.	Gertrude Beehler
		&
		Clarence Wm. Vail

9 Ch. of David H. Beers

6 Emeline Beers		David H. Beers	Newtown, Conn.
6 *William H. "	ch.	&	
6 Lucy Ann "		Lucy Fairchild Beers, 95 years old July 16, 1918	" "

7 Edwin Wheeler	ch.	Emeline Beers & Charles Wheeler	Bethel, Conn.
7 Clarence "			" "

7 Julia Beers Duncomb	ch.	Lucy A. Beers & Geo. F. Duncombe	Newtown, Conn
7 Julia B. Duncomb	m.	Rev. Walter Aiken	

Ch. of Dr. 5Moses Botsford Beers

6 Phebe Beers	ch.	Loraine Curtis & Dr. M. Botsford Beers	Hersey, Mich.
7 Albert Newland	ch.	Phebe Beers & J. Selwyn Newland	" "

Ch. of 5Horace Beers and Emily Terrill

6 Sophia Emily Beers	m. William Kellogg	Brookfield, Conn.
6 *Herbert Booth "	Drowned in Housatonic River Aug. 9, 1878.	
6 *Edward Terrill "	Drowned in Housatonic River Aug. 9, 1878.	
6 Frederick Horace "	m. Florence Mapes	

7 Florence E. Kellogg	ch.	Sophia B. Beers & William J. Kellogg	Brookfield, Conn.
7 Herbert Beers "			" "

8 Lina Mansfield	ch.	Florence E. Kellogg & Arthur Mansfield	Brookfield, Conn.

7 Muriel W. Beers	ch.	Florence A. Mapes & Frederick H. Beers	
7 Hazel "			" "

1 Samuel, 2Nathan, 3Nathan Jr., 3Ebenezer, 3Ezekiel.   Newtown, Conn.

Ch. of 3Ezekiel and Polly Candee 1st wife

4 Lucy Beers	m.	Edward Fairchild	New Milford, Conn.
4 Annette "	m.	1st David Botsford 2nd William Botsford	" " " "

5 *Charles B. Botsford	ch.	Annette Beers & David Botsford	New Milford, Conn.
5 David B. "			" "

6 *William Allen "	ch.	Minnie C. Allen & Charles B. Botsford	
6 Lena Annette "			" "

Ch. of Ezekiel Beers and Nancy Johnson 2nd wife,   Newtown, Conn.

4 *Amos "	m.	Jeannette Pierpoint 1st	" "
4 *Theodore "	unm. "	Susan Frances Peck 2nd	

Ch. of Ezekiel Beers and Mrs. Sally Morris Beers, 3rd wife   "

4 *Sylvester "		d. unm.	
4 *Nancy "	m.	Edwin Clarke (See Clarke)	
4 *Julius Augustus "	twins m.	Sarah E. Warner	Monroe, Conn.
4 *Julia Augusta "	m.	Rev. Wm. C. Saxton	Vineland, N. J.

Ch. Julius A. Beers and Sarah Warner   Monroe, Conn
5 Carrie Fenn   "   m. Edwin Sutliffe   "   "
5 Morris Daniel   "   m. Ada Sophia Curtis   "   "

                              Carrie Fenn Beers   "   "
6 Lois Adelaide Sutliffe ch.   &
                              Edwin Sutliffe

                              Lois Adelaide Sutliffe   "   "
7 Edwin Warner   ch.   &
                              Stanley Harold Warner   "   "

6 Preston Morris Beers   Ada Sophia Curtis   Newtown, Conn.
6 Irving Curtis   "   . ch.   &
                              Morris D. Beers

   3 Samuel Beers son of 2 Nathan married Anna Peck   Newtown, Conn.
4 Henry Beers   m. 1st Betsey Glover, 2nd Julia Beers   "   "
4 Amariah   "   "   Betsey Curtis   "   "
4 Charles   "   "
   Henry called Harry, 1st President Newtown Savings Bank.

5 *Julia E. Beers   Julia Beers
5 *Booth G.   "   ch.   &
5 Charlotte   "   Harry Beers

   Charlotte Beers married 1st. A. R. T. Nichols   Greenfield Hill, Conn.
               "   2nd Edward Gebhard   Schoharie, N. Y.
3 Samuel   "   Jr.   m. Charlotte Booth

   Their Ch.

4 Sally Maria Beers   unm.
4 Julia   "   m. Harry Beers
4 David B.   "   " Margaret Pray
4 Charlotte   "   " unmarried.
4 Harriet   "   " George B. Beers   Ithaca, N. Y.
5 *Rev. John Samuel "   Was Gen Missionary of W. Mass.
5 *Emma E.   d. young   Margaret Pray   Brookfield, Conn.
5 *George d. 16 yrs.   ch.   &
5 *Emma S.   "   David B. Beers   Newtown, Conn.

6 Charlotte Louise "
6 George Emerson   "
6 John Howard   "   M. Josephine Wakeman Greenfield Hill Ct.
6 Susan Wakeman   "   ch.   &
6 Henry Sherman   "   Rev. John S. Beers d. Natick, Mass.
6 Eleanor Margaret "

7 Henry Sherman   "   Margaret Lowry
                          ch.   &
7 Margaret Lowry   "   George Emerson Beers

BIRCH

1 William Birch m. Catherine Hubbell daughter of Peter Hubbell 1750
   Their Ch.

2 Ezra, Nehemiah, Sarah, Delight, Catherine, William, Lamson.

3 *David Meeker Birch   Polly Nichols 1st wife Newtown, Conn.
3 *William Nichols "   ch.   &
3 *Polly Ann   "   Lamson Birch   "   "
3 Sally Maria   "

GENEALOGICAL SECTION

Birch	Betty Perry 2nd wife,	Newtown, Conn.
	Hannah Thompson Lake	
	Widow of Ezra Lake 3rd wife	" "
	Joanna Glover Botsford	" "
	Widow of Henry Botsford 4th wife	"
	Mary Ann (Glover) Glover	
	Widow of James Glover 5th wife	"

Mary Ann Glover, 5th wife of Lamson Birch lived to the age of 102 years.

4 *Cornelia Curtis
4 *Jane " ch. Sally M. Birch & Philo Curtis " "

Ch. 3Polly Ann Birch and Philo Lake   Newtown, Conn.

4 *Catherine Lake   m. Amos Hard   " "
4 *Hannah Ann "   " John S. Hubbard   Meriden, Conn.
4 *Ezra Birch "   " Melissa Saxton
4 *Lamson Birch "   " Sarah M. Beers 1st   Newtown, Conn.
                                 Sylvia M. Beers 2nd

5 Chester Hard   ch. Catherine Lake & Amos Hard

5 *John Beers Hubbard   ch John S. Hubbard & Hannah A. Lake

5 Nora B. Lake   Twins   ch. Melissa Saxton   East Randolph, N. Y.
5 *Ora "   & Ezra B. Lake   Cherry Creek, N. Y.

Ch. Lamson B. Lake and Sarah M. Beers 1st wife   Newtown, Conn.

5 Carrie Louise Lake   m. Frank A. Mallet (no ch.)   Monroe "
5 *Frederick Beers "   d. in young manhood
5 Katherine Augusta"   m. William C. Johnson (no ch.) Newtown, "

5 Grace Elizabeth "   ch. Sylvia M. Beers 2nd wife   Passaic, N. J.
5 Florence Amelia "   & Lamson B. Lake   " "

Ch. Chester Hard and Ida Harkness   Painesville, Ohio

5 Elmo Amos Hard   n. Eva Kenney   " "
5 Cora "   d. young.   " "
5 Florence Esther "   " Elmer B. Kimmel   " "
6 Harkness Gould "   In U. S. Service.
Corp Harkness G. Hard C. G. 23rd. Engineers in France.

BLACKMAN or BLAKEMAN

The Commemorative Biographical Record states:

1 "John Blackman b. 1685 grandson of Rev. Adam Blakeman of Stratford, was one of a company of fifty-two who purchased the township of Newtown of the Colonial Government and removed there in 1713. He m. Abigail Beers.

Their Children:

2 Martha   Blackman b. 1714 m. Abel Botsford   Newtown, Conn
2 Abigail   " " 1716 " Samuel Beers (see Beers)   " "
2 Capt. John   " " 1720 " Margery Glover   " "
2 Ebenezer   " " 1723 " Mary Smith   Brookfield, Conn.
2 Joseph   " " 1726 " Elizabeth Glover   Newtown, Conn.
2 James   " " 1730 " Huldah Griffin   " "

3 John son of Capt. 2John m. Diamah Seeley   " "

GENEALOGICAL SECTION

4 Simeon Seeley son of 3John m. Lucy Northrop,   Newtown, Conn.
  Their Ch.
5 *Eliza   Blackman   m. Charles Sherman (no ch.) Danbury, "
5 *Harriet   "   " Robert N. Hawley (See Hawley) Newtown
5 *Sarah   "   " Andrew Sherman   Bethel, Conn.
5 *Sophia   "   " Dr. Ransom Lyon   "   "
5 *Emeline   "   " Robert Adams Clarke   "   "
                      (See Freegrace Adams)
6 Mary Helen Sherman   m. Leonard Smith (no ch.)

6 Frederick   Sarah Blackman
                     ch.   &&
                          Andrew Sherman
   "   "   m. Lillian Stearley   Bethel, Conn.
                                           "   "

6 *Edward Lyon   Sophia Blackman
                     ch.   &&
                          Dr. Ransom Lyon   Bethel, Conn.

2 Ch. Ebenezer Blackman and Mary Smith
3 Mary   Blackman   m. Turner   Brookfield, Conn.
3 Philo   "   " Eunice Peck   "   "
3 Lois   "
3 Anna   "   " Liverius Hawley   "   "
3 Niram   "   " Phebe Sanford   "   "
3 Ebenezer   "   " Abagail Goodrich   "   "

4 Ebenezer   "   Eunice Peck   Brookfield, Conn.
4 Ammon Booth "   ch.   &&
5 Mary   "   3Philo Blackman
5 Nirom   "   Abigail Goodrich   Amenia, N. Y.
5 Hiram   "   ch. &&
5 William   "   Ebenezer Blackman   Brookfield, Conn.

6 Philo Booth   "   Caroline Skidmore 1st wife
                     ch. &&
                         Ammon B. Blackman   Brookfield, Conn.
                         Eliza Weed Sherman 2nd wife   "   "

4 Benjamin Hawley   3Anna Blackman
                     ch. &&
                         Liverius Hawley   "   "

5 Henry B.   "   ch. Betsey Peck   "   "
                         &&
  "   "   "   m. Benjamin Hawley   "   "
                      Esther Skidmore
                     (See Skidmore record)

6 Frederick   Roe
6 Sarah A.   "   5Mary Blackman   Brookfield, Conn.
6 Alva D.   "   ch. &&
6 William B.   "   Harvey Roe
6 Mary B.   "

7 Irving Roe Vail   Mary Blackman Roe   Danbury, Conn.
7 Grace Elizabeth " ch. &&
                       Frederick Vail

1 John   Blackman   m. Abigail Beers
2 Ebenezer   "   " Mary Smith
3 Nirom   "   " Phebe Sanford
  Their Ch.
4 Irena   Blackman m. Alfred Platt   Waterbury, Conn.
4 Esther   "   " Starr Ferry   Bethel   "
4 Maria   "   " David Northrop   Brookfield   "
4 Clark   "
4 Seabury   "   " Anna Booth   Newtown, Conn.

GENEALOGICAL SECTION

5 Clark	Ferry			
5 Oris S.	"		Esther Bleckman	
5 Leroy	"	ch.	&	
5 Maria Esther	"		Starr Ferry	Bethel, Conn.

Senator Orris S. Ferry, born Aug. 15, 1823. Elected in 1859 to Thirty-sixth Congress. At opening of Civil War was Colonel of Fifth Regiment, Conn. Volunteers. Commissioned Brigadier General by President Lincoln March 17, 1862. Elected U. S. Senator by Conn. Legislature in 1866; re-elected in 1872. Died at Norwalk, Conn. Nov. 21, 1875.

6 Legrand	Randall			Salt Lake City, Utah
6 Clarke	"			
6 *Leroy	"		Maria E. Ferry	Bethel, Conn.
6 Orris	"	ch.	&	"
6 *Charlotte	"		Charles Randall	Roxbury "
6 *Sarah	"			New Milford "

			Alice Couch 1st wife	Norwalk "
7 Alice Couch	"	ch.	&	
			Leroy Randall	New Milford "
		m.	George Allen	

7 Lee Randall	"		Mary Potter 2nd wife	New Milford, Conn.
7 Mary Ethel	"	ch.	&	
			Leroy Randall	" "

5 Emily Northrop			Maria Blackman	
5 Julia	"	ch.	&	
5 Esther	"		David Northrop	
"	"	m.	1st Ely Booth	Dayton Ohio
		"	2nd Henry Andrews	Brookfield, Conn.

Desc. of 4 Seabury son of 3 Niram

		Anna Booth	
5 *Pheobe Jane Blackman	ch.	&	Newtown, Conn.
		Seabury Blackman	" "

6 *Katherine Wolf Glidden				
6 *Clarence	"		Phoebe Jane Blackman	
6 Estella M.	"	ch.	&	Milwaukee, Wis.
6 Jennie Seabury	"		Carlos Glidden	" "
6 Minnie Maud	"		Pratt Institute	Brooklyn, N. Y.

Carlos Glidden assisted financially by C. Latham Sholes, invented the first successful typewriter; the one known as the Remington. It was at first called the Sholes and Glidden type-writer, and the No. 1, machine bears that name. The name Sholes was placed first in deference to his years. He was much older than Mr. Glidden.

7 Glidden	Perkins		Estella M. Glidden
7 Stella Frances	"	ch.	&
7 Marion Glidden	"		George Francis Perkins

7 Marion Glidden Perkins m. Horace Glenwood Gemmill

4 David S. son of 3 John, b. 1782, m. Fanny Peck.

5 Isaac	Blackman		Fanny Peck	Newtown, Conn.
5 Sally	"	ch.	&	" "
5 Ebenezer	"		David S. Blackman	" "
6 James M.	"		Sally Bennett	" "
6 Fanny	"	ch.	&	
6 Isaac Percy	"		Ebenezer Blackman	Passaic, N. J.
			Sarah Wilkins	Boston, Mass.
7 Lucy F.	"	ch.	&	
7 Maude H.	"		James M. Blackman	Newtown, Conn.

7 Pauline T.   Blackman   Jessie P. Mitchell   Passaic, N. J.
7 Olive M.   "   ch.   &
                                Isaac Percy Blackman   "   "

3 3Ebenezer, 4John, 5Joseph, 6Joseph, 6Daniel.
6 Joseph Blackman   m. Huldah Toucey   Newtown, Conn
  Their Ch.   gr. dau. Rev. Thomas Toucey

7 *James Glover   "   Newtown, Conn.
7 *John Toucey   "   m. Sally Baldwin   "   "
7 *Ziba   "   " Augusta Blakeslee   "   "
7 *Donald   "   " Louisa Platt   "   "
7 *Joseph   "   " Mary Botsford Bailey   "   "
7 *Maria   "   " Abner Peck Blakeslee   Plymouth, Conn.
                               Removed to Des Moines, Iowa

  Des. of Ziba (see Blakeslee line.)

  Des. of Donald and Louisa Platt

8 *Maria Louise Blackman m. Wm. D. B. Ferris (See Ferris) Newtown,
8 *Harriet Brown   "   " 1st wife David Curtis New Haven, Conn.
8 Sarah Elizabeth   "   " 2nd wife   "   " (see Curtis) "   "

  Desc. of 7Joseph Blackman and Mary Botsford Bailey

8 *Julia Esther Blackman   d. in girlhood
8 Ann Elizabeth   "   Mary Botsford Bailey   Newtown, Conn.
8 Joseph Albert   "   ch.   &
8 Mary Frances   "   Joseph Blackman   "   "

  Ch. Joseph Albert Blackman and Mary Warner:

9 Mary Elizabeth Blackman   unm.   Danbury, Conn.
9 Stanley Joseph   "   m. Sarah Miner   South Britain   "
9 Albert Francis   "   unm.   Newtown,   "
9 Henry Warner   "   m. Caroline Clark   New Britain   "
9 Eva Hutchinson   "   m. Clarence Naramore   Bridgeport   "

10 Clarence   Naramore   Eva Hutchinson Blackman   Bridgeport
10 Mary Blackman "   ch.   &
                                Clarence B. Naramore   "

  Ch. Rev. F. W. Barnett and Mary Frances Blackman   Newtown, Conn.

9 Rev. Francis Blackman Barnett, Rector of Christ Church, Ridley Park
Philadelphia, Pa., Chaplain in U. S. Army in France.

9 Mary Pritchard Barnett
9 Rev. Joseph Noyes   "   Lieut. in U. S. Service in France
9 Lieut. William Edward"   Now in France

10 Dorothy Barnett   Emily Hale   Ridley Park
10 Francis   "   ch.   &
10 Walter   "   Rev. F. B. Barnett   Phila., Pa.

6 Daniel Blackman   m. Lois Skidmore   Newtown, Conn.
  Their Ch.
7 Lucy   "   m. John Curtis (See Curtis)   "   "
7 Letty   "   unm.
7 Esther   "   m. Dibble Camp (See Camp)   "   "
7 Sybil   "   unm.
7 Polly Ann   "   m. Dibble Fairchild (See Fairchild)   "
7 Harriet   "   unm.

1 James   "   m. Sylvia Hitchcock
2 Samuel   "   m. Eunice Skidmore

GENEALOGICAL SECTION

Their Ch.
3	James Blackman	m.	Hannah Turner	Newtown, Conn
3	Abel Beers	"	" Lucy Maria Barnum	Bethel "
3	Lucy	"	" William Guyer	" "
3	Lacy	"	" Clara Lyon	Bridgeport "
3	Marietta	"	" Wilson Lyon	Redding "
3	Bennett	"	" Hepsa Shepard	Newtown, "
3	Clark	"	" Sarah Ann Shepard	" "

Ch. Hannah Turner and James Blackman

4	*Eliza Blackman	m.	Henry Stevens	
4	*Reuben Starr "	"	Elizabeth Lake	
4	*Mary "	"	Thaddeus Hollister	Bethel "
4	*Margaret "	"	James Baldwin	Danbury, Conn.
4	*Cornelia "	"	2nd wife, Clark T. Jackson, Brookfield, "
4	*Caroline Blackman	m.	Thomas Bristol no ch.	Brookfield, Conn.
4	James Leroy "	"	Elizabeth Barlow 1st	Redding "
			Elizabeth Austin Bennett 2nd	
4	*Frances "	"	1st wife, Clark T. Jackson, Brookfield "

Ch. Eliza Blackman and Henry Stevens.

5	Hattie Stevens	m.	Eliad Taylor	Waterbury, "
5	Charles "	"	Helen Osborne	" "
5	James "	"	Lary Durant (no ch.)	
5	*George "	"	Bertha Ward (no ch.)	

6 Ruth Taylor		Hattie Stevens	Waterbury, Conn.
6 Daniel " unm	ch.	&	
6 Harry " unm.		Eliad Taylor	" "
6 Eliza "			

7 Harriet Houghton		Eliza Taylor	Waterbury, Conn.
7 Franklin "	ch.	&	
		Frank Houghton	

6 Annie Stevens		Helen Osborne	Danbury, Conn.
6 Bertha "	ch.	&	
		Charles Stevens	

7 Charles Andrews	ch.	Annie Stevens & Leroy Andrews	

7 Jennette Morgan			
7 Helen "		Bertha Stevens	
7 Marion "	ch.	&	
7 Frances "		Frank Morgan	Danbury, Conn.
7 Starr "			
7 Gladys "			

5 Florence E. Blackman			Newtown, Conn.
5 Charles J. "		Elizabeth Lake	" "
5 Henry S. "	ch.	&	
5 Eliza S. "		Reuben S. Blackman	" "

6 John S. Drew	ch.	Florence E. Blackman & Frank Drew	Newtown, Conn.

7 Eleanor "	ch.	Grace Lockard & John Drew	Bridgeport, "
7 Elizabeth "			

6 Lottie E. Blackman	ch.	Augusta Blackman & Charles J. Blackman	Newtown, Conn. " "

GENEALOGICAL SECTION

7 Laura Ruffels	ch.	Lottie E. Blackman, & Frank Ruffels ..	Newtown, Conn. " "
7 Wm. Clark "			
6 Flora E. Blackman	ch.	Catherine Foster & Henry S. Blackman	Danbury, Conn.
6 Arthur S. "			
6 Herbert M. "			
7 Catherine Virginia Cook	ch.	Flora E. Blackman & Irving Cook	
7 Arthur Starr, Ch.		6 Arthur S. Blackman	
6 Edward Leverich	m.	Maud Cody Lieut. in U. S. Army	Egg Harbor, Wis.
6 Pierce "			
6 Earl "	ch.	Eliza Blackman & James W. Leverich	Sparta, Wis.
6 Florence "			
6 Harriet "			
6 Jesse "			
6 Grace "			
3 Ella Holister	ch.	4 Mary Blackman & Thaddeus Hollister	Bethel "
m. Adolph Tumerell			

Ch. 4 Margaret Blackman and James Baldwin

5 *Mary Eliza Baldwin	m.	Wm. Wheeler no ch.	
5 William D. "	"	Annie Monroe	Danbury, Conn.
5 Jennie "	"	Wm. Godfrey	" "
5 John "	"	Lottie Pierce no ch.	Hartford, Conn.
5 Robert "	"	Carrie Gordon	
5 *Dwight "	"	Lottie Peete	
5 *Louis "	"	unm.	
6 Louis "	ch.	Annie Monroe & Wm. D. Baldwin	Danbury, Conn. " "
6 William "			
6 Eugenie "			
7 Catherine Schafer"	ch.	Catherine Schafer & 6 Louis Baldwin	" "
7 Robert "			
6 Margaret Godfrey	ch.	Jennie Baldwin & Wm. Godfrey	Danbury, Conn. " "
6 Robert Gordon Baldwin	ch.	Carrie Gordon & Robert Baldwin	" "
6 Hazel "			" "
6 Dwight "	ch.	Lottie Peete & Dwight Baldwin	" "
6 Dorothy "			
5 Charles Jackson m. Maude Crosby (no ch.)	ch.	Frances Blackman 1st wife &.. Clark T. Jackson	Newtown, Ct.
5 *Cornelia Jackson m. W. J. Beehler (no ch.)	ch.	Cornelia Blackman 2nd wife & Clark T. Jackson	Brookfield, Ct
5 *Starr Blackman	ch.	Elizabeth Barlow 1st wife & James Leroy Blackman Elizabeth Austin Bennett 2nd wife	Redding, Conn.
5 Bessie "			
5 Lloyd "			

GENEALOGICAL SECTION

5 Bessie   Blackman   m. Aaron Sanford (no ch.)   Redding, Conn.

6 Amy Elizabeth "   ch. Gertrude Von Gal & Lloyd Blackman   Redding, Conn.

3 Lucy Maria Barnum and Abel Beers Blackman

4 George Blackman   Bethel, Conn.
4 Theodore "   "   "
4 Elizabeth "   m. Joel Seymour   "   "
4 *Augusta "   " Edwin Short 1st wife   "   "
4 Lucy "   " George Osborn   "   "
4 Mary "   " Edwin Short 2nd wife   "   "

5 Rev. William S. Short   ch. Augusta Blackman 1st wife & Edwin Short
5 Grace "

6 Carrie E. "
6 Edwin T. "   Lottie A. Wheeler
6 Seabury T. "   ch.   &
6 Wm. Frederick "   Rev. Wm. S. Short   Santa Rosa, Calif.

6 Lucy E.   Spittle   5Grace Short   Astoria, Oregon
6 Samuel "   ch.   &
6 John "   Frank Spittle   "   "

4 Lucy Blackman and William Guyer

5 Henry Guyer   William Guyer
6 Esther "   ch.   &
5 Juliette "   Lusy Blackman

Clara Lyon and 3Lacey Blackman

4 Smith Blackman
4 Henry "
4 Hart "
4 Monroe "
4 Eunice Ann "   Mrs. Charles Way
4 Lorintha "   " Elmer Shepard
4 Emily "   " David Bulkley
4 Annis "

3 Ch. Marietta Blackman and Wilson Lyon

5 Susan Lyon   Mrs. George Lane
5 William "

4 *Susan J. Blackman   Hepsa Shepard 1st wife   Newtown, Conn.
4 John H. "   ch.   &
                    Bennett Blackman   "   "
                    Elizabeth Platt 2nd wife

5 Bennett Short   Susan J. Blackman
5 Julia "   ch.   &
                    Rufus Short   Bethel, Conn.

6 Royal Ferry   Julia Short   "   "
6 Leonard "   ch.   &
6 Harold "   Theodore Ferry   "   "
6 Ruth "

Sarah Ann Shepard and 3Clark Blackman   Newtown, Conn.

4 *Samuel Ambrose Blackman m. Anna A. Barnum   "   "
4 Mary Augusta "   m. Charles Blackman   "   "
4 Charlotte E. "   " 3rd wife, Clark T. Jackson

5 Clark	Blackman	m.	Roberta Neville,	Newtown, Conn.
5 Dr. Claude	"	ch.	Anna A. Barnum &	" "
5 Frank	"		Samuel A. Blackman	" "
6 Clara	"		Clara Williams	New Milford, Conn.
6 Gordon	"	ch.	&	
6 Phyllis	"		Dr. Claude Blackman	
6 Allen	"	ch.	Florence Edwards & Frank Blackman	
5 Sarah L. Jackson m. Arthur H. Osmon		ch.	Charlotte E. Blackman 3rd wife & Clark T. Jackson	Brookfield, Conn.

BLAKESLEE.

"Ziba Blakeslee is said to have been a most skilled workman and manufactured all kinds of jewelry. His advertisement in the Farmers Journal, Dec. 22, 1792, shows that he carried on at the head of the Street in Newtown, the goldsmith's business in all its branches; cast bells for Churches, made and repaired surveyor's instruments, church clocks and clocks of all kinds."

1 Ziba	Blakeslee	m.	Mehitable Botsford	Newtown, Conn.
2 Charles	"	"	Jane Botsford	Woodbury, "
2 William	"	"	Chloe Fairman	Newtown, Conn.
2 Augusta	"	"	Ziba Blackman	" "
Ch. William	"	&	Chloe Fairman	" "
3 *James Beach	"	m.	Susan J. Beers	" "
3 *Eliza Maria	"	"	Henry Beers Glover	" "
3 *Charles Fairman	"	"	Ella M. Hugus	
3 *Sophia Augusta	"	"	Daniel G. Hammond	Brooklyn, N. Y.
3 *William Ziba	"	"	Eliza Dingman	
3 *Mary Jane	"		d. in infancy	
3 *Geo. Benjamin	"		unm.	Newtown, Conn.
3 *Mary 2nd	"		unm.	" "
3 Sarah Grace	"	"	Samuel Curtis Glover	" "
4 *Carrie	"		Susan J. Beers	" "
4 *Annie	"	ch.	& James B. Blakeslee	St. Petersburg, Pa.

Ch. Charles F. Blakeslee and Ella Hugus   Franklin, Pa.

4 Florence Glover	"	m.	Rollin Coleman Smith	Los Angeles, Calf.
4 Charles Fairman	"	"	Marion Aida Coulter	" " "
5 Florence Blakeslee Smith			Florence G. Blakeslee	" " "
5 Charles Blakeslee	"	ch.	&	
5 Rollin Coleman	"		Rollin C. Smith	

Charles Blakeslee Smith in Signal Service Corps. in France

4 *Mary Grace Hammond				
4 Eva	"		Sophia A. Blakeslee	Brooklyn, N. Y.
4 Ella	"	ch.	&	
4 Sophie	"		Daniel Hammond	
4 Daniel	"			
5 *Grace Northrop			Mary Grace Hammond	Newtown, Conn.
5 Eleanor	"	ch.	&	
5 Nelson	"		*Charles H. Northrop	

Ch. 3William Z. Blakeslee and Eliza Dingman   Butler, Penn.

4 William S. Blakeslee		m.	Dorothy McKean	" "
4 Irene	"	"	John V. Ritts	" "
4 *Isaac	"		d. young	

GENEALOGICAL SECTION

5 Dorothy Irene Blakeslee	Dorothy McKean,	Butler, Penn.
5 Dorothy Irene " ch.	&	" "
	William S. Blakeslee	
Ch. Irene "	& John V. Ritts	" "
5 Elias Ritts	m. Helen Hunt Here	" "
5 Maud A. "	" Frank Craig Dickson	" "
5 Leonard "	" Gladys Clark	" "
4 Curtis Glover	ch. Sarah Grace Blakeslee & Samuel Curtis Glover	Newtown, Conn.

Ch. 2 Augusta Blakeslee and Ziba Blackman — Newtown, Conn.

3 *Sarah Blackman	m. Dr. Monroe Judson	" "
3 *John "	d. in young manhood	" "
3 *Eliza "	" Delos Smith (no ch.)	" "
3 *Mary "	" William H. Taylor	
3 Hattie "	" James Turney	
3 Martha "	d. young	

Ch. Sarah "	& Dr. Monroe Judson	
4 Martha Judson	m. E. P. Taylor	Oakland, Calif.
4 John "		

Ch. Martha Judson	& E. P. Taylor	" "
5 Mary Judson Taylor	m. John Adolph Breitling	" "
5 Harriet Benedict "	" Julius Young	" "
5 Florence Barker "	" James Scott Ireland	" "
	Desc. of Sir Walter Scott	" "

6 John Judson Breitling	ch. Mary J. Taylor & John A. Breitling	
6 Edward Taylor Young	ch. Harriet B. Taylor & Julius Young	
6 Martha Ireland	Florence Barker Taylor	
6 Anita " ch.	&	
6 Jane "	James Scott Ireland	" "

3 Mary Blakeslee Blackman	m. Wm. H. Taylor	San Francisco, Cal.
Their Ch.		
4 Dr. Walter Judson Taylor and wife		Sacramento, Calif.
5 John Meister Taylor		
5 Elinor "	ch. Dr. Walter Judson Taylor	" "
5 Walter Judson Jr. "		
4 Maud Blackman Turney	ch. Hattie Blackman & James Turney	Astoria, Oregon
5 Mabel Taylor Woolsey	ch. Maud B. Turney & Ammon J. Taylor	Seattle, Oregon

BOOTH

1 Richard Booth first settler of the name in Stratford in 1640.
   m. Elizabeth Hawley
2 Sergeant John, son of 1Richard born 1653 m. Dorothy Hawley. He served in the Pequot War.
3 Jonathan, son of Sergt. John b. 1681 m. Hester Galpin and came to Newtown in 1707.
4 Lieut. Daniel son of 3Jonathan b. 1704 m. Eunice Bennett.
5 Daniel son of Lieut. Daniel, b. 1730, m. Huldah Thompson

 Their Ch.

6 *Parthena	Booth	m.	Jabez Hawley (See Hawley)	Newtown, Ct.	
6 *Thompson	"	"	Eunice Coburn	"	"
6 *Daniel	"	"	Sabra Sherman	"	"
6 *Joseph	"	"	Clara Blackman	"	"
6 *Phebe	"		unm.		
6 *Huldah	"	"	Cyrus Sherman (See Sherman)	"	"
6 *Naomi	"		unm.	"	"
6 *Nichols	"		died young	"	"
6 Sabra	"		unm.	"	"

 Ch. Daniel Booth and Sabra Sherman

7 Julia Ann	Booth	m.	Cyrenius Beecher (no ch.)	Wakeman, Ohio	
7 Daniel Lewis	"	"	1st Emelia Randall	Bridgewater, Conn.	
			2nd Jane Ann Peck	Newtown, Conn.	
7 Sarah Irene	"		unm.		
7 Mary Charlotte	"	"	George Smith	Bridgewater	"
7 Walter Sherman	"	"	Catherine Eliza Peters	Kent	"

 Ch. Daniel L. " & Emelia Randall 1st wife Bridgewater "

8 Daniel Theodore	"	m.	*Mary Nelson	Long Beach, Cal.
8 *Nathan Randall	"	"	Fidelia Hamm	Bridgewater, Conn.
8 *Justin Sherman	"		Killed in Civil War at Mission Ridge.	
8 *Susan Emelia	"	"	George Fowler	Bridgewater, Conn.

 Ch. Daniel L. " & Jane Ann Peck 2nd wife Newtown, Conn.

8 *Emeline Jane	"	m.	Rev. Joseph Hillmer	Winona, Minn.
8 Lewis Abner	"	"		Watertown, S. Dakota
8 *Richard Botsford	"		died young	Faribault, Minn.
8 Joseph Peck	"			" "

8 Rev. Daniel Theodore Booth m. Mary Nelson
 Rev. Mr. Booth 83 years old in 1918 living in Long Beach, California.

9 Grace Emelia Booth		m	William D. Higgins
9 Julia Esther	"		
9 Mary Seabury	"		
9 Lawrence Nelson	"		
9 Sarah Irene	"	"	Samuel C. Tompkins
9 Daniel Norman	"	twins	
9 Gertrude Theodora	"	twins	
9 William Robert	"	twins	
9 Margaret Louise	"	twins m.	John Clarkson Mann
9 Mary Esther Nelson	"	"	Franklin H. Baxley

10 John Booth Higgins		Grace Emelia Booth
10 Lawrence Gilbert "	ch.	&
		Wm. D. Higgins
10 Eleanor Laurane Tompkins		Sarah Irene Booth
10 Margaret Louise "	ch.	&
10 Allen Coles "		Samual Coles Tompkins

GENEALOGICAL SECTION

10 Margaret Mary Mann   ch.   Margaret Louise Booth
                                             &
                                             John Clarkson Mann

9 Jennie Aloisia Monica Hilmer
9 Joseph Booth   "   Emeline Jane Booth   Winona Minn.
9 Nonna Theresa   "   ch.   &
9 Elsie Corinne   "   Rev. J. J. Hillmer, Prof. of Ancient
                                                                                           Languages at University.

10 Joseph Lawrence   "
10 Thurston Booth   "
10 Marjorie Marie   "   Bertha Gressins
10 Edgar Thompson   "   ch.   &
10 Herbert Julius   "   Joseph Booth Hillmer Wessington Springs
10 Ralph Gressins   "   S. Dakota.

10 Bernice Lorraine Bagley   Nonna Theresa Hillmer
10 Lucile   "   ch.   &
                                           Chester A. Bagley   Denver Colo.

10 Helen Beverly Meile   Elsie Corinne Hillmer   New Ulm., Minn.
10 Alice Jane   "   ch.   &
                                            Adolph G. Meile

8 Julia Frances Smith   George Smith   "   "
8 Ada Apphia   "   ch.   &
                                       Mary Charlotte Booth Bridgewater, Conn.

9 Mary Charlotte Turrill   Frederick Jay Turrill
9 Dr. Henry Smith "   ch.   &
   m. Edith Josephine Ferris.   Julia Frances Smith   "   "
                                Medical Adviser at Kent School, Kent, Conn.,

10 Elizabeth Bentley   ch.   Mary Charlotte Turrill
                                         &
                                         Charles Prentice Bentley

                                         Ada Apphia Smith   Brigdewater, Conn.
9 Grace Carson Mead   ch.   &
                                         Carson Beers Mead   "   "

10*Joseph Carson Wellwood ch. &
10 Francis Caldwell "   Grace Carson Mead   "   "
                                         Frank Wellwood

Joseph Carson Wellwood enlisted in 1st Conn. Ambulance Co. Changed in England to 102nd Ambulance Co. 26th Div. 101st. Sanitary Train and promoted to 104th Field Hospital. Died of Scarlet fever in France Feb. 17th 1918, aged 19 yrs. 9 mos.

8 *Harriet Gertrude Booth   b. Canaan, Conn.
8 *John Peters   "   Catherine E. Peters   Kent, Conn.
8 Walter Sherman, Jr. "   ch.   &
8 *Henry Whipple   "   Walter S. Booth   Rochester, Minn.
8 William Hull   "

9 Catherine Elizabeth Abel   Harriet G. Booth   Minneapolis, Minn.
9 Marie Albertine   "   ch.   &
     "   "   Wilhelm August Abel
                                 m.   Rev. Wm. E. Warren

9 Lillie May Booth   Nettie Amelia Nelson 1st wife   Rochester,
9 William Henry "   ch.   &   Minn.
                                         Walter S. Booth Jr.   "   "

                                         Bertha M. Townsend 2nd wife "   "
9 Corinne   "   ch.   &
                                         Walter S. Booth, Jr.

GENEALOGICAL SECTION

```
   4Lieut. Daniel, 5Ezra, 6Austin, 7Cyrus A.        Newtown, Conn.
6 Austin Booth         m. Abigail Botsford              "    "
   Their Ch.

7 Ezra    Booth       m. Sophia Whalley           Vergennes, Vt.
7 Cyrus A.  "         "  Catherine White 1st wife      "    "
7 Henry     "         "  Sarah Brace White 2nd wife    "    "
8 William White Booth     Catherine White 1st wife
8 Charles Austin  "   ch.          &
                          Cyrus A. Booth

9 Harriet Mabel   "       Elizabeth Lane
9 Marion Elizabeth "  ch.          &
                          William W. Booth

                          Harriet M. Booth
10 Donald Clark       ch.          &
                          Geo. K. Clark

10 William Booth Bunn     Marion E. Booth
10 Elizabeth     "    ch.          &
                          Albert C. Bunn

9 Harry H. Booth          Flora Burge            Richmond Hill, L. I.
9 Charles L.  "       ch.          &
9 Catherine   "           Charles A. Booth

                          Mary Rich
10 Jane       "       ch.          &
                          Harry H. Booth

10 Ralph   Heuch Jr.      Catherine Booth
10 Flora Jane    "    ch.          &
10 Charles Booth "        Ralph Heuch

8 Sarah White Booth       Sarah Grace White 2nd wife
8 John Henry   "      ch.          &
                          Cyrus Booth

9 Rev. John Booth Clark   Sarah White Booth      Rosebud, S. Dakota
9 Rev. David William "ch.          &             Rapid City
9 Corp. Hobart Hare  "    Rev. A. B. Clark       Hot Springs S. Dakota
   Now in France

9 John Parkhurst Booth    Maria Parkhurst
9 Robert Cyrus    "   ch.          &
9 Catherine       "       John Henry Booth

7 Ch. Ezra Booth and Sophia Whalley              Vergennes, Vt.
8 *William  Booth     m. Thrirza Field           Ferresbury, Vt.
8 *Lucy     "         "  Solomon Williams        Charlotte, Vt.
8 *Ellen    "         "  David C. Peck           Newtown, Conn.
8 Richard   "         "  Carrie Barnes           Vergennes, Vt.
8 Ada       "         "  Wallace Higbee          Charlotte, Vt.
8 Austin    "         "  Louise Porter           Ferrisburg Vt.

                          Thirza Field           Waltham, Vt.
9 Arthur E.   "       ch.          &                 "    "
9 Agnes F.    "           William Booth
                      m. David C. Peck 2nd wife

10 William W.  "
10 Fred A.     "
10 Hermon T.   "          Mary A. Ward               "    "
10 Ezra W.     "      ch.          &                 "    "
10 Ralph F.    "          Arthur E. Booth
10 Margaret E. "                                  Shelburne, Vt.
```

9 Alice Williams			Charlotte, Vt.
9 Ezra Booth "	*Lucy Booth		" "
9 Flora "	ch. &		
9 John "	Solomon Williams		" "
10 Marsh Byington	Alice Williams		
10 Hazel "	ch. &		
10 Janice "	Burton Byington		
10 Charles Williams	Jessie Elliott		
10 Harold "	ch. ch. &		
	Ezra B. Williams		
9 *Ada Booth Peck	Ellen Booth		Newtown, Conn.
9 *Cora E. "	ch. &		" "
	David C. Peck		
9 Fred R. Booth	Carrie Barnes ch. & Richard Booth		
10 Lucy "	Susan Merritt		" "
10 Rachel "	ch. & Fred B. Booth		
9 Mabel Higbee m. Henry Hill	Ada Booth ch. & Wallace Higbee		New York, City
9 Herbert A. Booth	Louise Porter ch. & Austin Booth		Ferrisburg Vt. " "
10 Flora "	Alice Wilkins		" "
10 Austin "	ch. &		
10 Richard "	Herbert A. Booth		" "

Ch. Seabury Booth and Lucinda Sanford:

7 Anna Booth	m.	Seabury Blackman (See Blackman)	Brookfield, Conn.
7 Lewis "	"	Harriet	
7 William "	"	Mary Rice	Bridgeport, Conn.
7 Carlos "	"	Elizabeth Fairchild	Newtown, Conn.
7 Henry "	"		St. Louis Mo.
7 Charles "	"	Emily Gregory	Bridgeport, Conn.
7 Ely "	"	Esther Northrop	Dayton, Ohio

Ch. Carlos Booth and Elizabeth Fairchild   Newtown, Conn.

8 Luncinda Booth	m.	Henry Cook	
8 *Henry Sanford "	unm.		
8 *Levi Burtis "	m.	Sophia Clark	Newtown, Conn.
8 *Charles "	unm.		
8 *Anna Elizabeth "	m.	John Blackman (no ch.)	" "
8 *Emily Louise "	"	Charles Canfield (no ch.)	" "
8 Carlos Tracy "	"	Lillie Robinson	
8 *Cora Frances "	"	Elliott M. Peck (See Peck)	" "

9 Harry Cook		Lucinda Booth	Newtown, Conn.
9 *Lillian "	ch.	&	
9 Bertha "		Henry Cook	
10 Harry Cook Mitchell m. Sarah Beers	ch.	Bertha Cook & Amos Mitchell	Hartford, Conn.
9 Philo Clarke Booth	ch.	Sophia Clarke & Levi Burtis Booth	" "

GENEALOGICAL SECTION

   Ch. Cora Frances Booth and Elliott M. Peck
9 Eugene Marshall Peck   m. Florence Clark   Brookfield, Conn.
9 Tracy "   " Maude Estelle Ives   Newtown, Conn.
9 Cora May "   " Clifford Russell

10 Benjamin Russell   Cora May Peck
10 Anna May "   ch. &
10 Sterling "   Clifford Russell

   Ch. Charles Booth and Emily Gregory   Bridgeport, Conn.
8 Rev. Robert C. Booth   m. Mary Carter   New York, N. Y.
9 Robert "   their Ch.
8 Louise "   m. Capt. Albert W. Peck   Newtown, Conn.
(For desc. see Peck record.)

6 Joseph Booth m. Clara Blackman.

   Their Ch.
7 *Elmer Booth   m. Ann Curtis
7 *Nichols "   " Antoinnette Pray (ch. d. in early life)
7 *Josiah "   " Sarah Morehouse (no ch.) Newtown, Conn.
7 *Charlotte "   unm.
7 *Daniel "   unm.

8 *Sarah "   *Ann Curtis   " "
8 *Mary Ann "   ch. &
                *Elmer Booth   " "

9 Harriet Somers Bronson   Mary Ann Booth   Oxford, Conn.
9 Ann Tomlinson "   ch. &
9 *Mary Esther "   David W. Bronson   " "
9 Anna T. Downs   Bridgeport, Conn.

10 Mary Booth Cramer   Harriet S. Bronson
10 Fannie Bristol "   ch. &
10 Wm Bronson "   *Burnett A. Cramer

11 Cecil Johnston   Mary Booth Cramer   Redlands, Cal.
                ch. &
                *August Johnston

11 William T. Forden Jr.
11 *Winston Dent "   Fannie Bristol Cramer   Ansonia, Conn.
11 Louise Dent "   ch. &
11 Sterling Cramer "   William T. Forden   " "
11 Raymond Burnett "

11 John Richard Cramer   Elsie A. Richards
11 Baby Girl 1918 "   ch. &
                Wm. Bronson Cramer   Douglas, Arizona
                Assayer of Metals in Govt. Employ.

1 Philo Booth   m. Aurelia Hard   Newtown, Conn.
   Their Ch.
2 Charles Booth   m. Miss Candee (no desc.)   " "
2 Dr. Cyreneus "   " Sarah Edmond

1 Andrew Booth m. Anna   " "
   Their Ch.
2 Orville Booth   m. Annis Blackman   " "
2 Russell "   unm.   " "
2 Delana "   m. Newell Brinsmade (no ch.) Trumbull "
2 Elon "   unm.   Newtown, Conn.

He amassed a fortune at his trade as Stone Mason, and often proudly made the statement that he never spent a cent for a book or a newspaper. Poor man!

Ch. Orville Booth and Annis Blackman   Newtown, Conn.

3 Susan Booth   m. Stiles Belfield
3 John W.   "   " Mary Northrop
3 Homer   "
3 Sophia   "   unm.

BOTSFORD

1 Henry Botsford came from Leicestershire England to New England and settled in Milford, Conn. in 1639. He was the Progenitor of Newtown's Botsford Families.

2 Elnathan, 3Sergeant John, 1st Newtown settler in 1680.
4 Gideon, son Sergt. John and Hepsibah Camp

5 Amos, 5Gideon, 5Clement ch. Bethia 1st wife
                                &
                               4Gideon son of 3John

5 5Vine, Bethia, 5Annis   ch. Miriam 2nd wife
                                &
                               4Gideon Botsford

5 Gideon, m. Pulchrea Fairman.

Their Ch.

6 Richard   Botsford   m. Annis Peck
6 Gideon Bennett "   " Elizabeth Farmer   Woodbury, Conn
6 Jane   "   "
6 Dr. Amos   "   " Betsey Clarke   Greenville, N. Y.
6 Marcus   "   " Betty Perry 1st wife Huldah Lake 2nd wife
6 Damaris   "   " Cyrus Fairchiild   (see Fairchild record)
6 William   "   " Delia Curtis
6 Ursula   "   " Ethel Dibble   Danbury, Conn.
6 Polly Ann   "   " Cyrus Camp   (see Camp record)
6 Rev. David   "   unm. (see ministers) Newtown, Conn.

Ch. 6Richard Botsford and Annis Peck   Newtown, Conn.

7 Gideon Burtis   "   m. Sophia Hard   "   "
7 Sarah, Ann   "   " Frederick Dibble   "   "

                           Sophia Hard
8 Sophia   "   ch.   &   "   "
                           Gideon B. Botsford

                           Sophia Botsford
9 Harriet B. Camp   ch. &   "   "
9 Gideon B.   "   Marcus B. Camp   "   "

Ch. Sarah Ann Botsford and Frederick Dibble   Newtown, Conn.

8 Margaret Dibble   m. Isaac Lake   "   "
8 Mary Curtis   "   " Fred Dunham   "   "
8 Annis   "   " Lyman Stone, no ch. "   "
8 Burtis   "   d. at 15 yrs.
8 Samuel E.   "   m. Elizabeth Davis   New Haven, Conn
8 Fred B.   "   " Sarah Clinton 1st. wife
   "   "   "   " Emily Dibble 2nd. wife.

Ch. Margaret Dibble and Isaac Lake.   Newtown, Conn

9 Frederick Lake   m. Ella Oliver, no ch. "   "
9 *Anabelle   "   " Howard Banks   Bethel, Conn.
9 *Robert   "   " Julia Warner, no ch. "   "
9 *Richard   "   " d. in infancy.

GENEALOGICAL SECTION

Ch. Annabelle Lake and Howard Banks

10 Clara Banks	m.	Wallace Banks	Bethel, Conn.
10 Willard "		d. young.	
10 Paul Frederick "		d. young.	
10 Leola Banks	m.	Spencer Heady	" "
10 Lloyd "			" "
10 Mayla "			" "

11 Eleanor Banks — ch. Clara Banks & Wallace Banks

11 Allen Heady — ch. Leola Banks & Spencer Heady.

9 Carrie Dunham
9 Samuel " — ch. Mary Curtis Dibble & Fred Dunham

9 Eva Dibble — ch. Sarah Clinton 1st. wife & Fred B. Dibble

9 Burton " — ch. Emily Dibble, 2nd wife.

Ch. Samuel E. Dibble and Elizabeth Davis   New Haven, Conn

9 C. Elmer Dibble			Seattle, Wash.
9 Ethel G "	unm.		E. Haven, Conn.
9 Eleanor E. "	m.	Robert Eggleston	Up. Montclair, N.J.
9 Samuel Edward " 2nd	"	Nora Sage	Pittsburg, Pa.
9 Lewis A. Dibble	"	Lillian Kneranger	Naugatuck, Conn.
9 Albert B. "	"	Mabel Homan	New Haven, Conn.
9 Marguirite "	"	Elihu Wing	Lieut., M. D. in Navy
9 Ruth Botsford "	"	Morton Alderage	Worcester, Mass.
9 Donald "	"	Roberta Preston	Waterbury, Conn.
9 J. Mansfield "	unm.		In U. S. Infantry, France
9 Benjamin "	unm.		In U. S. Infantry, France
9 Elizabeth "	unm.		East Haven, Conn.

10 Dorothy Eggleston
10 Eleanor E. " — ch. Eleanor E. Dibble &
10 Mary " Robert Eggleston   Montclair, N. J.

10 Davis Sage Dibble — ch. Nora Sage &   Pittsburg, Pa.
10 Samuel E. " 3rd. Samuel E. Dibble, 2nd.

10 Doris Dibble
10 Jane " — ch. Lillian Kneranger & Lewis A. Dibble   Naugatuck, Conn.

10 Dorothy Homan Dibble — ch. Mabel Homan & Albert Dibble   New Haven, Conn.

10 Barbara Sherwood Dibble — ch. Roberta Preston & Donald Dibble   Waterbury, Conn.

10 Ruth Bailey Alderage — ch. Ruth Dibble & Morton Alderage   Worcester, Mass.

3John, 4Gideon, 5Clement, m. Mary Baldwin.

6 *Lucinda Botsford		m. Ichabod Noble	New Milford, Conn.
6 *Sally	"	unm.	
6 *Mary Ann	"	" Isaac Birch	Newtown, Conn.
6 *Hersey	"	" John Dibble	Bethel, Conn.
6 *Jabez Baldwin	"	Anner Smith	
6 *Dr. Russell B.	"	" Eliza Whittlesey, (See Doctors)	

Ch. 6Jabez Baldwin Botsford and Anner Smith

Clement Botsford, M. D., born August 25th, 1814, was the son of Jabez Baldwin and Anner (Smith) Botsford, of Newtown, Conn. He graduated from Yale College in 1838, and soon after was married to Caroline Montgomery, of Bloomingburg, N. Y., where he went to engage in his work. No better words can express the appreciation in which he was held than an extract from the "Sullivan County Whig" of February 11th, 1848.

"He was universally esteemed as a man and a physician, and his loss has deeply affected the entire community. For ten years he has been arduously engaged in the duties of his profession and has worn out his own in trying to save the lives of others. Among the poorer classes especially, his loss will be deeply felt, as he was attentive to their afflictions and charitable to their wants. In all the relations of life the conduct of the deceased was marked by the strictest integrity and the highest sense of moral bearing. He possessed correct business habits and was a careful and successful practitioner. We believe that he lived a true and manly life, and died the death of the Christian." (Rec'd to late for insertion with "Doctors").

7 *Clement Botsford M. D.	m.	Caroline Montgomery	
7 *John Smith	"	" Harriet Nichols (no ch.)	Huntington, Ct.
7 *George R.	"	" Sophia Botsford (no ch.)	Newtown, Conn.
7 *Mary E.	"	" Charles Nichols (no ch.)	" "
7 *Charlotte	"	" Henry Russell Weed	
8 Minnie M. Weed		ch. Charlotte Botsford & Henry R. Weed	New Haven, Conn
8 Clara L.	"		
7 *Carolina Eliza Botsford	ch.	Eliza Whittlesey & Dr. Russell B. Botsford	Danbury, Conn.
8 Sarah W. Bacon		ch. Caroline E. Botsford & John W. Bacon	" "
8 Eliza W.	"		" "
8 John R.	"		" "
9 Christine R. Rundle		ch. Eliza Bacon & G. Mortimer Rundle	" "
9 Marguerite B.	"		" "
9 Christine R.	"	m. McLean	" "

Ch. 6Gideon Bennett Botsford and Mary Elizabeth Farmer, Woodbury,Ct.

7 Jane Botsford	m.	1st Charles Blakeslee (no ch.)	Newtown, "
	"	2nd Mr. Sprague	Petersburg, Va.
7 Harriet	"	" Albert Seeley Blackman	
7 Lucius	"	" Adaline Hubbell	
7 Edgar	"	unm.	
7 William	"	" Annette Beers Botsford (See Beers)	
7 Charles	"		
7 Frederick	"	" Betsey Canfield	New Haven, Conn.
7 David	"	" Annette Beers (See Beers)	New Milford "

Ch. Harriet Botsford and Albert Seeley Blackman

8 *Theodore Blackman	m.	Evaline Wygant 1st wife	
8 *Charles	"	" Esther Grace Mann 2nd wife	
8 *Edwin	"	unm.	
8 Benjamin Knower	"	" Elizabeth Collier	Schenectady, N. Y.
8 *Mary Elizabeth	"	" *Henry Martin Bishop	New Haven, Conn.
8 Albert Seeley	"	" Annie Jones	

GENEALOGICAL SECTION

  Ch. Theodore Blackman and Evaline Wygant   New Milford, Conn.

9 Willis Wygant " m. Delia Townsend
9 Evaline Jane " " Victor Morell

8 Ch. Benjamin K. Blackman and Elizabeth Collier,   Schenectady, N. Y.

9 Edwin Carlton " m. Lora Crego Chicago, Ill.
9 Harold Ross " " Ada Tomlinson Hope Mountain, N. J.

  Ch. Mary E. Blackman and Henry Bishop New Haven, Conn.

9 Mary Harriet Bishop unm. Worcester, Mass.
9 George Herbert " m. Annie Neary
9 Edith Elizabeth "
9 *Frederick Henry "
9 Charles Albert " m. Ruth Scallon (no ch.)

6 William Botsford m. Delia Curtis

 Their Ch.

7 Elizabeth " m. Rufus Watson Catskill, N. Y.
7 Mary " " Rev. John Betts Glastonbury, Conn.

8 Emma Watson   Elizabeth Botsford Albany, N. Y.
8 *Elizabeth " ch. &
       Rufus Watson

9 Eugene Burlingame   Albany, N. Y.
9 Elizabeth " Emma Watson " "
9 Frances " ch. & " "
9 Westcott " Burlingame " "

8 *John Beach Betts Mary Botsford Hartford, Conn.
8 Edw. Herbert " ch. &
8 Mary " Rev. John Betts " "

7 Lucius Botsford m. Adaline Hubbell Coxsackie, N. Y.

8 Phoebe Jane " m. Henry Custo Van Bergen

9 *Phillip Van Bergen Phoebe Jane Botsford Albany, N. Y.
9 *Lucius Botsford " ch. &
       Henry Custo Van Bergen

       Julia Van Ness
10 Bessie " ch. &
       Phillip Van Bergen
      m Vanderheyden

10 Nellie Coles " Margaret Barhyte " "
10 Henry Custo " ch. &
       Lucius Botsford Van Bergen
10 Nellie Coles " m. George Frank Ackerman Albany, N. Y.

       Margaret Briner Ebert New York, City
11 Robert Ebert " ch. &
       Henry Custo Van Bergen

       *Mary Botsford Greenville, N. Y.
8 Dr. Charles P. McCabe ch. &
       Dr. McCabe

9 Dorothy Kerr McCabe Miss Elliott
9 Phillip " ch. &
       Dr. C. P. McCabe

Moses Botsford b. 1750 m. Huldah Winton.
2 Theophilus Botsford m. Lucy Ann Peck Newtown, Conn.
2 Daniel " " Lucinda Candee " "
Their ch.
2 Phoebe " " Ebenezer Beers (See Beers) " "
2 Sally " " Harry Downs " "
2 Aurelia " " Isaac Peck (see Peck) " "

3 *Julia " Theophilus Botsford " "
3 *Mary " ch. & " "
3 *William " Lucy Ann Peck " "

4 *William Skidmore Julia Botsford " "
4 *Robert " ch. &
4 *Mary Caroline " d. 1918 John Russell Skidmore

4 *Julia Esther Blackman Mary Botsford " "
4 Joseph Albert " ch. &
4 Ann Elizabeth " Joseph Blackman " "
4 Mary Frances " See Blackman record

4 Henry Booth Botsford Mary Sophia Terrill " "
4 Frank Terrill " ch. &
  William Botsford

5 Frank Leroy " Elizabeth Saunders 1st wife Los Angles Cal
5 Lulu Kate " ch. &
  Henry B. Botsford

4 *Frank T. " m. Adelaide Tanner (no ch.) San Diego, Cal
  d. Arizona

2 Daniel " m. Lucinda Candee Newtown, Conn.
Their ch.
3 *Huldah " " Albert Turney " "
3 Sophia " " Wheeler Blakeman " "
3 *Emily (twins)" " Walter Northrop (see Northrop) "
3 *Emeline (twins)" " James Corwin
3 *Moses " " Mary Beers
3 *Jabez " " Elizabeth Clark

Ch. of Sophia and Wheeler Blakeman " "
4 Eugene Blakeman m. Maggie Bond 1st California, Mo.
  " Jennie Beach, 2nd
4 Lucena " " Ephraim Brisco Newtown, Conn.
4 Arthur " " Anna Hurley California, Mo
4 Edson "
4 Carrie " unm.

4 Daniel Botsford
4 Nelson " Mary Beers
4 Lena " ch. &
4 Inez " Moses Botsford

4 Nellie "
4 Willis " *Elizabeth Clark Staten Island
4 Laura " ch. &
4 Elizabeth " 3 *Jabez Botsford " "
4 Jabez "

Ch. Ephraim Brisco and Lucena Blakeman Newtown, Conn

5 *Eugene Brisco d. in boyhood
5 Charles " unm. Shelton, Conn.
8 George " unm. Newtown, Conn
5 Jessie " unm.
5 Inez " m. George Quinn Shelton, Conn
5 *Carrie " " Elmer Spencer
5 Eva " unm.

GENEALOGICAL SECTION

6 Catherine Quinn   ch. Inez Brisco   Shelton, Conn.
6 Myrtle "   &   "   "
                             George Quinn

6 Eugene Spencer   ch. Carrie Brisco
6 Hazel "   &   "   "
                           Elmer Spencer

1 Jared Botsford b. 1745 Ann his wife.

   Their Ch.
2 Henry   Botsford   m. Joanna Birch   "   "
2 Philo   "   "   Hannah Nichols
3 Capt. Edwin   "   "   Julia Summers   "   "

   Their Ch.
4 *Oliver   "   "   *Elizabeth Bray
4 *Henry   "   "   *Rebecca Johnson 1st. (no ch.) "   "
                          Julia Hook 2nd

5 George   "   Elizabeth Bray
5 *Nellie   "   ch.   &
5 Morris   "   Oliver Botsford

2 Desc. of Lieut. 2Philo Botsford and Hannah Nichols
3 Austin son of Philo   m. Volucia B. Glover   "   "

   Their Ch.
4 *Caroline   Botsford   m. Edward Parsons   New Haven, Conn.
4 *Philo G.   "   "   Charlotte Hinman
4 *Richard   "   "   Ellen Bundy   Elgin, Ill.
4 *Jerome   "   "   Emily Northrop
4 Eugene   "   "   Jane Blakeman   Newtown, Conn.
4 *James   "   "   d. unm.   "   "
4 Austin N.   "   "   Mollie Scott   "   "
4 Alosia   "   "   Reuben Johnson   Fort Dodge, Iowa.
4 *Amelia   "   "   Sidney Frost   New Haven, Conn.

5 Ella Parsons   *4Caroline Botsford   New Haven, Conn.
5 Jennie "   ch.   &
5 Caroline "   Edward Parsons

5 Carl   Botsford   Ellen Bundy   Elgin, Ill.
5 *Alosia   "   ch.   &
                         Richard Botsford

   Ch. Jerome Botsford and Emily Northrop

5 *Henry   Botsford   m. Ella Couch   Newtown, Conn.
5 Samuel   "   "   Ella Couch Botsford   New Haven, "
5 *Homer   "   d. in boyhood
5 Adella   "   In Gov't. employ in Washington, D. C.
5 Charlotte   "   unm.
5 Emily   "   "   K. Lester Coleman   New Haven, Conn.

6 Leonard Austin   ch. Ella Couch   Bridgeport, Conn.
                              &
                          Henry Botsford

   Ch. Samuel Botsford and Ella Couch Botsford   New Haven, Conn.

6 Gertrude Elizabeth "   m. Emerson Setchel   Whitestone, L. I.
6 Herbert Clayton   "   m. Florence Morgan   Monroe, Conn.
6 Robert Couch   "   "   Ella B. Collard   New Haven, Conn.
6 Emily Frances   "   Teacher in Mt. Holyoke College, Mass.

7 Alice Evelyn   "   ch. Lottie Dickenson   Bridgeport, Conn.
7 Richard Austin   "   &
                          Leonard A. Botsford   "   "

GENEALOGICAL SECTION

7 Clarence Emerson Setchel   Gertrude E. Botsford
7 Ruth Elizabeth "   ch. &
7 Gertrude Mary "   Emerson Setchel

Ch. Emily Botsford and K. Lester Coleman   New Haven, Conn.

6 Willis Coleman   m. Alice Bronson   Roxbury, Conn.
6 Margery "   New Haven, Conn.
6 Clayton "   In U. S. Service   New Haven, Conn.
6 Jerome "   In U. S. Naval Reserve   " "
6 Walter "
6 Louise "

7 Lester Coleman   Alice Bronson
                 ch. &
7 Barbara "   Willis Coleman

Ch. 4 Eugene Botsford and Jane Blakeman.

5 Ida J. Botsford   m. Stephen Mallette Sanford   Easton, Conn.
5 N. Alosia "   " Banks Goodsell
5 *Charles B. "   unm.
5 Eugene R. "   " *Ida Lamphear   Newtown, Conn.
5 Cora A. "   " Austin Ferry
5 *Bertha M. "   " Arthur G. Warner
5 Elsie P. "   unm.
5 Austin N. "   " Elizabeth Goodwin

6 Clara Elsie Sanford   Ida J. Botsford
                 ch. &
                 Stephen M. Sanford

6 Harold E. Botsford
6 Mayla "   Ida Lamphear
6 Charles W. "   ch. &
6 Philo G. "   Eugene R. Botsford
6 Richard L. "

7 Edna "   Ludwina Mager
                 ch. &
7 Jean "   Harold E. Botsford   Nichols, Conn.

7 Carl Botsford Rasmussen   Mayla Botsford
                 ch. &
7 Shirley "   George Rasmussen

6 Earl Botsford Warner
6 George T. "   Bertha G. Botsford
6 Russell G. "   ch. &   New Haven, Conn.
6 Marion "   Arthur G. Warner

7 Arthur Page Warner   Marion Page
                 ch. &
7 Margaret W. "   Earl Botsford Warner

7 George T. "   m. Emma O. De Bann   Minneapolis,
7 Russell G. "   " Vera Chandler

6 Bertha G. Ferry   Cora A. Botsford
6 Hazel "   ch. &   Bridgeport, Conn.
6 Pearl "   Austin Ferry
6 Bertha G. Ferry   m. George Lattin

7 Pearl Green   Hazel Ferry   " "
                 ch. &
                 Carl Green

5 Reuben Johnson, Jr.   Alosia Botsford
                 ch. &   New Haven, Conn.
                 Reuben Johnson

6 Reuben Johnson 3rd   Harriet Setchel   " " "
                 ch. &
6 Richard "   Reuben Johnson, Jr.

GENEALOGICAL SECTION

5 Geis   Botsford   Mollie Scott   Fort Dodge Iowa
5 *Scott   "   ch.   &   "   "   "
5 *Richard   "   Austin N. Botsford   "   "   "

1 Chauncey Botsford was an early settler in Newtown and a large land owner. He m. Mary Peck.

Their Ch.

2 David   Botsford   Newtown, Conn.
2 George   "   m. Harriet Jennings   "   "
2 Narcissa   "   " Philo Beers   "   "

Ch. George Botsford and Harriet Jennings

3 *Mariette   "   m. John R. Tomlinson   "   "
3 *Israel twins "   Served in Civil War
3 *Lemuel twins "   Served in Civil War
3 *Charles   "
3 Susan   "   m. Edward Taylor   "   "
3 Anna E.   "   " Edson Wilson   "   "
3 *Stanley "   " Julia Tomlinson   "   "
3 Hattie   "   " Noyes Thompson   "   "
3 Edward twins "   " Emma G. Peet   "   "
3 Frederick "   " Ella Barnes   "   "
3 *Phebe   "   d. in infancy.

Ch. 3Mariette Botsford and John R. Tomlinson

4 Carrie   Tomlinson m. Alfred Briscoe (see Briscoe) "   "
4 Robert Sherman "   " 1st Hattie Croffutt
                          " 2nd Christine Kleine Suffield, Conn.
4 John Lewis   "   " Lila Platt   Claremont, Calif.

Ch. Robert S. Tomlinson and Christine Klein   Suffield, Conn.

5 *Ruth Lillian   "
5 Charlotte Agnes "   m. Dr. Russell Barber Street
                               in U. S. Service in France
6 Russell Barber Street Jr. Their Ch.

Ch. John L. Tomlinson and Lila Platt   Claremont, Calif.

5 Alberta   "   m. Benjamin Wilson

Ch. 3Susan Botsford and Edward Taylor

4 4 George Francis Taylor m. Lorena Glover   Sandy Hook, Conn.

Ch. 3Stanley Botsford and Julia Tomlinson,   Wallingford, Conn.

4 Rowland Stanley "

Ch. 3Edward Botsford and Emma G. Peet   Stepney, Conn.

4 *Lina   "   "   "
4 *Lilla   "   m. Emma Martha Mattegat   "   "
4 Stanley   "
4 Effie   "

Ch. Stanley Botsford and Emma M. Mattegat   "   "

5 Alice Isabelle " twins
5 *Ida Emma   " twins
5 Laura May   "

Ch. 3Frederick Botsford and Ella Barnes   Newtown, "

4 Ruby   "
4 Paul   "

BRISCOE

2 Nathaniel Briscoe b. 1629 was an early settler in Milford. His descendants probably came to Newtown as the names James and Nathaniel are found in the list of pioneers of 1712.

3 Nathaniel m. Mary Camp in 1672.
4 James son of 3Nathaniel b. 1673.
5 Lieut. Nathaniel son of 4James b. 1708, Newtown, Conn.

He owned a large amount of real estate; the homestead he occupied is now a part of the Newtown cemetery. He served as Selectman for 10 years between 1743 and 1777.

In 1768 he and Capt. Amos Botsford gave the bell to the Cong. Church which is now in use.

5 Lieut. Nathanial Briscoe   m. Eunice Hurd Johnson   Newtown, Conn.

Their Ch.

6 Eunice	Briscoe	m.	Thompson Booth	Bridgewater, Conn.
6 Isaac	"	"	Anna Sherman	Newtown, Conn.
6 Nathaniel	"	"	Hannah Leach	" "
		"	2nd Sally Raymond	" "

Ch. Nathaniel Briscoe and Hannah Leach

7 Susan	"	m.	Alfred Wixon
7 Mary	"	"	Joseph G. Ferris

Ch. Nathaniel Briscoe and Sally D. Raymond

7 Bradley D.	"	m.	Mary C. Glover
7 Miranda	"	"	Duranzel Hall

Ch. Bradley D. Briscoe and Mary C. Glover

8 Alfred	"	m.	Carrie Tomlinson	Bethel, Conn.
8 Ella	"	"	Walter B. Welton	(See Foote record)
8 Esther	"	"	Ormel Morgan (See Morgan)	

Ch. Alfred Briscoe and Carrie Tomlinson

9 Florence	"	m.	F. S. Wood	Fairfield, Conn.
9 Howard	"	"	Emma E. Sherman	Bethel, "

10 Howard E. Wood   ch.   Florence Briscoe & F. S. Wood   Fairfield, "

10 Helen Ruth Briscoe
10 Harold Russell "   ch.   Emma E. Sherman & Howard Briscoe   Bethel, Conn.

Ch. Isaac   "   & Anna Sherman   Newtown, Conn.

7 Amy	"	m.	William Tomlinson	" "
7 Lewis	"	"	Jane E. Pettis	" "
7 Charles	"	"	Mary Davison	" "
7 Harriet	"	"	Horace Dibble	New Haven, Conn.
7 Polly	"	"	David Glover (See Glover)	Newtown, Ct.
7 Sally	"	"	Curtis Frost	Bridgewater Conn.
7 Caroline	"	"	Peter Warren Fairchild	(See Fairchild)

Ch. Lewis Briscoe and Jane E. Pettis

8 *Isaac	"	m.	*Cornelia Fairchild	" "
8 *Cornelia	"	"	*Edward Crofut	" "
8 *Gustavus	"	"	Susan Taylor	" "
8 *Louisa S.	"	"	*Leroy Taylor	" "
8 *Charles L.	"	"	Jennette Taylor	" "

GENEALOGICAL SECTION

9 Alfred Briscoe	ch.	Cornelia Fairchild & Isaac Briscoe	(See Fairchild) " "
9 *Jennie "			" "
10 Jennie "	ch.	Agnes Tomlinson & Alfred Briscoe	" "
10 Louis "			" "
9 Wilbur "	ch.	Jennette Taylor & Charles L. Briscoe	" "
9 Frances "			" "
9 *Sherman Crofut	ch.	Cornelia Brisco & Edward Crofut	

Ch. 7 Charles Briscoe and Mary Davison " "

8 Harriet "		Henry Mygatt	California
8 Mary "		unm.	
8 Charles H. "	"	1st Anna J. Traver	See Newtown's lawyers
	"	2nd Alice Bradley	Thompsonville, Conn.
8 Willis "		d. in Panama	

Ch. Judge Chas. H. Briscoe and Anna J. Traver 1st wife

9 Willis Briscoe	m.	Jessie Bradley Drew	
9 Anna T. "	"	Rev. David Lewis Sanford	
9 Alice M. "	"	Rev. J. Francis George	Essex, N. Y.

Ch. Rev. David L. Sanford and Anna T. Briscoe

10 Helen Traver Sanford	m.	Dr. Wm. Richard Brown	Phila., Pa.
10 *Alice Amelia "	"	Albert Truax	Hartford, Conn.
10 Charles Briscoe "	"	Katherine Uri	Thompsonville "
10 Edgar Lewis "		unm.	" "
10 John Beach "		unm.	" "
10 Arthur Hall "		unm.	" "
10 David Platt "		unm.	" "

11 William Richard Brown	ch.	Helen Traver Sanford & Dr. Wm. Richard Brown,	Phila., Pa.
11 Charles Briscoe Sanford Jr.	ch.	Katherine Uri & Chas. Briscoe Sanford,	Thompsonville, Ct.
11 Anna Winslow Truax	ch.	Albert Truax & Alice A. Sanford	" "
11 Albert Winslow "			

Ch. Rev. J. Francis George and Alice M. Briscoe. Essex, N. Y.

10 Willis George twins
10 *Nelson "   Drowned in 1916.

CAMP

First Camp settled in 1707.

1 Lieut. Samuel Camp	m.	Rebecca Caafield	Newtown, Conn.
2 Lemuel "	"	Alice Leavenworth	

Some of their Ch.

3 Joel Camp	m.	Ellen Jackson	" "
3 Samuel "		Killed in French War.	
3 Phebe "	"	Cyrenius Hard	" "
3 Hoppie "	"	Amiel Peck	" "
3 Alice "	"	Sims	" "
3 Clarissa "	"	Josiah Blackman	" "

Ch. Joel Camp & Ellen Jackson
4 Deborah " m. Matthew Sherman Newtown, Conn.
4 Lemuel " " Sarah Dibble Bethel, Conn.
4 John " " Wife not known
4 Susan " " Joseph Wheeler Newtown, Conn.
4 Phebe " " unm.
4 Silas " "
4 Samuel in war of 1812.

Ch. Lemuel Camp and Sarah Dibble
5 Joel Trowbridge Camp m. Polly Fairchild Newtown, Conn.
5 Cyrus " " Polly Ann Botsford " "
5 Polly " " Samuel Fairchild (no ch.) " "
5 Adah " " Beers Fairchild 2nd wife " "
5 Maria " " John Smith 2nd wife " "
5 Beach " " Catherine H. Foote " "
5 Dibble " " Esther Blackman " "
5 Hiram " " Eliza Barnum
5 Sarah Ann " " Zachariah Clarke (see Clark) " "
5 Mary Ann " unm.

Ch. Joel T. " & Polly Fairchild " "
6 Lemuel F. " & Sarah J. Lake
6 *Edwin " " Hannah Hawley (no ch.) " "
6 *Lucia " " John R. Smith (no ch.) " "
6 Samuel B. " " Caroline C. Lake " "

Ch. Lemual F. " & Sarah J. Lake
7 *Carrie A. " d. young
7 Alma M. " m. Charles B. Johnson (See Johnson record)
7 Mary Alice " " Edmund Platt
7 Amos T. " " Cornelia Sherwood
7 Sarah A. " " Asa Hawley (See Hawley record)

Ch. Mary Alice " & Edmund C. Platt
8 Percival Camp Platt in France in U. S. Hospital service.
Ch. Amos T. Camp and Cornelia Sherwood
8 *Lyman Fairchild Camp d. in infancy

Ch. Samuel B. " & Caroline C. Lake
7 Edwin Beers " (Samuel Camp in 1918 is in his 91st year)
7* Frank Bennett " d. young

Ch. Cyrus " & Polly Ann Botsford
6 *Marcus " m. Sophia Botsford Newtown, Conn.
6 *Sarah M. " unm. " "
6 *Gideon B. " unm.

7 *Harriet B. " Sophia Botsford " "
7 *Gideon B. " ch. &
Marcus Camp

Ch. Dibble " m. Esther Blackman
6 Hobart " m. Juliette Hawley
6 Emily " " Henry Dikeman (See Dikeman) " "
6 Daniel " " Augusta Nichols

Ch. Hobart " & Juliette Hawley " "
7 *Anna L. " d. in childhood
7 *Susan A. " d. unm.
7 Robert N. "

Ch. Daniel Camp		& Augusta Nichols	
7 Esther L. "		unm. A successful teacher in Albany N. Y.	
7 Grace "		m. Dr. Clyde Anderson	Pittsburg, Pa.
8 Donald Anderson		Grace Camp	" "
8 Elizabeth "	ch.	&	" "
8 Duncan "		Dr. Clyde Anderson	" "
Ch. Beach Camp		& Catherine H. Foote	Newtown, Conn.
6 *Dr. William "		m. *Ophelia Randall	Roxbury, Conn.
6 *Julia Ann "		" *Ogden Tuttle	Minneapolis, Minn.
6 Jane Eliza "		" *Ezra L. Johnson (See Johnson)	
6 *Katherine F. "		unm.	
Ch. Dr. Wm. "		& *Ophelia Randall	Kent, Conn.
7 *William H. "		m. Jane Adam	Canaan, Conn.
7 Marion Barlow Tuttle			
7 *Henry Ogden "		*Julia Ann Camp	Minneapolis, Minn.
7 *William Beach "	ch.	&	
7 Lauren Steele "		*Ogden Tuttle	" "
In U. S. Service			
Ch. Hiram Camp		& Eliza Barnum	Newtown, Conn.
6 Lydia Jane "		d. when 17 years old	" "
6 Sarah Esther "		m. Wm. G. Hard (no ch.)	" "
6 *George Beach "		unm. Served in Civil War	" "
6 *Henry Barnum "		unm.	

Desc. of Silas Camp son of Joel

5 Emma Camp		m. Isaac Barnum	Bethel, Conn.
5 Marietta "		" Amos Hard	Newtown, Conn.
5 Edson "		unm.	" "
Ch. Emma "		& Isaac Barnum	Bethel, Conn.
6 *Edwin Barnum			
6 *William "		d. in prison during Civil War	" "
6 *Jerome "			
6 Emma "		.m Charles Grumman	" "
Their Ch.			
7 Minnie Grumman		m. William Wildman	" "
7 Anna "		m. J. B. Lynn	" "
7 William "		" Agnes Tomlinson	" "
7 Clifford "		" Edna Haines	" "
8 Cleon Wildman			" "
8 Leroy "			
8 Lester "		Minnie Grumman	" "
8 Grace "	ch.	&	
8 Nellie "		William Wildman	" "
8 Alice "			
8 Richard Lynn			
8 Bertha "		Annie Grumman	" "
8 Lawrence "	ch.	&	
8 Bernard "		J. B. Lynn	" "
8 Raymond Grumman		Agnes Tomlinson	" "
8 Leland "	ch.	&	
		William Grumman	" "
8 Frances "		Edna Haines	" "
8 Louise "	ch.	&	
8 Florence "		Clifford Grumman	
8 Helen "			
6 William G. Hard	ch.	Marietta Camp & Amos Hard (See Hard)	

CHAMBERS

1 Thomas Chambers settled in Newtown, 1736. He had 12 children. Name of wife unkown.

2 Mary Chambers		m.	Dr. William Warner
2 Asa "		"	1st Adams
" "		"	2nd Mrs. Elizabeth Osborn Clifford
2 Jesse "			d. in British Army
2 Nathan "		" "	" "
2 James "			d. in American Service
2 Jemima "		m.	Dr. Benjamin Warner

3 Thomas Osborn Chambers ch. Elizabeth Osborn Clifford
&
" " " Asa Chambers
m. Sarah Curtis

Their Ch.

4 Henry R. Chambers	m.	Emeline Munson
4 Dr. Cornelius "		d. unm. Newbern, N. C.
4 Jane Elizabeth "	"	Eli J. Morris
4 Frederick "	"	Betsey Morris Burritt
5 Susie Sturges "	"	
5 Jennie Morris "		
5 *Sarah Burritt "	ch.	Betsey M. Burritt &
5 Elizabeth Burritt "		Frederick Chambers

CLARKE

1 James Clarke was one of the signers of the Fundamental Articles of Agreement when New Haven was settled in 1639.

2 James Jr., earliest Clarke settler in Fairfield County.
m. Deborah Peacock, 1662.

3 James, b. 1664,	"	Jane Griffen	
4 Zachariah (1) b. 1702	"	Eunice Staples	Newtown, Conn.
5 Zachariah (2) b. 1739	"	Mary Bacon	" "
6 James, b. 1769	"	Polly Sherman	" "
6 Zachariah, b. 1771	"	Hannah Toucey	" "

Ch. James Clark and Polly Sherman

7 Grandison	"	m.	Hannah Hard
7 Everett	"	"	Ann Barnum	Bethel, Conn.
7 Eliza	"	"	Levi Edwards	Trumbull, Conn.
7 Polly	"	"	Abijah Hard	Newtown, Conn.
7 John	"	"	Mary Curtis 1st wife
		"	Sally French 2nd wife	Monroe, Conn.
7 William	"	"	Nancy Adams	Newtown, Conn.
7 Zachariah	"	"	Sarah Ann Camp	" "
7 Anna Maria	"	"	Charles C. Warner (See Warner)
7 Huldah	"	"	James B. Beers (see Beers) B'klyn, N. Y.

Ch. Grandison " & Hannah Hard

8 George	"	m.	Jane Warner
8 Mary	"	"	Charles Webster (no ch.) Newtown, Conn.

9 Homer G. " ch. Jane Warner " "
&
George Clarke " "

10 *Mabel " ch. *Elizabeth Wheeler, 1st wife " "
&
10 George " Homer G. Clarke " "
Sarah W. Hall, 2nd wife

GENEALOGICAL SECTION

8 *Rev. James Starr Clarke ch. Ann Barnum   Bethel, Conn.
          &
          Everett Clarke   "   "

For many years the successful Principal of a school for boys at Tivoli on the Hudson, N. Y.

8 *Abel French Clarke   ch. Sally French   Newtown, Conn.
          &
          John Clarke
8 *Abel French Clarke   m. Florence Glover 1st wife Newtown, Conn.
 "   "   "   "   "   Adella Van Name 2nd wife, New York

8 Robert A. Clarke   ch. Nancy Adams   Newtown, Conn.
          &
          William Clarke
See Freegrace Adams' record

8 Lemuel Beach Clarke   ch. *Sarah Ann Camp, 1st. wife, Newtown, Ct.
8 *Sherman Beers "   &
          Zachariah Clarke   Danbury, Conn.
          Sarah Ann Gregory 2nd wife

9 Jennie   "   ch. Mary Osborn   "   "
9 Frederick   "   &
          Lemuel B. Clarke   "   "

10 Bertha Mary   "   ch. &
10 Frederick Beers "   Frederick Clarke

11 Ruth Daisy Plue   ch. Bertha M. Clarke   "   "
11 Lois Vivian   "   &
          Silas Raymond Plue   "   "

6 Zachariah Clarke b. 1771   m. Hannah Toucey

    Their Ch.

7 Sally   Clarke   m. Daniel Connelly   Newtown, Conn.
7 Oliver   "   unm. Died of small pox in New York
7 Maria   "   m. Harry Hawley 1st. m.   Ridgefield, Conn.
    See Skidmore record   Rufus Skidmore 2nd m. Brookfield,   "
7 Walter   Clarke   "   Dimah Ann Beers   Newtown, Conn.
7 Charles   "   "   Betsey Ann Fairchild   "   "
7 Emma   "   "   William Hill   Redding,   "
7 William   "   "   Elizabeth Lewis   Monroe   "
7 Philo   "   "   Sarah Minerva Beers   Newtown, Conn.

8 *Eli B.   "   Dimah Ann Beers   "   "
8 *Edwin   "   ch. &
8 *Emma J.   "   Walter Clarke

9 E. Beers   "   ch. Nancy Beers 1st wife
9 Julia L.   "   &
          Edwin Clarke

9 *Mattie Eugenie "   ch. Mattie A. Parker 2nd wife
9 *Edwin Parker   "   &
          Edwin Clarke

10 Samuel E. B. Clark   ch. Elizabeth Bowers   Minneapolis, Minn.
          &
  "   "   "   "   m. E. Beers Clarke   "   "
          m. Alcetta Gilbert

9 *Samuel Clarke Peck
9 Walter Toucey   "   Emma J. Clarke   Newtown, Conn.
9 Elizabeth Fayerweather " ch. &
9 Susan Emma   "   George B. Peck   Brooklyn, N. Y.

10	Priscilla Burdick		Susan Emma Peck	
10	Ruth Mac Bride "	ch.	&	
10	Merrill Clarke "		Willard Merrill Burdick	S. Orange, N. J.
10	Elisabeth Chester Peck		Elisabeth Chester Backus	
10	Samuel Clarke "	ch.	&	Schenectady, N. Y.
			Walter T. Peck	

Ch. 7 Charles Clarke and Betsey Ann Fairchild

8	*Robert Toucey Clarke	m.	Harriette Eliza Peck	Brookfield, Conn.
8	*Emily "		unm.	
8	Rev. Sylvester "	"	Annie Dalrymple	Newark, N. J.
8	*Elizabeth "	"	David Beecher	Shelton, Conn.
8	*Charles W. "		d. young	Newtown, Conn.
8	*William H. "		d. young	" "

	Ch. Robert T. "	&	Harriette Eliza Peck	Brookfield, Conn.
9	*Henry Peck "	m.	Julia C. Hurd, 1st.	
		"	Mary J. Macfie 2nd	
9	Mary Toucey "	"	William C. Haight	Bridgeport, Conn.
9	Charles Robert "	"	Martha E. Griffen	Brookfield, "

10	Nancy Barnum "		*Julia C. Hurd 1st wife	" "
10	Julia H. "	ch.	&	
			Henry Peck Clarke	Brevard, N. Carolina

			*Mary J. Macfie 2nd wife	
10	Harry F. "	ch.	&	
			Henry Peck Clarke	
10	Nancey Barnum "	m.	Henry N. Carrier	Brevard N. Carolina

10	Alton Clarke Haight		7 Mary Toucey Clarke	Bridgeport, Conn.
10	Marian Toucey "	ch.	&	
			William C. Haight	" "

10	Philip Griffen Clarke		Martha E. Griffen	Brookfield, Conn.
10	Elizabeth "	ch.	&	
10	Charles R., Jr. "		Charles R. Clarke	Bridgeport, Conn.

9	Annie Fairchild Clarke		Anna Dalrymple	Newark, N. J.
9	Grace Dalrymple "	ch.	&	
9	Robert Toucey "		Rev. Sylvester Clarke	Bridgeport, Conn.
			See Ministers	

0	Jessie Beecher twins		*Elizabeth Clarke	Newtown, Conn.
9	*Bessie "	ch.	&	
			David Beecher	Shelton, Conn.
			7 Emma Clarke	Newtown, Conn.
8	*Rev. William Toucey Hill	ch.	&	
			William H. Hill	Redding, Conn.

9	Emma Elizabeth Hill			
9	William Burr "		Jane C. Burr	Middletown, Conn.
9	*Cyrus Foss "	ch.	&	
9	Ellen Toucey "		Rev. Wm. T. Hill	New Haven, Conn.

			Illie C. Clapp	Brooklyn, N. Y.
9	William Burr jr., "	ch.	&	
			William Burr Hill	New York, N. Y.

10	Cyrus Giles "		Kate S. Giles	Chicago, Ill.
	In 1917 an aviator in France	ch.	&	
			Cyrus Foss Hill	" "

	Ch. Philo Clarke	&	Sarah Minerva Beers	Brookfield, Conn.
8	*Hannah Sophia Clarke	m.	Levi Burtis Booth	
8	*Emma Francis "		d. in young womanhood	Newtown, Conn.
8	*Flora M. "	m.	Alfred Walker	Ossining, N. Y

9 Philo Clarke Booth	ch.	Hanah Sophia Clarke & Levi Burtis Booth	Newtown, Conn. " "
9 Clarke Skidmore Walker	ch.	Flora Clarke & Alfred Walker	Newtown, Conn.

COBURN

1 Daniel Coburn and Sarah Johnson			Newtown, Conn.
2 Charles Coburn	ch.	Sarah Johnson & Daniel Coburn	" " " "
3 Emma " 3 *William " 3 *Charles "	ch.	Nabby Johnson & Charles Coburn	" "
4 Mary Hilliard	ch.	Emma Coburn & *Edward Hilliard	Easton, Penn.
5 Edward Hart Greene Jr.	ch.	Mary Hilliard & Edward Hart Greene	
4 Clarence Wooster Coburn	ch.	Frances Wooster & William Coburn	SanFrancisco, Cal.
4 Henry Coburn 4 Mary " 4 Erwin " 4 Edwin Rogers "	ch.	*Helen Messinger & Charles Coburn	
5 Clarence Wooster Coburn Jr.	ch.	Jennie Greathouse & Clarence W. Coburn	San Francisco, Cal.
5 Harry Coburn 5 Minnie "	ch.	Henry Coburn	Easton, Penn.
5 Julia Merrill 5 Rev. Richard Nye " 5 Rev. Charles Coburn " 5 Philip S. " Jr.	ch.	4*Mary Coburn & Rev. Phillip S. Merrill	Rochester, N. Y. New Castle, Penn. Philadelphia, Penn.
6 Dorothy Sweeting 6 Margaret "	ch.	Julia Merrill & Ralph Sweeting	Rochester, N. Y.
6 Richard Nye Merrill, Jr. 6 John Estey "	ch.	Agnes Estey & Rev. Richard Nye Merrill,	Miami, Florida " "
5 Emily Middaugh Coburn 5 Margaret "	ch.	Elizabeth Middaugh & Erwin Coburn	Newark, N. J.
4 Edwin Rogers Coburn	m.	Julia Hackman	Easton, Penn.

CURTIS

1 Elizabeth, "Widow Curtis," of Stratford
2 William her son b. 1618 in England m. 1st Mary.
   2nd Sarah Morris Goodrich.
3 Josiah, 1662 b. Stratford m. Abigail Judson, 2nd Mary Beach
4 Benjamin m. Elizabeth Birdsey
4 Matthew m. 1st Phebe Judson, 2nd Abigail Thompson
   They were first Curtis settlers in Newtown, 1716

Ch. Matthew Curtis	& Phebe Judson	Newtown, Conn.
5 Phebe "	m. John Beach Jr.	" "
5 Niram "	" Mabel	
5 Matthew 2nd. "	" Hannah Ford	
5 Stiles "	" Hannah Bishop	
5 Josiah "	" Ann Ford	
Son of Matthew "	& Abigail Thompson	
5 Gold "	m. Elizabeth Gold	Fairfield, Conn.

Their Ch.		
6 Abigail "	" Cyrus Hard (See Hard)	Newtown, Conn.
5 Betsey "	unm.	
6 Deborah "	" Hermon Warner (See Warner) "	"
6 Gould "	" Joanna Peck	" "
6 Marilla "	unm.	
6 John G. "	" Lucy Blackman	" "
6 Phebe "	unm.	
6 Hezekiah "	" Marcia Glover	" "
6 David "	" Jeannette Shelton	Monroe, "
6 Daniel "	" Elizabeth Beach	Trumbull "

Ch. Gould "	& Joanna Peck	Newtown, Conn.
7 *Mary "	m. Cyrenius Beers	Chicago, Ill.
7 *Samuel "	" Mary Nichols 1st	Newtown, Conn.
"	Betsey Curtis Hinman 2nd Southbury	"
"	Mary Curtis Wheeler 3rd. New Haven	"
7 *Elizabeth "	" Robert C. Peck 1st	Newtown, "
"	" Simeon B. Peck 2nd	" "
7 *Sarah "	" Dr. Monroe Judson 2nd wife	" "

Ch. Mary "	& Cyrenius Beers	Chicago, Ill
8 Mary Curtis Beers	m. Orrington C. Foster	" "
8 Charles Gould "	" Louisa Wilson	" "
8 Rissa "	" Augustus Warner	" "

Ch. Mary Curtis Beers	& Orrington C. Foster	" "
9 George B. Foster	m. Margarite Johnson	" "
9 Orrington "	" Mary Ehlin	" "
9 Mary Susan "	" Dr. John Marrurre	" "

	Marguerite Johnson t	" "
10 Marguerite "	ch. &	
	George B. Foster	" "
	Mary Ehlin	" "
10 Elizabeth "	ch. &	
	Orrington Foster	" "
10 John Marrurre	Mary Susan Foster	" "
10 Katherine "	ch. &	" "
10 Mary "	Dr. John Marrurre	" "
	Louisa Wilson	" "
9 Catherine E. Beers	ch. &	
	Charles Gould Beers	" "

GENEALOGICAL SECTION

9 Charles Curtis Warner		Rissa Beers	Chicago, Ill.
9 Raymond "	ch.	&	
9 Catherine "		Augustas Warner	
Ch. Samuel Curtis	&	Mary Nichols	Newtown, Conn.
8 Henry Gould Curtis	m.	Anna Beers	" "
8 Julia "	"	Henry S. Hawley	" "
Ch. 8 Henry G. Curtis	&	Anna Beers	
9 Harry Beers "	m.	Laura Trulock	
9 William R. "	"	Bertha Niles George	
10 Henry Gould "		Bertha Niles George	" "
10 Nelson George "	ch.	&	
		William R. Curtis	" "
9 Curtis Hawley		Julia Curtis	" "
9 Mary Nichols "	ch.	&	
		Henry S. Hawley	" "
10 Hobart Warner		Mary Nichols Hawley	" "
10 Austin "	ch.	&	
10 Henry Hawley "		Hobart Glover Warner	

Dec. 6 John Curtis and Lucy Blackman

7 Daniel Curtis	m.	Mary A. Brown	Erie, Pa.
7 Simeon "		unm.	
7 John Gould "	"	Mary Chambers	Erie, Pa.
7 Robert "	"	d. in infancy	
7 David "	"	1st Harriet Blackman	New Haven, Conn.
	"	2nd Sarah E. Blackman	" "
Ch. Daniel "	&	Mary Brown	Erie, Pa.
8 *Jennie "		d. in infancy	
8 John Simeon "	m.	Grace Bemis	Erie, Pa.
8 George H. "	"	Annie Hitchcock (no ch.)	
8 Uri Balcom "	"	Martha A. Doiers (no ch.)	
8 Mary A. "	"	Rev. Karl Klass	Seattle, Wash.
Ch. John S. "	&	Grace Bemis	Campbell, N. Y.
9 Daniel B. "			" "
8 John Simeon "			
9 Daniel G. "			
9 Harriet Eldred "	ch.	Jane Eldred & Daniel G. Curtis	
9 Mary Klass		Mary A. Curtis	Seattle, Washington
9 Karl "	ch.	&	
9 Georgianna "		Rev. Karl Klass	" "
8 *Charlotta Augusta Curtis	ch.	*Harriet Blackman 1st & David Curtis	New Haven, Conn. " "
8 *Hattie Louise Curtis	ch.	Sarah E. Blackman 2nd wife & David Curtis	" " " "

Desc. through 6 Hezekiah Curtis and Marcia Glover

7 Henry Curtis	m.	Fannie Parker	Seattle, Washington
7 Benjamin "	"	Laura Lewis	Newtown, Conn.
7 Betsey "	"	1st Daniel Hinman (no ch.)	" "
	"	2nd Samuel Curtis (no ch.)	" "
7 Mary "	"	1st James Wheeler (no ch.)	New Haven
		2nd Samuel Curtis	

```
          Ch. Henry Curtis         &  Fannie Parker
8 *Charles         "            m.  Pearl Hunt (no ch.)      Dubuqe, Iowa
8 Florence         "             "  Mr. Cone (no ch)            "     "
8 Hobart H.        "
8 Jennie           "                Laura Lewis              Newtown, Conn.
8 Frederick        "          ch.        &
8 Newton M.        "                Benjamin Curtis          Passaic, N. J.

                                    Ruth Amelia Nichols     Newtown, Conn.
9 Marion           "          ch.         &
                                    Hobart H. Curtis
     "             "            m.  Clayton Hawley          Monroe, Conn.

6 Desc. through David Curtis and Jennet Shelton    Painted Post, N. Y.

7 *Jane Marilla Curtis              d. Newtown, sixteen yrs. of age.
7 *Infant Son                       d. in infancy
7 *Antoinette      "            m.  Charles H. Erwin( no ch.)   "     "
7 Phebe Minerva    "             "  Charles G. Thompson      Campbell  "
7 Josiah           "            m.  Caroline Sophia Smith

     Their Ch.
8 Carrie Jennet    "            m.  1st Louis Patterson     New York, N. Y.
                                 "  2nd Alfred Lublin           "     "
8 Minnie Antoinette"             "  Frank E. Smedley (no ch.) Addison, "
8 Bertha Jane      "                unm.
8 *José Richmond   "                d. young

     Ch. Carrie Jennet "         &  Louis Patterson
9 Curtis Patterson "            m.  Carla Owen
9 Janet Curtis Patterson         "  Lynn Taylor

                                    Janet Curtis Patterson   Addison, N. J.
10 Allan Curtis Taylor        ch.         &
10 Curtis Sheldon  "             "  Lynn Taylor

4 Matthew and 4Benjamin first in Newtown, 1716.

     Ch. 4Benjamin Curtis        &  Elizabeth Birdsey       Newtown, Conn.
5 Nehemiah         "            m.  Martha Clark                "     "
5 Phebe            "             "  Daniel Morehouse            "     "
5 Eunice           "             "  Amos Hard                   "     "
5 Elizabeth        "             "  Capt. John Glover           "     "
5 Benjamin         "             "  1st Phedima Nichols         "     "
                                 "  2nd Mary Devine             "     "
                                 "  3rd. Phebe Toucey           "     "
5 Abijah           "             "  Sarah Birdsey               "     "
5 Sarah            "             "  Nirom Hard

     Ch. 5Benjamin "             &  Phedima Nichols             "     "
6 Philo            "            m.  Huldah Hubbell              "     "

     Ch. Benjamin  "             &  Mary Devine
6 Artemisia        "            m.  Linus Sherman (see Sherman)
6 Alfred Devine    "             "  Sarah Hard
6 Epenitus         "             "  Salina Hard                 "     "

     Ch. Philo     "             &  Huldah Hubbell              "     "
7 Philo            "            m.  Sally Maria Birch           "     "
7 Polly            "             "  John Glover (see Glover)    "     "
7 Betsey           "             "  Amariah Beers (see Beers)   "     "
7 Huldah           "             "  Chauncey Hatch              "     "
```

GENEALOGICAL SECTION

	Ch. Alfred Devine Curtis	&	Sarah Hard	Newtown, Conn.
7	*Sophia "		unm.	" "
7	*Nirom "	m.	Matilda Rogers 1st m.	" "
7	*Phebe "	"	Joseph Nettleton (See Beach)	" "
7	*Cyrenius "	"	Christa Ann Beardsley	Monroe, Conn.
7	*Alfred "	"	Matilda Rogers Curtis 2nd m.	Newtown, "
7	*Edwin A. "	"	Matilda Rogers Curtis 3rd m.	"

	Ch. Nirom "	&	Matilda Rogers	
8	*Julia M. L. "	m.	Rev. Curtis Woodruff	New York, N. Y.

She was "W. M. L. Jay," authoress of "Shiloh" and numerous poems.

	Ch. 6Epenitus Curtis	&	Salina Hard	
7	Susan "	m.	Anson Smith	Brookfield, Conn.
7	Charles "		unm.	
7	Henry Francis "	"	Lany McDaniel	Marysville, Tenn.

	Ch. Henry F. "	&	Lany McDaniel	
8	*Jasper "		d. in Civil War	New Orleans, La.
8	Susan "		unm.	Marysville, Tenn.
8	Henry William "	m.	Ida Whitlow	Knoxville, Tenn.
8	Charles "	"	Rachel Barnum	Danbury, Conn.
8	Salina "	"	Richard Randall	Shelton "
8	*Lany Elizabeth "		unm.	Los Angeles, Cal.
8	*Sarah "		unm.	Knoxville, Tenn.
8	*Frances "		unm.	" "

9	Lucy McDaniel "	ch.	Ida Whitlow & Henry Wm. Curtis	
9	Henry William "			

9	Henry Barnum "	ch.	Rachel Barnum & Charles Curtis	New Fairfield, Conn.
9	Anna "			

9	Richard Curtis Randall		Salina Curtis & Richard Randall	Shelton, Conn.
9	Elizabeth "	ch.		" "
9	Keith Meade "			
9	Miriam Flint "			
9	Richard Curtis "	m.	Florence Valentine	" "

8	Cornelia Curtis	ch.	Sally Maria Birch & Philo Curtis	Newtown, Conn.
8	Jane "			

	Ch. 7Cyrenius Curtis	&	Christa Ann Beardsley	Monroe, Conn.
8	Joseph "	m.	Jane Eliza Tyler	" "
8	Sarah Matilda "	"	Frederick W. Curtis	
8	Phebe Ann "	"	James A. Wilson	Bridgeport, Conn.
8	Bertha Celia "		unm.	

	Ch. Phebe Ann "	&	James A. Wilson	
9	Lynn W. Wilson	m.	1st Maude Blakmey	" "
		"	2nd Alice Peckham Booth	
9	Clyde Curtiss "		d. young	
9	Justin A. "	m.	Lucy MacDonald (no ch.)	" "
9	Leigh H. "	"	1st Edith Henna	
		"	2nd Florence Yoder (no ch.)	
9	Enid Lynnette "	"	Bradford Tilden Seney	" "

10	Curtis A. Wilson	ch.	Maude Blamey & Lynn W. Wilson	" "
10	Alan W. "			

GENEALOGICAL SECTION

10 Wilson Tilden Seney		ch.	Enid Lynnette Wilson	Bridgeport, Conn.
10 Clyde Curtis	"		& Bradford Tilden Seney	" "

Ch. 5 Abijah	Curtis	&	Sarah Birdsey	Newtown, Conn.
6 John	"	m.	Hannah Beach	" "
6 Benjamin	"	"	Mehitable (no desc.)	" "
6 Maj. Abijah Birdsey	"	"	Anna Glover	" "

Their Ch.

7 Marcia	"	"	John Beach (See Beach)
7 Horatio Nelson	"	"	Marcia Nefus — Rochester, N. Y.
7 Charlotte	"	"	Nichols Booth Lake (See Lake)
7 Anna	"	"	Simeon Nichols (See Nichols)
7 Joseph B.	"	"	Betsey Platt — Newtown, Conn.
7 Birdsey G.	"	"	Louisa Ketcham — Beloit, Wis.
7 Caroline	"	"	Simeon B. Peck (see Peck)
7 Ira L.	"	"	Marietta Glover — Newtown, Conn.

8 *Julianna	"	ch.	Betsey Platt & Joseph B. Curtis
8 *Sarah Frances	"		

Ch. Ira L. " & Marietta Glover " "

8 *Elizabeth	"	m.	Daniel W. Parker	Bedford, Ind.
8 *Juliette	"	"	Winthrop Foote (no ch.)	" "

Ch. Elizabeth " & Daniel Parker

9 Cora Parker		m.	T. J. Leonard (no ch.)	Springville, Ind.
9 Alfred Curtis	"	"	Gertrude Bowden	Bedford "

10 Mabel	"	ch.	Gertrude Bowder & Alfred Curtis Parker
10 Harriet	"		

DIKEMAN

Nathaniel Dikeman   m. Experience Hawley 1791, Newtown, Conn.

Their Ch.

2 Mary Ann	"	"	Taylor Judd	
2 Polly	"	"	Samuel Starr	Bethel "
2 Ira	"	"	Betsey Hurd	Cheshire "
2 Maria	"	"	Ebenezer Beers (no ch.)	Newtown, Conn.
2 Ebenezer	"	"	Julia Fairchild	" "
2 Sylvia	"	"	Abram K. Fairchild (see Fairchild)	"
2 Betsey	"	"	Norman Beers (see Beers)	Newtown, Conn.
2 Charles	"	"	Mary Matilda Benedict	" "
2 Harriet	"	"	Walter Parmelee	" "

Ch. Mary Ann Dikeman & Taylor Judd   Bethel, "

3 *Maria Judd	m.	Daniel Gregory	" "
3 *Catherine "	m.	William Dikeman	" "
3 *Arsina "	"	Benjamin Gregory	" "
3 Juliette "	"	Stiles Smith	" "
3 *William "	"	Elizabeth Seeley	" "
3 *Mary "	"	John Stone	" "
3 *Louisa "	"	Ira Manley	" "

Ch. Polly Dikeman   m. Samuel Starr

3 *Eliza Starr	"	Adolph H. Upson	Bethel, "
3 Dr. Alfred "	"	Mary Alice Nichols (no ch.)	New York.
3 *Ira "	"	Jane Hutton	

GENEALOGICAL SECTION

```
Ch. 2 Ira Dikeman          m.  Betsey Hurd
3 *Homer        "          "   Lydia Ann Northrop (no ch.) New Haven,
3 Mary          "          "       Doolittle
3 Sylvia        "          "   John Bishop              Cheshire, Conn.
3 Hattie        "          "   Elbert Sprang 1st        New Haven, Conn.
                           "   Howard 2nd               Chicago, Ill.
3 *Theodore     "              unm.

   Ch. Ebenezer "           "  Julia Fairchild 1st wife  Newtown, Conn.
3 *Henry        "           "  Emily Camp                   "      "
3 Sophia        "           "  George E. Porter          New Haven,  "

   Ch. Ebenezer "          &   Betsey Maria Dikeman, 2nd wife
3 *Martha       "           "  Alfred Tyrill
3 Oscar         "           "  Lillian Russell           New Haven,   "
3 Emma          "              unm.                          "       "

4 *Arthur Dikeman              Emily Camp                Newtown, Conn.
4 Julia         "         ch.      &
4 Lillian       "              Henry Dikeman                "       "

4 Dwight Tyrill                Martha Dikeman            New Haven, Conn.
4 *Gertrude  "            ch.      &
                               Alfred Tyrill                 "       "

5 Raymond Tyrill
5 Dorothy    "            ch.      &
5 Phyllis    "                 Dwight Tyrill                 "       "

5 Reginald Reid                *Gertrude Tyrill              "       "
5 Marion    "             ch.      &
                               William Reid

4 *Russell Dikeman             Lillian Russell           New Haven, Conn.
4 Mildred       "         ch.      &
                               Oscar Dikeman                 "       "

5 Henry Dikeman Stoddard
5 Russell Buddington  "        Mildred Dikeman,          Woodbridge, Conn.
5 William             "   ch.      &
5 Marcia              "        Clifford Ives Stoddard        "       "

2 Ch. *Charles Dikeman    &    Mary Matilda Benedict     Danbury, Conn.
3 Jane Dikeman            m.   Theodore Sanford              "       "
3 Sarah     "             "    John Hodge                    "       "

   Ch. Harriet Dikeman    m.   Walter Parmelee           Wallingford  "
3 Edwin Somers Parmelee   m.   Mary A. Treat                 "       "
3 Bruce Leavenworth  "    "    Martha Treat                  "       "

   Ch. Edwin S. Parmelee  "    Mary A. Treat                 "       "
4 Jennie Maria       "    "    Seymour Gilbert Baldwin       "       "
4 *Harriet Elizabeth "    "    Robert Culm Canby         Phila. Pa.
4 Mary Rebecca       "    "    James McIntosh Jones      Petersburg, Va.
4 Eva Treat          "         unm.                      Wallingford, Conn.
4 Sarah Edwina       "    "    Daniel Hervey Havens      Meriden     "

   Ch. Jennie Maria   "   &    Seymour G. Baldwin
5 *Edwin Seymour Baldwin       d. at 3 mos.
5 Mary Eliza          "   m.   Rufus Town Stephenson     Springfield, O.
5 Walter Parmelee     "   "    Marguerite Doyle          East Haven, Conn.
5 Elizabeth Gilbert   "        unm.

                               Mary Eliza Baldwin
6 Seymour Towne Stephenson ch.     &
                               Rufus Towne Stephenson
```

GENEALOGICAL SECTION

6 John Doyle Baldwin	ch.	Marguerite Doyle & Walter Parmelee Baldwin
5 Daniel Parmelee Havens 5 Mary Edwina " 5 William Edwin "	ch.	Sarah Edwina Parmelee Meriden, Conn. & Daniel Mervey Havens " "
3 Bruce Leavenworth Parmelee	m.	Martha Jane Treat Wallingford, Conn.
4 Fannie Augusta Parmelee	m.	Fred Markham " "

Their Ch.

5 Evelina Augusta Markham	m.	Willett Ives
5 Esther Jane "		unm.
5 Fred		unm.
6 Ruth Ives	ch.	Evelina Augusta Markham " " & Willett Ives

Ch. 3 Maria Judd   & William Dikeman

4 George Dikeman	m.	Kittie Jones Bethel, Conn.
4 Orson "	"	
4 Hannah Maria "		unm.
4 Mary Ann "	"	Henry Griffin
4 Anna Gregory	ch.	Catherine Judd & Daniel Gregory " "
" "	m.	Ferris Mead (no ch.)
4 Juliette " 4 Harriet R. " 4 *Martha A. " 4 *Arthur R. " 4 *Henry R. "	ch.	Arsina Judd & Benjamin Gregory Sandy Hook, Conn.
5 Grace Louise Hubbell 5 Charles Gregory "	ch.	Harriet R. Gregory & Luman Leroy Hubbell Danbury, Conn.
6 Leland Hubbell Lyon 6 Roger Adams " 6 Fred Gregory " 6 Marion Louise " 6 Harriet Grace "	ch.	Grace Louise Hubbell " " & G. Fred Lyon
6 Luman George Hubbell 6 Catherine Annette "	ch.	Mary Louise Modeman " " & Charles G. Hubbell
7 Leland Hahn Lyon	ch.	Alice Hahn " " & Leland Hubbell Lyon " "
4 Ch. Martha A. Gregory	&	Joseph B. Bloomer
5 Emma J. Bloomer	m.	Arthur A. Mead
5 Hattie A. "	"	Elmo Bateman " "
6 Joseph Blomer Bateman	ch.	Hattie A. Bloomer & Elmo Bateman
4 Henry Smith 4 *William " 4 Cortez " 4 *Jane Ann " 4 Cortez "	ch. m.	Juliette Judd & Stiles Smith Bethel, Conn. Cora B. Ferry

4 Ch. Henry Smith	&	Minnie Bruin	
5 Grace "	m.	John Killingbeck	Bethel, Conn.
5 Florence "	"	Gerald Hall	
5 Georgia "	"	Burton Orton	
5 Frederick "		unm.	
3 Ch. William Judd	m.	Elizabeth Seeley	
4 *John "		d. unm.	
4 Elizabeth "	m.	Runyon	
4 Alice "		unm.	
4 Lloyd Taylor "	m.		
4 Estella "		unm.	
4 *Ida "	m.	Charles Ray	
5 Virginia Ray		Ida Judd	
5 Alice "	ch.	&	
5 George "		Charles Ray	
3 Ch. Louise Judd	m.	Ira Manley	
4 Henry Manley	"	unknown	
4 Eveline "	"	Fred H. Richmond	
4 Howard "	"	Mary Reynolds	

EDMOND

See Newtown's Lawyers.			
1 Judge William Edmond	m.	1st Elizabeth Chandler	Newtown, Conn.
2 Mary E. "		Their Ch.	
1 Judge William "	m.	2nd Elizabeth Payne	" "
Their Ch.			
2 Elizabeth P. "	"	Holbrook Curtis	Waterbury "
2 Sarah "	"	Dr. Cyreniuh Booth	Newtown, "
2 William P. "			
2 Ann "		unm.	
2 Robert "		unm.	
3 Wiilliam Edmond Curtis	ch.	Elizabeth P. Edmond & Holbrook Curtis	Waterbury " Watertown, "
3 William Edmond "	m.	Mary Ann Scoville	
Their Ch.			
4 William Edmond Curtis, Jr.			
4 Henry Holbrook "	m.	Josephine Allen	Brooklyn, N. Y.
4 Frederick Kingsbury "	"	Marion Scott Hare	N. Y. City, N. Y.
Ch. Sarah Edmond	&	Dr. Cyrenius Booth	
3 *Mary Booth	m.	Henry Sanford	Newtown, Conn.
Sarah "	"	Marcus C. Hawley	" "
*Dr. William "		unm. (See Doctors)	" "
Ch. Mary "	&	Henry Sanford	" "
4 Annie Sanford		unm.	" "
4 Sarah "	m.	Robert C. Beers	" "
5 Henry Sanford Beers	ch.	Sarah Sanford & Robert C. Beers	" " " "
5 Robert Edmond "			
4 *William B. Hawley			
4 Mary "		Sarah Booth	" "
4 *William 2nd "	ch.	&	" "
*Harry C. "		Marcus C. Hawley	" "

GENEALOGICAL SECTION

FAIRCHILD

1 Thomas Fairchild came from England in 1638-9 and settled in Stratford in 1639 d. in 1670. The name was originally Fairbairn.
2 Edward, 2 Samuel, 2 Thomas, sons of 1 Thomas.
3 Edward first Fairchild settler in Newtown in 1705.
4 Ebenezer, 4 Jonathan, 4 James, sons of 3 Edward.
5 Peter, 5 Clement, 5 Truman, sons of 4 Ebenezer.
5 Josiah, 5 Zadoc, sons of 4 Jonathan.

5 Peter Fairchild, son of 4 Ebenezer m. Eunice Bulkley. She was a desc. of Gen. Warren of Revolutionary fame. Peter was a soldier in the war of the Revolution having served seven years. He was at Putnam Park during one winter with Gen. Putnam. He was a Corporal and it is said he served for a time on the staff of Gen. Washington.

[handwritten margin note: Son of Samuel, First son of Thomas 1.]
[handwritten margin note: also Zechariah f of David of Newton f of Agur]

	Ch. of 5 Peter Fairchild	&	Eunice Bulkley
6	Marcus	" m.	Susan Underhill Foote
6	Fanny	" "	Hawley Fairchild son of 5 Zadoc
6	Rufus	" "	Mary Windom Picken
6	William B.	" "	Sarah Hoffman
6	Nabby	" "	James B. Fairchild
6	Walter	" "	Abigail Jennings (no desc.)
6	Hermon	" "	Clara Dibble
6	Peter Warren	" "	Caroline Briscoe

	Ch. 6 Marcus	" "	Susan Underhill Foote
7	*Fayette	" "	Mary Jane Spring
7	*Horatio	"	Accidentally shot.

8	*Isabella	"		
8	Oscar	"	Mary Jane Spring	Naugatuck, Conn.
8	*Lillian	" ch.	&	
8	*Bernice	"	Fayette Fairchild	

			Mabel Atwood 1st wife	" "
9	Iza May	" ch.	&	
			Oscar Fairchild	

			Alice J. Beardsley 2nd wife	" "
9	Pearl	" ch.	&	
			Oscar Fairchild	

6 Fanny Fairchild dau. of Peter m. 6 Hawley Fairchild

			6 Fanny Fairchild	Newtown, Conn.
7	Harriet	" ch.	&	
			6 Hawley Fairchild	

			Harriet Fairchild	" "
8	*Edwin Benedict	"	&	
8	Emily "	ch.	George Benedict	
8	*Delia "			

			Cornelia Morse	Bethel "
9	*Hattie "	ch.	&	
			Edwin Benedict	

			Delia Benedict	Newtown, "
9	Lena "	ch.	&	
9	*George Lewis "		Lewis Beers Fairchild	

			Lena Fairchild	
10	George Hull		&	
10	Ruth "	ch.	Matthew Hull	
10	Emily "			

5 Silas son of 4 James	m.	Sarah Godfrey	Newtown, Conn.
6 Joseph son of 5 Silas	"	Electa Fairchild 1st wife	

GENEALOGICAL SECTION

Their Ch.
7 Polly Ann Fairchild   m. Beman Fairchild
7 Philo   "

   Ch. 6 Joseph   "   & Amarillis Dibble 2nd wife
7 Aurinda   "   m. Mizenus Hard
7 Electa   "   " Augustine Thayer   New Milford, Conn.
7 Sarah   "   " John Gale   Bethel, "
7 Mary   "   " Charles Stevens   " "
7 Laura Ann   "   " Barlow Stevens   Bridgeport "
7 James   "   " Evelyn Wallace   Newtown, "
7 Dr. S. Bradley   "   " Sarah McKinney   Woodbury "

6 Joseph   "   " Patience Judson Wheeler 3rd wife

7 Amarillis Gale   Sarah Fairchild   Bethel "
7 Angeline "   ch.   &
              John Gale

8 Florence Sherman, M.D.   Angeline Fairchild Gale
8 William "   ch.   &
              William Sherman

6 *Rufus Fairchild   m. Mary W. Pickens   New York, N. Y.
7 They had a daughter who m. a Zogbaum
8 Rufus Fairchild Zogbaum became an eminent artist. His specialty was battle scenes during the Civil War.

6 *Nabby Fairchild   m. 5 James Fairchild son of 4 James
   Their Ch.
7 *Mary E.   "   m. Capt. Wason   Bridgeport, Conn.
7 *Sarah   "   " William Mayuard (no ch.) Newtown, "
7 *Susan   "   " David Andrews   " "
7 *Smith   "   d. in Civil War

8 Frederick Andrews
8 Rufus "   Susan Fairchild   " "
8 William "   ch.   &
8 Elizabeth "   David Andrews Killed in Civil War

9 Susan "   Jennie Butcher   Newtown, Conn.
9 Fannie "   ch.   &
              Frederick Andrews   " "

6 Ch. Hermon Fairchild   & Clara Dibble   " "
7 *Hannah Dibble "   m. Charles Henry Peck   " "
7 *Edwin "   d. in young manhood   " "

*Lewis Henry Peck   Hannah D. Fairchild   " "
    Adopted   ch.   &
Arthur Treat Nettleton   Charles Henry Peck
" " "   m. *Jennie Morris   " "

Ch. 6 Peter Warren Fairchild & Caroline Briscoe   " "
7 *Emily Fairchild   m. Charles Gray (no ch.)   " "
6 Juliette "   " Hosea B. Northrop (see Northrop) rec.)
7 Robert "   " Frances Smith   Stamford "
7 *Margaret "   " Benjamin Lewis   " "
7 Jerome "   d. in Civil War
7 *Albert Warren "   " Mary Greene 1st   Newtown, Conn.
              Mrs. Victoria Burritt 2nd   Stepney "

8 Arthur Fairchild   Mary Green 1st wife   Newtown, Conn.
8 Adelaide "   ch.   &
              Albert W. Fairchild

GENEALOGICAL SECTION

9 Arthur Warren Fairchild   Emily Hazen Smith   Newtown, Conn.
9 Robert Dunning "   ch.   &
9 Mary Hazen "   Arthur Fairchild " "

Sergt. Arthur W. Fairchild in France, Oct. 1917. In Med. Dept.
   Robert D. in France May 1918.

9 Edith Fairchild Wilson   Adelaide Fairchild
9 Edna Louise "   ch.   &
    Ernest Wilson

5 Clement Fairchild son of 4 Ebenezer m. Sarah Platt   Newtown, Conn.

   Their Ch.
6 Lucinda Fairchild   m.   John Williams   Brookfield "
6 Beman "   "   Polly Ann Fairchild   " "
6 Hiram "   "   1st Sarah Northrop   " "
    2nd Betsey Gelston   " "
6 Lucia "   "   Asel Beebe   Bethel, "

   No desc. located.

5 Truman Fairchild son of 4 Ebenezer m. Sarah Sherman   Newtown, Conn.

   Their Ch.
6 Araunah Fairchild   m.   1st Esther Bryant   " "
    2nd Anna Beers (no ch.)
6 Abraham K. Fairchild   m.   Sylvia Dikeman

   Their Ch.
7 *Harriet Catherine "   m.   John Nichols (see Nichols) " "
7 *George S. "   "   unm.
7 *Nathaniel Perry "   "   Abby Bartram   " "
7 *Sarah "   "   unm.
7 Henry Hobart "   "   Lydia Platt   " "

   Ch. Henry H. Fairchild   &   Lydia Platt   " "
8 George S. "   "   Florence Sirine   " "
8 William H. "   "   Nettie Ward   " "
8 Alice P. "   "   Ernest Sherman   Stepney, "
8 *Hobart C. "   "   Mary L. Botsford   Newtown, "
8 Sarah L. "   "   Arthur L. Sirine   Bethel, "
8 Edwin C. "   "   Grace McDowell   " "
8 Perry E. "   "   Belle Smith   " "

9 George S. Jr. "   Florence Sirine   " "
9 Julia "   ch.   &
9 *Louise "   George S. Fairchild   " "
9 Ivan O. "   " "

9 Ruth H. "   Nettie Ward   " "
9 Arthur W. "   ch.   &
    William H. Fairchild

    Alice P. Fairchild   Stepney, "
9 Arthur E. Sherman   ch.   &
    Ernest S. Sherman

    Mary L. Botsford   Newtown "
9 May L. Fairchild   ch.   &
    *Hobart C. Fairchild
" " "   m.   Louis Bedat

9 Grace L. Sirine   Sarah L. Fairchild   Bethel "
9 *Arthur E. "   ch.   &
9 Fairchild J. "   Arthur L. Sirine   " "

9 Geraldine Fairchild   Belle Smith   " "
9 Elliott R. "   ch.   &
    Perry E. Fairchild   " "

GENEALOGICAL SECTION

10 George S. Curtis 3rd.	ch. George S. Fairchild Jr. & Jessie M. Stucklan	Bethel, Conn. " "
10 May L. "		" "
10 Pearl H. Cable	ch. Ruth H. Fairchild & Harvey Cable	" "
10 George H. "		" "
10 Florence Thompson	ch. Julia Fairchild & David Thompson	" "
10 Harold H. Fairchild	ch. Mary Hawley & Ivan O. Fairchild	" "
10 Dorthea "		" "
10 Beatrica "		" "

Ch. of 5 Josiah Fairchild & Betsey Wheeler

6 Adoniram Fairchild	m. Polly Dibble	Newtown, Conn.
6 Wheeler "	" Betsey Botsford	" "
6 Jonathan Sturges "	" Lucy Wheeler	" "
6 Ira "	" Jerusha Hall	" "
6 Betsey Ann "	" Levi Weed	Bethel "
6 Cyrus "	" Damaris Botsford	" "

Ch. 6 Adoniram " & Polly Dibble

7 *Dibble "	m. Polly Blackman	" "
7 Josiah "	" Phebe Booth	" "
7 Horace "	" Laura Taylor	" "
7 Florilla "	" 1st Daniel Leavenworth	" "
7 Polly Ann "	" William Hinman	Monroe, "

Ch. 7 Dibble Fairchild & Polly Blackman

8 *Elizabeth "	d. at twenty one years	
8 *Lilly Delia "	d. sixteen years	" "
8 *Jane Ann "	m. William Kellogg (no ch.)	" "
8 *Theodore "	" Maria Bryant	Canada
9 Jane "	ch. Maria Bryant & Theodore Fairchild	"
9 William "		"
9 Carrie "		"
8 Mariette "	ch. Phebe Booth & 7 Josiah Fairchild	Newtown, Conn.
8 Josiah Booth "		" "
8 Mariette Fairchild	m. Glover Hawley (See Hawley)	" "

7 Ch. of 7 Horace Fairchild m. Laura Taylor

8 Harriet "		" "
8 Martha "		
8 Adoniram "	m. Phebe Summers. A diver. Lost his life diving.	
8 Reuben "		

Ch. Adoniram and Phebe Summers

9 Benjamin Fairchild	m. Marion Siditer	Brooklyn, N. Y.
9 Anna "	unm.	
9 *Ada "	m. Dr. Charles Penny	Stepney, Conn.
9 Edith "	unm.	
9 David "	unm.	
10 *Benjamin H. "	ch. Marion Siditer & Benjamin Fairchild	Brooklyn, N. Y.
10 Edith "		
10 *Walter "		
10 Anna "		

GENEALOGICAL SECTION

Ch. 7 Polly Ann Fairchild	&	William Hinman	Monroe, Conn.
8 John S. Hinman	m.	Mary Turney	
8 Kate L. "	"	Jackson Lake	
8 Emma J. "		unm.	
8 Arthur W. "	"	Lydia O. Lane	Monroe "
8 *Anna "	"	Bruce Griffen	Shelton, "
9 Florence Lake	ch.	Kate L. Hinman & Jackson Lake	Monroe "
9 Rev. Clarence "			" "
9 Lydia Lane Hinman Benedict	ch.	Lydia O. Lane & Arthur Wm. Hinman	" "

Ch. Levi Weed	&	Betsey Ann Fairchild	Bethel, "
7 Eliza Ann "	m.	Charles Sherman	Brookfield, "
7 Edwin "	"	Susan Tripp	New Haven
7 Josiah Austin "	"	Jeannette Treat	
7 Granville "	"	Phebe Dann	
7 Harrison "	"	Elizabeth Platt	
7 Henry Russell "	"	Charlotte Botsford	
8 Maria Sherman	ch.	Eliza Ann Weed & Charles Sherman	
9 Carrie Twiss " " m. H. F. Burgess	ch.	Maria Sherman & Gustavus Twiss	
8 Emma Weed " " m. J. W. Drum	ch.	Susan Tripp & Edwin Weed	
8 Charles T. Weed		Jeannette Treat	
8 Jennie " " "	ch. m.	& J. Austin Weed H. C. McKnight	
8 Smith G. Weed	ch.	Phebe Dann & Granville Weed	
8 I. De Witt "		Elizabeth Platt	
8 H. Harrison "	ch.	& H. Harrison Weed	
8 Elizabeth " " "	m.	A. J. Ward	
8 Minnie M. " 8 Clara L. "	ch.	Charlotte Botsford & Henry Russell Weed	
5 Zadoc son of 4 Jonathan	m.	1st Mary Griffen " 2nd Abiah Wheeler	

Ch. 5 Zadoc Fairchild	&	Mary Griffen	Newtown, Conn.
6 Hawley "	m.	Fanny Fairchild	" "
6 Ezra "	"	Anna Shepard	" "
6 Ziba "	"	Sally Morehouse	" "
6 Clark "	"	Charlotte Beecher	" "
6 Lewis "	"	Betsey Botsford Fairchild	" "
6 Levi "	"	Anna Shepard	" "
6 Samuel "	"	Polly Camp (no ch.)	" "
6 Burtis "	"	Hannah Wakelee (no ch.)	" "
6 Beers "	"	1st Esther Toucey (no ch.) 2nd Adah Camp	" "
6 Moss "	"	Eliza Fairchild	" "
6 Polly "	"	Trowbridge Camp (see Camp)	" "
6 Eunice "	"	Judd	Bethel "

GENEALOGICAL SECTION 61

Ch. Ezra Fairchild	m.	Anna Shepard	Newtown, Conn.
7 Sophia "	"	Stephen Allen	Woodbury "
7 Lucretia "	"	George Redstone	Newtown, "
7 Eliza "		unm.	
7 Catherine "	"	Charles B. Glover (see Glover record)	
7 Charles "	"	Jerusha Edmonds	Newtown, Conn.
8 Julius Henry Allen	ch.	Sophia Fairchild & Stephen Allen	Woodbury, "
9 Howard Sanford " 9 Arthur Stephen "	ch.	Lillian Amelia Sanford & Julius H. Allen	" " " "
6 Ziba Fairchild	m.	Sally Morehouse	Newtown, Conn.
Their Ch.			
7 Edmund "	"	Harriet Whitney 1st wife	" "
" "	"	Lois Peck 2nd wife	" "
7 David Wheeler "	"	Emeline Wetmore	" "
7 Le Grand "	"	Emily Whitney	" "
7 Samuel "		no desc. located	
8 *Lucy A. "	ch.	Harriet Whitney 1st wife & Edmond Fairchild	" "
8 *Julia A. "			" "
8 *Julia A. 2nd "	ch.	Lois Peck 2nd wife & Edmund Fairchild	" "
9 Edgar Northrop 9 George " 9 Lucy "	ch.	Lucy A. Fairchild & Edgar Northrop	" " " " " "
9 Homer Baldwin	ch.	Lucy Fairchild Northrop & Baldwin	" "
10 Aurelia Wetmore Northrop 10 Edgar Whitney "	ch.	Florence Wetmore 2nd wife & Edgar Northrop Cora St. John 1st wife	" " " " " "
10 Mary Northrop 10 Georgia " 10 Helen "	ch.	Annie Warren & George Northrop	" " " "
10 Lucy A. Baldwin 10 Ruth " 10 Carlton "	ch.	Annie Hawley & Homer Baldwin	Stratford " " " " "
10 Allan Mc Gregor	ch.	Lucy Northrop & Albert Mc Gregor	" "
9 Lois Bulkley 9 Edmond "	ch.	Julia A. Fairchild & Eugene Bulkley	Newtown. " " "
7 Ch 7 David Wheeler	&	Emeline Wetmore	" "
8 Mary Jane Fairchild	m.	William Lawrence	Bethel "
8 Augustine "	"	E. A. Goodemote	" "
8 Sarah M. "	"	Myron Colby	
8 Henry W. "	"	unknown	
8 Arthur "		d. young	Newtown, "
8 Julia "		d. young	" "

GENEALOGICAL SECTION

Ch. 7 Le Grand Fairchild son of Ziba and Emily Whitney, Newtown, Conn.

8 *J. Botsford	"	m.	Emma Jane Jennings	" "
8 *Julius Burr	"		unm.	
8 *Emily Aurelia	"	"	1st Jacob Mayhew	Bethel "
			2nd John Gay	Newtown, "
9 Mary Ella	"		Emma J. Jennings	" "
9 Jennie Louise	"	ch.	&	
9 *Emma Irene	"		J. Botsford Fairchild	" "
10 Willis Arndt	"	ch.	Jennie L. Fairchild & Richard Arndt	" "

6 Ch. Levi Fairchild son of Zadoc and Anna Shepard

7 Elizabeth	"	m.	Carlos Booth (see Booth)	" "
7 Delia	"	"	Henry Terrill (see Terrill record)	
7 Levi Beers	"	"	Louisa Sanford	Bethel, "
6 Moss son of Zadoc		m.	Eliza Fairchild	" "
7 Cornelia Fairchild	"	"	Isaac Briscoe (see Briscoe)	" "
7 Mariette	"	"	William Babbitt	Bridgewater "
7 Clarinda	"	"	Ammon Taylor	Newtown, "
7 Lewis Beers	"	"	Delia Benedict	" "

See desc. Fanny Fairchild

Ch. 6 Wheeler son of 5 Josiah m. Betsey Botsford " "

7 Boyle Fairchild		m.	Julia A. Hatch	" "
7 Josiah Beach	"	"	Eliza Dibble	" "
7 Lucy Ann	"	"	John Hawley (see Hawley)	Brookfield "
7 Laura	"	"	Sallu P. Barnum	Newtown, "
7 Betsey Ann	"	"	Charles Clarke (see Clarke)	" "
7 Jane	"	"	Betts	Woodbury "

Ch. 7 Boyle Fairchild & Julia A. Hatch Newtown, "

8 David W.	"	m.	Mary Gregory	Danbury, "
8 George Hatch 2nd	"	m.	Jane D. Parrot	
8 Dr. Josiah Beach	"	"	1st Jane McLean Wade	
		"	Mary E. Waterbury	
8 Elijah Boyle D.D.S.	"	"	Emroy Alma Blinn	
8 Catherine	"	"	William Hart Davis	Monroe, "

Ch. 8 David " & Mary Gregory Danbury, "

9 *Alfred Boyle	"		unm.
9 Julia Gertrude	"	m.	Charles Cristadora
9 Mary Kate	"	"	Harris Richardson
9 Charles Gregory	"	"	Ada Vandewater

Ch. Charles Cristadora & Julia Gertrude Fairchild

10 Agnes Gertrude "
10 Bertha Corinne "
10 Charles Clarence "
10 Harold "

Ch. Harris Richardson & Mary Kate Fairchild

10 Gertrude	"	m.	Austin Angell
10 Walter	"	"	Theresa Bates Walley

11 Harris Angell
11 Benjamin " ch. Gertrude Richardson & Austin Angell

11 Russell Richardson
11 Harris 2nd " ch. Theresa Bates Walley Walter Richardson

GENEALOGICAL SECTION

Ch. George Hatch Fairchild & Jane D. Parrot
9 *Mary Hatch Fairchild
9 George William "
9 Jane Francis " m. Nelson Miles Beach
9 Julia Alice "
9 George Hatch "
9 Julia Anna " m. Robert T. Patterson
9 Sherman "
9 Fannie Parrot " " Frederick R. Drake
9 David Allen "

10 Herman Kissam Beach ch. Jane F. Fairchild
10 Nelson Miles Jr. " & Nelson Miles Beach

10 Allen Fairchild Drake ch. Fannie P. Fairchild
& Frederick R. Drake

11 Herman Beach ch. Bertha Rigmar Lynge
11 William " & Herman Kissam Beach

Ch. 8 Dr. Josiah B. Fairchild and Jane McLean Wade
9 William Wade Fairchild
9 Kate "

10 Bertha " ch. Clara
& William Wade Fairchild

11 Twin daughter ch. Bertha Fairchild
11 Twin son & Arthur L. Roberts

7 Josiah Beach son of 6 Wheeler m. Eliza Dibble   Newtown, Conn
  Their Ch.
8 *Catherine Fairchild   m. Robert Van Keuren   East Aurora, N. Y.
8 Susan A.   "   unm.   Bridgeport, Conn.
8 Mortimer   "   m. Elizabeth Agnes Kelly   "   "
9 *Robert Mortimer Fairchild m. Lillian May Wilson   "   "
9 Mortimer Van Keuren   m. Katie Schaaf
9 Robert Fairchild "   " Maude Felt

10 Katherine Louise "   Katie Schaaf   East Aurora, N. Y.
10 Robert Mortimer "   ch. &
                             Mortimer Van Keuren

8 Mary Catherine Barnum   Laura Fairchild   Newtown, Conn.
8 David   "   ch. &
8 Sarah Frances   "   Sallu Pell Barnum   "   "

9 Mary Barnum   ch. Mary Louise Seymour
                              &
                             David Barnum
  "   "   m. Arthur Frederick MacArthur

Ch. 6 Jonathan Sturgis Fairchild and Lucy Wheeler
7 *Joseph Bennett Fairchild .m. Phebe Shepard
7 *Mary   "   " Charles Skidmore (no ch.) Newtown Conn.
7 *Henry   "   " Caroline Booth 1st   "   "
                 "   " Elizabeth Peck 2nd   "   "
7 *Emeline   "   " Edwin Terrill (see Terrill) Brookfield "
7 *William   "   " Adaline Johnson   Newtown,   "
7 Lucy   "   " David Beers (se Beers)   "   "

7 Ch. Joseph Bennett Fairchild and Phebe Shepard
8 Sarah M.	"	m.	William E. Duncomb	Redding, Conn.
8 George	"	"	Mary Clark (no ch.)	Southbury "
8 Jonathan Sturgis	"	"	Nellie Morse	
8 Ambrose S.	"		unm.	
8 Elmer W.	"		unm.	
8 Esther B.	"	"	Charles J. Merritt	Medina, N. Y.
8 Henry W.	"	"	Anna Green	

8 Ch. Sarah Fairchild and Wm. E. Duncomb   Redding, Conn.
| 9 David S. Duncombe | m. | Lydia Lane Lockwood | Knoxville, Tenn. |
| 9 George F. " | m. | Lucy Beers | Newtown, Conn. |

10 Wm. Millington Duncombe			New York, N. Y.
10 Frederick Howe "		Lydia Lane Lockwood	Newtown, Conn.
10 Raynor Sanford "	ch.	&	Mount Vernon, N. Y.
10 David Sanford "		David S. Duncomb	Albany, N. Y.

| 11 Frederick Taylor " | ch. | Mabel Taylor & | Newtown, Conn. |
| 11 Raynor Lockwood " | | Frederick H. Duncombe | |

| 10 Julia Beers " | ch. | Lucy Beers & George F. Duncombe | |
| " " " | m. | Rev. Walter Aiken | Torrington, Conn. |

| 9 *Ida Merritt | ch. | Esther Fairchild & | |
| 9 *Charles H. " | | Charles J. Merritt | Chicago, Ill. |

| 10 Margery " | ch. | Annie Crawford & | " " |
| 10 Crawford " | | Charles H. Merritt | " " |

Ch. 7 Henry Fairchild and Caroline Booth   Newtown, Conn.
| 8 Jane Elizabeth | " | m. | Col. Julius W. Knowlton | Bridgeport " |
| 8 Anna Frances | " | " | Andrew C. Moore | Newtown, Conn. |

| 9 *Willie Knowlton | ch. | Jane E. Fairchild & | |
| 9 *Waldo " | | Col. J. W. Knowlton | Bridgeport, Conn. |

9 Henry Fairchild Moore			Newtown, Conn.
9 Arthur Hill "	ch.	Anna F. Fairchild &	
9 Elsie May "		Andrew C. Moore	" "
9 Henry F. "	m.	Lillian Bonner	

10 Evelyn Frances "			
10 Mildred Jane "		Ethel Holroyed	
10 Arthur Holroyd "	ch.	&	
10 Ralph Fairchild "		Arthur H. Moore	Bridgeport, Conn.

Ch. 7 William Fairchild   &   Adaline Johnson   Newtown, Conn.
8 *Charles Johnson "		unm.	
8 Julia Merrit "	m.	George C. Stahl	Toledo, Ohio
8 *William Henry "	"	Nellie A. Hartshorn	Newtown, Conn.

| 9 William F. Stahl | ch. | *Julia M. Fairchild & George C. Stahl | Tulsa, Okla |

| 10 Winifred Elizabeth Stahl | ch. | Elizabeth Thornton & Wm. F. Stahl | " " |

GENEALOGICAL SECTION

Ch. Wm. H. Fairchild & Nellie A. Hartshorne
9 Dean Drummond Fairchild m. Ada May Allen Cold Spring Harbor, N. Y.
9 Raymond " " Pearl Harrison Depew, N. Y.
9 Nellie Hartshorne " " *Samuel E. Speed Albany, "
" " Speed " 2nd, Horatio T. Allen Waterbury, Conn.

10 Burgess Johnson Speed ch. Nellie H. Fairchild Milford, Conn.
10 Nellie Hartshorne " " &
 *Samuel E. Speed Milford, Conn.

8 James Fairchild son of 7 James was in Colonial Army Newtown, Conn.

Ch. James Fairchild and Mary Beers " "

9 Kiah B. was a teacher in Newtown. He enlisted in U. S. Army in 1809, was Sergt. in war of 1812; later raised to rank of Capt.

9 Capt. Kiah Fairchild m. Polly Hubbell Newtown, Conn.

Their Ch.

10 Matthew Fairchild m. Mary Booth " "
10 Burton " " Amy Wayland " "
10 Maria " " 1st Newton Benedict " "
10 Mary " 2nd Wheeler Drew " "
10 Lucinda " "

Ch. Matthew Fairchild and Mary Booth " "

11 Julia "
11 Jane "
11 Ellen " m. W. W. Courter Bridgeport, "
11 George " " Jane Marilla Warner
11 Emma "
11 William "
11 Clarence " Lives in San Francisco

Ch. Burton Fairchild and Amy Wayland Newtown, Conn.

David Burton

11 George Newton " m. Mary J. Sherman Bethel, "
11 Col. Robert Bruce " unm. Bridgeport "
11 Frank Harrison " " "

Ch. George N. Fairchild and Mary J. Sherman

12 George Burton " m. Martha B. Farnum Bethel, "
12 Anna M. " m. Stuart Kyle " "

Col. Robert B. Fairchild, a Newtown boy, was left an orphan when eleven years of age by the death of his mother; the father having been killed while blasting rocks several years earlier. He lived with Rufus Couch of Bethel a few years, then went to Bridgeport, where he became a salesman with Birdsey & Co. At the breaking out of the Civil War he enlisted in 23rd Conn. Vols.; was taken prisoner in Louisiana when Capt. Julius Sanford and his company were captured. At the time of his death he was Colonel of 4th Reg. C. N. G. and was in a fair way to be promoted to the highest military position in the State.

He was for seventeen years Supt. of S. School of Washington Park M. E. Church, Bridgeport and exerted untold influence for good.

FAIRMAN

1 Richard Fairman b. 1708 m. Jane Botsford

Their Ch.

2 Ichabod Fairman m. Rebecca Glover Newtown, Conn.

Their Ch.

3 Henry " " "
3 Patience "
3 James Beach " m. 1st Polly Peck " "
 " 2nd Nancy Betsey Peck
3 Pulchrea " " Gideon Botsford (See Botsford record)
3 Jane "
3 Dorcas "

Ch. James B. Fairman and Polly Peck Newtown, Conn.
4 Chloe " m. Ziba Blakeslee (see Blakeslee record)
Ch. James B. Fairman & Nancy Betsey Peck Newtown, Conn.
4 Polly " unm. " "
4 Charles " m. Eliza Morehouse " "
4 Maria " unm. " "
4 William " m. Sarah Dunn Adams New York, City
4 James " " Mary Louise Doolittle New Haven, Conn.
4 Zerah " " Sarah Bennett " "

Ch. Charles " & Eliza Morehouse " "
5 Franklin " m. Mary Jane Sherman Chicago, Ill.
5 Matilda Eliza " d. in infancy Newtown, Conn.
5 Daniel Beach " d. in infancy " "
5 Daniel 2nd " m. Lucinda L. Southwick Chicago, Ill
5*Matilda 2nd " " James J. Noble " "
5*James " twins unm.
5*Jane " twins unm.
5*Arthur " m. Sohpia B. Seibert Manhattan, Kan.
5*Elizabeth " m. Rev. Geo. W. Patten Chicago, Ill.
5*Anna " unm.
5 Eva 2nd wife " m. James J. Noble " "
5*Drusus " d. in boyhood Newtown, Conn.

Ch. Franklin Fairman and Mary Jane Sherman Chicago, Ill.
6 Matilda Louise "
6 Frank S. " d. in young manhood " "
6 Marion "

Ch. Daniel B. Fairman and Lucinda L. Southwick Chicago, Ill
6 Charles Chauncey " m. Sarah Overman " "
6 Clarence " " Margaret Miller " "

Ch. Charles C. Fairman and Sarah Overman Detroit, Mich.
7 Ruth " m. Allen Ray Johnston Chicago, Ill.
7 Helen "
7 Hazel " " Ralph Doyle " "
7 Charles Chauncey "

Ch. Ruth Fairman and Allen Ray Johnston " "
8 Kenneth Allen Johnston
8 Richard Lloyd "
8 Robert Fairman "

8 Dorothy Doyle ch. Hazel Fairman " "
 &
 Ralph Doyle

7 Daniel Beach Fairman ch. Margaret Miller " "
7 Margaret " &
 Clarence Fairman

FRANKLIN FAIRMAN

Franklin Fairman was born at Newtown, Conn. June 22nd, 1833. He attended the public schools and the academy, but when only sixteen years old, he entered the employ of his uncle, James Fairman of New Haven. Later he was employed in the printing office of the N. Y. Independent, but in 1855 sought larger opportunities in Chicago. He at once entered the service of the Ill. C. R. R. and from 1874 until 1900 was Chief Freight Clerk and Auditor of Freight Accounts. In 1900 he was made Auditor and held that position until 1903, when he was retired by age limitation. For years he was one of the forceful figures of railroad circles centering in Chicago. In the early 80's he became much interested in Fraternal Life Insurance, joining the National Union in which he was a very efficient worker and held the highest and most responsible positions until the time of his death.

In 1888 while President of the Lincoln Council, he inaugurated the public annual commemoration of Lincoln's birth-day and from this beginning the day has become a legal holiday in Ills. and the U. S.

In early life he was a member of the Congregational Church, but became much interested in the Reformed Episcopal Church in Chicago, and later in St. Paul's Episcopal Kenwood. The Kenwood Club of which he was an early member, gave him social diversion. He was much interested in the Art Institute and was very fond of music.

In politics he was a staunch Republican.

			Matilda Fairman	Chicago, Ill.
6	Mary Eliza Noble	ch.	&	" "
			James J. Noble	

Ch. 4 Arthur Fairman and Sophie Seibert — Manhattan, Kansas

6	Charles Edward Fairman	m.	Mary Marshall	
6	Anna	"		Joplin, Missouri
6	Margarita	"		
6	Arthur	"		
6	Jennie	"		
6	Hobart twins	"		Manhattan, Kansas
6	Seibert twins	"		
7	Laura Virginia	"		" "
7	Marjorie Jane	"	ch. Mary Marshall & Charles E. Fairman	
7	Mary	"		

			Eva Fairman	Chicago, Ill.
6	Alden Charles Noble	ch.	&	
			James J. Noble	

			Helen Parker Harlan	New York, N. Y.
7	Althea Noble	ch.	&	
			Alden C. Noble	

Ch. 4 William Fairman and Sarah Dunn Adams — New York, N. Y.

| 6 | *William James | " | m. Blanche Helfenstein | |

Ch. 3 James Fairman and Mary Louise Doolittle — New Haven, Conn.

| 5 | Caroline Elizabeth | " | m. Leslie Moulthrop | Short Beach, Conn. |
| 5 | *James Yale | " | " Suzie Chaffee | New Haven, " |

Ch. Caroline E. Fairman and Leslie Moulthrop

6	Caroline Louise Moulthrop	m. Walter Peck Stanley	Atlanta, Georgia
6	Berkeley	"	
6	Alice Fairman	" m. Alfred Russell Burr	New Haven, Conn.

Ch. James Yale Fairman and Suzie Chaffee

| 6 | Ruth Lillian | " | m. Graham Fellows Thompson | " " |
| 6 | Hortense Victoria | " | " James Franklin Cowan | Wellsley Hills, Mass. |

		Ruth Lillian Fairman	
7	Graham F. Thompson Jr.	ch. &	
		Graham Fellows Thompson, New Haven, Ct.	

		Hortense Fairman,	Wellsley Hills, Mass.
7	James Franklin Cowan, Jr.	&	
		James F. Cowan	

In Y. M. C. A. in U. S. Service. Has charge of work in different camps.

			Sarah Bennett,	Newtown, Conn.
5	Sarah Elizabeth Fairman	ch.	&	
			Zerah Fairman,	Bridgeport, "

FERRIS

Jeffrey Ferris, ancestor of the many Ferris families in New England, was made a freeman in Boston in 1635.

He m. Susannah Lockwood *2nd wife, Judy Feake-Palmer*

Their ch. James, Peter, Joseph, Mary, John. *by 1st wife Mary*

1 Peter, desc. of Jeffrey, bought a farm in Newtown in 1711.
  He m. Martha Northrop

GENEALOGICAL SECTION

2 Joseph Ferris m. Abigail Sherman

Being a conscientious adherent of the Church of England, he went to Nova Scotia during the war of the Revolution. His wife saved the farm from confiscation.

Their ch.

3 Daniel Ferris	m. Jerusha Glover	Newtown, Conn.
3 Martha "	m. Abel Hurd	Brookfield, "
3 Ruth "	desc. not located	

..Ch. Daniel Ferris and Jerusha Glover

4 Jerusha "	m. Dr. Rufus Skidmore,	Newtown, Conn.
4 Glover "	m. Mary Briscoe	

Ch. Jerusha Ferris and Dr. Rufus Skidmore (See Doctors)

5 Jane A. Skidmore   m. Barak Burr (no ch.)   Fairfield, Conn.

She placed in Trinity Church a beautiful window in memory of Joseph Ferris, her gr. grandfather.

5 Marietta Skidmore b. 1825 m. Alanson Lyon, living, 1918 Redding, Conn.
5 Martha E. "   m. James Johnson,   Bridgeport, Conn.

See Skidmore record for other desc. of Dr. Rufus.

4 Peter Hurd	ch. Martha Ferris, & Abel Hurd,	Brookfield, Conn.
4 Jabez "		" "

Ch. Jabez Hurd and Lucy H. Blackman

5 George S. Hurd	m. Mary Taylor,	Danbury, Conn.
5 Bernice "	m. Zerah Skidmore	Bethlehem "
5 Philo "	m. Melinda Tomlinson,	Bridgeport, "
5 Hester "	m. Abel Sherman Hawley (See Hawley)	Newtown, "
5 Samuel Ferris Hurd	m. Julia Tomlinson	Bridgeport, "
5 Rhoda Ferris	m. Abraham Shepard	Brookfield, '

1 Squire Zachariah Ferris

2 Abel "	m. Abiah———	Newtown, Conn.
3 Gideon Baldwin "	m. Charlotte Northrop,	" "

Their ch.

4 Harriet "	m. Starr Skidmore,	Brookfield, Conn.
4 Wm. David Baldwin Ferris	m. Maria E. Blackman	Newtown, Conn.

Their ch.

5 George B. Ferris	m. Bertha Clark	Newtown, Conn.
5 Charles D. "	m. 1st Mary Sherwood	" "
	m. 2nd Ophelia Thornhill,	Brookfield, Conn.
5 Hattie Louise "	m. Dr. Thomas Wallace	Warren, Pa.

6 Elsie Clark   Ferris
6 Herbert Curtis   "
6 Capt. George Mallett "   ch. Bertha Clark   Brookfield, Conn.
   In U. S. Service   &
6 Arthur Judson   "   George B. Ferris
6 Charles Blackman "

7 Herbert Curtis Jr. Ferris   ch. Lucy Wright   Bridgeport, Conn.
7 Dorothy Wilson   "   &
                                   Herbert C. Ferris

6 Charles   Ferris   Newtown, Conn.
6 William   "   "   "

6 Florence Ferris		Ophelia Thornhill	Newtown, Conn.
6 Donald "	ch.	&	
6 Louise "		Charles D. Ferris	" "
6 Sarah "			
6 George Wight "			

6 Romaine Wallace	ch.	Hattie L. Ferris & Dr. Thomas Wallace	Warren, Penn.

Nathan Ferris	m.	Abiah Skidmore	Newtown, Conn.

Their Ch.
Thomas S. Ferris
Abraham Booth "   m. Phoebe Ferris   " "
Betsey   "   " Louis Beers Prindle (see Prindle) " "

FOOTE

Nathaniel, first Foote settler in Wethersfield, Conn. 1593.
1 Daniel first Foote settler in Newtown in 1716.
2 James   m. Adah Stilson
3 Rhesa Foote   m. Polly Hawley

Their Ch.
4 *Julia Maria Foote   m. Charles Stilson (no ch.)
4 *Catherine Hawley " " Beach Camp (See Camp)
4 *George Lewis   " " Minerva Tuttle
4 *Frederick William " " Vashti Butler Thompson   Elizabeth, N. J.
4 *Mary   " " Rev. Henry V. Gardner d. E. Aurora, N. Y.
4 *Harriet   " " Rev. William Atwill
4 *Robert   " " d. on ninth birthday
4 *Dr. Henry Hawley "   unm.
4 *Jane Elizabeth   " " Walter B. Welton   Bridgewater, Conn.
For desc. of Catherine see Camp and Johnson

Ch. Rev. George L. Foote and Minerva Tuttle
5 *George   "   d. in infancy,   Roxbury, Conn.
5 *Harriet Minerva   " m. Rt. Rev. Daniel S. Tuttle St. Louis, Mo.
5 *Rev. George Wm.   " " Sarah Ellen Pidsley   San Jose, Cal.
5 *Rev. Henry Lewis   " " 1st Christine Carr   Salt Lake City, Utah
                                 2nd Ellen Wiggin   Holyoke, Mass.
                                 3rd Harriet Risley   Marblehead Mass.
5 Mary Tuttle   " m. Rev. G. D. B. Miller   St. Louis, Mo.
5 *Frederick Rhesa   "   unm.
5 Sarah Katherine   " " Abel White   Salt Lake City, Utah
5 *Charles Edgar   "   unm.

Ch. Harriet M. Foote and Rt. Rev. Daniel S. Tuttle   St. Louis, Mo.
6 Dr. George Marvine Tuttle m. Grace Dean Wallace Salt Lake City, Utah
6 *Herbert Edward   " " Willie Lea
6 Arthur Lemuel   " " Mary Eliza Hackley   "   "
6 Christine   " " Stanley Matthews Ramsey Cincinnati, O.

7 Daniel Sylvester 2nd "   Grace Dean Wallace   St. Louis, Mo.
7 Wallace   " ch. &
                                Dr. George M. Tuttle   "   "

7 Mary Eilzabeth   " ch. Willie Lea
                                &
                                Herbert E. Tuttle

7 Arthur Lemuel Jr.,   " ch. Mary Eliza Hackley
                                &
                                Arthur L. Tuttle

GENEALOGICAL SECTION

7 William McCreery Ramsey   Christine Tuttle   Cincinnatti, Ohio
7 Harriet Tuttle " ch. &
7 Christine Frances "   Stanley M. Ramsey " "
7 Virginia Foote "

                 Sarah Ellen Pidsley   San Jose, Calif.
6*Christine Foote   ch. &
                 Rev. George W. Foote

Ch. 4 Frederick Wm. Foote and Vashti Butler Thompson,   Elizabeth, N. J.
5*Julia Magie   Foote   unm.   " "
5 Frances Meeker "   m. *William Boyce Eakin,   " "
5*Frederick Wm. Jr. "   m. Sara Fitz Randolph DePuy,   New York
5*Louis Thompson "   unm.   Elizabeth, N. J.
5*George Rhesa "   d. in infancy   " "
5 Anna Butler "   unm.   " "
5 Harriet "   m. Wm. Pennington Toler
5 Mary Roberts "   m. John Burnside Value
5*Henry Hawley "   m. Ada Henderson   Elizabeth, N. J.

Ch. Frances M. Foote and *Wm. Boyce Eakin   Elizabeth, N. J.
6 Elizabeth Buttler Eakin   " "
6 William Boyce "   m. Mary Winchester   " "
6 Corp. Frederick Foote "
6 Constant Mattheiu "
6 Corp. Fred'k. F. Eakin, wounded at Chateau Thierry, has recovered and is with 2nd Engineers—regulars in Army of Occupation in Germany.

Ch. William Boyce Eakin and Mary Winchester   Elizabeth, N. J.
7 Arthur Rutherford "   " "
7 William Boyce, Jr. "   " "
7 Patricia "   " "

Ch. Frederick Wm. Foote and Sara FitzRandolph DePuy,   New York
6 Nathaniel Niles "   m. Katherine Andrews   " "
6 Isabel DePuy "   m. Holmes Agnew   " "
6 Sara Randolph "   m. Robert Sayle Hill   " "
6 Florence Butler "   " "

                      Katharine Andrews
7 Frederick Wm. "   ch. &   " "
                      Nathaniel Niles Foote

                      Sara Randolph Foote   " "
7 Robert Sayle Hill, Jr.   ch. &
                      Robert Sayle Hill

                      Mary Roberts Foote
6 Burnside Rene Value   ch. &
6 Mary Foote "   John Burnside Value

                      Mary Foote Value
7 Alfred Pearce Dennis Jr.   ch. &
7 John Value "   Alfred Pearce Dennis

                      Ada Henderson   Elizabeth, N. J.
6 Maud Bryan Foote   ch. &
                      Henry H. Foote

Ch. Mary Foote and Rev. Henry V. Gardner, Newtown, Conn., b. Hartford,
5 Ella Jane Gardner   m. Dr. Charles R. Hart,   Bethel, Conn.
5*Rev. Charles H. "   m. 1st Annie Parker   Utica, N. Y.
                          m. 2nd Margaret Jackson   Omaha, Neb.
5 Marietta "   twins   unm.
5*Henrietta "   twins   d. in infancy
5 Harriet Foote "   m. Edward Burroughs   Long. Hill, Conn.
5 Mary Watson "   "   Thomas H. Dobson   Brockport, N. Y.
5*Rev. George E. "   "   Jessie Lewis   Lowville "

FREDERICK W. FOOTE

Born at Newtown Oct. 23, 1816, for many years conducted a boys' school in Elizabeth, N. J. Many prominent business men in the city said they had never been a day to any other school before going to College or business. After many years as an educator he relinquished that work and became owner and editor of "The New Jersey Journal", which in a short time became "The Elizabeth Daily Journal", of which he was owner and editor at his death, March 18th, 1879.

i

REV. CHARLES H. GARDNER

Son of Rev. Henry V. and Mary Foote Gardner. At his death Aug. 8th, 1896, Dean of Trinity Cathedral, Omaha, Neb. His mother, born in Newtown, sister of Rev. Geo. L. Foote, was associated with him in the founding of Newtown Academy in 1837 and was assistant to other principals after Mr. Foote left to become rector of Christ Ch. Roxbury, Conn.

Five of the six sons of Dean Gardner were in the war with the Allies.

5 *Frederick Gardner   m. Nellie Roberts   E. Aurora, N. Y.

Ch. Ella Jane Gardner and Dr. Charles R. Hart   Bethel, Conn.

6 Martha   Hart   m. George Dimond   "   "
6 Bertha   "   "   Eugene Stone   "   "
6 *Charles Gardner "   "   Grace Roosevelt Fowler   Durham   "
6 Ella Gertrude "   unm.
6 Ruth Helen   "   unm. In Hospital Service.

Ch. of Martha Hart and George Dimond

7 Charles Henry Dimond   m. Minnabelle Burlingham Niagara Falls N. Y.
7 George Gardner   "
7 Leonard Alfred   "   "   Florence Schultz   "   "

                             Minnabelle Burlingham   "   "
8 Marjorie Jane Dimond ch.   &
                             Charles H. Dimond   "   "

7 *Herman Stone   Bertha Hart   Bethel, Conn.
7 *Mary   "   ch.   &
7 *Philip   "   Eugene Stone   "   "

7 Constance Worthington Hart Grace Roosevelt Fowler   Durham, Conn.
7 Gertrude Van Ness   " ch.   &
                              Chas Gardner Hart
    Mrs. Hart is great grand daughter of Noah Webster

Ch. *Rev. Charles H. Gardner and Annie Parker 1st wife Utica, N. Y.

6 Irvine Parker Gardner   m. Harriet Evelyn Jackson
6 William Thaw   "   " Emma Melissa Jenkins
6 Charles Henry   "

Ch. *Rev. Chas. H. Gardner and Margaret Jackson, 2nd wife, Washington, D. C.
Dean of Cathedral at Omaha, Nebraska.

6 Arthur   Gardner   (Yale 1910 Sheff.) In U. S. Service 2nd
                             Lieut. in Tank Corps, 1917.
6 Anson Blake   "   Yale 1913, B. A. Harvard Graduate Engin-
                             eer School and Boston Tech. 1915. 1st
                             Lieut. Ordnance Engineer, Machine Gun
                             and Small Arms division, 1917.
6 Edward   "   Training for Aviation ground section
                             Machine Gun division, 1917.

                             Harriet Evelyn Jackson
7 Marjorie Evelyn   ch.   &
                             Irvine Parker Gardner

                             Emma M. Jenkins
7 Wilhelmina Thaw   ch.   &
                             William T. Gardner

6 *Robert   Burroughs   Harriet Foote Gardner   Trumbull, Conn
6 Lucius   "   ch.   &
6 Mary Sylvia   "   m.   Edward Burroughs   Trumbull, Conn.
7 Dorothy Grace "   Annie Falls   Bridgeport, Conn.
7 George Norman "   ch.   &
7 Earl   "   Lucius Burroughs

Ch. Mary Watson Gardner and Thomas H. Dobson Brockport, N. Y.

6 Harold Gardner Dobson   m. Helen Wadsworth   "   "
6 Eleanor Mary   "   Training for U. S. Service as Nurse
                                                      San Francisco, Cal.
6 George Gardner   "   In Aviation Section of Signal Corps
                         m. Bertha McNaugton.
6 Rodney Hiram   "   In U. S. Submarine Chaser, 24

7 Harold Wadsworth Dobson ch.	Helen Wadsworth & Harold G. Dobson	Brockport, N. Y. " "
7 Helen Barbara "		
6 Ray Frederick Gardner	Nellie Roberts & Frederick Gardner	E. Aurora, N. Y. " "
6 Mildred " ch.		
6 Henrietta "		

Ch. 4 Harriet Foote and Rev. William Atwill.

5 Joseph Atwill	not located
5 *William "	d. young
5 *George Edgar "	d young

5 *George Nelson Welton		
5 Walter Beach "	Jane E. Foote & Walter B. Welton	Newtown, Conn. Bridgewater, Conn.
5 *Henry Hobart " ch.		
5 *Jane "		

6 Leonard Briscoe Welton ch.	Ella J. Briscoe & Walter B. Welton	White Plains, N. Y.

GLOVER

Henry Glover came to Boston in 1636, d. at New Haven, 1689.
1 John son of Henry, b. 1648 m. Joanna Daniels
2 John, first Glover settler in Newtown, b. 1674 d. 1752. m. 1700, 1st Marjorie Hubbard. 2nd 1707, Bathia Beach Bickley.

As early as 1710, John Glover is spoken of as "fast becoming an extensive land owner" and his signature is affixed to town records as Town Clerk in 1712-13.

Ch. 2 John Glover and Marporie Hubbard		Newtown, Conn.
3 John Glover	m. Elizabeth Bennett	" "
3 Henry "	" Prudence Stoddard	" "

Ch. John Glover and Bathia Beach Bickley		" "
3 Benjamin Glover	m. Mollie Bunnell	" "
3 John served in Revolutionary War		

Ch. Elizabeth Bennett and John Glover		
4 Marjory Glover	m. David Blackman	" "
4 Elizabeth "	" Joseph Blackman	" "
4 Bathiah "	" John Camp	" "
4 John "	" Elizabeth Curtis	" "
4 James "	" Eunice Booth	" "

Ch. 3 Henry Glover and Prudence Stoddard		" "
4 Henry Glover	m. 1st Julia Bassett.	2nd Anna Sanford
4 Simeon "	"	Newtown, Conn.
4 Esther "	d. young	" "
4 Prudence "	d. young	" "
4 Silas "	d. young	" "
4 Anadine "	m. ——— Bradfield	" "
4 Elias "	" 1st Nancy Beers.	2nd Joanna Northrop.
4 Rev. Solomon "	Mary Northrop	

5 Esther " ch.	Julia Bassett & Henry Glover	Newtown, Conn. " "
5 Esther "	m. Abel Toucey	" "

GENEALOGICAL SECTION

3 Benjamin Glover   m. Mollie Bunnell   Newtown, Conn.

Their Ch.

4 Huldah Glover   m. Joseph Prindle   " "
4 Mary   "   " William Hawley   " "
4 Bathia   "   " Joseph Tomlinson
4 Rebecca   "   " Ichabod Fairman (see Fairman)   "
4 Benjamin   "   " Phoebe Sanford

4 Rev. Solomon Glover son of 3Henry, m. Mary Northrop. b. 1750, d. 1842, age 92 years.

Their ch.

5 Joanna Glover   m. Henry Botsford (See Botsford)
                                                              Newtown, Conn.
5 Mary Ann   "   " James Glover
5 Silas Norman   "   " Nancy Morris   " "
5 Ziba   "   " Marinda Griswold
5 Maria   "   " Ambrose Beach   " "
5 Silas Norman,   m. Nancy Morris.

Their ch.

6 Roxy A. Glover   m. John Beers (See Beers)
6 Eunice Maria   "   " Charles Blackman
6 Mary E.   "   " Charles Beers (See Beers)
6 Betsey A.   "   " Abel Prindle (See Prindle)
6 Silas N.   "   died young
6 Daniel B.   "   " "
6 Nancy Anadine "   m. James Henderson

7 Annie Eliza Henderson   Nancy A. Glover
7 Julia Frances "   ch.   &
                                   James Henderson
7 Annie E. Henderson   m. 1st Dr. William Burhans, Bridgeport, Conn.
   "   "   " 2nd Dr. Edwin Eames

8 Wallace Works   Julia F. Henderson   Milford, "
                          ch.   &
In Aviation Corps U. S. Service William Wallace Works

4 John Glover   m. Elizabeth Curtis

Their ch.

5 James Glover   m. 5Mary Ann Glover
5 Zalmon   "   m. Phoebe Beach
5 Josiah   "   " Rebecca Booth
5 Benjamin Curtis "   " Clara Peck
5 Betsey   "   " Sylvanus Noble
5 Phoebe   "   " Samuel Wheeler

Ch. Zalmon Glover and Phoebe Beach

6 Lucy Ann Glover   m. Anson Abner Nettleton (See Nettleton in Beach record.)
6 John   "   " Lucy Beers 1st wife
                     Polly Curtis 2nd "
6 Villeroy   "   " Susan Hard

5 *Wm. Beach Glover   Lucy Beers 1st. wife
                     ch.   &
                     John Glover   Sandy Hook, Conn.

5 *Julietta "   Polly Curtis 2nd wife
                     ch.   &
5 *Marrietta "   John Glover   " " "

GENEALOGICAL SECTION

6 Esther Sophia Glover   Harriet Ann Peck, 1st wife Sandy Hook, Ct.
6 Smith Peck " ch. &
6 *John E. "   Wm. B. Glover " " "
                5 Susan Nichols 2nd wife " " "

Ch. Smith P. Glover and Marie Antoinnette Tomlinson " " "
7 *William Tomlinson Glover
7 Lorena Tomlinson " m. George Francis Taylor (no ch.)
7 Harriet Peck " " Charles Lawrence Warner

                Harriet Peck Glover   Vicksburg, Miss.
8 Lawrence Glover Warner ch. &
                Charles Lawrence Warner " "

6 *Elizabeth Curtis   Marietta Glover   Newtown, Conn.
6 *Juliette " ch. &
                Ira Lawrence Curtis " "

7 Cora   Parker   Elizabeth Curtis   Bedford, Ind.
7 Alfred Curtis " ch. &
                Daniel W. Parker

                Gertrude Bowden
8 Mabel " ch. &
8 Harriet "   Alfred C. Parker

7 Cora " m. Thomas J. Leonard (no ch.) Springoille "

6 *Juliette Curtis   m. Winthrop Foote (no ch.) Bedford, "

6 Mary Josephine Hawley   Julietta Glover,   Danbury, Conn.
6 Helen Sophia " ch. &
                Isaac H. Hawley " "

7 Herson Clark Osborne   Mary Josephine Hawley   Oxford, Conn.
7 Arthur Ray " ch. &
7 Thomas Elmer "   Thomas Smith Osborne " "

                Calista Johnson Crane
8 Florence Josephine " ch. &
                Herson C. Osborne

                Helen S. Hawley,   North Haven, Conn.
7 Ruth Juliette Warner, ch. &
                Orin Delos Warner " " "

                Phebe Beach   Newtown, Conn.
4 Villeroy Glover ch. &
                Zalmon Glover " "

                Susan Hard " "
5 Sarah Esther " ch. &
                Villeroy Glover " "

6 *Frank B. Nichols   Sarah E. Glover " "
6 *Grace " ch. &
8 Ruth Amelia "   *Philo Nichols

                Ruth A. Nichols " "
7 Marion Nichols Curtis ch. &
                Hobart H. Curtis
" " " m. Clayton B. Hawley

5 *Josiah Glover, son of 4 John, m. Rebecca Booth.

    Their ch.

6 *Betsey Glover   m. Henry Beers
6 Abel Booth "   m. Maria Nichols

7 *Eliza Maria Glover   Maria Nichols
7 *Henry Beers "   ch.   &
                                 Abiel Booth Glover

8 *William Booth   Glover
8 *Florence Stanley   "   Eliza Maria Blakeslee
8 *Mary Blakeslee   "   ch.   &
8 *Maria Nichols   "   Henry Beers Glover
8 *Florence Stanley   m. Abel French Clarke.

9 Flornece Beecher   Mary Blakeslee Glover
9 Marguerite "   ch.   &
9 *Glover "   William J. Beecher

5 *Benjamin Curtis Glover, son of 4John, m. Clara Peck

    Their Ch.

6 *Samuel   Glover   unm.
6 *Marcia   "   m. Hezekiah Curtis (See Curtis)
6 *Walter   "   " Marcia Botsford
6 *Benjamin N.   "   " Harriet A. Lake

7 *Samuel Curtis Glover
7 *John Birdsey   "   Marcia Botsford   Newtown, Conn.
7*Henry Botsford   "   ch.   &
7 *Sophia   "   Walter Glover   "   "
7 *Betsey   "

                                Sarah Grace Blakeslee   "   "
8 Samuel Curtis Glover   ch.   &
                                Samuel C. Glover

7 *Birdsey C. Glover   Harriet Lake   "   "
7 *Walter Henry "   ch.   &
7*Lemuel P.   "   Benjamin N. Glover   "   "

8 Bessie Glover   Sarah E. Northrop   "   "
8 *Emma "   ch.   &
8 Florence "   Birdsey C. Glover   "   "

9 David Glover Taylor   Bessie Glover   Bethel,   "
9 Florence "   ch.   &
9 Birdsey "   David Taylor

8 William B. Glover   Sarah M. Northrop   Newtown, "
8 Norman "   ch.   &
     "   Walter H. Glover   "   "
                           m. Emily Jones (no ch.)

Walter LeRoy Glover   Lydia Ann Benedict   "   "
Agnes Northrop "   ch.   &
Wm. DeForest "   William B. Glover   "   "

    Ch. 5Mary Ann Glover and 5James Glover

6 Flora Glover   m. Alonzo Beers (See Beers) Brookfield, Ct.
6 Granville Stoddard Glover "   Mary Hawley   Newtown, Conn.
6 Charlotte   "   "   Squire Van Smith   Brookfield, Conn.
6 Sophia (1st wife)   "   "   Botsford Terrill (Se Terrill)Newtown, Ct.
6 Julia (2nd wife)   "   "   Botsford Terrill (See Terrill) "   "
6 Norman Booth   "   "   Esther Hawley, 1st   "   "
                               Amelia Gilbert 2nd
6 Volusia   "   "   Austin Botsford (See Botsford) "   "
6 Mary Ann   "   "   unm.
6 Emma   "   "   George Foote
6 James Nelson   "   "   Sally Wetmore   "   "
6 George Heman   "   "   Elmira Page   "   "

GENEALOGICAL SECTION

7 Ann Elizabeth Glover	ch.	Mary Hawley Newtown, Conn.
7 Charlotte "		&
7 Jabez Hawley "		Granville S. Glover " "
8 Mary Charlotte Gilbert	ch.	Ann Elizabeth Glover
		&
		Henry D. Gilbert Kent, Conn.
9 Carrie Louise Stone	ch.	Mary Charlotte Gilbert " "
9 Mary Grace "		&
		Wm. K. Stone " "
10 Eleanor Grace Chase	ch.	Carrie L. Stone " "
		&
		Edwin M. Chase " "
10 Florence Gilbert Chase		
10 Mildred Kellogg "		Mary Grace Stone " "
10 Grace Mary "	ch.	&
10 Russell Stone "		Alva R. Chase " "
10 Pauline Harriet "		
8 *Carrie Glover	ch.	Mary E. Peck Newtown, Conn.
8 Mary Effie "		&
		Jabez H. Glover
9 Harold Glover Betts		Mary Effie Glover
9 Helen May "	ch.	&
9 *Arthur Berhila "		James A. Betts
10 John Doremus Betts	ch.	Mabel Doremus
		&
		Harold G. Betts
10 W. L. Kimball, Jr.	ch.	Helen May Betts
		&
		Atty. W. L. Kimball

6 Henry Glover, son of 5Henry m. Zeziah Johnson

   Their ch.

7 David Glover	m.	Polly Briscoe
7 Lossie "	m.	Austin Hurd
7 Emeline "	m.	Benjamin Hawley (See Hawley)
7 Grandison "		

   Ch. David Glover and Polly Briscoe

8 *Charles B. Glover	m.	Catherine Fairchild, 1st wife
8 *Mary C. "	m.	Bradley Briscoe (See Briscoe
8 *Delia "	m.	William Hoy, 2nd wife
8 *Jane Ann "	m.	Isaac Harris
8 Ann Eliza "	m.	Thomas Judson
8 Lewis Henry "		
8 George G. "		
8 Harriet Dibble "	m.	George Clark

9 Annie Glover	ch.	Catherine Fairchild, 1st wife
9 Martha "		&
		Charles B. Glover
		Frances Botsford, nd wife
9 Jennie Glover	ch.	Sarah Davis, 3rd wife
		&
		Charles B. Glover
10 Lulu Canfield		Jennie Glover
10 George "	ch.	&
10 Pearl "		William Canfield

GENEALOGICAL SECTION

6 Roswell Glover, son 5James and 5Mary Ann Glover

7 Roswell Booth Glover   ch.   Polly Ann Ferris   Newtown, Conn.
&
Roswell Glover   "   "

8 Harriet Jane Glover   Polly Ann Robertson   Danbury, Conn.
8 *Ida Ann "   ch.   &
8 *Lemuel Francis "   Roswell B. Glover   "   "

9 *Mabel Louise Hoyt
9 *Julia Banks "   Harriet Jane Glover   "   "
9 *Annie Isabelle "   ch.   &
9 Leon Glover "   George Banks Hoyt   "   "

10 Barbara Elizabeth Martin
10 Julia Isabelle "   Mabel Louise Hoyt
10 Harry Hoyt "   ch.   &
10 Frederic Arthur "   Frederic Arthur Martin

10 Christine Ella Lacey   ch.   Julia Banks Hoyt
&
Dwight Aaron Lacey

10 Frederic Couse Bennetto   Annie Isabella Hoyt
10 Josephine Harriet "   ch.   &
Frederic Couse Bennetto

7 Booth F. Glover   New Orleans, La.
7 E. Leroy "   Esther M. Hawley 1st wife
7 Mary S. "   ch.   &
7 William H. "   6Norman B. Golver   Newtown, Conn.

7 Julia F. "   ch.   Amelia Gilbert 2nd wife
&
Norman B. Glover

7 Julia F. "   m.   Henry Beers (See Beers)

" " "   Elizabeth G. Bartram   New Britain, Conn.
8 Charles B. "   ch.   &
William H. Glover

9 William H. Jr. "   ch.   Mary E. Bishop   "   "
&
Charles B. Glover

4 Simeon Glover son of 3Henry m. 1st Olive Booth

5 Ebenezer Booth Glover   ch.   Olive Booth
&
Simeon Glover
d. in U. S. Service at New London in 1815.

5 Harry Glover   Rachel ——— 2nd wife
5 Charles "   ch.   &
5 Olive "   Simeon Glover
5 Ives "

5 Melora "
              Mary Gregory 3rd wife
5 Henry "   ch.   &
Simeon Glover

6 Julia Maria Glover   ch.   Julia Hull
&
Ives Glover

6 *Sarah "
6 *Mary see Lake "
6 *Martin V. B. "   d. in hospital during Civil War.

6 Henry Glover
6 David "

7 Edith   Smith
7 Herbert   "   Sarah Glover
7 Leonard   "   ch.   &
7 Ida   "   Charles Smith

7 John H.   Glover
7 James C.   "
7 Thomas L.   "   Ella Clark
7 Elmer C.   "   ch.   &
7 Frederick   "   Henry Glover. Served in Civil War.
7 Benjamin   "
7 Harlod   "   Now, Feb. 1918 in Soldier's Home, Norton, Ct.
7 Ethel   "

HALL

1 Alexander Hall   m. Rebecca Colburn
            Their Ch.
2 Daniel   Hall   m. Sarah Judson
2 Mary   "   "   John Cocoran
2 Charlotte   "   "   John Parmelee
2 Rebecca   "   "   John A. Sayre
2 Alexander, Jr. "   "   Sarah Bradley
2 *James   "
2 *Polly Jane   "   "   1st Jerome T. Judson
                      "   2nd George Miles Grant
2 *Anna Eliza   "   "   Amos Shepard
2 *Henry Clay   "   "   Emily J. Andrews
2 *James Peck   "   "   Margaret Carr

3 *Ann M.   "   Sarah Judson   Derby, Conn.
3 Charles H.   "   ch.   &
3 William F.   "   Daniel Hall
3 Daniel A.   "   Waterville, Conn.

3 Charlotte Ellen Corcoran   Mary Hall
3 *Charles   "   ch.   &
3 *Frederick   "   John Corcoran

3 John Sidney Parmelee   New Haven, Conn.
3 Ella Douglas   "   "   "
3 *Anna Rebecca   "   Charlotte Hall
3 *Charlotte Rachel " ch.   &
3 *Mary Jane   "   John Parmelee

4 Raymond Hall Lewis   Southington, Conn.
4 Howard Bishop   "   Urbana, Ill.
4 *Ruth Parmelee   "   Charlotte R. Parmelee
4 Charlotte Mansfield " ch.   &
4 Esther Douglas   "   Fred A. Lewis   Southington, Conn.

                           Mildred Eaton
5 Charlotte Barber Lewis ch.   &
                           Howard B. Lewis   Urbana, Ill.

                           Ella D. Parmelee
4 *William Thorpe Babcock ch.   &
4 *Alexander Hall   "   George J. Babcock

5 *Douglas Armstrong "   Bertha Woods   Denver, Col.
5 Theodore Wood   " ch.   &
5 George Parmelee   "   Alexander H. Babcock   "   "

GENEALOGICAL SECTION

5 William Thorpe Babcock	ch.	May E. Pavey & William T. Babcock	New London, Conn.
3 *Frederick Augustus Sayre 3 *Charles Albarnus " 3 *Helena Anna " 3 *Alice Rebecca "	ch. m.	Rebecca Hall 2nd & John A. Sayre Frederick J. Brenner	
4 Virginia Dee Sayre 4 Clarence Charles " 4 Evelyn Bernice Sayre	gr. ch.	Rebecca Hall 2nd & John A. Sayre	Sacramento, Cal. San Francisco, Cal.
4 *Ruth Alice Brenner	ch.	Alice Rebecca Sayre & Fred J. Brenner	Charles City, Iowa
4 Clarence Charles Sayre Their Ch.	m.	Eva Cuneo	
5 *Ruth Louise Dasch Hull 5 Eleanor Virginia " 5 Richard Brenner "	gr. gr. ch. ch.	Rebecca Hall & John A. Sayre Ruth Alice Brenner & Dwight C. Hull	Charles City, Iowa
3 Alexander Morris Hall 3 Charles Bradley "	ch.	Sarah Bradley & Alexander Hall, Jr.	Boston, Mass. Springfield, Mass.
4 Sarah Elizabeth Hall	ch.	Martha E. Davis & Alexander M. Hall	Patterson, N. Y.
5 Anna Louise Austin	ch.	Sarah E. Hall & J. Clayton Austin	Patterson, N. Y.
3 Charlotte Emma Judson m Austin Mansfield	ch.	Polly Jane Hall & Jerome T. Judson 1st George Miles Grant, 2nd.	New Haven, Conn.
3 William Henry Shepard 3 *Jane Mary " 3 Albert Amos " 3 Robert John " 3 Anna Louise "	ch.	*Anna Eliza Hall & Amos Shepard	Wheaton, Ill. Chicago, Ill. " " " "
4 Amos Birdsey Shepard	ch.	Emily Day & William H. Shepard	Charles City, Iowa
4 Maryette Shepard Wallace m. Spickerman	ch.	Jane Mary Shepard & Wm. B. Wallace	DeKalb, Ill.
4 Marjorie Shepard	ch.	Margaret Cotton & Albert Amos Shepard	Chicago, Ill.
4 Robert Shepard Hale 4 Herbert Francis " 4 Albert William "	ch.	Anna Louise Shepard & Charles H. Hale	" " " "

3 *Edward Henry Hall   ch. Emily J. Andrews & Henry Clay Hall   Aurora, Missouri
3 Arthur Burnside "

4 Arthur Hall   ch. Arthur Burnside Hall   "   "

3 Birdsey James Hall
   m.   ch. Margaret Carr & James Peck Hall
Hattie Hart

4 Foster Hall
   m.   ch. Birdsey James Hall & Hattie Hart   New Haven, Conn.
Irene Ahrons

HARD

The old records show that 1James Hard served as Selectman of Newtown in 1713.

2 James Hard b. 1695   m. Hannah Kimberly   Newtown, Conn.
3 Abner Hard son of 2James m. Hannah Beers   "   "

Their Ch.

4 Niram Hard	m.	Sarah Curtis	" "
4 Cyrenius "	"	Phoebe Camp	" "
4 John "	"	Mary Nettleton	" "
4 Abigail "	"	Josiah Beardsley	" "
4 Currence "	"	David Botswick	Monroe, Conn.
4 Ann "	"	Ebenezer Beers	Newtown, Conn.
4 Zilpha "	"	Zalmon Peck (see Peck)	" "
4 Abner "	"	Lucena Nichols	" "
4 Mary "	"	2nd Ebenezer Beers	" "

Ch. Niram Hard and Sarah Curtis

5 Sarah "	m.	Alfred Divine Curtis	" "
5 Benjamin "	"	Mabel Tomlinson	" "
5 Cyrus "	"	Abigail Curtis	" "

6 Charles T. "
6 Susan "   ch. Mabel Tomlinson & Benjamin Hard
6 Sarah "

7 Benjamin1st "
7 Benjamin2nd "
7 Josephine M. "   ch. Eliza Ann Greaton & Charles T. Hard
7 James "
7 Susan G. "
7 Villeroy G. "

8 Benjamin Francis Hard   ch. Annie Crane & Benjamin Hard

9 Anna Hard
9 Ella "   ch. & Benjamin F. Hard
9 Elmer Francis "

8 Villeroy Glover Hard, Jr.
8 Elmer "   m. Harriet Watts
8 Sylvester "   Catherine E. Ming
8 *Jesse "   ch. & Villeroy Hard
8 *Mabel "

9 Emily Althea Hard   ch. Margaret Williams & Sylvester Hard

GENEALOGICAL SECTION

7 Sarah Esther Glover	ch.	Susan Hard & Villeroy Glover	Newtown, Conn. " "
8 Frank B. Nichols 8 *Grace " 8 Ruth Amelia "	ch.	Sarah Esther Glover & *Philo Nichols	" "
9 Marion Nichols Curtis	ch.	Ruth A. Nichols & Hobart H. Curtis	" "
6 *William Hard 6 *Amos " 6 *Sophia "	ch.	Abigail Curtis 5Cyrus Hard	" "
7 Sophia H. Botsford	ch.	Sophia Hard & Gideon Burtis Botsford	" "
8 *Harriet Botsford Camp 8 *Gideon Burtis "	ch.	Sophia Hard Botsford & Marcus Camp	" "
7 *Elizabeth Hard 7 William Gould "	ch.	Mariette Camp 1st wife & Amos Hard	" "
7 Chester Hard	ch.	Catherine Lake 2nd wife & Amos Hard	" "
8 Katie Nichols Hard 8 Charlotte " 8 *William "	ch.	*Sarah Erwin 1st wife & William G. Hard Sarah Esther Camp 2nd wife	" "
9 Stanley Hard Bedient	ch.	Charlotte Hard & James Bedient	Norwalk, Conn.

Ch. 7Chester Hard and Ida Harkness   Painesville, Ohio

8 Elmo Amos Hard	m.	Eva Kenney	" "
8 *Cora "		d. young	" "
8 Florence Esther "	m.	Elmer B. Kimmel	" "
8 Harkness Gould "		Corp. in U. S. Service, Co. G. 23rd Engineers	

HAWLEY

1 Joseph Hawley b. 1603, at Derbyshire, England, came to America, 1629, later came to Stratford, d. 1690.
2 Samuel, son of Joseph, b. 1652.
3 Samuel, Jr., son of Samuel, b. 1674.
4 Benjamin, son of Samuel, Jr., b. 1694, came to a place he called "Lands' end" which has ever since retained that name.   Newtown, Conn.
5 Benjamin, Jr., 5Abel, 5William, sons 4Benjamin   Newtown, Conn.
6 Jabez, son of Benjamin, Jr., m. Parthena Booth   " "

Ch. Parthena Booth and Jabez Hawley.

7 Sally Hawley	m.	Philo Beers	Michigan
7 Anna "		unm.	Newtown, Conn.
7 Mary "	m.	Granville Glover (see Glover)	" "
7 Benjamin "	"	Emeline Glover	" "
7 Daniel Booth Hawley	"	Olive Hawley	" "
7 Isaac Nichols "	"	Avis Shepard	Brookfield, Conn.

GENEALOGICAL SECTION

7 Robert Nichols Hawley   m. Harriet Blackman   Newtown, Conn.

8 Mary Beers   ch. Sally Hawley & Philo Beers

" "   m. Ingersoll
9 Robert Ingersoll   ch. & Mary Beers
Inventor of Ingersoll watch

7 Benjamin Hawley m. Emeline Glover
Their ch.
8 *Mary Hawley   unm.   Newtown, Conn.
8 *Frederick "   m. Ella Burritt   " "
8 *Susan "   " John R. Smith (See Lake record)
8 Juliette "   " Hobart Camp (See Camp record)
8 *William "   " Mary Francis Terrill   Brookfield, Conn.
8 Annie "   " Duane Stone   New Milford, Conn.
8 Margaret "   " Homer White (no ch.) Huntington, Conn.
8 Sarah "   " Homer Lake   Brookfield, Conn.

Ch. Mary F. Terrill and William Hawley   Newtown, Conn.

9 Edward "   Killed by cars
9 William Hawley   d. in infancy   " "
9 Annie "   m. Homer Baldwin   " "
9 *Ernest "   " Cornelia Young   " "
9 William 2nd "   " *Fanny V. Daniels (no ch.) " "
9 *Carlton "
9 Harry "   died young
9 Helen "   accidentally killed
   unm.

10 Lucy A. Baldwin   Annie Hawley   Stratford, Conn.
10 Ruth "   ch. &
10 Carlton "   Homer Baldwin

10 Ernest Hawley   ch. Cornelia Young & Ernest Hawley   Newtown, Conn.   " "

9 Florence Stone   ch. Annie Hawley & Duane Stone   New Milford, Conn.

9 Eugene Lake   Sarah Hawley   Brookfield, Conn.
9 Herbert "   ch. & Homer Lake

Ch. Daniel Booth Hawley and Olive Hawley

8 *Esther A. Hawley   m. *Rev. Jonathan Elbridge Goodhue,
   Rector St. Mark's Ch.   Newark, N. J.
8 Elmer B. "   " Cornelia Belle Estey   Chicago, Ill.
8 *Henry S. "   " Julia Curtis   Newtown, Conn.

9 Mary Helen Goodhue   unm.   Courtland, N. Y.
9 *Willis Elbridge "   Esther A. Hawley
9 Marion Louise "   ch. & Rev. Jonathan E. Goodhue

10 Stephen F. Sherman, 3rd   Marion L. Goodhue   Bridgeport, Conn.
10 Jonathan Elbridge "   ch. &
   Rev. Stephen F. Sherman, Jr.,
   Rector St. John's Ch.   Bridgeport "

9 S. Curtis Hawley   Julia Curtis   Newtown, Conn.
9 Mary Nichols Hawley   ch. & Henry S. Hawley   " "

GENEALOGICAL SECTION

10 Hobart G. Warner, Jr.　　Mary N. Hawley　　Newtown, Conn.
10 Austin　"　　ch.　&
10 Henry Hawley　"　　Hobart G. Warner　　"　"

7 *Isaac Nichols Hawley m. *Avis Shepard

Their ch.

8 *Edson N. Hawley　　m.　Margaret Nichols
8 Homer A.　"　　　"　Grace Nichols
8 *Edgar F.　"　　　"　Sarah McMahon
8 *Arthur　"　　　d. young

Ch. Edson N Hawley and Margaret Nichols　　Brookfield, Conn.
9 Clara Bertha　Hawley　　d. in infancy
9 Arthur Shepard　"　　m.　Marie Isabel McDonald　Syracuse, N. Y.
9 Julia Nichols　"　　Nurse in Pittsburg, Pa.
9 Clarence Beach　"　　m.　Mary Esther Wilson　"　"
9 John Beach　"　　"　Maud Addis　　Matheson, Col.

Ch. Homer A. Hawley and Grace Nichols　　Pittsfield, Mass.
9 Willis Nichols　Hawley　d. in U. S. service in Spanish War
9 Sarah Louise　"
9 Maj. James Shepard　"　in U. S. service in France

Ch. Edgar F. Hawley and Sarah McMahon
9 Jessie McMahon　Hawley m. Ray Leach　　New Milford, Conn.
9 George Shepard　"　　"　Jessina White　　Bridgeport, Conn.
9 Florence Avis　"

Ch. Arthur S. Hawley and Marie Isabel McDonald　Syracuse, N. Y.
10 Margaret Elizabeth Hawley
10 Isabel Louise　"

Ch. Clarence B. Hawley and Mary Esther Wilson　"　"
10 *Helen　Hawley
10 Alys May　"　twins
10 Florence Isabel　"
10 Ruth Nichols　"

Ch. John B. Hawley and Maud Addis　　Matheson, Col.
10 John Beach Jr., Hawley
10 Clara Jean　"

7 *Robert Nichols Hawley　m. *Harriet Blackman　Newtown, Conn.

Their ch.

8 Angeline E.　"　　m.　Frederick Beers (See Beers record)
8 *Robert S.　"　　"　Ida E. Stoddard　　Newtown, Conn.
8 Harriet S.　"　　"　William F. Hurd　　Bridgeport, Conn.

9 *Asa H.　Hawley　　Ida E. Stoddard　　Newtown, Conn.
9 Julia M.　"　　ch.　&
9 Robert N.　"　　Robert S. Hawley
9 Collis S.　"

10 Mildred C. Hawley　　Sarah Anna Camp　　Newtown, Conn.
10 Mabel S.　"　　ch.　&
　　　　　　　　　　Asa H. Hawley

　　　　　　　　　　Harriet S. Hawley　　Bridgeport, Conn.
9 William Hurd　　ch.　&
　　　　　　　　　　William Hurd

6 Jotham, 5Abel, 4Benjamin, 3Samuel, Jr., 2Samuel, 1Joseph

7 Abel Sherman Hawley　　Olive Terrill　　Newtown, Conn.
7 Tyrus　"　　ch.　&
　　　　　　　　　　Jotham Hawley

Ch. Abel Sherman Hawley and Hester Hurd

8 *Isaac Herson Hawley　m. Juliette Glover　　"　"
8 *Olive　"　　"　Daniel Booth Hawley　　"　"

GENEALOGICAL SECTION

8 Mariette Hawley	m.	Judson Marsh	Danbury, Conn.
8 *Ferris Hurd "	unm.		Newtown, Conn.

8 Jotham Burr Hawley			Hartford, Conn.
8 *Royal DeForest "		Sally Lewis	" "
8 Mary Caroline "	ch.	&	" "
8 Marshall "		Tyrus Hawley	" "

Danbury, Conn.

6 Joseph, 5William, 4Benjamin, 3Samuel, Jr., 2Samuel, 1Joseph

7 William Hawley		early went to Carthage, Ill.	
7 Hon. John N. "	m.	1st Harriet Norton	Brookfield, Conn.
7 Glover "	"	Mariette Fairchild	Newtown, Conn.

Glover Hawley made the first cast iron plough in Newtown. He and his brother, William invented the principle of the corn-sheller still in use. He went to California in 1849 for gold, returning in 1851.

8 Asa Norton Hawley ch. Harriet Norton and John N. Hawley Newtown, Ct.
8 John N. Hawley, Jr. ch. Lucy Fairchild and John N. Hawley, Brookfield, Ct.

8 Asa N. Hawley	m.	Julia Stoddard	Brookfield, Conn.
9 Charles B. Hawley		Clarissa Keeler	New York, N. Y.
9 Rev. Franklin K. Hawley "	ch.	&	
9 Clara F. "		John N. Hawley	Brookfield, Conn.

10 John T. Hawley		Julia Alice Terrill	
10 Ruth F. "	ch.	&	
		Rev. Franklin K. Hawley	" "

10 David H. Keeler		Clara F. Hawley	" "
10 Ray D. "	ch.	&	
		C. W. Keeler	" "

Ch. Mariette Fairchild and Glover Hawley.

8 *William E. Hawley	d. in Army during Civil War		
8 Martha E. "	m.	Minot Blakeman	Bridgeport, Conn.
9 Mariette H. "	"	Martin Lum	Redlands, Calif.

9 William D. Lum		Mariette Hawley	
9 Mabel A. "	ch.	&	
9 Mariette H. "		Martin Lum	

7 Charles, 6Daniel, 5William, 4Benjamin, 3Samuel, Jr., 2Samuel, 1Joseph

8 Charles Seeley Hawley	ch.	Anna Merwin	Brookfield, Conn.
8 Sidney E. "		&	
		Charles Hawley	Bridgeport, Conn.

Sidney E. Hawley, Fairfield Co. sheriff several terms.
Sidney E. Hawley m. 1st Sarah A. Roe, 2nd Amelia Northrop.

HUBBELL

Peter Hubbell having been given a large tract of land in Newtown by his father Lieut. Richard Hubbell and his wife Rebecca Morehouse, settled there in 1709, kept the first hotel and was granted the first Ferry. Newtown's first business meeting was held at his house Sept., 1711 when it was voted that Peter Hubbell should be Newtown's first Town Clerk.

Peter Hubbell m. Katherine Wheeler   Newtown, Conn.
Their Ch.

2 Ephraim Hubbell	m.	Johanna Gaylord	" "
2 Peter "	"	Hepzibah ————	" "
2 Capt. Ezra "	"		" "
2 Sarah "	"	Alexander Bryan	" "

GENEALOGICAL SECTION

2 Jebediah Hubbell   m. 1st Abigail Northrop   Newtown, Conn.
                                2nd Susanna Hickok   "   "
                                3rd Mary Hurlbert   "   "
                                4th Eunice Johnson   "   "
                                5th Mrs. Chloe Bemen   "   "
                        m. his 5th wife when 87 years and lived with
                           her 12 years   "   "
2 Matthew   Hubbell   m. Abiah Wolcott   "   "
2 Gideon   "
2 Comfort   "   "   Susanna Baxter   "   "
2 Katharine   "   "   William Birch (see Birch)   "   "
2 Enoch   "   "   Sarah ———
2 Silas   "   "   Elizabeth Edmond

Ch. Matthew Hubbell and Abiah Wolcott
3 Ann   "   b. in Newtown
3 Annah   "   b. in Newtown
3 Silas   "   killed in Revolutionary War
3 Wolcott Hubbell was one of the Minute Men of Berkshire Co., Mass. and
     fought in the battle of Bennington. Was State Senator of Berkshire
     Co. and many years Judge of the Courts of Berkshire Co.

Ch. Wolcott Hubbell and Mary Curtis   Lanesboro, Mass.
4 Silas   "   m. Sarah Henderson
4 Wolcott, 2nd   "   "   Mary Elizabeth Woolsey   "   "
4 Julius Caesar   "   "   Anna Moore ..
4 Algernon Sidney "   "   Julia Ann Jackson

Their ch.
5 George Wolcott Hubbell   m. Cornelia Churchill
5 Julia Jackson   "   "   Rev. Chas. R. Treat

Ch. George Wolcott Hubbell and Cornelia Churchill
6 Grace C. Hubbell   m. Dr. Henry C. Rowland
6 George Wolcott Hubbell, Jr. is of the 5th generation to occupy the Hub-
     bell homestead built by his great, great grandfather, Matthew Hubbell
     in 1768 in Lanesboro, Mass.

Ch. 4Wolcott 2nd, Hubbell and Mary E. Woolsey
5 George H. Hubbell   m. Mary A. Smith
Their ch.
6 William Wolcott Hubbell   m. Sarah Austin
Their ch.
7 Alida Taylor   Hubbell
7 Annie Austin   "
7 Arthur Rutkom   "
7 Austin Eberly   "
7 Laura Livingston   "
7 Nellie Grant   "
7 Melancthon Woolsey "

Ch. 2Comfort Hubbell and Susanna Baxter
3 John Hubbell   m. Parillas Foote   Newtown, **Conn.**
Their ch.
4 Philena Hubbell   m. Dr. John Judson   "   "
Their ch.
5 Dr. George Judson   m. Jane Bidwell (no ch.)   "   "
5 Dr. Monroe   "   "   1st Sarah Blackman   "   "
                               2nd Sarah Curtis (no ch.)
5 Jerome   "   unm.
5 John   "   "   1st Cornelia Peck   "   "
Their ch.
6 Anna Cornelia   "   "   Henry Tucker   "   "

Ch. John Judson and Julia Colt, 2nd wife
6 Grace   "   m. Herbert Clarke   Brooklyn, N. Y.
6 Jerome   "

Ch. Dr. Monroe Judson and Sarah Blackman   Newtown, Conn.
6 Martha   "   m. E. P. Taylor   Oakland, Calif.
Their ch.
7 Mary Judson   Taylor   m. John Adolph Breitling   "   "
7 Harriet Benedict   "   "   Julius Young   "   "

7 Florence Barker Taylor   m. James Scott Ireland   Oakland, Calif.
  Ch. Mary Judson Taylor and John Adolph Breitling   "   "
8 John Judson Breitling   "   "
  Ch. Harriet Benedict Taylor and Julius Young
7 Edward Taylor Young   "   "
  Ch. Florence Barker Taylor and James Scott Ireland   "   "
8 Martha Ireland   "   "
8 Anita   "   "   "
8 Jane   "   "   "
  James Scott Ireland is a descendant of Sir Walter Scott.   "   "

JOHNSON

1 Robert Johnson came from Yorkshire England, no date given.
2 Thomas drowned in New Haven, Harbor in 1640
3 Thomas and Jeremiah sons of 2Thomas,
  Jeremiah m. Sarah Hotchkiss.
4 Ebenezer son of 3Jeremiah, b. 1679 at Derby d. at Newtown 1768. He was one of the witnesses of the deed given by the Indians in 1705.

Of all the Johnson names that figure in the Conn. Colonial Records, no name is so prominent as that of Ebenezer Johnson, who settled in the town of Derby; admitted as an Elector there in 1678; was first appointed to the General Court as the deputy from Derby, in May, 1685; the same year was confirmed as Lieut. of the Derby Trained Band. He had already done service in the field, for the same year the General Court granted him four pounds English money for services done in the Pequot war. In 1689 was chosen Captain of volunteers to go forth against the Indian enemy, with liberty to drum for volunteers under him in every plantation in Fairfield and New Haven counties. In 1697 he was made captain of a second expedition. In May, 1698 the Court granted him six pounds cash for money he expended at Albany out of his own estate to satisfy for damage done by soldiers under his command. In 1702 was appointed one of a committee to settle the line between the colonies of Rhode Island and Connecticut. In 1704 appointed as Sergt. Major and commissioned as such for New Haven county. In 1709 "upon consideration of the age and long service of Major Ebenezer Johnson, the General Court does excuse and release him from any furthur labor in that post;" although in 1710 he was appointed Lieut. Colonel of forces upon the expedition to Port Royal and Nova Scotia.

1 Ebenezer m. Hannah Tomlinson and had two sons, Abraham b. 1715 and Ichabod, b. 1719.
2 Ichabod Johnson m. Elizabeth
  Their Ch.
3 John, Hannah, Jerusha, Ebenezer, Abel, Mary, Mabel, Hulda, Enos.

Of these we have located only descendants of oldest.

3 John Johnson   m. 1st Dorothy Hurd
                           " 2nd Sarah Northrop
  Their Ch.

4 Abram   Johnson   d. young
4 Isaac   "   m. Hinman (no dec.)
4 Jacob   "   " Jerusha Northrop   Newtown, Conn.
4 Ezra   "   " Rebecca Northrop   "   "
4 Clarissa   "   " 1st Samuel Northrop   "   "
                          " 2nd ——— Banks   "   "
4 Joseph   "   " Huldah Judson   Easton   "
4 Ebenezer   "   " Hepsa Shelton
4 John   "   " Clarissa Peck   Newtown, Conn.
4 Lucy   "   " Levi Drew (no ch.)
4 Daniel   "   " Lamira Wheeler   Brookfield, "
4 Elias   "   " Hepsa Judson   Newtown, Conn.
4 Abraham   "   " Sarah Briscoe   "   "
4 Dolly   "   " Eli Briscoe   "   "

GENEALOGICAL SECTION

4 Sally Johnson	m.	John Fayerweather	Danbury, Conn.
4 Eli "	"	1st Sally Watkins	
	"	2nd Betsey Baldwin	Lyons, N. Y.
4 Benjamin "	"	Dorcas Morse	
	"	2nd Jane Thompson	

Desc. of 4 Isaac not located. He went to Ballston, Spa, N. Y.

4 Jacob Johnson   m. Jerusha Northrop
Their Ch.

5 Walter Johnson	m.	Emma Bennett	Newtown, Conn.
5 Isaac "	"	Marietta Hinman	Southbury, Conn.
5 Nancy "	"	Thomas Stillman	Bridgeport, "
5 Clarissa "		unm. deaf and dumb	" "

Ch. Walter Johnson and Emma Bennett   Newtown, Conn.

6 Juliette W. "	m.	1st Jerome Somers	" "
		2nd Stephen S. Hanford	
6 Mary Jerusha "	"	Joseph W. Birdsey	Bridgeport, "
6 Elizabeth "	"	Isaac Turney	Easton, "
6 Orville "	"	Jane Durant	Newtown, "

Ch. Juliette Johnson and Jerome Somers   " "

7 Lucy Amanda Somers   m. Leon Woodford   Bridgeport, "
Their Ch.

8 Leona Woodford   m. Elmer Osborne   " "
Their Ch.

9 Marjorie Osborne   " "
9 Hazel "   " "

Ch. Juliette Johnson Somers and Stephen S. Hanford, Bridgeport, "

7 Emma L. Hanford   m. Chas. S. Thompson   " "
7 Nellie J. "   m. Henry R. Kimberley   " "

Ch. Emma L. Hanford and Chas. S. Thompson   " "
8 Grace W. Thompson   " "
8 Mabel L. "   " "

Ch. Nellie J. Hanford and Henry R. Kimberley   " "
8 Helen Kimberley   m. Robert D. Goddard   " "
Their Ch.
9 Katharine K. Goddard   " "
9 Dorothy J. "   " "
9 Robert D. Jr. "   " "

Ch. 6Mary Jerusha Johnson and Joseph W. Birdsey   " "

7 Helen L. Birdsey   m. Franklyn Burton   Ansonia, "
Their Ch.
8 Ruth   Burton   " "
8 Franklin, Jr. "   m. Anna Peck
Their Ch.
9 Elizabeth Burton
9 Helen "

5 Ch. Isaac Johnson and Marietta Hinman   Southbury, Conn.
6 Marietta "   m. Isaac Jay Allen   " "
Their Ch.
7 Ella   Allen   m. George W. Smith (no ch.)   Milford, "
7 Minnie   "   "   George B. Russell   Southbury, "
7 Horatio Treat   "   "   1st *Mary B. White (no ch.) Waterbury, "
            "   2nd. Nellie Fairchild Speed

Ch. Minnie Allen and George B. Russell   Southbury, "

8 *Lulu Russell   d. in girlhood
8 Allen B.   "   " Marian Ambler   Southbury, Conn.

Ch. 5 Nancy Johnson and Thomas Stillman   Bridgeport, "
6 Mary E. Stillman   m. 1st E. W. Pond   "   "
                         " 2nd E. Smith Hubbell   "   "
6 Amelia   "   unm.
6 *Franklin P. "   m. Emma M. Wilson
   Their Ch.
7 Ray W. Stillman   " Elizabeth Meleady
7 *William T.   "   " Helena Radcliffe   Shelton, Conn.
   In U. S. Service
Wm. T. Stillman was one of seven who lost their lives Aug. 13th, 1918 when the oil tanker Richard R. Kellogg was blown up off Barnegat.

Ch. Mary E. Stillman and E. W. Pond
7 Lillian S. Pond   m. Dr. G. F. Williams
   Their Ch.
8 Frances S. Williams

4 Ezra Hurd Johnson   m. Rebecca Northrop   Newtown, "
   Their Ch.
5 *Charles   Johnson   " Julia Merritt   "   "
5 *John   "   " Mary Dibble   "   "

Ch. Charles Johnson and Julia Merritt
6 Adaline   "   m. Wm. Fairchild (see Fairchild) " "
6 *Ezra Levan   "   " Jane Eliza Camp   "   "
   Their Ch.
7 William Camp   "   " Katherine A. Lake (no ch.) "   "
7 Charles Beach " twins " Alma M. Camp   "   "
7 *Levan Merritt "   " Nellie A. Hartshorne   "   "
7 Rt. Rev. Fred. F. "   " 1st Susan Lynn Beers   "   "
                         " 2nd Elizabeth Louise Beers "   "
7 Dora Northrop "   " John C. Keeler   Bethel, "
   Adopted dau.

Ch. Charles B. Johnson and Alma M. Camp   Newtown, "
8 Ruth Rebecca   "   m. Sereno F. King   Milford, "
8 Elsie Merritt "   Newtown, "
8 Frank R. Lemuel "   Trinity College Hartford, 1917
   Master St. Paul's School Concord, New Hampshire.

Ch. Ruth R. Johnson and Sereno F. King   Milford, Conn.
9 *Sarah   King   "   "
9 Irene Alma   "   "   "
9 Howard Randall "   "   "

Ch.* Levan M. Johnson and Nellie Hartshorne   Painesville, Ohio
L. M. Johnson fatally injured by an enraged bull, d. May 14, 1917. " "
8 Earl Levan   "   Supt. Stock Farm   "   "
8 Merritt Camp   "   In U. S. Service Camp Decatur, Great Lakes, Ill.
8 Ralph Emerson "   d. in childhod

Ch. Rt. Rev. Frederick F. Johnson and Susan Lynn Beers, St. Louis, Mo.
8 Frederick Foote Johnson Jr.

Ch. Dora N. Johnson and John C. Keeler   Seymour, Conn.
8 Katherine Johnson Keeler   "   "
8 Irene Elizabeth   " twins   "   "
   Ch. John Johnson and Mary Dibble
6 *Betsey Rebecca Johnson   d. unm.
6 *Edward Dibble   "   d. in young manhood
6 *Emily   "   d. in infancy

GENEALOGICAL SECTION

Ch. 4Clarissa Johnson   m. 1st Samuel Northrop   Newtown, Conn.
Their Ch.
5 Rebecca Northrop   m. Walter Northrop
5 Isaac   "   Went to Wilmington, N. C.

4 Joseph Johnson   m. Huldah Judson
Their Ch.
5 Zenas   Johnson   m. Anna Sherwood   Easton, Conn.
5 Albert   "   " Mary Louise Wheeler   Monroe, "
5 Sophia   "   " Marcus McEwen   "   "

Ch. Zenas Johnson and Anna Sherwood
6 Elizabeth   Johnson   m. Rev. Hawley Sanford   Redding, "
6 Mary Sophia   "   " Thomas Burr Fanton   Danbury, "
6 David   "   " Jane Clark   Redding, "
6 Joseph   "   " Martha Nickerson   Bridgeport, "

Desc. of 6Elizabeth Johnson and Rev. Hawley Sanford   Jesup, Iowa
7 Mary Louisa Sanford   m. *John T. Burrell   "   "
7 Alsimore Meade "   "   Amanda Gilbert   Milwaukee, Wis.
7 Wilbur Young   "   "   Nancy Beckley   Waterloo, Iowa
7 Harriet Anna   "   "   Charles Webster   "   "
7 John S.   "   "   Callie Moore   Memphis, Tenn.
7 Nellie E.   "   "   Charles A. Paul   Huntington, Beach, Cal.
7 Martha Jane   "   "   *William H. Gilbert   Rock Island, Ill.
7 Charles H.   "   "   Luella Velvin   Atlanta, Ga.

Ch. Mary Louisa Sanford and John T. Burrell
8 Clarence J. Burrell   m. 1st Linda Underwood   Overland, Cal.
                             2nd Laura Keller
8 Frank T.   "   m. Ethel McClain   Jesup, Iowa
8 *Mary Louise   "   "   A. Clinton Sayles   West Branch, "
8 Myrta Elizabeth "   "   George Arnold   Jesup, "
8 Jay S.   "   "   Cora Sabin   Birch Island, Minn.
8 Blanche   "   unm.   Jesup, Iowa

Ch. Clarence J. Burrell and Linda Underwood 1st.
9 Paul D.   "   In U. S. Artillery Serivce, Overland, Cal.
9 Gates U.   "   "   "
9 Philip   "   ch. Laura Keller 2nd wife   "   "

Ch. *Mary L. Burrell and A. Clinton Sayles   West Branch, Iowa
9 Margaret   Sayles
9 Burrell C.   "

Ch. Jay S. Burrell and Cora Sabin
9 Robert Sabin "   Birch Island, Minn.

Ch. Alsimore M. Sanford and Amanda Gilbert   Milwaukee, Wis.
8 Harold   "   Rochester, Minn.
8 Arthur H.   "   m. Margaret Seager   "   "
Their Ch.
9 Raymond   "
9 Hawley   "   m. Alice Tynan   St. Paul, "
Their Ch.
10 Wilber O.   "   "   "
10 Earl H.   "   "   "

Ch. 7Wilbur Young Sanford and Nancy Beckley   Sioux City, Iowa
8 Rollin E.   "   m. Nina Akin   Waterloo, "
8 Jay G.   "   " Ora Edwards   Sioux City, "
8 Hawley   "   "   "
8 Edna M.   "   "   "

Ch. Rollin E. Sanford and Nina Akin   Waterloo, "
9 Bernita   "   "   "

GENEALOGICAL SECTION

4 Ebenezer Johnson son of 3John m. Hepsa Shelton — Derby, Conn.
   Their Ch.
5 Edwin Clark Johnson m. Sarah Grace Hubbell " "
5 Lucy " " William Shelton

   Ch. Edwin C. Johnson and Sarah Grace Hubbell
6 Mary Jeannette Johnson m. Herbert P. Smith North Haven, Conn.
   Their Ch.
7 Mabel Grace Smith m. Harry C. Beers
7 Ellsworth Johnson " " Mabel E. Greenwood
7 Herbert William " " Gertrude Tooke
7 Martha Jeannette "

   Ch. Mabel Grace Smith and Harry C. Beers Lanesboro, Mass.
8 Sherman Johnson Beers
8 Jeannette Elizabeth "

   Ch. Herbert W. Smith and Gertrude Tooke
8 Mary Parker Smith
8 Herbert Wm., Jr. "

   Ch. 5Lucy Johnson and William Shelton White Hills, Conn.
6 Charlotte Shelton m. Charles Hubbell " "
6 Charles " " Cornelia Hubbell " "

   Ch. Charlotte Shelton and Charles Hubbell
7 Amanda Hubbell m. George P. Bidwell
7 Theresa " " William H. Jones
7 Warren C. " " Annie Shelton
   Their Ch.
8 Elsie M. Hubbell
8 Sterling B. " m. Elma Buckingham
   Their Ch.
9 Elinor S. Hubbell
9 Virginia "

   Ch. Amanda Hubbell and George P. Bidwell
8 Charles H. Bidwell m. May Bidwell
   Their Ch.
9 Bodford Bidwell

   Ch. William H. Jones and Theresa Hubbell
8 Helen C. Jones
8 Philip H. " m. Joan Newell
   Their Ch.
9 Newell Jones

   Ch. 6Charles Shelton and Cornelia Hubbell
7 William Shelton
7 Edwin C. " m. Alice French
   Their Ch.
8 Lester M. Shelton

4 John Johnson son of 3John m. Clarissa Peck Newtown, Conn.
   Their Ch.
5 Cornelia Johnson " David H. Belden, 1st wife " "
5 Susan Jane " " David H. Belden, 2nd wife " "
   David H. " " 1st Esther Beers (no ch.) " "
                 " 2nd Rebecca Beers (no ch.) " "

6 Susan Jane Belden m. Rev. Dr. Berry Litchfield, Conn.

GENEALOGICAL SECTION

6 Susan Jane Belden   ch.   5Cornelia Johnson & David H. Belden

Ch. 5Susan J. Johnson and David H. Belden

6 Cornelia Belden	m.	Dr. Maddox	
6 Clarissa "	unm.		Newtown, Conn.
6 David "	m.	Elizabeth Farrell	San Jose, Calif.

An eminent lawyer, See Lawyers, Newtown, Conn.

6 John Belden   desc. not located

7 John Johnson Berry, M. D. ch.   Susan J. Belden & Rev. Dr. Berry   Portsmouth, N. H.

He with Mrs. Belden published a memorial volumne of David Belden of San Jose, Calif.

4 Daniel Johnson m. Lamira Wheeler

Their Ch.

5 Emeline Johnson	m.	Barzillai Kellogg	Brookfield, Conn.
5 Elizabeth "	"	Washburn (no ch.)	Brooklyn, N. Y.

Ch. Emeline Johnson and Barzillai Kellogg   Brookfield Conn.

6 *Angeline Lamira Kellogg	m.	Benjamin Griffin	" "
6 *William Johnson	" "	Sophia E. Beers	" "
6 *Florence Ann	" "	Charles S. Hawes	Bridgeport, Conn.
6 *Charles Daniel H.	" "	Annie S. Terrill	" "
6 *Emeline	"	unm.	Brookfield, Conn.
6 Sarah E.	"	unm.	" "
6 *Elizabeth Washburn	"	unm.	" "

Ch. Angeline L. Kellogg and Benjamin Griffin

7 Edward Griffin	m.	Ida Rogers	
7 Ernest Barzillai twins	" "	Tillie M. Beach	
7 *Edith Emeline	" "	Dr. Howard P. Mansfield	
7 Martha Elizabeth	" "	Charles R. Clarke	Bridgeport, Conn.
7 Henry Washburn	" "	Janet Hodge	
7 Florence Sophia	"		

Ch. Ernest B. Griffin and Tillie M. Beach

8 Helen Edith Griffin

Ch. Edith E. Griffin and Dr. Howard Mansfield

8 Ernest Griffin Mansfield

Ch. Martha Griffin and Charles R. Clarke   Bridgeport, Conn.

8 Philip Griffin Clarke   " "
8 Elizabeth "   " "
8 Charles Robert, Jr. "   " "

Ch. Henry W. Griffin and Janet Hodge

8 Marjorie Angeline Griffin

Ch. Wm. J. Kellogg and Sophia Beers   Brookfield, Conn.

7 Florence Emily Kellogg	m.	Arthur S. Mansfield	" "
7 Herbert Beers	"	Mary Amelia Bateman	Pittsfield, Mass.

Their Ch.

8 Genevieve Kellogg   " "
8 Eloise "   " "
8 Ruth "   " "

Ch. Florence E. Kellogg and Arthur Mansfield   Brookfield, Conn.

8 Lina Beers Mansfield

Ch. Florence A. Kellogg and Charles E. Hawes

7 Grace Florence Hawes   Brooklyn, N. Y.

Ch. Chas. D. H. Kellogg and Annie S. Terrill   Bridgeport, Conn.

7 Hanford Barzillai Kellogg m. Emma Roy   " "
7 Stanley Terrill " " Nellie G. Clarke   " "
7 Louise Fairchild " " Willard M. Taylor   " "
7 Charles D. H. Jr. "
7 Mary Skidmore " " Arthur J. Millington   " "

Ch. Hanford B. Kellogg and Emma Roy

8 Hanford B. Jr. "

Ch. Stanley T. Kellogg and Nellie G. Clarke   Bridgeport, Conn.

8 Clarke Terrill "

Ch. Louise F. Kellogg and Willard M. Taylor   " "

8 Dorothy Taylor twin
8 Doris " "
8 Mary Elizabeth "

4 Elias Johnson son of 3 John m. Hepsa Judson

Their Ch.

5 *Cornelia Johnson m. John Knowles   Bridgeport, Conn.
5 *Henry M. " " Lois Jones (no ch.)   " "
5 *Stiles Wheeler " " Henrietta Hanly (no ch.)   " "

Ch. Cornelia Johnson and John Knowles

6 Cornelia Knowles m. Francis E. Fitch   Passaic, N. J.

Their Ch.

7 Mallory Knowles Fitch d. 1904 aged 26 yrs.   " "
7 John Knowles " m. Lillian Whitehead   " "
7 *Marion " d. 1916 aged 33 yrs.

Ch. John Knowles Fitch and Lillian Whitehead

8 John Knowles Jr. Fitch   " "
8 Marjorie "   " "
8 Muriel "   " "

4 Sally Johnson dau. 3 John m. John Fayerweather

Their Ch.

5 *Walter B. Fayerweather m. Abby Post Austin   Danbury, Conn.
5 *John " " Abigail Oakley
5 *William " unm.
5 Julia " m. Samuel B. Peck   Newtown, Conn.

Ch. Walter B. Fayerweather and Abby Post Austin   Danbury, Conn.

6 Ellen G. Fayerweather m. Daniel Barnes
6 S. Isabelle " " Capt. Chas. Colcord   " "

7 Margaret Barnes ch. Ella G. Fayerweather & Daniel Barnes

7 Margaret Barnes m. 1st Geo. Wilson
    " " " 2nd Walter Clifford

8 Walter Wilson ch. Margaret Barnes & George Wilson

8 Charles G. Clifford ch. Margaret Barnes & Walter Clifford

9 Clifford Barnes ch. Elsie Wilkins & Walter Wilson Barnes

Ch. John Fayerweather and Abigail Oakley

6 *Julia Fayerweather   m.   Seelye
6 *Oakley   "   "   Lavinia Cook

Their Ch.
7 *John   Fayerweather
7 Blanche   "
7 Frederick   "
7 Charles   "

Ch. 5Julia Fayerweather and Samuel B. Peck   Sandy Hook, Conn.

6 *Julia   Peck   unm.   "   "
6 *George   "   m. Emma J. Clarke   Newtown, Conn.
6 Edward S. "   " Lilla Lockitt   Patchogue L. I.

Ch. George Peck and Emma J. Clarke   Brooklyn, N. Y.

7 *Samuel Clarke   Peck   d. in young manhood
7 Elizabeth Fayerweather "   unm.   Schenectady, N. Y.
7 Walter Toucey   "   m. Elizabeth Chester Backus   "   "
7 Susan   "   "   Willard Merrill Burdick   "   "

Their Ch.
8 Priscilla   Burdick   "   "
8 Ruth MacBride   "   "   "
8 Merrill Clarke   "   "   "

Ch. Walter T. Peck and Elizabeth Chester Backus   "   "

8 Elizabeth Chester   Peck   "   "
8 Samuel Clarke   "   "   "

Ch. Edward S. Peck and Lilla Lockitt   Patchogue L. I.

7 Edward Stanley   Peck   "   "
7 *Grace   "

4 Eli Johnson son of 3John   m. Sally Watkins   Ballsten Spa, N. Y.
  Their Ch.
5 Louisa Johnson   m. Rev. M. Williams   "   "
  Their Ch.
6 Emma   Williams   m. Chas T. Dunwell   "   "
6 Allan S.   "

7 Elsie   Dunwell   Emma Williams
7 James   "   ch.   &
7 Ruth   "   Chas T. Dunwell

4 Benjamin Johnson son of 3John m. Dorcas Morse
  Their Ch.
5 Lucy   Johnson   m.   Kline
5 Benjamin   "

6 William Kline   ch. Lucy Johnson Kline
6 Benjamin Johnson   ch. 5Benjamin (no desc. located)

KIMBERLY

The name Kimberly appearing so often in Newtown's early records has disappeared from the names of the present generation, but the descendants in Newtown of Abraham 2nd, 3rd and 4th are very numerous.

1 Thomas Kimberly came from London and was one of the founders of the New Haven Colony.

2 Eleazer Kimberly is said to have been the first white male child born in New Haven.

2 Abraham Kimberly 1st   m. Hannah

3 Abraham " 2nd " Abigail Fitch   Newtown, Conn,

Their Ch.

4 Hannah	Kimberly	"	James Hard (See Hard)	"	"
4 Abigail	"	"	John Lake (see Lake)	"	"
4 Gideon	"	"	Mary Osborne	"	"
4 Abraham 3rd	"	"	Abigail Adams	"	"
4 Sarah	"	"	3Joseph Prindle (see Prindle)	"	"

Ch. Abraham 3rd Kimberly and Abigail Adams

5 Anah	Kimberly	m.	John Dunning		
5 Sarah	"	"	Ebenezer Fairchild (see Fairchild)		
5 Abiah	"	"	Michael Dunning		
5 Fitch	Kimberly	m.	Abigail Woodruff		
5 Abraham 4th	"	"	Tamar Burritt	Newtown, Conn	"
5 Sabra	"	"	Joel Prindle	"	"

Ch. Abraham Kimberly 4th and Tamar Burritt

6 Mary	Kimberly	m.	George Northrop		
6 Abel Burritt	"	"	Currence Prindle	"	"
6 Polly	"	"	Ephraim Platt (see Platt)		
7 Betsy Ann	"	"	Abram Prindle		

Fitch Kimberly and his brother Abraham 4th served in the French War in 1756; also Abraham 4th was appointed by the Assembly Jan. 7th, 1777, "Lieut. of the Western Alarm List Company in the town of Newtown in the 16th Regt. of this state. Fitch Kimberly served as private in Revolutionary War.

LAKE

Desc. of 1Thomas Lake and Sarah Peat

2 John Lake, b. 1688 m. Abigail Kimberly dau. of Abigail Fitch and Abraham Kimberly, settled in Newtown early in 1700.

Their Ch.

3 Sarah	Lake	m.	Ebenezar Bristol
3 Charity	"	"	Nehemiah Skidmore
3 Nathaniel	"		
3 Ephraim	"	"	Mary Bristol
3 Thomas	"	"	Betty Jackson
3 Abigail	"	"	Thomas Lattin

Ch. Thomas Lake and Betty Jackson

4 Ezra	Lake	m.	Hannah Thompson
4 John	"	"	Susanna Hubbell
4 Peter	"	"	Temperance Thompson
4 David	"		
4 Isaac	"	"	no desc.

Ch. Ezra Lake and Hannah Thompson

5 Philo Lake   m. Polly Ann Birch

Their Ch.

6 *Hannah Ann	Lake	m.	John S. Hubbard	Meriden, Conn.
6 *Catharine	"	"	Amos Hard (see Hard)	
6 *Ezra Birch	"	"	Melissa Saxton	

GENEALOGICAL SECTION

6 *Lamson Birch Lake " 1st Sarah M. Beers
                                       2nd Sylvia M. Beers

   Ch. Hannah A. Lake and John S. Hubbard   Meriden, Conn.

7 John B. Hubbard   d. in young manhood   "   "

   Ch. Ezra Birch Lake and Melissa Saxton

7 Nora Belle Lake twins   Cherry Creek, N. Y.
7 *Ora E.   "   twins   d. in infancy

   Ch. Lamson B. Lake and Sarah M. Beers 1st wife   Newtown, Conn.

7 Carrie Louise   Lake   m. Frank Mallett no ch.   Monroe, Conn.
7 Frederick Beers   "   d. in young manhood   Newtown, Conn.
7 Katherine Augusta   "   m. Wm. C. Johnson no ch.   "   "

   Ch. Lamson B. Lake and Sylvia M. Beers   "   "

7 Grace Elizabeth   Lake   unm.   Passaic, N. J.
7 Florence Amelia   "   unm.   "   "

   4 ch. John Lake and Susanna Hubbell   Newtown, Conn.

5 Legrand Seabury Lake   m. Deborah McLean   Newtown, Conn.
5 Walter   "   "   Polly Ferris   "   "
5 John   "   "   Maria Skidmore
5 Clara   "   "   Ornan Sherman (see Sherman)
                                                                          Danbury, Conn.
5 Susan   "   "   John R. Smith   Newtown, Conn.

   Ch. Walter Lake and Polly Ferris   "   "

6 Isaac   Lake   m. Margaret Dibble   "   "
6 D. Jackson "   "   Katharine Hinman   "   "
6 Ferris   "   desc. not located
6 Harriet   "   m. Moulthrop

   Ch. Isaac Lake and Margaret Dibble

7 Frederick   Lake   m. Ella Oliver no ch.   Newtown, Conn.
7 *Robert   "   "   Julia Warner no ch.
7 *Annabelle   "   "   Howard Banks   Bethel, Conn.

   Ch. D. Jackson Lake and Katharine Hinman   Monroe, Conn.

7 Rev. Clarence Lake   Colusa, Calif.
7 Florence   "

5 Ch. Susan Lake and John R. Smith   Newtown, Conn.

6 John Russell Smith   m. 1st Lucia Camp   "   "
                                   2nd Susan Hawley   "   "
6 Eliza   "   "   Marcus Camp, ch. d. in infancy
6 Susan   "   "   Henry Weed no ch

   Ch. John R. Smith and Susan Hawley   Newtown, Conn.

7 Mary Eliza Smith   m. H. Wilbur Bristol   Bridgeport, Conn.
8 Laura Bristol, their ch.

   Ch. 4Peter Lake and Temperance Thompson

5 Nichols Booth Lake   m. Charlotte Curtis   Newtown Conn.
5 Thompson   "   desc. not located
5 Amos   "   m. 1st Catharine Blackman   Bethlehem, "
                          "   2nd Mary Ann Bennett   "   "
5 Abbie   "   "   Abraham Ferris Shepard   Brookfield, "

   Ch. Nichols B. Lake and Charlotte Curtis

GENEALOGICAL SECTION

6 Joseph Thompson Lake m. Hannah R. Smith .. Newtown, Conn.
6 Birdsey Curtis " " Jane Sherman 1st
                        " Phebe Warren Peck 2nd New Haven, "
6 Mary A. " " Robert S. Peck (see Peck) Newtown, "
6 Daniel B. " desc not located

    Ch. Joseph T. Lake and Hannah R. Smith   "   "

7 Mary Josephine Lake m. Chas. F. Beardsley   "   "
7 Nettie " d. in childhood

    Ch. Mary Josephine Lake and Charles F. Beardsley   " "

8 Clarence Lake Beardsley m. Viola May Gamsby New Haven, "
8 Paul Joseph " unm.

    Ch. Birdsey C. Lake and Jane Sherman   "   "

7 Ives Levi Lake
7 Birdsey Curtis Jr. "

    Ch. Amos Lake and Catharine Blackman 1st wife Bethlehem, "

6 Norman Lake m. Louisa Beach   "   "
6 Julia " " Joseph Hawley   "   "

    Ch. Amos Lake and Mary Ann Bennet 2nd wife   " "

6 Walter B. Lake m. Alma Nettleton
6 Benjamin " " Hannah Bradley   "   "
6 Peter " " Susan Pierce
6 Mary Lake m. Thomas Bennett no ch. Nunda, N. Y.
6 Sarah Jane " " Lemuel Camp (see Camp) Newtown, Conn.
6 Horation Nelson " unm.
6 Caroline Cynthia " " Samuel B. Camp (see Camp) " "

    Ch. Norman Lake and Louisa Beach Bethlehem, "

7 Elizabeth Lake
7 Ellen "
7 Norton B. "
7 Herbert W. " m. Jennie Belden Waterbury, "
7 Arthur B. "
7 George Tuttle "

    Ch. 6Walter B. Lake and Alma Nettleton Bethlehem, Conn.

7 Amos Caleb Lake m. Amanda Bloss   "   "
7 Royal Bennett " " Josephine Bacon Torrington, "

    Ch. Benjamin Lake and Hannah Bradley Bethlehem, "

7 *Annie Bradley Lake d. unm.

    Ch. 6Peter Lake and Susan Pierce Northfield

7 Franklin Rudolph Lake m. Jennie Beach
7 Origen Toucey "

    Ch. Herbert W. Lake and Jennie Belden Waterbury, "

8 G. Irving Lake
8 Arthur "
8 Frederick "
8 Gordon "

    Ch. 7Amos Caleb Lake and Amanda Bloss Bethlehem, Conn.

8 *Elsie Lake
8 Ina "
8 Walter "

GENEALOGICAL SECTION

Ch. 7 Royal Lake and Josephine Bacon — Torrington, Conn.
8 Edna Lake
8 Robert "
8 Edith "

Ch. 7 Frank R. Lake and Jennie Beach — Thomaston, "
8 Grace Lake
8 Clara "

Ch. 6 Julia Lake and Joseph Hawley
7 Catherine Sophia Hawley
7 Hannah Adelaide " m. Edwin Camp no ch. — Newtown, Conn.
7 Philo " " — Bridgewater "
7 Sarah Elizabeth "
7 Amos Lake " " Mary Bills — Hawleyville, "
7 Hobart Melville " " Flora Trumbull
7 Franklin Joseph " "

Ch. Amos L. Hawley and Mary Bills — " "
8 Ernest Hawley m. Cornelia Morehouse — " "

5 Lyman Lake son 4 David m. Abba Foote 1st. — Newtown, "
" Sophia Hawley 2nd.

Ch. Lyman Lake and Abba Foote
6 3 Charles " m. — Danbury "
6 Julia A. " " Henry W. Oliver — Brooklyn, N. Y.
6 *Lamira " " Mason Thorpe — Danbury, Conn.
6 *Nelson " " Mary A. Glover — Newtown, "

Ch. Lyman Lake and Sophia Hawley — " "
6 *Abba Lake unm. — Newtown, Conn.
6 *Elizabeth " m. Reuben Starr Blackman (See Blackman)

Ch. Charles Lake and wife — Danbury, Conn.
7 Ella " m. Frost — " "
7 Frank "

Ch. 6 Julia A. Lake and Henry W. Oliver
7 *Wallace L. Oliver m. Amelia Brown
7 *Eugene H. " " *Ida Crawford
7 *Addie J. " d. in infancy
7 Charles A. " " Jennie Stephenson
7 Ella J. " " Frederick Lake — Newtown, "
7 Carrie E. " unm. — " "
Mrs. Julia A. Oliver 92 years, Oct. 1918. — " "

Ch. Lamira Lake and Mason Thorpe
7 Emma D. Thorpe m. *John Walling — Danbury, "
7 Julia E. " " Orlando Starr — " "

Ch. Nelson Lake and Mary A. Glover — Newtown, "
7 Edward G. "
7 *Wilbur "
7 Martin N. "
7 Robert A. "
7 *Ada " m. Lucius G. Norton
7 Anna " " U. S. Booth
7 *Julia " " Albert Cole

Ch. Edward G. Lake and wife
8 Ada " m. Charles Buell
8 Anna " " 2nd wife Charles Bacbath
8 *Mary Belle " " 1st wife Charles McBath

Ch. Martin H Lake and wife

8 Rose	"	m.	Devine
8 Nelson	"		In U. S. Service in Army
8 Robert	"		In U. S. Service in Army
8 Harry	"		

Ch. Robert A. Lake and wife

8 Arthur L.　　"　　　　　In U. S. Service in Army
8 Doris A.　　"
8 Mary A.　　"

Ch. *Julia Lake and Albert Cole

8 Julia　　　Cole
8 Edith　　　"
8 Albert　　　"
8 Richard　　"

Ch. Anna Lake and U. S. Booth

8 Jessie Booth　　　　m. Hummiston
8 Rachel "
8 Harold "
8 Herbert "
8 Arthur "
8 Clarence "　　　　　　In U. S. Serivce

MERRITT

1 John Merritt came from the north of Ireland to Stratford date unknown. He was frozen to death on Stratford Beach. His son John settled in Newtown on what is still known as Merritt Hill.

2 John Merritt m. Deborah Wheeler.

The town records show that their son 3Abijah Merritt filled many offices of public trust. He m. Hannah Sanford.

Their Ch.

4 Julia	Merritt	m.	Charles Johnson (See Johnson)	
4 Levan Wheeler	"	"	Cynthia Patience Loomis	Medina, N. Y.

Their Ch.

5 *Charles Johnson Merritt	m.	1st Esther Fairchild	Newtown, Conn.	
		2nd Julia Chase	Medina, N. Y.	
5 Julia	"	d. unm.	Washington, D. C.	
5 *Henry	"	d. in childhood	Medina, N. Y.	
5 Cynthia A.	"	unm.	Washington, D. C.	
5 *Elsie Henrietta	"	d. unm.	Medina, N. Y.	
5 *Henry Sanford	"	m. 1st Urilla Swingley Phelps	Elkader, Iowa	
		2nd Ella Havens	" "	
5 *Lee Wheeler	"	d. in young manhood	Medina, N. Y.	

Ch. Charles J. Merritt and Esther Fairchild　　　Chicago, Ill.

6 *Ida　　　　　"　　d. in childhood　　　　" "
6 *Charles Henry　"　m. Annie Crawford　　　" "

Their Ch.

7 Marjorie Merritt　　　　　　　　　　Urbana, Ohio
7 Crawford　　"　　　　　　　　　　　" "

Ch. Henry S. Merritt and Urilla S. Phelps　　　Elkader, Iowa

6 Frank Henry　　"　　m. Bertha Emory
6 James Levan　　"　　"　Irene　　　　　　Seattle, Wash.

Ch. Frank H. Merritt and Bertha Emory　　　Milford, Iowa

7 Ruth　　　　　"　　　　　　　　　　　" "

HON. DANIEL N. MORGAN

See Page 101 (Genealogical Section)

GENEALOGICAL SECTION

7 Bernadine Merritt — Milford, Iowa
 Ch. Henry S. Merritt and Ella Havens — Elkader "
6 Isaac Havens " m. Mary Ethel Carpenter — Denver, Colo.
 Their Ch.
7 Helen Merritt — " "
7 Robert Homer " — " "

MORGAN

1 Zedekiah Morgan was in the Revolutionary War and a field in Hopewell district in Newtown where he kept cavalry horses, is still called "Cavalry field." So says Hon. D. N. Morgan.

2 Hezekiah Morgan, son of 1 Zedekiah Morgan — Newtown, Conn.
6   m. Elizabeth Sanford   6th in descent from Rev. John Beach

7 Ezra Morgan   Elizabeth Sanford   Newtown, Conn.
7 Fanny   "   ch.   &
7 Zera   '   Hezekiah Morgan   "   "
7 *Ezra Morgan   m. Hannah Nash   Westport, Conn.
 Their ch.

8 Elizabeth S   Morgan m. Rufus D. Cable   "   "
8 *Mary Camp   "   d. unm.   Newtown, Conn.
8 Daniel Nash   "   m. Medora Huganen Judson Huntington, Conn.
8 *Harriet Louise "   d. unm.   Newtown, Conn.
8 *Cornelia Jane   "   d. unm.   "   "
8 *Hannah Sophia   "   d. young   "   "
8 *Frederick Ezra "   d. in boyhood   "   "
8 *Edward Kemper   "   m. Charlotte Adelaide Judson Bridgeport, "

Ch. Elizabeth S. Morgan and Rufus D. Cable

9 Mary Eilzabeth Cable   m. Marcus B. Butler   Westport, Conn.
9 Hannah Louise   "   m. Edward F. Buchner   Baltimore, Md.
9 Antoinette Cornelia " m. Rev. George A. Robson E. Lansing Mich.
10 Dorothy Morgan Butler   Mary E. Cable   Bridgeport, Conn.
10 Virginia Lacey   " ch.   &
10 Marcus Bayard, Jr. "   Marcus B. Butler   "   "
 U. S. N.
10 Edward F. Buchner, Jr.   Baltimore, Md.
10 Morgan Mallory   "   Hannah Louise Cable "   "
10 Elizabeth Sanford " ch.   &
10 Margaret Louise   "   Edward F. Buchner   "   "
10 Janet Elizabeth Robson   Antoinete C. Cable East Lansing, Mich.
10 Edward John   "   ch.   &
10 Faith   "   Rev. George A. Robson "   "

Ch. Medora Judson and D. N. Morgan.   Bridgeport, Conn.

9 Mary Huntington Morgan m. Daniel Edwards Brinsmade Shelton, Conn.
9 *Florence Newton   "   d. in infancy   Bridgeport, Conn.
9 William Judson   " m. Helen Jeanette Brinsmade "   '
                           Helen Jeannete Brinsmade "   "
10 Marjorie Brinsmade   ch.   &
                           William Judson Morgan   "   "

HON. DANIEL NASH MORGAN

Besides those Newtown born who became lawyers, doctors or clergymen, some attained prominence in other and equally large fields.

Hon. Daniel Nash Morgan, son of Hannah Nash and Ezra Morgan, was born Aug. 18, 1844; received his education at the public school, Newtown Academy, and Bethel Institute.

He was assistant in his father's country store until attaining his majority, when he assumed control for one year. Like most country stores in those days it was the custom to sell by the dram, pint, quart or gallon, spirituous liquors to customers. Upon assuming control of the business, he caused to be emptied into the ditch all containers of the liquor; and when later he became a partner in the old stand of David H. Johnson, of the firm of Morgan and Booth he made it one of the conditions that no liquor should be sold.

Upon removing to Bridgeport he was elected Mayor, 1880-1884; for thirteen years was Parish Clerk of Trinity Parish, Bridgeport, then Junior and later Senior Warden. He was President of Bridgeport Hospital, President of City National Bank, 1887-1893, President of Mechanics and Farmers Bank, State Senator from 14th disrict 1885-86, and again in 1892, and was United States Treasurer from June 1, 1893 to July 1, 1897. He is a Mason and connected with many offices of trust in the city of Bridgeport.

9 Daniel Judson Morgan		Charlote Adelaide Judson	
9 Frederick Edward "	ch.	&	Bridgeport, Conn.
		Edward Kemper Morgan	"
8 Charles Morgan		Sally Underhill	Newtown, Conn.
8 Rev. Henry "	ch.	&	
		Zera Morgan	Boston, Mass.
9 Henry P. Morgan		Polly Peck	Newtown, Conn.
9 Ormel "	ch.	&	
9 Merwin D. "		Charles Morgan	" "
9 Edith L. "			
10 Arthur Briscoe Morgan	ch.	Esther P. Briscoe	" "
10 Grace Edith "		&	
		Ormel E. Morgan	" "
9 Agnes Banks		Sophia Bradley	Redding, Conn.
9 Elizabeth "	ch.	&	
9 Alma L. "		Charles Morgan Banks	" "
10 Eva Banks Whitehead	ch.	Agnes Banks	Redding, Conn.
		&	
		Henry Whitehead	
11 Hazel Elaine Sherwood	ch.	Eva Whitehead	
		&	
		James Arthur Sherwood	Easton, Conn.
10 Charles Henry Lee		Alma Louise Banks	Redding, Conn.
10 Julian "	ch.	&	
10 Coley Fanton "		Francis Coley Lee	" "
10 Elsie May Cook		Edith Louise Morgan	
10 Flora Edith "	ch.	&	
10 William M. "		William James Cook	
10 Edward R. "			

MORRIS

First Morris settler in Newtown.
1 Daniel b. 1750 m. Mary Salter Burritt.

Their ch.

2 Sally Morris		1st Sylvester Beers (See Beers)	
		2nd Ezekial Beers	Newtown, Conn
2 Eli Gould "	m.	Lydia Bennett	" "
2 Polly "	m.	John Blackman	" "
2 Nancy "	m.	Silas Norman Glover	" "
2 Eunice "		(See Glover)	
	m.	John Blackman 2nd	" "

Ch. Eli Gould Morris and Lydia Bennett

3 *Eli James	Morris	m.	Jane Chambers	Newtown, Conn.
3 Luzon Burritt	"	m.	Eugenia Tuttle	New Haven, Conn.
3 *Martha Jane	"		A successful teacher, unm.	Newtown, Conn.

Luzon B. Morris elected Governor of Conn. 1892. Took office Jan. 1893

Ch. Luzon B. Morris and Eugenia Tuttle (see Lawyers.)

4 Dr. Robert Tuttle	Morris	m.	Aimee Reynaud	New York
4 Mary Seymour	"	m.	Charles Millard Pratt	Brooklyn, N. Y.
4 Helen Harrison	"	m.	Arthur T. Hadley	New Haven, Conn.
4 Emily Eugenia	"	unm.		
4 Charles Gould	"	m.	Elisabeth Woodbridge	New Haven
4 Ray	"	m.	Katherine Grinnell	New York, N. Y.

5 Eugenia R. Morris   ch. Aimee Reynaud & Dr. Robert T. Morris   New York

Ch. Chas. Millard Pratt and Mary Seymour Morris   Brooklyn, N. Y.

5 Morris	Pratt			
5 Lieut. Theodore	"	m.	Laura Merrick (no ch.)	New Orleans, La.
5 Margaret R.	"	m.	Frank J. Frost	St. Louis, Mo.
5 Katherine E.	"	"	Burton P. Twitchell	Nordhoff, Calif.
5 Lieut. Richardson	"		Infantry in France	

6 Morris Pratt Frost   ch. Margaret R. Pratt & Frank J. Frost   St. Louis, Mo.

Ch. Arthur T. Hadley and Helen Harrison Morris

6 Maj. Morris	Hadley	youngest Maj. in the Army Art. in France	
6 Capt. Hamilton	"	Aviation in France	
6 Laura Beaumont	"		
Arthur T.	"	President Yale University	New Haven and Newtown

5 Laura Wylie	Morris			
5 Woodbridge Edward	"			
5 Martha Cartwright	"	ch.	Elizabeth Woodbridge & Charles G. Morris	New Haven and Newtown
5 Daniel Luzon	"			
5 Charles Lester	"			
5 Elisabeth Woodbridge	"			

5 Virginia	Morris		Katharine Grinnell & Ray Morris	
5 Grinnell	"	ch.		
5 Stephen Burritt	"			New York

NICHOLS

Richard Nichols	m.	Comfort Sherman	Newtown, Conn.
First Nichols settler in Newtown			" "
1 Nathaniel Nichols	m.	Ann Booth	" "

Of their ten children

2 Esther	Nichols	m.	John Holbrook, Jr.	Derby, Conn.
2 Peter	"	m.	Rebecca Camp	Newtown, Conn.
2 Phedima	"	m.	Benjamin Curtis	" "
2 Richard	"	m.	Abigail Gold	" "
2 Theophilus	"	m.	Sarah Meeker	" "

Ch. Esther Nichols and John Holbrook, Jr.   Derby, Conn.

3 Abel Holbrook	m.	Hannah Clark	Oxford "

GENEALOGICAL SECTION

4 Abel Holbrook Jr.	m.	Olive Pierce	Southbury, Conn.
5 Esther "	"	Chas. Lawrence Mitchell	" "

Their Ch.

6 Frank Mitchell	"	Emma Judson	Newtown, Conn.
6 Nellie "	"	Charles Parsons	" "
6 Jessie Pauline "	"	J. Percy Blackman	" "
6 Vivan "	"	Alice Babcock	" "

Ch. Frank Mitchell and Emma Judson

7 Laura Mitchell	m.	George Camp	Waterbury "
7 Wallace "	"	Edith Ganung	" "

Ch. Laura Mitchell and George Camp

8 Merwin Camp	" "
8 Nelson "	

Ch. Nellie Mitchell and Charles Parsons — Newtown, Conn.

7 Herbert Parsons	m.	Florence Watson	Albany, N. Y.
7 Birdsey "	"	Vivian Wetmore (see Wetmore)	
7 Ethel "	"	1st Chas. Finch	Albany, N. Y.
		2nd Lindsay Polly	" "
7 Pearl "	"	Wm. Stevens	

Ch. Herbert Parsons and Florence Watson — Albany, N. Y.

8 Ruth Nichols Parsons

Ch. Ethel Parsons and Charles Finch

8 Esther Finch

Ch. Pearl Parsons and Wm. Stevens

8 William Stevens
8 Heman "

Ch. Jessie Pauline Mitchell and J. Percy Blackman — Newtown, Conn.

7 Pauline Frances Blackman	(b. Newtown)	Passaic, N. J.
7 Olive Mitchell "	(b. Newtown)	Passaic, N. J.

Ch. 2Peter Nichols and Rebecca Camp

3 Phedima Nichols	m.	Simeon Beers	" "
3 Nathaniel "	m.	Grace Sherman	" "
3 Sarah "	m.	Reuben Hull Booth	Danbury, Conn.
3 Polly "	m.	Lamson Birch (See Birch)	Newtown, Conn.

Ch. 3Nathaniel Nichols and Grace Sherman

4 Henry Nichols	m.	Sarah Blackman	" "

Their Ch.

5 *David M. Nichols	m.	1st Caroline Crane	New York, N. Y.
		2nd Phebe Crane Tompkins	" "
5 *Mary "	m.	Samuel Curtis (See Curtis)	Newtown, Ct.
5 *Philo "	m.	Sarah Esther Glover	" "

Their ch.

6 Frank B. Nichols		d. in infancy	" "
6 Grace "		d. in infancy	" "
6 Ruth Amelia "	m.	Hobart H. Curtis (See Curtis)	" "

Ch. David M. " and Caroline Crane — New York, N. Y.

6 John Henry " " "

GENEALOGICAL SECTION

    Ch. David M. Nichols   and Phebe Crane Tompkins   New York, N. Y.
6 David Arthor   "   "   "

2 Ch. Theophilus Nichols and Sarah Meeker   Newtown, Conn.
3 Capt. James Nichols   m. Lucy Beach   "   "
    Their Ch.
4 Theophilus B.   Nichols   Lost at sea no ch.
4 Isaac   "   m. 1st Betsey Platt   "   "
    "   "   2nd Louisa Bartlett   "   "
4 William   "
4 Drusus   "   " Rebecca B. Graves   English Prairie, Ind.
4 Rev. Abel   "   " Elizabeth Saunders no ch., Lost at sea
4 Thaddeus H.   "   no ch.
4 James A. F.   "   Killed at Fort Wayne, Ind.
4 John   "   m. Julia Ann Sheldon
4 Philo   "   " Melinda Carr   La Grange, Ind.
4 Susan   "   " Wm. B. Glover no ch. Sandy Hook, Conn.

    Ch. 4Isaac Nichols and Betsey Platt 1st wife   Newtown, "
5 Henry   Nichols   m. Elizabeth Sharp   Orland, Ind.
5 James   "   " Isabella Starkweather   Hartford, Conn.
5 William   "   Drowned in Taunton Pond
5 Mary Betsey   "   d. in young womanhood

    Ch. Isaac Nichols and Louisa Bartlett, 2nd wife   Newtown, Conn.
5 Augusta   Nichols   m. Daniel Camp (see Camp)   "   "
5 Sarah   "   " Silas N. Beers (see Beers)   "   "
5 Margaret   "   " Edson Hawley (see Hawley)Brookfield"
5 Beach   "   " Adelia Fairchild   Newtown, "
5 Louisa   "   d. unm.
5 William   "   d. in boyhood   "   "
5 Arthur   "   d. in infancy   "   "
5 Grace   "   m. Homer Hawley (see Hawley) "   "

    Ch. 5Henry Nichols and Elizabeth Sharp   Orland, Ind.
6 Arthur   Nichols   m. Belle Canse   "   "
6 Emma   "   " Charles M. Clark   Friend, Nebr.
6 Fred   "   " Elizabeth Jellay   La Grange, Ind.
6 *Alice   "   " Benjamin Barber   "   "
6 *Fanny   "   "   "   "
6 Lizzie   "   " Rev. Alvin Weaver   Jonesboro, "
6 Susan   "   James A. Turner   Fenton, Mich.
6 *James   "   "   "
6 *Willie   "   "   "
6 *Anna   "   m. Huestis Beers   "   "
6 *Margie   "   " Charles Dirrim   "   "

    Ch. Arthur Nichols and Belle Canse   Orland, Ind.
7 Clara   "   m. Earl Faulk   "   "
    Their Ch.   Herbert Faulk   "   "
7 Ray   Nichols   "   "
7 Mabel   "   "   "
7 Ralph   "   "   "
7 Julia   "   "   "
7 Martha Alice   "   "   "
7 Mary   "

7 Ch. Fred Nichols and Elizabeth Jellay   La Grange, Ind.
7 Walter   Nichols   Orland, Ind.
7 Margie   "   "   "
7 Harry   "   "   "

GENEALOGICAL SECTION

  Ch. Lizzie Nichols and Rev. Alvin Weaver   Jonesboro, Ind.
7 *Charles C. Weaver   " "
7 Martha "   " "

  Ch. Susan Nichols and James A. Turner   Fenton, Mich.
7 Fanny Nichols   Turner   " "
7 Stanley Raymond   "   " "
7 James Donald   "   " "
7 Anna Louise   "   " "

  Ch. Anna Nichols and Huestis Beers   La Grange, Ind.
7 Bruce   Beers   " "
7 Henry   "   " "
7 Homer   "   " "

  Ch. Margie Nichols and Charles Dirrim   " "
7 William Dirrim   " "

  Ch. 5James Nichols and Isabelle Starkweather   Hartford, Conn.
6 James Loomis Nichols   accidentally shot in boyhood " "
6 Helen C. "   m. Harry A. Smith   " "
  Their Ch.
7 James Nichols   Smith
7 Harriet Helen   "

5 Beach Nichols   m. Adelia Fairchild   Newtown, Conn.
  Their Ch.
6 Harriet   Nichols   m. Dr. Henry Nichols   New Haven, Conn.
6 James Beach   "   "   Bessie Louise Dickinson   Roxbury, "
  Their Ch.
7 Helen Rachel   Nichols   Newtown, Conn.
7 Bessie Louise   "   " "

  Ch. 4 Drusus Nichols and Rebecca B. Graves   Sherman, Conn.
5 *Charles Graves Nichols m. Ella Burnell   English Prairie, Ind.
  Their Ch.
6 *Drusus Burnell   Nichols "   Jane Louise Shipman   " "
6 Mary   "   " "
6 Charles Stuart   "   " "
6 Samuel Burnell   "   m. Mary A. Samson   Homer, N. Y.
6 *Frank Morse   "   "   Rachel May Kenyon   Lima, Ind.
6 *Gunther C.   "   "   Grace Pauline Tryall   La Grange, Ind.

  Ch. Drusus B. Nichols and Jane Louise Shipman   Chicago, Ill.
7 James Howe   Nichols m. Edith French   Baker, Oregon
7 Drusus Holbrook   "   "   Irene Anna Whiting   Duluth, Minn.
7 Marion Williams   "   "   Chas. H. Evenson   Baker, Oregon

  Ch. Frank Morse Nichols and Rachel May Kenyon   Lima, Ind.
7 Charles Kenyon   "   " "
7 Frank Morse, Jr.,   "   " "

  Ch. Gunther C. Nichols and Grace Pauline Tryall   La Grange, Ind.
7 Margaret Ellen   "   " "

  Ch. Marion W. Nichols and Chas. H. Evenson   Baker, Oregon

GENEALOGICAL SECTION

8 Eleanor Nichols Evenson   Baker, Oregon

   Ch. 4Philo Nichols and Melinda Carr   La Grange, Ind.

5 Lucy Alice Nichols   m. Joseph W. Talmage   "   "

   Their Ch.

6 Mary Nichols Talmage   "   "

   Ch. 1Peter Nichols

2 Theophilus Nichols   m. Lucinda Noble   New Milford, Conn.
2 Peter   "   m. Polly Blackman   Newtown, Conn.
2 Hester   "   m. William Edwards   "   "
2 Margery   "   m. David Griffin   "   "
2 Sally   "   unm.
2 Simeon   "   m. Anna Curtis   "   "
2 John B.   "   m. Harriet Fairchild   "   "

   Ch. Theophilus Nichols and Lucinda Noble

3 *Charlotte Nichols   unm.
3 *William N.   "   m. Belle Blackman
3 *Ann   "   d. young
3 *Frances   "   m. Rev. George Rumney   Bethel, Conn.
3 *Henry T.   "   m. Abigail Skidmore   Newtown, Conn.

   Ch. William N. Nichols and Belle Blackman

4 William T. Nichols   m. Helen Hull
4 Henry D.   "

   Ch. 3Henry T. Nichols and Abigail Skidmore   Newtown, Conn.

4 Dr. Henry S.   Nichols   m. Harriet Nichols   New Haven, Conn.
4 Philo Hurd   "   unm.   Bridgeport, Conn.
4 Stella L.   "   m. Frederick Hall   "   "
4 Jessie A.   "   d. young
4 Walter Monroe "   m. Eva Birdsall   "   "
4 Arthur   "   d. young

   Ch. Dr. Henry S. Nichols and Harriet Nichols   New Haven, Conn.

5 Jessie Nichols   m. William Gilbert   New Haven, Conn.

   Their ch.

6 Margery Nichols Gilbert   "   "
6 Janet Nichols   "   "   "

   Ch. Stella Nichols and Frederick Hall   Bridgeport, Conn.

5 Pauline Nichols Hall   "   "
5 *Harold Hatch   "   "   "
5 Ruth Skidmore   "   "   "

   Ch. Walter M. Nichols and Eva Birdsall   "   "

5 Hazel Nichols   "   "

   Ch. 2Peter Nichols and Polly Blackman

3 *Harriet Nichols   m. Smith Botsford(no ch.) Huntington, Conn.
3 *Charles B.   "   m. Mary Botsford (no ch.) Newtown, Conn.
3 *Julia Ann   "   unm.   "   "

   Ch. 2Margery Nichols and David W. Griffen   "   "

3 *John Griffin   m. Julia Summers   "   "

   Their ch.

4 *George Griffin   m. Isabel Gilbert   Shelton, Conn.
4 Bruce N.   "   m. 1st *Annie Hinman
                           2nd Ida Daulley
4 Sarah   "   m. Marshall Sears

5 Clarence Sears, their ch.

   Ch. Bruce Griffin and Ida Dawley   Shelton, Conn.

5 Clarence Griffin   " "
5 John C.   "   " "

2   Ch. Simeon Nichols and Anna Curtis   Newtown, Conn.

3 Mary Alice Nichols   m. Dr. Alfred Starr (no ch.) Brooklyn, Conn.
3 George   "   unm.
3 Charlotte   "   m. Henry C. Miles   Milford, Conn.
3 Caroline   "   d. in girlhood   " "

   Ch. Charlotte Nichols and Henry C. Miles   " "

4 Henry C. C. Miles   " "

   Ch. 2John B. Nichols and Harriet Fairchild   Newtown, Conn.

3 Catharine Nichols   m. Charles Bouton (no ch.) Bethel, Conn.
3 George H.   "   m. Elizabeth Gunn   " "
3 John F.   "   m. Kate M. Schoonmaker   " "

   Ch. George H. Nichols and Elizabeth Gunn

4 George C. Nichols   " "
4 Julia E.   "   " "
4 *Mary   "   " "

   Ch. John F. Nichols and Kate M. Schoonmaker   " "

4 S. Alice Nichols   " "
4 John L.   "   " "
4 Kate S.   "   " "
4 Chas. B.   "   " "
4 Grace   "   " "

   Gr. Ch. George H. Nichols and Elizabeth Gunn   " "

5 Louise Steck Nichols   Bethel, Conn.
5 Mary   "   " "
5 George Richard "   " "
5 Philip   "   " "

NORTHROP

1 Jospeh Northrop first Northrop settler in Milford about 1640,
  m. Mary Norton.

2 Jeremiah their son b. 1654 m. Phoebe ——
   Their two sons first of the name in Newtown had home lots assigned to
   them in 1712.   Newtown, Conn.

3 Lieut. John Northrop   m. Mary Porter   " "
3 Benjamin   "   " Sarah Platt   " "

   Ch. 3Lieut. John Northrop and Mary Porter   " "

4 Jonathan Northrop   m. Ruth Booth   " "
4 Ruth   "   " Peter Ferris   " "
4 Mary   "   " Daniel Sherman   " "
4 John Jr.   "   " Lois Northrop   " "

   Lieut. John and John Jr. held the office of Town Clerk for 25 years.

GENEALOGICAL SECTION

Of the ten ch. of John Jr. and Lois Northrop.
5 Peter Northrop	m.	Lucy Sherman	Newtown, Conn.	
5 Mary "	"	Solomon Glover (See Glover)	"	"
5 Amy "	"	John Sanford (See Sanford)	"	"
5 John "	"	Nabby Baldwin	"	"

Ch. Peter Northrop annd Lucy Sherman " "
6 Walter Northrop	m.	1st Rebecca Northrop	"	"
	"	2nd Sally Platt	"	"
	"	3rd Mrs. Volucia Botsford	"	"
	"	4th Mrs. Emily L. Hoyt	"	"
6 Norman "	"	Eliza Selleck	"	"

Ch. Walter Northrop and Rebecca Northrop
7 *Charles Northrop	m.	Sophia Amelia Banks		
7 *Norman "		d. in infancy		

Ch. Walter Northrop and Sally Platt
7 *Walter Northrop, Jr.	m.	Emily Botsford	"	"
7 *Norman2 "	"	Julia Sanford		
7 *William N. "	"	Julia Lamberton	"	"
7 *Jerome "	"	Sarah Stuart	"	"

Ch. Walter Northrop and Emily Botsford " "
8 Sarah Eliza Northrop	m.	Birdsey Glover (See Glover)	"	"
8 *Annie Belle "	m.	Orrin B. Smith	Bethel, Conn.	
8 *Emeline A. "	"	William Rowell	Newtown, Conn.	

Ch. Norman Northrop and Julia Sanford " "
8 Sarah Maria Northrop	m.	Walter Glover (See Glover)	"	"
8 *Charles Wm. "	"	Alice Kewes	"	"
9 Maud A. Northrop	ch.	Alice Kewes & Charles W. Northrop	"	"
9 Julia Loretta "			"	"
8 *Charles Henry Northrop	ch.	Julia Lamberton & Wm. N. Northrop	"	"
8 John J. "			"	"
8 Mary Hattie "			"	"
9 *Mary Grace Northrop	ch.	Mary Grace Hammond & Charles H. Northrop	Newtown, Conn.	
9 Eleanor Louise "			"	"
9 Nelson William "			"	"
9 John Arthur Northrop	ch.	Hazel Pierce & John J. Northrop	"	"
9 Cora "			"	"
8 *Nellie L. Northrop	ch.	Sarah Stuart & Jerome Northrop	"	"
8 Sarah Frances "			"	"
8 Sarah Frances Northrop	m.	John Schermerhorn	"	"

5 Ch. John Northrop and Nabby Baldwin Newtown, Conn.
6 Nancy Northrop	m.	Capt. Oliver Northrop	"	"
6 Alonzo "	"	Mary Ann Skidmore	"	"
6 Nelson "	"	Mrs. Abigail Walker	"	"
6 David "	"	Sarah Emily Johnson	"	"
3 Benjamin Northrop	"	Sarah Platt	"	"

Of their eleven ch.
4 Benjamin Northrop Jr.	"	Sarah Prindle	"	"
4 Nathaniel "	"	1st Esther Gould	"	"
	"	2nd Rebecca	"	"

GENEALOGICAL SECTION

Ch. 4 Nathaniel Northrop and Esther Gould

5 Grace Northrop	m.	William Birch	Newtown, Conn.
5 Samuel "	"	Clarissa Johnson	" "
5 Jerusha "	"	Jacob Johnson (See Johnson)	" "

Ch. Samuel Northrop and Clarissa Johnson

6 Rebecca Northrop	m.	Walter Northrop	" "
6 Isaac "		Went to Wilmington N. C.	

Ch. 4 Benjamin Northrop and Sarah Prindle

5 Alanson Northrop	m.	Lydia Hull	" "

Their ch.

6 Oliver Northrop	m.	Nanny Northrop	" "
6 Cyrenius "	"	Phoebe Ann Parmelee	" "
6 Lydia Ann "	"	Timothy Benedict	" "
6 Elizur "	"	1st Charlotte Johnson	" "
		2nd Delia Sherwood	" "

Ch. Oliver Northrop and Nanny Northrop

7 Heman Northrop	m.	Fanny Dimon	" "
7 Horatio "	"	Louisa French	" "
7 Hosea "	"	Juliette Fairchild	" "

Ch. Heman Northrop and Fanny Dimon

8 *Annie Eliza Northrop	m.	Francis W. Platt	Waterbury, Conn.
8 *Lucy Amelia "	unm.		
8 George Wilbur "	"	Frances E. Merrill	Newtown, Conn.

Their ch.

9 Raymond G. Northrop			" "
9 *Roland D. "	m.	Caroline Tucker	
9 Mabel F. "	m.	John Gilbert	
10 Francis T. "	ch.	Caroline Tucker & Roland Northrop	" "

Ch. Horatio Northrop and Louisa French

8 Ella Louise Northrop	m.	Laura Skidmore (no ch.)	
8 *Oliver "	"	Mary Elizabeth Mallett	
8 Turney "	"	Novella Thorp	Easton, Conn.
9 Edith Hazel Northrop	ch.	Mary E. Mallett & Oliver Northrop	" "
9 Moses Stanley Northrop	ch.	Novella Thorp & Turney Northrop	" "
9 Elliot Sherwood "			

Ch. Hosea Northrop and Juliette Fairchild — Newtown, Conn.

8 Caroline E. Northrop	m.	Frederick C. Sanford	" "
8 Annie C. "	"	Arthur Wilson	
9 *Juliette F. Sanford	ch.	Caroline E. Northrop & Frederick C. Sanford	
9 Eva L. "			
10 Albert Sanford Boyson	ch.	Eva L. Sanford & Albert Boyson	

9 Annie Caroline Wilson
9 Mildred " ch. Annie C. Northrop & Arthur Wilson

Ch. Cyrenius Northrop and Phebe Ann Parmelee

7 *Mary Elizabeth Northrop   d. unm.
7 *Horace   "   m. Sylvia Nichols
7 *Lydia Ann   "   " Homer Dikeman (no ch.)

8 *Mary Elizabeth Northrop
8 Emma Jane   "
8 Lydia Augusta "   ch. Sylvia Nichols & Horace Northrop
8 Clara Louise   "
8 William Nichols "

Ch. Elizur Northrop and Charlotte Johnson

7 Juliette Northrop   m. Dr. Wm. H. Bronson
7 Emily   "   " Jerome Botsford (See Botsford)
7 Harriet   "   " Dr. Oliver M. Allen
7 Charlotte   "   " Hiram Pulling

Ch. Elizur Northrop   & Delia Sherwood 2nd wife

7 John Northrop   m. Mary Tomlinson
7 Phebe Ann Northrop " Prosper Beach

PARMELEE

Stephen Parmelee was born in Guilford, Conn., in 1699, and moved to Newtown early in 1700.

1 Stephen Parmelee   m. Elizabeth Baldwin
2 Nathaniel b. 1694   " Althea Whitmore

Their Ch.

3 Rufus   Parmelee   " Diama Bundy no ch.   Newtown, Conn.
3 Olive   "   " Burr Turney   "   "
3 Levi   "   " Polly Beers   "   "
3 Hiram   "   " Betsey Winton   "   "
3 Eloise   "   " Bradley Hull   "   "
3 Hermon   "   m. 1st Polly Fairweather Newtown, Conn.
             " 2nd Polly Peck
3 Polly Ann   "   " David Corning

Ch. Levi Parmelee and Polly Beers

4 *Julia Ann Parmelee   m. Charles Short   Derby, Conn.
4 *Grandison   "   " Phebe Lattin no ch.   Newtown, Conn.
4 *George   "   " 1st Rebecca Benedict no ch. " "
                         " 2nd Ada Summers no ch.   " "
4 *Theodore   "   " 1st Margaret Morehouse no ch. " "
                         " 2nd Lydia Patterson no ch.
4 *Fanny   "   " George French

Ch. Julia A. Parmelee and Charles Short

5 *Edwin   Short   m. 1st Augusta Blackman   Bethel, Conn.
                     " 2nd Mary Blackman (see Blackman) "
5 *Mary   "   d. unm.   Bethel, Conn.
5 *Rufus   "   " Susan Blackman   " "
5 *Louise   "   " Robert Brown
5 Alfred   "   " 1st Sarah Warner   Plymouth, Conn.
                     " 2nd Sarah Wilson no ch.
                     " 3rd Sarah Whitaker no ch

5 Emily	Short	m.	Robert Dauchy	Bethel, Conn.
5 *Levi	"	"	Emily Durant	" "
5 Arletta	"	"	George Welch	Meriden, Conn.
5 Charles	"	"	Irene Ferry	

Ch. Rufus Short and Susan Blackman

6 Julia	Short	m.	Theodore M. Ferry
6 Bennett	"	"	Laura Kyle

Ch. Julia Short and Theodore Ferry

7 Royal   Ferry
7 Harold   "
7 Leonard   "
7 Ruth   "

Ch. Bennett Short and Laura Kyle

7 Rufus   Short
7 Julia   "
7 Helen   "
7 Samuel   "
7 Bennett   "

Ch. Louise Short and Robert Brown

6 Robert	Brown		
6 Alfred W.	"	m.	Hattie Haugh

Their Ch.

7 Leon   Brown
7 Edward   "

6 *Jessie Short   Ch. Sarah Warner & Alfred Short

Ch. Emily Short and Robert Dauchy   Bethel, Conn.

6 Samuel E.	Dauchy	m.	Sophia Comstock	Westfield, N. J.
6 William O.	"	"	Emma Foulds	Stamford, Conn.

Catherine S.   "   ch. Sophia Comstock & Samuel E. Dauchy

7 Leila G.   Dauchy ch. Emma Foulds & William O. Dauchy

6 Frank Short ch. Emily Durant & Levi Short

Ch. Arletta Short and George Welch   Meriden, Conn.

6 George	Welch		
6 *Gertrude	"		d. in young womanhood " "

Ch. Charles Short and Irene Ferry   Bethel, "

6 Mabel	Short	m.	George A. Osborne
6 Susie	"	"	James G. Matthews
6 Charles	"	"	Ruth K. Hamm

Ch. Mabel Short and George A. Osborne

7 Marion Irene   Osborn
7 Elizabeth Grace   "

Ch. Susie Short and James G. Matthews

7 James Gordon Matthews
7 Susie Gay "
7 Jean Short "

3 ch. Hiram Parmelee and Betsey Winton   Newtown, Conn.

4 John	Parmelee	m.	Mary B. Sherman	" "
5 David	"		their ch.	" "

3 Ch. Hermon Parmelee and Polly Fairweather   " "

4 Peter Parmelee   m. Abba J. Leavenworth no ch. " "

Ch. Hermon Parmelee and Polly Peck

4 Marietta	Parmelee	m.	Abram J. Whitney	Bethel, Conn.
4 Sarah	"	"	Jerome Green	" "
4 *Angeline	"	"	Chas Hubbell	Stepney, "
4 Emma	"	"	Chas Barnum	Norwalk, "

PECK

1Joseph Peck and 2Joseph resided in Milford having removed there from New Haven in 1649.

Of the many children of 2Joseph only 3Joseph, 3Ephraim and 3Heth came to Newtown.

The name of 3Joseph appears as Town Clerk on many of the early records.

3 Joseph Peck	m.	Abigail Baldwin	Newtown, Conn.
3 Ephraim "	m.	Sarah Ford	" "
3 Heth "	m.	Hannah Camp	" "

Ch. of 3Joseph

4 Joseph Peck	m.	Rebecca Shepard	" "
4 Moses "	m.	Elizabeth Baldwin	" "
4 John "	m.	Bethiah Booth	" "

Ch. of 3Ephraim

4 Henry Peck	m.	1st Ann Smith 2nd Hannah Leavenworth	" "
4 Ephraim "	m.	Sarah Porter	
4 Gideon "	m.	Abiah Smith	
4 Ebenezer "	m.	Sarah Booth	

Ch. of 3Heth

4 Heth Peck	m.	Mary Skidmore	Newtown, Conn.
4 Samuel "	m.	Sarah Skidmore	" "
4 Amos "	m.	Sarah Lobdell	" "

Ch. of 4Joseph

5 Violet Peck	m.	Job Northrop	" "
5 Grace "	m.	Jotham Sherman, 1st wife	" "
5 John "	m.	Emily Burritt	" "
5 David "	m.	Mary Stilson	" "

Ch. of 5David

6 David Peck   m. Prudence Glover

Ch. of 6David

GENEALOGICAL SECTION

7 Dillison Peck   m. Sarah Ann Crofut

   Their ch.

8 Augustus Peck   m. Louise Gillette   Newtown, Conn.
8 Eliza Jane   "   m. George Botsford   "   "

   Ch. Augustus Peck and Louisa Gillette   "   "

9 Ella   Peck   m. Cornelius B. Taylor   "   "
9 Bertha   "   m. Carlos Stilson (no ch.) "   "

   Ch. Ella Peck and Cornelius Taylor   "   "

10 Mabel Taylor   m. Frederick Duncombe   "   "
10*Jessie   "   m. Leonard M. Johnson   "   "

   Ch. Mabel Taylor and Frederick Duncombe

11 Frederick Taylor Duncombe
11 Raynor Lockwood   "

   Ch. *Jessie Taylor and Leonard M. Johnson   "   "

11 Byron Taylor Johnson

   Ch. 8Eliza J. Peck and George Botsford

9 Mary Botsford   m. Hobart Fairchild (See Fairchild)

   Ch. 4Moses, son of 3Joseph

5 Enos Peck   m. Sibyl Griffen   Newtown, Conn.
5 Dan   "   m. Hannah Peck
  Son of 4Henry
5 Zalmon Peck   m. Zilpha Hard, 1st   "   "
                    Mrs. Sarah Booth, 2nd

   Their ch.

6 Zerah S. Peck   m. Clara Smith   Brookfield, Conn.
6 Ezekiel   "   m. Sarah Ann Johnson, 1st Newtown, Conn.
                    Betsey Briscoe, 2nd

   Ch. Zerah S. Peck and Clara Smith

7 Ralph B. Peck   m. Caroline Merwin   Brookfield, Conn.
7 Harriet   "   m. Wm. B. Glover   Newtown, Conn.
7 Sophia   "   m. John Cornwall   Bridgeport, Conn.

   Ch. 6Ezekiel, son of 5Zalmon

7 Zilpha Peck   m. Alva B. Beecher   Newtown, Conn.
7 Zalmon Peck   m Polly Lum   Newtown, Conn.
   Served as postmaster 26 years.

   Their ch.

8 Henry S. Peck   m. Isabella Barton   Waterbury, Conn
   Served in civil war.
8 Austin L. Peck   m. Susan Root   Hartford, Conn.
   Served in Civil War.
8 Mary Frances Peck   m. *Col. R. Cheves   Macon, Ga.
                    Served in Civil War.

9 Florence Peck   Isabella Barton
9 Burton   "   ch.   &
                    Henry S. Peck

9 Edward A. Peck   Susan Root
9 Harry H.   "   ch.   &
9 Theodore   "   Austin L. Peck

Ch. of 4Ephraim

5 Nathan Peck	m.	Hulda Fabrique	Newtown, Conn.
5 Levirus "	m.	Anna Wheeler	" "
5 Isaac "	m.	Lucy Ferris	" "

Ch. 4Gideon, son of 3Ephraim

5 Oliver Peck	m.	Lucy Sickles	" "
5 Gideon "	m.	Betsey Briscoe	" "
5 Abner "	m.	Jane Botsford	" "

Ch. 4Ebenezer

5 Eunice Peck	m.	Philo Blackman. (See Blackman)	Brookfield, Conn.
5 James "	m.	Sarah Coburn dau. d. in young womanhood	Newtown, Conn.

Ch. of 4Heth

5 Elnathan "   m. Jerusha Blackman, 1st   "   "
              Sarah Beers Merwin, 2nd   "   "

Ch. 4Samuel, son of 3Heth.

5 Isaac Peck	m.	Aurelia Botsford	" "
5 Annis "	m.	Richard Botsford (See Botsford)	"
5 Clarissa "	m.	Benjamin C. Glover (See Glover)	"
5 David "	m.	Rebecca Beers, 1st	Newtown, Conn.
	m.	Mrs. Harriet Booth, 2nd	" "
5 Joanna "	m.	Gould Curtis (See Curtis)	" "

Ch. 5David

6 Simeon B. Peck   m. Caroline Curtis, 1st   "   "
                      Elizabeth Curtis Peck, 2nd   "   "

7 *Abner   Peck   Montgomery, Ala.
7 *Henry   "   Caroline Curtis
7 David Curtis "   ch.   &
                           Simeon B. Peck   Newtown, Conn.

                           Elizabeth Curtis Peck   "   "
7 Charles Gould "   ch.   &
                           Simeon B. Peck   "   "

Ch. Abner Peck and Mary Smith, 1st wife   Montgomery, Ala.

8 Caroline Rebecca Peck   m. Charles F. Ashurst   Savannah, Ga.

Ch. Abner Peck and Sarah E. C. Thompson, 2nd wife

8 Clara Pauline Peck   m. Chester Curtis (no ch.)

8 William Dingley Peck   m. Eugenia Dillard, 1st   Montgomery, Ala.
                             Mrs. Edson, 2nd
8 Charlotte Curtis "   m. A. L. Greene, (no ch.) Atlanta, Ga.

Ch. Caroline R. Peck and Chas. F. Ashurst

9 Julia Ashurst   m. F. M. Oliver
9 Mable   "   m. R. B. Flinn
9 *Charles Curtis Ashurst

10 Joseph McDonald Oliver   Julia Ashurst   Savannah, Ga.
10 Frances Whitington " ch.   &
10 Caroline Louise   "   F. M. Oliver   Savannah, Ga.

GENEALOGICAL SECTION

10 William Flinn	ch.	Mable Ashurst & R. B. Flinn	New York, N. Y.
9 Emily Peck 9 Weenona "	ch.	Eugenia Dillard 1st wife & William Dingley Peck	Montgomery, Ala.
9 Margaret "	ch.	Mrs. Edson, 2nd wife & William Dingley Peck	
8 *Ada Peck 8 *Cora "	ch.	Helen Booth, 1st wife & David C. Peck Agnes Booth, 2nd wife	Newtown, Conn. " "

Ch. 5Dan, son 4Moses   Newtown, Conn.

6 Marcia Peck	unm.		" "
6 Charles "	m.	Freelove Nash	" "
6 Hezekiah "	"	Maria W. Hubbell	" "
6 Hermon "	"	Maria Hawley	" "
6 Lorin "	"	Jane Ann Lawrence	" "
7 *Charles Henry Peck " " "	ch.	Freelove Nash & Charles Peck	" " " "
*Lewis Henry Peck Drowned in Housatonic river Arthur Treat Nettleton	m.	Hannah D. Fairchild Adopted by Hannah D. Fairchild & Adopted by Charles H. Peck	" " " " " " " "
" " "	m.	*Jennie Morris	" "
7 John Howard Peck	ch.	Maria W. Hubbell & Hezekiah Peck	Brookfield, Conn. Newtown, Conn.
John Howard Peck	m.	Amie Burr	

Ch. Hermon Peck and Maria Hawley   Newtown, Conn.

7 *Sylvia Peck	m.	Edward T. Clark	" "
7 *Elizabeth "	"	James Ashman Morris	Bridgeport "
7 *Edward "		Died at 18 years.	
7 Hermon H. "	m.	Emma French	Newtown, Conn.
8 *Frank Clark	ch.	Sylvia Peck & Edward T. Clark	" "
8 *Edward, infant son 8 Annie Morris	ch.	Elizabeth Peck & James A. Morris	Bridgeport, "
8 Sylvia Marion Peck	ch.	Emma French & Hermon H. Peck	Newtown, Conn. " "
7 Arthur L. Peck 7 Edward "	ch.	Jane Ann Lawrence & Lorrin Peck	" " " "
8 Edith Peck 8 *Arthur, Jr. "	ch.	Cornelia Lamberton & Arthur L. Peck	" " " "

GENEALOGICAL SECTION

9 Ethel May Peck		Newtown, Conn.
9 Harold Arthur "	ch. Bertha Mead & Arthur Peck, Jr.	" "
9 Evelyn Marion "		" "
8 Ada Marsh Peck		Brookfield, Conn.
8 Alice Judd "	ch. Stella Judd & Edward Peck	" "
8 George "		" "
9 George Hatch	ch. Ada Marsh Peck & George Hatch	" "
9 Edward Burr	ch. Alice Judd Peck & Willis Burr	" "
9 Dorothy Peck		" "
9 Alice "		
9 George "	ch. Miriam Smith & George Peck	" "
9 Miriam "		
9 Marguerite "		

Ch. 5Abner, son 4Gideon

6 George C. Peck	m. Ann Tomlinson	
6 Jane Ann "	" Daniel Lewis Booth (See Booth)	

Ch. George C. Peck and Ann Tomlinson   Newtown, Conn.

7 John F. Peck served in Civil War; was 2nd Lieut.; promoted to 1st Lieut. Captured June 24, 1863.

7 *Lieut. John F. Peck	m. Nellie Ackley	
7 *Gideon "	unm.	
7 Homer A. "	" Mary Ann Tuthill	
7 Cornelius "	" Mary Brown (no ch.)	
7 Abbie L. "	unm. Librarian for many years of Beach Memorial Library.	
7 Harriet M. "	unm.	
8 Ira J. "	ch. Nellie Ackley & Lieut. John F. Peck	
8 Myra Ackley "		
" " "	m. John Curtis Medcalf	
8 George Anna Eliot Peck	ch. Mary Ann Tuthill & Homer A. Peck	
8 Louise H. "		
9 Elizabeth Eliot Higby	ch. Louise H. Peck & Edward J. Higby	

Ch. 5Isaac Peck, son of 4Samuel

6 Jabez Botsford Peck	m. Henrietta Jarvis	Newtown, Conn.
6 Harriet "	" Charles Beers (See Beers)	" "
6 Robert C. "	" 1st Abigail Booth (no ch.)	" "
	" 2nd Mary Lake (see Lake)	" "
	" 3rd Elizabeth Curtis (See Curtis)	"
6 Sarah E. "	" George Beers (See Beers)	Newtown, Conn.

Ch. 6Jabez Botsford Peck and Henrietta Jarvis   " "

7 *Charles A. Peck	m. Mary E. Oliver	Brooklyn, N. Y.
7 *Elizabeth J. "	" Samuel J. Pinckney	" "
7 *Albert W. "	" Louise Booth	Newtown, Conn.
7 *Nelson J. "	d. in service of his country in Civil War.	

GENEALOGICAL SECTION

8 Charles B. Peck	Mary E. Oliver	Brooklyn, N. Y.
8 *William J. " ch.	&	" "
8 Mary E. "	Charles A. Peck	" "
8 *Henry W. Pinckney	Elizabeth J. Peck	" "
8 Jennie E. " ch.	&	" "
8 *Elizabeth T. "	Samuel J. Pinckney	" "
8 Robert N. Peck	Louisa W. Booth	Bridgeport, Conn.
8 Dr. Charles H. Peck ch.	&	
8 Grace L. "	Capt. Albert W. Peck	Newtown, Conn.
8 Albert W. Jr. "	With Mackay Unit of Roosevelt Hospital in France.	

Capt. Peck enlisted as private in Co. D, 17th Conn. V. I., July 1862. Was soon made Sergeant; was next made 2nd Lieut. and after the battle of Chancellorsville was promoted to be 1st Lieut. His next promotion was June 29, 1865 when he became Captain. He is now, March 1918, proud of the fact that two of his sons and one grandson are doing great things in France for their country and the Allies against Germany. He died at Port Chester, N. Y. April, 1918.

9 Eugene Curtis Peck	Helen Curtis	New Britain, Conn.
9 Louise " ch.	&	
9 Margaret "	Robert N. Peck	
9 *Charles Howard Peck,Jr.	Betsey Chaffee	
9 Nelson Chaffee " ch.	&	
9 Dexter "	Dr. Charles H. Peck	

Dr. Charles H. Peck, as Director of the Mackay Unit of the Roosevelt Hospital of New York City, comprising a large company of Surgeons, Physicians and Nurses, sailed July 2, 1917 for France to establish a Base Hospital close to the American Headquarters in France. His oldest son, Charles Howard Peck, Jr. and his younger brother, Albert W. Peck, Jr., Capt. Albert Peck's youngest son, accompanied him. Since his arrival in France, Dr. Charles H. Peck has been appointed Asst. General Director of Surgery of the American Expeditionary Forces in France. Newtown feels honored by the honor so worthily bestowed upon him. Charles Howard Jr. d. in hospital in France, March, 1918.

Dr. Peck was commissioned Lieut. Col. while in France. Since returning to U. S. he received, August 24th 1918, his commission as Colonel.

9 *Eugenia Minor	Grace L. Peck	Port Chester, N. Y.
9 Ralph " ch.	&	
9 Marion "	James Minor	

Ch. 5Isaac, son 4Eph.

6 *Polly Ann Peck	m. Ebenezer Griffen	Newtown, Conn.
6 *Fanny "	m. David Blackman	" "
6 *Lucy "	m. Gershom Dimon	" "
6 *Levi "	m. Marcia Beers	" "
	Marcia Beers	Newtown, Conn.
7 *Cornelia Peck ch.	&	
	Levi Peck	" "
	Cornelia Peck	" "
8 Anna Cornelia Judson ch.	&	
	John Judson	
8 Anna Cornelia Judson	m. Henry Tucker	

Ch. 5Levirus, son 4Eph.

6 Thomas W. Peck	m. Sarah Ann Toucey	" "
6 Polly "	m. Jeremiah Beers (See Beers)	" "
6 Richard "	unm.	

GENEALOGICAL SECTION

Ch. 6Thomas Wheeler Peck and Sarah Ann Toucey, 1st wife.
Theodosia Coe, 2nd wife

7	*Fanny Peck	m.	Noah Smith	
7	*Alosia "	m.	Harley Sanford	Bridgewater, Conn.
7	*Richard W. "	m.	Sarah Cadwelder	Hillsville, Pa.
7	*Abel T. "	m.	Huldah Hawley	Newtown, Conn.
7	*John B. "	m.	Charlotte Colt	" "

Ch. John B. Peck and Charlotte Colt " "

| 8 | Fanny C. Peck | m. | Levi C. Morris | " " |
| 8 | John R. " | m. | Fanny Taylor | " " |

Ch. Fanny C. Peck and Levi C. Morris " "

9	Curtis Peck Morris	m.	Mabel Denton	Bridgeport, Conn.
9	Mabel "	m.	Howell Wright	Cleveland, Ohio
9	Levi Phillips "	m.	Maylah Hawley Hallock	Bridgeport, Conn.

With American army in France.

10 Curtis Denton Morris ch. Mabel Denton
& Curtis P. Morris " "

10 Edwin Kingsbury Wright Mabel Morris Cleveland, Ohio
10 Francis Howell " ch. &
10 Morris " Howell Wright " "

Ch. John R. Peck and Fanny Taylor

| 9 | Harley Taylor Peck | m. | Augusta Campbell | |
| 9 | Ethel " | m. | Jesse Woodhill | |

With American Army in France

9	*Richard "	d. in infancy	
9	James "	With American Army in France	
9	Wesley "	m. Louise Mary Dubret	Newtown, Conn.

10 Harley Taylor Peck, Jr. Augusta Campbell
10 John Murray " ch. &
10 Katherine Campbell Peck Harley T. Peck

Ch. 5John, son of 4Joseph

6	Comfort Peck	m.	Oliver Toucey (See Toucey)
6	Lavinia "	"	Joseph Burritt
6	Clara "	"	John Johnson (See Johnson)

Ch. 5David, son of 4Joseph Newtown, Conn.

6	David Peck	m.	Prudence Glover	" "
6	Hannah "	"	Chauncey Botsford (See Botsford)	
6	Daniel "	"	Sally Ann Sherwood	Newtown, Conn.

Ch. 5Enos, son of 4Moses " "

| 6 | Wooster Peck | m. | Elizabeth Marshall | " " |
| 6 | Esther " | " | Rufus Somers | " " |

Ch. 6Wooster Peck, and Elizabeth Marshall

7	Elizabeth Peck	m.	Henry Fairchild (no ch.)	Newtown, Conn.
7	Elliott M. "	"	Jane Gray	
7	Henrietta M. "	"	Frederick Lathrop	Roxbury, "

Ch. Elliott M. Peck and Jane Gray

8	Fanny Peck	m.	Charles Sherman	Monroe "
8	Henry "	"	Margaret Reynolds	
8	Elliott "	"	1st Cora Booth	Newtown, "
		"	2nd Flora Curtis	

GENEALOGICAL SECTION

8 William Peck	m.	1st Jane Colgan	
	"	2nd Dorothy Vincent	
8 John Somers "	"	Minnie B. Hubbell	Brookfield, Conn.
8 Dr. George "			New Rochelle, N. Y.

9 Elliott Marshal Peck
9 Marion "
9 Dorothy "   ch.   Margaret Reynolds
9 John "   &
                             Henry Peck   Newtown, "

9 Jennie Peck   ch.   Jane Colgan   "   "
                             &
                             William Peck   "   "

Ch. Elliot Peck and Cora Booth 1st wife   "   "

9 Eugene Marshall Peck m. Florence Clarke (no. ch)   "   "
9 Tracy Booth "   "   Maude Estelle Ives (no. ch.) "   "
9 Cora May "   "   Clifford Russell   "   "

9 Madge Peck   ch.   Flora Curtis 2nd wife
9 Dr. Earl "   &
                             Elliot Peck (See Doctors)

10 Benjamin Russell   Cora May Peck
10 Anna May "   ch.   &
10 Sterling "   Clifford Russell

10 Elliott Peck Brown ch. Madge Peck   Newtown, Conn.
                             &
                             Homer Brown

Ch. 7 Henrietta Peck and Frederick Lathrop b.   Roxbury, Conn.

8 James Marshall Lathrop m. *Kate A. Lawrence   "   "
8 Emma Frances "   "   Rev. David Evan Jones   Ellington, "
8 Annette Augusta "   "   Walter H. Young   Hebron, Va.
8 *Frederick Amasa "   d. in 15th year   "   "
8 Herbert Wooster "   "   1st Laura Young   "   "
                               2nd Sarah Beck   "   "

9 *Marie Henrietta Jones ch. Emma F. Lathrop   Ellington, Conn.
9 Gwendolin M. "   &
                                Rev. David E. Jones   "   "

10 David Allen Giddings
10 Edwin Lathrop "   Gwendolin M. Jones   Hartford, "
10 Frances Keep "   ch.   &
10 Mary Marshall "   David Allen Giddings   "   "

9 Jessie Florence Young
9 Chas. W. Russell "
9 Mary Marshall "   ch.   Annette A. Lathrop   Hebron, Va.
9 Walter Fred. Lear "   &
9 Annette V. H. "   Walter H. Young   "   "

PERRY

Desc. of 1 Dr. Bennett Perry. (See Doctors)   Newtown, Conn.

2 Sally Perry m. Hon. Curtis Hinman   Southbury, Conn.
   Their Ch.

3 Caroline P. Hinman   m. Barnabas Root   Thomaston, Conn.

3 *Robert Curtis "
3 *Catherine E. "

GENEALOGICAL SECTION

Ch. Caroline P. Hinman and Barnabas Root — Thomaston, Conn.

4 *Charles W. Root
4 Edward Curtis "   m. Amelia Renfree   "   "
4 *Howard Perry "

Ch. Edward Curtis Root and Amelia Renfree

5 *Walter Edward Root
5 Lena Caroline   "   m. Rev. Louis I. Belden   Hartford, Conn.
5 Fannie Maria   "   " Dr. John M. Robinson   Duluth, Minn.
5 Grace Mary   "   " Edward Hotchkiss   Thomaston, Conn.
5 *Ethel   "
5 *Theodore Edward "

Ch. Lena Caroline Root and Rev. Louis I. Belden, Hartford, Conn.

6*Beulah   Belden
6 Edward Root   "
6 Richard Louis   "
6 Francis Root   "
6 Elizabeth   "

Ch. Grace Mary Root and Edward Hotchkiss — Thomaston, Conn.

6 Gardner Hinman Hotchkiss
6 Hayden Renfree   "
6 Dorothy Grace   "
6 Stanley Root   "
6 Frances Amelia   "

PLATT

Richard Platt came to this country from England in 1638 and settled in Milford. Among the capstones of the Memorial Bridge in Milford is one with this inscription:

"Deacon Richard Platt
Obit, 1684,
Mary His Wife."

It is stated that it was placed there "by the liberality and thoughtfulness of two of his descendants. Prof. Johnson T. Platt of New Haven, and Theron E. Platt of Newtown.

2 Isaac son of 1Richard   m. Elizabeth Wood
3 Jonas   Platt   m. Sarah Scudder
4 Obadiah   "   " 1st Mary Smith
5 Obadiah   "   " 2nd Thankful Scudder
6 Jarvis   "   " Ann Nichols
7 David   "   " Lucretia Toucey
8 Philo Toucey "   " Jeanette Tuttle
9 Johnson T. "   " Mary Jay Pettee (See Newtown Lawyers)
9 Theron E.   "   " Mary E. Russell   Newtown, Conn.
    Their son
10 Philo T.   "   " Elsie Sanford

11 Raymond Platt   ch.   Elsie Sanford
                            &
                            Philo T. Platt

GENEALOGICAL SECTION

1 "Richard Platt and Mary his wife were among the original proprietors of Newtown."

2 Josiah	Platt	m.	Sarah Canfield	
3 Josiah	"	"	Sarah Sanford	
4 Nathan	"	"	Ruby Smith	
5 Levi Smith	"	"	Patty Hawley	Bethel, Conn.

Ch. Levi Smith and Patty Hawley

6 Emmon	Platt		unm.
6 Mary Ann	"		unm.
6 William	"	m.	Fanny Sherman Newtown, Conn.
6 Lorin	"	"	Sarah Sherman
6 Elizabeth	"	"	Harrison Weed (See Fairchild record)

Ch. William Platt and Fanny Sherman   Newtown, Conn.

7 *Francis William Platt		m.	Annie Northrop	" "
7 *Emily Jane	"			
7 Charles Smith	"	"	Ella Eoline Ingraham	North Adams, Mass
7 *Fannie E.	"		d. young	
7 *Roger Sherman	"		d. at 18 years.	Newtown, Conn.
8 Charles Roy	Platt		Ella E. Ingraham	
8 Arthur Ingraham	"	ch.	&	
8 Agnes Electra	"		Prof. Charles S. Platt	" "

Many years organist of Trinity Church.

8 Arthur Ingraham "   m. Elizabeth Walker Rylands, Bridgeport Ct.

1 Ephraim	Platt	m.	Polly Kimberley	Newtown, Conn.

Their Ch.

2 Harry	"	"	1st Tryphena Crofut	" "
			2nd Hannah Barnum	" "
			3rd Julia Perkins	" "
2 Bennett	"	"	Augusta Shepard	" "
2 Charlotte	"	"	Capt. Hart Shepard	" "
2 Laura	"	"	William Scudder	Kalamazoo, Mich.

Ch. Harry Platt and Tryphena Crofut

3 Jerome	Platt	m.	1st Martha Joyce	Newtown, Conn.
3 Jerome	"		2nd Ida McLaughlin	New York, N. Y.
3 Charles	"	m.	—— Bassett	
3 Elizabeth	"	"	Bennett Blackman	Newtown, Conn.

Ch. Jerome Platt and Martha Joyce   "   "

4 Caroline	Platt	m.	1st Ambrose Taylor	Bridgeport "
		"	2nd George Soper	New York, N. Y.
4 Alice	"	"	Dr. W. Downs	" "
4 Lillian	"	"	Frank Bennett	" "
4 Henry	"			
4 Edmund	"	"	Alice Camp	Newtown, Conn.

5 Jerome Bennett	ch.	Lillian Platt & Frank Bennett Newtown, Conn.
5 Percival Camp Platt	ch.	Alice Camp & Edmund Platt Newtown, Conn.

Percival Camp Platt in U. S. Hospital Service under Dr. Charles H. Peck Assistant Director of Surgery of American Expeditionary Forces in France.

GENEALOGICAL SECTION

1 Eli Platt   m. Betsey Underhill   Newtown, Conn.
  Their Ch.
2 Wanzer Platt
2 Louisa "   " Donald Blackman (see Blackman)
2 Horace "   " Mabel Hill   Newtown, Conn.
  Ch. Horace Platt and Mabel Hill   "   "
3 Gershom Platt   m. Mary Sherwood (no ch.)   "   "
3 Moses Hill "   " Frances Crane   Redding, Conn.
3 Francis Wm. "   Mary Sweezey   Newtown, Conn.

4 Howard Crane Platt
4 Arthur "   ch. Frances Crane   Redding, Conn.
4 Clarence "   &
4 Francis Horace "   Moses Hill Platt

4 Charles Wilbur "
4 Elliott Hill "   ch. Mary Sweezey   Newtown, Conn.
4 May Adella "   &
4 Russell Lawrence "   Francis Wm. Platt

John Platt was an early settler in Newtown. The records show that he conveyed land in the town to his sons, Ebenezer, John and Moses in 1741. Probably the Moses whose family record was dicovered some time ago in Nora, Ill.

"December 6th 1770, Moses Platt and Hannah Judson joined in marriage, I in the 24th year of my age, she in her 18th."

Mehitable	Platt	b. Jan. 10th, 1772
Anna	"	b. Oct. 28th, 1775
Agur	"	b. Oct. 31st, 1775
Polly	"	b. Sept. 13th, 1777
Betsey	"	b. Aug. 24th, 1779
David	"	b. Sept. 6th, 1781
Sally	"	b. March 2nd, 1783
Moses	"	b. Jan. 29th, 1785
Prarnel	"	b. Nov. 8th, 1786
Mercy	"	b. March 31st, 1788
		m. Lieut. Thomas Toucey
Ely	"	b. Aug. 24th, 1789
		died Jan. 12th, 1790
Ely 2nd	"	b. Sept. 13th, 1790
		died Jan. 2nd, 1791
Judson	"	b. Nov. 8th, 1791
		m. Laura Mallory
Zerah	"	b. Feb. 5th, 1793
Livy	"	b. Dec. 22nd, 1795
Betsey	"	died Oct. 25th, 1796, aged 17 yrs.
Betsey&Nanie	"	b. Nov. 28th, 1798
Betsey	"	m. Isaac Nichols (see Nichols)
Nanie	"	died Jan. 26th, 1799
Hannah	"	died Sept. 11th, 1816

aged 63 yrs. 11 mo. and 11 days, the mother of seventeen children.
Moses Platt   died Sept. 18th, 1819
aged 73 yrs.
Judson Platt   son of Moses & Hannah Platt
" "   m. Laura Mallory
  Their Ch.
Emily Platt   m. 1st Eli Morris
  Their Ch.
Levi C. Morris   m. Fannie C. Peck (See Peck)
*Jennie "   " Arthur Treat Nettleton
Emily Platt Morris   " 2nd George Couch
  George Couch, their ch.

PRINDLE

1 William Prindle m. Mary Desborough

2 Ebenezer Prindle was born at New Haven, Conn. in 1661, m. Elizabeth Hubby. They first removed to Milford, Conn. in 1703. Then removed to Newtown, in 1709-10. He was one of the original proprietors of Newtown in 1710. The minutes of town meetings contain many references to Ebenezer Prindle as a prominent citizen as well as to his children.

2 Joseph, b. 1663, in New Haven is believed to have been with Rev. Samuel Johnson one of the founders of the Episcopal Church in West Haven.
He m. Mary Brown.

3 Samuel, m. Mary Smith. His father deeded him land in Newtown in 1715.
3 Joseph jr., son of 2Joseph, m. Elizabeth Thomas   Newtown, Conn.
3 Joseph Prindle son of 2Ebenezer m. 1st Mary Adams   "   "

    2nd Sarah Kimberly

4 Ann ch. 3Joseph and Mary Adams m. Thomas Sharpe   "   "

      ch. 3Joseph and Sarah Kimberly   "   "

4 Mary	Prindle	m. John Skidmore (See Skidmore)	" "
4 Sarah	"	m. Benjamin Northrop	(See Northrop)
4 Capt. Joseph	"	m. Huldah Glover	Newtown, Conn.
4 Lieut. Abel	"	m. Amaryllis Toucey	
4 Joel	"	m. Sabra Kimberly	
4 Jonathan	"	m. Damaris Peck	Newtown, Conn.
4 Experience	"	m. Jeptha Hubbell	" "
4 Ebenezer	"		
4 Eliada	"	m. Sarah Beers	
4 Nathan	"	m. Ann Bristol	" "
4 Joanna	"	m. 1st Zachariah Brinsmade	
		2nd Richard Peet	

4 Ch. Capt. Joseph Prindle and Huldah Glover   Newtown, Conn.

5 Zada	Prindle	m. David Hinman	" "
5 Phedemia	"	m. Clark Baldwin	" "
5 Cyrus	"	m. Polly Beers	" "
5 Lazarus	"	m. Joanna Glover	" "
5 Philemon	"	m. Nannie Ferris	" "
5 Huldah	"	m. Joel Sanford	New Milford, Conn.

    Ch. Cyrus Prindle and Polly Beers   Newtown, Conn.

6 *Lewis Beers	Prindle	m. Betty Ferris	" "
6 *Maria	"	unm.	
6 *Polly Ann	"	unm.	

    Ch. Lewis B. Prindle and Betty Ferris   Newtown, Conn.

7 *Albert Lewis	Prindle	m. Polly Ann Thorpe	" "
7 *Maria	"	m. Daniel Picket	Bethel, Conn.
7 *William Beers	"	m. Maria Shepard	Newtown, Conn.
7 *Angeline	"	m. 1st Czar Plumb; 2nd Homer Hayes; 3rd Harson Twitchell; 4th C. C. Warner.	
7 *Mary	"	m. Samuel W. Trowbridge	Newtown, Conn.

8 Sarah Maria   "   ch. Polly Ann Thorpe & Albert L. Prindle

    "   "   m. Asaph Hodges   Waterbury, Conn

    Their Ch.

9 Miriam	Hodges	d. in infancy	" "
9 Albert E.	"	m. Nellie Hughes	" "

GENEALOGICAL SECTION

9 William M. Hodges	m.	Miriam H. Miller	Waterbury, Conn.
9 George Frederick " twins	unm.		" "
9 Mary Faustina " twins	unm.		
9 Charles Howard "	unm.		
9 Samuel Lewis "	unm.		

8 Mary A. Pickett   ch.   Maria Prindle & Daniel Pickett   Bethel, Conn.

9 Myron Clark
9 Charles "
9 Clarence "   ch.   Mary Ann Pickett & Levi S. Clark   Cleveland, Ohio
9 Mary "   " "

8 William Hurd   ch.   Maria Shepard & 7William Beers Prindle   Newtown, Conn.

William Hurd   m.   Elizabeth Ford

8 *Charles Trowbridge
8 *Julia Frances "   ch.   Mary Prindle & Samuel Wm. Trowbridge   Waterbury, Conn.
8 Frank W. "

9 Frederick J. Trowbridge
9 William "
9 Florence "   ch.   Katherine Jarvis & Frank W. Trowbridge
9 Amy "

4 Lieut. Abel Prindle, son of 3Joseph, m. Amaryllis Toucey, dau,
Rev. Thomas Toucey. Was killed at the battle of Bennington, 1777.
Their Ch.

5 Armenal Prindle	m.	Asa Stoddard	Newtown, Conn.
5 Phebe "	unm.		
5 Currence "	m.	Nathan Preston	
5 Josiah "	unm.		

Ch. Jonathan Prindle and Damaris Peck   "   "

5 Abel Prindle	m.	Ruth Griffen	" "
5 Keziah "	m.	Capt. Enos Johnson	" "
5 Jerusha "	m.	Abel Stilson	" "
5 Sarah "	m.	Daniel Terrill	" "

6 *Mary Ann Prindle
6 *Abel Booth "   ch.   Ruth Griffen & Abel Prindle   "   "

7 Julia M. Prindle
7 *Robert Morris "   ch.   Betsey A. Glover & Abel B. Prindle   "   "

6 Ichabod Johnson   ch.   5Keziah Prindle & Capt. Enos Johnson

5 Huldah Prindle   m.   Joel Sanford   New Milford, Conn.
Their Ch.

6 Harriet Sanford	m.	Oliver Mead	
6 Judge David Curtis	m.	1st Caroline Merwin no ch.	" "
" " "	m.	2nd Amelia Selima Seymour	" "
" " "	m.	3rd Emily Bull	" "
6 Julia Maria Sanford	m.	Albert Gaylord	" "
6 Charles Grandison Sanford	unm.		

7 Henry Seymour Sanford	ch.	Amelia Selima Seymour, & David C. Sanford	New Milford, Ct.
7 Sarah Northrop Sanford 7 Caroline Selina "	ch.	Emily Bull & Judge David C. Sanford	" " " "
7 Sarah Northrop "	m.	William D. Black, no ch.	New York, N. Y.
7 Henry Seymour "	m.	Sophie Claflin Daniels	New Milford, Conn.

Their Ch.

8 Jennie Daniels "	m.	William Black Pell	" "
8 David Curtis "	m.	Goldie A. McMahon	" "
8 Henry Seymour "	m.	Alice Bostwick Buck	" "
9 David Curtis, Jr. "	ch.	Goldie A. McMahon & David C. Sanford	" "

6Zenas, 5Zalmon, 4Joel, 3Joseph, 2Ebenezer, 1William

4 Joel Prindle	m. Sabra Kimberly	Newtown, Conn.
5 Zalmon "	m. Mary Williams	
6 Zenas "	m. Hannah Cogswell	
7 Hawley "	m. Olive Andrew	
8 Franklin Cogswell Prindle,	Rear Admiral, Retired Civil Engineer, U. S. Navy, Washington, D. C.	
	m. 1st Gertrude Alida Stickle	" "
	m. 2nd Sarah Amelia Cranston	
	m. 3rd Mrs. Fidelia E. Mead	" "

Ch. Gertrude Alida Stickles and Franklin Cogswell Prindle.

9 Roscoe Stickles Prindle		New York, N. Y.
9 *Olive twin "	d. at Philadelphia, Pa.	
9 Minnie twin "	d. at Philadelphia, Pa.	
9 *Frank C. "	d. at Brooklyn, N. Y.	
9 Harry Augustus "	m. Frederica Patterson	
9 Gertrude Elizabeth "	m. Francis Gilbert	
9 Allan "	d. E. Arlington, Vt.	

5Elijah, Jr., 4Elijah, 3Joseph, Jr., 2Joseph, 1William   Newtown, Conn.

2 Joseph Prindle	m. Mary Brown	
3 Joseph, Jr. "	m. Elizabeth Thomas	
4 Elijah "	m. Elizabeth Benham	
5 Elijah, Jr "	m. Sally Ward	
6 Harriet "	m. George Tuttle	New Haven, Conn.
7 *George H. Tuttle	m. Bessie Stanwood Collins	
8 Roger Walker Tuttle	m. Lillian May Hopton	
8 Marjorie Allison Tuttle		

7 George H. Tuttle of Tuttle, Morehouse & Taylor, New Haven, Conn., was instantly killed by a trolley car May, 1918.

SANFORD

1 Thomas Sanford came from England to Boston, Mass., in 1631, to Dorchester, Mass., in 1634, to Milford, Conn., in 1639.

Ch. Thomas Sanford and Sarah his wife

GENEALOGICAL SECTION

2 Samuel   Sanford   m. Hannah Bronson
2 Ephraim   "   " Mary Powell

Ch. Samuel Sanford and Hannah Bronson

3 Samuel first settler in Newtown in 1711, m. Esther Baldwin

Their Ch.

4 Samuel3   Sanford   m. Hannah Gilbert   Newtown, Conn.
4 John   "   " 1st Rebecca Northrop   "   "
                          2nd Abiah Deming   "   "
5 John Jr.   "   " Amy Northrop   "   "

Their Ch.

6 David   "   unm.   "   "
6 Elijah   "   " Abigail E. Townsend   "   "
6 Charlotte   "   " Rev. Birdsey G. Noble   Bridgeport, Conn.

Ch. Elijah Sanford and Abigail Townsend

7 Juliet   Sanford   m. George A. Townsend   New Haven, Conn.
7 David   "   " Emily A. Townsend   "   "
7 Elizabeth C. "   " Edmund T. H. Gibson   Brooklyn, N. Y.

Ch. David Sanford and Emily A. Townsend   Newtown, Conn.

8 John Townsend   Sanford m. Hattie Mills
8 *William Isaac   "   " Annie Manning
8 *Jane Elizabeth   "   " Rev. Wm. H. Moore   "   "
8 *George Morton   "   d. in boyhood   "   "
8 *Grace Stanfield   "   d. unm.   "   "
8 Paul James   "

Ch. Elizabeth C. Sanford and Edmund T. H. Gibson   Brooklyn, N. Y.

8 Edmund T. H. Gibson, Jr. m. Frances P. Burbank   "   "
8 Charles Dana   "   " Mamie Tugwell   "   "
8 John Cotton   "   d. unm.
8 Emily C.   "   d. unm.
8 Elizabeth C.   "   d. unm.
8 Wm. Hamilton   "   " Emma L. Blanchard   Washington, Conn.
He was a celebrated Naturalist and Artist

8 Juliet   Gibson   m. Clarence Meigs Noble   Bridgeport, Conn.
8 Henry Stockwell "   " Augusta Louise Foust
8 Hubert Temple   "

5 Ch. Samuel Sanford and Abiah Dunning, 1st wife   Newtown, Conn.

6 Isaac Sanford   m. Anna Bristol   "   "

Their Ch.

7 Elias B. Sanford   " 1st Sally Lockwood   "   "
                       " Lucretia Fayerweather   "   "

Their Ch.

8 Rev. Isaac   Sanford   Middlefield, Conn.
8 Lockwood   "   New Haven,   "
8 Joseph B.   "   Preston, Penna.
8 Edson   "   In Civil War   Meriden, Conn.
8 *Ann   "   m. Rev. James Taylor   Newtown,   "
8 Luman   "   In Civil War   Gibson, Penn.
8 Elias   "   In Civil War   Salisbury, Conn.

5 ch. 4Samuel Sanford and Charity Foote Bristol 2nd wife Newtown, Conn.

GENEALOGICAL SECTION

6 Josiah Sanford m. Polly Johnson — Newtown, Conn.

Their Ch.

7 *Edwin Sanford — d. in young manhood — " "
7 *Capt. Julius, In Civil War — Mary Parsons, — " "
7 *Henry " " Mary Booth — " "
7 *Frederick " unm. — " "
7 *Charlotte " m. George B. Wheeler (see Wheeler) Dyersville, Iowa
7 Margaret " " Albert Northrop — Pittsburg, Penn.
7 *Josiah " unm. — Newtown, Conn.
7 *Augusta " unm. — " "

Ch. Capt. Julius Sanford and Mary Parsons

8 *Ellen Louise Sanford m. Sherwood Thompson — New Haven, Conn.
8 Gertrude " " Clarence Bolmer — " "

Ch. Henry Sanford and Mary Booth — Newtown, Conn.

8 Annie Sanford unm. — " "
8 Sarah " m. Robert Beers (see Beers) — " "

2 ch. Ephraim Sanford and Mary Powell

3 Samuel Sanford m. Esther Baldwin — Newtown, Conn.

Their Ch.

4 Jonathon Sanford m. 1st Phebe Platt — " "
 " 2nd Hannah Platt — " "

Their Ch.

5 Jonathan Jr., Sanford m. Rebecca — " "

Their Ch.

6 *Lavina Sanford — " "
6 *Lucretia " m. Daniel Scott no ch. — Winsted, Conn.
6 *Hannah " twins " Abijah Merritt (see Merritt
6 *Zalmon " twins " Hannah Curtis — Newtown, Conn.
6 *Abba " Foote no ch. — " "
6 *Huldah " — " "
6 *Polly " m. Oliver Peck no ch. — " "
6 *Lucinda " " Seabury Booth (see Booth) — " "

Ch. Zalmon Sanford and Hannah Curtis — " "

7 *John Albert Sanford unm. — " "
7 *Julia " m. Bethel Booth no ch.

SCUDDER

The "Commemorative Biographic Record" states that Capt. Isaac Scudder was born in Newtown, April, 11th, 1776. "He was the leading carpenter and builder of the country in his day. The first Methodist Church dedicated in 1831 was constructed by him.

1 Capt Isaac Scudder m. Sarah Banks — Newtown, Conn.

Their Ch.

2 *Isaac B. Scudder m. 1st Lucinda Hickock — Bethel, Conn.
2 *William " " Laura Platt
2 *Samuel " m. Mary Miller — Cedar Rapids

3 *Lucinda " ch. Lucinda Hickock & Isaac Scudder

Ch. 2 Isaac Scudder and Betsey Skidmore 2nd wife

3 *Sarah Scudder m. Charles Lamoureaux Rochester, N. Y.
3 *Samuel Starr " " Jennie Wright
3 *Lucy " " 1st Henry Lake Brookfield, Conn.
                    2nd William Smith Lamoureaux

4 Lillian Lamoureaux

Their ch.

Ch. Sarah Scudder and Charles Lamoureaux

4 *Lucy Lamoureaux unm.
4 *Julia " unm.
4 Susan " m. Harry Fairman
4 Hattie " " George Atkinson

5 *Rev. Charles Fairman ch. Susan Lamoureaux
 &
 Harry Fairman

Ch. Hattie Lamoureaux and George Atkinson

5 May Atkinson m. Delos Rose
5 Herbert " " Martha Bowlby
5 Ward "

4 Susan Jane Scudder   Jennie Wright
4 Mary Elizabeth "   ch.   &
4 Frances Carolyn "   Samuel S. Scudder   Newtown, Conn.

5 Paul Scudder Smith   Frances Carolyn Scudder " "
5 Earl Wright "   ch.   &
5 *Robert Stedman "   Arthur J. Smith " "

4 *William Lake   Lucy Scudder 1st m. Brookfield, Conn.
                ch.   &
                    Henry Lake

4 Lillian M. Lamoureaux   Lucy Scudder Lake 2nd m.
                ch.   &
                    William Lamoureaux

3 Theodore Scudder   Laura Platt
3 *Emma "   ch.   &
                    William Scudder

4 Addie Scudder   Sarah Robinson
4 Fanny "   ch.   &
                    Theodore Scudder

4 Flora Milham   Emma Scudder
                ch.   &
                    William Milham

SHEPARD

1 John Shepard m. Mary Parsons and moved to Newtown, 1737.

2 Abraham Shepard m. Rhoda Ferris

Their Ch.

3 Betty "
3 Truman "
3 Lazarus "
3 Nathan "
3 Samuel "

3 Sueton   Shepard   m. Dymah Ann Hurd
3 Abraham Ferris "   " Abba Lake   Brookfield, Conn.
3 Rufus   "   " Lucy Ann Peck

   Ch. Sueton Shepard and Dymah Ann Hurd   Newtown, Conn.

4 Harriet   Shepard   d. young
4 Mary   "   m. Lyman Smith   Nunda, N. Y.
4 Elizabeth Jane   "   " Damman Blackman
4 Delia   "   " Benjamin White
4 Lazarus Clarke   "   " Emily Strong
4 Juliaette   "   unm.
4 Maria   "   " Wm. B. Prindle (see Prindle) Newtown, Ct.
4 Samuel Ferris   "   " Sarah Maria Weed
4 Grant   "   d. young

3 Ch. Abraham F. Shepard and Abba Lake

4 Avis   "   m. Isaac N. Hawley (See Hawley)
4 Edson   "   " Jane Terrill   Brookfield, Conn.
4 Rev. Peter Lake   "   " Mary Anne Burr

   Ch. Rufus Shepard and Lucy Ann Peck

4 *Frances Sophia Shepard   unm.
4 Anne Elizabeth   "   unm.
4 **Caroline W.   "   m. Cornelius C. Corson (no ch.)   New York
4 *George W.   "

   Ch. Edson Shepard and Jane Terrill   Brookfield, Conn.

5 *Carrie   "   m. Daniel G. Beers 1st wife Newtown, Conn.
5 Eugene   "   m. Adelaide Street

   Ch. Rev Peter Lake Shepard and Mary Anne Burr Saybrook, Conn.

5 Horace B. Shepard   d. in young manhood
5 Mary Hard   "
5 Anne Campbell   "
5 Margaret McLeod "
5 Louis Jennings   "
5 Finley Johnson   "   m. Helen Gould   New York, N. Y.

   Rev. Peter L. Shepard was for many years Principal of a Church School for boys at Saybrook, Conn.

SHERMAN

1 Daniel Sherman, b. 1668, m. Rebecca Wheeler and settled in Newtown at an early date. Was selectman in Newtown, in 1738.

   Of their six ch.

2 Samuel   m. Elizabeth   Newtown, Conn.

   Of their eight ch.

3 Jotham   m. 1st Grace Peck   "   "
                               " 2nd Amy Beers   "   "
                               " 3rd Cynthia Beers   "   "
                               " 4th Rhoda   "   "

   Ch. 3Jotham Sherman and Grace Peck   "   "

4 Lewis   "   m. Sarah Glover   "   "
4 Samuel   "   " Betty Hawley   "   "
4 Rufus   "   " Amy Booth   "   "
4 Sabra   "   " Stephen Burwell   "   "

GENEALOGICAL SECTION

Ch. 3 Jotham Sherman and Amy Beers   Newtown, Conn.
4 Grace   "   m. Nathaniel Nichols   "   "
4 Jotham Beers   "   " Hephsibah Sherman   "   "
4 Cyrus Beers   "   " Huldah M. Booth   "   "

Ch. Lewis Sherman and Sarah Glover   "   "
5 Esther   "   m. Eben Tyrrill (See Tyrrill)   "   "
5 Sabra   "   " Daniel Booth (See Booth)   "   "
5 Anna   "   " Isaac Briscoe (See Briscoe)   "   "
5 Justin   "   " Senea Sherman   Wakeman, Ohio
5 Marcia   "   " N. S. Beers   Bridgewater, Conn.
5 Ornan   "   " Clara Lake   Danbury, "

Ch. Justin Sherman and Senea Sherman
6 Lewis J.   "   Wakeman, Ohio
6 Nathan G.   "   m. Elizabeth Otis

Their Ch.
7 Mary Nancy   "   m. B. A. Hayes   Toledo, Ohio

Their Ch.
8 *Rutherford B. Hayes   "   "
8 Sherman Otis   "   "   "
8 Webb Cook   "   "   "
8 Walter J.   "   "   "

Ch. Marcia Sherman and N. S. Beers   Bridgewater, Conn.
6 Sylvia Beers   m. Lewis Frost   "   "
6 Philo S.   "   " Susan Tomlinson   "   "

Their Ch.   "   "
7 Estelle J.   "   "   "
7 Carrie A.   "   "   "

5 Marcia Sherman Beers d. Dec.1890, nearly 102 years old.   "   "

Ch. 5 Ornan Sherman and Clara Lake   Danbury, "
6 Charles L.   "   m. Eliza Blackman (no ch.)   "   "
6 Fanny   "   " William Platt   Newtown, "
6 Harriet   "   unm.
6 Jane   "   " Lorin L. Platt   Waterbury, "
6 Sarah   "   " Alfred L. Platt   "   "
6 Phebe   "   " Winters Day Somers   Leominster, Mass.
6 Clara   "   " William Hoy (no ch.)   Newtown, Conn.
6 Samuel Justin   "   " 1st Caroline A. Benedict   Danbury, "
                       " 2nd Sarah E. Wildman
                       " 3rd Jane A. Lockwood

Three others d. in infancy

Ch. Fanny Sherman and William Platt   Newtown, Conn.
7 Frank Platt   m. Annie Northrop (no ch.)   Waterbury, "
7 Charles S.   "   " Ella E. Ingraham   Newtown, "
7 Emily   "   no desc.
7 Roger   "   d. in boyhood   "   "

Ch. Charles S. Platt and Ella E. Ingraham   New York
8 Roy   "   "   "
8 Arthur Ingraham   "   m. Elizabeth Walker Rylands Bridgeport, Ct.
8 Agnes Electra   "   New York, N. Y.

Ch. Phebe Sherman and Winters Day Somers   Leominster, Mass.
7 Julia Frances Somers   "   "
7 Clara Medora   "   m. Alexander Sinclair Paton   "   "

Their Ch. Leominster, Mass.
8 Phebe Sherman Paton m. Ferderick Langley Perry Redding, Conn.
8 Somers Sinclair " " "
8 Agnes Frances " " "
8 Pauline Parmelee " " Harry Fulton Sturges " "
8 Clara Lake " " "

Ch. Phebe S. Paton and Frederick L. Perry " "

9 Frances Irene Perry " "
9 Alender Paton " " "

Ch. 4Samuel Sherman and Betty Hawley Brookfield, Conn.

5 Lucy " m. Eli Baldwin " "
5 Betsey " " Eleazer Hawley " "
5 Lemuel " " Brittania McManus no ch. " "
5 Vashti " unm.
5 Amy " " Lemuel Peck no ch. " "
5 Abel " " Sarah Bradley " "
5 Sally Minerva " " Rev. Benj. Benham " "

Ch. 5Abel Sherman and Sarah Bradley " "

6 Hon. Samuel " m. Mercedes Montejo, Puerto Principe, Cuba

Ch. Sally M. Sherman and Rev. Benj. Benham Brookfield, Conn.

6 Candace Vashti Brittania McManus Benham " "
    m. Dr. Augustus Boream " "

Their Ch. " "

7 Anna Boream " "
7 Benjamin " " "
7 Florence " " "

Ch. 4Rufus Sherman and Amy Booth " "

5 Olive " m. Eldrad Ruggles " "

Their Ch. " "

6 Sherman Booth Ruggles " Sarah Oakley " "

Their Ch.

7 Elizabeth Ruggles " Charles Randall Bridgewater, Conn.
7 *Henry B. " " Emma E. Cole Kent "
7 *Almon B. " " Susan Shelton Southbury, "
7 *Olive J. " d. in girlhood.

Ch. Elizabeth Ruggles and Charles Randall

8 Dr. William Randall m. Hattie L. Beers Shelton "
8 Grace Elizabeth " " Alfred Charles Sperry " "

Ch. Dr. William Randall and Hattie L. Beers " "

9 Harold Beers " m. Helen Davis " "
9 Helen Starr " " Charles R. Williams " "

Ch. Harold B. Randall and Helen Davis " "

10 Harriet Elizabeth "
10 Jean "

Ch. Henry B. Ruggles and Emma E. Cole Kent, "

8 Henrietta Ruggles Shelton, "

Ch. Almon Ruggles and Susan Shelton Redlands, Cal.

8 Annie " m. Albert Welton " "

GENEALOGICAL SECTION

8 Henry   Ruggles   unm.   Redlands, Calif.
8 Elizabeth   "   unm.   "   "
8 Nellie   "   unm.   "   "
8 Frederick   "   m.   Mary Barton   "   "
8 Charles   "   "   Amelia Smith   San Francisco, Cal.
8 Susan   "   "   Claude Rhoades   Redlands   "

Ch. Annie Ruggles and Albert Welton

9 Harold   Welton   m.   Isabel Elliott   "   "

9 Frances   "   Harold Welton
10 Margaret Isbell "   ch.   &
                                  Isabel Elliott

Ch. Charles Ruggles and Amelia Smith   San Francisco, Cal.

9 Gertrude   "   "   "
9 Priscilla   "   "   "
9 Louise   "   "   "
9 Elizabeth   "   "   "

Ch. Frederick Ruggles and Mary Barton   Redlands, Cal.

9 Almon Barton   "

Ch. 4Jotham B. Sherman and Hepsibah Sherman

5 Major Charles   "   m.   Sally Foot desc. not located Newtown, Ct.
5 Harry   "   "   Flora Sherman   "   "

Their Ch.

5 George Hubbell "   "   Eliza Stilson   Noroton, Conn.
Was in Civil War d at Soldier's Home.
5 Nancy Sherman   m.   George Andrews   Bethel, Conn.

Their Ch.

6 George Edward Andrews
6 Caroline Frances   "
6 Nancy Amelia   "
6 Henry Ashton   "
6 Elgin Sherman   "
6 Martha Eliza   "
6 Lillie Eudora   "
6 Jennie Thomas   "
6 Fred Thomas   "
6 Gertie C.   "
6 Clifford Stowe   "

Ch. 4 Cyrus Sherman and Huldah Matilda Booth   Newtown, Conn.

5 Jotham   "   m.   Mary Ann Bostwick   "   "
5 Cyrus Beers   "   "   Caroline Beers (no ch.)   "   "
5 Mary   "   "   E. Benedict Price   Norwalk   "

Ch. Jotham Sherman and Mary Ann Bostwick   Newtown, Conn.

6 Mary Jane   "   m.   Franklin Fairman (see Fairman) Chicago,
6 Cyrus Lynson   "   d. in young manhood   Newtown, Conn.
6 Frances Augusta "   d. in childhood

Ch. Mary Sherman and E. B. Price   Norwalk   "

6 Dr. Sherman Price   m.   Ellen Beardsley Clark   "   "

Their Ch.

7 Jannet Alden Price

1 Benjamin, 2Job, 3John, 4Daniel, 5Linus   Newtown, Conn.

5 Linus Sherman   m. Artemisia Curtis

   Their Ch.

6 Daniel Sherman   Has three ch. living in the West
6 Hannah   "   m. Nathan Prince
6 Aurelia   "   " William S. Whiting   Urbana, Ohio
6 Phebe   "   " Hermon Beers, See Beers, Newtown, Conn.

   Ch. Hannah Sherman and Nathan Prince

7 *Nathan   Prince
7 Hannah Sherman   "   m. Charles Robertson
7 *Mary Louisa   "

   Ch. Aurelia Sherman and Wm. S. Whiting

7 *Stephen Betts Whiting m. Kate Draper
7 *Sarah Maria   "   m. John Church
7 *William Samuel   "
7 *Edward Sherman   "
7 *Charles Wilcox   "

   Ch. Sarah M. Whiting and John Church

8 Lewis Whiting Church
8 Stephen Betts   "   Seymour, Conn.

SKIDMORE

Lieut. 4Thomas Skidmore son of John 3rd was born at Stratford in 1693, and with his wife Martha settled in Newtown as early as 1715. He was ensign of the military "train-band" of Newtown in 1723.

   Ch. of Thomas Skidmore and wife Martha

5 Nehemiah Skidmore   m. Charity Kimberly Lake
5 Jedidah   "   m. Ensign Richard Hubbell (see Hubbell)
5 Thomas   " Jr.   " Cynthia Beers
5 John   "   " Mary Prindle
5 Mary   "   " Heth Peck Jr. (See Peck)
5 Comfort   "   " Lieut Amos Terrill (See Terrill)
5 Martha   "   " Unknown
5 Rebecca   "   " Unknown

   Ch. 5Nehemiah Skidmore and Charity Kimberly Lake

6 Elnathan Skidmore   m. Eunice Wakeley
6 Sarah   "   " Samuel Peck (See Peck)
6 Joanna   "   " unm.
6 Lemuel   "   " Annie Burtis
6 Amos   "   " Esther H. Blackman

   Ch. 5Lieut. Thomas Jr. and Cynthia Beers

6 Dr. James Skidmore   m. Polly Sherman
6 Daniel   "   " Currance Baldwin
6 John   "   " Polly Baldwin
6 Abiah   "   " Nathan Ferris
6 Amy   "   " Ebenezer Sherman
6 Anne   "   " James Bristol
6 Zada   "   " Mr. Nash
6 Mary   "   " Sueton Baldwin

   Ch. 6Amos Skidmore and Esther Hitchcock Blackman

7 Wheeler   "   m. 1, Miss Lake, 2, Lucy Lake Brookfield, Ct.
7 James Blackman "   d. unm.
7 Hannah A.   "   " Philo Baldwin

GENEALOGICAL SECTION

7 Rufus   Skidmore   m. 1st Esther Terrill
                                          2nd Maria Clark Hawley

Ch. Wheeler Skidmore and 1st Miss Lake   Brookfield, Conn.

8 Burtis Skidmore,   m. Hannah Bradley (no ch.) Newtown, Conn.

Ch. Wheeler Skidmore and Lucy Lake   Brookfield, Conn.

8 Betsey   "   m. Isaac B. Scudder (See Scudder)
8 Starr   "   m. Harriet Ferris (no ch.) Brookfield, Conn.

Ch. Rufus Skidmore and Esther Terrill   "   "

8 Eliza   "   m. Alfred Walker   Ossining, N. Y.

Their Ch.

9 Abigail E. Walker   d. young
9 Emmon Terrill "   m. Mary Halliday   Elmira, N. Y.
9 James Nelson "   m. Jennie Ogden   Sing Sing, N. Y.
9 William Rufus "   unm.   Elmira, N. Y.
9 Lizzie   " twins   m. William I. Townsend   Ossining, N. Y.
9 Alfred Jr.   " twins   m. Flora Clarke   Newtown, Conn.

10 Jennie Ogden Walker ch.   Jennie Ogden
                                              &
                                              James N. Walker   Elmira, N. Y.
" " "   m. Hon. Charles H. Knipp

10 Clarke Skidmore Walker ch.   Flora Clarke   Newtown, Conn.
                                                &
                                                Alfred Walker, Jr.   Ossining, N. Y.

7 Rufus Skidmore   m. 2nd Maria C. Hawley   Brookfield, Conn.

Their Ch.

8 Esther Maria Skidmore   m. Henry B. Hawley   "   "
8 *William Henry "   m. Julia G. Williams   "   "

Ch. Esther M. Skidmore and Henry B. Hawley   "   "

9 Emily Carrie Hawley   Author of "Skidmore Genealogy" " "
9 William Henry "   m. Victoria Barnum Adams
9 Dr. George Rufus "   m. Alice B. Beebe   Brooklyn, N. Y.
9 Benjamin "   d. in infancy
9 Grace Skidmore "   d. in infancy
9 Henry Benjamin " twins   unm.   Danbury, Conn.
9 Lucius Skidmore " twins   unm.   Brookfield, Conn.

Ch. Julia G. Williams and William H. Skidmore   "   "

9 *William Rufus Skidmore   d. in infancy   "   "
9 Julia Wilhelmine "   unm. engaged in teaching   "   "
9 Anna Theodora "   unm. engaged in teaching   Newark, N. J.

Ch. 6 Dr. James Skidmore son Lieut. Thomas, Jr. and Polly Sherman

7 Dr. Rufus Skidmore   m. Jerusha Ferris (See doctors) Newtown, Ct.

Their Ch.

8 Jane Ann Skidmore   m. Barak Burr (no ch.)   Fairfield, Conn.
8 Marietta "   m. Alanson Lyon   Redding, Conn.
8 Elizabeth "   m. James Johnson (no ch.) Bridgeport, Conn.

Ch. Marietta Skidmore and Alanson Lyon
    She is living (1918) aged 93 years.

9 Mary Ella Lyon   m. Hobart Brinsmade   St. Louis, Mo.
9 Rufus Alanson "   unm.   Redding, Conn.
9 *Elizabeth F. "   d. young
9 Jennie L. "   m. John C. Read   "   "

10 Robert Bruce Brinsmade		Mary Ella Lyon	
10 Louis Lyon "	ch.	&	
		Hobart Brinsmade	St. Louis, Mo.
11 Virginia Skidmore "		Helen Christine Steenboch	Pueblo, Mex.
11 Robert Turgott "	ch.	&	
11 Harold Steenbock "		Robert Bruce Brinsmade	" "
11 Akbar Lyon "			
11 Eleanor Louise "		Claribel Green	St. Louis, Mo.
11 Hobart Louis "	ch.	&	
		Louis Brinsmade	" "
10 Herbert Read		Jennie L. Lyon	Redding, Conn.
10 Elizabeth Skidmore "	ch.	&	
10 Ferris Lyon "		John C. Read	" "

Ch. Elnathan Skidmore and Eunice Wakeley   Newtown, Conn.

7 Lois Skidmore   m. Daniel Blackman (See Blackman)

6 Abel Skidmore son of 5 John Skidmore and Mary Prindle Newtown, Conn.

Ch. Abel Skidmore and Bethia Glover

7 Daniel	"	m. Marjory Blackman	
7 Zerah	"	m. Bernice Hurd	Bethlehem, Conn.
7 Glover	"	m. Sarah Blackman	Newtown, Conn.
7 Bennett	"	m. Eliza Berry	" "
7 Annis	"	m. Henry Jackson	" "
7 Eunice Ann	"	m. Samuel Blackman (see Blackman)	" "
7 Mary Ann	"	m. Glover Botsford	Newtown, Conn.
7 Maria	"	m. John Lake	" "
7 Abel Booth	"	m. Lucy Berry	" "
7 John	"	m. Molly Wheeler	" "
7 Charles	"	m. Mary Fairchild no ch.	" "

8 *Lauren Skidmore son of Daniel and 1st wife Marjory Blackman   "
                                " d. unm.

8 Lauren B. Skidmore 2nd		Sarah Ann Dibble, 2nd wife " "
8 *Sarah Ann "	ch.	&
		Daniel Skidmore

8 Lauren   "   m. Ella Northrop (no ch.)   " "

Ch. 7 Zerah Skidmore and Bernice Hurd   Bethlehem, Conn.

8 Homer	"	m. Annis N. Raymond	" "
8 Julia	"	m. Roswell Morse	" "
8 Wealthy	"	m. Lucius Shelton	" "
8 Philo Hurd	"	m. Abigail Ives	Cheshire, Conn.

Ch. Philo Hurd Skidmore and Abigail Ives   Newtown, Conn.

9 *Stella Amelia Skidmore	m. Edward L. Beard	Cambridge, Mass.
9 Julius Wordsworth "	m. Marion E. Lewis	Bridgeport, Conn.
9 Abigail Louise "	m. Henry Nichols (See Nichols)	Newtown, Ct.
9 *Philo Hurd Jr. "	m. Irene Brown	Bridgeport, Conn.
9 *William A. "	d. young	
9 *Edward Ives "	d. young	
9 *Herbert Monroe "	d. at twenty-two years	Newtown, "

Ch. Stella A. Skidmore and Edward L. Beard   Cambridge, Mass.

10 Bessie Woodbury Beard	unm.	
10 Florence "	unm.	
10 Mabel Montgomery "	m. Francis Mitchell Smith	Providence, R.I.
10 Amy Wentworth "	m. George S. Chappell	Pelham Manor, N. Y.
10 Edward Leonard Jr. "		Cambridge, Mass.

GENEALOGICAL SECTION

11 Caroline Rhodes Smith 11 Francis Mitchell " Jr.	ch.	Mabel M. Beard & Francis M. Smith Providence, R. I.
11 *Barbara Chappell 11 George Shepard " Jr.	ch.	Amy Wentworth Beard & George S. Chappell, Pelham Manor, N. Y.
10 Lewis P. Skidmore 10 Maud Bernice "	ch.	Marion Lewis Bridgeport, Conn. & Julius Skidmore " "
10 Nellie Skidmore 10 Laurie " 10 *Amy " 10 *Philo Hurd 3rd " 10 Preston "	ch.	Irene Brown " " & Philo Hurd Skidmore, Jr " "

7 Glover Skidmore   m. Sarah Blackman   Newtown, Conn.
  Their Ch.
8 John Russell Skidmore   m. Julia Botsford   " "
8 Caroline   "   m. Ammon B. Blackman   Brookfield, Conn.
  Ch. John R. Skidmore and Julia Botsford
9 *William Botsford "   d. young
9 *William Russell "   unm.
9 *Robert Edwin   "   m. Grace Walker, no desc.
9 *Mary Caroline   "   d. 1918 unm.

9 Philo Booth Blackman	ch.	Caroline Skidmore & Ammon B. Blackman
10 William H. Blackman	ch.	Antoinette Carpenter & Philo B. Blackman

7 John   Skidmore   m. Molly Wheeler   Newtown, Conn.
8 Elizabeth M. "   m. Samuel Thornhill
  Their Ch.
9 *Emma E. Thornhill   m. *Charles E. Beers   Brookfield, Conn.
9 John   "   m. Anna Tibbals   " "
9 Amelia B.   "   m. George W. Stuart   Newtown, Conn.
9 Fannie O.   "   m. Charles D. Ferris (see Ferris) " "

  Ch. Charles E. Beers and Emma Thornhill   Brookfield, "
10 Hattie E. Beers   m. Peter H. Fennell   " "
10 Edgar H.   "   m. Georgia M. Ferry   Newtown, "
10 Susie O.   "   m. John A. Carlson
10 Clara I.   "   m. Leonard A. Taylor   Detroit, Mich.
10 Clinton T.   "   m. Grace E. Stapleberg

11 Emma M. Fennell 11 Henry B. " 11 Joseph B. " 11 *Charles E. Beers 11 Dorothy "	ch.	Hattie E. Beers Brookfield, Conn. & Peter H. Fennell
11 Ruth " 11 Morris " 11 Helen "	ch.	Georgia M. Ferry & Edgar E. Beers
11 Emily Elizabeth Carlson	ch.	Susie O. Beers Newtown, " & John Carlson

11 Harold B. Taylor	ch.	Clara I. Beers & Leonard A. Taylor	Detroit, Mich.
11 *Lina M. "			
11 Harold G. Beers	ch.	Grace E. Stapleberg & Clinton T. Beers	
10 George F. Stuart	ch.	Amelia B. Thornhill & George W. Stuart	Newtown, Conn.

STILSON

1Vincent Stilson of Scotch-English descent originally settled in Milford
2Vincent Stilson, Jr. came to Newtown early in the settlement of the town.

He m. Abigail Peck, Newtown, Conn.

Their Ch.

3Abel, Elnathan, Jean, Parthenia, John, Sarah Ann   Newtown, Conn.

The original house, added to in 1812 by 3Abel, is still standing (1918), the oldest house in town; owned and occupied by James Egan.

3 Abel Stilson	m.	Jerusha Prindle	Newtown, Conn.

Their Ch.

4 Dothy J. Stilson		d. young	
4 David "	m.	Betsey St. John	Easton, Conn.
4 Abel, Jr "	m.	Sarah Wetmore	Newtown, Conn.
4 Elnathan "	m.	Polly Wetmore	" "
4 Anan "		d. young	
4 Jonathan "	m.	Ellen Wells	" "
4 Sarah A. "		unm.	
4 Isaac "		unm.	
4 Asa "		unm.	

Ch. 4David Stilson and Betsey St. John   Easton, Conn.

5 Mary Ann Stilson	m.	David Hawley	Trumbull, Conn.
5 Phoebe Ann "	m.	Philo B. Sherwood, 1st wife	
5 Jerusha "	3rd wife	of Philo B. Sherwood,	Redding, Conn.
5 Abby "	m.	Perkins French	Easton, Conn.
5 John "	m.	Mary E. Sherman	Newtown, Conn.
5 Betsey "	m.	Henry Wakeman	Easton, Conn.
5 Horace "		unm.	Newtown, Conn.
5 Sidney "		unm.	" "
5 Alfred "		unm.	" "

Ch. 4Abel Stilson, Jr. and Sarah Wetmore   " "

5 *Dr. Joseph Stilson		Residence unknown	
5 *Polly Ann "		unm.	" "
5 *Abel 3rd "		unm.	" "
5 *Mary A. "		unm.	" "
5 *Anan "	m.	1st Georgiana Merchant	
6 Gertrude Stilson	ch.	2nd Sarah Stoddard & Anan Stilson	
7 Marion Lawrence	ch.	Gertrude Stilson & Wilder F. Lawrence	
7 Stilson "			

GENEALOGICAL SECTION

4 Elnathan Stilson	m.	Polly Wetmore	Newtown, Conn.
Their Ch.			
5 William Stilson	m.	Martha Ward	" "
5 Phebe Ann "		unm.	" "
5 Antoinnette "	m.	James Henderson	" "
6 David Henderson	ch.	Antoinnette Stilson & James Henderson	Milford, Conn. Newtown, Conn.
6 *Abel Stilson		Martha Ward	" "
6 George "	ch.	&	
6 John "		William Stilson	" "
6 Frank "		No descendants	
Ch. 5 Mary Ann Stilson	m.	David Hawley	Trumbull, Conn.
6 Frances Hawley	m.	John Hunt (no ch.)	
6 Mary "	m.	Edward Borroughs (no ch.)	" "
6 Emmeline "	m.	Harlan Phillips	" "
6 Josephine "	m.	Birdsey Thompson	" "
6 Joseph "	m.	Lenora Toucey (no ch.)	" "
6 Julia "		unm.	" "
5 Phebe Ann Stilson	m.	Philo B. Sherwood	Easton, Conn.
Their Ch.			
6 Phebe Ann Sherwood	m.	William Patchin	Redding, Conn.
5 Jerusha Stilson, 3rd wife Philo B. Sherwood			
Their Ch.			
6 *Eugene "		d. in infancy	
6 Juliet Sherwood	m.	Hobart Mallet (no ch.)	Trumbull, Conn.
6 Hannah "	m.	Charles Sanford	Redding, Conn.
6 Lavinia "	m.	William Ward (no ch.)	" "
6 Ella "	m.	George Gillette	
6 Mary "		2nd wife Wm. Ward (no ch.)	" "
6 Milfred "	m.	Charles Ferris	Easton, Conn.
6 John "	m.	Minnie Odgen	" "
7 Elsie Sanford	ch.	Hannah Sherwood & Charles Sanford	Redding, Conn. " "
7 Lucy "			
8 Raymond Platt	ch.	Philo Platt & Elsie Sanford	Newtown, Conn.
8 Earl George Sanford	ch.	Lucy Sanford & George Sanford	Redding, Conn.
7 Willard Gillette	ch.	Ella Sherwood & George Gillette	" "
8 George Sterling	ch.	Dorothy Mallette & Willard Gillette	
7 Minnie Sherwood	ch.	Minnie Odgen & John Sherwood	

8 John Sherwood Edwards ch. Minnie Sherwood
&
Erwin Edwards

7 Mary Sherwood Ferris m. Arthur Wheeler

Ch. 5 Abby Stilson   m. Perkins French   Easton, Conn.
6 Harriet French   unm.   "   "
6 Electa   "   m. Jerome Nichols   "   "
6 Emma   "   m. Hermon H. Peck   Newtown, Conn.
6 John   "   unm.
6 Charles   "   m. Emily Nichols   Monroe, Conn.
6 Antoinette "   m. Wilbur Tomlinson   Danbury, Conn.
6 *George   "   d. in infancy

6 Ch. 6 Electa French and Jerome Nichols   Monroe, Conn.

7 Charles Nichols   m. Lillian Hull   "   "
7 Flora   "   m. Horace Lyon (no ch.)
7 Elsie   "   unm.
7 Mildred   "   m. George Sturges (no ch.) "   "
7 Jerome   "   d. in infancy

8 Perkins French Nichols ch. Lillian Hull   "   "
                              &   In U. S. S. in France
8 Irma French   "   Charles Nichols   "   "

7 Sylvia Marion Peck   ch. Emma French   Newtown, Conn.
                              &
                              Hermon H. Peck

7 Inez French   Emily Nichols   Monroe, Conn.
7 Harry   "   ch. &
7 John   "   Charles French
7 Sidney "

6 Carlos D. Stilson   ch. Mary Sherman   Newtown, Conn.
                              &
                              John Stilson

  Carlos D. Stilson   m. Bertha Peck (no ch.

SUMMERS

1 Abijah Summers   m. Phebe Pixlee, 1776
  Their Ch.
2 Daniel Summers   " Sally Gilbert
  Their Ch.
3 David Summers   " Jane Avery
  Their Ch.
4 Phebe A.   Summers   " Adoniram Fairchild (see Fairchild)
4 Harriet   "   " W. Waterhouse served in Navy Civil War
4 Mary   "   " Irving Goodsell (see Hubbell)
4 Julia   "   " Smith Lewis
4 John H.   "   " Ella Mellen   Newtown, Conn.
4 *Charles   "   d. young
4 Ella   "   " Thomas Perkins   "   "
4 Ada   "   " George Parmelee (no ch.)
4 Lizzie   "   " Chauncy Wakeman
4 Andrew J.   "   " Martha Towell   Newtown, Conn.
4 *George   "

Ch. Harriet Summers and Wm. Waterhouse — Newtown, Conn.

5 *Laura Waterhouse
5 Ernest "
5 Fannie " m. Reginald Smith
5 Alice " unm.
5 Irving " m. Blanche Boucher " "

6 Lucile " ch. Blanche Boucher & Irving Waterhouse

Ch. Julia Summers and Smith Lewis

5 *Irene Lewis

Ch. John H. Summers and Ella Mellen — Newtown, Conn.

5 George Summers

Ch. Ella Summers and Thomas Perkins " "

5 Harry Perkins
5 Adoniram "
5 Raymond "

Ch. Lizzie Summers and Chauncy Wakeman

5 Arthur Wakeman " "
5 Angeline "

Ch. Andrew J. Summers and Martha Towell

5 E. Marion Summers
5 Bertha E. " m. George Hartley — New Rochelle, N. Y.
5 Maude N. "

Ch. Bertha Summers and George Hartley — Newtown, Conn.

6 Marian Elizabeth Hartley

George Hartley took part in the Revolution in Hayti in 1914, and received a medal. Also was in the Mexican trouble in service during the war. Was subordinate officer on S. S. George Washington which conveyed President Wilson to Peace Conference.

TAYLOR

1 Stephen Taylor m. Betsey Hull, 1786

Their Ch.

2 David Taylor
2 Jabez "
2 Alonzo " m. Louisa Peck
2 Sherman "
2 Thomas B. "
2 Hannah " m. Elizen Hayes
2 Aurilla " " E. Granniss
2 Philo "
2 Sally " " William Taylor
2 Polly " " Wait Plumb
2 Rebecca "

Ch. Alonzo Taylor and Louisa Peck

3 Lucy Taylor m. Birdsey McEwen
3 Francis " " Nellie R. Perry

3 Edward   Taylor   m. Susan S. Botsford
3 Marcia   "   d. unm.

Ch. Edward Taylor and Susan S. Botsford

4 George Francis Taylor   m. Lorena Glover

Alonzo Taylor was a successful teacher; one of the best of the local teachers of the time.

Edward Taylor for many years the popular proprietor of the Sandy Hook Hotel and held many offices in the town.

George F. Taylor for many years of the firm of Taylor, Curtis & Co. has retired from active mecantile business.

TERRILL

1 Roger	Terrill	m.	Patience Foote	Newtown, Conn.
2 James	"	"	Esther Booth	" "
3 Abel Booth	"	"	Sophia Botsford	" "

Their Ch.

4 Mary Sophia Terrill		"	Wm. Botsford (see Botsford)	" "
4 Emily	"	"	Horace Beers see Beers	Brookfield Conn.
4 Caroline	"	"	Daniel Morris Beers no ch.	Vineland N. Y.
4 Hannah M.	"	"	Wm. Terrill	Newtown, Conn.
4 James	"	unm.		

2 Reuben   "   m.
3 Botsford   "   "   1st Sophia Glover

Their Ch.

4 *Edwin	Terrill	m.	Emeline Fairchild	Brookfield, Conn.
4 *Jane	"	"	Edson Shepard (see Shepard)	" "
4 *Henry	"	"	Delia Fairchild	Newtown, Conn.

Ch. 3Botsford Terrill and Julia Glover 2nd wife

4 *William Terrill		m.	Hannah Terrill	" "
4 *Frederick	"	"	Elizabeth Wilcox (no ch.)	
4 *Beach	"		Desc. not located.	

Ch. Edwin Terrill and Emeline Fairchild   Brookfield, Conn.

5 Mary Frances Terrill	m.	Wm. Hawley (see Hawley)	Newtown "
5 Alice	"	" Rev. Frank Hawley (see Hawley)	
5 Annie	"	m. Chas. D. H. Kellogg (see Johnson)	

Ch. Henry Terrill and Delia Fairchild   Newtown, Conn.

5 *Robert Terrill		d. young
5 Mortimer	"	m. Ella J. Clarke (see Adams) Ansonia, Conn.

Ch. William Terrill and Hannah Terrill   Newtown, Conn.

5 *Ella J.	Terrill	unm.	" "
5 William B.	"		" "
5 *Emily F.	"	unm.	
5 Frederick A.	"		Los Angeles, Cal.
5 Reuben B.	"	unm.	" "
5 Henry B.	"		Bridgeport, Conn.

Ch. Frederick A. Terrill,   Los Angeles, Cal.

6 Josephine A. Terrill			" "
6 Carolin F.	"		" "

TOUCEY

Richard Toucey came from England to Saybrook, date not certainly known. Thomas Toucey, his son, came to America in 1679. Thomas Toucey, Jr. b. 1688 joined in 1709 the little colony of settlers in Newtown. See Newtown's first settled minister, 1713.

1 Rev. Thomas Toucey   m. Hannah Clark

Their Ch.

2 Hannah	Toucey	m. Josiah Hooker (no ch.)	
2 Arminal	"	m. Donald Grant	Newtown, Conn.
2 Elizabeth	"	m. John Cooke	
2 Oliver	"	m. Deborah Wilcox	" "
2 Mehitable	"	m. Agur Judson	Huntington. Conn,
2 Sarah	"	m. Ebenezer Ford	
2 John	"	m. Rebecca Booth	Newtown, Conn.
2 Ann	"	m. Daniel Baldwin	
2 Lieut. Thomas	"	m. Mercy Platt	" "
2 Zalmon	"	m. Jerusha Booth	" "
2 Amaryllis	"	m. Lieut. Abel Prindle	" "

(See Prindle")

Lieut. Abel Prindle was killed at the battle of Bennington, 1777.

Ch. Arminal Toucey and Donald Grant

3 Sueton	Grant,	b. 1744, d. 1760	Buried Newtown Cemetery
3 Elizabeth	"	b. 1746, d. 1762	" " "
3 Donald	"	b. 1747, d. 1767	" " "
3 Thomas	"	b. 1751, d. in infancy	" " "
3 Thomas, 2nd	"	b. 1753 d. in infancy	" " "

See "Inscriptions and Epitaphs"

3 Hannah Grant   m. Stephen Mix Mitchell   New Haven, Conn.

Their Ch.

4 Elizabeth	Mitchell	m. Stephen Chester	
4 Capt. Donald Grant Mitchell			
4 Stephen Mix, Jr. Mitchell	m. Sophia Coit		New Haven, Conn.
4 Judge Walter	"		
4 Julia	"	m. Daniel Buck	
4 Harriet	"		
4 Rev. Alfred	"	m. Lucretia Woodbridge	

Rev. Alfred Mitchell was the father of

5 Donald Grant Mitchell, "Ike Marvel"   Westville, Conn.
Author of "Reveries of a Bachelor."

Ch. 3 Oliver Toucey and Deborah Wilcox

4 Philo	Toucey	m. Esther Shelton	Newtown, Conn.
4 Isaac	"	m. Sarah Burwell	" "
4 Zalmon	"	m. Phebe Booth	" "
4 Oliver, Jr.	"	m. Comfort Peck	" "
4 Hannah	"	m. Zechariah Clarke (See Clarke)	

Ch. Philo Toucey and Esther Shelton

5 Lucretia	Toucey	m. David Platt (See Platt)	Newtown, Conn.
5 Esther	"	m. Israel Beardsley (See Beardsley)	
5 Flora	"	m. Asa B. Beardsley	" " " "

Ch. 4 Oliver, Jr. Toucey and Comfort Peck   Newtown, Conn.

5 Hon. Isaac Toucey   m. Catherine Burrell (no ch.) d. Hartford, Ct.

See "Lawyers, Newtown born"

Ch. 2 John Toucey and Rebecca Booth   Newtown, Conn.

GENEALOGICAL SECTION

3 Abel Toucey	m. Esther Glover	Newtown, Conn.
3 Donald "	m. Betty Ferris	" "
3 Rebecca "	m. Eli Beers (See Beers)	" "
3 Huldah "	m. Joseph Blackman (See Blackman)	

Ch. 3 Abel Toucey and Esther Glover

4 Sarah Ann Toucey	m. Thomas W. Peck (See Peck)	
4 Marcia "	m. Jeremiah Hubbell (See Hubbell)	

Their Ch.

5 Ruamy Hubbell	m. Benjamin Burr
5 William "	m. Jane E. Winton

Their ch. (See Hubbell)

Ch. Donald Toucey and Betty Ferris — Newtown, Conn.

4 Laura Toucey	m. Jacob Beers (no ch.)	" "
4 Samuel "	m. Harriet Birch	" "
4 Sinclair "	m. Sylvia Beers	

Their Ch.

5 *Henry Sinclair Toucey	d. unm	New York, N. Y.
5 *Edward "	d. unm.	" " "
5 *Mary Beers "	d. unm.	" " "

Ch. 2 Zalmon Toucey and Jerusha Booth

3 Lazarus Toucey	m. Lucretia Wood	
3 Donald Grant "	m. Lucretia Beers	
3 Phebe "	m. Ebenezer Turner	Ithaca, N. Y.
3 Jerusha "	m. Peter Finch	Newtown, Conn.
3 Sarah "	m. Samuel C. Blackman	" "
3 Joseph "	m. Hannah Curtis	
3 Mary "	m. Dr. Nathan Thompson	Galway, N. Y.

Ch. 3 Donald Grant Toucey and Lucretia Beers

4 Ann Eliza Toucey	m. Richard Mansfield White

Their Ch.

5 Richard Grant White	New York, N. Y.

Ch. 3 Phebe Toucey and Ebenezer Turner — Ithaca, N. Y.

4 Mary Blackman Turner	m. Edward Starr (no ch.)	Newtown, Conn.
4 David Booth "	m. Susan Enders	Ithaca,, N. Y.
4 Ebenezer, Jr. "	m. Mary E. Williams	" "
4 Phebe Jane "	m. 1st. Samuel Bates (no ch.)	" "
	m. 2nd John McGraw (no ch.)	" "

Ch. David Booth Turner and Susan Enders — Ithaca, N. Y.

5 Florine Enders Turner	m. Richard Starr Dana

Their Ch.

6 Richard Turner Dana	" "
6 David T. Dana	" "

Ch. Ebenezer Turner and Mary E. Williams — Ithaca, N. Y.

5 Samuel Bates Turner	d. in infancy
5 John Williams "	d. in infancy
5 Mary Elizabeth "	d. in infancy
5 Ebenezer Toucey Turner	m. Martha Thompson Mairs — Galway, N. Y.

Ch. 3 Sarah Toucey and Samuel C. Blackman — Newtown, Conn.

GENEALOGICAL SECTION

4 Caroline Blackman   Newtown, Conn.
4 Sarah   "   "   "
4 George   "   m. Eliza W. Richmond   Waterbury, Conn.
4 Samuel G.   "   m. Miss Field   "   "
4 Alfred   "   m. Abby Beers   "   "

   Ch. 3Polly (Mary) Toucey and Dr. Nathan Thompson   Galway, N. Y.
4 Emma Thompson   m. Thomas Mairs   "   "

   Their Ch.

5 Nathan Thompson Mairs   "   "
5 Margaret Montgomery "   "   "
5 Julia Montgomery   "   "   "
5 Martha Thompson   " m. Ebenezer Toucey Turner   "   "
5 Charles Frederick   "   "   "

TYRRILL

   Ch. 5Esther Sherman and Eben Tyrrill   Newtown, Conn.
6 Sally Tyrrill   m. Andrew Shelton (no ch.)   "   "
6 Abby   "   " Burton Clark   "   "
6 Isaac   "   " Harriet S. Blake   "   "

   Ch. Abba Tyrrill and Burton Clarke
7 Edward Clarke   m. 1st Sylvia Peck   "   "
  "   "   " 2nd Susan Burritt Hyde
7 Juliette Clarke   " George Northrop   Roxbury   "

   Ch. Edward Clarke and Sylvia Peck   Newtown, Conn.
8 Frank Clarke   d. in childhood   "   "

   Ch. Juliette Clarke and George Northrop
8 Grace Northrop   d. in childhood.   Bridgeport, Conn.
8 Mary   "   m. Frank Allen   "   "

   Their Ch.
9 Marjorie Allen

   Ch. 6Isaac Tyrrill and Harrriet S. Blake   Newtown, Conn.
7 Elmer Tyrrill   m. Letitia Clingan
7 Alfred   "   " Martha Dikeman   New Haven   "

   Their Ch.
8 *Gertrude Tyrrill   m. Wm. Reid   "   "
8 Dwight   "   m. Anna ———

9 Reginald Reid   Gertrude Tyrrill
9 Marion   "   ch.   &
                           William Reid

   Ch. Dwight Tyrrill and Anna.
9 Raymond Tyrrill
9 Dorothy   "
9 Phyllis   "

WARNER

5 Dr. William, 4Dr. Eph., Jr., 3Dr. Ephraim, 2John Jr., 1John of Hartford.
5 Dr. William Warner   m. Mary Chambers of Newtown

GENEALOGICAL SECTION

9 William Warner   ch. William Warner and wife
9 Mabel "

   Their Ch.

6 Austin Warner   no desc. located
6 Loretta "   no desc. located
6 Hermon "   m. Rebecca Camp, 1st
             Deborah Curtis, 2nd   Newtown, Conn.

7 Charles Camp Warner, son of Hermon Warner and Rebecca Camp, served as Probate Judge 17 years; selectman six terms; was Town Clerk from 1863 to 1870; representative in State Legislature several terms; also a Justice of the Peace. He m. 1st Ann Maria Clarke.
             2nd Angeline Prindle Twitchell

   Ch. by 1st m.

8 *James Hobart Warner   m. Flora Jane Beers   Newtown, Conn.
8 *Austin W. "   m. Belle T. Lawrence   Vicksburg, Miss.
8 *Augustus "   m. Rissa J. Beers   Chicago, Ill.

   Ch. J. Hobart Warner and Flora Jane Beers   Newtown, Conn.

9 Mary S. Warner   unm.
9 *Howard C. "   d. in young manhood
9 Paul B. "   m. Anna Teresa Driggs
9 Florence A. "   a successful teacher   New Britain, Conn.
9 Hobart Glover "   m. Mary Hawley   Newtown, Conn.
9 *William A. "   d. in infancy

10 Sherman Driggs Warner   Anna Teresa Driggs
10 Flora Teresa "   ch. &
             Paul B. Warner

10 Hobart G. Jr., Warner   Mary Hawley   Newtown, Conn.
10 Austin "   ch. &
10 Henry Hawley "   Hobart G. Warner

   Ch. Austin W. Warner and Belle T. Lawrence   Vicksburg, Miss.

9 C. Lawrence Warner   m. Harriet P. Glover
9 Jessie C. "   unm.
9 Austin "   m. Milly Elizabeth Carter   Port Gibson, Miss.
9 Howard S. "   Capt. in U. S. Service at San Antonio, Texas

                         Harriet P. Glover   Vicksburg, Miss.
10 Glover Lawrence Warner   ch. &
                         C. Lawrence Warner

9 Charles C. Warner   Rissa Beers
9 Raymond "   ch. &
9 Catherine "   Augustus Warner   Chicago, Ill.

6   Ch. Hermon Warner and Deborah Curtis, 2nd wife   Newtown, Conn.

7 John Warner   m. Jane Lord   New Haven, Conn.
9 David C. "   unm.

8 Jane Marilla Warner   Jane Lord
8 William "   ch. &
             John Warner

                    Jane Marilla Warner
9 *Laura Fairchild   ch. &
                    George Fairchild

                    Jane M. Warner Fairchild
9 Elgin Squires   ch. &
                         Squires

WETMORE

1 James Wetmore

2 Ephraim P.	Wetmore	m.	Sophia Griffen	Newtown, Conn.	
2 Sarah	"	"	Abel Stilson (see Stilson)	"	"
2 Polly	"	"	Elnathan Stilson (see Stilson)	"	"

Ch. Ephraim Wetmore and Sophia Griffen " "

3 Mary Jane	Wetmore	m.	Wheeler Wilcoxen	Stratford, Conn.	
3 Emeline	"	"	Wheeler Fairchild (see Fairchild)		
3 Sarah	"		unm.	Newtown, Conn.	
3 Cyrus	"	"	Sylvia Glover	Brookfield, Conn.	
3 Lemuel P.	"	"	Sarah Anna Reed	"	"
3 Henrietta	"	"	Walter Simpson		
3 Harriet	"	"	Parmelee		
3 Roxy	"	"	1st Frederick Henderson	Newtown, Conn.	
		"	2nd Chas. Middlebrook	Trumbull, Conn.	
3 Cornelia	"	"	William Simpson		

Ch. Cyrus Wetmore and Sylvia Glover

4 Frank E.	Wetmore	m.	1st Isabella Wickham	Newtown, Conn.	
	"		2nd Mattie Holden		
4 Julia A.	"	"	George McLean		
4 Charles P.	"	"	Augusta Warner		
4 Albert A.	"				

Ch. Frank E Wetmore and Isabelle Wickham " "

5 Florence E.	Wetmore	m.	Edgar F. Northrop		
5 Edward	"	"	Rosa Blendenbacher	"	"
5 Vivian	"	"	Birdsey Parsons		

Ch. Lemuel P. Wetmore and Sarah Anna Reed   Brookfield, Conn.

5 Helen	Wetmore	m.	John Bateman
5 *Mary	"		
5 John C.	"		
5 Vernon C.	"		

Ch. Florence Wetmore and Edgar F. Northrop   Newtown, Conn.

6 *Aurelia W.	Northrop
6 Edgar W.	"

Ch. Vivian Wetmore and Birdsey Parsons " "

6 Isabella W.	Parsons
6 Sylvia G.	"
6 Ellen	"
6 Frances	"
6 Bradford Mitchell	"

Ch. Frank E. Wetmore and Mattie Holden " "

5 James Russell Wetmore
5 Julia Elender "

WHEELER

2 Obadiah Wheeler son of 1Thomas Wheeler of Milford, came to Newtown, before 1739. In that year he was commissioned by the Governor of the Colony of Connecticut, 1st Lieut. of the 2nd Company of "Trainband" of Newtown. He m.

3 Joseph Wheeler son of Obadiah, was commissioned Capt. of 2nd Company of "Trainband" in Newtown, by William Pitkin. Captain General and Commander in 1766.

He married Keziah Botsford.

Ch. Joseph Wheeler and Keziah Botsford

4 John	Wheeler			
4 Joseph B.	"	m.	Anna Botsford	Newtown, Conn.
4 Ely	"	"	Ann Terrill	

Ch. Joseph B. Wheeler and Anna Botsford

5 Lucy	Wheeler	m.	Sturges Fairchild(see Fairchild)
5 John Botsford	"	"	Polly Blackman
5 Anne Maria	"	"	William Hoyt
5 Molly	"	"	John Skidmore

Ch. John B. Wheeler and Polly Blackman   Newtown, Conn.

6 Russell	Wheeler	m.	Lydia Ann Botsford	" "
6 Sally	"	"	Elizur Keeler	" "

Their Ch.

7 Homer   Keeler   "   Martha Drake   Waterbury, Conn.

Ch. Russell Wheeler and Lydia Ann Botsford

7 John B.	Wheeler	m.	Mary Wilcox	Newtown, "
7 Ellen	"		d. in childhood	" "

Ch. John B. Wheeler and Mary Wilcox   " "

8 Hervey W.	"	m.	Nellie Hubbell, 1st wife	" "
9 Russell	"	ch.	&	" "
			Hervey W. Wheeler	
			Mary Hubbell, 2nd wife	
9 Ruth	"	ch.	&	" "
			Hervey W. Wheeler	" "

4 Ely Wheeler, son of 3Joseph m. Anna Terrill

Their Ch.

5 Joseph Davis Wheeler   m. 1st Miss Bradley

Their Ch.
Bradley	"	m.	Sabra
6 Joseph B.	"	"	Clarissa Dick, no ch.

Ch. 5Joseph D. Wheeler and Delia Bradley, 2nd wife

6 George B.   "   m. Charlottte Sanford

Their Ch.

7 Emily Alice	"	m.	George M. McKee	Dyersville, Iowa
7 Hattie	"	m.	Walter McKee (no ch.)	Minneapolis, Minn.

Their Ch.

8 *Estelle	McKee		
8 *Hattie	"		
8 Walter Howard	"	m.	1st. Grace Hall
			2nd Grace Lee
8 Gertrude	"	m.	Otis Harn
8 Ernest W.	"	m.	Adaline Consuela Vetter
8 Charlotte Elizabeth McKee		m.	Elgar C. Martin

Ch. Gertrude McKee and Otis Harn

JOSEPH TALCOTT Esq;
Governour and Commander in Chief of His Majesty's Colony of Connecticut in New-England,

To _____ Gent. Greeting.

YOU being by the General Assembly of this Colony, Accepted to be _____ of the _____ Company or Trainband in the Town of _____ Reposing special Trust and Confidence in your Loyalty, Courage and good Conduct, I do, by Virtue of the Letters Patents from the Crown of England to this Corporation, Me thereunto Enabling, Appoint and Impower you to take the said Trainband into your Care and Charge, as Their _____ Carefully and Diligently to discharge that Trust, Exercising your Inferiour Officers and _____ in the use of their Arms, according to the Discipline of War, keeping them in good Order and Government, and Commanding Them to Obey You as Their _____ for His Majesty's Service. And You are to observe all such Orders and Directions, as from Time to Time you shall Receive, either from Me, or from other your Superiour Officer, pursuant to the Trust hereby Reposed in You. Given under my Hand and the Seal of this Colony, in _____ the _____ Day of _____ In the _____ Year of the Reign of Our Sovereign Lord GEORGE the Second, KING of Great-Britain, &c. Annoque Domini, 1739

By his Honour's Command,

WILLIAM PITKIN, Esq.
Captain-General, and Commander in Chief, of His Majesty's Colony of Connecticut, in NEW-ENGLAND.

To Joseph Whaler. Gent. Greeting.

YOU being by the General Assembly of this Colony, accepted to be Captain of the second Company or Train band in the town of Newtown. Reposing special Trust and Confidence in your Loyalty, Courage and good Conduct, I do, by Virtue of the Letters Patents from the Crown of England, to this Corporation, Me thereunto enabling, appoint and impower you to take the said Trainband into your Care and Charge, as their Captain carefully and diligently to discharge that Trust; exercising the inferior Officers and Soldiers in the Use of their Arms, according to the Discipline of War, Keeping them in good Order and Government; and commanding them to obey you as their Captain for his Majesty's Service. And you are to observe all such Orders and Directions as from Time to Time you shall receive either from Me, or from other your superior Officer, pursuant to the Trust hereby reposed in you. Given under my Hand and the Seal of this Colony, in Newtown the 27 Day of October In the 7th Year of the Reign of Our Sovereign Lord GEORGE the Third, King of Great-Britain, &c. Annoque Domini, 1766

By His Honor's Command

GENEALOGICAL SECTION

9 Richard Eugene Harn

Ch. Ernest Wheeler McKee and Adaline Consuela Vetter

9 Doris Olive McKee

8 Lieut. Com. Ernest McKee was graduated from Naval Academy, Annapolis, in 1908. Was Commander of the Governor's private ship when the U. S. took over the Danish Islands(now Virgin Islands). Is now, 1918, Lieut. Commander on the battleship Utah.

1 Obadiah Wheeler b, 1784 m. Patience Judson 1804

   Their Ch.

2 Norman Wheeler   b. 1806
2 Russell   "   b. 1810
2 John J.   "   b. 1812
2 Betsey   "   b. 1819 m. Nathan Couch

   Their Ch.

3. Ella M. Couch m. 1st Henry Botsford.
              m. 2nd Samuel J. Botsford (see Botsford)
3 George Couch m. Emily Platt Morris.

   Their Ch.

4 George Couch

WHITNEY

1 James Whitney born in Stratford came to Newtown in 1771. He m. Eunice Johnson. Of their twelve children only Philo lived in Newtown.

He was a blacksmith, his shop being at the head of Newtown street at (the foot of Mt. Pleasant). Ives Glover the well known blacksmith of South Center learned his trade of him.

2 Philo Whitney   m. 1st Jerusha Wheeler
                                  2nd Aurelia Wheeler.

Ch. of Philo Whitney and Jerusha Wheeler

3 *Harriet   "   m. Edmund Fairchild (See Fairchild)
3 *Joseph Botsford   "
3 *James Wheeler   "   m. Anna Maria Lewis
3 *Emily   "   " Legrand Fairchild (See Fairchild)
3 Aurelia   "   " Oliver Warner Moore (no ch.)
3 Ruth Ann   "   " 1st Truman Hubbell   Bethel, Conn.
                        " 2nd Mark Leavenworth Hubbell
3 Abraham Johnson   "   " Marietta Parmalee   Bethel, Conn.

Ch. James W. Whitney and Anna Maria Lewis

4 Anna Maria   "   Staten Island
4 Joseph Botsford   "   Brooklyn, N. Y.
4 *Isabella Lewis   "   d. young

Ch. *Ruth A. Whitney and Mark L. Hubbell   Bethel, Conn.

4 Truman Johnson Hubbell   "   "
4 Mary Estella   "   "   "
4 Philo Whitney   "   "   "

Ch. *Abram Johnson Whitney and Marietta Parmalee   "   "

4 Harriet Aurelia Whitney
4 James Wheeler   "   Ohio
4 Frederick Moore   "   Rochester, N. Y.
4 Bertha Belle   "   Bethel, Conn.

LIST OF ILLUSTRATIONS

Ezra L. Johnson 73 yrs. of age
                            Frontispiece
Jane Eliza Johnson, 82 yrs. of age.

	Page
Jane Eliza Camp, facing page..	10
Ezra Levan Johnson " "	10
Ezra L. Johnson, facing page..	11
Jane E. Johnson, " "	11
Quanneapague (2 views).......	18
South Main Street.............	19
Smith-Scudder Residence	19
Johnson House................	51
Rev. Wm. H. Moore...........	78
Rev. Henry B. Smith..........	78
Rev. James P. Hoyt...........	79
Rev. Otis W. Barker..........	79
Rev. Edward O. Grisbrook.....	79
Congregational Church	79
Old Newtown, facing..........	80
Memorial Boulder, facing......	81
Rev. Daniel Burhans D. D......	84
Rev. Newton E. Marble D. D...	84
Trinity Episcopal Church......	85
Silas N. Beers................	85
The Two Churches 1793 & 1870	85
Rev. George T. Linsley........	86
Rev. James H. George.........	87
Rev. William C. Cravner.......	87
Beach Camp	87
Daniel G. Beers...............	87
Rev. Francis W. Barnett.......	88
The three sons of Rev. F. W. Barnett	88
Rev. David Botsford...........	89
Rev. George L. Foote..........	89
Rev. Sylvester Clark...........	90
Rt. Rev. Frederick F. Johnson..	91
William B. Prindle.............	92
St. John's Church..............	93
Methodist Church	93
Rev. Otis Olney Wright........	94
St. Rose Church...............	95
Rev. James McCartan..........	95
Mrs. Mary Ann Birch..........	141
Caleb Baldwin Inn.............	144
William A. Leonard...........	145

	Page
Willson M. Reynolds..........	171
Governor Isaac Toucey........	199
Governor Luzon B. Morris.....	201
William J. Beecher............	203
Frederick P. Marble...........	203
Dr. Monroe Judson............	211
Dr. Charles H. Peck...........	213
Miss Susan J. Scudder.........	230
Mrs. Edith G. Mitchell........	231
Prof. Charles S. Platt.........	234
Main St. Looking South......	235
Beach Memorial Library.......	235
Newtown Savings Bank........	236
Simeon B. Peck...............	237
Philo Clarke	238
David C. Peck.................	238
Arthur T. Nettleton...........	240
Cornelius B. Taylor...........	241
Masonic Temple...............	242
Capt. Julius Sanford...........	245
Louis T. Briscoe..............	246
Fabric Fire Hose Co...........	248
Dennis C. Gately..............	248
Wm. T. Cole...................	249
Office of Newtown Bee.......	250
Reuben H. Smith..............	250
Allison P. Smith...............	251
Arthur J. Smith...............	251
Zalmon S. Peck................	252
Factory of S. Curtis and Son...	260
Residence of Wm. T. Cole....	262
The Country Club.............	263

MILITARY RECORD SECTION

Dr. Wm. C. Wile.............	274
Edward Troy.................	275

GENEALOGICAL SECTION

Franklin Fairman.............	66
Frederick W. Foote...........	70
Rev. Charles H. Gardner.......	71
Daniel N. Morgan............	100
Wheeler Commissions.........	148

* FAMILY NAMES

CONTRIBUTORS' LIST

Mrs. Franklin Fairman...Chicago
Dr. Charles H. Peck.......................................New York and Newtown
Alfred Walker...Newtown
The Misses Beecher..Newtown
Arthur Reynolds...Newtown
Willson M. Reynolds...Newtown
Congregational Church Society...Newtown
Frederick I. Marble..Lowell, Mass.
Mrs. S. N. Beers...Pittsfield, Mass.
Trinity Parish..Newtown
Mrs. George F. Taylor..Sandy Hook
Mrs. Frank H. Mitchell..Newtown
Mrs. Julia Hawley..Sandy Hook
Rev. George T. Linsley..Hartford, Conn.
Miss Grace Clark..Bridgeport, Conn.
Miss Anna McCartan..Newtown
Mrs. William K. Stone...Kent, Conn.
William Camp and Charles Beach Johnson..................................Newtown
Levan Merritt Johnson..Painesville, Ohio
Earle Levan and Merritt Camp Johnson...........................Painesville, Ohio
Rt. Rev. and Mrs. Frederick Foote Johnson..................St. Louis, Missouri
Mrs. Harriet Foote Toles.................................Elizabeth, New Jersey
Clarence L. Beardsley..New Haven, Conn.
Mrs William A. Leonard..Newtown
Theron E. Platt...Newtown
Charles G. Morris..New Haven, Conn.
Mrs. Stanley M. Ramsey..Cincinnati, Ohio
Miss Susan J. Scudder...Newtown
Mrs. Edith G. Mitchell..Newtown
William T. Cole...Newtown
Mrs. Charles S. Platt..New York
Newtown Savings Bank..Newtown
David C. Peck...Newtown
Arthur T. Nettleton...Newtown
Cornelius B. Taylor...Newtown
Hiram Chapter and Lodge..Sandy Hook
Mrs. Clarence Bolmer...New Haven, Conn.
William R. Curtis...Newtown
Mrs. Dennis C. Gateley...Mamaroneck, N. Y.
Mrs. William Samuel Johnson....................................Mamaroneck, N. Y.
Newtown Bee...Newtown
Mrs. Mary F. P. Cheves...Macon, Georgia
Miss Mary E. Hawley...Newtown
Miss Alice Wile...Danbury, Conn.
Mr. Edward Troy..Sandy Hook
Hon. Daniel N. Morgan...Bridgeport, Conn.
John B. Wheeler...Newtown
Mrs. Charles H. Gardner.......................................Washington, D. C.
Frederick P. Sherman...Monroe, Conn.
Mrs. E. P. Taylor..Oakland, Cal.
David Curtis...New Haven, Conn.
In dear and loving memory of our daughter, Hattie L. Curtis.

CONTENTS

	Page
Foreword	3
Mr. Johnson's Own Foreword	4
Reuben Hazen Smith's Tribute	7
The Bridgeport Farmer's Tribute	9
The Newtown Bee's Tribute	9
Resolutions by Vestry of Trinity Church	11
His Epitaph	12
Copy of Deed	13
Quiomph's Purchase	14
Bearing Each Others Burdens	17
Quanneapague	18
First Grist Mill	21
First Sawmill	24
Granting Town Rights	25
Pitching for Land	29
Pitching for Meadow Land	32
Newtown's First Meeting House	35
Newtown's Town Houses	43
Sabbath Day Houses	44
Disputes Over Town Lines	45
Brookfield's Origin	48
Layout of Country Roads	50
Newtown's First Call for a Minister	53
Mr. Phineas Fisk	53
Newtown's First Settled Minister	54
Mr. Thomas Tousey	54
Newtown's Second Settled Minister	59
Rev. John Beach	59
Rev. Elisha Kent	63
Rev. David Judson	69
Rev. Zephaniah Smith	74
Rev. John Clark	74
Rev. Wm. Mitchell	75
Rev. N. M. Urmston	75
Rev. Alexander Leadbetter	76
Rev. Jason Atwater	78
Rev. Wm. H. Moore	78
Rev. Wm. M. Arms	78
Rev. Daniel W. Fox	78
Rev. Henry Bagg Smith	78
Rev. James P. Hoyt	79
Rev. Samuel Delzell	79
Rev. Otis W. Barker	79
Rev. Ralph Danforth	79
Rev. Alexander Steele	79
Rev. T. J. Lee	79
Episcopal Churches	80
Rev. John Beach	81
Rev. Philo Perry	83
Rev. Daniel Burhans	84
Rev. Samuel C. Stratton	84
Rev. S. S. Stocking	84
Rev. Horace Hills	84
Rev. Dr. Wm. M. Carmichael	84
Rev. Benj. W. Stone	84
Rev. Dr. Newton E. Marble	84
Building of Fourth Church Edifice	85
Rev. Thomas W. Haskins	85
Rev. Governeur Morris Wilkins	86
Rev. George Thomas Linsley	86
Rev. James Hardin George	87
Resolutions Adopted by Vestry of Trinity Church on Death of Chas. S. Platt	88
Rector's Assistants	88
Rev. Wm. Ackley	88
Rev. Thomas Mallaby	88
Rev. Francis W. Barnett	88
Those Newtown Born Who Entered the Ministry	89
Rev. David Botsford	89
Rev. Abel Nichols	89
Rev. George L. Foote	89
Rev. Sylvester Clarke D. D.	90
Rev. Arthur Thomas Parsons	91
Rev. Edward Egan	91
Rt. Rev. Frederick Foote Johnson	91
Rev. James Hardin George Jr.	92
St. Jame's Church	93
St. John's Church	93
The Methodist Church	94
The Baptist Church	95
St. Rose's Church	95
Sandemanian Church	95

SCHOOL DISTRICTS

North Center	96
Middle	99
Taunton and Zoar	100
Land's End	101
Palestine	102
Hanover	103
South Center, Kettletown, Deep Brook	104
Lake George	105
Flat Swamp and Sandy Hook	106
Pohatuck	107
Bear Hills and Middle Gate	108
Gray's Plain and Head of Meadow	109
Wapping	110
Gregory's Orchard and Walker's Farms	111
Toddy Hill and Huntington	112
Walnut Tree Hill	113
Hopewell	114
Half Way River	115
The Southerly Highway	116
Those Who Took Freeman's Oath, 1742 to 1796	119 to 121
Those Who Took Freeman's Oath, Also Those Who Took "Oath of Fidelity", 177-1791	121 to 124
Those Who Took Freeman's Oath, 1778-1833	124-130
Newtown During The Revolution	130-138
Passing of French Soldiers Through Newtown	139
The Roadside Tavern	143

CONTENTS

	Page		Page
Care and Keep of Newtown's Dependents	147	Dr. John Judson	210
Bridgeport and Uewtown Turnpike Co.	152	Dr. Cyrenius H. Booth	210
Old Days of the Stage Coach	157	Dr. William Edmond Booth	210
Highway Reconstruction	159	Dr. Thomas Dutton	210
Building, Equipment, Running Expenses etc. of the Housatonic Railroad 1835-1843	165-170	Dr. Russell B. Botsford	211
		Dr. George Judson	211
		Dr. Monroe Judson	211
		Dr. Erastus Erwin	211
		Dr. Moses Botsford Beers	212
Newtown's Post Offices and Post Masters 1800-1912	170	Dr. Henry Hawley Foote	212
Restrictions to Domestic Animals	176	Dr. William Camp	212
		Dr. James W. Gordon	212
Newtown's Sheep Industry	180	Dr. Ralph N. Betts	212
God's Acre	189	Dr. Andrew Egan	213
Epitaphs and Inscriptions	192	Dr. Charles Howard Peck	213
Newtown's Lawyers	198	Dr. Earle Peck	214
Judge William Edmond	198	Dr. Clement Botsford 34 of Genealogical Section	
Samuel Curtis Blackman	198	Grand Levy for 1739	214
Asa Chapman	198	Grand Levy for 1769	217
Holbrook Curtis	198	Ratable Estates for 1809	221
Reuben Booth	199	Newtown Borough	222
Henry Dutton	199	Newtown's Fire Companies, 1803-1913	224
Hon. Isaac Toucey	199	Newtown Academy, 1837-1902	226
David Hull Belden	199	Newtown High School, 1902-1917	231
Charles Chapman	200		
David B. Beers	200	The John Beach Memorial Library	233
Isaac M. Sturges	200	Sandy Hook Free Library	235
Alfred Blackman	200	Newtown Savings Bank	236
Hon. Amos S. Treat	200	Free Masonry in Newtown	240
Judge Daniel Blackman	201	The Rubber Industry	248
Julius B. Curtis	201	The Newtown Bee	250
Luzon B. Morris	201	Pohtatuck Grange	252
Richard Botsford	201	The Domestic Economy of our Mothers	253
Judge James Nichols	202	Berkshire	260
Hon. Charles H. Briscoe	202	The Men's Club	261
Judge David Belden	202	The Water Company	263
Austin N. Botsford	202	The Country Club	263
Johnson Tuttle Platt	202	A 40 Year Lease of Mountain Land in Sandy Hook	264
Julius C. Cable	203		
William J. Beecher	203	The Conservation of Timber	267
Charles H. Northrop	203	Newtown's Military Record	269
Frederick Parker Marble	203	The Red Cross Work	281
Nichols Curtis Downs	204	Complete Record of Soldiers of 1812	283
James M. Betts	204		
Doctors of the Old School and of Later Years	205	Index to Newtown's Military Record	285
Dr. Lemuel Thomas	205		
Dr. Gideon Shepherd	205	Preface and Index to Genealogical Section	149 pages
Dr. Bennett Perry	207		
Dr. Oliver Bancroft	209		
Dr. Rufus Skidmore	209		

In the Index to the Main Book the following Errata occurs on **page 194**, it should read Mr. Daniel Booth instead of David.

Newtown, Connectic[ut]
1705-1918

The Story of the Book.

It was the fond hope of Ezra L. Johnson to accede to the expres[s request] of many friends that he place in permanent form for the benefit of f[uture gen]erations, the articles published in The Newtown Bee that he had dug [from] early records of the town.

Mind and body failed at the same time, and he passed away [in] 1914.

In 1916, being in sound health and with a reasonably clear mind, [it occur]red to me that as I had always assisted in preparing the papers for publi[cation] I might be able to carry out his wishes. The response to a card, issued [to de]termine whether there would be sufficient encouragement to undertak[e the] work, was so cordial, that, with the able assistance of Reuben Hazel S[mith,] formerly editor and owner of The Newtown Bee, the work was commence[d.]

Some hint of its historical character can be obtained from some extra[cts.] Extract from Copy of Deed given in 1705 to the Colony of Connecticut: "Kn[ow] all men by these present, we, Masquash, Massumpas, Nunnewauk, all belon[g]ing to Pootatuck in Colony of Connecticut, for and in consideration of fou[r] guns, four broadcloth coats, four blankets, four ruffelly shirts, four collars, te[n] shirts, ten pair of stockings, forty pounds of lead, ten pounds of powder and forty knives.......... by these presents do freely and absolutely Give, Grant, Bargain, Sell, Alienate, Convey and Confirm unto William Junos, Justus Bush and Samuel Hawley, all now residents in Stratford, a tract of land.......... containing in length eight miles and in breadth five miles, etc.

From the Table of Contents: First Grist Mill, First Saw Mill, Granting Town Rights, Pitching for Land, Newtown's First Meeting House, Newtown's Town Houses, Sabbath Day Houses, Layout of Country Roads, First Call for a Minister, First Settled Minister, Rev Thomas Tousey; Second Settled Minister Rev John Beach; Episcopal Churches, First Rector, Rev John Beach; Those

CPSIA information can be obtained at www.ICGtesting.com
Printed in the USA
LVOW11s0339110713

342388LV00004B/79/P